Mastering

Advanced English Language

MACMILLAN MASTER SERIES

Accounting
Advanced English Language
Advanced Pure Mathematics
Arabic
Banking
Basic Management
Biology
British Politics
Business Administration
Business Communication
Business Law
C Programming
Catering Theory
Chemistry
COBOL Programming
Communication
Databases
Economic and Social History
Economics
Electrical Engineering
Electronic and Electrical Calculations
Electronics
English as a Foreign Language
English Grammar
English Language
English Literature
French
French 2
German

German 2
Global Information Systems
Human Biology
Internet
Italian
Italian 2
Japanese
Manufacturing
Marketing
Mathematics
Mathematics for Electrical and
    Electronic Engineering
Modern British History
Modern European History
Modern World History
Pascal Programming
Philosophy
Photography
Physics
Psychology
Science
Social Welfare
Sociology
Spanish
Spanish 2
Statistics
Study Skills
Visual Basic

Macmillan Master Series
Series Standing Order ISBN 0–333–69343–4
(outside North America only)

You can receive future titles in this series as they are published by placing a standing order.
Please contact your bookseller or, in case of difficulty, write to us at the address below with
your name and address, the title of the series and the ISBN quoted above.

Customer Services Department, Macmillan Distribution Ltd
Houndmills, Basingstoke, Hampshire RG21 6XS, England

Mastering

Advanced English Language

Sara Thorne

MACMILLAN

First published 1997 by
MACMILLAN PRESS LTD
Houndmills, Basingstoke, Hampshire RG21 6XS
and London
Companies and representatives
throughout the world

ISBN 0–333–62832–2

A catalogue record for this book is available
from the British Library.

10   9   8   7   6   5   4
06   05   04   03   02   01   00   99

Printed in Hong Kong

Contents

Preface   ix
Acknowledgements   xi
Abbreviations   xii

I   Reference – the structure of English

1   The structure of English   3
  1.1   What is grammar?   3
  1.2   Word classes   4
  1.3   The structure of words: morphology   22
  1.4   Function and form   26
  1.5   Phrases   27
  1.6   Clauses   33
  1.7   Sentences   37
  1.8   Mood   42
  1.9   Cohesion   43

2   Phonetics and phonology   48
  2.1   The reason for studying phonetics and phonology   48
  2.2   Phonetics   48
  2.3   Phonology   62

3   Style   72
  3.1   Focus   72
  3.2   Rhetoric   74

4   How to use your knowledge   83
  4.1   Grammar   83
  4.2   Phonetics and phonology   85
  4.3   Style   86
  4.4   What to aim for   87

II Language issues – aspects of English

5 **Some basic concepts** 91
  5.1 A starting point 91
  5.2 Standard English and Received Pronunciation 91
  5.3 Attitudes to language 92
  5.4 Audience, purpose and context 93
  5.5 Register 95
  5.6 Spoken and written English 97
  5.7 Using the basic concepts 101

6 **English: a living language** 102
  6.1 English: a living language 102
  6.2 What changes language? 103
  6.3 The changing faces of English 104
  6.4 The democratic nature of language change 116

7 **Historical change** 117
  7.1 The reason for studying historical change 117
  7.2 The importance of text analysis 117
  7.3 The Old English period 118
  7.4 The Middle English period 121
  7.5 The Early Modern English period 126
  7.6 The Modern English period 129
  7.7 What to look for when dating a text 132

8 **Language variation: regional and social** 137
  8.1 Regional and social variation 137
  8.2 Accent 139
  8.3 Dialect 155
  8.4 Accent and dialect levelling 161
  8.5 What to look for in British accents and dialects 162

9 **Child language – learning to talk** 164
  9.1 The nature of child language acquisition 164
  9.2 The theories of language acquisition 164
  9.3 The function of communication 167
  9.4 Features of child language 167
  9.5 Types of child language 174
  9.6 What to look for in examples of child language 186

III Varieties – English in use

10 **Spoken English** 193
  10.1 The nature of spoken language 193
  10.2 The function of spoken language 194
  10.3 Features of spoken language 194
  10.4 Different kinds of spoken language 204
  10.5 What to look for in spoken language 226

11 The language of newspapers   229
11.1   The nature of newspaper language   229
11.2   The function of newspaper language   233
11.3   Features of newspaper language   234
11.4   Types of newspaper reports   242
11.5   What to look for in newspapers   254

12 The language of advertising   257
12.1   The nature of advertising   257
12.2   The function of advertising   259
12.3   Features of advertising language   260
12.4   Types of advertising   265
12.5   What to look for in the language of advertising   280

13 The language of literature – narrative prose   283
13.1   The nature of narrative prose   283
13.2   The function of narrative prose   283
13.3   Features of narrative prose   283
13.4   Different kinds of authorial intention   286
13.5   What to look for in the language of narrative prose   304

14 The language of literature – poetry   307
14.1   The nature of poetry   307
14.2   The function of poetry   307
14.3   Features of poetry   307
14.4   Different kinds of poetic intention   312
14.5   What to look for in the language of poetry   323

15 The language of the law   326
15.1   The nature of legal language   326
15.2   The function of legal language   327
15.3   Features of written legal language   327
15.4   Types of legal language   330
15.5   What to look for in the language of the law   344

16 The language of the Church   346
16.1   The nature of the language of the Church   346
16.2   The function of the language of the Church   347
16.3   Features of the language of the Church   347
16.4   Types of Church language   352
16.5   What to look for in the language of the Church   365

17 The language of politics   368
17.1   The nature of political language   368
17.2   The function of political language   369
17.3   Features of political language   369
17.4   Types of political language   373
17.5   What to look for in the language of politics   395

18 The language of broadcasting   398
18.1   The nature of broadcasting language   398

18.2	The function of broadcasting	399
18.3	Features of broadcasting language	400
18.4	Different kinds of broadcasting language	403
18.5	What to look for in the language of broadcasting	427

19 Other varieties 430

19.1	How to classify other varieties	430
19.2	Instruction texts	430
19.3	Information texts	434
19.4	Personal texts	438
19.5	Narrative texts	443
19.6	What to look for in an unfamiliar variety of English	448

20 How to use your knowledge 450

20.1	Analysis	450
20.2	Original writing	450
20.3	Tackling a coursework project	451
20.4	Tackling examination questions	452
20.5	Preparing for an examination	454

IV Appendices

A	**Answers to activities**	459
B	**Glossary**	466
C	**Wider reading**	479
Index		481

Preface

This book examines the ever-changing faces of English, introducing you to examples of historical, social and cultural change. It also provides you with practical guidelines for identifying the ways in which writers and speakers adapt language and structure according to their purpose. It encourages you to look at everyday examples of spoken and written English and to 'deconstruct' them – speech and writing are no longer seen as polished end products, but as linguistic structures that have been put together in a particular way to influence us.

Because English is a living language it continues to change, and its flexibility is a source of fascination. As well as studying language topics and analytical approaches, the linguist has a wealth of material in everyday life. Language students can broaden the range of their study by keeping up to date with contemporary debate, by observing the spoken and written English around them, and by drawing on personal experience.

In order to help you work in an organised way, this book is divided into three distinct areas: reference; language topics; and different types of spoken and written English. Part I summarises the main grammatical, phonetic, phonological and stylistic knowledge you will need in reading the rest of the book. It is important to understand the terminology used because it is a linguistic code which helps you to discuss topics and examples concisely. Part II focuses on key linguistic issues; and Part III suggests ways of tackling a range of spoken and written examples. Each part is divided into logical subsections which focus on one element at a time: the general information provides a background; the activities test understanding; the wide range of source material introduces real examples of English in use; the commentaries suggest possible responses to the tasks set; and the lists of points to look for provide a systematic procedure for analysing unseen material. Two sections deal exclusively with the best ways to use your linguistic knowledge, offering general advice and practical approaches to written work.

The book synthesises the skills and knowledge needed to study language effectively. Because language cannot be divided neatly into discrete topics, there are inevitably points of contact at which different topics and varieties overlap. Be an active reader, therefore, cross-referencing and making connections so that your consideration of language is wide ranging. The book has been designed to enable you to get the most out of your study. Dip into it, using the contents list and the index to help you focus on key sections – it is not necessary to read sequentially. The book can be used as a core reference, as a revision guide both during and at the end of an advanced-level course, or as a secondary text supporting work covered in school or college. The general reader, on the other hand, can use it to develop personal interests.

Language study is challenging, thought-provoking and compulsive – once you start looking below the surface of words to the ways in which meaning is constructed, it is difficult to stop. I hope that this book will help you to focus your interests by providing a framework for your study, but above all I hope that it will help you enjoy words and the ways in which we use them.

SARA THORNE

Acknowledgements

The author and publishers wish to thank the following for permission to use copyright material: Carcanet Press Ltd for Robert Graves, 'The Face in the Mirror'; Faber & Faber Ltd and Harcourt Brace & Company for T. S. Eliot, 'Preludes 1' from *Collected Poems 1909–1962*. Copyright © 1936 by Harcourt Brace & Company, copyright © 1963, 1964 by T. S. Eliot; Guardian Newspapers Ltd for headlines from various issues of *The Guardian* and *The Observer*; The Controller of Her Majesty's Stationery Office for material from a Central Criminal Court judgment; David Higham Associates on behalf of the Estate of the author for an extract from Louis MacNeice, 'Prayer Before Birth', from *Collected Poems*, Faber & Faber; Newspaper Publishing plc for extracts from various issues of *The Independent*; Mirror Syndication International for material from various issues of *The People* and *The Sunday Mirror*; Laurence Pollinger Ltd on behalf of the Estate of Frieda Lawrence Ravagli and Viking Penguin, a division of Penguin Books USA, for an extract from D. H. Lawrence, 'Discord in Childhood', from *The Complete Poems of D. H. Lawrence*, eds, V. de Sola Pinto & F. W. Roberts. Copyright © 1964, 1971 by Angelo Ravagli and C. M. Weekley, Executors of the Estate of Frieda Lawrence Ravagli; Rex Features Ltd for headlines from various issues of *The Sun*; Solo Syndication Ltd for a headline from *The Daily Mail*.

Every effort has been made to trace the copyright holders but if any have been inadvertently overlooked the publishers will be pleased to make the necessary arrangement at the first opportunity.

The author would like to thank all the people who have helped at each stage in the preparation of this book.

Abbreviations

A	adverbial	IPA	International Phonetic Alphabet
ACl	adverbial clause	It	Italian
Adj	adjective		
AdjP	adjective phrase	l., ll.	line, lines
Adv	adverb	L	Latin
AdvP	adverb phrase	LAD	language acquisition device
AFr	Anglo-French	lex	lexical verb
art	article	LME	Late Modern English
aux	auxiliary verb		
AV	Authorised Version	m	pre-modifier
		MCl	main clause
BAE	Black American English	ME	Middle English
BCP	Book of Common Prayer	mod	modal verb
BEV	Black English Vernacular	ModE	Modern English
		MRP	Modified Received Pronunciation
C	complement		
CD-Rom	compact disk – read-only memory		
Cl	clause	N	noun
Co	complement – object	NCl	noun clause
ComCl	comment clause	neg	negative
CompCl	comparative clause	NFCl	non-finite clause
CompP	comparative phrase	NP	noun phrase
conj	conjunction	N-SE	non-standard English
Cs	complement – subject	nuc	nucleus
		num	number
det	determiner		
dumS	dummy subject	O	object
		Od	object – direct
EME	Early Modern English	OE	Old English
		OFr	Old French
Fr	French	Oi	object – indirect
		ON	Old Norse
h	head word		
H	head	P	predicator

(P)	delayed main clause predicator	SCl	subordinate clause
past pa	past participle	sconj	subordinating conjunction
PH	pre-head	SE	Standard English
pre-det	pre-determiner	Sp	Spanish
prep	preposition		
PrepP	prepositional phrase	thatCl	that clause
pres pa	present participle	T	tail
prim	primary verb	TS	tonic syllable
pron	pronoun		
		V	verb
q	qualifier or post-modifier	VlessCl	verbless clause
		V/N	verbal noun
RelCl	relative clause	voc	vocative
rel pron	relative pronoun	VP	verb phrase
RP	Received Pronunciation		
		whCl	wh-clause
S	subject		
(S)	delayed subject	$\emptyset$	omitted word(s) or clause
SAE	Standard American English		element(s)

Reference – the structure of English

1 The structure of English

1.1 What is grammar?

To focus your study of language, you need to learn about grammar. You already **know** instinctively about the grammar of English: you read, speak and write English, only occasionally making mistakes. This section will move beyond your intuitive knowledge so that you can begin to **talk about** grammar in context.

Whether we speak or write, we must arrange our words in certain patterns if we are to be understood. An explicit knowledge of the patterns we use instinctively will help you to recognise usage that conforms to our expectations and usage that does not. By analysing the structure of words and sentences, linguists can begin to discuss **what** speakers or writers are trying to communicate and **how** they do so.

For linguists, GRAMMAR is a study of the **organisation of language**. It involves taking language structures apart in order to see the ways in which we can communicate effectively in a range of situations and for a range of purposes. Linguists look closely at the ways in which words and sentences are made up of different units. They break words down into their smallest component parts so that they can describe the ways in which they are constructed (MORPHOLOGY), and they look at the ways words are combined to create sentences (SYNTAX). Both speakers and writers use grammatical patterns to organise what they wish to say or write. Although speech and writing are characterised by different grammatical structures, the basic process of analysis is the same. Linguists are interested in the structures of words and sentences in both spoken and written DISCOURSE (any continuous use of language which is longer than one sentence).

By studying grammar, you will become able to evaluate the flexibility and variety of both written and spoken language use. Grammatical knowledge can also make you a more effective writer because you will be more aware of what you can do in order to achieve certain effects.

For analysis, language is usually divided into different levels. Within each of these levels, there are certain rules and patterns describing how the elements can be combined and how they relate to the elements of other levels. Language is said to have a RANK SCALE because the levels can be arranged hierarchically: a word is made up of groups of letters; a phrase is made up of groups of words; a clause is made up of groups of phrases; and a sentence is made up of groups of clauses.

1.2 Word classes

In order to be able to discuss the way words work together in a sentence, it is useful to be able to classify them. You are probably familiar with names like nouns, adjectives, verbs and adverbs and this section will aim to help you develop a more detailed knowledge of each of these word classes. A knowledge of word classes is useful because it allows linguists to look closely at the kinds of words speakers and writers choose and the effects they create.

There are two types of word class: open and closed.

- **OPEN CLASS WORDS** New words can be added to nouns, verbs, adjectives and adverbs as they become necessary, developing language to match changes in the society around us. The computer age, for example, has introduced words like *hardware*, *software*, *CD-Rom* and *spreadsheet*; the 1980s introduced words like *Rambo*, *kissogram* and *wimp*. Open class words are often called **lexical words** and have a clearly definable meaning.
- **CLOSED CLASS WORDS** New words are rarely added because pronouns (e.g. *I*, *you*, *she*, *he*, *it*, *his*, *hers*, *ours*), prepositions (*up*, *down*, *over*, *under*, *round*, *of*, *at*, *in*), determiners (*the*, *a*, *this*, *some*, *many*) and conjunctions (*and*, *or*, *but*, *if*, *because*) have a fixed, limited number of words. Closed class words are often called **STRUCTURAL WORDS**, **FUNCTION WORDS** or **GRAMMATICAL WORDS** because they enable us to build up language grammatically.

Open class words

Nouns

NOUNS (N) are traditionally known as **naming words**; they name people, places and things. You can test a word to see whether it is a noun:

- by trying to place 'the' in front if it ('the ____');
- by seeing whether it will fit into the structure 'do you know about ____?'

Although some words will not fit into these structures even though they are nouns, these tests provide a starting point.

Nouns can be divided in several ways.

Common and proper nouns

COMMON NOUNS classify things into types or general categories.

▨ car dog flower chair

PROPER NOUNS refer to specific people and places and are usually written with an initial capital letter. They do not often appear after the determiners *a* and *the*.

▨ Steven Spielberg England Wales Robin Hood

Concrete and abstract nouns

CONCRETE NOUNS refer to physical things like people, objects and places, things that can be observed and measured.

▨ guitar table clothes

ABSTRACT NOUNS refer to ideas, processes, occasions, times and qualities; they cannot be touched or seen.

▨ happiness   week   birth   confinement

Count and non-count nouns

COUNT NOUNS can be counted and therefore have a plural form; they cannot be used after the determiner *much*.

▌ one lorry → two lorries
one pen → two pens
one cup → two cups

NON-COUNT NOUNS refer to substances and qualities that cannot be counted. They have no plural form and cannot follow the determiner *a*; many of them, however, can follow the determiner *much*.

▨ silver   information   hockey   traffic

Some nouns are both count and non-count.

▌ joy (non-count)   the *joys* of spring (count)
water (non-count)   still *waters* run deep (count)

Plurals

In written language, regular nouns add *-s* to mark the **PLURAL**. Many nouns, however, are irregular and therefore follow alternative patterns.
    Nouns ending in *-y* form their plurals by changing the *-y* into *-ies*.

▨ story → *stories*   penny → *pennies*

Nouns ending in *-o*, *-s*, *-sh*, *-ss*, *-tch*, and *-x* often form their plurals by adding *-es*.

▨ mistress → *mistresses*   box → *boxes*   flash → *flashes*

Nouns ending in *-f* (except *-ff*) or *-fe* change to *-ves* in the plural.

▨ hoof → *hooves* (or sometimes *hoofs*)   life → *lives*

Some nouns form a plural by changing a vowel or by using a suffix other than *-s*.

▨ mouse → *mice*   tooth → *teeth*   ox → *oxen*   child → *children*

Some nouns are the same in the singular and the plural.

▨ sheep   fish (or sometimes *fishes*)

COLLECTIVE NOUNS, although singular in form, refer to groups of people, animals and things.

▨ crowd   family   committee

Possessives

In written language, *'s* or *'* is added to the noun to mark possession. The following rules govern use of the **POSSESSIVE ENDING** in written English.
    Add an apostrophe and an *-s* to singular nouns to form the possessive.

▨ a *baby* → a *baby's* bottle   an *engine* → an *engine's* design

Add an apostrophe to regular plurals.

■ the *cars* → the *cars'* colours   the *pictures* → the *pictures'* frames

Add an apostrophe and an -*s* to irregular plurals.

■ the *children* → the *children's* games   the *oxen* → the *oxen's* strength

Singular nouns ending in -*s* usually add an apostrophe and an -*s*.

■ Dylan *Thomas's* poetry   King *Louis's* throne

The overall classification

For purposes of analysis, it is useful to see the relationship between these sub-categories of the open word class 'nouns'. The diagram in Figure 1.1 summarises the ways in which nouns can be classified.

Figure 1.1   The classification of nouns

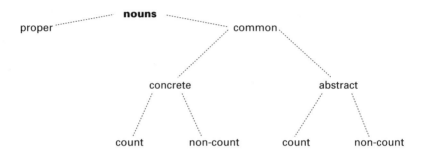

ACTIVITY 1.1   Answers on page 459.

1   Read through the extract below and list all the nouns.

December 1984

Monday December 24th

CHRISTMAS EVE

Something dead strange has happened to Christmas. It's just not the same as it used to be when I was a kid. In fact I've never really got over the trauma of finding out that my parents had been lying to me annually about the existence of Santa Claus.

To me then, at the age of eleven, Santa Claus was a bit like God, all-seeing, all-knowing, but without the lousy things that God allows to happen: earthquakes, famines, motorway crashes. I would lie in bed under the blankets (how crude the word blankets sounds today when we are all conversant with the Tog rating of continental quilts), my heart pounding and palms sweaty in anticipation of the virgin Beano album.

Sue Townsend, <u>True Confessions of Adrian Albert Mole</u>

2 Classify the following nouns, deciding whether they are proper or common nouns, concrete or abstract.

a	parents	f	heart
b	Christmas	g	Santa Claus
c	existence	h	trauma
d	quilt	i	bed
e	Beano	j	anticipation

Adjectives

ADJECTIVES (**Adj**) are traditionally known as **describing words**. They provide extra information about nouns by giving details of physical qualities like colour and shape, and of psychological qualities like emotions; and by providing evaluative judgements.

> some *green* leaves   a *heavy* sack   a *funny* film   a *good* story
> a *foolish* excuse

Adjectives specify a noun's FIELD OF REFERENCE: that is, they narrow the range of meaning by providing us with specific detail. You can test a word to see whether it is an adjective:

- by placing it between *the* and a noun;
- by placing *very* before it.

> the *old* tree   very *sad*

Adjectives have the following characteristics.

Position in relation to nouns

Adjectives can be used in two positions: before a noun (**ATTRIBUTIVE ADJECTIVES**), and after the verb *to be* and other **COPULA VERBS** (or **copular verbs**) or **LINKING VERBS** like *to become* and *to seem* (**PREDICATIVE ADJECTIVES**).

> Attributive: the *large* balloon   a *pure white* stallion
> Predicative: the balloon is *large*   the essay was *very good*

Grading

Adjectives can be GRADED so that nouns can be compared.

> a *big* car   a *bigger* car   the *biggest* car

Monosyllabic and disyllabic adjectives form the COMPARATIVE by adding *-er*, and the SUPERLATIVE by adding *-est*.

> long → *longer* → *longest*   sad → *sadder* → *saddest*
> happy → *happier* → *happiest*   clever → *cleverer* → *cleverest*

Polysyllabic and some disyllabic adjectives form the **comparative** by using *more* and the **superlative** by using *most* before the adjective.

> *more* fortunate → *most* fortunate   *more* grateful → *most* grateful

Irregularity

Some adjectives are **irregular**, as the following patterns show.

▨ bad → *worse* → *worst*   good → *better* → *best*

Words from other word classes

Sometimes words from other word classes do the job of an adjective.

▨ the *running* boy (V)   the *garden* wall (N)

In examples like this, a noun and a verb give extra details about the nouns *boy* and *wall*. The verb *running* and the noun *garden* are not adjectives, even though they occur in the same position as an adjective and are describing the *boy* and the *wall*. Linguists call any word describing a noun a MODIFIER: this takes account of the fact that not all words used will be from the adjective word class.

ACTIVITY 1.2   Answers on page 459.

1   Read the following extract and underline all the modifiers.

> The gloomy day became a glorious evening as the ancient crimson sun dropped to the far horizon. As it began to sink lower and lower, the sea became redder and redder. It was calm, the calmest sea I'd seen for a long time, and the tiny waves rolled to the seaweed-edged shoreline. I walked to the glowing dunes and sat and watched the flying gulls dip and glide as they searched for food left by the careless tourists, both young and old. I closed my eyes and listened to the harsh sounds of the gulls as they fought for rotting scraps. The beauty of the evening contrasted with my solemn mood. I was lonely, sad and despairing because my customary companion, my large golden dog, had disappeared and there now seemed little hope of his return.

2   Try to categorise the modifiers under the following headings:
    a   descriptive adjectives;
    b   size or distance adjectives;
    c   age adjectives;
    d   colour adjectives;

    e   comparative and superlative adjectives;
    f   noun or verb modifiers.

Verbs

VERBS (V) are traditionally known as **doing words**, but this does not cover all their possible meanings. A more accurate definition would be that verbs can express **actions** and **states**. STATIVE VERBS express states of being or processes in which there is no obvious action; they are not often used as commands and do not usually occur after the verb *to be* with an *-ing* ending.

▨ to know   to believe   to remember   to realise   to suppose   to appear

DYNAMIC VERBS express a wide range of actions which may be physical, like *jump*; mental, like *think*; or perceptual, like *see*. They can be used as commands and occur after the verb *to be* with an *-ing* ending.

▨ to buy → buy! → buying

TRANSITIVE VERBS have to be followed by an **OBJECT** (the person or thing to which the action of the verb is done) to complete their meaning.

■ I *carried* the baby.   They *found* the lost ring.   We can *make* a Christmas cake.

INTRANSITIVE VERBS do not need to be followed by an object to make sense. Many verbs describing position, like *to sit* and *to lie*, and motion, like *to run* and *to go*, are intransitive – the verb will often be followed by a description of place or destination.

■ It *happened*.   The children *laughed*.   The girl *went* to the cinema.

It is important to realise that many verbs can be both transitive and intransitive.

■ I was *eating*. I was *eating* cake.   He is *writing*. He is *writing* a story.

You can test to see whether a word is a verb:

• by adding an *-ing* ending;
• by placing it after *I* or *we*.

Verbs have the following characteristics.

Regular verbs

Regular verbs have four forms:

Example (*base form*)	Infinitive (*to + base form*)	Third person singular present tense	Past tense and past participle	Present participle
walk	*to* walk	walk*s*	walk*ed*	walk*ing*

Irregular verbs

Irregular verbs often have five forms:

Example (*base form*)	Infinitive (*to + base form*)	Third person singular present tense	Past tense	Present participle (pres pa)	Past participle (past pa)
show	*to* show	show*s*	show*ed*	show*ing*	*have* shown
write	*to* write	write*s*	wr*o*te	writ*ing*	*have* writ*ten*
give	*to* give	give*s*	g*a*ve	giv*ing*	*have* given
put	*to* put	put*s*	put	put*ting*	*have* put

Types of verbs

There are two main types of verbs: lexical and auxiliary. **LEXICAL VERBS** (**lex**) express the **meaning** in a verb phrase.

■   the boy *ran* to school   the dog *jumped* and *frisked*

AUXILIARY VERBS (**aux**) can be used to construct different timescales, questions and negatives, to add emphasis or to give information about the mood or attitude of a speaker or writer. The **PRIMARY VERBS** (**prim**) *to be*, *to have*, and *to do* can act as auxiliaries.

I *have* gone.   The girl *has* swum.   *Do* you want to go to bed?
I *did* not watch television.   The baby *does* want food.

The **MODAL VERBS** (**mod**) *can* and *could*, *may* and *might*, *must*, *shall* and *should*, and *will* and *would* convey a range of attitudes and moods about the likelihood of an event taking place.

Ability: I *can* swim.
Intention: You *will* do as you are told.
Necessity/obligation: You *must* go at once. You *should* do as you are told.
Permission: *Can* I leave the classroom, please? *May* I leave the room?
Prediction: He *will* come today, I'm sure. I *shall* finish tonight.
Possibility: I *can* go. I *may* go.

Past and present tenses

There are two **TENSES** in English: the present and the past. The **PRESENT TENSE** has two forms: the **BASE FORM** (a verb which has no ending or vowel change) is used with *I*, *you*, *we* and *they*; while for *he*, *she* and *it*, an -*s*/-*es* ending is added to the base form.

I *live* at home.   They *enjoy* going to the cinema.
He *lives* in town.   She *enjoys* going to the theatre.

The present tense can be used to describe states of affairs and events that occur on a regular basis. It is also used in spontaneous sports commentaries, proverbs and sayings.

I *know* about dinosaurs.   He *goes* to work by bus.
And he *takes* the ball and *runs* down the wing towards the goal. He *cuts* infield, *shoots* and *scores* – the game *is* over, the champions *win* the day!
A bird in the hand *is* worth two in the bush.   A stitch in time *saves* nine.

The **PAST TENSE** for regular verbs has only one form: in most cases, -*ed* is added to the base form of the verb. It refers to actions and states that took place in the past; it is sometimes used to record indirect or reported speech; and it can be used to refer to something hypothetical.

I *loved* my primary school.   We *missed* the bus for school.
He *said* that the girl *stayed* for tea. She *replied* that they *played* happily.
If I *walked* faster, perhaps I could win. I would go home, if there *was* a bus.

Many verbs are **irregular** and do not form the past tense by adding -*ed*. You use these irregular verbs in your speech and writing automatically, but you now need to become more conscious of their forms.

be → I *was*; we *were*   *become* → *became*
freeze → *froze*   *hear* → *heard*
catch → *caught*   *swim* → *swam*
hit → *hit*   *spell* → *spelt* (or *spelled*)

Future time

In order to create a sense of **FUTURE TIME**, English can use a range of structures.

1   The simple present.

I *leave* tomorrow.   She *starts* next week.

2   The modal verbs *shall* or *will* + *base form verb*.

▓   I *shall* go to town later.   They *will* go on holiday soon.

3   *be going* + *infinitive*.

▓   I *am going* to visit France next year. We *are going* to travel by train.

4   *to be* + *present participle*.

▓   The programme *is starting* in ten minutes.   The tide *is ebbing* now.

5   *will* or *shall* + *to be* + *present participle*.

▓   I *shall be writing* again next week.   We *will be waiting* for you.

Aspect

ASPECT describes the timescale of a verb – it establishes whether the action or state of a verb is complete or in progress. There are two types of aspect: the perfect (or perfective) and the progressive. The **PERFECT ASPECT** is constructed using the auxiliary *have* + *past participle*. The **PRESENT PERFECT** (*has* or *have* + *past participle*) is used for any action continuing in the present or having relevance in the present.

▓   We *have eaten* in this restaurant for years. [We still do.]

The **PAST PERFECT** (*had* + *past participle*) describes a previous time in the past.

▓   The building *had decayed* years ago.

The **PROGRESSIVE ASPECT** is constructed using the auxiliary *be* + *present participle* or the auxiliaries *have* + *be* + *present participle*. The progressive aspect implies that an activity is ongoing and is probably not complete.

Present progressive: The boys *are playing* football.
Past progressive: The ladies *were playing* tennis.
Present perfect progressive: The lions *have been roaring* wildly all day.
Past perfect progressive: The weeds *had been growing* throughout the summer.

Voice

The action of a verb and the person(s) or thing(s) responsible for it can be conveyed in two ways using **VOICE**: the active voice and the passive voice.

The **ACTIVE VOICE** is most common: it expresses the action of the verb, directly linking it to the person or thing carrying out the action.

▓   The car stopped suddenly.   The girl picked up a book.

The **PASSIVE VOICE** changes the focus of the sentence by reordering the elements. The basic structure of the passive is as follows:

1   the **subject** or actor of the active sentence (the person or thing **doing** the verb) is moved to the end of the passive sentence and becomes the optional passive **agent** (i.e. *by* + *subject* of active sentence);
2   the **object** of the active sentence (the person or thing **receiving the action** of the verb) is moved to the front of the passive sentence and becomes the **subject**;
3   the active verb is replaced by a verb in the passive form: *to be* + *past participle* or *have* + *to be* + *past participle*.

| Active: | The police hit the rioter. |
| Passive: | The rioter *was hit* [by the police]. |

| Active: | The young child threw the ball and broke the window. |
| Passive: | The ball *was thrown* and the window *was broken* [by the child]. |

Because the passive voice allows us to take the subject from the front of the sentence and replace it with something that is not the actor, we are able to change the focus of the active sentence. The passive is used for a variety of reasons:

1   Using *by + actor*, the subject can be delayed to the end of the sentence; this can create suspense.

The murder *was committed* by the infamous Mr Smith.

2   If the actor is a long phrase that seems awkward at the start of the sentence, it can be placed at the end for fluency.

A tremendous meal *was prepared* and [*was*] *served* by the cooks and waiters from the local hotel who trained at the college.

3   By omitting the *by + actor*, it is possible to exclude the person or thing responsible for the action of the verb.

Despite the explosion, nuclear power *was reported* [by the government] to be quite safe.

Finite and non-finite verbs

Verbs can be classified into two main types: finite and non-finite. FINITE VERBS change their form to show contrasts of number, tense and person. NON-FINITE VERBS never change their form.

Finite verbs:	she *lives* in Europe; she previously *lived* in America (contrast of tense)
	he *eats*; they *eat*; I *am*; you *are* (contrast of number/person)
Non-finite verbs:	(*is*) *living* (-*ing* participles)
	(*has*) *lived* (-*ed* past participles)
	live (base form of the verb)
	to live (the infinitive).

It is important to recognise the difference between the **past tense** and the **past participle** of regular verbs since both have an -*ed* ending. The past tense is finite because it is showing a change of tense; the past participle usually follows an auxiliary and does not change its form.

ACTIVITY 1.3   *Answers on pages 459–60.*

Complete the following exercises to test your knowledge of verbs.

1   Underline the verbs and decide whether each is a lexical or an auxiliary verb.
    a   She had gone to town.
    b   They had a picnic in the country.
    c   I can do the work.
    d   Did you like the concert?

2   List the verbs in the following sentences and decide whether each is finite or non-finite.
    Then use the diagram in Figure 1.2 to describe their forms exactly.

Figure 1.2   The classification of verbs

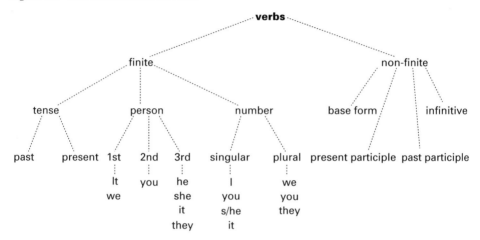

The boy *runs* to school.
    runs: finite; present tense; third person; singular.

    a   The eagles flapped their wings.   f   We chased the intruder.
    b   She laughs at herself.   g   You have been silly.
    c   You have gone mad.   h   What has been happening?
    d   I carried the child away.   i   Does he know?
    e   The frog was croaking loudly.

3   Re-write the following active sentences in the passive voice, including the passive agent.
    a   The strong waves lifted the boat above the dangerous sandbank.
    b   The monks rang the bells to warn the surrounding villagers of the impending
        danger.
    c   After the disturbance, the police shut the pub.

4   Rewrite the following active sentences in the passive, omitting the passive agent.
    Comment on the effect created in each case.
    a   The police beat the Black South African prisoners.
    b   The bully left the child face down in the playground.
    c   The scientists discovered the way to split the atom and created the first atom bomb.

Read the passage below and answer the questions that follow it.

Wednesday December 26th

BOXING DAY

I was woken at dawn by the sound of Grandad Sugden's rusty Ford Escort refusing to start. I know I should have gone down into the street and helped to push it but Grandma Sugden seemed to be doing all right on her own. It must be all those years of flinging sacks of potatoes about. My parents were wisely pretending to be asleep . . .

Went back to sleep but the dog licked me awake at 9.30, so I took it for a walk past Pandora's house. Her dad's Volvo wasn't in the drive so they must still be staying with their rich relations. On the way I passed Barry Kent, who was kicking a football up against the wall of the old people's home. He seemed full of seasonal good will for once and I stopped to talk with him. He asked what I'd had for Christmas . . .

Sue Townsend, <u>True Confessions of Adrian Albert Mole</u>

1 Underline all the verbs in the extract.

2 Find examples of the following:
   a two lexical verbs; d two primary auxiliary verbs;
   b two stative verbs; e two modal auxiliary verbs.
   c two dynamic verbs;

3 Find an example of the passive voice and rewrite the sentence in the active voice.

4 Find one example of the progressive aspect and one of the perfective aspect.

5 Find one example of the present tense and one of the past tense.

6 Find two examples of a finite verb and two examples of a non-finite verb.

Adverbs

ADVERBS (Adv) are modifying words. They give information about time, place and manner and can express a speaker's attitude to or evaluation of what is being said. They can modify:

- Verbs: The car drove *slowly.*
- Adjectives: The house was *very* pretty.
- Other adverbs: The painting was painted *particularly* carefully.
- Sentences: *Certainly*, the work will be completed on time.
  I went home; my friend, *meanwhile*, stayed to chat.

CIRCUMSTANCE ADVERBS (or **ADJUNCTS**) modify verbs, giving details of circumstances like time, manner and place.

Manner:	He was sleeping *well*; the cat was fighting *furiously.*
Time:	You must go to school *now*; *afterwards*, you can go swimming.
Frequency:	I *always* visit my grandmother on Sundays; I *never* stay at home.
Place:	Go *there* to get a coat; *upstairs* they have shirts too.

- To test for an adverb of manner, ask yourself the question 'how?'
- To test for an adverb of time, ask yourself the question 'when?'
- To test for an adverb of frequency, ask yourself the question 'how often?'
- To test for an adverb of place, ask yourself the question 'where?'

DEGREE ADVERBS (or **MODIFIERS**) modify adjectives or adverbs.

▓ Degree: It is *very* good to see you; I *really* missed you; I'm *so* glad to be back.

- To test for an adverb of degree, ask yourself the question 'to what degree?'

SENTENCE ADVERBS (**disjuncts** and **conjuncts**) modify a whole sentence. **DISJUNCTS** express speakers' or writers' attitudes, allowing them to comment on what is being said or written; **CONJUNCTS** can be used to link sentences.

▓ Linking: *Firstly*, I intend to go away; *however*, I will write postcards.
Attitude: I could *perhaps* do the work, but *surely* you could get someone else.

Adverbs have the following characteristics.

Forming adverbs

Many adverbs are formed by adding -*ly* to adjectives:

▓ calm (Adj) → calm*ly* (Adv)   shabby (Adj) → shabb*ily* (Adv)
gentle (Adj) → gent*ly* (Adv)

Comparatives and superlatives

Like adjectives, adverbs can have **COMPARATIVE** and **SUPERLATIVE** forms. Although some can take the -*er* and -*est* endings, most require the use of *more* and *most*.

▓ early → earl*ier* → earl*iest*
loudly → *more* loudly → *most* loudly
crucially → *more* crucially → *most* crucially

Irregular adverbs

Some adverbs are **irregular**.

▓ badly → *worse* → *worst*   little → *less* → *least*
much → *more* → *most*   well → *better* → *best*

Position

There are three main **positions** for adverbs.

1 The front of the sentence.

▓ *Actually*, I have loved this place for a long time.

2 The middle of a sentence: after the first auxiliary, after the verb *to be* as a lexical verb, or before the lexical verb.

▓ I have *actually* loved this place for a long time.
I am *actually* in love with this place.
I *actually* loved the place.

3   The end of the sentence.

▪ I loved the place *actually*.

Distinguishing adjectives and adverbs

Sometimes the same word can be both an **adjective** and an **adverb**. In order to distinguish between them, it is important to look at the **context** of the word and its **function** in a sentence.

▪ The *fast* train from London to Cardiff leaves at three o'clock.
▪ The sprinter took the bend *fast*.

▪ The bed was *hard* and gave me a bad night's sleep.
▪ After faltering, the horse hit the fence *hard*.

In the first and third sentences, the words *fast* and *hard* modify nouns. The first is an attributive adjective, coming before the noun it modifies; the second is a predicative adjective, coming after the verb *to be*. In the second and fourth sentences, the words *fast* and *hard* modify verbs. These are both circumstance adverbs which are in the end position.

ACTIVITY 1.5   Answers on page 460.

Underline the adverbs in the following passage and identify them as:

1   circumstance adverbs;
2   degree adverbs;
3   sentence adverbs.

The sun shone brightly there on that crisp December morning. Nevertheless, I could not help feeling that the day would not go well. Again and again, I was aware of the completely isolated nature of the spot here and anxiously I waited for the others to arrive. I knew I was being really silly, but generally my intuitions were correct. I had found recently that things happened as I knew they would. It made me very suspicious and often I would look around warily. Sometimes, however, I was wrong and I hoped desperately that I was being over-sensitive this time. I tried to relax and to think about something else. What would take my mind off my premonitions? Perhaps the beauty of the day could make me forget. Actually, I was here on holiday and I had to make sure that I enjoyed my stay properly.

Closed class words

Pronouns

PRONOUNS (**pron**) are used instead of nouns, noun phrases or noun clauses. There are seven main types of pronouns.

Personal pronouns

SUBJECT PRONOUNS are used when it is clear who the **actor** of the sentence is:

- First person singular: *I*
- Second person singular: *you*
- Third person singular: *he/she/it*

- First person plural: *we*
- Second person plural: *you*
- Third person plural: *they*

> The next-door neighbour visited today. *She* was in a good mood.
> Children should always be seen and not heard. *You* should be seen and not heard.

When a pronoun replaces the noun that receives the action of the verb (object), an **OBJECT PRONOUN** is used:

- First person singular: *me*
- Second person singular: *you*
- Third person singular: *him/her/it*

- First person plural: *us*
- Second person plural: *you*
- Third person plural: *them*

> The people carried their parcels indoors. The people carried *them* indoors.
> Give your brother the book. Give *him* the book.

Possessive pronouns

POSSESSIVE PRONOUNS are used when you need to show possession of something:

- First person singular: *mine*
- Second person singular: *yours*
- Third person singular: *his/hers*

- First person plural: *ours*
- Second person plural: *yours*
- Third person plural: *theirs*

> It is my book. It is *mine*.
> We think it is our choice. We think it is *ours*.
> They told us that it was their taxi. They told us it was *theirs*.

Reflexive pronouns

REFLEXIVE PRONOUNS are used when the **same** person is the actor (subject) and **receiver** of the action (object) in a sentence. They can also be used to create emphasis:

- First person singular: *myself*
- Second person singular: *yourself*
- Third person singular: *himself/ herself/itself*

- First person plural: *ourselves*
- Second person plural: *yourselves*
- Third person plural: *themselves*

> You should wash *yourself* carefully.
> You *yourself* know how dangerous it is.
> He said he saw her worry *herself* unnecessarily.

Demonstrative pronouns

DEMONSTRATIVE PRONOUNS are used to 'point' to the relationship between the speaker and a person or a thing. They are said to have a **'deictic' function**. There are four demonstrative pronouns:

- *this* and *these* point to something that is close to the speaker;
- *that* and *those* point to something that is distant from the speaker.

> I like the apples. I like *these*.   The lady over there is my aunt. *That* is my aunt.

Interrogative or question pronouns

INTERROGATIVE or **QUESTION PRONOUNS** are used to ask questions. There are five types: *what, which, who, whom* and *whose.*

> *Who* did you visit today?
> *What* do you think the time is?
> To *whom* did you address your letter?

Relative pronouns

RELATIVE PRONOUNS follow directly the nouns they describe. They introduce relative clauses, although sometimes the pronoun itself is omitted. There are five forms: *that, which, who, whom* and *whose.*

> The man *who* has white hair lives close to me.
> I went to the library to return the book *that* you got out for me.
> I saw a car *which* drove the wrong way down a one-way street.

Indefinite pronouns

INDEFINITE PRONOUNS have a less certain reference point than the other pronouns listed here. There are two types:

- *of* **PRONOUNS** *all of, both of, each of, either of, neither of* and *some of* – these are always followed by an object pronoun;

> I want the books. I want *all of* them.
> I will buy a shirt and a jacket. I will buy *both of* them.

- **COMPOUND PRONOUNS** *every, some, any* and *no* + *-thing, -one* and *-body.*

> They don't want dinner. They don't want *anything.*
> We live near no other people. We live near *nobody.*

ACTIVITY 1.6   *Answers on page 460.*

List the pronouns in the following passage and identify them as:

1 personal pronouns;	5 interrogative pronouns;
2 possessive pronouns;	6 relative pronouns;
3 reflexive pronouns;	7 indefinite pronouns.
4 demonstrative pronouns;	

> We enjoyed our days at the beach that summer. It had been glorious weather and everyone had relished the warmth and light after the harshness of a long winter which had seemed endless. Some ran the length of the sand to the sea; some lay peacefully on their towels. I decided to paddle, and covered myself in suntan lotion before walking lazily to the sea which shimmered before me. Why was it not like this all the time? Everything seemed perfect. The day was ours to do with as we wished. As I turned back to the beach, a small boy sat on my towel.
>
> 'Get off,' I shouted. 'That is mine.' He stood up suddenly and shouted something. Who could he be talking to? Then I saw the girl a short distance away. He had clearly thought the towel was hers.

I lay back down and closed my eyes to think of the girl that I had met earlier in the day. What was she doing now, I wondered? I still had her book and I would have to return it to her.

Determiners

DETERMINERS (**det**) precede nouns. There are five main types.

Articles

ARTICLES can be definite (*the*) or indefinite (*a* or *an*). The former specifies something particular, while the latter does not.

- *the* dog *a* dog   *the* house *a* house

Possessive determiners

POSSESSIVE DETERMINERS are used to suggest ownership of a noun. There are seven forms: *my*, *your*, *his*, *her*, *its*, *our* and *their*.

- *my* book   *our* suitcases   *their* motives

Demonstrative determiners

DEMONSTRATIVE DETERMINERS express a contrast, establishing either a close or a more distant relationship.

- *This* week is going slowly.
  The shop assistant said that she wanted *these* things kept aside for her.

Indefinite determiners

INDEFINITE DETERMINERS convey a range of meanings. The most common ones are: *all*, *some*, *any* and *no*; *every*, *each*, *either*, *neither*, *one* and *another*; *both*, *several* and *enough*; *many*, *more*, *most*, *few*, *little*, *fewer*, *less*, *fewest* and *least*.

- *Some* grapes would be nice.   *Every* adult must take some responsibility.
  Several children are expected today.   *More* chocolate, anybody?

Numbers

If NUMBERS precede a noun, they are functioning as determiners. Both **cardinal** (*one*, *two*, *three* and so on) and **ordinal** (*first*, *second*, *third* and so on) can be used as determiners.

- The *first* visitor will receive a present.   *Six* sheep have escaped from the farm.

Context

Because there is a considerable overlap between pronouns and determiners, it is important to look closely at the context to distinguish between the two. A **determiner precedes** a noun, while a **pronoun replaces** a noun, noun phrase or noun clause.

- *That* book is worth reading.   *That* is worth reading.
  det   pron

- *Both* children are really hard workers.   *Both* are really hard workers.
  det   pron

List the determiners in the following passage and try to classify them under the headings below:

1 articles: definite and indefinite;   4 indefinite determiners;
2 possessive determiners;   5 numbers.
3 demonstrative determiners;

> The old lady reached the doorstep of her home and put her bag down to search for a key in her pocket. This search was always the worst part of any trip out. However hard she tried, she could never find either key – she always carried one key for the front door and one key for the backdoor in case of emergencies. On many occasions she had been sure that both keys were lost. But this time was an exception.
>
> She skilfully slotted one key into the lock and turned it carefully. In two minutes she was indoors, but for the second time that day, she drew her breath sharply. Every day recently she had had some visitors, but enough was enough. There was more mess than even she could bear and for the rest of that day, she concentrated on making her home her own again.

Prepositions

PREPOSITIONS (prep) describe relationships that exist between elements in sentences. They convey the following relationships:

- Place: *at, on, by* and *opposite.*
- Direction: *towards, past, out of, to* and *through.*
- Time: *at, before, in* and *on.*
- Comparison: *as . . . as* and *like.*
- Source: *from* and *out of.*
- Purpose: *for.*

It is important to be aware that some words that have the **form** of a preposition do not have the same **function**.

■ The girl read *in* the library.   The rioters kicked *in* the door.

The form of the preposition *in* is identical in each case, but the function is different. In the first sentence, *in* describes where the girl is reading – it is therefore a preposition of place. In the second sentence, however, *in* is directly related to the verb *kicked* – in this case, it is called a **PARTICLE**.

Decide whether the words <u>underlined</u> in the following sentences are prepositions or particles.

1 Steven threw <u>out</u> the rubbish.
2 Judith ran <u>into</u> the bedroom.
3 The pilot flew <u>out of</u> the local airport.
4 Will you carry <u>on</u> preparing the meal?
5 The warring factions gave <u>in</u> to the demands of the United Nations.

6 The sea rolled inexorably <u>towards</u> the defensive wall.
7 The car broke <u>down</u> at the traffic lights.
8 The plane rose high <u>above</u> me, but I could still remember the moment of take-off.
9 It's difficult to be a single-parent family and to bring <u>up</u> two children alone.
10 I turned to my companion and we went <u>down to</u> the basement.
11 They cleared <u>out</u> the attic ready for moving-day.

Conjunctions

CONJUNCTIONS (**conj**) are joining words, and there are two types.

Co-ordinating conjunctions

CO-ORDINATING CONJUNCTIONS (*and, but, or, neither ... nor* and *either ... or*) link lexical units of equal value.

The girl *and* the boy.   They saw *and* understood.
  N   N   V   V

The dog was gentle *and* friendly.   The day was wet *and* the trip was ruined.
          Adj   Adj   sentence   sentence

Subordinating conjunctions

SUBORDINATING CONJUNCTIONS join a subordinate clause to a main clause. They often give information on *when, where, why, how* or *if* an action takes place. A clause introduced by a subordinating conjunction cannot stand alone. The list below contains some of the main subordinating conjunctions.

- Time: *when(ever), while, as, before, until, after, since, once* and *when;*
- Place: *where* and *wherever;*
- Purpose: *so that* and *in order that;*
- Reason: *because, as* and *since;*
- Condition: *if* and *unless;*
- Contrast: *although, while* and *whereas;*
- Comparison: *as, than, like, as if* and *as though.*

I love going to the theatre *because* it makes texts studied in college come alive.
Whenever we visit France, I remember that first holiday.
I want to study at the moment, *so that* I can go to university.
I go to restaurants *where* I can get a good vegetarian meal.
If they travel at a reasonable speed, they should be here by evening.
The woman looked *as if* she was going to shout.
While she loved her new home, she still yearned for her old cottage.

ACTIVITY 1.9   *Answers on page 461.*

Read through the passage below and choose an appropriate conjunction to fill each of the gaps in the text. Identify the type of conjunction used in each case.

> ___1___ the doctor hurried from one bed to another, the nurses went about their tasks calmly. They had beds to make ___2___ medicine to allocate, ___3___ it was all part of the daily routine. ___4___ they were accustomed to being shorthanded, they found ways to divide the tasks. ___5___ they were really busy, things went quite smoothly.
>
> The ward was full at the moment, ___6___ they all knew that there were at least two patients waiting for admission. It always seemed to happen these days – ___7___ a bed was vacated, it was stripped and filled within half an hour. ___8___ the nurses looked, they saw the need for more beds, more facilities and above all, more nurses. ___9___ they had to cope with the cuts, they had to think only of the job in hand. It was not worth wasting energy on bewailing the conditions in which they had to work, ___10___ they needed all their strength to cope with their long shifts. It was better ___11___ working on a production line, surely!

1.3   The structure of words: morphology

A knowledge of morphology will be useful when you study the history of language, **ETYMOLOGY** (the study of the origin of words) and **PHONOLOGY** (the study of the sounds of a language). **MORPHOLOGY** is the study of **MORPHEMES**, the smallest units of grammar.

Free and bound morphemes

There are two kinds of morphemes: free morphemes and bound morphemes. A **FREE MORPHEME** can stand alone and is understandable in isolation:

> ■ boy (N)   happy (Adj)   run (V)

A **BOUND MORPHEME** cannot occur alone:

> ■ *-ly   un-   -ish*

These bound morphemes are also called **AFFIXES**, and can occur at the beginning or the end of a free morpheme.

Prefixes

A **PREFIX** precedes a free morpheme.

> ■ *un*kind   *dis*like

Suffixes

A **SUFFIX** follows a free morpheme.

> ■ kind*ness*   lean*ing*

Words can have multiple affixes (*un* + *like* + *li* + *hood*).

ACTIVITY 1.10 *Answers on page 461.*

Divide the words below into bound and free morphemes, bearing in mind that the addition of suffixes sometimes changes the spelling of free morphemes.

1	unjustifiable;	5	negativity;
2	summative;	6	unlikely;
3	midnight;	7	pitiful.
4	daily;		

Derivational and inflectional morphology

Bound morphemes are used in two distinctive ways: they can be used to create new words (**DERIVATIONAL MORPHOLOGY**) or to change the form of words (**INFLECTIONAL MORPHOLOGY**).

Derivational morphology

Words can be created by using prefixes, suffixes or both:

> *un*real, *re*draft (prefixes)
> sad*ly*, boy*ish* (suffixes)
> *un*accept*able*, *sub*conscious*ly* (affixes)

Although it is always important to look closely at words in context, it is still possible to make some generalisations about the words created by prefixation, suffixation and affixation.

Prefixes

Prefixes alter the meaning of a word, but they do not always change the word class.

Prefix	*Word class of free morpheme*	*Word class of of created word*
hyper-	tension (N)	hypertension (N)
be-	devil (N)	bedevil (V)
re-	style (V)	restyle (V)

Suffixes

Suffixes usually, but not always, change the class of the free morpheme to which they are attached:

Word class of free morpheme	*Suffix*	*Word class of of created word*
exploit (V)	-ation	exploitation (N)
joy (N)	-ful	joyful (Adj)
friend (N)	-ship	friendship (N)

Suffixes associated with nouns

Words ending with the bound morphemes *-acy*, *-ation*, *-er/-or*, *-ess*, *-ity*, *-ment*, *-ness* and *-ship* are usually nouns.

> diplom*acy*   similar*ity*   jubil*ation*   compart*ment*   writ*er*   sad*ness*
> conduct*or*   relation*ship*   poet*ess*

Suffixes associated with adjectives

Words with suffixes like *-able*, *-ful*, *-ical*, *-less*, *-like*, *-ous* and *-y* are usually adjectives.

> a *profitable* account   an *animal-like* noise   a *gloomy* day
> a *courageous* child   a *theatrical* show   a *godless* society

Suffixes associated with verbs

Words with the suffixes *-ise* or *-ize* are usually verbs.

> dramat*ise*   democrat*ise*

Suffixes associated with adverbs

Words with the suffix *-ly* are usually adverbs.

> the bus moved off *slowly*   the dog ate *eagerly*

Words formed from two free morphemes

Words can also be formed by the **compounding** (adding together) of two free morphemes.

> *duty* + *free* → *duty-free*   *sign* + *post* → *signpost*

ACTIVITY 1.11   Answers on page 461.

Add appropriate bound morphemes to the underlined words in order to derive new words.

1   Add a prefix to the verb <u>present</u>.
2   Add a suffix to the noun <u>hospital</u>.
3   Make an adverb by adding the appropriate suffix to the adjective <u>calm</u>.
4   Add an appropriate suffix to the noun <u>child</u> to create an adjective.
5   Make a noun by adding an appropriate ending to the following: <u>glorify</u>, <u>audit</u> and <u>act</u>.

Inflectional morphology

Open-class words can be altered by adding a suffix. However, while derivational morphology often involves a change in word class, inflectional morphology **never** does.

In written English, inflection can mark the following.

Plurals

The **plural** of nouns.

Free morpheme	Bound morpheme	Inflected word
cat	-s	cats
book	-s	books
gas	-es	gases
penny	-ies	pennies

Possessives

The **possessive** of all nouns.

Free morpheme	Bound morpheme	Inflected word
girl	-'s	the girl's jumper
children	-'s	the children's toys
adults	-'	the adults' books

Present tense

The **present tense** of regular third person singular verbs.

Free morpheme	Bound morpheme	Inflected word
run	-s	he runs
cry	-ies	the baby cries

Present participle

The **present participle** form of verbs.

Free morpheme	Bound morpheme	Inflected word
do	-ing	doing
justify	-ing	justifying

Past tense and past participle

The **past tense** and **past participle** of regular verbs.

Free morpheme	Bound morpheme	Inflected word
walk	-ed	walked
dress	-ed	dressed

ACTIVITY 1.12   Answers on pages 461–2.

List the suffixes in the example below and try to identify the kind of inflection used.

1   sailors;   4   dreaming;
2   viewed;   5   the dog's bone;
3   the girls' bags;   6   the tiger snarls.

ACTIVITY 1.13   Answers on page 462.

For each of the examples below, list the free and bound morphemes and then identify:

a   the word class of each example;
b   the word class of each free morpheme;
c   whether derivational or inflectional morphemes have been used.

morality (N)   Free morpheme = *moral* (Adj); bound morpheme = *-ity*;
derivational morphology (change of word class – words ending with
the suffix *-ity* are nouns).

lives (V)   Free morpheme = *live* (V); bound morpheme = *-s*; inflectional
morphology (inflection marking a third person singular present
tense verb).

1   greatness   6   illogical
2   multigym   7   predetermination
3   declaration   8   horrifying
4   delimited   9   institutionalise
5   inter-rivalry   10 reassesses

1.4   Function and form

It is important to look at more than just the word class of a word because the same word can perform quite different jobs in a sentence.

(a) At seven o'clock, the man will *light* the bonfire.
(b) When I was cleaning, the *light* fell on the floor and broke.
(c) This room is very *light*.

In each of these sentences, the appearance of the word *light* is identical, but the job the word does is different. In example (a), *light* is a lexical verb preceded by a modal auxiliary *will*; in example (b), it is a noun preceded by the determiner *the*; in example (c), it is a predicative adjective following the copula verb *is*.

Linguists analyse words in terms of both their **FORM** (word class) and their **FUNCTION** (the job they fulfil). By describing words in this way, linguistic analysis can be very precise – it allows linguists to focus specifically on the words chosen and the results created by different writers and speakers.

(a) a *costumed* concert performance
(b) the *award-winning* dramatisation of the novel by Roald Dahl
(c) one of the biggest *floating* book shops in the world

Each of the words in italic print is a verb in form although each is functioning as a modifier. In examples (a) and (b) the verb modifiers *costumed* and *award-winning* help the promoters to convey the nature of the event concisely. In example (c), the verb modifier *floating* is dramatic because it is followed by the nouns *book shops*. It makes an effective advertisement for the ship's book shop because they are not words we are accustomed to seeing together – they attract attention because of their novelty.

When linguists analyse phrases (groups of words), an awareness of function and form is important because it enables them to describe exactly what words are doing and how particular effects are created. There are three key terms that describe the function of words in a phrase: the HEAD WORD (**h**) is the main word; words that come before the head word and modify or change it in some way are called PRE-MODIFIERS (**m**); and words that provide extra information after the head word are called POST-MODIFIERS or QUALIFIERS (**q**). By using these terms, it is possible to describe the function of individual words in a phrase exactly.

1.5 Phrases

A PHRASE is a single word or a group of words that act together as a unit but that do not usually contain a finite verb.

Noun phrases

A NOUN PHRASE (**NP**) usually begins with a determiner and normally has a **noun** as its most important word. It can act as a **subject**, and **object** or a **complement** in a clause (see Section 1.6). Noun phrases have the following characteristics.

Nouns and pronouns as head words

The HEAD WORD or main word of a noun phrase is usually a **noun**, but it can be a **pronoun**.

The baby is crawling over *the grass.*	*He* is crawling over *it.*
NP NP	NP NP
det N det N	pron pron

Adjectives as head words

Sometimes **adjectives** can function as the head word of a noun phrase.

The old often get a raw deal.
NP
det   Adj

Constituents of a noun phrase

A noun phrase can be made up of either a **single noun** or a **noun** with one or more **pre-modifiers** and **post-modifiers** or **qualifiers**.

h		h		m	h		m	h	FUNCTION
Dogs eat *bones.*				*The girls* are picking *the flowers.*				
NP		NP		NP			NP		FORM
N		N		det	N		det	N	

m	m	h	q		m	m	h	q	FUNCTION
The beautiful sky of blue rose above *the glimmering sea of green.*									
NP						NP			FORM
det	Adj	N	prep	Adj	det	V	N	prep	Adj

Pre-modification

Pre-modification can take the following forms.

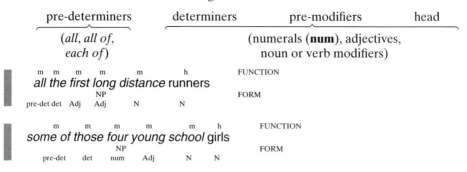

pre-determiners	determiners	pre-modifiers	head
(*all*, *all of*, *each of*)		(numerals (**num**), adjectives, noun or verb modifiers)	

						FUNCTION
m	m	m	m	m	h	
all the first long distance runners						
NP						FORM
pre-det	det	Adj	Adj	N	N	

					FUNCTION
m	m	m	m	m	h	
some of those four young school girls						
NP						FORM
pre-det	det	num	Adj	N	N	

Post-modification

Post-modification or **qualification** can take the following forms.

Prepositional phrases

A PREPOSITIONAL PHRASE (**PrepP**) will always begin with a **preposition**.

m	h	q	FUNCTION
the baby	*on the floor*		
	NP		FORM
det	N	PrepP	

Non-finite clauses

A NON-FINITE CLAUSE (**NFCl**) will always begin with a **non-finite verb** (see Section 1.6).

m	h	q		h	q	FUNCTION
the baby	*chewing his rattle*		time	*to go home*		
	NP			NP		FORM
det	N	NFCl		N	NFCl	

m	h	q	FUNCTION
a man	*called Jack*		
	NP		FORM
det	N	NFCl	

Relative clauses

A RELATIVE CLAUSE (**RelCl**) which will usually begin with a **relative pronoun** (see Section 1.6).

m	h	q	FUNCTION
the baby	*who was chewing his rattle*		
	NP		FORM
det	N	RelCl	

ACTIVITY 1.14 *Answers on page 462.*

Read the following passage, then list all the noun phrases and try to identify:

1 the head word of each noun phrase;
2 the kind of modification (pre- or post-) used.

The first summer's day burst through my curtains unexpectedly. The new dawn's sunlight highlighted the paths of dust which lay on the ancient sea chest. The scratches paid tribute to a life of hardship and I couldn't help wondering about the interesting stories which were linked to the marks. The drowned men who had owned this chest could tell their own versions of events, but I would never know them.

I turned lazily towards the wall, but I was merely met by another withered mark of the past. This time, I was confronted by the faded rose wallpaper. The memory of another place slowly filtered through my hazy mind, forcing me to make connections. I remembered that first disturbing visit to the ruined cottage and its ongoing effects. This second historical link waiting for me, unexpectedly, stirred me at last.

ACTIVITY 1.15 *Answers on pages 462–3.*

Analyse the following noun phrases from the extract in terms of function and form.

1   the interesting stories which were linked to the marks;
2   their own versions of events;
3   the wall;
4   the faded rose wallpaper;
5   This second historical link waiting for me.

Adjective phrases

An **ADJECTIVE PHRASE** (**AdjP**) has an **adjective** as its main word. Adjective phrases have the following characteristics.

Adjectives as head words

The **head word** of an adjective phrase is an **adjective**. While attributive adjectives precede nouns as pre-modifiers in a noun phrase, predicative adjectives follow nouns (often after a copula verb) and are the head words of adjective phrases.

>   h   FUNCTION
> The sky grew *black*.
>   AdjP   FORM

>   h   FUNCTION
> The horse was *black* and stood out against the whiteness of the snow.
>   AdjP   FORM

Pre-modification

Adverbs and some **adjectives** can pre-modify an adjective.

> m   h   m   h   m   h   FUNCTION
> *very* bold   *extremely* dangerous   *pure* white
>   AdjP   AdjP   AdjP   FORM
> Adv   Adj   Adv   Adj   Adj   Adj

Post-modification

Post-modification of adjective phrases can take the following forms.

Prepositional phrases

A **prepositional phrase** will always begin with a **preposition**.

```
     h    q              FUNCTION
  afraid of ghosts
          AdjP           FORM
    Adj   PrepP
```

Non-finite infinitive clauses

A **non-finite infinitive clause** will always begin with an **infinitive**.

```
      h    q             FUNCTION
  anxious to please
           AdjP          FORM
    Adj    NFCl
```

Noun clauses

A NOUN CLAUSE (**NCl**) will always start with the **pronoun** *that*, although this may be **omitted** (marked in analysis by the symbol ∅).

```
    h   q                FUNCTION
  sure that he'll get lost
          AdjP           FORM
   Adj   NCl
```

```
    h       q            FUNCTION
  sure (∅) he'll get lost
          AdjP           FORM
   Adj      NCl
```

ACTIVITY 1.16   *Answers on page 463.*

Read the following passage and then list the adjective phrases and analyse them in terms of function and form. The first example is completed for you.

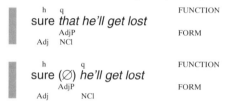

```
    m      h   q         FUNCTION
  very glad to meet him.
            AdjP         FORM
   Adv    Adj  NFCl
```

I was <u>very glad to meet him</u> on that winter's day. The snow, deep and white, fell quickly, covering the ground like a blanket. He seemed rather sad, but quite sure of his need for company. He was very sincere about the purpose of his journey – he wanted to visit the place, isolated and very bleak though it was, to remind himself of everything that had happened. Surprisingly fierce, he justified his arrival, quite certain that he had made the right decision. As we walked, however, he became so unbelievably withdrawn that I could not agree with his interpretations of events. He was unsure and rather quiet, and I was certain he wished he had not come.

Verb phrases

A VERB PHRASE (**VP**) generally has a **lexical verb** as its main verb. It can be made up of one lexical verb, or one or more auxiliary verbs and a lexical verb. Verb phrases have the following characteristics.

Lexical verbs as head words

A verb phrase may consist of one **lexical verb** as a head word.

Auxiliary verbs

A verb phrase may have up to four **auxiliary verbs** – the lexical verb will always be the last element in a verb phrase.

Phrasal verbs

Some verb phrases are made up of a verb and an adverb. They are called PHRASAL VERBS.

> I have *gone off* tomatoes.   The manager *brought up* the same arguments.
> VP   VP
> V   Adv   V   Adv

Many phrasal verbs can stand alone, they do not need anything to follow them (*look up*, *break down*).

Prepositional verbs

Some verb phrases are made up of a verb and a preposition or particle. They are called PREPOSITIONAL VERBS.

> I *looked at* the pictures.   He *stood against* his opponent.
> VP   VP
> V   prep   V   prep

Prepositional verbs cannot stand alone: they must be followed by a **noun phrase**.

Phrasal and prepositional verbs are common in informal speech and writing. They can often be replaced by one lexical item.

Prepositional phrases

A PREPOSITIONAL PHRASE (**PrepP**) has a **preposition** as its main word. It will normally be followed by a noun phrase. Prepositional phrases add extra information and are therefore optional – they can be omitted without affecting the meaning. They have the following characteristics.

Post-modification

Prepositional phrases are used to **post-modify** other phrases.

	m	h	q					FUNCTION
	the boys	*from the town*		rather unhappy	*about the prospect*			
		NP			AdjP			FORM
	det	N	PrepP	Adv	Adj	PrepP		

Adverbials

Prepositional phrases can function as **adverbials** in a sentence, providing information about time, manner and place (see Section 1.6).

		A		A		A	FUNCTION
	We went	*to town*	*in the afternoon*.	The girls sat	*in the shade*.		
		PrepP	PrepP		PrepP		FORM
		prep NP	prep NP		prep NP		

Adverb phrases

An ADVERB PHRASE (**AdvP**) has an **adverb** as its main word. Adverb phrases have the following general characteristics.

Adverbs as head words

The **head word** of an adverb phrase is an adverb.

	h		m	h	FUNCTION
	the child laughed *loudly*	the crowd jostled	*very*	*impatiently*	
	AdvP		AdvP		FORM
	Adv		Adv	Adv	

Extra information

Adverb phrases provide **extra information** – if omitted a sentence will still make sense.

	h		FUNCTION
	The choir sing *gloriously*. The choir sing.		
	AdvP		FORM
	Adv		

Adverbials

Adverb phrases can function as **adverbials** in a sentence, providing information about time, manner and place.

	A			A		FUNCTION
	We visited France *recently*.	They go to the cinema	*quite*	*regularly*.		
	AdvP			AdvP		FORM
	Adv		Adv	Adv		

1.6 Clauses

CLAUSES (**Cl**) are the main structures used to compose sentences. A sentence will be made up of at least one MAIN CLAUSE (a clause that makes sense on its own and that is not dependent on or part of another clause); it may also contain one or more SUBORDINATE CLAUSES (a clause that cannot stand on its own and that is dependent on the main clause). Clauses may be **finite** (containing a verb marked for tense, number and person); **non-finite** (containing a present participle, a past participle or an infinitive); or **verbless** (containing no verb).

Finite clause:	(The guests *arrived* late).
Non-finite clause:	(*Arriving* late), the guests crowded around the door noisily.
Verbless clause:	(Well I never)!

Clause elements

There are five types of CLAUSE ELEMENT and each has a different **function** and **site** (position within the clause).

Subject

The SUBJECT (**S**) normally describes the person who or thing which does the action of the verb. It is also called the **actor** of a sentence. You can check which part of the clause is a subject by asking *who?* or *what?* is responsible for the action or process of the verb.

Kinds of subject

The subject is usually a **noun phrase** or a **pronoun**, but it can also be a **clause**.

(*The girl*) was a good swimmer. (*She*) was a good swimmer.

(*What I look forward to*) is a restful Christmas.

Position in the clause

The subject usually **precedes** the verb in a statement.

(*The whole family*) went to town.

Position in a question

The subject **follows** the auxiliary verb in a question.

Did (*the girl*) go to town?

Effect on the verb

The subject dictates the form of the verb.

(I) *go* to town. (The old lady) *goes* to town.

Effect on the object or complement

The subject sometimes controls the form of the **object** or **complement** in a sentence.

> (She) cut *herself*. (They) cut *themselves*.

with S marked above "She" and "They".

Verb

Verbs (**P**) can express a range of meanings – actions, processes, states and so on. They are the most important clause element: they cannot be omitted, except in a minor sentence.

> *Like father, like son.*

Only a **verb phrase** can fill the verb site of a clause.

> I *should go* to town.

Object

The **object** (**O**) describes something that is **directly affected** by the verb. You can check which part of a clause is in the **direct object** (**Od**) site by asking *who?* or *what?* is affected by the action or process of the verb.

> The dog ate (*the bone*).

with Od marked above "the bone".

Indirect objects

The object can also be something that is **indirectly affected** by the verb. Usually an **indirect object** (**Oi**) will **precede** the direct object, but it may instead **follow** the direct object. You can check whether an object is indirect by placing it after the direct object and putting *to* before it.

> The child gave (*her friend*) (a present). The child gave (a present) (*to her friend*).

with Oi above "her friend", Od above "a present", Od above "a present", Oi above "to her friend".

Kinds of object

The object is usually a **noun phrase** or a **pronoun**. If the object is a pronoun, it may have a distinctive form.

> The rain soaked (*the boy*). The rain soaked (*him*).

with Od marked above "the boy" and "him".

> He gave (*the visitors*) a cup of tea. He gave (*them*) a cup of tea.

with Oi marked above "the visitors" and "them".

Position in the clause

The object normally **follows** the verb.

Complement

The **complement** (**C**) gives **extra information** about the **subject** (**Cs**) or about the **object** (**Co**).

> The sun was (*bright*).   The teacher considered his pupil (*a genius*).

with Cs marked above "bright", Co marked above "a genius".

Kinds of complement

The complement can be an **adjective phrase**, a **noun phrase**, a **pronoun**, a **numeral** or a **clause**.

> The musician was (*excellent*).   The man thought the wine (*a bargain*). FUNCTION
> Cs · AdjP   Co · NP · FORM

> The book is (*his*).   The old lady was (*ninety*). FUNCTION
> Cs · pron   Cs · num · FORM

> This field is (*where the battle took place*). FUNCTION
> Cs · Cl · FORM

Position in the clause

The complement usually **follows** a verb (*appear, seem, become, be*).

> The man felt (*gloomy*).   The garden had become (*overgrown*).
> Cs   Cs

Adverbials

ADVERBIALS (**A**) give information about time, manner and place. You can check which part of a clause is an adverbial by asking questions like *how?*, *when?*, *where?* and *how often?*

Kinds of adverbial

Adverbials can be **adverb phrases**, **prepositional phrases**, **noun phrases** or **clauses**.

> They went (*to town*) (*yesterday*). They went (*to town*) (*on Saturdays*). FUNCTION
> A · PrepP   A · AdvP   A · PrepP   A · PrepP · FORM

> They went (*to town*) (*last week*). They went (*to town*) (*when it rained*). FUNCTION
> A · PrepP   A · NP   A · PrepP   A · Cl · FORM

Number of adverbials

More than one adverbial can be added to a clause.

> (*Twice a week*) the boy ran (*to his grandmother's house*) (*for tea*). FUNCTION
> A · NP   A · PrepP   A · PrepP · FORM

Position in the clause

An adverbial can change its **position** in order to create different kinds of emphasis.

> (*Actually*), we went (*to the library*) (*on Mondays*).
> A   A   A

> (*On Mondays*), we (*actually*) went (*to the library*).
> A   A   A

Clause structure

Most clauses will have a **subject** and a **verb**. Other clause elements are **optional** and will be used depending upon the information and the kind of verb selected.

It is useful to distinguish between the **form** or **word class** of a verb and the **grammatical role** or **function** of a verb phrase in a clause. In clause analysis, therefore, linguists call the verb site the **predicator (P)**.

S	P		S	P	Od	FUNCTION
(I)	(run).		(The children)	(will need)	(some food).	
NP	VP		NP	VP	NP	FORM
pron	V		det	N	aux	lex	det	N	

Clause types

There are seven types of clause, in which the elements are combined in different ways.

Subject + verb

S · · · P
(They) (voted).

Subject + verb + direct object

S · · · P · · · Od
(They) (ate) (dinner).

Subject + verb + indirect object + direct object

S · · · P · · · Oi · · · Od
(Father Christmas) (gave) (each child) (a present).

Subject + verb + subject complement

S · · · P · · · Cs
(Snow) (is) (disruptive).

Subject + verb + direct object + object complement

S · · · P · · · Od · · · Co
(The government) (considered) (its election promises) (inappropriate).

Subject + verb + adverbial

S · · · P · · · A
(You) (must not go) (near the derelict house).

Subject + verb + direct object + adverbial

S · · · P · · · Od · · · A
(They) (packed) (their bags) (for school).

ACTIVITY 1.17 *Answers on page 463.*

Try to identify the clause elements in the following passage. The first sentence is completed for you. Use the following abbreviations:

S	subject	C	complement
P	verb	A	adverbial
Od	direct object	conj	coordinating conjunction
Oi	indirect object	neg	negative

A · · · · · · · · · · · · · · · S · · · · · · · · · · · · P · · · C
(After William the Conqueror), (the next King of England) (was) (his son

William). He was a very strong and good-looking man, but he had a red face and rather reddish hair. He was not a good man and was cruel to his people. Like his father, he enjoyed hunting animals. One day the Red King's arrow just missed a big deer. William was very excited and called out to his friend, Walter. Walter fired an arrow, but by accident it stuck in the King's eye and he fell dead. Walter was very frightened and he rode away. The King's body lay in the forest all day. In the evening it was carried away in a workman's cart and buried in the big church at a town called Winchester.

1.7 Sentences

A SENTENCE is a grammatical construction that makes sense on its own. In writing, it begins with a capital letter and ends with a **full stop** or an **exclamation** or **question mark**. This section will help you to recognise and describe the different kinds of sentences. Before beginning work on sentence structure, it would be useful to look back over the information on word classes, phrases, clause elements and clause types.

Simple sentences

A SIMPLE SENTENCE contains just **one clause**. It has only **one finite verb** and is described as a MAIN CLAUSE (**MCl**).

■ (The cook) (ate).
    S   P

■ (The cook) (ate) (dinner).
    S   P   Od

■ (The cook) (made) (the guests) (dinner).
    S   P   Oi   Od

■ (The cook) (became) (hot).
    S   P   Cs

■ (The cook) (thought) (the guests) (rude).
    S   P   Od   Co

■ (The cook) (worked) (quickly).
    S   P   A

■ (The cook) (made) (a large stew) (for the evening meal).
    S   P   Od   A

Compound sentences

A COMPOUND SENTENCE contains **two or more simple sentences** linked by CO-ORDINATING CONJUNCTIONS (*and, or, but*). Each clause in a compound sentence carries equal weight and makes sense on its own – they can therefore both be described as **main clauses**. Sentences will often be linked like this because they share content in some way.

■ (The girl) (weeded) (borders) *and* (removed) (dead flowers) (from the roses).
 MCl S   P   Od   MCl P   Od   A
                            conj

■ (The children) (often) (watched) (television) *but* (they) (preferred) (the cinema).
 MCl   S   A   P   Od   MCl S   P   Od
                               conj

| MCl | S | P | A | MCl | S | P | Od |
(We) (could go) (to the park) *or* (we) (could visit) (the museum).
conj

When two sentences are linked, it is usually better to avoid repetition. This can be achieved by using substitution or ellipsis.

Substitution

In **SUBSTITUTION**, a pronoun replaces a noun or a noun phrase.

| MCl | S | P | Od | MCl | S | P | A |
(The tearful boy) (took) (his coat) and (*he*) (left) (immediately).

| MCl | S | P | Od | A | MCl | S | P | A | C |
(Dickens) (wrote) (many stories) (in his lifetime) and (*he*) (is) (still) (popular).

Ellipsis

ELLIPSIS is the omission of an element of language. As long as the reader can easily recognise exactly what has been deleted, part of a sentence can be omitted to avoid repetition.

| MCl | A | S | P | Od | MCl | (∅) |
(Soon), (the Labour Party) (will run) (a leadership campaign) (and) [*the Labour*
conj

| P | Od |
Party] (will elect) (a new leader).

| MCl | S | P | A | MCl | (∅) |
(The latest film releases) (are publicised) (extensively) (but) [*the latest film*
conj

| P | C |
releases] (are not) (always successful).
neg

Recognising subordinate clauses

You can usually recognise a subordinate clause by identifying the **word class** of the first word in the clause. It may be a **SUBORDINATING CONJUNCTION** (**sconj**), a *wh-* word or a **non-finite verb**. It is important to remember that subordinate clauses can be used in all the clause sites except the verb. In other words, a subordinate clause can be used as a subject, an object, a complement or an adverbial.

| MCl | S | P | C |
(*That* John Major leads the Conservative Party) (is) (a well-known fact).
SCl–NCl
(sconj)

| MCl | S | P | Od |
(I) (know) (*who* sent me the valentine card).
SCl–RelCl
(rel pron)

| MCl | S | P | C |
(The prospective candidates) (were) (*what* we had hoped for).
SCl–NCl
(*wh-* word)

| MCl | S | P | Od | A |
(We) (will discuss) (the new house) (*when* we know *if* we've sold this one).
SCl–ACl   SCl–ACl
(sconj)   (sconj)

In assessing the **role** of the subordinate clause, always check whether it functions as the **whole** of a clause element or just as **part** of the clause element.

MCl S   P   Od
    (I) (know) (the boy *who* sent me the valentine card).
                                SCl–RelCl

MCl S   P   Od
    (I) (know) (*what* to do next).
                        SCl–NCl

In the first example, the subordinate clause could be omitted and part of the object would still remain: *the boy*. The function of the relative clause is to **post-modify** the head noun. In the second example, the subordinate clause stands as the **object** on its own. If it were omitted, the sentence would have no object.

Complex sentences

Clauses in COMPLEX SENTENCES do not have equal value. One is a **main clause** and the one or more other clauses are called **subordinate** or **dependent clauses**. A subordinate clause does not make sense standing on its own.

There are six types of subordinate clause.

Noun clauses

A NOUN CLAUSE (**NCl**) can fill the subject or object site of a clause. There are two main kinds of noun clause.

That-clauses

A THAT-CLAUSE (**thatCl**) will begin with the pronoun *that*, although this may be elided.

MCl S   P   O
    (I) (decided) (*that* the essay was too long).
                        SCl–NCl

Wh-clauses

A WH-CLAUSE (**whCl**) will begin with a *wh-* word.

MCl S   P   O
    (I) (wonder) (*what* I can do).
                        SCl–NCl

Adverbial clauses

An ADVERBIAL CLAUSE (**ACl**) functions as an adverbial within the main clause. It answers questions such as *when?*, *why?* and *what for?* An adverbial clause can be recognised by the **subordinating conjunction** that marks its beginning (*if*, *because*, *unless*, *where*, etc.).

MCl S   P   A   MCl   A   S   P   O
    (I) (went) (*when* I saw the time).   (*Because* I left late), (I) (missed) (the train).
                        SCl–ACl   SCl–ACl

Relative clauses

A RELATIVE CLAUSE (**RelCl**) adds extra information about one of the nouns in the main clause. The beginning of a relative clause is usually marked by a **relative pronoun** (*who*, *whose*, *which* and *that*), although it can be omitted. Relative clauses follow the nouns they post-modify or qualify.

MCl   S   P   C
(The man *who* lives next door) (is) (deaf).
           SCl–RelCl

MCl   S   P   O
(Our friend) (likes) (stories *that* come from other countries).
                       SCl–RelCl

Comparative clauses

A COMPARATIVE CLAUSE (**CompCl**) starts with *as* (**equal comparison**) or contains *than* (**unequal comparison**).

MCl S   P   C   MCl S   P   O
   (I) (am) (faster *than* he is).   (We) (took) (*as* many pictures as he did).
          SCl–CompCl   SCl–CompCl

Non-finite clauses

A NON-FINITE CLAUSE (**NFCl**) can be recognised by an **infinitive**, a **present participle** or a **past participle** at the beginning of the clause.

MCl S   P   O   MCl   A   S   P   C   A
   (I) (wanted) (*to go*).   (*Leaving* it all behind), (I) (was) (happy) (at last).
                  SCl–NFCl   SCl–NFCl

Verbless clauses

While VERBLESS MAIN CLAUSES (**VlessCl**) like *What about a cup of tea?*, *Good thing too!* and *Lovely weather!* are more likely to be used in informal speech, a VERBLESS SUB-ORDINATE CLAUSE is more likely to be used in formal written English.

MCl   A   S   P   A   P   O
(*Once alone*), (I) (cried).   (*If in doubt*), (call) (the freephone number).
SCl–VlessCl   SCl–VlessCl

Compound-complex sentences

Co-ordination and **subordination** can be used in the same sentence.

MCl   S   P   Od   MCl A   P
(The police) (needed) (to discover who had been seen) (and) (then) (hoped)
                   SCl–NFCl   SCl–RelCl   conj

    Od
(to arrest him).
SCl–NFCl

The first main clause here has two subordinate clauses in the object site. It is co-ordinated with another main clause of equal value which has one subordinate clause in the object site.

MCl   S   P   A   MCl P   A
(The lorry) (left) (when it had been loaded) (and) (returned) (after it had delivered
          SCl–ACl   conj   SCl–ACl

its load).

Each main clause in the sentence above contains a subordinate clause functioning as an adverbial. Each subordinate clause starts with a subordinating conjunction: *when* or *after*; the two main clauses are joined by a co-ordinating conjunction: *and*.

Major and minor sentences

All the sentences considered so far can be described as REGULAR or MAJOR SENTENCES because they are constructed using regular patterns.

Some sentences, however, do not follow expected patterns and these are called IRREGULAR or MINOR SENTENCES. Minor sentences lack some of the essential clause elements considered so far. They use unusual patterns which cannot easily be analysed. Minor sentences are often used in everyday conversation, on posters, in headlines, in advertisements and in slogans. You can check to see whether a sentence is minor by trying to change the verb into the past tense. If you can and the sentence still makes sense, it is probably a major rather than a minor sentence.

Minor sentences can be:

- **formulae** used in **social situations**: *hello, thanks, bye*;
- **interjections** used to express some kind of **emotion**: *ah!, tut tut!*;
- **abbreviated forms** often used on postcards or in spoken commentaries: *wish you were here, nearly there*;
- words or phrases used as **exclamations**, **questions** or **commands**: *what a day!, congratulations, never!, taxi*.

Analysing a sentence

In order to analyse a sentence, use the following process.

1 Underline the **verbs** in the sentence – if there are none, it is an example of a minor sentence.
2 Identify the main **lexical verb(s)** and mark the **main clause(s)**.
3 Label the **clause elements**.
4 Identify any **subordinate clauses** and decide whether they function as a whole or as a part of the clause element.
5 Identify the **type** of subordinate clause by identifying the word class of the first word. Table 1.1 summarises the kinds of words that appear in the initial position of a subordinate clause and the clause types in each case.

Table 1.1 The classification of subordinate clauses

Word in initial position	Clause type	Function
who, whose, which, that	Relative	Post-modify noun phrases
that, wh- words	Noun	Fill subject or object site
subordinating conjunctions	Adverbial	Answers questions such as *why?, when?, how?* and *where?*
as, than	Comparative	Making comparisons
to + verb, present participle, past participle	Non-finite	Can be used in subject, object or complement clause sites. More succinct than finite clauses as they use fewer words

ACTIVITY 1.18 *Answers on page 464.*

Underline the subordinate clauses in the following passage and try to identify their type. Remember that a subordinate clause can:

1 replace a whole clause site: subject, object, complement or adverbial;
2 post-modify a noun phrase;
3 add extra information to a complement, etc.

I shall always remember the day when we arrived at the new house. It was perfect. The weather was good and our spirits were high. Things did not remain the same for long because things were not quite what they seemed. Looking back, I now regret many things.

The first problem was the key which did not fit. Then the removal van did not arrive, leaving us stranded. With no furniture and no boxes, there was nothing for us to do. The fact that we were helpless was not too disturbing, but the sudden change in the weather was since we were stuck outside. The estate agent was sent for and the removal company phoned. Although we could do nothing for the moment, I felt obliged to act, rushing around like a headless chicken while the rain fell steadily.

The time passed slowly. Eventually, someone did bring a new key, so that we could go into the house and wait for the removal van in the dry. We had been assured that it was on its way at last!

The unpredictable day became a peaceful night as we settled into a bare and disorganised house. Our immediate problems were over, but we had not anticipated what was to come next . . .

1.8 Mood

The **MOOD** of a sentence shows the attitude of the speaker to the action or event referred to in the verb phrase: we can **tell** someone something, or **ask** them or **command** them to do something. There are three moods.

Declarative mood

The **DECLARATIVE MOOD** is used for making statements. You can recognise the declarative by checking whether the **subject** comes first in the clause and is followed by the **verb**. If the sentence is complex, the mood is determined by the main clause, so always look at that first.

■   S   P   C   A
(The old man) (was) (content) (in the park).

■   S   P   A   A
(The symphony orchestra) (played) (resoundingly) (in the new concert hall).

Interrogative mood

The **INTERROGATIVE MOOD** is used for addressing questions. You can recognise the interrogative by checking whether the **subject** follows the **auxiliary verbs** *do, have* or *be.*

P　　　　S　　　P　　　A　　　　　A
(Did) (the old man) (sit) (in the park) (contentedly)?
aux　　　　　　　　lex

P　　　　　　　S　　　　　　　P　　　A　　　　A
(Was) (the symphony orchestra) (playing) (well) (in the new concert hall)?
aux　　　　　　　　　　　　　　lex

In **speech**, if the word order is unchanged and INTONATION PATTERNS (the way the voice moves up and down) are used to indicate a question, the mood is said to be **declarative**. The only examples of the **interrogative** mood in which words are not inverted are in sentences in which **wh- words** fill the subject site.

S　　　　P　　　A　　　　　　S　　　　P　　　O
(What) (happens) (next)?　　(Who) (wants) (tea)?

Imperative mood

The IMPERATIVE MOOD is used for addressing commands or orders. You can recognise the imperative by checking that there is **no subject** and that the **verb** is in the **base form** (the unmarked form).

P　　　A　　　　　　　P　　　　A　　　　　　　　　A
(Sit) (in the park).　　(Vote) (in the European elections) (today)!

Sometimes the person addressed is named but not in the traditional subject site of the clause; instead, a VOCATIVE (**voc**) is used. This refers to the person to whom the sentence is addressed. A vocative has two functions:

• to call someone, in order to gain her or his attention;

Joseph, it's tea-time.　　It's your turn on the computer now, *Julie*.

• to address someone, expressing a particular social relationship or a personal attitude.

Waiter, there's a fly in my soup!　　*You fool*, what are you trying to do?

Vocatives are optional and can occur at the beginning, middle or end of the sentence. They can be:

• names: *Andrew*, *Sharon*;
• family titles: *Mummy*, *Dad*, *Aunt*;
• labels which reflect status or respect: *sir*, *madam*, *ladies and gentlemen*;
• professional titles: *nurse*, *doctor*, *teacher*;
• words reflecting evaluative judgements: *pig*, *darling*, *sweetheart*;
• *you* as an impolite term of address.

1.9 Cohesion

Language has a hierarchical structure. So far, you have studied words, phrases, clauses and sentences: these are divided in terms of their RANK. **Words** are described as having a **lower rank** and **sentences** as having a **higher rank**. This is because a sentence may be made up of more than one clause; clauses may be made up of more than one phrase; and phrases may be made up of more than one word.

You now need to think about the ways in which sentences are combined into larger units or DISCOURSE – the linguistic term used to describe spoken or written language that is longer than a sentence in length. In any study of COHESION, you will need to consider the ways in which sentences are linked to create text.

There are five forms of cohesion which it is useful to be able to recognise: lexical cohesion, substitution, ellipsis, referencing, and linking adverbs and conjunctions.

Lexical cohesion

LEXICAL COHESION is a kind of textual linking dependent on a writer or speaker's choice of words. A number of cohesive techniques can be used.

Collocations

In COLLOCATIONS, words are associated within **phrases**. Because they are often well known, they are predictable. Many can be described as IDIOMS and CLICHÉS.

▓ *home and dry   safe and sound   free and easy*

Repetition

In REPETITION either words or phrases are directly repeated or SYNONYMS (related words with a similar meaning) are used.

This little pig went to market,
This little pig stayed at home,
This little pig had roast beef . . .

Superordinates and hyponyms

SUPERORDINATES are **general words**; HYPONYMS are **subdivisions** of the general categorisation. Both these types of words can be used to provide cohesion.

Superordinate: *dog*   Hyponyms: *alsatian, poodle, spaniel*
Superordinate: *crockery*   Hyponyms: *plate, cup, bowl*

Many written or spoken texts have a clear content focus and could therefore be described as SUBJECT SPECIFIC.

I saw a *ship* a-sailing,
    A-sailing on the sea,
And oh, but it was laden
With pretty things for thee.
    There were comfits in the *cabin*,
        And apples in the *hold*.
    The *sails* were made of silk,
And the *masts* were all of gold

Traditional nursery rhyme

Substitution

In linking by SUBSTITUTION, one linguistic item is replaced by a shorter one. The substitution must always occur in the second clause if the meaning is to remain clear. Several parts of a sentence can be replaced.

Noun phrases

Personal pronouns can be substitutes for noun phrases in the subject or object clause sites. They should only be used if the identity of the person or thing is clear.

>   S   P   O   S   P   O
> (Joseph) (loves) (toy trains) (and) (Joseph) (has) (two toy trains).
>   conj

>   S   P   O   S   P   O
> (Joseph) (loves) (toy trains) (and) (*he*) (has) (two *of them*).
>   conj

Either the head or the whole of a noun phrase can also be replaced by the **indefinite pronouns** *one* or *some* or by the **noun phrase** *the same*.

> 'Would you like *a coffee*?' 'I'd love *one*.'
> 'I'd like *the vegetarian lasagne and salad*, please.' 'And I'll have *the same*.'

Equally, **superordinates** and **hyponyms** can be substitutes.

> *The alsatian* was large and the child was obviously afraid of *the dog*.
> *The flowers* were in abundance and people came from miles around to see *the newly blooming roses*.

Verb phrases

A verb phrase or a verb phrase plus object can be replaced by the **auxiliary verb** *do*.

> S   P   O   A   S   P   A
> (I) (*saw*) (*'The Piano'*) (last week). (I) (*did*) (yesterday).

>   S   P   O   S   P   A
> (Julie) (*likes*) (*swimming*) (and) (Mark) (*does*) (too).

Clauses

Clauses can be replaced using *so* as a substitute for a **positive clause** and *not* as a substitute for a **negative clause**.

> '*It's going to be sunny today*?' 'They say *so*.'
> 'I wonder if *I need to buy a new ticket*?' 'The driver said *not*.'

Ellipsis

In ELLIPSIS, part of a sentence is left out. It must be clear what the omitted words are, so that the sentence remains meaningful.

Noun phrases

The head of a simple noun phrase and the head and any modifiers or qualifiers in a complex noun phrase can be omitted.

>   S   P   C   (∅)   P
> (*The buttercups*) (were) (bright yellow) (and) [*the buttercups*] (stretched)
>   conj
>
> A
> (for miles).

>   S   P   A
> (*The black clouds of the impending storm*) (rose) (above us) (and) [*the black*
>   conj

$(\varnothing)$ ^{P} ^{A}
clouds of the impending storm] (loomed) (threateningly).

Verb phrases

Repeated lexical and auxiliary verbs can be omitted from a verb phrase.

The children *ate* jelly and ice-cream and the adults [*ate*] bread and cheese.
We were *shopping* in Cardiff and Lucy was [*shopping*] in Swansea.
We *had* visited the cinema and [*had*] looked around the museum.
They *have been* riding and [*have been*] surfing this week.

Clauses

Whole clauses can be omitted, usually within sentence boundaries rather than outside.

'Who was *playing the clarinet last night*?' 'Susan was [*playing the clarinet last night*].'

Referencing

REFERENCES cannot be interpreted alone because they **point** to something else in a discourse. **Pronouns** (also called SUBSTITUTE WORDS) are often used to make these references, but **comparative structures** expressing particular similarities or differences can also be used.

The girl loved reading, so *she* often visited the library.
The black horse ran fast, but *the white one* was faster.

There are three main kinds of reference.

Anaphoric references

ANAPHORIC REFERENCES point **backwards** in a text. In other words, the reader or listener must refer to a previous reference to make sense of the pronoun or comparative structure used.

The boy broke the window and then *he* ran away.

Cataphoric references

CATAPHORIC REFERENCES point **forwards** in a text. In other words, the reader or listener must refer to a future reference in order to understand the structure used.

This was *the life* – lying in the sun with the waves roaring in the background.
These are *the words* he used: 'I cannot stand it any longer and I'm leaving.'

Exophoric references

EXOPHORIC REFERENCES point **beyond** a text. In other words, the reader or listener must make a connection with something **outside** the discourse.

'I was *this* high then.'   '*That* boat over there is mine.'

A gesture or a context is needed to accompany each of these statements if it is to make sense.

Linking adverbs and conjunctions

LINKING ADVERBS and **CONJUNCTIONS** are joining words that provide links either within a sentence or within the larger context of discourse. There are four main types.

Additive adverbs and conjunctions

ADDITIVE ADVERBS and **CONJUNCTIONS** **add on** information, possibly as an afterthought: *and, furthermore, besides, incidentally*.

Adversative adverbs and conjunctions

ADVERSATIVE ADVERBS and **CONJUNCTIONS** help to create a contrast between the sentence they introduce and the preceding sentence: *yet, however, nevertheless, on the contrary*.

Causal adverbs and conjunctions

CAUSAL ADVERBS and **CONJUNCTIONS** link two clauses or sentences by suggesting that one has been the result of the other: *because, since, therefore, as a result, thus*.

Temporal adverbs and conjunctions

TEMPORAL ADVERBS and **CONJUNCTIONS** create a time link between one clause or sentence and another: *before, while, then, after that, at once, meanwhile*.

2 Phonetics and phonology

2.1 The reason for studying phonetics and phonology

Spoken language is a very important part of any linguistic study because it is so central to our everyday lives. A knowledge of grammar helps linguists to explain some distinctive features of each spoken variety, but it is also necessary to be able to describe the **sounds** of language. **PHONETICS** is the study of **spoken sounds**, and it focuses on the way in which sounds are produced. Instead of considering sound production in general, **PHONOLOGY** focuses on sounds in a particular language. It focuses on the ways in which sounds are combined to produce meaning.

The study of phonetics and phonology gives linguists the means to discuss a range of key areas in spoken language. It helps them focus their analysis in a wide range of contexts by providing an appropriate analytical framework. When studying spoken varieties, language students also need to be able to use appropriate terminology and analytical approaches. A knowledge of phonetics and phonology will help you to study:

- **accent** – social and regional variations in pronunciation can be transcribed exactly;
- **the history of English** – changes in pronunciation can be identified and described accurately;
- **child language** – immature pronunciation can be recorded as children experiment with new words;
- **informal conversation** – changes in speech linked to audience, purpose and context can be discussed precisely;
- **scripted speech** – the realism of speech on television and the radio can be analysed and compared with 'real' speech;
- **other spoken varieties** – key linguistic features of television advertisements, commentaries and public speeches can be identified.

The information here will help you to tackle these areas of your course. It is not necessary to learn the material systematically, but you should be able to use it as it will help you to discuss the sounds and characteristics of spoken English concisely.

2.2 Phonetics

Phonetics is the scientific study of the ways in which humans make sounds. It can be used to analyse any language and it attempts to describe, classify and transcribe **all** possible sounds.

Table 2.1 The International Phonetic Alphabet

	Bilabial	Labiodental	Dental, Alveolar, or Post-alveolar	Retroflex	Palato-alveolar	Palatal	Velar	Uvular	Labial-Palatal	Labial-Velar	Pharyngeal	Glottal
Nasal	m	ɱ	n	ɳ		ɲ	ŋ	ɴ				
Plosive	p b		t d	ʈ ɖ		c ɟ	k ɡ	q ɢ		k͡p ɡ͡b		ʔ
(Median) Fricative	ɸ β	f v	θ ð s z	ʂ ʐ	ʃ ʒ	ç ʝ	x ɣ	χ ʁ		ʍ	ħ ʕ	h ɦ
(Median) Approximant		ʋ	ɹ	ɻ		j	ɰ		ɥ	w		
Lateral Fricative			ɬ ɮ									
Lateral (Approximant)			l	ɭ		ʎ	ʟ					
Trill	ʙ		r					ʀ				
Tap or Flap			ɾ	ɽ				ʀ				
Ejective	p'		t'				k'					
Implosive	ɓ		ɗ				ɠ					
(Median) Click	ʘ		ǀ	ǃ								
Lateral Click			ǁ	ɺ								

(left margin, vertical): CONSONANTS (pulmonic air-stream mechanism) / (non-pulmonic air-stream)

DIACRITICS

- ̥ ° Voiceless n̥ d̥
- ̬ Voiced s̬ t̬
- ʰ Aspirated tʰ
- ̤ Breathy-voiced b̤ a̤
- ̪ Dental t̪
- ̫ Labialized t̫
- ̴ Velarized or Pharyngealized t̴, ɫ
- ̩ Syllabic n̩ l̩
- ̯ or ̑ Simultaneous sf (but see also under the heading Affricates)

- ˔ or ̝ Raised e̝, e̝ , e̝ ̞
- ˕ or ̞ Lowered e̞, e̞, e̞ ̝
- + or ̟ Advanced u̟, ə̟
- - or ̠ Retracted i̠, t̠
- ̈ Centralized ë
- ̃ Nasalized ã
- ˞ ɚ r-coloured a˞
- ː Long aː
- ˑ Half-long aˑ
- ̆ Non-syllabic ŭ
- ̹ More rounded ɔ̹
- ̜ Less rounded y̜

OTHER SYMBOLS

- ɕ, ʑ Alveolo-palatal fricatives
- ʃ, ʒ Palatalized ʃ, ʒ
- ɺ Alveolar fricative trill
- ɺ Alveolar lateral flap
- ɧ Simultaneous ʃ and x
- ʃˢ Variety of ʃ resembling s, etc.
- ɪ = i
- ʊ = u
- ɝ = Variety of ə
- ɚ = r-coloured ə

VOWELS

	Front		Back		Front		Back	
	Unrounded				*Rounded*			
Close	i	ɨ	ɯ		y	ʉ	u	
Half-close	e		ɤ		ø	ɵ	o	
Half-open	ɛ	ə	ʌ		œ		ɔ	
Open	æ a	a	ɑ			ɶ	ɒ	

STRESS, TONE (PITCH)

ˈ stress, placed at beginning of stressed syllable: ˌ secondary stress: ˉ high level pitch, high tone: ˍ low level: ˊ high rising: ˎ low rising: ˋ high falling: ˏ low falling: ˆ rise-fall: ˇ fall-rise.

AFFRICATES can be written as digraphs, as ligatures, or with slur marks; thus ts, tʃ, dʒ: t͡s t͡ʃ d͡ʒ: ʦ tʃ ʤ: ts tʃ dʒ. c, ɟ may occasionally be used for tʃ, dʒ.

PHONETICS AND PHONOLOGY 49

There are three key areas:

- the **way** sounds are made by the vocal organs – ARTICULATION:
- the **physical properties** of sounds as they travel from the mouth to the ear – TRANS-MISSION;
- the way in which the ear and the brain **receive** and **respond** to sounds – RECEPTION.

The main focus in this section will be on **articulation**, since it is useful to understand the way in which the speech organs create sound.

In **Received Pronunciation** (**RP** – see Section 5.2), there are 44 recognisable sounds: 24 consonant sounds and 20 vowel sounds. Because the Roman alphabet used for recording written English does not reflect this range, linguists use a specially designed PHONETIC ALPHABET which tries to classify each variation. The idea of creating a phonetic alphabet was first proposed by Otto Jespersen (1860–1943) in 1886, and the first version of the INTERNATIONAL PHONETIC ALPHABET (**IPA**) was published in 1888. The aim of the system was to create a separate symbol for each sound which could then be used in any language in which the sound appeared. In order to make it accessible, the symbols of the Roman alphabet were used as often as possible. DIACRITICS – marks or points slightly altering the sound quality of the original symbol – were added to some symbols to give a greater range of sounds. Alongside these some new symbols were created. The IPA has been altered and extended several times (most recently in 1989) but is still used by linguists throughout the world.

Table 2.1 records all the IPA symbols: it classifies each sound according to the way that it is physically produced. The list of diacritics and other symbols provides linguists with the means to record all kinds of variations in the sound quality. In your study of language, you are unlikely to need such a wide range of symbols: this section will therefore introduce you to the basic sounds and symbols that will be useful in recording the sounds of English.

The symbols of the International Phonetic Alphabet record the 'sound' of words exactly. They allow linguists to distinguish between words that **look** similar in traditional orthography, but that **sound** quite different. Words transcribed phonetically are enclosed in square brackets to show that the focus is on the **way** that sounds are made.

cough [kɒf]	enough [ɪnʌf]
dough [dəʊ]	through [θruː]

The articulators – the organs of speech

To understand **how** we speak, linguists need to know something about the organs involved in the production of sound and the way in which these move. When we make sounds, we alter the flow of breath through the mouth and nose by moving the tongue and other organs related to the production of sound. By describing the process involved in the creation of each sound, linguists are able to classify and analyse the particular sounds making up a language. Figure 2.1 identifies the main ARTICULATORS.

Air passes from the LUNGS through the LARYNX and into the VOCAL TRACT. Here the VOCAL CORDS produce two kinds of sounds. When spread apart, the air can pass between them without obstruction to make sounds which are described as VOICELESS. If you place your fingers on your larynx and say *pick* and *fish* you will feel no vibrations. When the vocal cords are drawn together, however, the air from the lungs has to push them apart, creating a vibration. This produces a VOICED sound – try saying *big* and *visit*. The opening between the vocal cords is called the GLOTTIS – when the cords are apart, the glottis is said to be **open**; when they are pressed together, the glottis is said to be **closed**.

Figure 2.1 The organs of speech

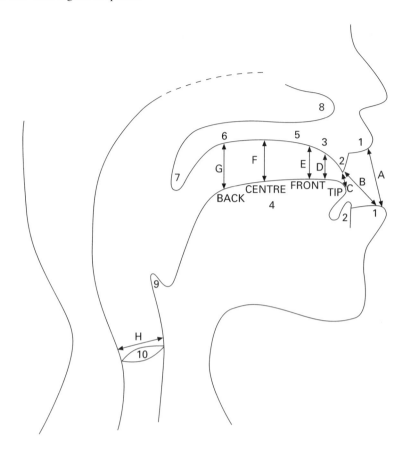

Key to the organs of speech

1 lips
2 teeth
3 alveolar ridge
4 tongue
5 hard palate
6 soft palate (velum)
7 uvula
8 nasal cavity
9 epiglottis
10 vocal cords

Key to the places of articulation

A bilabial
B labio-dental
C dental
D alveolar
E palato-alveolar
F palatal
G velar
H glottal

Having passed through the vocal cords, the air is then affected by the speech organs. The TONGUE, SOFT PALATE and LIPS, for instance, move to produce a range of sounds. The resonance of these sounds is influenced by the shape of the ORAL and NASAL SPACES through which the air passes.

Some of the articulators, like the UPPER TEETH, the ALVEOLAR RIDGE and the HARD PALATE, are described as **passive** because they do not move. Other articulators are described as **active** because they move to change the spaces through which the air passes. The **soft palate** in normal breathing is lowered so that air can pass through the nasal cavity easily. In speech, however, it can be raised to force air through the mouth;

lowered to allow air to escape through the mouth and nose; or lowered with the mouth closed so that air is forced through the nose. The LIPS may be closed or held open in a range of positions. The JAW controls the size of the gap between the teeth and the position of the lips. The TONGUE is the most important vocal organ – because it is so flexible, it helps to create a wide range of sounds.

ACTIVITY 2.1

In English, many consonants (all the letters of the alphabet except a, e, i, o and u) form pairs of sounds in which one is voiced and the other voiceless. The distinction between voiced and voiceless sounds is important because it enables us to distinguish between words that would otherwise be phonetically the same.

Read through the list of consonantal sounds (IPA symbols are enclosed in square brackets) and accompanying words. Try singing each one aloud and compile a list of those that can be sung and those that cannot. Then create pairs by deciding which voiceless sounds can be made into voiced sounds by doing nothing but opening the vocal cords.

1	thth [θ] – thank;	6	nnnn [n] – neck;
2	ssss [s] – snake;	7	mmmm [m] – monkey;
3	vvvv [v] – vase;	8	zhzh [ʒ] – treasure;
4	zzzz [z] – zoo;	9	ffff [f] – fast;
5	shsh [ʃ] – shoe;	10	thth [ð] – there.

COMMENTARY

To sing aloud, the vocal cords must vibrate. Any consonant that can be sung is therefore likely to be a voiced sound. From your experimentation, you should have found that the following consonants are voiced: [v], [z], [n], [m], [ʒ], [ð]. The sounds in your other list are all voiceless consonants: [ʃ], [s], [f] and [θ]. By changing the voiceless sounds into voiced sounds, it is possible to recognise pairs: [ʃ] → [ʒ]; [s] → [z]; [f] → [v]; and [θ] → [ð]. In some examples, the sound of two words may be almost identical except for the fact that a particular consonant is voiced or voiceless – the distinction in sound can help us to recognise semantic differences.

> sue (voiceless) → zoo (voiced)   wreath (voiceless) → wreathe (voiced)
> fast (voiceless) → vast (voiced)

The basic division of sounds into voiced and voiceless depending on the position of the vocal cords is one of ways in which linguists can classify speech sounds. But each of the voiced and voiceless sounds is quite different from the others, so linguists use other methods of description to categorise sounds more precisely.

Consonants

The place of articulation

In addition to dividing consonant sounds (sounds made by completely or partially blocking the flow of air) into the categories of voiced and voiceless, they can be classified by the speech organs used to articulate them. The PLACE OF ARTICULATION describes where the airstream is stopped in the mouth. To describe the place of articulation, linguists need to be able to refer to the main articulators named in Figure 2.1. The following list records the speech organs used in the production of RP consonants.

As you read, experiment with the sounds, thinking about the position of the speech organs and whether the vocal cords are apart (voiceless) or together (voiced).

Bilabials

BILABIALS are sounds formed using both lips.

[p]	*p*ig	(voiceless)	[b]	*b*ig	(voiced)
[m]	*m*ilk	(voiced)			

The place of articulation for the sound [w] in words like *well* can be described as bilabial, but some linguists class it as a SEMI-VOWEL.

Labiodentals

LABIODENTALS are sounds formed using the lower lip and upper teeth.

[f]	*f*lower	(voiceless)	[v]	*v*ase	(voiced)

Dentals

DENTALS are sounds formed by placing the tip of the tongue behind the upper front teeth or between the teeth.

[θ]	*th*in	(voiceless)	[ð]	*th*ere	(voiced)
	tee*th*			tee*th*e	

Alveolars

ALVEOLARS are sounds formed by placing the tip of the tongue on the alveolar ridge just behind the upper teeth.

[t]	*t*in	(voiceless)	[d]	*d*in	(voiced)
[s]	*s*in	(voiceless)	[z]	*z*ip	(voiced)
[n]	*n*ip	(voiced)	[l]	*l*ip	(voiced)

Because the tongue is curled back when the consonant [r] is articulated, it does not actually touch the alveolar ridge. Linguists sometimes therefore describe [r] as a POST-ALVEOLAR SOUND.

[r]	*r*ip	(voiced)

Palato-alveolars

PALATO-ALVEOLARS are sounds formed by placing the tongue at the front of the hard palate near the alveolar ridge.

[ʃ]	*sh*in	(voiceless)	[tʃ]	*ch*ips	(voiceless)
	*s*ugar			*ch*in	
[ʒ]	plea*s*ure	(voiced)	[dʒ]	tru*dge*	(voiced)
				*g*em	

Palatal

A PALATAL is a sound formed by putting the tongue against the middle of the palate.

[j]	*y*ou	(voiced)
	*y*et	

Velars

VELARS are sounds formed using the soft palate and the tongue.

[k]	*k*ick	(voiceless)	[g]	*g*et	(voiced)
	*c*ar				
[ŋ]	si*ng*	(voiced)			
	to*ng*ue				

Glottals

GLOTTALS are two sounds that can be produced without using the tongue or other articulators. The glottis can be opened so that there is no obstruction to the air in the mouth.

[h]	*h*igh	(voiceless glottal)
	*h*orse	

Alternatively, the glottis can be briefly closed completely and then released.

[ʔ]	bo*tt*le	(as pronounced with a Cockney accent)
	bi*tt*er	

The manner of articulation

Having classified sounds as voiced or voiceless and by the place of articulation, linguists also refer to the MANNER OF ARTICULATION or the **way** in which consonants are produced. This enables them to distinguish between sounds that although quite different may be produced in the same part of the mouth and that may both be voiced or voiceless.

[d] and [z] are both voiced alveolars
[b] and [m] are both voiced bilabials

To describe the manner of articulation, linguists focus on what happens to the airstream after it has passed through the vocal cords. It may be stopped, partly blocked or allowed to move freely. Sounds that are completely blocked in the mouth are called STOPS; sounds in which the airstream is uninterrupted or only partly interrupted in the mouth are called CONTINUANTS. All sounds are either stops or continuants.

The following list records what happens to the airstream once it has entered the mouth. As you read, experiment with the sounds, thinking about the passage of air, the position of the speech organs, and whether the vocal cords are together or apart.

Plosives

PLOSIVES are sounds produced by stopping the airstream. A blockage may be created by the movement of one articulator against another, or by the movement of two articulators against each other. The air trapped by the blockage is then released suddenly, making a noise loud enough to be heard.

[p]   [b]   [t]   [d]   [k]   [g]

The consonants [p], [t] and [k] are always voiceless; the others are usually voiced, but may be only partly voiced when they occur in initial or final position (the beginning and end of words). The glottal stop [ʔ] is also a plosive, but it is less important than the others because it is usually just an alternative pronunciation for [p], [t] and [k].

Fricatives

FRICATIVES are sounds produced by a partial blockage of the airstream resulting in friction as the air is forced through the small gap. Fricatives are continuants: it is possible to continue making each sound until all the air in the lungs has been exhausted.

▓ [f]   [v]   [θ] (*thing*)   [ð] (*this*)   [s]   [z]   [ʃ]   [ʒ] (*pleasure*)   [h]

Other than the glottal [h], the fricatives in the English language are paired according to their place of articulation. For each type, there is one voiced and one voiceless consonant: the labiodental [f] is voiceless while [v] is voiced; the dental [θ] is voiceless while [ð] is voiced; the alveolar [s] is voiceless while [z] is voiced; and the palato-alveolar [ʃ] is voiceless while [ʒ] is voiced.

The consonant [h] alters depending upon the vowel it precedes. Some linguists therefore describe it phonetically as a **VOICELESS VOWEL**. Nevertheless, it behaves like a consonant because it almost always precedes a vowel. When it appears between voiced sounds, it too is voiced.

Affricates

AFFRICATES are sounds produced by combining a brief blockage of the airstream with an obstructed release which causes some friction. Like the plosives, these are called stops.

▓ [tʃ] (*church*)   [dʒ] (*judge*)

Nasals

NASALS are sounds produced when the soft palate is lowered and the airstream is forced into the nasal cavity. Although the airstream continues to flow in the production of these sounds, they are called stops because a blockage in the mouth prevents air escaping orally.

▓ [m]   [n]   [ŋ]

While [m] and [n] frequently occur in the word-initial position, [ŋ] cannot. In RP, if [ŋ] is at the end of a morpheme, it usually occurs without a following [g].

▓ banger (ba*ng* + er) = [bæŋə]

If it is in the middle of a morpheme, it is usually pronounced.

▓ bingo = [bɪŋgəʊ]

In the word-final position, it is rarely followed by [g] except in some regional accents.

▓ bring = [brɪŋ] RP; [brɪŋg] regional

Laterals

[l] can be described as a **LATERAL** consonant because the passage of air through the mouth is along the sides of the tongue rather than along the centre. This is caused by a blockage created where the centre or front of the tongue makes contact with the front of the alveolar ridge behind the upper front teeth.

The consonant [l] sounds different depending upon its position in a word: [l] before a vowel sounds quite different to [l] in other positions.

▓ *l*eg, *l*og, *l*ag (clear *l*)   mea*l*, ti*ll*, betraya*l* (dark *l*)

Varying pronunciations of a consonant are called **ALLOPHONES**. Another allophone occurs when [l] follows [p] or [k] at the beginning of a stressed syllable – in words like *place* or *klaxon* the consonant is not voiced as it is in other words.

Approximants or frictionless consonants

The sounds [r], [w] and [j] are described as APPROXIMANTS or FRICTIONLESS CONTINU-ANTS because although they are consonants they do not adopt the articulator positions of the plosives, nasals or fricatives.

The consonant [r] is articulated with the tip of the tongue near the alveolar area, but the tip never actually touches the ridge as it would in the production of [t] or [d]. The tongue is usually curled backwards, and this positions it slightly further back than in the alveolar sounds – [r] is therefore often described as a POST-ALVEOLAR APPROXI-MANT. If [r] is preceded by [p], [t] or [k], it becomes voiceless.

■ tray [treɪ]   print [prɪnt]

If it is in the initial position or is preceded by anything other than [p], [t] or [k], it is voiced.

■ read [riːd]   abrasive [əbreɪsɪv]

If a word is spelt with a final *r* or if the letter *r* is followed by a consonant, the *r* is not pronounced.

■ car [kɑː]   bears [beəs]

Some dialects pronounce [r] in the final position and before a final consonant – these are called **rhotic accents**. RP, however, is a **non-rhotic accent**.

The consonants [w] and [j] are sometimes described as SEMI-VOWELS. Although phonetically they may sound like a vowel, phonologically they are consonants, only occurring before vowels. They are produced when the tongue moves from one position to another, and are therefore sometimes called GLIDES.

Describing consonants

By using these three kinds of classification, it is possible to define the nature of a conso-nant very precisely. Linguists can record the exact production of a sound by describing:

1   the **positions of the vocal cords**: together or open;
2   the **place of articulation**: bilabial, labiodental, dental, alveolar, post-alveolar, palato-alveolar, palatal, velar or glottal;
3   the **manner of articulation**: plosive, fricative, affricate, nasal, lateral, approximant.

■ [d]   voiced alveolar plosive   [v]   voiceless labiodental fricative
  [w]   voiceless bilabial approximant

ACTIVITY 2.2   Answers on page 464.

Use the following exercises to check your understanding of the phonetic nature of conso-nants.

1   Say the following words and work out the place of articulation for the initial sound in each word:

a	fox	d	thing
b	night	e	shop
c	music	f	king

Table 2.2 The classification of consonants

	Manner of articulation											
	Plosives		Fricatives		Affricates		Nasals		Laterals		Approximants	
Place of articulation	VL	V	VL	V	VL	V	VL	V	VL	V	VL	V
Bilabial	p	b						m				w
Labiodental			f	v								
Dental			θ	ð								
Alveolar	t	d	s	z				n		l		
Post-alveolar												r
Palato-alveolar			ʃ	ʒ	tʃ	dʒ						
Palatal												j
Velars	k	g						ŋ				
Glottal	ʔ		h									

2   Say the following words and try to decide whether the final consonant is voiced or voiceless:

  a   shi<u>p</u>   d   teethi<u>ng</u>
  b   dit<u>ch</u>   e   fal<u>l</u>
  c   li<u>d</u>   f   nu<u>dge</u>

3   Define the following consonants by describing the position of the vocal cords and the place and manner of articulation. Use Table 2.2 to check your description.
  [k] voiceless velar plosive

  a   [g]   d   [p]
  b   [ʃ]   e   [m]
  c   [v]   f   [h]

Vowels

Pure vowels

Vowel sounds are produced by the **free flow of air** and the position of the **tongue**, which influences the shape of the space the air has to pass through. The method of description used for consonants needs to be adapted – it is not appropriate to talk about the place and manner of articulation. Instead linguists have to ask themselves three key questions about a vowel sound.

How high is the tongue?

The tongue's height may be described as CLOSE (**high**), HALF-CLOSE, OPEN (**low**) or HALF-OPEN – these relate to the closeness of the tongue to the roof of the mouth.

  [iː]   close vowel   [æ]   open vowel
  [ʊ]   half-close   [ɜː] half-open

Which part of the tongue is raised or lowered?

By raising or lowering different parts of the tongue different sounds are made. The parts of the tongue involved in making vowel sounds are the **FRONT**, **CENTRE** and **BACK**.

| [æ] | front | [ʌ] | centre |
| [ɑː] | back | | |

What is the position of the lips?

As well as defining vowels in terms of tongue height and the part of the tongue involved, linguists have to consider the shape of the lips. There are three main positions involved – **ROUNDED LIPS**, such that the corners of the lips come together and the lips are pushed forward; **SPREAD LIPS**, such that the corners of the lips move away from each other, as they do for a smile; **NEUTRAL**, in which the lips are not noticeably rounded or spread.

| [uː] | rounded | [ɜː] | neutral |
| [iː] | spread | | |

Vowels that are not marked with diacritics are described as **SHORT VOWELS**: [ɪ], [e], [æ], [ʌ], [ɒ], [ə] and [ʊ]. The **LONG VOWELS** are marked with diacritics /ː/, which denote length: [iː], [ɑː], [ɔː], [ɜː] and [uː]. It is important to remember, however, that the length of all vowels in English varies according to the context.

Describing pure vowels

By using these three areas of classification, it is possible to define the nature of a pure vowel sound precisely. Linguists can record the exact production of a sound by describing:

1 the **height of the tongue**;
2 the **part of the tongue**;
3 the **shape of the lips**.

[e] pet
   The **front** of the tongue is between **half-open** and **half-close** position with the lips **neutral**.

[ɔː] roar
   The **back** of the tongue is between **half-open** and **half-close** position with the lips **rounded**.

[iː] sleep
   The **front** of the tongue is raised in a **high** or **close** position with the lips **spread**.

Because vowel sounds are so variable, linguists need some points of reference. The **CARDINAL VOWELS** are not 'real' vowels, but are inflexible standards against which the vowel sounds of everyday usage are set. These eight sounds are formed using clearly contrasting tongue heights and parts of the tongue and are therefore often called **REFERENCE VOWELS**. Figure 2.2 records the way in which these eight key vowels are produced – linguists learn to make and recognise these vowels so that they can use them as a norm. By starting from the clearly defined positions of the cardinal vowels, they are then able to describe other vowels, comparing their production with those already marked on the chart.

Figure 2.2 The eight primary cardinal vowels

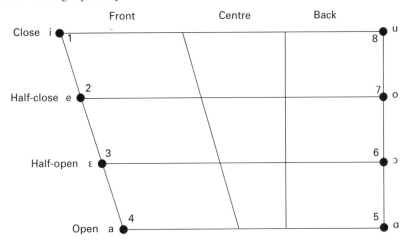

The cardinal vowels have been chosen as reference points because they occur at clear intervals around the chart, but many vowels do not fall so neatly into categories. In regional accents, for instance, it is usually the vowels that are noticeably different from RP, rather than the consonants. The same chart allows linguists to define the exact nature of an individual's vowel sounds by placing them at **any** appropriate point. For instance, a vowel sound may lie between half-close and close or between centre and back rather than at an exact intersection (see Figure 2.3).

Figure 2.3 Tongue positions for the pure vowels in English

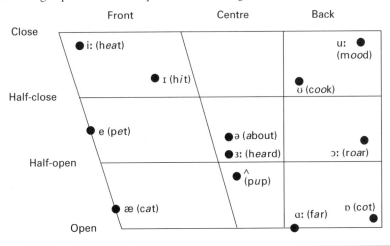

ACTIVITY 2.3 Answers on page 464.

Define the following cardinal vowels by describing:
  a   the height of the tongue;
  b   the part of the tongue raised or lowered.
  c   the shape of the lips.

1 [i]   2 [ɔ]   3 [a]   4 [o]   5 [u]

Table 2.3 The classification of pure vowels

Vowel sound	Height of tongue	Part of tongue	Lip shape	Length
iː	Close	Front	Spread	Long
ɪ	Just above half-close	Front	Loosely spread	Short
e	Between half-open and half-close	Front	Neutral	Short
æ	Just above open	Front	Neutral	Short
ʌ	Just below half-open	Centre	Neutral	Short
ɑː	Open	Back	Neutral	Long
ɒ	Open	Back	Slightly rounded	Short
ɔː	Between half-open and half-close	Back	Moderately rounded	Long
ə	Between half-open and half-close	Centre	Neutral	Short
ɜː	Between half-open and half-close	Centre	Neutral	Long
ʊ	Just above half-close	Back	Rounded	Short
uː	Close	Back	Closely rounded	Long

ACTIVITY 2.4   *Answers on page 464.*

Define the following IPA vowels by describing:
  a   the height of the tongue;
  b   the section involved in production of the sound;
  c   the shape of the lips.
Use Table 2.3 to check your description.

  [ɜː]   heard [hɜːd]
    The centre of the tongue is between half-open and half-close position with the
    lips in a neutral position; it is different from the eight cardinal vowels because
    the centre of the tongue rather than the front or back is raised.

1 [ʌ] abrupt   2 [iː] tree   3 [uː] beauty   4 [æ] camp

Compound vowels

Some vowels are described as COMPOUND VOWELS or DIPHTHONGS. These glide from
one vowel sound to another and involve a change in the position of the tongue – the
first part of the sound is always stronger than the second. Linguists describe these
vowels as either closing or centring, and this process can also be summarised in a chart
(see Figure 2.4).

Figure 2.4 Tongue positions for the compound vowels in English

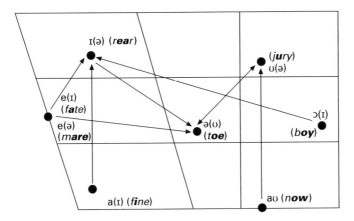

CENTRING DIPHTHONGS end in a [ə].

ear	[ɪə]	air	[eə]
cure	[ʊə]		

CLOSING DIPHTHONGS end in either [ɪ] or [ʊ]:

late	[eɪ]	home	[əʊ]
time	[aɪ]	cow	[aʊ]
voice	[ɔɪ]		

Using Figure 2.4, linguists can describe the ways in which these sounds are made.

[aɪ] high
The **front** of the tongue is just above **open** position, moving towards a **closed** position.

[ʊə] tour
The **back** of the tongue is just above **half-close** position, moving towards the **centre**.

ACTIVITY 2.5   *Answers on pages 464–5.*

By referring to Table 2.4, describe the following diphthongs in more detail.

[ɪə] fear
The front and then centre of the tongue move from just above half-close to between half-open and half-close position with the lips in a neutral position; it is a centring diphthong.

1 [eɪ] great   2 [əʊ] mode   3 [ʊə] cure   4 [aʊ] brow

Table 2.4 The classification of compound vowels

Vowel sound	Height of tongue	Part of tongue	Lip shape	Type
eɪ	Between half-open and half-close to just above half-close	Front	Neutral to loosely spread	Closing
aɪ	Just above open to just above half-close	Front	Neutral to loosely spread	Closing
ɔɪ	Between half-open and half-close to just above half-close	Back to front	Moderately rounded to loosely spread	Closing
aʊ	Open to just above half-close	Back	Neutral to rounded	Closing
əʊ	Between half-open and half-close to just above half-close	Centre to back	Neutral to rounded	Closing
ɪə	Just above half-close to between half-open and half-close	Front to centre	Loosely spread to neutral	Centring
eə	Between half-open and half-close and then lowered slightly	Front to centre	Neutral	Centring
ʊə	Just above half-close to between half-open and half-close	Back to centre	Rounded to neutral	Centring

2.3 Phonology

Ultimately, **phonetics** deals only with the physical properties of speech sounds – what sounds are. Linguists, however, also need to consider the meaningful combinations of sounds in spoken language. **PHONOLOGY** is the study of the sound system of a particular language and its specific organisation. It considers distinctive patterns of sound so that general statements can be made about a language system. Its focus is on the **function** of sounds – that is, their role in expressing meaning. Because of this it is sometimes called **functional phonetics**.

In a study of phonetics, the focus is on the pronunciation of sounds and on the way each sound is produced. Phonology is more interested in the way in which different sounds or **phonemes** change meaning.

The International Phonetic Alphabet includes a wide range of symbols because it aims to convey **all** sound. A phonetic transcription using IPA symbols indicates the physical details of pronunciation – it is not interested in the role of sounds in conveying meaning. Linguists use square brackets to distinguish between traditional orthography and phonetic symbols.

■ [t] a voiceless alveolar plosive   [d] a voiced alveolar plosive

A phonemic transcription, on the other hand, would use fewer IPA symbols and diacritics because it focuses on speech sounds which create meaning in a particular language. This kind of transcription is often described as **broad** – it focuses only on phonemes that convey different meanings, not on the physical process involved in the production of sounds.

> /t/, /d/ phonemes that change **meaning** – /ten/ can be contrasted in meaning with /den/

Phonemic transcriptions are marked by slant brackets to distinguish them from traditional orthography. They are not meant to be a faithful representation of pronunciation. The transcriptions in this book are **phonemic** and therefore use **slant brackets**. **Square brackets** are used only where the focus is on details of **articulation**.

The phonemic symbols needed to transcribe the sounds of English are as shown in Table 2.5. These symbols allow linguists to distinguish between the spoken and written word. They are a useful means of transcribing things like the immature pronunciation of a child or the regional pronunciation of a particular dialect. They will be used in the rest of this section to describe the sounds that make up the English language.

Table 2.5 Phonemic symbols

Consonants

/p/	pit, top		/ʃ/	shin, bush
/b/	ban, rub		/ʒ/	beige, treasure
/t/	ten, step		/tʃ/	cheap, latch
/d/	din, bad		/dʒ/	jeep, judge
/k/	cave, scar		/m/	mat, small
/g/	gave, big		/n/	net, snow
/s/	sit, loss		/ŋ/	bring, singer
/z/	zoo, easy		/h/	hit, behind
/f/	fan, rough		/w/	wit, one
/v/	van, love		/j/	yet, cure
/θ/	thin, athlete		/r/	rat, bran
/ð/	this, either		/l/	lot, pill

Vowels I – pure vowels

/æ/	cat, sat		/ɔ:/	port, talk
/ɑ:/	bar, heart		/ʊ/	put, wood
/i:/	beat, key		/u:/	boot, rude
/ɪ/	bit, busy		/ʌ/	but, blood
/e/	bet, many		/ɜ:/	bird, word
/ɒ/	pot, want		/ə/	about

Vowels II – diphthongs

/eɪ/	bay, late		/əʊ/	boat, know
/aɪ/	buy, die		/ɪə/	beer, here
/ɔɪ/	boy, noise		/eə/	bare, pear
/aʊ/	pout, cow		/ʊə/	jury, cure

Segmental phonology

The focus so far has been on individual sounds, but in spoken language sounds rarely occur on their own. In continuous speech, some sounds are elided, others merge into each other, and some are modified by the sounds that come before and after them – the boundaries are not distinct.

SEGMENTAL PHONOLOGY involves analysing the distinctive units or **phonemes** of speech – it is a means of reducing the large number of possible sounds to a set which have a clear function in a particular language. It is possible to find out which sound units or phonemes have a distinct function in English by considering the ways in which the substitution of certain phonemes in words changes the meaning. MINIMAL PAIRS are words that are identical in form except for one phoneme which occurs in the same position – they are words differentiated by each having only one sound different from the others.

▨ tar, bar, far   hike, hide, hire   bit, beat, bought, bat

In the first example, the phonemes /t/, /b/ and /f/ are used to change the meaning; in the second /k/, /d/ and /r/ and in the third the /ɪ/, /iː/, /ɔː/ and /æ/ perform the same function. The words in each list make up a MINIMAL SET.

Analysis of minimal pairs and sets enables linguists to establish patterns of the types of sound combinations possible in English. When a change in the pronunciation of a word results in a change of meaning, the two different segments can be described as two different phonemes. A change in the phonetic form, however, does not always result in a change in meaning. The substitution of a **glottal stop** for a medial position /t/, for example, does not create a new word.

▨ bottle [bɒʔl]

The glottal stop in English is therefore not a phoneme.

ACTIVITY 2.6   *Answers on page 465.*

The words below are minimal pairs which show that the phonemes /d/ and /t/ in English contrast in initial, medial and final positions.

Initial: *dot/tot*
Medial: *medal/metal*
Final: *cad/cat*

Find similar minimal pairs for the following phonemes in initial, medial and final positions.

1	/k/ and /g/	3	/s/ and /ʃ/
2	/m/ and /n/	4	/b/ and /v/

In studying the phonological properties of continuous speech, linguists have established certain distinctive features.

Assimilation

ASSIMILATION describes the process in which two phonemes occurring together are influenced by each other, making the sounds more alike. For example, a vowel preceding a nasal sound like [m] or [n] will become more nasal itself (indicated on a transcription with a diacritic ˜).

▨ p[ɪ̃]n pin   p[æ̃]n pan

Assimilation may alter the place of articulation, so an alveolar /t/ may become more like a dental when followed by a dental fricative /θ/:

■ that theatre

The position of the vocal cords can also be assimilated: a voiced plosive like /d/ can be devoiced (losing its voiced qualities) before a voiceless sound like /s/:

■ cold soup

Assimilation is particularly noticeable in conversational speech where utterances are unplanned and exchanges tend to be fast.

■ I can go   /aɪ kæn gəʊ/ → [aɪkəŋgəʊ]

In the example here, the pronunciation of the alveolar [n] and the velar [g] move closer together and the resulting sound is more like the velar [ŋ] + [g] rather than [n] + [g].

Some assimilations are inevitable and they should not automatically be seen as examples of lazy pronunciation. In segments where all speakers assimilate the sounds of particular phonemes, there is usually a physical reason for doing so. In other cases, individual speakers may modify sounds without a valid practical reason. While linguists see such modification as evidence that English is a living language, changing according to user, use and context, some people find such assimilation unacceptable.

ACTIVITY 2.7   *Answers on page 465.*

Read the following utterances and mark the points at which assimilation might occur. Try to record the changed sounds using a broad phonemic transcription.

look behind you   [bɪhaɪndʒ uː]
   The word-final /d/ becomes palato-alveolar affricate /dʒ/ before palatal
   approximant /j/, which disappears.

1   is the train coming?
2   what do you want?
3   he sails ships

Elision

In deliberate and controlled pronunciation the speaker will articulate all the sounds in a word, but in conversational speech many are often omitted. Just as assimilation changes the pronunciation of words at boundaries, so too does ELISION (the complete disappearance of a sound).

me and you   /miː ænd juː/ → [miːənjuː]
   The final /d/ phoneme has been lost and the stressed vowel phoneme /æ/ has
   been reduced to /ə/, the unstressed vowel sound called **schwa**.

It is possible to summarise the main kinds of elision in English spoken with an RP accent.

Initial-position /h/

An initial-position /h/ is often elided in informal speech.

■ what's the height?   [wɒtsðiaɪt]

Alveolar plosive followed by continuant consonant

Words ending with an alveolar plosive preceded by a continuant consonant (one which can be sung, like /s/, /f/, /ʃ/, /n/, /l/, /z/, /ð/, /v/) followed by a word with a consonant in the initial position, will often elide the final /t/ or /d/.

▪ next day [neksdeɪ]   last week [lɑːswiːk]

Plosive or affricate followed by /t/ or /d/

Words ending with a plosive or an affricate followed by a /t/ or /d/ will also often elide the final phoneme.

▪ pub door [pʌdɔː]   tick-tock [tɪtɒk]

/t/ or /d/ followed by /t/ or /d/

If one word ends with /t/ or /d/ and the next starts with /t/ or /d/, one consonant is elided to simplify pronunciation.

▪ you've got to [gɒtə]   sat down [sædaʊn]

Verbal negative contractions

In verbal negative contractions, the final /t/ is elided if the next word begins with another consonant.

▪ I can't come [kɑːnkʌm]

Liaison

This process also changes the pronunciation of words at boundary points, a change called LIAISON. A linking /r/ is inserted between words in continuous speech that end with a vowel or semi-vowel like the letter *w* and that are followed by another word with a vowel in the initial position.

▪ law and order /lɔː ænd ɔːdə/ → [lɔːrənɔːdə]

In some examples of liaison, the written form of an utterance does contain an *r*.

▪ here and there [hɪərənðeə]   the far east [ðəfɑːriːst]

In most, however, the inserted /r/ is no more than a vocalised link.

Reduction

REDUCTION tends to occur in monosyllabic function words or in unstressed syllables of words with more than one syllable. Pronunciation is again changed, but no longer at the boundaries of words – front and back vowels are replaced by weak central vowels like /ə/.

▪ of /ɒv/ → /əv/   have /hæv/ → /(h)əv/

ACTIVITY 2.8   *Answers on page 465.*

Identify any examples of assimilation, elision, liaison or reduction in the following utterances, and record the effects created in a broad phonemic transcription.

   I can't wait

elision of alveolar plosive /t/ in a negative contraction preceding the consonant /w/ [kɑːnweɪt]

1 she should have gone home
2 she'll be here in an hour or two
3 the train came in late

All these segmental features are common in connected speech – without them our spoken language would seem artificial in any but the most formal contexts. Broad transcriptions will usually identify only the most significant examples of assimilation, elision, liaison and reduction at word boundaries where pronunciation changes.

Non-segmental phonology – prosodics and paralinguistics

While segmental phonology focuses on segments (consonants and vowels) of spoken language, **PROSODICS** is interested in larger units – the form and function of connected utterances of speech. It is a study of the ways in which speakers:

- organise utterances into meaningful units, just as paragraphing and punctuation do in written language;
- make words more striking and memorable;
- use varying intonation patterns to convey different attitudes;
- change rhythm, pitch, pace and volume to express different moods and levels of interest in a subject;
- draw attention to key sections of an utterance by ordering clause elements in a certain way and by keeping new information distinct from things that are already known;
- interact with each other – signalling the end of turns, latching on, overlapping and so on.

Non-segmental phonology also includes a study of **PARALINGUISTICS**. This focuses on the way in which facial expressions and body language can be used alongside spoken utterances. Linguists are interested in the way smiles, frowns or gestures can either support or challenge the meaning conveyed by language. Vocalisations like giggles, sighs and coughs can also contribute to the meaning system.

In studying non-segmental phonology, linguists have established certain distinctive features.

Intonation

INTONATION describes variations in the sound quality of a speaker's voice. Because speakers rarely stay at one level, linguists listen to the **changes** in TONE. Tone can be described as **LEVEL** or **MOVING**, and moving tones can be identified as **RISING** (´) or **FALLING** (`). In transcription or a written record of spoken language, these variations can be marked with the appropriate symbols either at the beginning of the word or over the main vowel.

Level tone: yes or -yes
Falling tone: yes or `yes
Rising tone: yes or ´yes

Each variation performs a certain linguistic function: if you mark moving tones on a transcription, it is important to comment on their purpose. A level tone tends to be used in more restricted situations, and often conveys a feeling of routine – for example, calling out names from a list. Often a falling tone implies a sense of finality, while a rising tone suggests that something more is to follow. The mood of a sentence also affects the tone: interrogatives tend to use a rising tone, while declaratives adopt a falling tone.

▪ Statement: you want an àpple   Question: you want an ápple

Rising and falling tones can be combined to create more subtle effects too: a fall-rise pattern (ˇ) can suggest limited agreement of some kind, or can express surprise or disbelief; a rise-fall (ˆ) pattern can convey strong feelings of approval, disapproval or surprise.

▌ Fall-rise: pŏssibly or ˇpossibly
▌ Rise-fall: wêll or ˆwell

Intonation patterns can also mark GRAMMATICAL BOUNDARIES at the end of a phrase or clause. They help listeners to recognise the end of an utterance, just as punctuation in written discourse divides language into meaningful units. By drawing attention to key words, intonation can **distinguish between new and old information** in a speech encounter.

▌ wé saw a good film yesterday   Focus: the people involved
▌ we saw a góod film yesterday   Focus: the nature of the film

Intonation changes can structure a discourse by marking the **end** of a story on the television news or by hinting at scores in the football results. (Pauses (.) are discussed on page 71.)

▌ Cardiff City 2́ (.) Bristol Rovers 1̀
▌ And fìnally . . .

Intonation contributes to the **rhythm** of utterances.

▌ Humpty Dúmpty sat on the wàll,
▌ Humpty Dúmpty had a great fàll

Distinctive intonation patterns can make the spoken language of particular kinds of speakers easily identifiable. Preachers, 'rag and bone' men and auctioneers, for instance, each have a distinctive spoken style by which they can be immediately recognised.

▌ Evening Pòst   (street newspaper vendor)   lèt us pray . . .   (preacher)
▌ góing (.) góing (.) gòne   (auctioneer)

The PITCH of an utterance is closely related to intonation. It may be high, low or anywhere in between. Transcriptions use a variety of methods to record significant pitch changes.

• Solid lines at low, mid and high points mark the pitch, and dotted lines mark transition points.

▌ you know I don't like going there

• The symbols for different tones (falling, rising, and so on) are used at various heights to mark low, mid and high pitches.

▌ -you ´know I don't like goingˎ there

• Arrows are placed before and after the word in which movements up or down occur.

▌ you ↑know↑ I don't like going ↓there↓

The VOLUME of an utterance will often change in conjunction with variations in intonation and pitch. Usually, the louder the utterance, the more important the speaker considers the meaning to be. On a transcription, details about volume are recorded in marginal notes, with the start and end of the feature marked by inverted commas (*I 'will finish' on time*): **'forte'** (loud), **'piano'** (quiet); **'cresc'** (getting louder), **'dimin'** (getting quieter).

■ 'cresc' if I can't go 'now I'll scream'

To summarise, intonation enables speakers to express emotions and attitudes, therefore adding another layer of meaning to spoken language. It does this by emphasising particular parts of the utterance through variations in pitch and volume. Such variations help the listener to recognise key grammatical points in what is being said: the mood of a sentence; the relative importance of particular phrases, clauses or sentences; and so on. Semantically, it prepares the listener for contrasts or links in material and can signal what kind of a response is expected.

Rhythm

The English language has quite a regular pattern of stressed and unstressed syllables – in other words, the RHYTHM is regular. However, speakers often vary the **beat** of their language depending upon their audience, purpose and context. A formal debate, for instance, may require a very regular and conscious rhythmic pattern; a situation in which a speaker is ill at ease may cause hesitant and arrhythmic speech; and an informal conversation will probably fall between these two extremes.

Conversational features

Conversational features like **assimilation** and **elision** may alter the rhythm of speech. Equally, **liaison**, in which words are slurred rather than pronounced as distinct sound units, can change the pattern.

■ Elision: police /pəliːs/ → /pliːs/

Stress

STRESS can be used for emphasis both within an individual word and within larger units of spoken discourse. It is not usually produced by greater force of articulation, but by changing pitch on a syllable. To study stress in individual lexical items, it is important to be able to recognise SYLLABLES and SYLLABIC STRESS. Some syllables are described as WEAK because they are **unstressed**; others are described as STRONG because they are **stressed**.

There are four kinds of weak syllables in English and these are indicated in transcription by specific IPA symbols: the vowel schwa [ə]; a close front unrounded vowel [i], which is shorter than [iː]; a close back unrounded vowel [u], which is shorter than [uː]; and a syllabic consonant (a syllable with no vowel) like [l] or [n].

trader /treɪdə/   lovely /lʌvli/   to /tu/
muscle /mʌsl/   often /ɒfn/

In informal conversation, unstressed pronunciations are common since few people articulate each syllable distinctly.

A stressed syllable can be marked in transcription by placing a small vertical line ' just before the syllable it relates to. Stressed syllables are said to have PROMINENCE because they are usually louder and longer and have a noticeably different pitch from that of unstressed syllables. The primary stress in English may fall on any syllable.

> 'mo ther   First syllable stressed
> e 'la tion   Middle syllable stressed
> per 'haps   Final syllable stressed

A SECONDARY STRESS is marked by a small vertical line (ˌ) just before the syllable it relates to.

> ˌun 'sure (Adj):   First syllable carries secondary stress; second syllable carries
>   primary stress
>
> 'pro ˌgress (N):   First syllable carries primary stress; second syllable carries
>   secondary stress
>
> 'mon u ˌment (N):   First syllable carries primary stress; final syllable carries
>   secondary stress

Some linguists, however, use other typographical means to highlight stress: capitalisation, bold print or underlining.

English is basically a free stress language – it is possible for some words to differ only in their internal stress patterns.

> ˌex 'port (V)   'ex ˌport (N)

It is not easy to predict which syllable will be stressed, but in continuous utterances, stresses tend to be patterned quite regularly.

Tone units

Having established the stress points in individual words, linguists can divide the **utterances** into tone units. A TONE UNIT is a segment of information consisting of one or more syllables with a series of rises or falls in tone where there is one particularly marked syllable. This is called the TONIC SYLLABLE (**TS**) or NUCLEUS (**nuc**): it is stressed and carries a tone.

> you've had enough haven't you
>   TS
>   ˋ   FALLING TONE
>   STRESS (ye̲s)

As well as a tonic syllable, a tone unit consists of other key elements.

1   The **HEAD** (**H**) describes the section of an utterance from the first stressed syllable up to but not including the last stressed syllable.

>   H   TS
> (yo̲u must be) (ri̲ght)

2   The **PRE-HEAD** (**PH**) describes any unstressed syllables preceding the head.

>   PH   TS   PH   H   TS
> (in three) (we̲eks)   (oh) (wha̲t can I) (do̲)

3   The **TAIL** (**T**) describes any part of an utterance that follows the tonic syllable.

>   TS   T
> (whe̲re) (did you go)

By changing the tonic syllable, it is possible to change the focus of an utterance.

> PH   H   TS   T
> (I) (wa̲nt to visit the) (pa̲rk) (now)   Focus: the park rather than anywhere else
>
> PH   H   TS   T
> (I) (wa̲nt to) (vi̲sit) (the park now)   Focus: visit the park rather than drive past

STRESS PATTERNS are usually directly linked to the syntactic structure of a sentence. By understanding the nature of the stresses used in connected utterances, it is possible to understand the semantic intentions of the speaker.

4   Changes in PACE also affect the rhythm of spoken discourse. The speed of utterances is directly related to meaning and to the speaker's relationship with the topic – an **increase** in speed may indicate excitement or anticipation; a **decrease** in speed may mark a change in mood or a dramatic emphasis of some kind. Significant changes in pace are marked in the margin of a transcript using the following abbreviations based on musical annotations: **'alleg'** (fast), **'lento'** (slow); **'accel'** (getting faster), **'rall'** (getting slower).

▨   'accel'   I want to 'go out n<u>ow</u>'

Similarly an abrupt irregular delivery can be described as **'stacc'** and a drawled elongation of words can be marked **'leg'**.

5   In almost all spoken contexts, PAUSES are acceptable, although particularly long pauses can cause embarrassment. The frequency of their occurrence means that the rhythm of spoken language is often uneven. Very brief pauses, or **micropauses**, are marked on a transcription by the symbol **(.)**; longer pauses can be timed in seconds and marked in figures – for example, **(6)**. Pauses may mark the grammatical end of an utterance or indicate hesitation on the part of a speaker.

▨   well (.) I (.) I know I was (.) <u>meant</u> to do it (2) I just (.) forgot

Formal spoken discourse can use pauses to dramatise and stylise utterances – they will be exaggerated for effect. In informal speech encounters, however, pauses at the end of utterances are often omitted – because the audience is usually known, the participants take up cues rapidly.

Other kinds of pauses are also used frequently: VOICELESS HESITATIONS (silence); VOICED HESITATIONS like *um* and *er*, and WORD SEARCHING. These are called NORMAL NON-FLUENCY FEATURES and are distinctive characteristics of spontaneous speech. They are found in both formal and informal spoken contexts, but are more acceptable in the latter. Because such pauses are irregular, they tend to make spoken language arrhythmic.

To comment on the **rhythm** of spoken utterances, linguists focus on segmental features like assimilation, elision and liaison; and prosodic features like stress patterns within single words, the structure of tone units, the pace, the delivery, and the kinds of pauses used. These are all directly linked to meaning and work alongside the actual words uttered to make communication effective.

Paralinguistics

PARALINGUISTICS or BODY LANGUAGE can also reinforce the semantics of spoken discourse. Comments on such features are always directly related to the intentions of the speaker. Vocalisations like **giggling** may express nervousness, enjoyment or amusement; **sighs** may express sadness, agitation or annoyance. **Gesture** can reinforce or challenge the apparent meaning of words. Paralinguistic features are usually marked on a transcription in square brackets in italic print.

▨   SPEAKER A: I (.) well I hardly dare to say it [*giggling*] (.) I actually s<u>poke</u> to him
        today (.) can you believe it
▨   SPEAKER B: who (.) <u>him</u> [*pointing*] (.) wonders will never cease

By considering both language and paralinguistic features, linguists can analyse not only what is said, but the speaker's intentions too. They can identify any underlying tensions between what the actual words convey and what the paralinguistic features imply.

3 | *Style*

So far, you have considered the basic building blocks of spoken and written English and the ways in which these are **normally** used. However, language can be manipulated, and writers and speakers can draw our attention to key features of their discourse by using slightly different language patterns. There are two important stylistic areas you need to consider: **focus** and **rhetoric**.

3.1 Focus

In a traditional simple declarative sentence, the subject will come first, followed by the predicator and any other appropriate clause elements. In linguistic terms, whatever comes **first** in the sentence is called the THEME: usually this will be the **subject**. However, it is possible to change the FOCUS by using a range of devices.

Marked theme

Some elements of the clause can be moved to the front of a sentence, replacing the usual thematic subject. **Adverbials** are the most flexible clause elements and therefore thematic adverbials are most common. The device of placing a clause element other than the subject at the front of a sentence is called FRONTING or FOREGROUNDING. The clause element that has replaced the subject in the **initial position** is called a MARKED THEME.

Unmarked theme: (The train) (departed) (on time) (that morning).
S   P   A   A

Marked theme: (That morning), (the train) (departed) (on time).
A   S   P   A

Unmarked theme: (He) (came) (into the room) (at last).
S   P   A   A

Marked theme: (At last), (he) (came) (into the room).
A   S   P   A

It is also possible to make **objects** and **complements** marked themes. This is more common in spoken than in written English, where stress and intonation help to emphasise the theme. However, in literary language, writers can also change the expected order of objects and complements in order to create dramatic effects.

Unmarked theme:	(The garden) (was) (uncontrolled) (after years of neglect).

S P C A
(The garden) (was) (uncontrolled) (after years of neglect).

C P S A
Marked theme: (Uncontrolled) (was) (the garden) (after years of neglect).

S P O A A
Unmarked theme: '(Lynne) (brought) (five kittens) (home) (last night).'

O S P A A
Marked theme: '(Five kittens) (Lynne) (brought) (home) (last night).'

End focus

It is also possible to put new information towards the **end** of a sentence, thus emphasising the end rather than the beginning. This is described as END FOCUS.

S P Oi Od · · · S P Od Oi
(I) (gave) (John) (*a brand new pen*). (I) (gave) (a brand new pen) (*to John*).

Sometimes it is stylistically more fluent to place the longest clause element at the end of a sentence.

S A P O
(I) (quickly) (opened) (*the door of the unnamed, unknown and secret chamber*).

S P Od Oi
(I) (gave) (directions) (to *the tall, elegant and undoubtedly striking blonde woman*).

Existential 'there'

It is also possible to create an end focus by using the existential *there*. Such sentences often **point** to the general existence of some state of affairs and they are therefore called EXISTENTIAL SENTENCES. By using *there* as a dummy subject, the writer or speaker can delay introducing the real subject of the sentence. *There* is called a DUMMY SUBJECT, **dumS**, because it has no meaning in itself – instead, its function is to put the real subject in a more prominent position.

You can recognise existential sentences by looking out for the following pattern: *There* + *to be* + (S). *There* becomes the dummy subject at the front of the sentence; and the true subject of the statement, though syntactically a complement, becomes a DELAYED SUBJECT, **(S)**, which is given added emphasis because of its position.

S P C · · · dumS P (S)
(A great many people) (are) (worried). (There) (are) (a great many worried people).

S P A · · · dumS₂ P (S) A
(The guard) (was) (on the train). (There) (was) (a guard) (on the train).

The verb *to be* is not the only verb that can be used in this way. Others, such as *to arise* and *to occur*, can also follow the dummy subject *there*, but these are less common and are more likely to be found in literary language.

S A P · · · dumS A P (S)
(A strange event) (then) (occurred). (There) (then) (occurred) (a strange event).

Similar structures can be found in sentences where *it* is the dummy subject. There are two main patterns.

1   *It* + *be* + (S/O/A) + relative pronoun *that* + Cl.

dumS	P	(S)		P	Oi	Od

(It) (was) (Lucy) (that) (told) (me) (the news).

rel pron

2   *It* + P + (C/Oi/Od) + NCl.

dumS	P	Od	(S)

(It) (is) (no concern of yours) (what I really want).

SCl–NCl

These rearrangements of clause elements refocus the information, allowing writers and speakers to place emphasis on selected parts of sentences. The sentences from which these examples derive present the information in a less emphatic way:

S	P	Oi	Od

(Lucy) (told) (me) (the news).

S	P	Od

(What I really want) (is) (no concern of yours).

SCl–NCl

Passive voice

Another way to alter the focus of a sentence is to use the **passive voice** instead of the active. In an active sentence, the clause elements follow the usual pattern, but by using the passive, the writer can change the focus.

Active: (The bank-tellers) (counted up) (the change) (at closing time).

S   P   O   A

Passive: (The change) (was counted up) (at closing time) (by the bank-tellers).

S   P   A   A

The inclusion of the adverbial *by* + *agent* is not compulsory, and omitting it can also change the focus.

Active: (The boys) (made) (the beds), (while the girls collected water

S   P   O   A

SCl–ACl

and started the fire).

Passive + agent: (The beds) (were made) (by the boys), (while the water was

S   P   A

SCl–ACl

collected and the fire started) (by the girls).

A   A

In the passive sentence here, the focus is on the boys and girls because the position of the *by* + *agent* always creates end focus. By omitting the adverbial, however, emphasis is placed not on the people, but on the events.

Passive without agent: (The beds) (were made), (while the water was collected

S   P   A

SCl–ACl

and the fire started).

3.2   Rhetoric

RHETORIC is the art of persuasive discourse. It is used in everyday life to persuade people to do or believe things and in literature to help the readers to engage with and believe in the fictional world with which they are presented. The Greek philosopher Aristotle (384–322 BC) was perhaps one of the first people to define rhetoric, and he established three key types of persuasion.

- **ETHOS** is a form of persuasion which is dependent upon the individual **character of the speaker or writer** as it is this that will determine the viewpoint and tone chosen for the discourse.
- **PATHOS** is a form of persuasion which works on the **emotions of the audience**, directly appealing to their sensitivities.
- **LOGOS** is a form of persuasion which is based on **reasoned argument**; the structure is important since it will help convince the audience of the logic of what is being said or written.

Rhetoric, then, is the strategic use of language and structure to persuade or move a listener or reader. Language and structure are used tactically to influence the intended audience and it is possible to identify the techniques used to achieve certain effects. It is useful to categorise the most common techniques into four key areas.

Lexical choice

Always consider a writer's or speaker's **choice of words**. This may be influenced by the viewpoint and tone adopted for a particular subject or situation (ethos); it may be dictated by the particular emotive response a writer or speaker wishes to evoke in the audience (pathos); or it may be governed by the subject-specific nature of a topic which requires technical lexis (logos). Look closely at the kind of words selected and be prepared to assess which approach or approaches are used.

Sound patterning

Writers and speakers can use a range of devices for playing on the patterns and sounds of words to create certain stylistic effects. These are chosen to enhance the meaning to be conveyed to the audience. You should be able to recognise the following.

Alliteration

ALLITERATION is the repetition of a consonant, often in the initial position.

> Help Labour *B*uild a *B*etter *B*ritain.   *P*ick up a *P*enguin.
> Persil *W*ashes *W*hiter.

In advertisements, captions and headlines this device can be used to make the text more eye-catching and memorable.

Assonance

ASSONANCE is the repetition of a vowel in a medial position (an element that does not occur in the initial or the final position).

> The pallor of girls' br*ow*s shall be their pall;
> Their fl*ow*ers the tenderness of s*i*lent m*i*nds,
> And each slow dusk drawing-d*ow*n of bl*i*nds.
> > Wilfred Owen (1893–1918), 'Anthem for Doomed Youth'

This poetic device makes words sound sonorous and musical and is often used to create a grave or pensive tone.

Consonance

CONSONANCE: repetition of a consonant in the medial or final position.

■ Bea*nz* Mea*nz* Hei*nz*

This device can draw attention to a product name in advertising or enhance the meaning of literary language by creating a hard sound.

Onomatopoeia

ONOMATOPOEIA is the term used when the sound of a word directly links to its meaning.

> ... at night when the wind rose, the lash of the tree
> *Shrieked* and *slashed* the wind ...
> D. H. Lawrence (1885–1930), 'Discord in Childhood'

The emphasis on the sound quality of words focuses the reader's or listener's attention on the aural aspects of the discourse, thus creating another dimension to the meaning.

Rhyme

RHYME or **HALF-RHYME** are exact or partial repetitions of a sound, usually at the end of a poetic line.

> And you, my father, there on the sad *height*,
> Curse, bless, me now with your fierce tears, I pray.
> Do not go gentle into that good *night*.
> Rage, rage against the dying of the *light*.
> Dylan Thomas (1914–53), 'Do Not Go Gentle Into That Good Night'

This kind of sound patterning can be used to draw attention to certain words. It creates a kind of end focus and can be used in a conclusive way to signal the end of a poem or a speech in verse drama emphatically.

Metaphorical language

METAPHORICAL LANGUAGE is an important part of successful persuasive discourse because it allows a speaker or writer to combine everyday language with devices that create special semantic effects. Aim to be able to recognise the following.

Irony

IRONY is the use of a word, phrase or paragraph turned from its usual meaning to a contradictory or opposing one, usually to satirise or deflate the person or issue.

> I do therefore humbly offer it to public consideration, that of the hundred and twenty thousand children already computed, twenty thousand may be reserved for breed ... That the remaining hundred thousand may at a year old be offered in sale to the persons of quality, and fortune, through the kingdom, always advising the mother to let them suck plentifully in the last month, so as to render them plump, and fat for a good table. A child will make two dishes at an entertainment for friends, and when the family dines alone, the fore or hind quarters will make a reasonable dish, and seasoned

with a little pepper or salt will be very good boiled on the fourth day, especially in winter.

> Jonathan Swift (1667–1745), 'A Modest Proposal for preventing the
> children of poor people in Ireland from being a burden to their
> parents or country, and for making them beneficial to the public'

In this text, Swift adopts an ironic stance, suggesting that eating babies is the only way to tackle Ireland's problems of poverty and overpopulation. By making such an emotive proposal, Swift aims to draw attention to the failures of both England and Ireland in governing and providing for the people.

Metaphor

A **METAPHOR** describes one thing in terms of another, creating an implicit comparison.

> I remember sharing the last of my moist buns with a *boy* and a lion. *Tawny* and *savage*, with *cruel nails* and *capacious mouth*, the *little boy tore* and *devoured*.
>
> Dylan Thomas, 'Holiday Memory'

Metonymy

METONYMY is the term used when the name of an attribute or thing is substituted for the thing itself.

> the Stage = the theatrical profession   the Crown = the monarchy

Oxymoron

An **OXYMORON** uses two apparently contradictory words, put together to create a special effect.

> *delicious poison*   Robin Hood was an *honest thief*.

Paradox

A **PARADOX** consists of an apparently self-contradictory statement which contains some kind of deeper meaning below the surface.

> War is peace. Freedom is slavery.
>
> George Orwell (1903–50), *1984*

Personification

PERSONIFICATION is the term used when an object or idea is given human qualities.

> On the *parade ground* of language accidence, morphology, phonology, and semantics are *drills* the *words* perform individually, like *new recruits* being made to *march, halt* . . . the *squad drilled* by *Sergeant Major Grammar*.
>
> Philip Howard, *The State of the Language*

> The *winter evening settles down*
>
> T. S. Eliot (1888–1965), 'Preludes'

Simile

In a SIMILE two things are explicitly compared by using a marker such as the prepositions *like* or *as*.

> And the cold postman ... tingled down the tea-tray-slithered run of the chilly glinting hill. He went in his ice-bound boots *like a man on fishmonger's slabs*. He wagged his bag *like a frozen camel's hump* ...
>
> Dylan Thomas, 'A Child's Christmas in Wales'

Symbolism

SYMBOLISM is the use of an object to represent or stand for something else – *scales*, for instance, symbolise *justice*; a *dove* symbolises *peace*.

> S.O.S. – is there a *lifeboat*? Thankfully God has a *rescue plan*: Jesus Christ, God's Son, died on the cross to *throw* us a *life-line* and bridge the gap between man and God.
>
> Logos, promotion leaflet

Synecdoche

SYNECDOCHE is a rhetorical device in which the part stands for the whole, and something wider than the thing actually mentioned is intended.

> The prisoner was placed behind bars [in prison].

All of these devices allow writers and speakers to influence their audience's perceptions of the subject. By encouraging readers and listeners to make wider associations, writers and speakers can work on their emotions (pathos), and can also convey their own viewpoint (ethos) in a more personal way.

Structural devices

In order to be successful in persuading an audience, a writer or speaker not only uses devices to enhance the meaning, but also makes conscious decisions about the structural patterns of discourse. You should be able to comment on the following techniques.

Antithesis

ANTITHESIS is the technique of placing two words or ideas in opposition to create a contrary effect.

> Leeds was *working class*, was built on work; Watermouth was *bourgeois*, built on tourism, property, retirement, pensions, French chefs ... you could be anything here. *Radical philosophy* approved this, but here it was *bourgeois indulgence*.
>
> Malcolm Bradbury (1932–), *The History Man*

The opposition here is used to create a contrast between two places and two ways of life. The author undermines Watermouth by choosing words with connotations of superficiality and unnecessary luxury. He draws the reader's attention to this through the rhetorical techniques he uses.

Listing

If conjunctions are used to co-ordinate groups of words, a list is said to be **SYNDETIC**; if commas are used instead, the list is described as **ASYNDETIC**.

> [1] Only you can see, in the blinded bedrooms, the coms and petticoats over chairs, the jugs and basins, the glasses of teeth, Thou Shalt Not on the wall, and the yellowing dickybird-watching pictures of the dead. [2] Only you can hear and see, behind the eyes of the sleepers, the movements and countries and mazes and colours and dismays and rainbows and tunes and wishes and flight and fall and despairs and big seas of their dreams.
>
> Dylan Thomas, *Under Milk Wood*

Listing always has an accumulative effect and enables a writer or speaker to create a range of impressions. A list can convey confusion and chaos or logic and reason, depending on its context. Equally, a writer or speaker can build towards a climax, or defy expectations by concluding in an anti-climax.

In this example, Thomas uses listing in both sentences, but the effect achieved in each case is different. In sentence [1], the accumulation of objects creates a claustro-phobic atmosphere which mirrors the everyday lives of the inhabitants of Llareggub. In sentence [2], however, the use of syndetic co-ordination creates a sense of the freedom that they find in the limitless nature of their dreams.

Overstatement

OVERSTATEMENT or **HYPERBOLE** is a form of persuasive exaggeration.

> Prettier musings of *high-wrought love* and *eternal constancy* could never have passed along the streets of Bath, than Anne was sporting from Camden-place to Westgate-buildings. It was almost enough *to spread purification and perfume* all the way.
>
> Jane Austen (1775–1817), *Persuasion*

Austen's use of hyperbole here results in a parody (a comic imitation) of contemporary romantic novels. Exaggeration of this kind will often be adopted to create a comic or less than serious tone.

Understatement

UNDERSTATEMENT or **LITOTES** leaves the audience to recognise that the writer or speaker could have put the point more strongly.

> I have, myself, full confidence that if all do their duty, if nothing is neglected, and if the best arrangements are made ... we shall prove ourselves once again able to defend our island home, to ride out the storm of war, and to outlive the menace of tyranny ... *At any rate*, that is what we are going to *try* to do ...
>
> Winston Churchill (1874–1965)

There are two distinct tones here: the initially grand and very formal tone and the high-lighted informal one. The contrast between these suggests that the second sentence has been understated – Churchill could have said much more.

Puns

A PUN is a play upon words: HOMONYMS have the same sound and spelling but a different meaning, and HOMOPHONES have the same sound but a different spelling and meaning.

> And so to bed
>
> *Carmarthen Journal* (24 May 1995)

This headline plays on language in two ways: first, the journalist has used a well-known quotation from Samuel Pepys's diary (20 April 1660) to head an article about gardening; secondly, the homonym *bed* is used to attract attention to the article – at first sight, readers will probably not realise that the feature is about preparing flower 'beds' for summer 'bedding' plants.

Newspaper headlines often play with words in a more general way to attract attention. The following headline was designed to sensationalise an article about a politician's extra-marital affair:

> It's Paddy Pantsdown
>
> *The Sun* (6 February 1992)

By punning on the sound of Paddy Ashdown's name and by using a commonly known cliché, 'caught with your pants down', the journalist made front page news with a story that was hardly topical since the affair had taken place several years earlier.

Repetition

REPETITION of words, phrases, clauses or sentences draws attention to key ideas.

> Your £15 gift can help the children so much.
> Your £15 can help us to maintain our family care services . . .
> Your £15 can help to cover the cost of counselling a traumatised child . . .
> Your £15 can help fund our Child Protection Helpline . . .
> Your £15 can help a child whose life may be in danger . . .
>
> NSPCC Christmas Appeal leaflet (October 1995)

The repetition of the noun phrase *Your £15* and the verb phrase *can help* emphasises that donations do not have to be large – to many people £15 is a nominal sum of money, yet it enables the charity to provide a wide range of services. The repetition is persuasive because it is emotive – so little can achieve so much.

Syntax

Grammatical patterns are used to add variety to a discourse and to emphasise particular features. There is a range of syntactical elements that a writer or speaker can manipulate.

Grammatical function

The GRAMMATICAL FUNCTION of words can be changed.

> Young girls lie *bedded soft* or glide in their dreams, with rings and trousseaux, *bridesmaided* by glow-worms . . . The boys are dreaming *wicked* of the *bucking ranches* of the night and the *jolly-rodgered sea*.
>
> Dylan Thomas, *Under Milk Wood*

Thomas uses the highlighted words in unusual contexts. He takes the nouns *bed* and *bridesmaid* and turns them into verbs in order to create a sense of movement in the dreams of the girls. Equally, by using the adjectives *soft* and *wicked* where we would expect adverbs, he draws the audience's attention to the nature of these dreams. In the noun phrases *bucking ranches* and *jolly-rodgered sea*, Thomas has taken attributes associated with horses and the sea and used them as verb modifiers. This also creates a sense of movement and characterises the boys who are dreaming of stereotypical boys' things – cowboys and pirates.

When a writer takes a modifier expressing a quality or attribute of one thing and uses it in relation to another, the modifier is called a **TRANSFERRED EPITHET**.

Parallelism

In **PARALLELISM**, phrase, clause and sentence structures are repeated to give a sense of balance and reason to a discourse.

> Labour will win by being the party of democratic renewal: demolishing unaccountable quangos, devolving power to the nations and regions of Britain and providing a Bill of Rights.
>
> > Tony Blair, campaign address for the election of a new Labour leader
> > and deputy leader

Here three parallel non-finite clauses (*demolishing . . .*, *devolving . . .* and *providing . . .*) provide concrete evidence to explain exactly what the noun phrase *the party of democratic renewal* means. The tripling is rhetorical, aiming to convince readers of the logical and democratic approach of the Labour Party.

Sentence structure

A varied choice of sentence types will draw the reader or listener into the discourse. A writer or speaker must think about the use of simple, complex and branching sentences.

SIMPLE SENTENCES can suggest an innocence and naïvety of style.

> (The Vances) (lived) (in number seven). (They) (had) (a different father and
>
> mother). (They) (were) (Eileen's father and mother).
>
> > James Joyce (1882–1941), *A Portrait of the Artist as a Young Man*

The simple sentences here portray a style that is reminiscent of a child. Joyce, in a book which is charting the path of Stephen Daedalus' growth from childhood to adulthood, varies his style to suit the age of his main character at each stage of his development.

COMPLEX SENTENCES can withhold information until a certain point in the discourse, or subordinate some ideas to others which seem more important.

> MCl
> (We shall all agree *that* the fundamental aspect of the novel is its story-telling
> SCl–NCl
>
> MCl   MCl
> aspect,) (*but*) (we shall voice our assent in different tones), (*and*) (it is on the
> conj   conj
>
> precise tone of voice [*which*] we employ now that our subsequent conclusions
> SCl–RelCl   SCl–RelCl
>
> will depend).
>
> > E. M. Forster (1879–1970), *Aspects of the Novel*

The complexity of the sentence here is directly related to the number of clauses: there is one subordinate clause introduced by the subordinating conjunction *that*; there is one post-modifying relative clause with the relative pronoun *which* omitted, and one clause that is introduced by the relative pronoun *that*; and there are three clauses linked by the co-ordinating conjunctions *but* and *and*. This intricate structure reflects the nature of the book from which the sentence is taken – a text discussing the key elements of novels accompanied by analysis of various examples. Forster is dealing with **ideas** and **theories** and therefore his sentence structure is inevitably complex.

BRANCHING is the arrangement and order of subordinate and main clauses in a discourse. The **order** determines whether left or right branching has been used. LEFT BRANCHING forces the reader or listener to wait for the main clause by using subordination at the beginning of a sentence. The results can often be dramatic because the reader or listener has to wait for all the information. This device is better suited to writing than to speech because of the demands it makes on the memory.

> Every body has their taste in noises as well as in other matters ... When Lady Russell, not long afterwards, was entering Bath on a wet afternoon and driving through the long course of streets from the Old Bridge to Camden-place, amidst the dash of other carriages, the heavy rumble of carts and drays, the bawling of newsmen, muffin-men and milkmen, and the ceaseless clink of pattens, *she made no complaint.*
>
> Jane Austen, *Persuasion*

Austen uses left branching to convey a sense of the hustle and bustle of town life in Bath. The description leading up to the main clause creates a negative view of Bath and the reader does not anticipate that Lady Russell will relish the atmosphere. By forcing the reader to wait for the main clause at the end of a very long sentence, Austen suggests that she herself does not see Bath in the same way that Lady Russell does.

RIGHT BRANCHING gives the important information first and then supplies a commentary on it or additional information. It can often seem more natural because it deals with information cumulatively and in what seems to be a more logical order: it provides the main clause first, before any embedded subordinate clauses.

> *There is in the Midlands a single-line tramway system* which boldly leaves the country-town and plunges off into the black, industrial countryside, up hill and down dale, through the long ugly villages of workmen's houses, over canals and railways, past churches perched high and nobly over the smoke and shadows ...
>
> D. H. Lawrence, 'Tickets, Please'

Lawrence's use of right branching creates a different kind of effect from Austen's use of left branching. The reader is immediately presented with the main information and what follows is an elaboration. The very pattern of the subordinate clauses reflects the nature of the journey on which the reader is taken, while the connotations of the verb *plunges* reinforce the readers' sense of isolation as they journey through the bleak industrial landscape.

4 How to use your knowledge

The information covered in Part I should be used as a reference point and you should be prepared to dip into it to build up a technical knowledge base. The exercises that accompany each section are drills to test your understanding of the key concepts, but your study of language will require you to do more than just recognise grammatical, phonetic, phonological and stylistic features. You will instead need to learn how to **use** the knowledge you have gained. The suggestions below should prepare you for the sections of the book that follow, showing you how a knowledge of grammar, phonetics, phonology and style can be used in a variety of contexts.

4.1 Grammar

Words and phrases

Sometimes it is useful to consider the ways in which words and phrases are used. You will not, however, be required merely to identify all the nouns, adjectives and so on. Instead, you will have to think about why a writer or speaker has made certain lexical choices. Your first step should be to text mark any words or lexical sets that seem to be particularly effective: comment on their **connotations**, **context** and **register**. In your analysis of phrases, you need to discuss the **function** and **form** of key examples, considering the importance and effect of modifiers and qualifiers. At all times, try to comment on the effects created, focusing on the **purpose**, **audience** and **context** of the variety you are analysing.

Table 4.1 records the abbreviations you should be able to use in your analysis at the level of words and phrases.

Table 4.1 Abbreviations

Word classes

N	noun	prim	primary verb
Adj	adjective	mod	modal verb
V	verb	lex	lexical verb
Adv	adverb	aux	auxiliary verb
pron	pronoun	pres pa	present participle
det	determiner	past pa	past participle

prep	preposition	conj	conjunction

Phrases

NP	noun phrase	PrepP	prepositional phrase
AdjP	adjective phrase	m	modifier
VP	verb phrase	h	head word
AdvP	adverb phrase	q	post-modifier or qualifier

Clauses and sentences

Within any discourse analysis, a consideration of clauses and sentences or utterances is central. You need to understand how **clause elements** and **main** and **subordinate clauses** are used, and the ways in which writers and speakers can manipulate these to create certain effects. You will not have to identify the type of every clause or sentence or utterance, but you should be able to discuss key examples. Writers and speakers use clauses and sentences or utterances in different ways; as you focus on a range of spoken and written varieties in the following chapters, you need to become accustomed to selecting appropriate examples for analysis. It is useful to identify examples of simple, compound, complex and compound-complex sentences or utterances because the choices writers or speakers make are often directly linked to their **purpose**, **audience** and **context**. You should always link the structures you describe to the **meaning** by considering both the **effects** created and the ways in which these relate to a writer's or speaker's **intentions**.

Table 4.2 records the abbreviations you should use in your analysis.

Table 4.2 Abbreviations

Clauses and sentences

S	subject	MCl	main clause
P	predicator	SCl	subordinate clause
C	complement	NCl	noun clause
Cs	subject complement	ACl	adverbial clause
Co	object complement	RelCl	relative clause
Od	direct object	CompCl	comparative clause
Oi	indirect object	NFCl	non-finite clause
A	adverbial	VlessCl	verbless clause

Cohesion

When analysing cohesion in a discourse, it is necessary to look for examples of all types of linking devices. For instance, writers and speakers inevitably use **pronoun referencing**, substituting pronouns for noun phrases to avoid repetition, and usually there is nothing out of the ordinary in this process. However, you should be prepared to identify and comment on examples where cohesion has been used to achieve distinctive effects. **Lexical sets** may be linked to a specific field or register which will help you to identify the subject matter or focus of a text. A writer's or speaker's **use of pronouns** instead of proper nouns may leave the identity of a character intentionally vague, so that a dramatic revelation can be made at a significant moment. Examples of repetition, **referencing** or **ellipsis** may be used to draw attention to some key element of the discourse. In any discussion, you must remember to link your comments to the writer's or speaker's **intentions**.

4.2 Phonetics and phonology

Phonetics

Phonetics focuses on the ways in which sounds are produced. It deals specifically with **the physical properties of sounds** and it does not look at the way sounds are combined to create meaning. It is useful to be able to describe **the place and the manner of articulation of consonants** and **the ways in which different vowel sounds are formed**. You should be able to use appropriate **IPA symbols** to record immature sounds used by children or characteristic regional variations. Equally, your knowledge of phonetics should enable you to discuss topics like the advantages and disadvantages of **traditional orthography** and **phonetic spelling**.

Phonetics is a complex area of language study and your course will only require you to show an understanding of some basic concepts. Try not to be daunted by the material contained in Chapter 2 – instead, aim to acquire a working knowledge so that you can describe the production of sounds in spoken English.

Phonology

Because you are studying sounds within a particular sound system – RP English – most of your work will be on areas associated with phonology. It is useful to be able to analyse the **phonological units** or **segments** of English: you should know about **minimal pairs** and the way these are used to convey meaning; you should be able to discuss the effects created by **elision**, **assimilation**, **liaison** and **reduction** in continuous speech; and you should have a basic knowledge of the **rhythm** and **intonation patterns** in spoken English. Identifying and commenting on features like these will help you to show how spoken language is quite different from written language. In addition, analysis of **vocalisations** and **gesture** will show how speakers either support or challenge the actual words they utter. By discussing segmental and non-segmental features and by considering speakers' attitudes and opinions, you will be able to demonstrate the complexity of spoken interaction.

Transcription

A phonetic transcription is marked by **square brackets**. It aims to reflect the nature of sounds exactly and uses the **International Phonetic Alphabet** to do so. Although many symbols are directly related to the Roman alphabet we use for written discourse, other symbols have been created or drawn from other alphabets to take account of the wide range of sounds that make up languages in general. In order to record the kind of sounds heard exactly, linguists have a range of **diacritics** and other symbols to describe any variations from the norm.

A phonemic transcription is less detailed – it focuses on the relationships between sounds rather than on a description of their exact quality. Because it analyses sounds in context, this kind of transcription considers the structure and meaning of sounds. A phonemic transcription is marked by **slant brackets** and uses a limited selection of the IPA symbols relating specifically to one particular language.

For your course, you will need to produce broad transcriptions which record the main phonological features of spoken discourse. You are unlikely to have to use complex systems of diacritics to mark things like aspiration, the nasalisation of vowels and voiceless or voiced syllables. However, if you have a personal interest in this area of spoken language, this can be developed in project work.

Linguists use a range of symbols to mark phonological features on their transcriptions: you need to decide on the ones that will suit you best. Table 4.3 records the annotations used to mark prosodic features on transcriptions in this book.

Table 4.3 Annotations used in transcriptions

/ /	slant brackets indicate that the transcription is more interested in the phonemic structure of an utterance than in the exact nature of the sounds articulated		
gó	rising tone	gò	falling tone
gô	rising-falling tone	gǒ	falling-rising tone
'alleg'	fast	'lento'	slow
'accel'	getting faster	'rall'	getting slower
'forte'	loud	'piano'	quiet
'cresc'	getting louder	'dimin'	getting quieter
'stacc'	clipped pronunciation	'leg'	drawled pronunciation
'alleg'	Gascoigne gets the ball and beats the defender (.) 'runs down the wing'		
'stacc'	'inside to Ince (.) on to Shearer (.) back (.) to Ince' (.) who shoots		
↑go↑	raised pitch	↓go↓	lowered pitch
<u>go</u>	word stress	a'bout	syllabic stress
d.	· incomplete word	(.)	micro-pause
(2)	timed pause	[*pointing*]	gesture
ₒh	in breath	h°	out breath
ʰ	heavy aspiration		
[*coughing*]	non-verbal vocalisation	ch<u>oo</u> ch<u>oo</u>	held word or syllables
(*indistinct*)	indistinct sound or word	g.go	stutters, false start
I'll come over later (.) give me a ring ‖ if you decide to go out ‖ yeah (.) great			overlapping speech
I'll come over later (.) give me a ring if you decide to go out = = yeah great			smooth latching of turns

4.3 Style

You will not find examples of all the stylistic techniques in a passage for analysis, but it is worth being able to recognise them when they do appear. Both spoken and written varieties of English use **focus**, distinctive **lexical choices**, **sound patterning**, **metaphorical language** and **structural devices** to influence their respective audiences. By analysing the stylistic techniques used, you can draw conclusions about the distinctive features of different varieties. Equally, you will be able to assess and evaluate exactly **what a writer or speaker is trying to achieve**. It is important to comment on the **semantic effects** of the devices you find: you will gain little credit for merely recognising them. Instead, once you have identified certain stylistic techniques, consider **why** the writer or speaker has chosen them and the ways in which these will **influence the reader or listener**.

4.4 What to aim for

You should refer to Part I of this book regularly, using the contents list, the index and the glossary to help you find your way around. The definitions, examples and exercises will provide you with a starting point since they introduce you to important linguistic terminology. As you read the following chapters, you will gain confidence in your technical knowledge – the source material and commentaries will provide you with concrete examples of the way to use theoretical information in practice. The analytical approaches to each variety will show you how to annotate and discuss unseen material, and how to use appropriate terminology in context.

Ultimately, you must aim to bring together your grammatical, phonetic and phonological, and stylistic knowledge so that you can comment on the distinctive characteristics of spoken and written English in an informed way. As a linguist, you must aim to identify the techniques different speakers and writers use to convey their message, and to discuss these linguistically.

PART II

Language issues – aspects of English

5 Some basic concepts

5.1 A starting point

As well as a general knowledge of the structure of spoken and written English, linguists use certain core concepts to classify language. The key terms introduced in this section will provide you with the necessary basis for linguistic analysis since they establish a background against which all kinds of language change and variety can be considered.

5.2 Standard English and Received Pronunciation

STANDARD ENGLISH (SE) is a form of English which has been accepted as a norm. It is the variety with which other forms of English are compared. Sometimes it is called a *dialect* although it is not linked to a specific region and has no regionally distinctive words or grammatical structures.

All language users adapt the form of their language according to where they are, what they are trying to communicate, and to whom they are speaking or writing. Even Standard English, therefore, exists in a variety of forms – spoken and written; formal and informal; personal and impersonal. Although most people speak either a regional variety of English or a mixture of Standard English and regional forms, Standard English provides the country with a unified means of communication. It is what we usually hear on the television and radio news, for instance, because it is a form that everyone can understand. In its written form, Standard English is found in print and in formal written varieties like essays and business letters. It is also called BBC ENGLISH or THE QUEEN'S ENGLISH, and for some people it is the symbol of 'good English'.

It is a prestigious language form because it is associated with government, the law, education, the Church and the financial world. It is the form taught to second-language speakers because it is universally understood and this perpetuates its cultural value.

Linguists are interested in the varieties of English we use and in order to describe them they use Standard English as a point of comparison. Any variety which does not use the same vocabulary or grammar as Standard English is called NON-STANDARD ENGLISH. By using this term, linguists can avoid value judgements – non-standard varieties of English are not wrong, but different.

Just as Standard English provides linguists with a convenient norm for describing variations in vocabulary and grammar, RECEIVED PRONUNCIATION (RP) provides a standard form of pronunciation. It is an accent often associated with the South-East where most RP speakers live, but unlike regional accents it is not confined by regional boundaries. In fact, RP tells you more about speakers' social and cultural backgrounds than about the region from which they come.

There are no linguistic reasons for describing RP as the 'best' accent, but socially it is associated with respectability, good education and high social status. It is prestigious because it is linked to the law, public schools and the Church. Second-language learners are often taught an RP accent, and it has been linked to the BBC since the early days of broadcasting.

Today, although RP still exists, only 2–3 per cent of the British population speak it in its original pure form. Now it most commonly exists as MODIFIED RECEIVED PRONUNCIATION (**MRP**), educated speakers having mixed characteristics of RP with regional forms. Speakers equally modify regional accents by moving towards a spoken form that they see as more prestigious, a form that they believe will improve their social status. The ESTUARY ENGLISH of the 1990s, for example, shows the way some regional speakers adapted their accent by using features of RP. Although it originated in the South-East, young people as far north as Hull now adopt Estuary English as a 'trendy' accent.

Because language change is constant, some people argue that RP will not survive in its original form. Social judgements about regional varieties have to some extent become less dogmatic and this inevitably affects the way that users view different accents. The use of RP is no longer a prerequisite to social status – BBC presenters, academics and politicians now often retain their regional accents, although probably in a modified form. Ultimately, the use of Standard English is socially more important than the use of RP.

5.3 Attitudes to language

There are two distinct approaches to language: PRESCRIPTIVISM and DESCRIPTIVISM. The **prescriptivists** believe that English is governed by a set of rules which dictate a 'proper' and 'correct' use of language. They believe that if the 'rules' are not obeyed, the speaker or writer is 'wrong'. The form of English they see as 'correct' has a high social prestige – it is associated with formal written and spoken language and is used in dictionaries, grammar books and language handbooks. Because prescriptivists regard one particular form of English as the 'best', they dislike linguistic change. They see it as a process of decay which erodes standards and leads to a debased form of English.

The **descriptivists**, on the other hand, observe language as it is spoken or written in different situations. They aim to describe the ways in which language varies according to the user, the use and the context. While prescriptivists dislike language change, descriptivists see it as inevitable. They recognise that a living language cannot be fixed, but will adapt to meet the demands of its users.

Despite this, descriptivists recognise the need for a standard form of language as a point of comparison. Although they believe that some usage is 'wrong' (*I in live town the*), they are more interested in describing variations from the standard as 'non-standard' than as 'incorrect'. In other words, they do make judgements, but these are based on a knowledge of audience, purpose and context.

5.4 Audience, purpose and context

All speakers and writers make decisions about the kinds of language they use – often subconsciously. They think about who they will be addressing (**audience**) and the kind of relationship they need to create. They assess the formality or informality of the occasion (**context**) and the reason for the speech or writing (**purpose**). Lexical choices are then a reflection of their assessment of the linguistic situation.

Each individual has a wide range of language forms called a PERSONAL REPERTOIRE. We draw on these, speaking and writing in different ways according to the impression we want to make – with friends we are informal and familiar; with employers or teachers we are polite and formal. By assessing what is expected of us according to our audience, purpose and context, we regularly make decisions about what is **appropriate** or suitable. The term APPROPRIATENESS offers linguists an alternative to the right/wrong approach of the prescriptivists. It encourages a recognition of the variety and flexibility of language, and recognises that there are different linguistic expectations for different situations.

Language can also be assessed for its ACCEPTABILITY – whether it is considered permissible or normal by ordinary users. Linguists use **acceptability tests** to assess what is and what is not acceptable and their results show that language users do not always agree. Variations in opinions are caused by geographical, cultural, social and personal factors. To a linguist, however, any form of language that is regularly in use in speech or writing is acceptable in an appropriate context.

ACTIVITY 5.1

Read through the following examples of informal spoken English and then answer the questions below.

a   Are the utterances acceptable or unacceptable to you?
b   If they are unacceptable, can you identify what does not seem normal?
c   To what extent would the acceptability of these utterances depend upon the formality or informality of the context?

Examples

1   I never do nothing on a Friday night.
2   I'm going to town now, me.
3   Don't forget to get off of the bus at the right stop.
4   Who did you speak to?
5   They always start Star Trek by saying 'To boldly go where no man has gone before'.
6   I was badder than my brother when I was little.
7   I met up with Julie when I went to town.
8   Tom forgot to pick me up and I was sat there for more than half an hour.
9   You'm all right now. You just need a good rest.
10   We was going shopping for mum when it happened.
11   The little boy fed hisself quite well for a toddler.
12   The temperature today will be 19° through 21°.
13   I can't make an appointment with the doctor while 5 o'clock.
14   The mouses were running everywhere last night.
15   The chairperson picked up her brief for the meeting.
16   I'm betterer than he is at writing stories.
17   I likes it better when my friend comes to play.

COMMENTARY

You may or may not have found examples that seemed unusual to you. Despite the fact that many of these utterances differ from the norm or standard, descriptivist linguists would say that they are all **acceptable** because they are real examples of everyday usage in British regional dialects. However, it is important to realise that they would not be **appropriate** in all contexts. The comments below summarise some of the grammatical and linguistic features to which you may have responded.

Verb forms will often be different from the standard in regional dialects. In utterance 8, the verb phrase *was sat* would be replaced in Standard English by the progressive *was sitting*. The use of the verb *to be* + *past participle* is associated with the passive voice and linguistic purists would argue that in this example the *by* + *agent* has been omitted from a passive construction – that is, *I was sat there ... by someone*. In utterance 10, there is evidence of a dialectal standardising process in which the first person plural past tense of the verb *to be* is replaced by the singular *was*. A similar process of standardisation occurs in utterance 17 – the verb *likes* has the *-s* inflection we would expect to see with the third person singular present tense. *You'm* in utterance 9 also standardises an irregular pattern: it is a dialectal contraction of *you are* in which the first person singular *am* is contracted to *-m* and applied to all parts of the verb. These are all common processes of regularisation, since dialects often simplify irregular patterns.

Other non-standard features linked to verbs can be seen in the use of a multiple negative in utterance 1. In Late Modern Standard English, the use of *never* and *nothing* together cancel each other out, although in earlier forms of English, listing of negatives was used for emphasis. The phrasal-prepositional verb *to meet up with* used in utterance 7 is a new combination and its meaning is still not yet stable. While some speakers use it to denote an accidental meeting, others would interpret it as an arranged meeting. This ambiguity is evidence of the way in which language change takes place – during the process of change, several variants often exist alongside each other. Finally, utterance 5 may or may not have seemed non-standard to you. Prescriptivists argue that an infinitive like *to go* is a lexical item and should not be split by a word placed in between. They would say that *to go boldly* is the 'correct' form, while descriptivists would argue that language is flexible and that *to boldly go* is far more dramatic in this context.

Pronouns are also often non-standard in regional dialects. In utterance 2, the object pronoun *me* is semantically redundant, but it is used in some dialects for emphasis. The reflexive pronoun *hisself* in utterance 11 also simplifies a pattern. Most reflexive pronouns are formed by adding *-self* or *-selves* to a possessive determiner: *my* + *self*; *your* + *self/selves*; *our* + *selves*. For the third person singular, however, *-self* is added to the object pronoun *him*. The dialectal form regularises the pattern by using the possessive determiner *his* + *self*.

Several examples here show how **prepositions** can be flexible in dialects. In utterance 3, the preposition *of* is not needed in Standard English to describe the direction of the movement since *off* denotes this itself. In utterances 12 and 13, Standard English would use a different preposition – *through* would be replaced by '*from* _____ *to* _____' (SE) and *while* by *until* (SE). This kind of dialectal substitution can cause problems in communication since speakers not familiar with the dialect could fail to understand the meaning. The utterance in example 4 may not have seemed unusual, but prescriptivists would argue that sentences should not end with a preposition. They would see *To whom did you speak?* as the 'correct' form, with the preposition moved to the initial position and an object pronoun form of the relative pronoun *who* following it. This structure is more common in writing than in speech.

Some **adjectival** use is also non-standard. Example 16 highlights the process of grading adjectives. In Standard English, mono- and many disyllabic adjectives add the inflection -er (slow + er, easy + (i)er); some disyllabic and all polysyllabic adjectives add more (more + recent; more + intelligent). Irregular adjectives do not follow this pattern, but instead have distinctive forms. The example here uses better, the irregular comparative form of good, adding the regular -er inflection as well. In utterance 6, an irregular comparative worse is standardised in the form of badder. This kind of simplification can be found in child language where a child recognises a language pattern and then overuses it by applying 'the rule' to irregular as well as regular words.

Some **nouns** may also be different in non-standard forms of English. In utterance 14 an irregular noun plural mice has been standardised as mouses. The regular -s inflection has been added where in Standard English the plural is marked by a change in the vowel. (In written language the consonant also changes, from s to c, but it is important to remember that these sound the same phonologically, and in speech would both be realised as /s/.) This is another instance of overextension in which a child assimilates a 'rule' and then overuses it. Finally, the use of chairperson in utterance 15 may or may not have attracted your attention. Purists may argue that the use of chairperson is unnecessary and awkward, but most people would prefer it since there is no need to distinguish between the sexes in this role.

The dialectal forms here may be **inappropriate** in some contexts, but in others they are **appropriate**. If they were used in informal contexts within regional boundaries where the audience was familiar with such variations, they would not cause problems in understanding. Modern linguists would not automatically describe them as 'wrong', therefore, but would assess the appropriateness of each utterance by considering the audience, purpose and context.

5.5 Register

REGISTER is a term used to describe variations in language according to use – lawyers use a legal register, doctors a medical register and priests a religious register. When analysing an example of spoken or written language, linguists ask questions about three key areas of register. The MODE can either be spoken or written, although subdivisions can be identified where a formal speech is written to be read aloud or a written record is made of spoken language. A letter to the Prime Minister and an informal conversation with a friend, for instance, would use different registers: one uses a written mode while the other uses a spoken one. The MANNER describes the relationship between the participants and the formality or informality of the context in which communication takes place. A written examination essay does not aim to create a personal relationship with an unknown examiner because it is a formal task, while a postcard to a friend is both informal and personal. The FIELD is linked to the subject matter – by looking at the kind of words used, linguists can come to conclusions about the topic or focus of communication. A medical field, for example, may use words like medicine, patient, asthma and inhalant, while a legal field may use judge, fixed penalty, sentence and witness.

By considering mode, manner and field, linguists can draw conclusions about the role and form of language in different contexts. Different varieties of English are characterised by distinctive features and 'register' is a logical starting point for analysis.

ACTIVITY 5.2

Some writers adopt different registers in order to create particular effects. The following extract is taken from Ulysses (1922), an experimental novel by James Joyce. It describes a June day in Dublin in 1904, mainly from the viewpoint of Leopold Bloom whose thoughts and activities are in some ways a parallel to the epic adventures of Homer's Ulysses.

The extract focuses on a conversation between friends in a pub. Read it through and try to identify where the changes in register occur. To help you, think about Joyce's use of:

1   direct speech and description;
2   religious language;
3   legal language;
4   informal and colloquial language.

1   – I know that fellow, says Joe, from bitter experience.
        – Cockburn. Dimsey, wife of David Dimsey, late of the admiralty: Miller, Tottenham, aged eightyfive: Welsh, June 12, at 35 Canning Street, Liverpool, Isabella Helen. How's that for a national press, eh, my brown son?
5   How's that for Martin Murphy the Bantry jobber?
        – Ah, well, says Joe, handing round the boose. Thanks be to God they had the start of us. Drink that, citizen.
        – I will, says he, honourable person.
        – Health, Joe, says I. And all down the form.
10   Ah! Ow! Don't be talking! I was blue mouldy for the want of that pint. Declare to God I could hear it hit the pit of my stomach with a click.
        And lo, as they quaffed their cup of joy, a godlike messenger came swiftly in, radiant as the eye of heaven, a comely youth, and behind him there passed an elder of noble gait and countenance, bearing the sacred scrolls of
15   law, and with him his lady wife, a dame of peerless lineage, fairest of her race.
        Little Alf Bergan popped in round the door and hid behind Barney's snug, squeezed up with the laughing, and who was sitting up there in the corner that I hadn't seen snoring drunk, blind to the world, only Bob Doran. I didn't
20   know what was up and Alf kept making signs out of the door. And begob what was it only that bloody old pantaloon Denis Breen in his bath slippers with two bloody big books tucked under his oxter and the wife hotfoot after him, unfortunate wretched woman trotting like a poodle. I thought Alf would split.
25   – Look at him, says he. Breen. He's traipsing all round Dublin with a post-card someone sent him with u.p.: up on it to take a li . . .
        And he doubled up.
        – Take a what? says I.
        – Libel action, says he, for ten thousand pounds.
30   – O hell! says I.
        The bloody mongrel began to growl that'd put the fear of God in you see-ing something was up but the citizen gave him a kick in the ribs.

                                                                        James Joyce, Ulysses

COMMENTARY

Changes in **mode** are noticeable where direct speech (spoken mode) becomes description (written mode) at lines 12, 27 and 31. The extract opens with spoken language and the **manner** is informal because these are friends drinking socially. The informality is marked by exclamations like *Ah!* (l. 10), *eh* (l. 4) and *Ow!* (l. 10). The use of shortened forms (contractions) like *How's* (l. 4), colloquial language like *boose* (l. 6) and dialect like *oxter* (l. 22) (Irish and Scots dialect for *armpit*) also reflect the informality of the manner. In the second line, however, one of the characters reads aloud from the births and deaths column of a newspaper. Information is provided in the almost note-like written form associated with obituaries placed in a newspaper personal column. The register changes again when Joyce uses another written style, drawing on the **field** of religion: *And lo* (l. 12), *the sacred scrolls of law* (ll. 14–15). Contrasting with this is the **field** of myth, which talks of a *godlike messenger* (l. 12) and *a dame of peerless lineage* (l. 15).

The result here is comic because Joyce's choice of **register** contrasts with the reality of his characters. By juxtaposing (setting one thing against another) *boose* (l. 6) with *quaffed their cup of joy* (l. 12), and *an elder of noble gait and countenance* (l. 14) with Denis Breen *in his bath slippers with two bloody big books tucked under his oxter* (ll. 21–2), Joyce encourages his reader to see both the comedy and the grandeur of ordinary life. This effect can also be seen in the contrasting descriptions of *Little Alf Bergan* (l. 17) as a *godlike messenger* (l. 12) and a *comely youth* (l. 13) and Denis Breen's wife, an *unfortunate wretched woman* (l. 23), as the *fairest of her race* (ll. 15–16).

The **field** of law is briefly used to establish another contrast. The references to *libel action* (l. 29) are juxtaposed with the informality of the context and the insignificant reason for the libel case. Finally, Joyce's repeated use of *bloody* (ll. 22, 31), establishing a realistic informal context, can be juxtaposed with his use of a literary **register** in describing Denis Breen's wife *trotting like a poodle* (l. 23). This is not a traditional simile, but nevertheless creates a vivid image for the reader.

By identifying register changes, the reader can see links between the grand world of myth and the ordinary world of Dublin. This enables Joyce to elevate the city of Dublin and its inhabitants through his mythological references, but also to satirise them because of the difference between myth and reality.

5.6 Spoken and written English

There are significant differences between speech and writing. For instance, a lawyer summing up in court uses language in a different way from a legal document like a will; the language of an estate agent discussing a valuation with a client wishing to sell property differs from an estate agent's written selling details; the language of a live television news interview differs from a tabloid newspaper report; the language of a television cookery programme differs from a cake recipe in a cookery book; and a child's explanation to her mother about why she wishes to miss gym at school will be different from the note the mother writes to the teacher. In each case, the register is different: the **mode** for some is spoken while for others it is written; the **manner** for some is more formal than others, which affects the kind of relationship created between participants; and the **field** varies depending on the subject matter. Just as we can write in a variety of ways, so we vary our speech according to our audience, purpose and context.

Many people believe that written language is more prestigious than spoken language – its form is likely to be closer to Standard English, it dominates education and is used as the language of public administration. In linguistic terms, however, neither speech nor writing can be seen as superior. Linguists are more interested in observing and describing all forms of language in use than in making social and cultural judgements with no linguistic basis.

Linguists' analysis of speech and writing has highlighted key differences between spoken and written language.

The nature of speech and writing

Spoken	Written
Speech is spontaneous and often transient. Most forms of everyday speech are not recorded for repeated listening, although in the age of the mass media much of what we hear on radio and television can be bought on cassette or video, or recorded for repeated home use.	Writing is permanent: the same text may be read repeatedly or by several different readers (e.g. a recipe; a newspaper).

Audience

Spoken	Written
Spoken encounters (conversations) usually take place **face-to-face** with a particular person or persons. A telephone conversation is a notable exception.	Written language may be intended for a particular reader (a postcard; a letter), but often it will be addressed to an **unknown audience** (a coursework essay; an anthology of poetry).
Speakers can use **paralinguistic features** as well as words to check that communication is meaningful.	There is **no immediate feedback** for a piece of written text. Equally, the time difference between the writing and reading of the text means that writers must make sure that there is no unintentional ambiguity.
Deictic expressions like *this one*, *over there* and *just now*, referring to the present situation, are common.	All **references** need to be built into the written text because the reading context will be different for each reader (a novel; DIY instructions).
Interruptions and **overlaps** allowing the addressee to participate are common (informal conversation; BBC Television's *Question Time*).	Communication is **one-way**. Although the reader may respond in a written or spoken form, the response is rarely immediate (the reply to a letter; an examiner's comments on an essay).

Style

Spoken	Written
Speech is not usually **planned** in advance and speakers tend to think ahead as they speak (informal conversation; 'Question Time' in Parliament).	Writing is often **pre-planned** and ideas can therefore be carefully organised (a poem; an opinion essay).
Speech often has a **loose structure**, marked by repetitions, rephrasing of ideas and comment clauses. Errors once uttered cannot be withdrawn.	Interruptions during the process of writing are not visible in a final copy. **Drafting** also means that errors can be corrected.
Lexis is often informal and there may be examples of a personal lexicon developed between familiar speakers (family conversation). In more formal contexts, vocabulary may be subject-specific (a political speech), but speech is still likely to be marked by contractions and comment clauses.	In many contexts informal **lexical** features like contractions will be unacceptable (a job application; an essay). Some lexical items will be rarely used in spoken language (chemical and mathematical equations).
Intonation and pauses are used to mark the **grammatical boundaries** of utterances. They are often long, with **multiple co-ordination**. **Subordination** is used but speakers have to make sure that embedded subordinate clauses do not place too many demands upon listeners who cannot easily reconsider an utterance.	Punctuation and layout are used to mark the **grammatical boundaries** of sentences. In more formal kinds of writing, sentences are often marked by **multiple subordination** and balanced **syntactical structures**.
Prosodic features like volume, pace, rhythm, tone and stress patterns as well as words communicate meaning.	Writers use **paragraphing** and **page** layout to organise their text. **Capitalisation** and **underlining** can be used for stress, while **question marks** and **exclamation marks** can be used to convey attitude.

Function

Spoken	Written
Speech is a useful **social tool** which can develop relationships and convey attitudes and opinions directly, and so on.	Written text is useful for recording **facts** and **ideas**; making **notes**; and developing large-scale **fiction**, and so on. Because they are more permanent than speech, written texts can be longer without causing communication problems.

Inevitably, a summary like this generalises the differences between speech and writing, but the distinctions here are a useful starting point. It is important, however, to be aware of the overlap between spoken and written forms. Written texts, for instance, can imitate spoken words, so that when spoken they sound spontaneous; likewise spoken texts can be transcribed. An informal conversation and a formal essay can be seen as two extremes – between these, there will be varying degrees of difference. In assessing the differences between spoken and written examples, linguists first establish the audience, purpose and context of the discourse. Having done this, they can consider the extent to which a text or an utterance is typical of speech or writing.

Society is invariably judgemental about language – people write to papers like *The Times* bewailing the poor standards of the 1990s. Prince Charles on several occasions has spoken of what he claims is a deterioration in standards, resulting from a supposedly sloppy attitude towards language and a lack of knowledge about it. At the centre of complaints like these lies the debate about the relative worth of spoken and written language.

Recently, emphasis has moved away from written language as the only mode of value. Traditionally, written language was seen as most significant because it was the medium for education and literature and was, therefore, prestigious. Now, however, schools both use and assess spoken language alongside written language. Our society is dependent upon the telephone, the television and the radio, all of which use spoken language in a variety of forms. Politicians often no longer deliver their speeches as formal written texts read aloud, but 'speak' them directly from notes.

While prescriptivists see speech as inferior because of its errors and hesitations, descriptivists use speech as the basis for much of their research. Not only does spoken language reflect how language is used in society, but language is first and foremost a spoken phenomenon with written language as a by-product.

ACTIVITY 5.3

Copy and complete Table 5.1 with appropriate examples, considering the general features of spoken and written language.

Table 5.1 Features of spoken and written language

Features	*Spoken*	*Written*
Level of formality		
• Formal	Politician's speech	Examination essay
• Informal	1	Shopping list
Level of permanence		
• Permanent	2	Novel
• Short-lived	Conversation with a neighbour over a garden wall	3
Use of Standard English		
• Standard English	BBC News	4
• Non-standard English	5	Use of non-standard language in literature

COMMENTARY

The table shows you how spoken and written language do not always appear at extreme ends of the scale – in many instances **formal speech**, for instance, will be marked by features of written language, and **informal writing** will have similarities with speech. The choices you made in each case will have been dictated by your instinctive knowledge of language and the way it is used.

As an example of informal speech (1) you could have chosen 'friends chatting in a nightclub'. The **context** is informal, the **participants** are familiar and the **purpose** is social. Permanent speech (2) is not typical of spoken language, but a taped police confession, for instance, will be repeatedly listened to by different people in different contexts. The **context** is formal, the **participants** may be known (other police officers) but they may also be unknown (a jury). The **purpose** is official.

Written lists like shopping lists and reminders of tasks to be completed are short-lived (3) because they are often destroyed once the job has been done. The **context** is usually informal and personal, the **audience** is often the writer alone and the **purpose** is informative. Most writing will use Standard English (4) because it tends to be formal. Students will choose Standard English for A-level work, for instance, because the **context** is formal and the **audience** is unknown. The **purpose** is to reveal academic knowledge and to demonstrate written skills. Non-standard speech (5) is common in any informal **context** where participants feel no pressure to conform to the standard. Often the **purpose** of communication will be social and the **audience** will be known. Equally, a television soap opera which aims to imitate life will use the appropriate regional accent and dialect according to the area in which it is set. In Channel 4's *Brookside*, for instance, the young people speak to each other informally in a Merseyside accent.

5.7 Using the basic concepts

All the terms used here play a central part in the study of English because they provide a means for linguists to classify different attitudes and varieties.

Different attitudes to language determine the way usage is classified – while a **prescriptivist** may say a particular usage is 'wrong', a **descriptivist** will describe it as **appropriate** or **inappropriate**. When faced with a range of spoken and written varieties of English, linguists need to establish the **register** (mode, manner and field) and to assess whether the language use is **standard** or **non-standard**. This kind of information enables linguists to avoid uninformed evaluative judgements, ensuring instead that analysis is based on **linguistic evidence**.

Because the terms highlighted here will be used frequently throughout the rest of this book, it is important to understand them before moving on.

6 English: a living language

6.1 English: a living language

Perhaps one of the first things to understand as you begin a study of the English language is that it is constantly changing. It is a **living language**, adapting to an ever-changing world which, in its turn, requires new and varied means of communication. The English language has embraced industrial, technological and social changes and we as users decide what will and what will not survive.

There are always people who yearn for the English language of the past. They believe that English now exists in a corrupted form, simplified and less subtle than its sophisticated antecedent. Their argument suggests that change is a new phenomenon running parallel to the breakdown of society. Taking this to its logical conclusion, we must therefore expect the English language to continue to deteriorate until it exists in a form no longer recognisable or comprehensible. The linguistic pessimists who view the English language in this way are concerned about several factors: supposedly decreasing standards of literacy marked by poor spelling and grammatically incomplete or 'incorrect' sentences; the use of informal spoken language in written contexts; allegedly inaccurate pronunciation; and the way in which international forms of English may affect British English in the future. The list of their complaints could be endless.

However, the debate is two-sided and while the critics bewail the lost glory of English, others see a flexibility and vitality in the adaptability of the English language. The people who believe in language as a democratic process see current linguistic developments broadening our world view: new words reflect new experiences, more liberal attitudes and a greater understanding of the world. Language cannot exist on its own since it is a product of the people who speak and write it daily, and therefore it develops to meet their **needs**. Certainly the English language is changing and certainly the rate of change is rapid, but that is merely a reflection of the society we live in. It does not automatically imply a downward spiral towards an impure and ineffective form of English. A study of the English language should be based on an awareness of these two crucial attitudes. In linguistic terms, the two views can be summarised as the **prescriptive** and the **descriptive** approaches to language.

Language change can be considered in either of two ways. If viewed from a historical perspective, the focus is on language as a constantly changing form. Linguists study the ways in which English has evolved from its early form (Old English) to its current form (Late Modern). This is called a DIACHRONIC APPROACH. If instead change is considered at a particular moment in time, a 'snapshot' is taken of English during a specific stage of its development. Linguists analyse a clearly defined period in order to identify characteristic features of English at that time. This is called a SYNCHRONIC APPROACH.

6.2 What changes language?

Because the sound of words and their order in sentences seems to vary very little, language appears to be quite static. Linguists have now demonstrated, however, that lexis, syntax and semantics are constantly in flux, changing from person to person and from place to place. Until quite recently, it was considered almost impossible to identify and record language changes because they were so gradual that they could easily go unnoticed. Now it is known that although the early stages of change are slow, once they have caught on and are used more regularly, change can be rapid.

Because language **patterns** remain constant, we can assume that change is not random. If change was arbitrary, the English language would eventually be made up of disjointed sequences which language users could not connect into sensible and meaningful patterns. If this was the case, people who see all linguistic change as cause for concern would be justified in their gloomy predictions for the future of the English language. However, linguistic research has shown that language users have a tendency to readjust patterns that have been disturbed. Because the basic function of language is to communicate, its users subconsciously protect its expressive capabilities.

Language change therefore can be seen as **systematic**. Social, historical, cultural or geographical influences can alter the words and structures that we use. These determinants can be described as 'triggers' because they stimulate change in distinctive ways:

- **Historical factors** Wars, invasions, industrial and technological changes all provide the context for the creation of new words.
- **Cultural transmission** Although each generation uses the form of language handed down by the previous generation, language is usually adapted and altered to suit the personal requirements of the next generation. Equally, a distinctive form of language can give a cultural group a sense of identity, uniting 'insiders' and alienating 'outsiders'.
- **Social factors** Education, social class, age, gender, ethnic background, occupation and personal identity will influence the words and grammar that individual speakers use.
- **Geographical location** The pronunciation of words (**accent**) and the kinds of words and grammatical structures used (**dialect**) will vary and change according to the region a speaker comes from.
- **The use of different registers** The words, grammatical structures and formats chosen will vary according to use. Different fields, like law, advertising and religion, will each have distinctive characteristic features.
- **The development of English as a world language** The power of the mass media, international trade, the blurring of international boundaries and easily accessible travel, all mean that English is affected by change both within the United Kingdom and beyond.

Linguists analysing the changing faces of English can categorise their findings by grouping together similar changes. A diachronic study of English will isolate the **historical changes** which have taken place over time. A society-based study of English will analyse **social changes** such as new technological development, changing attitudes and other social determinants affecting the kind of English we use. A cultural study of English will identify **cultural changes**, where groups of people with a distinctive heritage adapt a form of English to draw attention to their common background. A dialectal study of English will map out the **geographical changes** which result in regional variations. An international study of English will focus on **worldwide changes** to English as it is adapted to meet the needs of new first- and second-language speakers.

A study of different varieties of English will concentrate on **register changes** which alter the words, structures and formats of spoken and written English.

6.3 The changing faces of English

As a living language, English is constantly changing to meet the needs of its users. As soon as new forms are observed, described and recorded, other newer forms have appeared. Discussion of linguistic change can therefore never be complete – the summaries provided here merely outline some of the characteristic features in each case. Since historical (Chapter 7), geographical (Chapter 8) and register changes (Chapters 10–19) are considered later in this book, this section will try to pin down some of the social, cultural and worldwide changes that have resulted in distinctive forms of English.

Social changes: gender and language

While SEX describes the biological distinction between men and women, GENDER describes a cultural system by which society constructs different identities for men and women. Feminists believe that images of gender have developed in such a way that the masculine perspective is given a dominant position. They believe that society instils certain codes of behaviour in boys and girls from a young age: men are seen as logical, rational and objective, while women are emotional, intuitive and subjective; masculinity is associated with power and strength, and femininity with passivity and domesticity. Many people now believe that such stereotypical representations of gender should be challenged – individuals should not necessarily be expected to learn the behaviours and attitudes that society sees as appropriate to their sex.

The nature of language is at the very heart of this debate since it is language that teaches individuals to act in a certain way; it is language that reinforces society's expectations; and it is language that makes people powerful. SEXIST LANGUAGE reinforces stereotypical attitudes and expectations – it often implies male superiority. While men are *masterful*, women are *domineering*; while men *discuss*, women *chat* and *gossip*, and while men are *forceful*, women are *bossy*. Often words associated with men have positive connotations: they are *virile*, *manly* and *sporty*; words like *strength*, *independence* and *courage* are commonly linked to them. Women, on the other hand, are associated with *weakness* and with *emotional* and *erratic* behaviour; words like *frailty*, *dependence* and *vulnerability* are traditionally linked to them. Language use like this builds on a stereotypical view of women and men – it implies that differences between women and men are wholly based on gender rather than on individual personalities. Such language can suggest that women are inferior.

It is difficult to change these ingrained habits, but in an age of **political correctness** this kind of divisive language is often seen as quite unacceptable. Many workplaces now have 'equal opportunities' policies in which anti-sexist alternatives are offered as substitutes for the traditional male-dominated language of the office or shop floor. The *chairman* becomes a *chairperson*; *man-hours* become *work-hours*; a *master copy* becomes a *top copy*. For all the outdated terms marked by the generic term *man* there are viable alternatives.

Some people argue that language change must be actively promoted if the status quo is to be altered – that laws should define new acceptable terms of address; that positive discrimination should be used. Others believe that language will change automatically to reflect the new roles women have in society – because language is democratic, its users will dictate what is acceptable and what is not, and changes will follow naturally. The problem seems to be that although equal opportunity policies can suggest new lexical items to replace the older, more sexist alternatives, it is very difficult to change habits. While employers may insist on certain words being used in the workplace, society's underlying attitudes and expectations are far more difficult to challenge.

Research carried out by linguists suggests that not only is language use sexist, but the very roles men and women take in informal conversation are different. On a level of **discourse**:

- men are more likely to interrupt;
- men will often reject topics introduced by women, while women will talk about topics raised by men;
- women are more likely to use supportive minimal vocalisations like *mm* and *yeah*;
- while women are more likely to initiate conversations, they succeed less often because males are less willing to co-operate;
- men are more likely to use familiar terms of address even where the relative status and background of the speakers would seem to suggest that a formal, impersonal tone is more appropriate.

The **grammatical structures** used by women and men are also different:

- women use tag questions more frequently;
- modal verbs, modal adverbs like *probably* and *possibly*, and tentative verbs like *think* and *suppose* occur more often in women's utterances;
- men are more likely to use commands – where women do use them they are often framed as interrogatives like *Would you mind passing me that book?* or as hypothetical statements like *I wonder if you could pass me that book*.

Similarly, **lexical choices** often seem to be related to a speaker's gender:

- women are more likely to use evaluative adjectives like *wonderful*, *brilliant* and *great*;
- adverbs of degree like *so* and *very* are more common in women's speech;
- adjectives describing approximate amounts like *about* and *around* seem to be more common in women's utterances;
- reduplicated forms like *teeny-weeny* and *itsy-bitsy* are associated with women rather than men – because they are linked to baby talk, men see them as inappropriate;
- men are thought to use slang and swearing more frequently;
- women's speech is characterised by the frequency of politeness markers like *please* and *thanks*.

Phonological differences are seen in the fact that women are far more likely to use high-prestige forms and to adjust their accents to match other participants in a formal speech encounter. They are less likely to drop final consonants and to speak with a broad accent if they feel that they need to make a good impression.

Inevitably all the features outlined here are stereotypical because they imply that all women and all men speak in the same way. However, they are interesting to linguists because they illustrate that society's gender expectations influence far more than just the words we choose.

It is easy to see why sexist language is often seen as no more than a matter of lexical choice – it is an area in which linguistic inequality is more obvious than the gender biases that linguists identify in discourse and grammar. It is also the area in which change could be promoted most easily. For the people who wish to accelerate the process of change, it is possible to introduce lexical items as substitutes for the traditional sexist terms. Although lexis is the most accessible part of a language, unless lexical alternatives are set within the context of grammatical and discourse changes, attitudes will change only slowly.

Terms of address can provide a starting point for changing attitudes. Nameplates on office doors need no longer distinguish between *Dr D. B. King* and *Dr Dorothy B. King*; newspapers could standardise their references to males and females, avoiding descriptions of *bubbly blonde Debs* as opposed to *Mr Jackson*. In many contexts, there is no need to distinguish the gender of workers: *firefighter* replaces *fireman*; *conductor* replaces *conductress*; *officer* can be used for *policeman*; *businessperson* for *businessman*. Such changes in lexis reflect **social changes** – women are now part of the workforce at all levels and language needs to reflect this. Descriptions of the *working mother* or *working wife* are outdated because many women now combine domestic and occupational roles and the concept of a woman outside the home environment is no longer unusual.

Many words belittle women, making them seem no more than **sexual objects**. Although often meant to be friendly, in a formal context terms like *love* and *dear* can be offensive since they suggest that women do not have equal status with men. Other informal terms of address like *chicks*, *dolls* and *birds* also equate women with sexual objects. Where the words *master* and *mistress* were originally equivalents, the male term has gained far greater prestige. It is now used in a much wider sense – its connotations are positive, suggesting competence, authority and skill. Those associated with *mistress* on the other hand, are now negative – its field of reference has become narrower until it is now primarily associated with sexuality and illicit affairs.

The **generic *man*** is perhaps the word that causes most upset and for which many people have offered non-sexist alternatives. In Old English, *mann* meant *person*. This term was then accompanied by other distinct forms which marked differences in gender: *wer* (adult man); *wif* (adult woman); *wæpman* (adult male person); and *wifman* (adult female person). By 1850, an Act of Parliament had ruled that 'words importing the masculine gender shall be deemed and taken to include females'. However, many people feel that collocations like *political man* cannot possibly conjure up an image of political females as well as males. Similarly in a historical context, people who wish to actively promote language change believe that it is necessary to substitute phrases like *prehistoric people* for *prehistoric man*, *ancestors* for *forefathers*, and *human kind* for *mankind*.

Many other **collocations** use the generic *man*: *no man is an island*; *the man in the street*; *the common man*; *no-man's-land*; *an Englishman's home is his castle*. Although these are all meant to be inclusive, it is difficult to believe that speakers clearly visualise both men and women. Where *woman* is used in collocations, the connotations tend to be negative – phrases like *women of the night* and *woman driver* are pejorative. The **order of words** in compound phrases also presents a male-dominated view of the world: *husband and wife*; *boys and girls*; *Mr and Mrs*; *man and wife*. Some people would argue that the order of words does not matter, but in the sixteenth century the structure of these phrases was directly linked to the belief that men came before women in the natural order.

The use of the **third person singular pronoun *he*** also causes a lot of controversy. Sixteenth-century grammar books established its use – grammar books were written by men for school boys in a male-dominated society. In this context, the use of *he* was therefore logical: it reflected a literal reality. In the late twentieth century, it no longer reflects a society in which girls have equal access to free education and in which women are supposed to have equal employment opportunities. Although it is meant to be an inclusive reference, linguistic research suggests that in informal conversation, *he* is always a gender-specific reference.

Because English does not have an indefinite pronoun which could replace the supposedly inclusive *he*, many **new pronominal forms** have been suggested. The third person plural *they* which does not distinguish between genders is sometimes used, but purists complain that it is grammatically inaccurate to use it after a singular noun reference: *every person must now collect their ticket*. Another straightforward alternative is to use both the feminine and the masculine singular pronouns: *s/he, he/she*. More drastic measures have been suggested by some people, who propose new pronoun forms: *hesh* for *he/she*; *hirm* for *him/her*; *gen* for the generic *man*; *bod* for *anybody*. If these were to become realistic alternatives and not just gimmicks, it would be necessary to dictate their usage. Schools and government institutions would have to establish a new awareness of these as the 'standard' forms – they would have to enforce usage until it became the norm.

Gender and language are closely linked because it is through language that we communicate and construct models which help us to understand society. Sexist language can disparage and trivialise women and many people believe that the words we use should be carefully chosen to promote sexual equality – women can feel invisible because the English language defines everyone as male. Language does change as society places different demands upon it, and in time it would seem likely that it will encompass changes in women's roles. Inevitably this kind of evolution takes time – in the meantime, political correctness and equal-opportunities policies will endeavour to provide lexical alternatives. Behaviour that is more deeply engrained like female and male roles in discourse will take longer to alter – legislation cannot tackle this because it requires people to have linguistic knowledge and to develop different attitudes and expectations. Despite this, as social attitudes do change, language changes too.

ACTIVITY 6.1

The following examples are all marked by words or structures that reinforce a male-dominated perspective of society. Try to find alternatives which are gender-neutral and decide whether or not gender bias in language matters.

Examples

1 man-made
2 as a mammal, early man breastfed his young
3 manpower
4 Mr Legg runs a company in partnership with his wife
5 lady doctor
6 cameraman
7 the local Girl Guides were manning the sideshows
8 I'll have my girl type that immediately
9 the old masters are well represented in this gallery
10 one-man show
11 statesman

COMMENTARY

Gender-biased language does not present women and men as equal. Instead, it implicitly suggests that men are superior and therefore reinforces the gender roles that society assigns to males and females. The examples in this activity can be divided into three distinct categories: sexist language in the workplace; gender-biased terms of address; and uses of the generic *man*.

The language here associated with the **workplace** (examples 1, 3, 5 and 6) fails to take account of changing employment patterns – many of the words and phrases do not recognise that women are now likely to work alongside men in almost all occupations and at all levels. Nouns like *manpower* (3) can be replaced by a gender-neutral term like *staff* or *workforce* in order to reflect social changes in women's roles. Equally, a product labelled with an adjective like *man-made* (1) can more accurately be described as *synthetic* or *artificial*. Two other examples highlight the need for gender-neutral job titles: in most cases, there is no need to label male or female workers, so terms like *lady doctor* (5) and *cameraman* (6) should be replaced by *doctor* and *camera operator*. The alternatives offered are not cumbersome and substitution would cause no problems of understanding.

Another key area of gender bias can be seen in the **terms of address** (examples 4, 8 and 9) used to define people. These words limit our perceptions because of the connotations they carry. If a (male) boss refers to his personal secretary as *my girl* (8), for instance, he is reducing her role to something insignificant. She is diminished and becomes little more than an object owned by her employer. Similarly, the utterance in which one business partner is named as the *wife* (4) of the other may suggest that she is of minimal importance to the company. While her husband is formally named as *Mr Legg*, she is no more than an attribute of him. In both cases, the gender bias of the noun is underpinned by the use of a possessive determiner which defines the female as a possession of the male. The description of famous artists of the past as *old masters* (9) suggests that there are no women amongst them – the connotations of *master* are linked directly to our concept of successful men. Although many people would not agree that the use of *masters* in this context is as serious as some of the other examples of gender-biased language here, it is easy to replace it with a neutral description like *major artists*.

The use of the **generic *man*** (examples 2, 7, 10 and 11) is more controversial: many people feel that a male reference cannot possibly be all-inclusive. In collocations like a *one-man show* (10) and nouns like *statesman* (11), the generic *man* can be replaced by the general reference *person*: a *one-person show*; *statesperson*. Many people find this kind of substitution awkward, preferring alternatives like *leader* and *politician* to the compound created with *person*. In other cases, verbs derived from the generic *man* can be replaced quite easily: *manning* (7) becomes *staffing* or *running*. In some historical contexts, references to *man* can be contradictory – the example here (2) can easily be made meaningful. The noun phrase can be made gender-specific since it **was** the women who fed the babies: *early women*; or it can be made neutral by changing the word order and using the passive voice: *as mammals, the babies of early people were breastfed*.

In some cases it is possible to promote change by actively encouraging the use of alternatives: in the workplace, in textbooks and in the way that we name each other in everyday encounters. Inevitably, such change takes time and many people will continue to use more traditional forms. Despite this, because language does influence the way we see others, it is important that people are encouraged to recognise that there are alternatives. Language will continue to change to meet the needs of its users and will slowly reflect changing attitudes to gender roles, but positive action to enhance this natural change could help to challenge outdated, preconceived outlooks.

Cultural changes – Black English

Because of technological developments, increased travel opportunities and international multimedia links, it is possible that different languages and variants of the same language will in time become increasingly uniform. Despite this possibility, however, there are still many examples of linguistic diversity. In some instances, changes to a standard form of language are linked directly to social class or to the promotion and preservation of a particular cultural background or ethnic identity.

BLACK AMERICAN ENGLISH (**BAE**), for instance, is the language used by lower-class Blacks in urban communities. Probably 80 per cent of Black Americans can speak this variety, but as Blacks have become more integrated and as a Black middle class has developed, the language form used by the other 20 per cent has moved closer to Standard American English. BLACK ENGLISH VERNACULAR (**BEV**) is not a regional dialect because it is difficult to link it directly to a specific geographical area. Instead, it tends to be classified as a CULTURAL or SOCIAL VARIANT from the standard form. It is often described as a **'political' non-standard form** because as a distinct and separate variety of spoken English it is in direct conflict with STANDARD AMERICAN ENGLISH (**SAE**).

The history of Black English in America can be linked to the slave trade in the seventeenth, eighteenth and nineteenth centuries, when Africans were taken from their native lands to American plantations. There are different theories about the way in which Black English developed. Some people believe that because the slaves learned English from their masters as a second language, they passed on to their children a form of American English that was grammatically different from American Standard English. Because of racial segregation, the dialect features of this variety persisted and are still to be found in Late Modern Black English. Another view of the development of Black English suggests that many of its features are directly linked to West African languages. In the seventeenth and eighteenth centuries, African slaves who spoke the same languages were always kept apart, to prevent slave revolts. This meant that English was often the slaves' only common language. Rather than SAE, the slaves used a language made up of English and West African linguistic features: the vocabulary was dominated by English words and the grammatical structures were simplified.

So that English-speaking whites could communicate with Africans a CONTACT or PIDGIN LANGUAGE was developed. Pidgins are marginal languages created by people who need to communicate but have no common language. They are marked by a **simplified grammar** and a **small vocabulary** (about 700–2000 words); they have a **smaller range of functions** than either of the source languages from which they are formed. They can be distinguished from dialects because they are clearly made up from two source languages – parts of them will not be understandable to speakers who know only one of the source languages. Most pidgins are based on European languages (**English**, **French**, **Spanish**, **Dutch** and **Portuguese**), reflecting Europe's history of colonisation. Often when the original need for communication is no longer important, pidgin languages die – in Vietnam, for example **French Pidgin** no longer served any purpose when the French left and was therefore no longer used. Some, however, become so useful that they develop a more formal role, gaining official status and expanding to meet the needs of users. A language that develops in this way is called an EXPANDED PIDGIN or a LINGUA FRANCA. In Papua New Guinea, for instance, **Tok Pisin** is now recognised both as a primary language in urban centres and as a lingua franca in more remote areas.

When a pidgin becomes the main language of a community, it has to become more complex and be able to fulfil a wider range of functions. When later generations learn it as a first language, it is called a CREOLE. Creoles can develop in a variety of ways – if pidgin speakers can no longer use their first language, the pidgin will become a primary rather than an auxiliary language; in a community of mixed races, if the pidgin language is used in private contexts like the home as well as in public contexts, children will begin to learn it as a first language. For a pidgin language to become a creole, certain criteria must be met: the **vocabulary** has to be expanded: **grammatical structures** have to be able to communicate more complicated meanings; and **style** has to be adaptable.

There are two kinds of creole Englishes: **Atlantic** and **Pacific creoles**. Because Portuguese explorers had been trading in gold and people from the coast of West Africa since the early fifteenth century, later European traders found that many Africans used a simplified version of Portuguese. This formed the basis for a new pidgin, and English creoles are marked by the number of Portuguese words they still contain. The Atlantic varieties are connected to the languages of the West African coast.

The **grammatical structures** of creole languages tend to be marked by the following features.

- The absence of plural forms – creoles usually rely on the context to indicate whether or not a noun is plural. In Atlantic varieties, *dem* is often placed immediately after the noun.
- Third person singular pronouns are not marked for gender – *i* is used for *he*, *she* and *it*.
- Nouns can be marked for gender by adding *man* (man) or *meri* (woman).
- Verbs are not marked for person or tense – all verbs are used in the base form. Different timescales are indicated by the addition of auxiliary verbs like *did* or *been*, or by creole words like *baimbai* (by and by) for future time or *pinish* (finish) for past time.
- Multiple negatives are common.
- Some varieties distinguish between two kinds of *we*: *yumi* (you and me); *mipela* (me and other people, not including you).

Certain **lexical patterns** are distinctive:

- **REDUPLICATION** of words is used to extend a limited vocabulary: *ile* (hilly) → *ileile* (choppy sea).
- Reduplication can also distinguish between two words that sound similar: *sun* and *sand* would both be articulated as *san*, so *sand* is realised as *sansan*.
- Reiterated words are also used to intensify meanings, to mark continuity and to create emphasis: *smal* (small) → *smalsmal* (very small).
- Many nautical words were introduced in the first contact languages that evolved as a means of communication between the native language speakers and traders. In the creole varieties, these have modified their original terms of reference: *galley* (ship's kitchen) → *gali* (any kitchen).

In America, the pidgin English used on the slave plantations became a first-language creole. It was no longer just used for basic communication, but evolved so that it was central to the community. It was used in practical contexts for everyday communication; in ritual contexts for developing community worship; in celebrations and in oral storytelling traditions. Perhaps most importantly, it became a language of resistance since it was markedly different from the standard form of English used by the plantation owners. Creoles are often regarded as inferior by speakers who use a standard form of language.

In social terms, creole languages have no educational status, little social prestige and are usually spoken by people in the poorer social classes. Because they are linked to slavery and subjection, users are under pressure to adopt standard forms of language instead. The process by which creoles are modified by standard usage is called **DECRE-OLISATION**. As speakers adapt their language use, the original creole then exists in a variety of forms, all varying in different degrees from the standard. This range of creole forms is called the **POST-CREOLE CONTINUUM**. In some cases, speakers will automatically reassert the value of their first-language creole to challenge the superiority of the standard language that society wishes them to speak. This results in **HYPERCREOLISATION** – speakers use pure creole forms to emphasise their ethnic and cultural background.

Black English is not a creole, but its source lies in the pidgin and creole languages spoken by the African slaves on the plantations. Just as the history of the slave trade resulted in the development of social and cultural creole language forms, so too the social and cultural background of American Blacks resulted in the creation of Black English. Like the earlier creole languages, Black English differs from Standard American English in its vocabulary and grammatical patterns; it is an **ANTI-LANGUAGE** which is used as a challenge to the authority of society's accepted channels of communication.

An anti-language is an extreme version of a social dialect which is used by speakers who are on the edges of society – legally, financially, or culturally. The use of an alternative to the accepted standard reinforces **group identity** and emphasises that the users are outsiders. The use of Black English in America confirms Black solidarity and self-value in the face of segregation and white opposition. It creates links with the ancestral and cultural past of the speakers, while distancing them from mainstream society. Its distinctive grammatical patterns set it apart from American Standard English, challenging the accepted and ordered vision of life that the traditional language affirms. Its use can therefore be described as a **political statement** since it aims to challenge the status quo. Although commonly associated with Blacks in the lower social classes, educated people use Black English to convey political or cultural messages.

The **grammatical variations** from the standard that occur in Black English are rule-governed – that is, they are not haphazard, but follow distinctive patterns. The following features are typical of Black English.

- The copula verb (a linking verb) *to be* is omitted (*he good*).
- The base form of the verb *to be* is used as an auxiliary to express habitual action in the progressive aspect (*she be thinking*).
- Verbs in the present tense third person singular are not inflected with -*s* (*she eat*).
- The past participle of the verb *to be* is used to convey past activity when it still has a current relevance (*we been going there for years*).
- The auxiliary verb *do* is used with the past participle to imply a finished activity (*he done painted the room*).
- Plural nouns are uninflected (*two apple*).
- Multiple negation is common (*we don't go no more*).
- Pronoun usage differs from Standard English (*me take it to dem later*).

Pronunciations are also distinctive, and this affects the spelling of Black English when in a written form.

- Consonant clusters are simplified at the end of words, particularly where one of the consonants is an alveolar /t/, /d/, /s/ or /z/ (*ast* for *asked*).
- /θ/ is realised as /f/ or /t/, and /ð/ as /v/ or /d/ (*tink* for *think*; *de* for *the*).
- Vowel sounds reflect pronunciation (*git* for *get*; *mek* for *make*; *kus* for *curse*; *ketch* for *catch*).
- /r/ is deleted in intervocalic and final positions (*duing* /duːɪŋ/ for *during*).

There are other differences between Black English and Standard American English, but the features listed here demonstrate that changes to the standard language form are systematic and similar to other dialectal variations. This highlights the fact that Black English is not linguistically substandard. When described as primitive and illogical, the judgements being made are social, not linguistic.

By using Black English alongside the American standard, Black speakers can switch between two viable linguistic systems. The choice of language system becomes as important as the words uttered in conveying a political, social or cultural message.

ACTIVITY 6.2

Read the text below and comment on the following:

1 the different registers used;
2 features typical of Black English;
3 the message the writer is trying to convey.

White English in Blackface, or Who Do I Be?
GENEVA SMITHERMAN

1   Ain nothin in a long time lit up the English teaching profession like the current hassle over Black English. One finds beaucoup sociolinguistic research studies and language projects for the 'disadvantaged' on the scene in nearly every sizable black community in the country. And educators from K-Grad.
5   School bees debating whether: (1) blacks should learn and use only standard white English (hereafter referred to as WE); (2) blacks should command both dialects, i.e., be bi-dialectal (hereafter BD); (3) blacks should be allowed (??????) to use standard Black English (hereafter BE or BI). The appropriate choice having everything to do with American political reality, which is usu-
10   ally ignored, and nothing to do with the educational process, which is usually claimed. I say without qualification that we cannot talk about the Black Idiom apart from Black Culture and the Black Experience. Nor can we specify educational goals for blacks apart from considerations about the structure of (white) American society.
15   And we black folks is not gon take all that weight, for no one has empirically demonstrated that linguistic/stylistic features of BE impede educational progress in communication skills, or any other area of cognitive learning. Take reading. It's don been charged, but not actually verified, that BE interferes with mastery of reading skills. Yet beyond pointing out the gap between
20   the young brother/sistuh's phonological and syntactical patterns and those of the usually-middle-class-WE-speaking-teacher, this claim has not been validated. The distance between the two systems is, after all, short and is illuminated only by the fact that reading is taught *orally*. (Also get to the fact that preceding generations of BE-speaking folks learned to read, despite the
25   many classrooms in which the teacher spoke a dialect different from that of her students.)
        For example, a student who reads *den* for *then* probably pronounces initial /th/ as /d/ in most words. Or the one who reads *duing* for *during* probably deletes intervocalic and final /r/ in most words. So it is not that such students
30   can't read, they is simply employing the black phonological system. In the reading classrooms of today, what we bees needin is teachers with the proper attitudinal orientation who thus can distinguish actual reading problems from mere dialect differences. Or take the writing of an essay. The only percentage in writing a paper in WE spelling, punctuation, and usage is in
35   maybe eliciting a positive *attitudinal* response from a prescriptivist middle-class-aspirant-teacher. Dig on the fact that sheer 'correctness' does not a good writer make. And is it any point in dealing with the charge of BE speakers being 'non-verbal' or 'linguistically deficient' in oral communication skills – behind our many Raps who done disproved that in living, vibrant color?
40   What linguists and educators need to do at this juncture is to take serious cognizance of the Oral Tradition in Black Culture. The uniqueness of this

verbal style requires a language competence/performance model to fit the black scheme of things. Clearly BI speakers possess rich communication skills (i.e., are highly *competent* in using language), but as yet there bees no
45 criteria (evaluative, testing, or other instrument of measurement), based on black communication patterns, wherein BI speakers can demonstrate they competence (i.e., *performance*). Hence brothers and sisters fail on language performance tests and in English classrooms. Like, to amplify on what Nikki said, that's why we always lose, not only cause we don't know the rules, but
50 it ain't even our game.

Leonard Michaels and Christopher Ricks (eds), The State of the Language

COMMENTARY

The **field** of the essay focuses on the issue of language and education. **Lexical sets** based on each of these key areas are wide ranging. Subject specific linguistic terminology is used frequently: *dialects* (l. 7), *bi-dialectal* (l. 7), *prescriptivist* (l. 35), *intervocalic* (l. 29), *phonological system* (l. 30) and *phonological and syntactical patterns* (l. 20). The educational terminology is linked directly to speaking, reading and the assessment of skills: *cognitive learning* (l. 17), *oral communication skills* (l. 38), *language performance tests* (ll. 47–8), *actual reading problems* (ll. 32–3), *educational process* (l. 10), *educational progress* (ll. 16–17), *educational goals* (ll. 12–13) and *empirically demonstrated* (ll. 15–16). All these examples highlight the formal **mode** of the piece – it is written by an expert for other experts. Formal words are chosen where everyday alternatives would be equally acceptable: *employing* (l. 30) for *using*, *cognizance* for *notice* (l. 41), *hereafter* (l. 6), *wherein* (l. 46) and *juncture* (l. 40). However, this tone is not used throughout and an informal conversational register is juxtaposed with it on several occasions. The informal mode can be recognised in a variety of ways: words like *hassle* (l. 2), *ain't* (l. 50), *cause* (l. 49); phrases like *Also get to the fact. . .* (l. 23) and *Dig on the fact that. . .* (l. 36); ellipsis like *(there) Ain nothing* (l. 1); and words like *And. . .* (l. 15) and *Like. . .* (l. 48) in the initial position.

This juxtaposition of tones forces the reader to actively respond to the content. It encourages an intellectual focus on the issues being discussed. At first sight it would appear to be no more than an academic essay on the importance of *Black Culture* (l. 12) and the strengths of *Black English* (l. 2) or the *Black Idiom* (l. 11). The issues are brought to life, however, because the style as well as the content challenges preconceived attitudes towards 'standard white English' and Black English. A theoretical discussion of the way in which politics affects educational matters is made both personal and emotive.

The **noun phrases** are long and complex, providing a lot of information in a short space.

> m m m h q
> a positive attitudinal response from a prescriptivist middle-class-aspirant-teacher
> det Adj Adj N PrepP

(ll. 35–6)

This approach adds to the formality of the tone. Many of the verbs are also not associated with everyday conversation: *impede* (l. 16), *validated* (ll. 21–2), *eliciting* (l. 35) and *illuminated* (ll. 22–3). Other examples suggest, however, that the writer is not wholly serious, that she is challenging society's easy acceptance of white dominance. By using the French *beaucoup* (l. 2) alongside subject-specific lexis like *sociolinguistic research studies* (ll. 2–3), the writer seems to mock Standard American English.

There are certain features that mark this essay as **American English**: the spelling of *sizable* (l. 4), *color* (l. 39) and *cognizance* (l. 41); and a collocation like *The only percentage in. . .* (ll. 33–4). The **Black English** features, however, do more than identify this as American English – they provide concrete evidence of the writer's argument. Some **lexis** is commonly associated with Black speakers: *brother/sistuh's* (l. 20), *brothers and sisters* (l. 47) and *Raps* (l. 39). Certain **spellings** can be linked directly to Black English phonological features: *gon* (l. 15), *don* (l. 18), *nothin* (l. 1) and *sistuh* (l. 20). The **grammar** is also distinctive. Many of the verbs are marked in a distinctive way: non-agreement between subject and verb – *we black folks is not gon. . .* (l. 15) and *they is* (l. 30); the copula verb *to be* is used in non-standard forms – *School bees debating* (l. 5), *we bees needin* (l. 31), *there bees no criteria* (ll. 44–5); the dummy auxiliary *to do* is used to convey a sense of something that has been finished in the past – *It's don been charged* (l. 18) and *Raps who done disproved* (l. 39). In one instance, the pronoun system is simplified so that the personal pronoun *they* is used instead of the possessive determiner *their* (l. 46).

The writer's approach draws attention to the **message** underlying the stylistic variations. She clearly lists the three possible linguistic alternatives: Blacks should only use standard white English; they should be able to use both dialects; or society should 'allow' them to use Black English. Smitherman makes her views plain by enclosing six question marks in brackets after using the verb *allowed* (ll. 7–8) in the passive voice with its connotations of a superior authority granting permission to an inferior group. Having established her attitude implicitly in the beginning, she then develops her argument in a more concrete way. She emphasises that the battle over white and Black English is more to do with politics than education – because their language is directly linked to *Black Culture and the Black Experience* (l. 12), its use is a challenge to the white status quo. She points out that there is no evidence to suggest that Black English hinders educational progress – spoken language and reading are not adversely affected. Apparent reading problems are a result of a different phonological system, not an inability to learn. Smitherman suggests that Blacks fail on language performance tests because these are all designed for white speaking students and are not designed to show the Black students' skills. She concludes her argument by reminding readers of two things: the power of white English lies only in the social and educational attitudes to it; and the power of the *Oral Tradition in Black Culture* (l. 41) lies in its rich and vibrant communication skills.

The essay ends with the **metaphor** of a game in which Black English speakers are expected to compete without knowing the rules. This is an effective and dramatic end to an unusual and thought-provoking piece.

International changes – English as a world language

In the sixteenth century, there were under 5 million English speakers in the world – in the late twentieth century, there are 300–400 million first-language speakers and probably 1.5 billion English speakers worldwide. English is spoken in all five continents and is the recognised language of trade and international affairs.

Various **criteria** must be met if a language is to become a 'world' language: the number of first-language speakers must be high; users must be spread over a wide geographical area; and political and economic affairs must be stable so that the language can spread without large-scale opposition. Inevitably the source language changes as it comes into contact with new geographical and cultural environments. Linguistic pessimists believe that this process of change will ultimately make English no more than a series of overlapping dialects which will eventually become mutually incomprehensible. Other linguists believe that multimedia technology and the printed word will prevent such dramatic linguistic change. The Live Aid concert, for instance, was watched by a third of the world's population, while international pop stars like Michael Jackson and Madonna sell albums in huge numbers in twenty or more countries. These kinds of influences are stabilising forces which limit the changes taking place.

The world wide status of English is linked to the growth of the **British Empire** and the **colonisation** of places like India and Southern Africa from the seventeenth century onwards. In the military and commercial contacts that followed, native languages were often suppressed by the British rulers. The arrival of British settlers in North America in the early seventeenth century was also a significant stage in the development of English as a world language – by the end of the eighteenth century, English was the dominant language in North America.

The recognition of **English's role as a world language** has continued to grow. Linguists now believe that far from breaking away into mutually incomprehensible dialects, **world English** is developing a distinctive form of its own. This particular form of the language has no geographical markers and has been described as **standard international English**. It is used by international organisations like the European Free Trade Association (EFTA); by pilots and air traffic controllers at airports ('airspeak'); by international traders; and by police involved with international investigations ('police-speak'). Although each of these varieties has its own distinctive characteristics, linguists see the many common features as evidence that a 'standard world English' is emerging.

By looking at examples of world English it is possible to see the ways in which each variation changes the standard English that is spoken in the United Kingdom. In new environments, English acquires local nuances, particularly in its lexis. English, for instance, came to Australia with the first settlers in the eighteenth century and AUSTRALIAN ENGLISH emerged as the language evolved to fit its new historical, cultural and geographical circumstances. Many of the early settlers were convicts from the lower social classes who were more likely to use distinctive regional dialects, and it is therefore sometimes thought that the distinctive Australian accent resulted from the mix of UK regional accents handed down to descendants of the first English speakers. Australian English is marked by the number of Aboriginal words that have been assimilated into the language: *kangaroo*, *koala*, *billabong* (stagnant pool). These words filled gaps where there were no English equivalents for previously unknown plants, animals or geographical features. Television has made us familiar with examples of Australian English like *sheila* for a girl and *Pom* for someone from the UK.

AMERICAN ENGLISH is another distinct variety. Noah Webster's dictionary of American English in 1828 formalised the difference between UK English and American English spellings. It established American English as a separate form with its own spelling patterns: *color*, *theater*, *center* and *traveling*; and distinctive pronunciations: *missile* in American English rhymes with 'bristle' in UK English, and *momentary* has its stress on the third syllable (*mo men 'ta ry*, rather than '*mo men ta ry* as used traditionally in UK English – though the American version is now becoming more common in Britain too). Idioms like *have a nice day*, prepositions like *from...through* and lexis assimilated from America's immigrant population like *pastrami* and *bagel* are now often heard and sometimes used by UK English speakers. As with other versions of world English, much of our knowledge of American English comes from television and cinema.

Similarly, British Telecom **advertisements** with Maureen Lipman, and the Jewish ghost in the BBC television **situation comedy** *So Haunt Me*, use JEWISH ENGLISH. This has made mass audiences familiar with a linguistic device called FRONTING: *That you call a meal*. In this kind of structure, an inversion of the word order is used to create a mock emphasis of disbelief. Other forms of world English are not so common on our television screens, but are equally significant in terms of the international growth of the language. In India, there are about fifteen official languages and thousands of other dialect variations. Often, the only common language will be INDIAN ENGLISH. This too has developed distinctive features since it is usually learnt from books which rarely keep up to date with the subtleties of linguistic change. Indian English is, therefore, often considered to be very formal and dated. Words are sometimes used in a slightly unusual way – analogies are used to make new forms that have no parallel in UK English. Knowing the word *backside*, for instance, Indian English also uses *frontside*, *rightside* and *leftside*. Contracted phrases are also common, resulting in a kind of telegraphic talk: *key bunch* (bunch of keys) and *God-love* (love of God).

In countries where English is a second language, new formations are more common. Words can be humorous because they are almost but not quite what we are accustomed to. JAPANESE ENGLISH is known for its amusing 'misinterpretations', in which sandwiches are *sand witches*, the orchestra pit is an *orchestra box*, pedestrians are *passengers of foot* and motorists *tootle* their horns. Such variations from the source language, however, do not really cause problems of understanding.

Not all countries welcome the spread of English. It has been described as a **virus** by some linguists because it seems possible that it will replace the first language of many ethnic groups. At the height of European colonisation, there were approximately 1500 languages in the 'New World', but the majority have already died out. Even though there are attempts to revive and regenerate languages, ultimately the pressure of ethnic minorities to learn English makes their survival doubtful.

In **France**, the Académie Française is an official body which protects and regulates the French language. Speakers commonly use words like *le weekend, le fast food* and *le sandwich*, but recently objections have been raised about the way in which English words are infiltrating French. The Académie has banned the use of blended words like *un Walkman* and *un disc-jockey* on the radio – instead, the French equivalents *un baladeur* and *un animateur* must be used: failure to do so will result in a fine. Many of these words reflect the fact that the concept or product is not a part of French cultural tradition. When new products appear on the international markets, however, French purists argue that a new French word should be created. The safety airbag that is now fitted in many cars, for instance, is called *l'airbag* in French; many people believe a distinctive French word should be created to replace this blended word, since the process of creation would enrich French vocabulary, allowing the language to reflect changes in lifestyle as they occur.

6.4 The democratic nature of language change

Ultimately, as the history of language shows, it is very difficult to artificially control any language because language growth is organic, evolving to meet the demands users place upon it. Therefore, whatever linguists feel about the effects social, cultural and worldwide changes have on language, if the changes are useful they will probably survive. Those which have no real function, on the other hand, will perhaps be fashionable for a period before disappearing without trace. History would also suggest that English and its 'world' variations are highly unlikely to become mutually incomprehensible since the political and cultural developments of the twentieth century are bringing nations together rather than separating them.

Change is at the heart of a living language and by embracing it rather than fearing it, language users can benefit from the diversity that linguistic flexibility offers. The national and international dialects of English do not threaten but enrich the UK standard.

7 Historical change

7.1 The reason for studying historical change

In order to see how English has developed, it is important to think about the language both **synchronically** (as a snapshot of a particular moment) and **diachronically** (as part of a historical process). By concentrating on key periods and by analysing textual examples, it is possible to establish the characteristics of the English language at different times in its history and thus to see how older forms differ from the English we speak and write today. To focus your attention appropriately, for each period you will need to think about the changes in semantics, lexis, syntax, phonology and graphology.

To understand how and why the English language has become what it is, linguists study both the **causes** of change and the **characteristics** of English at key stages. For convenience, they refer to five distinct periods in the history of the English language: OLD ENGLISH (**OE**), 450–1150; MIDDLE ENGLISH (**ME**), 1150–1500; EARLY MODERN ENGLISH (**EME**), 1500–1700; MODERN ENGLISH (**ModE**), 1700–1900; and LATE MODERN ENGLISH (**LME**), 1900–1990s. These dates give a general indication of the different stages, but are only approximate since linguistic change does not take place neatly within boundaries. Linguists draw attention to the most significant linguistic features in each key period, and looking back it is easy to recognise the points at which each change occurs. However, it is important to remember that the process is gradual, often taking place over hundreds of years.

As the aim of this book is to give you practice in handling source material, this chapter will not cover the historical background of each period. This information can be found in many language textbooks, some of which are listed in Appendix C. Use the summaries following each extract to help you structure your reading and note-making.

7.2 The importance of text analysis

All that remains of earlier forms of English is to be found in surviving written documents. Linguists use these to build up a sense of what English was like. By analysing lexis, syntax and graphology, it is possible to chart how and why English changed. Some assumptions can also be made about the phonological structure of English, but until the age of recording, this can only be informed guesswork.

The Old English to Modern English periods will be represented here by prose texts. Close analysis of the examples highlights characteristic features of each key period, providing concrete evidence of the ways in which English was used. Inevitably, written examples can only hint at the nature of the language of everyday communication and literary language in particular is more likely to be manipulated and crafted to achieve certain effects. The constraints of poetic structure, for instance, can mean that word order is changed to achieve the right number of syllables in a line or to create a rhyme. Although poetic language has all the characteristic features of the period in which it was written, additional alterations may be linked to prosody (distinctive features of verse) rather than the nature of English at the time. By concentrating on prose, therefore, it is possible to understand more precisely the characteristic features of the language.

Surviving Old English poems like 'Beowulf' and 'The Seafarer' are marked by distinctive poetic features like half-line divisions and alliterative patterns. These features make Old English poetic language quite different from the English used in prose and speech. Non-fiction prose like the Anglo-Saxon Chronicle is not so consciously crafted. It recorded events in the form of a year-to-year diary. Early entries are list-like and are more likely to resemble everyday usage.

Middle English poems like Chaucer's *Canterbury Tales* and the anonymous *Gawain and the Green Knight* and Early Modern English plays by Shakespeare provide linguists with crucial information about literary language. It is prose texts, however, that highlight linguistic features of English at each stage of its development. *The Paston Letters*, for instance, were written by individuals during the Middle English and Early Modern English periods. Because they are examples of private correspondence, they provide linguists with evidence of the way in which ordinary people used English.

As a contrast, the Modern English texts cited here are examples of fictional prose. Since both are first person narratives (stories told from the point of view of a particular character), the writers are to some extent imitating individual style. Written language will usually be more formal than spoken language, but the narrative texts highlight some of the distinctive features of the period in real contexts.

By this stage in the history of English, there are few differences between the style and structure of Modern English and Late Modern English. No Late Modern English text is discussed here since the rest of the book will provide a range of examples for analysis.

7.3 The Old English period

It is by reading the surviving manuscripts of the Old English period that linguists have been able to ascertain so much about the lexis and grammar of Old English. The surviving alliterative poetry, the documentation of charters and wills, and the religious homilies all provide linguistic evidence for analysis.

Old English text

Alfred the Great saw the need for a compilation of important events and towards the end of the ninth century, he ordered that the Anglo-Saxon Chronicle should be written. This key historical document was continued for two centuries after his death. The fact that it was written in English helped to give the English people a sense of their own identity.

ACTIVITY 7.1

Read through the extract below and complete the questions that follow it.

from Cunewulf and Cyneheard

1 755 Hēr Cynewulf benam Sigebryht his rīces ond Westseaxna wiotan for unryhtum dǣdum, būton Hamtūnscīre; ond hē hæfde þa oþ hē ofslog þone aldormon þe him lengest wunode. Ond hiene þā Cynewulf on Andred ādrǣfde; ond hē þǣr wunade oþ þæt hiene ān swān ofstang æt Pryfetes
5 flōdan – ond hē wræc þone aldormon Cumbran.

Sweet's Anglo-Saxon Reader in Prose and Verse

1 Identify any unusual letter forms.
2 Make a list of all the Old English words that you think look familiar, and their Contemporary English equivalents. Record any changes in spelling.
3 List any words that appear to be inflected.
4 Using the Old English word list below, make a word-for-word translation of the extract.

Because Old English is an inflected language and because irregular patterns often change vowels, words in the text may appear in a slightly different form in the list.

ādrǣfan; ādrǣfde (past tense)	to drive
benǣman; benam (past tense)	to deprive
būton	except for
dǣd	deed/act
(e)aldor-man	prince/leader
habban; hæfde (past tense)	to have/to possess
Hamtūnscīre	Hampshire
hēr	in this year
hiene/hine	him
ofslēan; ofslog (past tense)	to slay
ofstingan; ofstang (past tense)	to stab to death
oþ þæt	until
Pryfetes flōde	the stream at Privett
rīce	kingdom
swān	swineherd
þa (adv)	then
þa (det)	the/that
þǣr (adv)	there
þe (pron)	who
þone	that
unryht	wrong/wicked
wiote	councillors
wrecan; wræc (past tense)	to take revenge
wunian; wunode/wunade (past tense)	to remain

5 Compare your version with the Contemporary English translation below and comment on any differences in lexis or syntax (word order).

1 757   In this year Cynewulf and the councillors of the West Saxons deprived Sigebryht of his kingdom because of his unjust acts, except for Hampshire; and he retained that until he killed the prince who stood by him longest; and then Cynewulf drove him into the Weald, and he lived there until a swineherd
5 stabbed him to death by the stream at Privett. He was taking revenge for Prince Cumbran.

COMMENTARY

Although some vowels are marked for length, most of this extract uses the letters of the **Roman alphabet**. It also, however, uses two of the Anglo-Saxon runes: þ and æ. It is these and unfamiliar words which make Old English seem so alien to modern readers. The words that are recognisable are all **closed-class words** with a grammatical function:

- determiners: *ān* (l. 4), *his* (l. 1);
- pronouns: *hē* (l. 5), *him* (l. 3);
- prepositions: *for* (l. 1), *on* (l. 3), *æt* (l. 4);
- conjunctions: *ond* (l. 2).

Some **open-class words** like the noun *dǣdum* (l. 2), the superlative adjective *lengest* (l. 3) and the adverb *þǣr* (l. 4) are also recognisable. Most of these words survive in an identical form in Late Modern English, but some have undergone minor changes in spelling: *deed* has replaced *dǣd* (l. 2); *at* has replaced *æt* (l. 4); *and* has replaced *ond* (l. 2); *longest* has replaced *lengest* (l. 3); and *there* has replaced *þǣr* (l. 4).

To produce a fluent Late Modern English version, **lexical and syntactical changes** have to be made to the original Old English text. The Old English preposition *for* (l. 1), for instance, can be replaced by the phrase *because of*, while the Old English adjective *unryhtum* (l. 2) is best conveyed by the Late Modern English *unjust*. While these alterations create greater fluency, other lexical changes **clarify meanings**. Old English *ofslog* (l. 2) is now archaic, so it needs to be replaced by a more general term *kill* to reflect changes in warfare. The Old English verb *wunian* (ll. 3, 4) is given a wider variety of meanings – the Late Modern English idiom *to stand by* is used with a distinctive meaning quite separate from *to live*, whereas Old English uses the same verb.

Because Late Modern English is dependent on **word order** to convey meaning, it is necessary to alter some of the Old English constructions. In the original text, the plural noun phrase *Westseaxna wiotan* (l. 1) has a nominative (subject) case inflection and therefore despite the fact that it is separated from the rest of the subject, *Cynewulf* (l. 1), it is possible to recognise its function. In Late Modern English, however, it is necessary to put the two phrases together. Similarly, to a modern reader the pronoun *hiene* (l. 3) may appear to be the subject of the sentence because of its position: *hiene þā Cynewulf* (l. 3) and *hiene an swān ofstang* (l. 4). However, because of its accusative (object) form, it must be translated as *him*.

Such changes emphasise both the development of the word stock and the simplification of inflections since the Old English period.

Summary

Examples of surviving Old English texts tell linguists something about the nature of English at the time.

Semantics

A modern reader cannot rely on understanding words in context since so many are alien to us: *būton* (l. 2) and *þone* (l. 2). Much of the writing seems to focus on battle and conflict: *ofslog* (l. 2), *ofstang* (l. 4) and *wræc* (l. 5).

Lexis

A few words have remained unchanged (particularly the closed-class words) while others can be recognised even though the spelling may be unfamiliar. The majority of the Old English word stock, however, has now disappeared in a process that started as words were borrowed from Latin and Old Norse: *benæman/benam* (l. 1) was displaced by *dēprivāre* (L); *ofslēan/ofslog* (l. 2) by *slā* (ON).

Grammar

The **word order** is reasonably close to that of Late Modern English, but because Old English was an inflected language, the order is more flexible. Modern readers therefore have to consider inflections carefully to work out the function of a particular word. For example, *his rīces* (l. 1) is marked by the genitive (possessive) singular neuter noun declension *-es* to indicate the possessive of *his kingdom*.

The system of Old English declension to mark case disappeared as the language was simplified – prepositions now imply relationships within a sentence. There were considerably more strong or irregular verbs in Old English than in Late Modern English and this too is evidence of the way in which language evolves. Language often simplifies usage, and irregular Old English past tense verbs that took a vowel change are often regular in Late Modern English: the irregular *ofstang* (l. 4) has been replaced by the regular *stabbed* and the irregular *benam* (l. 1) has been replaced by the regular *deprived*.

Phonology

Linguists can only make assumptions about the pronunciations of Old English, but from a study of surviving texts it is possible to identify a range of dialectal differences just as we have in Late Modern English. The stress was always on the first syllable of each word and contemporary versions of surviving manuscripts mark long vowels with ¯ to distinguish between the different sounds. There were no silent letters in Old English so an *-e* in the word-final position was pronounced. The Old English *flōde* for LME *stream*, for instance, would have been pronounced phonetically as [fləʊdə] rather than as the LME *flood* [flʌd]. Old English was very much part of the oral tradition in which literature was handed down from generation to generation in a spoken form. It used techniques like alliteration to emphasise the sound of the language.

Graphology

The Roman alphabet was used to record Old English in written forms, but additional runic symbols were added to mark sounds that were not represented. In contemporary versions, þ (thorn) and ð (eth) are still used to reflect a *th* sound, while the runic ƿ (wyn) and ʒ (yogh) are usually replaced by *w* and *g* or *j*. The æ symbol is used to convey a short *a* as in LME *cat* [kæt].

This brief summary highlights some key features of Old English. It is a synchronic study of English during the Old English period. In order to understand the way in which language changes over time, however, linguists consider Old English's relationship with other periods, undertaking a diachronic study of the historical process.

7.4 The Middle English period

Because French was the prestige language in the years after the Norman Conquest, most patronage of the arts focused on the production of French texts. However, the incentives were different in religious contexts and any literature recorded in English in the years 1150–1250 was almost exclusively religious: paraphrases of the Bible, interpretations of the Gospels, and so on. There was inevitably a range of popular literature in English, but because this will have been part of the oral culture little remains of the ballads of the time. After 1250, there is evidence that English was used to write romances, but our main experience of Middle English written texts comes from a period which is now often called 'the age of the great individual writers' and the text that you will now consider falls into this period (1350–1400).

Middle English text

Private letters still exist in quite large numbers from the fifteenth century onwards. The example you are about to read is taken from one of many letters saved by the Paston family over several generations. They are mostly personal records of everyday events, but perhaps the most interesting feature is in the actual form of English used to record these. Although the adoption of a standard form of the language had to some extent been stabilised and fixed, private correspondence like the letters of the Paston family did not yet reflect this. They provide evidence therefore of the extent to which official language policy filtered down to the people using English in less formal contexts.

ACTIVITY 7.2

Read the letter written by Margaret Paston to her husband John in 1442 or 1443 and answer the questions that follow it.

1 *To my ryght worchepful husbond, John Paston, dwellyng in the Inner Temple at London, in hast*

Ryth worchipful hosbon, I recomande me to yow, desyryng hertely to her of yowr wilfar, thanckyng God of yowr a mendyng of the grete dysese that ye
5 have hade; and I thancke yow for the letter that ye sent me, for be my trowthe my moder and I wer nowth in hertys es fro the tyme that we woste of yowr sekenesse, tyl we woste verely of your a mendyng.

James Gairdner (ed.), The Paston Letters

1 Comment on the content of the letter and what it tells you about the relationship between the writer and the addressee and the historical or social context.

2 Using the headings below, comment on the lexis:
   a the register and the lexical field;
   b the spelling and source of words;
   c the formal set phrases and collocation;
   d any idiosyncrasies.

3 Using the headings below, comment on the grammar:
   a the use of inflections;
   b pronoun forms;
   c verb forms.

COMMENTARY

The letter's **tone** conveys a strange mixture of the formal and the informal. Despite the fact that a wife is addressing her husband, the opening greeting is very formal: *To my* *ryght worchepful husbond, John Paston* (l. 1). Not only is Paston's full name used, but he is given his role of husband before he is named. This immediately suggests something about the respective social status of man and wife at this time – Margaret Paston clearly adopts a subservient position in the tone she uses.

The comments on John Paston's illness and on Margaret's and her mother's response to it suggest a time when health care was less developed and less widely available. The underlying suggestion is that any sickness can cause death and this indicates a quite different life expectancy from that of modern readers. The reference to God implies a society in which the Church has considerable influence and in which many people try to understand the inexplicable through religion and God's divine intentions.

The **register** too is an unusual mixture of formal and informal features. It is a written document, which means that it is not a transitory means of communication and is therefore associated with a more accurate and considered use of language than speech. Yet in its style and inconsistency, it seems more like a record of something that is being spoken. The **lexical field** is fairly narrow, concentrating on the relationship of a husband and wife and the illness from which he has just recovered.

The spelling in the letter seems quite unfamiliar to modern readers. The introduction of the printing press in 1476 began to fix English spelling, but this letter is the work of a private individual at a time when even the professional copyists did not always spell words in a standard way. The inconsistencies here could also be seen as the result of social attitudes towards the education of women who were far less likely to be instructed in a formal way at this time.

The **source** of words in this extract is typical of the Middle English period. Many, like *sekenesse* (*sickness*, l. 7), *hertely* (*heartily*, l. 3) and *trowthe* (*truth*, l. 6), can be traced back to the Old English word stock: *sēoc* or *sick*, *heorte* and *trēowth*. Others, like *hosbon* (*husband*, l. 3) and *tyme* (*time*, l. 6), have their source in Old Norse: *hūsbōndi* and *tīmī*. The significant difference between texts of the Old English and Middle English periods are the words like *recomande* (*recommend*, l. 3), *dysese* (*disease*, l. 4) and *letter* (l. 5) with their source in French: *recompenser*, *desaise* and *lettre*.

Many of the distinctive features of Middle English **spelling** are highlighted in this letter. The remains of the Old English inflection of nouns and adjectives can be seen in words like *grete* (l. 4) and *trowthe* (l. 6). In other examples, Late Modern usage of vowels like *i* and *u* is not yet settled: *ryght* (l. 1), *dwellyng* (l. 1) and *dysese* (l. 4); *yow* (l. 3) and *yowr* (l. 7). Other Late Modern English vowel patterns have also not yet emerged: some groups are simplified in words like *hertely* (*heartily*, l. 3) and *grete* (l. 4); others use a different vowel in words like *husbond* or *hosbon* (ll. 1, 3), *wilfar* (*welfare*, l. 4) and *dysese* (l. 4); and sometimes the final silent *-e* is omitted in words like *hast* (*haste*, l. 2), *wilfar* (l. 4) and *wer* (*were*, l. 6). Consonant patterns have changed less dramatically and are therefore closer to Late Modern English usage. Variations can be seen, however, in a word like *recomande* (l. 3), where Middle English has single consonants and Late Modern English has double.

The Middle English spelling used here is not only different from Late Modern English, but is inconsistent within the letter itself. Both the Late Modern English *husband* and *worshipful* are spelt in two ways: *husbond* (l. 1) and *hosbon* (l. 3); *worchepful* (l. 1) and *worchipful* (l. 3). Despite the emergence of a standard form of English, therefore, the spelling patterns of ordinary people do not always conform to it.

Although there are irregularities, few words remain completely incomprehensible: those that do should be commented upon. Probably one of the most unrecognisable words is *woste* (l. 6) which is the past tense form of the Middle English verb *witen*, *to know*. This is derived from the Old English *witan*, now obsolete and replaced by *to know*, derived from the Old English *cnāwan*. Other problems may have been caused by *nowth* (l. 6) which is representative of Late Modern English *mouth*. The spelling here perhaps reflects the confusion that sometimes occurred in the formation of *m* and *n*. Nevertheless the word can be understood from the collocation or set phrase *my heart in my mouth*, which is still used in Late Modern English. Equally, *es* (l. 6) can be deduced from its context as the Late Modern English *as*.

Although idiosyncratic – that is, reflective of the individual who has written the letter – there is no longer the great barrier of unfamiliarity that modern readers encounter when they face Old English texts. Spelling has begun to resemble the Late Modern English with which we are familiar.

Just as spelling has begun to move closer to Late Modern English patterns, so too has the **grammar**. Certain significant features, however, are still distinctive. Middle English is not a highly inflected language and this is evident here. The complex patterns used for Old English nouns and adjectives have been dramatically simplified. The possessive of the Middle English noun *herte*, for instance, is formed by the addition of the suffix *-s*. It would seem here (l. 6) that Margaret Paston has substituted *-ys* in order to mark the possessive. The use of inflections on adjectives is also far less complex than in Old English. Within this letter, *worchipful* (l. 3) is an example of the simplified Middle English inflections. Where Old English would have used an adjectival inflection on the modifier in the opening noun phrase, Middle English has dropped it. This suggests that final vowels were beginning to lose their pronunciation.

There is still evidence of a variety of pronoun forms because it was necessary to distinguish between the different kinds. In this letter, Margaret Paston uses *ye* (l. 5) for the subject pronoun in the second person, *yow* (l. 3) for the object, and *yowr* (l. 4) for the possessive determiner. A similar distinction can be seen in her use of *I* (l. 3) in the subject site, *me* (l. 3) in the object site, and *my* (l. 6) as a possessive determiner.

The verb forms cause few problems for the modern reader since they follow recognisable Late Modern English forms even though the spelling may be different. The present tense in the first person singular can be seen in the reflexive verb *I recomande me...* (l. 3) and in *I thancke* (l. 5). The past tense of the verb *to be* in the first person plural *wer* (l. 6) uses the same pattern as Late Modern English and the present participle adopts an *-yng* suffix which is a parallel to Late Modern English *-ing*. The perfect aspect is used in *have hade* (l. 5) and the infinitive form of *to her* (l. 3) uses the same Late Modern English structure of the preposition *to* + *base form verb*.

Summary

Examples of Middle English texts tell linguists something about the nature of English at the time.

Semantics

A modern reader can now rely on context to a large extent to understand any words that seem unfamiliar: *nowth in hertys* (l. 6) and *dysese* (l. 4). The number of texts surviving from this period is greater, so the registers and lexical fields linguists can study are more wide ranging. Since much of the literary work was dominated by the idea of courtly love and romance, epic adventure and religious thought, the lexis tended to reflect this. Private correspondence, on the other hand, offers the modern reader an insight into life and everyday affairs in the Middle English period.

Lexis

Most words are now recognisable although the spelling may be unfamiliar: *wer* (l. 6) and *thanckyng* (l. 4). In poems from the early part of the period, variations in the dialectal form can cause problems. The Northern forms of Middle English contained far more Old Norse and Old French words than the Midland dialect that formed the basis for Standard English and, since many of these are now obsolete, they can be a barrier to understanding.

Many of the words that have remained unchanged are closed-class words handed down directly from Old English: prepositions like *to* and *of*; determiners like *the* and *a*; and pronouns like *I* and *we*. The word stock was significantly different from Old English, however, because of the borrowings made from French: *desyryng* (l. 3) from the French *désirer*.

Grammar

As the period of levelled inflections, Middle English grammar was dominated by word order and this makes it far easier to understand. Plural nouns were still marked by a suffix, but the system had been simplified. Adjectives were inflected with *-e* in all cases until the final syllable was no longer pronounced and was eventually dropped from the spelling too. During the process of change, usage was inconsistent – some adjectives like *grete* (l. 4) would be marked with an inflection while others like *worchipful* (l. 3) were not. Pronouns, however, retained distinctive forms because it was still grammatically useful to distinguish between subject and object functions: *he* and *him*. Many verbs lost their strong forms and adopted the weak patterns, partly because English had for so long been a spoken language rather than a written one.

However, all these changes slowed down as the Midlands dialect was adopted as a standard form and as printing began to disseminate this standard to a far wider audience.

Phonology

The diversity of dialects at the beginning of the period was reflected in the range of pronunciations. If you listen to Middle English poems like *Gawain* and Chaucer's *Canterbury Tales* read aloud, they almost sound like two distinct languages rather than two forms of Middle English. Linguists believe that the spelling in each case is a a a very rough phonetic guide to the pronunciation of each dialect. Literary texts used distinctive sound patterning like rhyme and alliteration, following the oral traditions of Old English.

Graphology

Although the Roman alphabet was used predominantly, two runic symbols survived into the Middle English period: þ and ȝ. The 'thorn' þ survived longest in the initial position, while 'yogh' was retained after g had become established in vernacular texts. Most modern printers now substitute *th* and *g*.

There were two distinct forms of handwriting in use: the **cursive style** was common in charters, records and memoranda; the other form, in which the letters were separately written, was regularly used for literary texts and is often called the **book hand**. In handwritten manuscripts, letter forms were not as precise as they are in print and this meant that copyists sometimes mistook one letter for another. This led to some of the inconsistencies the modern reader recognises in Middle English spelling.

7.5 The Early Modern English period

The range of surviving texts from this period is vast: poetry, prose and drama exist alongside both public records and private correspondence. There is no longer any great linguistic barrier preventing a modern reader from understanding these. Linguists focus on the expanded vocabulary and the few grammatical features surviving which have since disappeared or have been standardised.

Early Modern English text

This next private letter is taken from the same collection as the letter in the Middle English section, but it was written sixty years after that of Margaret Paston. Archbishop Warham is writing to his cousin William Paston in 1503, about the death of his father.

ACTIVITY 7.3

Read the letter and jot down notes to answer the questions that follow it.

1
> *Archbishop Warham to William Paston*
> *To my cousyn Master William Paston*
> *September 6 1503*

Cousyn Paston, I recommaunde me unto you, and have received your letter,
5 by the which I undrestand of the deth of my cousyn your fadre, whose soule Jesu assoile. I wol counsaile and exhorte you to take it as wel and as paciently as ye can, seeyng that we al be mortal and borne to dey.

James Gairdner (ed.), The Paston Letters

1   Comment on the content of the letter and what it tells you about the relationship between the writer and the addressee.

2   Using the headings below, comment on the lexis:
   a   the register and the lexical field;
   b   the spelling;
   c   word sources;
   d   formal set phrases.

3   Using the headings below, comment on the grammar:
   a   the use of inflections;
   b   pronoun forms;
   c   verb forms;
   d   the order of sentence elements.

COMMENTARY

Clearly in dealing with death, the letter's **tone** has to be formal. Archbishop Warham is offering both personal and professional sympathy since he is writing as a cousin and in his role as religious adviser. He does not use his cousin's first name in the opening address, but begins the letter with *Cousyn Paston* (l. 4), which may suggest that they are not on close terms. Equally, he uses his official title, reinforcing his role rather than his family relationship.

The **register** is written and formal. However, since much of the advice offered is very personal, there is also a somewhat less official tone. The **lexical fields** can easily be divided: the religious field is marked by nouns like *soule* (l. 5), *Jesu* (l. 6) and *Archbishop* (l. 1) and the adjective *mortal* (l. 7); the field of death is conveyed by the noun *deth* (l. 5), the adjective *mortal* (l. 7) and the verb *dey* (l. 7). Inevitably the two fields overlap.

The **spelling** is more uniform than in Margaret Paston's letter of 1442, but some words have not yet adopted Late Modern spelling. The use of *i* and *y* is still different, but the writer is consistent: *cousyn* (l. 4) and *seeyng* (l. 7). Certain vowel groups also continue to be different from those used in Late Modern English. The simplification of *deth* (l. 5) is perhaps idiosyncratic, but the *au* in *recommaunde* (l. 4), the *ai* in *counsaile* (l. 6) and the *re* in *understand* (l. 5) could be related to French pronunciation and spelling. The use of the final *-e* is no longer inflectional since it is not pronounced. Its use here in words like *soule* (l. 5), *borne* (l. 7) and *assoile* (l. 6) may reflect the fact that private individuals were slower to adopt the standard form. However, since the letter is from an Archbishop, it is clearly an example of the writing of an educated man who would be more likely to have experience of the written standard. Other spelling irregularities are minor: single consonants where we would use double in *wel* (l. 6); different consonants with the same sound in *paciently* (l. 7); and some vowel variations in *wol* (l. 6).

There is evidence here of Latinate words which have been Anglicised by dropping the ending: *recommaunde* (l. 4) has its source in the Latin *commendāre*; *counsaile* (l. 6) was adopted via the French *conseil* but has a Latin root, *consilium*; and *exhorte* (l. 6) derives from the Latin infinitive *exhortāri*. There are French words that also have Latin links: the archaic *assoile* (l. 6) meaning to *absolve* (AFr *assoiler*, from the Latin *absolvēre*); and *paciently* (l. 7), from the French which was adopted from the Latin *patientia*. Nevertheless, the majority of the vocabulary here still derives from Old English: *fadre* (l. 5 – OE *fæder*); *soule* (l. 5 – OE *sāwol*); and *wol* (l. 6 – OE *willa*). The word *dey* (l. 7) is interesting because it is assumed to have come from an OE word *dēgan* of the Anglian dialect which has since been lost. Its other possible source would be in the Old Norse word *deyja*.

Set phrases are apparent both in the context of the letter and in the religious nature of the correspondence. The formulaic phrase *I recommaunde me unto you* (l. 4) was also used in the earlier Paston letter, and it would seem to be an example of written etiquette. The phrases *we al be mortal* and *borne to dey* (l. 7) can be linked to the teachings of the Church and the content of the letter.

The **grammar** is similar to that of Late Modern English and there are now only a few noteworthy features. Other than the final *-e* used at the end of some verbs and the noun *soule* (l. 5), inflections are not apparent. The examples already cited have no grammatical function and therefore cannot be described as inflections. Pronouns are now more or less standard, and both subject and object pronouns are used as in Late Modern English. There is, however, one use of the now archaic *ye* (l. 7) in the subject site. By the fifteenth century, it could be used as both subject and object and remained interchangeable until it disappeared from usage. Verb endings are standard and they are used in a variety of forms: perfect aspect (*have received*, l. 4); modal + the base form of the verb (*wol counsaile*, l. 6); the infinitive (*to take*, l. 6); and the present participle (*seeyng*, l. 7). The only non-standard example can be found in the use of *be* (l. 7) rather than the first person plural *are* which we would use in Late Modern English.

Sentence elements follow patterns we recognise from Late Modern English:

S	P	Od	Oi		P	Od
(I)	(recommaunde)	(me)	(unto you)	(and)	(have received)	(your letter. . .)

Each sentence has a structure in which several sub-clauses are embedded: *which...* (l. 5) and *whose...* (l. 5), relative clauses; *to take...* (l. 6), a non-finite clause; and *seeyng that...* (l. 7), an adverbial clause.

Summary

From looking at examples of early Modern English texts, linguists can draw certain conclusions about the nature of English at the time.

Semantics

There should now be few problems in understanding other than words that have not survived into the Late Modern English word stock, the occasional archaic word or words that have changed their meaning.

Lexis

This is probably the most important area of development at this time since the vocabulary was expanding significantly. It is important to be aware of the range of sources from which words were drawn: *explain* from *explānāre* (L), *chocolate* from *chocolate* (Sp) from the Nahuatl language of the Aztecs *chocólatl*; *detail* from *détailler* (Fr), and *violin* from *viola* (It).

There was wide-ranging debate about the quality of language and this led to the production of spelling texts which attempted to standardise the spelling of 'hard' words. Those which attempted to reform spelling failed because it proved impossible to impose an artificially created system on language. Other spelling books focused on current usage, which proved a far more logical approach to standardisation. It was these latter texts which recorded many of the spelling patterns that we now use. Purists objected to the wide-scale borrowing that was taking place and described the new foreign words as **inkhorn terms**. Nevertheless, many of these have survived into Late Modern English since they were introduced to fill a gap in the English language as it stood. The most important thing to remember about English at this time was that it had now been accepted as an appropriate language for academia and learning.

Grammar

There was almost nothing remaining of the earlier complexities of English inflection. The only ones left were those used to mark plurals and possessives on nouns and some verb endings. In the third person singular present tense, most verbs now used the *-s* inflection, although the archaic *-(e)th* was still in evidence in a few verbs. Double comparatives and superlatives were acceptable to create emphasis, as were multiple negatives. Pronouns were now used more or less as in Late Modern English.

Phonology

There was a dramatic change in the pronunciation of long vowels, which linguists still cannot fully explain. However, it meant that by the end of the period the pronunciation of Early Modern English was not far removed from that of Late Modern English.

Typographical features

The use of printing largely eliminated the need for handwritten manuscripts since now numerous identical copies of a single text could be distributed easily. In fact, publishing became a commercial venture, and this helped to reinforce the use of a standard written form across the country. The Roman alphabet was now used exclusively and therefore the surviving texts from this period are typographically very similar to those from our own.

7.6 The Modern English period

The texts of the Modern English period will cause few problems for the contemporary reader. There is a wide variety of poetry, prose and drama from which to draw examples. The biggest changes to English during the period were once again in the vocabulary. The only grammatical differences between Modern English and Late Modern English are the occasional change in word order or an unusual verb structure.

Modern English texts

The following extracts are taken from first person narratives in which the fictional 'I' character tells her or his own story. Inevitably, the prose is literary rather than spoken, but the author in each case creates a distinctive contemporary voice for the central character. The versions here have been modernised so that the spelling conforms to Late Modern patterns.

ACTIVITY 7.4

Read the texts carefully and identify and discuss linguistic features that mark the texts as non-standard in any way. Try to explain the features in relation to their historical context. You should refer to the word form, vocabulary and grammar where appropriate.

Text 1 (1722)

1   I went out now by daylight, and wandered about I knew not whither, and in
    search of I knew not what, when the devil put a snare in my way of a dread-
    ful nature indeed, and such a one as I have never had before or since. Going
    through Aldersgate Street, there was a pretty little child had been at a
5   dancing-school, and was agoing home all alone; and my prompter, like a true
    devil, set me upon this innocent creature. I talked to it, and it prattled to me
    again, and I took it by the hand and led it along till I came to a paved alley
    that goes into Bartholomew Close, and I led it in there. The child said, that
    was not its way home. I said, 'Yes, my dear, it is; I'll show you the way
10 home.' The child had a little necklace on of gold beads, and I had my eye
    upon that, and in the dark of the alley I stooped, pretending to mend the
    child's clog that was loose, and took off her necklace, and the child never felt
    it, and so led the child on again.

Daniel Defoe (?1660–1731), <u>Moll Flanders</u>

Text 2 (1860–1)

1   My father's family name being Pirrip, and my Christian name Philip, my infant
    tongue could make of both names nothing longer or more explicit than Pip.
    So, I called myself, Pip, and came to be called Pip.

I give Pirrip as my father's family name, on the authority of his tomb-
5 stone and my sister – Mrs. Joe Gargery, who married the blacksmith. As I
never saw my father or my mother, and never saw any likeness of either of
them for their days were long before the days of photographs, my first fan-
cies regarding what they were like, were unreasonably derived from their
tombstones. The shape of the letters on my father's, gave me an odd idea
10 that he was a square, stout, dark man, with curly black hair. From the character and turn of the inscription, '*Also Georgiana Wife of the Above*', I drew a
childish conclusion that my mother was freckled and sickly. To five little
stone lozenges, each about a foot and a half long, which were arranged in a
neat row beside their grave, and were sacred to the memory of five little
15 brothers of mine – who gave up trying to get a living exceedingly early in that
universal struggle – I am indebted for a belief I religiously entertained that
they had all been born on their backs with their hands in their trousers-
pockets, and had never taken them out in this state of existence.

Charles Dickens (1812–70), Great Expectations

COMMENTARY

Both the extracts are written in the first person, using the personal pronoun *I* to convey
a personal experience. In *Moll Flanders*, the reader is introduced to an uneducated
character who is writing about life as a pickpocket, while in *Great Expectations*, the
reader learns about Pip's background in a far more detailed way. Dickens uses a retrospective account in which his central character is looking back at his life and writing
from a point at which he has gained maturity. This means that the extract from *Great
Expectations* is far more complex than the straightforward recollection of events in
Defoe's narrative.

The **word forms** and the **word classes** now vary very little from Late Modern usage.
Both Dickens and Defoe use proper nouns to establish the credibility of their story: the
Moll Flanders extract draws on real London place names to create a sense of reality:
Aldersgate Street (l. 4), and *Bartholomew Close* (l. 8). Dickens is more interested in pre-
senting character in this extract, and therefore frequently uses names: *Pirrip* (l. 1), *Pip*
(l. 3), *Mrs. Joe Gargery* (l. 5), and *Georgiana* (l. 11). The majority of nouns in *Moll
Flanders* are concrete: *child* (l. 4), *hand* (l. 7) and *necklace* (l. 10). These reflect the ordinary nature of Moll's life, which is governed by the need to survive. By contrast,
Dickens's text uses more abstract nouns: *existence* (l. 18), *conclusion* (l. 12) and *memory* (l. 14). This is indicative of the reflective nature of the main character who is at a
time in his life when he wants to reconsider what has made him who he is.

Because these are taken from novels, the authors use a range of modifiers to create
atmosphere. Adjectival inflections are no longer used. Defoe's text:

m	m	h	m	m	h		m	m	h
a	dreadful	nature	a	dancing-school	(compound)		a	paved	alley
det	Adj	N	det	V	N		det	V	N

Dickens's text:

m	m	m	h	m	m	h		h
My	father's	family	name	my	first	fancies	my mother was	freckled
det	N	N	N	det	Adj	N		V (predicative)

Other word forms used now closely resemble Late Modern English usage. Pronouns
are varied in both the eighteenth and nineteenth centuries: *I* and *it*, personal pronouns;

mine and *its*, possessive pronouns. The latter example was established in the Early Modern English period and is clearly now used standardly.

The **vocabulary** used by Defoe may seem slightly dated to a contemporary reader. Lexis like the adverb *whither* (l. 1) and the preposition *upon* in the verb phrase *set me upon* (l. 6) are unlikely to be used in the same context now. Lexical sets also reflect the time: *devil* (l. 6) and *prompter* (l. 5) suggest the moral outlook, while *Street* (l. 4) and *alley* (l. 11) set the urban scene. Many of the words are of Old English origin: *snare* (l. 2 – OE *sneare*); and inevitably many derive from French and Latin sources: *prompter* (l. 5 – L *prōmptus*) and *alley* (l. 11 – OF *alee*). However, reflecting the increasingly cosmopolitan nature of the English word stock, *prattled* (l. 6) derives from the Low German *praten*.

Dickens's vocabulary moves even closer to that with which we are familiar in Late Modern English. The use of *photograph* (l. 7) is interesting because we can precisely date its introduction into English in 1839. Its derivation is typically classical, reflecting the technical nature of the processes involved: Greek *phōs/phōtos* (*light*) + *graphein* (*to draw*). The lexical sets centre on the key areas of the content: *family name* (l. 4) and *Christian name* (l. 1) focus on the issue of personal identity; *tombstones* (l. 9), *grave* (l. 14) and *existence* (l. 18) remind us of the fact that Pip is an orphan and that life expectancy at the time was not great.

Defoe's **grammar** is also close to our own, but there are specific examples that mark it as typical of the beginning of the Modern English period. In clauses like *I knew not* (l. 1) the author does not use the dummy auxiliary *do* with which we construct negatives in Late Modern English: *I did not know*. The use of the archaic *agoing* (l. 5) also dates the text. It was not until the nineteenth century that this form of the progressive was consistently shortened to *going*. The loosely co-ordinated sentences with embedded subordinate clauses reflect the way in which Defoe tries to imitate spoken language.

S	P	O		S	P	O	A		S	P	O	A
(I)	(talked to)	(it),	(and)	(it)	(prattled to)	(me)	(again),	(and)	(I)	(took)	(it)	(by the
			conj					conj				

	P	O	A		A
hand)	(and)	(led)	(it)	(along)	(till I came to a paved alley that goes into
	conj			SCl–ACl	SCl–RelCl

	S	P	O	A
Bartholomew Close),	(and)	(I)	(led)	(it)	(in there).
	conj			

The relative pronoun *that* (ll. 7–8) is used to post-modify the noun *alley*, while the subordinating conjunction *till* (l. 7) is used to introduce an adverbial clause of time. The Early Modern English period saw the introduction of the relative pronoun *who*, and although Defoe omits it in the clause *a pretty little child [who] had been...* (l. 4), the structure suggests that *who* is now used standardly. Finally, it is worth commenting on the range of verb forms in the extract: simple present (*it is*, l. 9); simple past (*I went*, l. 1); use of modals (*I'll show*, l. 9); the progressive (*was agoing*, l. 5); and the perfect aspect (*I have never had*, l. 3).

The grammar of *Great Expectations* is very similar to Late Modern English. There are only features worth commenting on in order to establish development from the 1722 extract. The relative pronoun *who* is used several times; the passive form of verbs also recurs: *were arranged* (l. 13); *had...been born* (l. 17); and the present participle now resembles Late Modern English usage: *being* (l. 1) and *regarding* (l. 8).

Summary

Examples of Modern English texts mean that linguists can draw certain conclusions about the nature of English between the years 1700 and 1900.

Semantics

Modern readers can now rely on understanding the meaning of words because of the similarities between Modern and Late Modern English.

Lexis

The word stock of English became increasingly cosmopolitan during the period as words were borrowed from a wider range of sources. Equally, technical, social and political developments were reflected in the lexis. Scholars continued to object to certain features of the language and many desired to perfect and fix English in order to prevent it becoming 'more corrupt'. Rules governing the language were stated and the beginning of 'prescriptive' grammar can be seen at this time.

Grammar

Few features are different from Late Modern English. Use of the progressive and the progressive passive became more common towards the end of the period. Changes taking place during this period were dictated by a semantic need – writers and speakers adapted structures that enabled them to convey more subtle shades of meaning.

Phonology

Pronunciation was remarkably similar to that in the present day. In some of the later literature of the period, writers tried to convey accent through the spelling. However, this was confined to dialogue in novels and to some regional poetry.

Graphology

No differences can be recorded here, but it is useful to remember the interest during the period in spelling reform. Many of the early schemes required either new phonetic alphabets or additional symbols in order to convey the phonetic sounds of English. None of the schemes had a lasting effect because the scale of the changes they required was too dramatic.

7.7 What to look for when dating a text

The following checklist can be used to identify characteristic features of English at each key stage of its development. There will not be examples of all the features listed in every textual extract, but the list can be used as a guide. For instance, you will only be able to discuss the sources of words if you have access to an appropriate dictionary or if an examination question provides you with etymological information. The points made here are general, so discussion of specific examples will need to be adapted to take account of the specific context, style and purpose.

The following are helpful questions to ask.

Register

1   What is the **mode**? – written.
2   What is the **manner**? – the relationship created between the writer and the reader: formal or informal? public or private? familiar or unfamiliar?
3   What is the **field**? – the subject matter and the purpose (to entertain, instruct, inform, record, etc.) will govern the kind of language used.

Old English texts

Graphological features

1   Are any **runes** from the Anglo-Saxon alphabet used? – æ, þ, ð, ʒ, ƿ?

Lexis

1   What **sources** of words can be identified? – Germanic? Celtic? Latin? Old Norse?
2   Are there any examples of **word creation**? – compounding? affixation?
3   Is there any evidence of **assimilation**? – Old English inflections like *-ian* (infinitive) or suffixes like *-dom* on loan words (words borrowed from other languages)?
4   Are there any words that have remained **unchanged** or **nearly unchanged** since the Old English period?

Grammar

1   Are there any noticeable **word endings**? – determiners? nouns? adjectives? pronouns?
2   Are there any **strong verbs** that are regular in Late Modern English?
3   Is the **word order** noticeably different from Late Modern English?

Middle English texts

Graphology/orthography

1   Is there any evidence of surviving Anglo-Saxon **runes**? – þ, ð, p, ʒ?
2   Has the Old English *sc* been replaced by *ss*, *sch*, or *sh* and *cw* by *qu*?
3   Are *u* and *v* and *i* and *y* still interchangeable?
4   Have Old English **marked long vowels** been replaced by **double vowels**?

Lexis

1   What new **sources** of words can be identified? – French? Latin?
2   Do the loan words appear in distinctive **lexical fields**? – administration? Church? law? military? social? art and learning? general?
3   Are any Old English words replaced by a **French equivalent**?
4   Is there any evidence of **word creation**? – affixation?
5   Could any of the words be described as **aureate terms** (borrowings of the fifteenth century which were seen as little more than stylistic borrowings or gildings)?

Grammar

1   Is there any evidence of **simplified inflections**? – nouns? adjectives? pronouns? determiners?
2   How are **plural nouns** marked? – *-s*? *-es*? *-en*?
3   Are there any Old English **strong verbs** that are regular in Late Modern English? – are the **past participle forms** weak or strong?

Emergence of a standard form

1   Has the standard form of English influenced the spelling?
2   Are there still examples of inconsistencies?

Early Modern English texts

Orthography

1   Are any words **unfamiliar**?
2   Are some words **recognisable** but with a different spelling from the Late Modern English version?
3   Is spelling still **inconsistent** or is there any evidence of **standardisation**?

Lexis

1   What **sources** of words can be identified? – Latin? French? Italian? Spanish? Portuguese?
2   Are any **archaic words** revived from earlier periods?
3· Are there any examples of **new coinages**?

Grammar

1   How is the **possessive** marked? – *-es*? *-ys*? *-'s*?
2   Are **comparatives** and **superlatives** used in a more flexible way than in Late Modern English?
3   Are **pronouns** noticeably different from Late Modern English or have they adopted the patterns still used today? – *ye* (subject), *you* (object)? *thou*, *thee* and *thy* (informal, familiar)? *you*, *ye* and *your* (respectful, unfamiliar)?
4   Is there any evidence that the **possessive pronoun** *its* and the **relative pronoun** *who* have been introduced?
5   Are **third person singular present tense verbs** inflected with *-s* or *-(e)th*?
6   Are there any **reflexive verbs**?
7   Is the **interrogative mood** constructed without the dummy auxiliary *do*?
8   Is the **dummy auxiliary *do* + *base form* verb** used where Late Modern English would use a progressive?
9   Are the **negatives** distinctive? – *not* placed before the verb? omission of the dummy auxiliary *do*? use of multiple negatives?

Modern English texts

Orthography

1   Is there any evidence that **spelling** is becoming more consistent?
2   Are there any **differences** between Modern English and Late Modern English spelling?

Lexis

1   In what areas is **new vocabulary** introduced? – general word stock? British Empire? trade? changes in society?

Grammar

1   Is there evidence that **verbs** are now used in a wider variety of forms? – use of the auxiliary *do* for emphasis? progressive? progressive passive?
2   Are there any examples of the **subjunctive** (in which the base form of the verb is used instead of a third person -*s* inflection)?

Late Modern English texts

Orthography

1   Is there any evidence of **changes** to standardised spelling? – American English? simplified spelling? artificial systems to match spelling to pronunciation?

Lexis

1   In what areas is **new vocabulary** introduced? – military? political? social? cultural? media? technological? scientific?
2   What are the **sources** of new words?
3   Are there any examples of **word creation**? – affixation? coinages? proper nouns? old words with new meanings? first usages?
4   Is there any evidence of **doublespeak** (language that is seen as confusing and obscuring rather than clarifying)? – official language? advertising?
5   Are there any examples of **ephemeral language** (language that continually changes to mirror social attitudes and groups), which mark the text as typical of its time? – slang? euphemism? idiom?

Grammar

1   Are there any examples of **prepositional usage** that differs from earlier periods?
2   Are any **transitive verbs** used intransitively?
3   Are there any other examples of **distinctive usage** – split infinitives? phrasal verbs?

Summary

Language change can be identified in three main areas: lexis, pronunciation and grammar. The changes taking place are gradual and go almost unnoticed by speakers and writers using the language from day to day. This gradual spread of change is called LEX-ICAL DIFFUSION. Because of the pace of change, it is very difficult to identify new forms as they emerge. Retrospectively, however, points of change can be seen quite distinctively. **Lexical change** is perhaps the most straightforward way in which a language can be altered: words are adapted, borrowed or created to meet new demands. Often additions to the existing word stock are linked directly to new objects, ideas, experiences or attitudes. The emergence of **sound changes** is more difficult to pinpoint because the spread of alternative pronunciations is very gradual. Some sound changes are adopted for physiological reasons – the new version is easier to say. Others may be due to the adoption of non-standard regional pronunciations beyond local boundaries as people move from area to area. At first a sound change will probably affect only a few words, but as the new pronunciation spreads, the old form will be replaced by the new. **Grammatical changes** usually involve regularisation or simplification which reduces the number of irregular forms. Since so much grammatical simplification has already taken place, grammatical change is unlikely to be dramatic in the twentieth century.

There are many **underlying tendencies** that cause language change – historical, social, cultural, political and economic forces have influenced English and made it what it is today. Language, however, has an inbuilt tendency to make **readjustments**, restoring disrupted patterns when change is too dramatic. It creates a balance between new and old forms to prevent problems in communication.

Change can be **conscious** or **subconscious**. New forms can spread through intentional imitation when certain pronunciations or words are **purposefully** adopted. Other changes **infiltrate** language – users are unaware of the new forms they adopt. While the change is in progress, several parallel forms will exist, until eventually one form will replace the existing variant forms.

Modern linguists recognise that English is always in **flux**, that it is almost impossible to fix it. Changes are inevitable, but because they take place slowly we hardly notice them in our everyday use of the language. It is only by looking back at written records that we can identify points of change. The new forms that appear do not always survive, but if they do they are consolidated as new generations of children learn them. Because language is changed by the people who use it, it is highly unlikely to break down into mutually incomprehensible dialects as the linguistic pessimists fear. In fact, where changes do occur, there will usually be valid linguistic reasons for them.

8 Language variation: regional and social

8.1 Regional and social variation

Not only does language change over time, it also has different forms that exist simultaneously. As children grow up in different communities and acquire language, for instance, they do not all learn one identical form of communication: instead, each learns a version that is distinctive to her or his particular **social**, **regional**, and **cultural background**. Children who acquire English as a first language in Britain will begin to speak in a variety that is used by the people around them – they will sound similar to these people, and they will use similar words and grammatical structures.

Language is constantly changing, not only from region to region and from social group to social group, but also from person to person. Even within one region, the words, grammatical structures and pronunciations of each individual may be different – and one individual may adopt slightly different kinds of pronunciations, words and grammatical structures depending upon the purpose of the communication, the audience and the context. In research, linguists must also take account of **idiosyncratic linguistic features** since although regional, social and cultural variants affect language usage, ultimately each member of the speech community will adopt a form of English that is in many ways personally distinctive.

As well as regional, social and personal characteristics, linguists also have to take into account a person's **age**, **gender**, **occupation** and **educational background**. The older speakers are the more likely they are to use traditional forms of language, while younger speakers are more likely to be influenced by current trends. Women are often thought to be more sensitive to 'standard' forms of language in formal contexts than men and tend therefore to be more likely to use SE and standard pronunciations. Not only do certain jobs have subject-specific lexis associated with them, but people with professional and non-professional jobs will tend to use language very differently: professional people are more likely to use the 'prestige' forms associated with SE and to some extent with RP; non-professional workers are more likely to use non-standard versions. Educational experience is directly linked to this occupational variation in language use – the longer individuals spend in education, the more likely they are to adopt standard lexis and grammar and the less likely they are to speak with a strong or broad regional accent.

The study of language variation is therefore very complex, and analysis of particular forms of English must include consideration of both general and personal variants. The variety people use may or may not be Standard English and linguists are interested both in the kinds of variants that change Standard English and in the changes themselves.

Having recognised that personal identity, social, cultural and educational background affect the kind of language an individual uses, linguists analyse the changes that these variants cause. By using **Standard English** and **Received Pronunciation** as norms, they can discuss variations in lexis, grammar and pronunciation. Rather than seeing any differences as examples of 'bad' English, however, they recognise all forms as equally valid in appropriate contexts.

In the nineteenth century, the phrase 'Standard English' was used to describe a form of English that was 'common' or 'universal' because it was a recognised system of writing. By the 1930s, however, it had become associated with social class and was seen by many as the language of the educated. In the 1933 'Supplement' to the *Oxford English Dictionary*, it was defined as a form of speech with cultural and social status which many users considered to be the 'best' form. The introduction of social judgements in the early part of the twentieth century made the concept of SE very emotive. By linking it to social class, feelings of social superiority and inferiority were reinforced in the very language that different people used. Describing SE as the 'best' implied that all other varieties were substandard and suddenly implicit judgements were made not only about the different versions of English, but also about the people who used them.

Most modern linguists try to avoid the political and class associations of SE. Instead, they see it as a form of national communication and treat it as a benchmark. Because it is not limited to any particular region, SE can act as a point of comparison for all other varieties of English, whether they are marked by personal, social or geographical variations.

Just as SE establishes a norm for the lexis and syntax of spoken and written language, so Received Pronunciation fulfils a similar function. It is a regionally neutral accent which is closely associated with public school education and high social class. Linguists can describe and classify the sounds heard in different versions of spoken English by comparing pronunciations of vowels and consonants in regional accents with the list of RP phonemes (Chapter 2).

As well as language forms changing, so too do **attitudes** to the different forms of English. Because young people tend to be most influenced by and involved in language changes, the role of education in maintaining 'standards' is much debated. Newspapers regularly report on falling standards of literacy, poor general knowledge and on the increase in 'lazy' and 'careless' speech – particularly among the young. Such coverage sensationalises issues by focusing on judgemental social perceptions while failing to take account of linguistic factors. Individual cases are presented as evidence for a general picture of linguistic doom and gloom.

In the wake of all the changes in education during the 1980s and 1990s, the Conservative government has focused attention on the nature of 'correct' English and on what should be taught in schools. The 1990s National Curriculum highlighted what children had to be taught about SE: it was the language of wide social communication and was generally required in formal contexts. Many people objected, fearing that non-standard varieties of English would be undermined on the basis of social rather than linguistic judgements. If this happened, they believed, children themselves would be made to feel worthless since language and identity are so closely interwoven. A revised version of the document in 1993 altered the focus slightly by stating that all children should be taught to use SE – implicitly suggesting that children were being offered choice rather than being forced to adopt only one form of language. A document drawn up by government advisers in 1994 goes one step further by establishing non-standard varieties of English in a position of respectability. When used in the right context, non-standard versions of spoken and written language are seen to be beneficial since they demonstrate to school pupils the richness of English. The original declaration that SE should be taught as a requirement for formal settings has been rephrased:

although children should be able to use SE when appropriate, they should also be free to adapt their language to suit any situation in which they find themselves. The 1994 document therefore recognises that there are many kinds of English which can be acceptable and that children already come to school as language experts, able to adopt one form of language for the home environment, another for their interaction with friends, and another for the classroom. This allows teachers to encourage young people to have the confidence to move between their different **repertoires** rather than just dictating the exclusive use of one form which is socially, not linguistically, seen as the 'best'.

Inevitably, social judgements will be made on the way in which people speak and write – communication is all about imparting information and a limited repertoire will be reflected in limited self-expression. A knowledge of SE is therefore crucial – it is the language of the media, of education, of the law courts and the Church, and in many contexts it is necessary to be able to use the universally recognised form of English. Nevertheless, in more personal situations it is often more appropriate to adapt language so that regional, social or cultural group identities can be developed. Rather than insisting that there is only one acceptable form of English, an education system needs to develop students' linguistic awareness of the different varieties of English and of the importance of audience, purpose and context. If children are actively involved in finding out about both standard and non-standard varieties, they will be able to make informed choices about the kinds of language they wish to use.

If the education system teaches children to be language experts then it has succeeded. If people can make conscious decisions about the appropriate kind of language for a particular situation, they will be proficient speakers and writers. If they can use regional, social and personal varieties alongside SE, then they will be active and effective participants in the language community.

8.2 Accent

ACCENT refers only to pronunciation that indicates where a person is from, geographically or socially. A **regional accent** links a speaker to a specific area in which certain kinds of pronunciations are heard; a **social accent** relates to the cultural and educational background of a speaker. Speakers of RP are often described as having no accent, but in the field of linguistics, everyone has some kind of accent. RP is therefore just one of many English accents, despite the fact that it is not linked to a specific region. When pronunciation differs dramatically from RP, speakers are said to have a **broad accent**.

Change occurs far more quickly in spoken language than in written. Pronunciation is therefore extremely variable. Research has shown that one speaker rarely says the same words in precisely the same way twice and pronunciation is altered constantly to suit the context. Even RP speakers do not all pronounce words identically. For instance, in RP a word like *poor* used to be pronounced as a diphthong, /pʊə/; in modified RP, it is pronounced as a monophthong (a simple vowel sound): /pɔː/.

When linguists analyse accents, they consider three key areas: **personal accent**; **social accent**; and **regional accent**. By focusing on relevant features under these headings, they can then come to conclusions about the kind of pronunciations an individual or a group uses. Often the regional elements of an accent will be dominant, but a particular regional variety is often modified by an individual speaker's personal style or cultural background.

Personal accents

Individual pronunciation changes may be linked to different contexts or moods, or to physical reasons like a sore throat or a mouth full of food. Whether consciously or subconsciously, speakers make decisions each time they participate in a speech encounter. In a formal context, speakers are far more likely to articulate words carefully – elision, assimilation, liaison and reduction (see Chapter 2) will be less prominent. In informal interaction, speech will often be quicker and the articulation will be less precise – some sounds will disappear or will be modified.

Formal context	Informal context	
green gate	/griːŋgeɪt/	(assimilation)
here and now	/hɪərənaʊ/	(liaison)
first stop	/fɜːstɒp/	(elision)
I could have done it	I could /həv/ done it	(reduction)

All of these segmental phonological features affect a speaker's accent to a greater or lesser degree. Such changes will be more apparent and more frequent in conversation than in an interview, for instance, but there will be examples of these features in almost every speaker's utterances in some context or another.

Linguists are interested in the ways individual speakers alter their language according to their situation. Some speakers are very aware of changing contexts and their accent may alter significantly depending upon the relationship between participants. CONVERGENCE describes the process of accent change in which two speakers modify their accents in order to become more similar. Usually a speaker with a non-standard accent will standardise pronunciation in order to sound more like an RP speaker, but equally the existence of modified RP is evidence that RP can also be altered by regional and social influences. DIVERGENCE reflects an opposite movement in which accents become further apart – this will usually only happen in a situation where a community is isolated from the influence of other communities. On a small scale, it can occur where two speakers take part in a hostile speech encounter, both exaggerating their different accents in order to emphasise their opposing positions – an RP speaker may exaggerate 'standard' sounds, while a speaker with marked regional pronunciation may adopt a 'broad' accent.

The most important thing about a personal accent is that it will rarely impede understanding. Most people at some point will adopt the characteristics of informal speech and linguists study both the reasons for this and the kinds of modifications that take place.

Social accents

When linguists consider the 'social' elements of an individual's accent, they are interested in things like the speaker's class, educational background, occupation and gender. Speakers in the lower social classes tend to have left formal education earlier and to have non-professional rather than professional jobs. They are far more likely to have a regional accent and to have speech marked by informal segmental features like elision and assimilation. Speakers from higher social classes are more likely to have stayed in education and to have professional jobs – they are therefore more likely to speak RP or modified RP.

People who wish to be upwardly mobile tend to modify their accent in order to resemble RP more closely, and this inevitably reinforces the prestige of RP. Speakers who are trying to emulate RP often **overcompensate**: in making sure that the phoneme /h/ is pronounced in the initial position, for instance, a speaker may also pronounce it where it is not needed. This process is called HYPERCORRECTION.

Attitudes in society change and in the 1990s it is common to hear both modified RP and regional accents on radio and television. Politicians often have regional accents: the Labour MP Austin Mitchell has a Yorkshire accent, for example, and the Conservative MP Teddy Taylor has a Scottish accent. Comedians like Paul Merton (South), Alexei Sayle (Liverpudlian) and Billy Connolly (Scottish) do not use RP; while some celebrities, such as the musician Nigel Kennedy, purposely reject RP in favour of a non-standard accent. Despite this, many people still modify their regional pronunciation in order to acquire social prestige.

Regional accents

In order to deal with accents in a practical way, linguists often divide the country into several very broad areas. The map in Figure 8.1 shows the broad regions that will be

Figure 8.1 The main accent and dialect regions of the United Kingdom

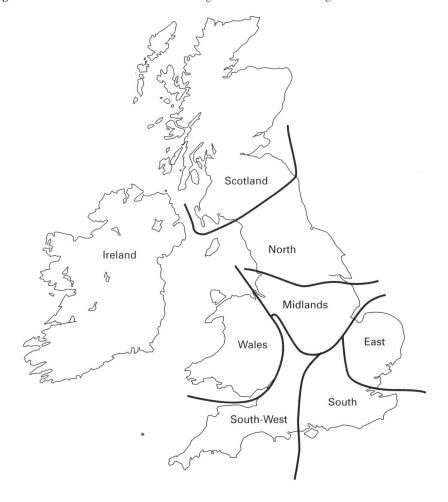

used here. Each line marked on a map to divide the country into areas defining differ-ent accents or dialects is called an ISOGLOSS. When you cross an isogloss, you pass from one accent or dialect type to another. Although the boundaries in Figure 8.1 are gen-eral, differences across each isogloss are more significant than variations within each area.

The following list summarises the **main pronunciation differences** which can be identified between RP and other English accents. It provides a starting point for analy-sis of regional accents in Britain and shows how they contrast with RP.

Consonants

The phoneme /h/

While RP pronounces the phoneme /h/ in the initial position, most regional dialects do not. This means that some minimal pairs sound the same: /eə/ might be *air* or *hair*; /iːt/ might be *eat* or *heat*; /ɪə/ might be *ear* or *hear/here*.

The phoneme /ŋ/

The phoneme /ŋ/ may vary in one of two ways in regional accents. In almost all infor-mal spoken discourse, accents other than RP will pronounce the phoneme /ŋ/ as /n/ in the final position: /kraɪɪn/ *crying*, /siːɪn/ *seeing*, /rʌnɪn/ *running*. In some parts of the Midlands and the North, speakers pronounce a final /g/ phoneme, thus articulating /ŋg/ at the end of words: /kraɪɪŋg/ *crying*, /siːɪŋg/ *seeing*, /rʌnɪŋg/, *running*.

Consonant followed by /uː/

In RP, certain words beginning with a consonant followed by the pure vowel /uː/ are pronounced with a /j/: /njuːz/ *news*, /mjuːzɪk/ *music*, /fjuːz/ *fuse*. This pronunciation is a remnant of earlier forms of English in which far more words were pronounced with the the /j/. Nowadays even RP pronunciation does not include the /j/ in words beginning with /r/, and it is dying out in words beginning with /s/. Some RP speakers, however, will still articulate *suit* as /sjuːt/. In some regional accents, the loss of the phoneme /j/ is common in many more words: /buːtɪfʊl/ for the RP /bjuːtɪfʊl/ *beautiful*, and /tuːb/ for the RP /tjuːb/ *tube*.

The post-vocalic /r/

In Chapter 2, the process of liaison described the way in which speakers insert a linking /r/ between words that end with a vowel sound and are followed by another word with a vowel in the initial position: /heərɔɪl/ *hair oil*. All accents including RP pronounce the **post-vocalic /r/** after a vowel, but RP would only pronounce it at word boundaries: while RP would pronounce *sawing* as /sɔːɪŋ/, a regional variant would be /sɔːrɪŋ/. In the speech of older regional speakers, the post-vocalic /r/ still occurs in words ending with a vowel sound: *tar* would be pronounced /taː/ in RP and /taːr/ by an older speaker in a rural community.

The glottal stop

In RP, the **glottal stop** is used on very few occasions, but in regional dialects it is com-mon, particularly amongst young people in urban areas. It frequently occurs as an **allo-phone** (a variation in the articulation of a particular phoneme) of /t/ in the medial and final position: *water* would be pronounced /wɔːtə/ in RP and /wɔːʔə/ in a non-standard accent.

Vowels

The phoneme /iː/

In RP, words ending with -y, -ey or -ee are pronounced with the phoneme /ɪ/: /pɪtɪ/ *pity*, /hʌnɪ/ *honey*, /bɪ/ *bee*. Northern accents also use /ɪ/: /tʃærɪtɪ/ *charity*, /nɔːrməlɪ/ *normally*, while Southern accents tend to use /iː/: /rɪəliː/ *really*.

Vowel *a*

In RP, the vowel *a* is pronounced as /ɑː/ rather than /æ/ when it precedes a voiceless fricative (/f/, /θ/ or /s/) or a consonant cluster with the phonemes /m/ or /n/ in the initial position: /grɑːs/ *grass*, /bɑːθ/ *bath*, /trɑːns/ *trance*, /sɑːmpl/ *sample*. Most Northern accents, however, will use the short /æ/: /græs/, /bæθ/, /træns/, /sæmpl/.

Phoneme inventory

Some vowels that occur in RP are absent from regional dialects. It is therefore possible to distinguish between dialects by creating a **PHONEME INVENTORY** – a list of the phonemes that are or are not used. The phonemes /ʌ/ and /ʊ/ both occur in RP; in many regional dialects, however, only /ʊ/ is used: /ʃʊt/ and /bʊt/ for RP /ʃʌt/ and /bʌt/. Some older regional dialect speakers use /uː/ to distinguish between pairs of words that would otherwise sound the same: RP /tʊk/ *took* may be pronounced as /tʊk/ or /tuːk/ in a regional accent; RP /tʌk/ *tuck* may be pronounced as /tʊk/ in regional accents.

By studying **transcripts of speakers** from different parts of Britain, it is possible to see accent variations in context. The following examples will help you to identify the differences between RP and regional accents and to build up an awareness of some distinctive accent characteristics. Each transcript represents a specific accent, but in a general sense they can be seen as illustrative of the broader areas represented on the map in Figure 8.1.

The transcriptions are broad and do not aim to describe the exact articulation of sounds. Instead, they aim to give an overall sense of the speakers' accents in a simplified form. Phonemic symbols are used to record pronunciations that differ significantly from RP. To show where vowels are either more open or closed than RP, the following IPA diacritics will be used: ⊥ tongue raised; ⊤ tongue lowered; /ː/ long vowel.

To help you read the transcriptions easily, a written version using traditional orthography and conventional punctuation will precede each monologue (Activities 8.2–8.5). In the dialogue, the written version will record only the non-standard accent of the second speaker (Activity 8.1).

ACTIVITY 8.1

The following transcript records a conversation between two speakers who grew up in Yorkshire. Although both speakers have lived away from Yorkshire for a number of years, Speaker 2 has largely retained his accent, while Speaker 1 consciously modified his pronunciations.

Read through the script and rewrite the words transcribed phonemically in SE. Then comment on:

1 distinctive pronunciations of consonants;
2 distinctive pronunciations of vowels;
3 the main differences between the accents of the two speakers.

Written version (Speaker 2 only)

As we remember it. As we remember it. What, thirty-eight years ago. It was a very busy town, full of steel works. Now, to my knowledge, most of the steel works have gone. Shopping centres have. Covered shopping centres have taken their place and a large sports area. Also all the houses have gone. Where the people have gone, I've no idea. They've gone somewhere, but where I don't know. It used to be a nice. It's a large town, but it used to be a nice safe place to be in because as a child, well not as as a child but a young fellow, I used to do a lot of cycling into Derbyshire and camping on the week-ends. No problem. Used to get spuds off the farmer for little jobs around the farm or whatever. Yes. Just a mass of smoke. Lots of smoke. Actually it was a dirty, sooty place. Yes. Through Sheffield. Oh yes, yes. I worked there. Um I know the place. That's. That was called then, when I when I left school, The English Steel Corporation. The full length of the railway. No there was two. There was one. There was two businesses, but one ran the full length of the railway, from what we used to call the Wicker Arches right out to the other side of Sheffield into Rotherham. There I first started in the building trade there.

Spoken version

1 SPEAKER 1: we'll talk about Sheffield =
   SPEAKER 2: = /əz/ we remember it =
   SPEAKER 1: = as we ‖ remember it
   SPEAKER 2:   ‖ /əz/ we remember it (.) what (.) /θɜːtɪ eːt/ years /əgɔː/
5   (.) it was a ‖ very busy ↑tówn↑ (.) full of steel wórks (.) nòw (.) to
   SPEAKER 1:   ‖ yes umm
   SPEAKER 2: my knowlèdge (.) /mɔːst/ of the steel works have ↑gone↑ (.)
             /ʃɒpɪn/ centres have (.) /kʊvəd ʃɒpɪn/ centres have /teːkən/ their
             ↑/pleːs/↑ and a large sports ↓areá↓ (.) /ɒlsɒ/ all the /aʊzəz
10   əv/ ‖ gone (.) where the people /əv/ gone I've no idea =
   SPEAKER 1:   ‖ yeah
   SPEAKER 1: = have they gone somewhére =
   SPEAKER 2: = they've gone /sʊmweər/ (.) but where I don't knòw (.) it used
             to be /ə/ nice (1) it's a large town (.) but it used to be a nice
15   /seːf pleːs/ (.) to bé ìn (.) /kɒs əz/ a child (1) well not /əz/
             as a child but a /jʊŋ felə/ (.) I used to do a /lɒtə saɛklɪn/ into
             /daːbɪʃə/ and /kæmpɪn/ on the weekends (.) ‖ no próblem (.) used
   SPEAKER 1:   ‖ mm
   SPEAKER 2 to get spuds off ‖ the /faːmə/ (laughs) (.) for little jobs round the
20 SPEAKER 1:   ‖ yes
   SPEAKER 2: /fáːrm/ or /wɒ'tevə/ =
   SPEAKER 1: = and when you went into Derbyshire did you look down on
             Shéffield =
   SPEAKER 2: = yes =
25 SPEAKER 1: = what did you see thére =
   SPEAKER 2: = just a mass of ↑/smɔːk/↑ (.) lots of ‖ ↓/smɔːk/↓ (.) actually it was a
   SPEAKER 1:   ‖ yeah mm

SPEAKER 2: dirty, /sʊtɪ̬/ ‖ /plɛ̬ːs/
SPEAKER 1: ‖ um (.) I remember (.) the train to Scar ‖ borough (.)
30 SPEAKER 2: ‖ yeah
SPEAKER 1: every now and again it would be diverted thro ‖ ugh Sheffield and
SPEAKER 2: ‖ through Sheffield
SPEAKER 1: along the side of the railway track (.) there'd be sort of these
           arched (1) buildings (.) with furnaces inside ‖ all the way along
35 SPEAKER 2: ‖ oh yeah
SPEAKER 1: it ‖ looked like ‖ hell
SPEAKER 2: ‖ yeah ‖ I worked there (.) um I /nɔː/ the /plɛ̬ːs/ that's (.)
           that was called then (.) when I when I left school (.) The
           English Steel /kɔ̬ːpərɛ̬ːʃən/ =
40 SPEAKER 1: = it was /wɒn wɒn/ (.) I remember it on the right hand
           ‖ side of the /rɛ̬ːlwɛ̬ː/ (.) oh so it was just /wɒn/ business (.) =
SPEAKER 2: ‖ the full length
SPEAKER 2: = no there was two (.) there was /wʊn/ (.) there was two
           búsinesses (.) but ‖ /wʊn/ ran the full length of the ‖ /rɛ̬ːlwɛ̬ː/ (.)
45 SPEAKER 1: ‖ yeah ‖ um
SPEAKER 2: from what we used to call the Wicker Arches ‖ right out to the other
SPEAKER 1: ‖ yeah
SPEAKER 2: side of ‖ Sheffield (1) into /ˈrɒð̬ˌrəm/ ‖ thère (.) I first /staːtɪd/ in the
SPEAKER 1: ‖ um ‖ yeah
50 SPEAKER 2: building /trɛ̬ːd/ there

COMMENTARY

The two speakers talk about Sheffield as they remember it. The **context** is informal and friendly and the interaction reflects this – the speakers are clearly known to each other and there is a lot of supportive affirmation (see Chapter 10 for discussion of the terms used in conversation analysis): *mm, yeah*. **Turn-taking** is relaxed: although Speaker 2 is dominant and takes longer turns, Speaker 1 initiates the topic and adds new information where appropriate.

The regional variations in the pronunciation of vowels is most likely to differ from RP, but there are some **consonantal features** which are typical of Yorkshire accents. The dropping of /h/ in /aʊzəz/ *houses* (l. 9) and /əv/ *have* (l. 10) and the pronunciation of the *-ing* inflection as /ɪn/ in /ʃɒpɪn/ *shopping* (l. 8) and /kæmpɪn/ *camping* (l. 17) are both common in many accents and typical of a Yorkshire accent.

Many of the RP **pure vowels** are realised in a slightly different way – usually they are closer than in RP. In words like /daːbɪʃə/ *Derbyshire* (l. 17), /faːmə/ *farmer* (l. 19) and /staːtɪd/ *started* (l. 48), the pure vowel /ɑː/ is articulated with the tongue raised, creating a harder and shorter sound. Another distinctive feature of Yorkshire accents appears in the absence of /ʌ/ in the phoneme inventory. In words like /kʊvəd/ *covered* (l. 8), /sʊmweər/ *somewhere* (l. 13) and /jʊŋ/ *young* (l. 16), /ʌ/ is articulated as the closer /ʊ/. The following pure vowels are also realised with the tongue raised: /ɜː/ in words like /θɜːtɪ/ *thirty* (l. 4); /æ/ becomes the unstressed vowel /ə/ in /əz/ *as* (l. 4); and /ɔː/ in words like /kɔːpərɛ̬ːʃən/ *Corporation* (l. 39). The *-y* at the end of words is pronounced as /ɪ/ in /sʊtɪ/ *sooty* (l. 28).

Yorkshire accents articulate **RP diphthongs** in distinctive ways. In some cases, they become narrower so that the two sounds of the diphthong are less distinct or become a monophthong. For instance, /eɪ/ RP is realised as a long pure vowel /ẹː/ in words like /tẹːkən/ *taken* (l. 8), /plẹːs/ *place* (l. 9), /ẹːt/ *eight* (l. 4), /sẹːf/ *safe* (l. 15), /rẹːlwẹː/ *railway* (l. 41) and /trẹːd/ *trade* (l. 50); /əʊ/ is realised as /ɔː/ in /əgɔː/ *ago* (l. 4), /mɔːst/ *most* (l. 7), /smɔːk/ *smoke* (l. 26), and /nɔː/ *know* (l. 37).

Speaker 2 no longer has a broad Yorkshire accent, but his pronunciations are characteristic – the narrow diphthongs; the close pure vowels; and the realisation of *-ing* as /ɪn/. Other non-standard pronunciations are linked to the stress patterns of Yorkshire accents: /wɒ'tevə/ *whatever* (l. 21) and /'rɒð,rəm/ *Rotherham* (l. 48).

Although both speakers will have had the same accent in the past, Speaker 1 has consciously altered his pronunciation. He uses a modified RP and so his regional accent is more difficult to pinpoint. However, occasionally his realisation of a sound falls between the two accents. This is an example of **hypercorrection** – in aiming to pronounce a word in RP, the speaker produces a form that differs from the norm. For instance, the typically Yorkshire pronunciation of *nothing* would be replaced by a form that does not exist in RP. The RP /nʌθɪŋ/ would become /nʊθɪŋ/ in a Yorkshire accent: the half-close back vowel /ʊ/ would be replaced by an open back vowel /ɒ/ in the process of realising the RP half-open central vowel /ʌ/. A similar process of hypercorrection occurs when Speaker 1 says /wɒn/ *one* (l. 40), which in RP is realised as /wʌn/.

From looking at this transcript, it is possible to list the following **characteristics** of a **Yorkshire accent**:

1   The phoneme /h/ is dropped in the initial position.
2   The *-ing* inflection is articulated as /ɪn/.
3   The pure vowel /ɑː/ is articulated with the tongue raised /aː/, so that it is closer than in RP.
4   The phoneme /ʌ/ is absent from the phoneme inventory – it is articulated as /ʊ/.
5   Words ending in *-y*, *-ey* or *-ee* are pronounced as /ɪ/.
6   Diphthongs are often narrower than in RP: /eɪ/ becomes /ẹː/; /əʊ/ becomes /ɔː/; /aɪ/ becomes /aɛ/.

Although each accent within the 'Northern' area will be different, many will display the kinds of pronunciation features highlighted here.

ACTIVITY 8.2

This next recording was made in an informal context – the participants were known to each other and topics emerged spontaneously as the conversation developed. The extract here focuses on a speaker who moved from the Midlands four years ago, but lived in Birmingham up to that point. Although she does not have a broad accent and most pronunciations are close to RP, there is still evidence of a Birmingham accent, particularly in the realisation of vowels.

Read through the transcript and try to identify characteristic features of Midlands accents. Try to suggest reasons why the speaker may have lost a strong accent.

Written version

I queued from three in the morning for Bob Dylan and mother thought I was crazy, but I ended up a few rows back. Mother said 'if it was Joan Baez I could understand'. So I queued from four o'clock the previous afternoon for Joan Baez. I was at the front of the queue. Queued for seventeen hours and I got her a ticket as well. But I met Bob Dylan. Fifth of May 1965. Yeh.

Although I was a few rows back, I went back stage and I held his jacket there while he did an encore.

Spoken version

1   I /kjaʊd/ from three in the morning for Bob Dylan and /mʊðə/ thought I was
/kræɪzəi/ but I ended up a few /rʌʊs/ back (.) /mʊðə/ said if it was Joan Baez I
could /ʊndəstænd/ (.) so I /kjaʊd/ from four o'clock the previous /æftənaʊn/
for Joan Baez (.) I was at the /frʊnt/ of the /kjaʊ/ (.) /kjaʊd/ for /sevəntəin/
5   hours (.) and I got her a /tikit/ as well (.) but I met Bob Dylan (.) fifth of /mæɪ
nɔɪntəin sɪxti-fɔɪv/ (.) yeh (.) although I was a few /rʌʊs/ back I went back
/stæɪdʒ/ and I held his jacket /ð̞ɜ:/ while he did an encore

COMMENTARY

There are examples here where **RP pure vowels** sound closer: the RP /ɪ/ is realised closer to /i/ in /tikit/ *ticket* (l. 5); the RP /ʌ/ becomes /ʊ/ in /mʊðə/ *mother* (l. 1) and /frʊnt/ *front* (l. 4), and the RP /ɑ:/ becomes /æ/ in /æftənaʊn/ *afternoon* (l. 3). Many of the sounds are wider than in RP: /u:/ becomes /aʊ/ in /kjaʊ/ *queue* (l. 1) and /æftənaʊn/; /i:/ becomes /əi/ in /sevəntəin/ *seventeen* (l. 4). A similar widening is seen in the diphthongs: /aɪ/ RP becomes /fɔɪv/ *five* (l. 6); /əʊ/ RP becomes /rʌʊs/ *rows* (l. 2); /eɪ/ RP becomes /stæɪdʒ/ *stage* (l. 7), /mæɪ/ *May* (l. 5) and /kræɪzəi/ *crazy* (l. 2); and /eə/ RP becomes /ð̞ɜ:/ *there* (l. 7).

The speaker is a professional, so despite the fact that she has lived almost all her life in Birmingham, her accent has been modified. Her educational and occupational background means that most sounds are similar to those of RP; even where pronunciations are different, the accent is not broad.

From looking at this transcript, it is possible to list the following **characteristics** of the **Birmingham accent**:

1   The phonemes /æ/ and /ɑ:/ are both articulated as /æ/.
2   The phoneme /ʌ/ is absent from the phoneme inventory – it is instead articulated as /ʊ/.
3   Some pure vowels become diphthongs: /u:/ becomes /aʊ/; and /i:/ becomes /əi/.
4   Many diphthongs are wide (the movement between the two vowels is greater than in RP): /eɪ/ becomes /æɪ/; /əʊ/ becomes /ʌʊ/; and /aɪ/ becomes /ɔɪ/.
5   Other vowels are also distinctive: /ɪ/ becomes /i/ and /eə/ becomes /ɜ̞:/.

In a broad Birmingham accent, you could also expect to find the following pronunciations:

1   /h/ is usually absent;
2   -*ing* is realised as /ɪn/ and sometimes as /ŋg/;
3   /ɔ:/ becomes /ʌʊə/.

Although each accent within the 'Midlands' area will be different, many will display the kinds of pronunciation features highlighted here.

ACTIVITY 8.3

The speaker in the next transcript is an old man who has lived in Norfolk all his life. His accent is broad and there are quite marked differences between his pronunciations and those of RP. The phonemic transcriptions pick out the words that illustrate his accent most effectively.

The extract takes the form of a spontaneous oral narrative in which the speaker talks to his great-nieces about a walk he took them on when they were younger. The context is informal and the speaker is in the dominant position – he chooses the topics and dictates the length of turns.

Read through the written version which follows and try to rewrite the phonemic transcriptions in SE. Then comment on:

1   consonantal features that are typical of this Eastern accent;
2   vowel variations that are typical of this Eastern accent.

Finally, try to suggest some reasons why the speaker may have such a broad accent.

Written version

> Well, one day my great-nieces they came over there with their mother and course they wanted me to show them round the village. Well there wasn't much to show them. I show them round the church, round the mission room and the village green and then I I said, 'Well, we'll go and have a look round the crematorium. They've got some really nice gardens round there.' So off we went and they weren't very old. I suppose one was about three, another was about six and another about nine. Anyway, we they were lovely gardens. We enjoyed it and they had little bridges to go over the dykes with. But Charlotte there, the middle one, she thought she was cleverer than the others. She tried jumping the dyke and when I looked, she'd jumped into it. Course she come out of there with all her socks, her boots wet so I had to take her socks off and she had to walk home like that and then when we got home, well I hunted some more socks out for her and she'd got them on when her ma saw her or I wouldn't have been popular. Anyway, everything went all right and they jolly well enjoyed theirselves.

Spoken version

1   well one /dæɪ/ my great /neəsəs/ they came over there with their /mɑːðə/ (.)
    and /kɔːs/ they wanted me to /ʃʊ əm/ round the village (.) well there /wɔːnt/
    much to /ʃʊ əm/ (.) I /ʃʊ em/ round the /tʃʌtʃ/ (.) round the /mɪʃən rʊm/ and the
    village /greən/ (.) and ↑then↑ I (.) I said well we'll go and have a look round
5   the /kremə'tɔːrəm/ they've got some really nice /gɑːdəns/ round ↓there↓ (.) so
    /ɔːf/ we went (.) and they /wɔːnt veəriː/ old (.) I /spo/ one was bout three (.)
    /nʌðə/ was about six (.) and /nʌðə/ one bout /nɔɪn/ (.) anyway we they were
    lovely /gɑːdəns/ we enjoyed it and they had little bridges to go over the
    /dɔɪks/ with (.) but Charlotte there (.) the middle one (.) she thought she was
10 /klevrə/ than the others she tried /dʒʌmpən/ the /dɔɪk/ (1) and when I looked
    (.) she'd jumped ↑/ɪntɪt/↑ (.) course she come out of there with all her /sɑːks/
    her boots wet so I /æd/ to /tæɪk/ her /sɑːks ɔːf/ (.) and she had to walk /əʊm/
    like /æt/ (.) and then when we got /hʊm/ well I hunted some more /sɑːks/ out
    for her and she'd got them on when her /mɑː sɔːrə/ or I /wɔːnt əv bɪn popələ/
15 (.) anyway /evriːθən/ went /ɔːrɔɪt/ and they jolly well enjoyed theirselves

COMMENTARY

Many of the **consonants** illustrate distinctive features of a Norfolk accent. The pronunciation of the *-ing* inflection as /ən/ is common and can be illustrated by examples like /dʒʌmpən/ *jumping* (l. 10) and /evriːθən/ *everything* (l. 15). Norfolk accents do not always elide the initial position /h/, and this can be seen in the speaker's inconsistent pronunciations of one word: /əʊm/ and /hʊm/ *home* (l. 13). He also elides the phoneme /j/ preceding the /uː/ in *popular* (l. 14): /pɒpjuːlə/ RP becomes /pɒpələ/ in a Norfolk accent. On several occasions the phoneme /ð/ in the initial position is elided: /æt/ *that* (l. 13) and /əm/ *them* (l. 2).

The vowels are more significantly different from RP. Many of the RP **pure vowels** are realised as longer sounds or as diphthongs: /ɒ/ becomes /ɔː/ in /wɔːnt/ *wasn't* (l. 2) and /ɔːf/ *off* (l. 12); /ʌ/ becomes /ɑː/ in /mɑːðə/ *mother* (l. 1); /ʊ/ becomes /ɔː/ in /wɔːnt/ *wouldn't* (l. 14); /iː/ becomes /eə/ in /neəsəs/ *nieces* (l. 1) and /greən/ *green* (l. 4); and /e/ becomes /eə/ in /veəriː/ (l. 6). Other variations can be identified in /tʃʌtʃ/ *church* (l. 3) where RP would use the phoneme /ɜː/ and /rʊm/ *room* (l. 3) where RP would use /uː/. Words ending with *-y* are pronounced as /iː/ in /veəriː/ *very* (l. 6).

Diphthongs are also modified: /eɪ/ becomes /æɪ/ in /dæɪ/ *day* (l. 1) and /tæɪk/ *take* (l. 12) and /aɪ/ becomes /ɔɪ/ in /dɔɪk/ *dyke* (l. 10) and /ɔːrɔɪt/ *all right* (l. 15). Some diphthongs are realised as monophthongs: /əʊ/ becomes /uː/ in /ʃuː/ *show* (l. 2) and /ʊ/ in /hʊm/ *home* (l. 13). Many of the vowel sounds are made with the back of the tongue raised or lowered rather than the centre or front used to articulate them in RP.

Phonological features like elision and reduction are also characteristic of Norfolk accents. Unstressed syllables at word boundaries are dropped and words are merged as in /ɪntɪt/ for *into it* (l. 11) and /wɔːnt əv/ for *wouldn't have* (l. 14). Liaison can be seen in the merging of word boundaries like /sɔːrə/ *saw her* (l. 14). Within words, unstressed syllables are elided: /kremə'tɔːrəm/ *crematorium* (l. 5) and /klevrə/ *cleverer* (l. 10). The stress patterns within longer utterances are also distinctive in Norfolk accents – stressed syllables tend to be held (marked by double underlining on the transcript) while unstressed syllables are very short: /gɑːdəns/ *gardens* (l. 5) and /nʌðə/ *another* (l. 7).

The speaker's educational and occupational background have not taken him outside the isogloss boundaries for the Eastern accent for any significant length of time, so his accent has not been modified by contact with speakers who have different pronunciation systems. The words transcribed phonemically here therefore illustrate both regional and social characteristics of his accent. Some pronunciations are idosyncratic, illustrating personal features of the speaker's accent.

From looking at this transcript, it is possible to list the following **characteristics** of a **Norfolk accent**:

1 The phoneme /h/ is sometimes dropped in the initial position.
2 The *-ing* inflection is realised as /ən/.
3 The semi-vowel or approximant /j/ is lost after consonants.
4 Words ending with *-y*, *-ey* or *-ee* are pronounced with the phoneme /iː/.
5 RP /uː/ is sometimes realised as /ʊ/.
6 Some pure vowels are longer than in RP: /ɒ/ becomes /ɔː/ and /ʌ/ becomes /ɑː/.
7 Some pure vowels are realised as diphthongs: /iː/ and /e/ become /eə/.
8 Some diphthongs are also modified: /eɪ/ becomes /æɪ/; /aɪ/ becomes /ɔɪ/; and /əʊ/ becomes /ʊ/.

Although each accent within the 'Eastern' area will be different, many will display the kinds of pronunciation features highlighted here.

ACTIVITY 8.4

The following monologue is taken from an informal conversation between two people who are well known to each other. Having been born within the sound of Bow Bells, the speaker is a true Cockney and although he has lived away from London for a number of years, his accent is still broad.

Read through the transcript below and identify the pronunciations that mark the speaker as a Londoner. The transcription is broad and phonemic symbols are only used to highlight the pronunciations that are most obviously typical of Cockney accents.

Written version

> I was born in Bow, you know, London. That's the East End. Er, I worked in the market as a barrow boy. That was my first job. I went to school till I was fifteen like and that was boys, a boys' school. Boxing and football and that was it and the education was er terrible, you know. I tried to join the army when I was sixteen and er left the Smoke and er joined the Welsh Regiment and they sent me up to, you know, Shrewsbury. I was up there for a bit and then I went to the Gulf. I fought there for a bit and I went to Ireland. We was the first Regiment to go into Ireland. That was sixty-eight. I had one tour in Ireland and that turned me right off. I applied to join the Air Force then. Cor, I've got a lovely history I have. In the Air Force for five years. I see a bit of the world. I went to Singapore and I went to Alaska. Absolutely superb. I mean, I'd go back there tomorrow if I could live there. Lovely place. Ah, then after my five years, I come out and believe it or not, I joined the Police Force and I was a copper for twelve years and um as I say, I enjoyed some of it. You know, it's all right, but where I come from in London, there is a thing between coppers and people. There is more of a gel, do you know. Down here, when I joined, they were trying to do away with the gelling and putting them in cars to get them away from the people. I can't hack that lark. I always still like to be hands on. I still like to see people and talk to people. So I come out in eighty-four and since then I've been trying to find some form of employment. I've done silly jobs in between, but nothing constructive.

Spoken version

1   I was /bəʊn/ in /bæʊ/ (.) /jə næʊ/ (.) /lændən/ (.) that's the East /eɪnd/ (.) er I
    worked in the market as a /bærə bóy/ (.) that was my first job (.) I /wen/ to
    /skuːʊ/ til I was fifteen /lɔɪk/ and that was boys (.) /əʊ bɔɪskuːʊ/ (.) /boksɪn/
    and /fʊtbəʊ/ and that was it (.) and the education was er /terɪbʊ/ (.) /jə næʊ/
5   (.) I tried to join the army when I was síxteen (.) and er left the /smæʊk/ and
    er joined the /weʊʃ/ Regiment and they sent /mɪ/ up to /jə næʊ/ Shrewsbury
    (.) I was up there for a /bɪ/ and then I went to the /gæʊf/ (.) I /fəʊt/ there for a
    /bɪ/ and I /wen/ to Ireland (.) we was the first Regiment to go into Ireland (.)
    that was ooo /síxtiː æɪʔ/ (.) I had one tour in Ireland and that turned me right
10 /ɔːf/ (.) I applied to join the /eə fəʊs/ then (.) cor I've got a /lævli: ɪstriː/ I /əv/ (.)
    in the /eə fəʊs/ for /fɒɪv jɜːs/ (.) I see a bit /əvə/ world (.) I /wen/ to Singapore
    and I /wen/ to Aláska (.) absolutely superb (.) I mean (.) I'd go back there
    /təmɒrə/ if I could live there (.) /lævliː/ place (.) ahh (.) then after /mɪ fɒɪv yɜːs/
    I come /aːt/ and believe it or not I joined the police /fəʊs/ and I was a /kɒpə/
15 for twelve /jɜːs/ and um as I say I enjoyed ↑some↑ of it (.) /jə næʊ/ it's /əʊrɒɪt/

but where I come from in /lændən/ (.) there is /ə/ thing between /kɒpəs/ and /pʰiːpʊ/ (.) there is more of a /dʒəʊ dʒənæʊ/ (.) down /ɪə/ when I joined they were /trɒɪn/ to do /əwæɪ/ with the /dʒelɪn/ and /pʊtɪn əm/ in cars to get them /əwæɪ/ from the /pʰiːpʊ/ (.) I can't /ek̦/ that lark (.) I /əwæɪs/ still /lɒɪk/ to be
20 /end̦s/ on (.) I still /lɒɪk/ to see /pʰiːpʊ/ and talk to /pʰiːpʊ/ (.) so I come /aːʔ/ in /æɪʔiː fʊə/ (.) and since then I've been /trɒɪɪn/ to find some form of employ-ment (.) I've done silly jobs in between but /nʌfɪŋk/ constructive

---

COMMENTARY

The **consonant** variations are distinctive. The phoneme /h/ in the initial position is elided on almost all occasions: /ɪstriː/ *history* (l. 10), /ev/ *have* (l. 10), /ek̦/ *hack* (l. 19) and /end̦s/ *hands* (l. 20). The realisation of the *-ing* inflection as /ɪn/ is also common: /boksɪn/ *boxing* (l. 3), /dʒelɪn/ *gelling* (l. 18) and /pʊtɪn/ *putting* (l. 18). The pronuncia-tion of the suffix at the end of *nothing* is also typical of a Cockney accent: /nʌfɪŋk/ (l. 22). Glottal stops can be seen in /æɪʔ/ *eight* (l. 9) and /aːt/ *out* (l. 20) and the lack of distinction between /θ/ and /f/ is illustrated in /nʌfɪŋk/ (l. 22). The heavy aspiration of /p/ associated with Cockney accents occurs in the words /pʰiːpʊ/ *people* (l. 17). There are also many examples of the ways in which Cockney accents pronounce /l/ in differ-ent positions within a word. It is realised as a vowel: after a vowel – /skuːʊ/ *school* (l. 3), /əʊwæɪs/ *always* (l. 19) and /dʒeʊ/ *gel* (l. 17); before a consonant – /weʊʃ/ *Welsh* (l. 6); and when it occurs in a syllable on its own – /terɪbʊ/ *terrible* (l. 4). After /ɔː/ in the final position, however, /l/ is elided: /fʊtbəʊ/ *football* (l. 4), /əʊ/ *all* (l. 3) and /əʊrɒɪt/ *all right* (l. 15).

As in many other regional accents, Cockney accents pronounce *-y*, *-ey* and *-ee* at the end of words as /iː/: /sɪxtiː/ *sixty* (l. 9) and /æɪʔiː/ *eighty* (l. 21). Other vowels, how-ever, are more distinctive. The **pure vowels** of RP are significantly different: /æ/ is realised as /e̦/ in /end̦s/ *hands* (l. 20) and /ek̦/ *hack* (l. 19); /ʌ/ is realised as /æ/ in /lævliː/ *lovely* (l. 10), /lændən/ *London* (l. 1) and /gæʊf/ *Gulf* (l. 7). Some pure vowels are artic-ulated as diphthongs: /e/ as /eɪ/ in /eɪnd/ *end* (l. 1); /ɔː/ as /əʊ/ in /bəʊn/ *born* (l. 1), /fəʊs/ *Force* (l. 11) and /fəʊt/ *fought* (l. 7), and /ɔː/ in the final position as /ʊə/ in /fʊə/ *four* (l. 21).

Diphthongs also change their sounds – they tend to be wider than in RP. In Cockney accents, /eɪ/ becomes /æɪ/ in /əwæɪ/ *away* (l. 18); /əʊ/ becomes /æʊ/ in /bæʊ/ *Bow* (l. 1), /næʊ/ *know* (l. 6) and /smæʊk/ *Smoke* (l. 5); /aɪ/ becomes /ɒɪ/ in /fɒɪv/ *five* (l. 13) and /trɒɪɪn/ *trying* (l. 21); and /aʊ/ becomes /aː/ in /aːt/ *out* (l. 14). Two other dis-tinctive vowel sounds here occur in /jɜːs/ *years* (l. 15) for RP /jɪəs/ and /ɔːf/ *off* (l. 10) for RP /ɒf/.

Many other variations occur in the pronunciation patterns illustrated by this speaker. These can often be linked to features of **informal spoken language**. The replacement of unstressed vowels with a schwa is common: /bærə/ *barrow* (l. 2), /əvə/ *of the* (l. 11), /təmɒrə/ *tomorrow* (l. 13) and /kɒpə/ *copper* (l. 14). Equally, the elision of final consonants is typical of conversation: /bɪ/ *bit* (l. 7) and /wen/ *went* (l. 12). In infor-mal speech, /ð/ is sometimes elided when it appears in the initial position: /əm/ *them* (l. 18). Vowels are often shortened in grammatical function words like /mɪ/ *me* (l. 13) and /jə/ *you* (l. 1). Finally, word boundaries are sometimes blurred: /bɒɪskuːʊ/ *boys' school* (l. 3) and /dʒənæʊ/ *do you know* (l. 17).

From looking at this transcript, it is possible to list the following **characteristics** of a **Cockney accent**.

1 The phoneme /h/ is often elided.

2 The -ing inflection is realised as /ɪn/, while words ending with the suffix -thing are pronounced /ɪŋk/.
3 Glottal stops are common.
4 The distinction between /θ/ and /f/ is often lost (a similar process occurs with /ð/ and /v/).
5 The phoneme /ð/ in the initial position is elided or may be pronounced as /d/.
6 The phoneme /p/ is heavily aspirated in the initial position.
7 The phoneme /l/ is replaced in a distinctive way: in the final position, after a vowel, before a consonant in the same syllable or in a discrete syllable, it is realised as a vowel, /ʊ/; when /l/ follows /ɔː/ it is elided.
8 Words ending in -y, -ey, -ee tend to be realised as /iː/.
9 Some pure vowels sound slightly different to RP: /æ/ becomes /ɛ/; /e/ becomes /eɪ/; /ʌ/ becomes /æ/.
10 Some diphthongs are wider: /eɪ/ becomes /æɪ/; /əʊ/ becomes /æʊ/; /aɪ/ becomes /ɒɪ/; /aʊ/ becomes /aː/.
11 When /ɔː/ is in the final position, it is realised as /ʊə/; in a non-final position, it becomes /əʊ/.

Although the Cockney accent is distinctive and other Southern accents will be different in many ways, some of the pronunciation features highlighted here will be found in other 'Southern' accents.

ACTIVITY 8.5

Read the following oral narrative about a local gardening competition which is held in a group of villages outside Cardiff in the county of Mid Glamorgan. The speaker has lived in the area all his life and his accent, although not broad, displays many of the accent features associated with South Wales. The transcription is broad and marks only the pronunciations that are significantly different from RP.

Having read the transcription, rewrite the words transcribed phonemically and try to assess the ways in which they are different from RP. Then comment on:

1 the distinctive consonantal features of this Welsh accent;
2 the distinctive vowel sounds of this Welsh accent.

Written version

Who started the garden competition? I'm not sure. It may have been requested via the Taffs Well Horticultural Society, I'm not sure, and then run by the Taff Ely Council, broken up into various areas: Taffs Well, Nantgarw, Ty Rhiw. The judges. In total, I'd say there's about ten judges who er try to er judge an area that they don't actually come from. Me and er myself and Dave judge Taffs Well because we're from Gwaelod-y-Garth, you see and er various people from Taffs Well will judge Nantgarw and so forth and you're judging gardens against hanging baskets. It's a difficult one that. I always maintain that particularly if you've got a corner plot, nicely set, you're way in front of something that's got a small frontage or even no frontage. So that the wording of the actual schedule regarding garden or sort of hanging baskets, you know, must be really a separate thing. We have had trouble with this. It's a er er. It's difficult to define um and put down in words erm. For a judge to judge a garden when you go along and see a so-called garden is very limited to the fact that it's just er out on the pavement with no garden at all with a few containers and hanging and climbing plants which is really unfair to that to them people who have put a lot of effort in but are very limited at the end of the day.

Spoken version

1   who /staːtɪd/ the /gaːdən/ cómpetition (.) I'm not /ʃʊwə/ (.) it /me̞ av/ been /rəkwe̞stɪd/ via the Taffs Well /hɔːtɪkəltrəl/ Society (.) I'm not /ʃʊwə/ (.) and then run by the Taff Ely Cóuncil (.) /brɔːkən/ up into /ve̞ərɪəs e̞ərɪəs/ (.) Taffs Well (.) Nantgárw (.) Ty Rhíw (3) the judges (.) in /tɔːtəl/ I'd say there's about
5   (3) could be about °h te̞n judges (1) who er /traɪ/ to er judge an /e̞ərɪə/ that they /dɔːnt/ actually come fróm (.) me and er (.) myself and (.) Dave judge Taffs Well because we're from Gwaelod-y-Garth you sée (2) and er /ve̞ərɪəs/ people from Taffs Well will judge (.) Nantgárw and /sɔː/ forth (2) and you're judging /gaːdəns/ against /æŋɪn baːskɪts/ (.) /ɪs/ a difficult one /æt/ (.) I
10 always maintain that (.) /paːtɪkuliː/ if you've got a corner plot (.) /na̠ɪsliː/ set (.) you're way in front of /sʌmθɪn/ that's got a small frontage (1) or even /nɔː/ fróntage (.) so that the /wɜ̠ːdɪn/ of the actual /ʃeduːl/ (.) /regaːdɪn gaːdən/ or sort of (.) /æŋɪn baːskɪts/ (.) you /nɔː/ (.) must be /riːliː/ (.) a separate thing (2) we have /æd/ trouble with /ɪs/ (.) /ɪs/ a er er (.) /ɪs/ difficult to defíne (.) um
15 and put down in /wɜ̠ːdz/ erm (.) for a judge to judge (.) a /gaːdən/ (.) and when you /gɔː/ along and see a /sɔː/ called /gaːdən/ (.) is very limited (1) to the fact that it's just er out (.) on the /pe̞vmənt/ with /nɔː gaːdən/ at all (.) with a few containers and /æŋɪn/ and climbing ↑/plænts/↑ (.) which is /riːliː/ unfair to that (.) to them people (.) who've put a /lɒrə/ effort in but are very limited at
20 the end of the day

COMMENTARY

Because the discourse takes place in a relaxed environment, many of the features asso-ciated with informal conversation are present. The liaison that occurs in the phrase /lɒrə/ *lot of* (l. 19) is an example of a **segmental phonological feature** which alters the pronunciation of words at boundary points. This kind of word linkage is common to many accents and does not illustrate a characteristic of a Welsh accent. Similarly, the elided /ð/ in /ɪs/ *this* (l. 14) and /æt/ *that* (l. 9) and the elided /t/ in /ɪs/ *it's* (l. 9) are com-mon to many accents.

Other **consonantal** features can, however, be described as typically Welsh. The dropped /h/, for instance, is common: /æv/ *have* (l. 1), /æd/ *had* (l. 14) and /æŋɪn/ *hang-ing* (l. 9). The speaker does not elide /h/ consistently – it is usually only elided when it occurs in an unstressed position. The pronunciation of the inflection *-ing* is consistently /ɪn/: /sʌmθɪn/ *something* (l. 11), /æŋɪn/ *hanging* (l. 9) and /wɜːdɪn/ *wording* (l. 12). The /j/ phoneme that RP realises in front of /uː/ is absent: /paːtɪkuliː/ *particularly* (l. 10).

As would be expected, the most significant variations from RP come in the **vowels**. Words ending with *-y* are pronounced as /iː/: /riːliː/ *really* (l. 18) and /na̠ɪsliː/ *nicely* (l. 10). Many of the RP **pure vowels** are produced with the tongue raised so that the sound is closer: /ɑː/ becomes /aː/ in /staːtɪd/ *started* (l. 1), /gaːdən/ *garden* (l. 1), /baːskɪts/ *baskets* (l. 9) and /regaːdɪn/ *regarding* (l. 12); /e/ in /rəkwe̞stɪd/ *requested* (l. 2); and /ɜː/ in /wɜːds/ *words* (l. 15). The long RP /ɑː/ is shortened to /æ/ in words like /plænts/ *plants* (l. 18) and /ʌ/ is pronounced as /ə/ in words like /hɔːtɪkəltrəl/ *Horticultural* (l. 2).

Diphthongs are usually either narrow or are realised as monophthongs. Sounds like /eɪ/ in /meɪ̈/ *may* (l. 1) and /pe̞vmənt/ *pavement* (l. 17), /eə/ in /ve̞ərɪəs/ *various* (l. 3) and /e̞ərɪəs/ *areas* (l. 3) and /aɪ/ in /traɪ̈/ *try* (l. 5) and /naɪ̈sliː/ *nicely* (l. 10) are all closer than the equivalent RP vowel sounds. The RP diphthong /əʊ/ becomes a monothong /ɔː/ in words like /brɔːkən/ *broken* (l. 3), /tɔːtəl/ *total* (l. 4), /dɔːnt/ *don't* (l. 6), /sɔː/ *so* (l. 8), /nɔː/ *no* (l. 11) and *know* (l. 13) and /gɔː/ *go* (l. 16). Another distinctive feature of a Welsh accent is the broadening of diphthongs so that the two sounds are quite distinct: /ʃuwə/ for RP /ʃʊə/ *sure* (l. 1).

The most distinctive features of the speaker's accent can be seen in the close pure vowel sounds, the narrow diphthongs, the dropped /h/ in unstressed positions and the pronunciation of *-ing* and /juː/. The frequency with which utterances end with a rising tone is also characteristic of Welsh accents. Although not illustrated in this transcript, the plosives /d/, /b/ and /g/ are aspirated in the initial position, while /p/, /t/ and /k/ are aspirated in all positions /pʰɒpʰ/ *pop*).

From looking at this transcript, it is possible to list the following **characteristics** of a **South Wales accent**.

1   The phoneme /h/ is dropped.
2   The *-ing* inflection is realised as /ɪn/.
3   The semi-vowel or approximant /j/ is dropped before /uː/; in some words it is replaced by /ɪu/.
4   Words ending in *-y*, *-ey* and *-ee* are realised as /iː/.
5   The phoneme /ʌ/ is pronounced as /ə/.
6   The phonemes /æ/ and /ɑː/ are distinguished by length rather than height; /ɑː/ is less open than in RP, and is realised as /aː/.
7   The phonemes /ɜː/ and /e/ closer than in RP.
8   Many diphthongs like /eɪ/, /eə/ and /aɪ/ are narrow (marked ⊥ on the transcript); others are realised as monothongs: /əʊ/ becomes /ɔː/ and /eɪ/ becomes /e/.
9   Some diphthongs are broadened so that the two sounds of the RP glide are quite distinct: /ʊə/ becomes /ʊwə/ and /ɪə/ becomes /ɪjə/.

Although the Cardiff accent is quite different both from rural South Wales and from North Wales accents, some of the pronunciation features highlighted here will be found in other Welsh accents.

Summary

Although the guidelines in this section cover the distinctive accent features of particular accents, many speakers will not exhibit all the characteristics. Linguists have to consider the following possibilities when assessing **why a speaker does not conform to expected accentual patterns**.

1   speakers may have lost a broad accent by moving away from the area in which they grew up;
2   the speakers' educational experience may have made their accent more like RP (modified RP);
3   the context in which the speech is taking place may be formal and speakers may be consciously or subconsciously modifying their speech (convergence);
4   the speakers' occupations may have moved them up a social class and they may therefore be adopting the speech behaviour associated with a higher social class;
5   exposure to the media and travel may have modified strong accentual features.

If an accent is very **broad**, linguists need to consider the following possibilities:

1   speakers may have lived in one particular area for a long time with little contact with other speech communities;
2   speakers may be old and their accents may retain features that are not as common among the younger people of the speech community;
3   speakers may be purposely adopting broad accentual features either to identify themselves within a particular group or to consciously alienate other speakers who do not speak in the same way;
4   speakers may belong to a lower social class or may have chosen to leave education early.

The **study of accents** is very complex. Whole books have been written on individual accents and linguists spend years researching single areas. The summaries here deal only with very basic differences between the main accents of the United Kingdom, acting as an introduction to characteristic features of regional pronunciation.

8.3 Dialect

A DIALECT is a subdivision of a language which is identified by variations in **lexis** and **grammar**. The different dialects of English may vary **socially** or **regionally** just as accents do, but despite variations they will remain largely comprehensible to other English speakers.

English is made up of a number of regional dialects which correspond more or less to the broad regions established in Figure 8.1. Linguists can identify the main characteristics of different regions, and the isoglosses establish boundaries which group together non-standard dialect forms with similar distinctive linguistic features. Inevitably, there are some overlaps – although non-standard lexis tends to be located in specific regions, non-standard grammatical features are similar across boundaries.

Regional variation can be seen in the dialectal differences between town and country. In rural areas, non-standard dialects are often stronger because the arrival of newcomers who use different dialects is less common. Urban areas, on the other hand, are far more likely to contain a linguistic mix. When people move round the country for employment, they introduce new dialects into the local speech community. Equally, **age** can affect the kind of dialect used. The broadest non-standard dialects tend to be spoken by older members of a community who have had little prolonged contact with other dialect users. Younger people, however, are exposed to a wider range of language forms, particularly Standard English. They are therefore less likely to speak the broad non-standard dialects of their grandparents. Instead they will use a dialect form which is modified in the direction of Standard English.

Some linguists believe that non-standard dialects are dying out. This may be the case with some of the older rural forms of English, but many new forms of English are appearing to replace them. This is particularly true of urban areas. The linguistic diversity of cities provides the right conditions for the emergence of new dialects, clearly illustrating that language is always in flux and that change is inevitable.

As urban centres grow and as educational and occupational opportunities offer more people the chance to move between social classes, non-standard dialects can be defined on a **social** rather than regional basis. The use of particular words and grammatical structure can be linked directly to specific social groups or classes. For instance, people of a lower social class are more likely to use the third person singular present tense inflection in all parts of the verb: *I goes* and *we goes*; while people of a higher social class are more likely to use a standard agreement of subject and verb: *I go* and *we go.* This kind of differentiation in use is clearly linked to educational and occupational background – the longer people stay in formal education, the more likely they are to use Standard English.

Although non-standard dialects are most commonly associated with spoken language, non-standard usage of words and grammatical structures can also be seen in **written work**. Most people will use Standard English rather than a non-standard dialect in formal writing because it is the language form used and taught in education. Informal writing may contain non-standard dialect features because it is the written variety that most closely approximates the spoken word. Novelists or poets may also choose to write in non-standard English in order to create certain effects.

It is important to remember that Standard English is one of the many dialectal forms of English. As the dominant variety, it is used for writing, but its choice as the prestige form is based on social rather than linguistic judgements.

Lexical variation

Within different geographical regions, words often develop that are unique to a certain community. These may be incomprehensible to people from another area, although when heard in context other English speakers will probably be able to work out an approximate meaning.

> *nobby*: smart, brilliant, really good; *cutch*: cuddle (South Wales dialect)
> *loke*: path leading up to a house; *dyke*: ditch (Norfolk dialect)

Some words, like *borrow/lend* and *teach/learn*, are used non-standardly in more than one dialect. Because non-standard dialects are predominantly spoken, colloquial words and collocations are common: *and all, like I said, and that, and everything, cos.*

It is useful to distinguish between non-standard dialect words and informal conversational words and phrases: the latter tend to be used across isogloss boundaries, while the former can usually be quite clearly linked to a particular region.

Grammatical variation

Many of the non-standard grammar features that can be identified occur across boundaries – verbs and pronouns are particularly likely to vary from the standard. The following list summarises the main variations that occur in non-standard English dialects (N-SE). Where appropriate, reference is made to the specific regions associated with a feature.

Nouns

The plural of a noun is usually formed by adding the inflection *-s*. However, in many phrases that contain a noun of measurement and a cardinal number, no plural inflection is used. This occurs in many regional dialects: *three mile* and *six pound*. In some dialects, a few plurals are still formed using the archaic inflection /n/: *housen*. The /n/ inflection used in this dialectal form accounts for the plural of *children*, which is one of the few remaining irregular plurals in SE. In Middle English the singular noun was *childre* which was made plural with the addition of the /n/ inflection. In some regional non-standard dialect forms, the archaic *childer* is still used.

Adjectives

Some adjectives in SE end in *-en* (*golden, silken, wooden* and *olden*) – these are all that remain of the OE system of case inflections. A few regional dialects in the South-West, however, still use archaic inflections on some adjectives: *papern*. In SE, the comparative and superlative are formed either by adding the suffixes *-er/-est* to an adjective, or by using *more/most* before an adjective. In many non-standard regional dialects, both forms are used simultaneously: *the more fiercer dog* and *the most coldest wind*.

Adverbs

In many non-standard dialects, the adverb *-ly* inflection is not used. This means that regular adverbs and adjectives have exactly the same form – they can, however, still be distinguished by their position and function.

FUNCTION	m		A	
	the *slow* bus	the bus drove *slow*	[slow*ly* (SE)]	
FORM	Adj		Adv	

Prepositions

Prepositions of place tend to vary from the standard forms in many of the regional dialects: *I went up town* (*to* SE); *It's along of a mile away* (*about* SE). In some cases, usage is so widespread that the non-standard versions are now often described as informal SE: *We got off of the bus* (*off* SE); *I got it off Julie* (*from* SE). In Northern dialects, *till* is used for SE *to* – for example, *she's going till the theatre*. In the South-West, the preposition *to* which accompanies verbs in the infinitive form often appears as *for to* – for example, *tell me how for to do it*. In some areas, the *to* is elided – for example, *tell me how for do it*. There are a few phrases in which the *for. . .to* structure is still used in SE: for example, *for me to understand* and *the idea is for us all to get involved*. In dialects, this construction is used more extensively in places where it is no longer accepted in SE.

Conjunctions

In Northern dialects *while* is used for SE *until* – for example, *I'm going while dinner-time*; and *without* is used for SE *unless* – for example, *you can't go without you tidy up*.

Pronouns

Pronominal forms vary significantly in non-standard dialects. **Subject** and **object personal pronouns** are often interchangeable, particularly in the dialects of the South-West: *she went out, didn't her; have you seen she?* This usage seems to be governed by rules: the object pronoun tends to be used in the subject site only when there is no emphasis; the subject pronoun is used in the object site when emphasis is needed. The pronouns that occur in unstressed positions often take the following weak forms: *ee* (*you*), *er* (*he* in the subject site), *n* (*he* in the object site), *er* (*she*), *us* (*we*) and *m* (*they*). In Northern dialects, the first person plural object pronoun is used for both singular and plural references: *give it us*. This usage occurs in standard colloquial English in some collocations like *give us a kiss* or *do us a favour*. Informal (*thou, thee*) and formal (*you*) second person pronouns are widespread. The possessive pronouns *hisn, hern, ourn, yourn* and *theirn* are also common except in the North.

In SE, **reflexive pronouns** are formed by adding *-self* or *-selves* to either the personal object pronouns or to possessive determiners.

Object pronouns	Possessive determiners	Reflexive pronouns
me	my	*my*self
you	your	*your*self
		*your*selves
him	his	*him*self
her	hers	*her*self
it	its	*it*self
us	our	*our*selves
them	their	*them*selves

SE is not consistent and many dialects use non-standard forms which actually standard-ise the system – they base all the forms on the **possessive determiner** + **-*self/-selves*** structure: *hisself*, *itsself* and *theirselves*.

Relative pronouns are frequently non-standard in regional dialects. Where SE uses *who* or *that* for people and *which* or *that* for non-human things, non-standard dialects will often use *which* for people and *what* for both human and non-human things: *the man which I described is here* and *the house what I live in is big*.

Demonstrative pronouns are also frequently non-standard: where SE uses *those*, many regional dialects will use *them* or *they* – for instance, *them horses are wild* or *they horses are wild*. In Northern dialects, the demonstrative *yon* is added to the SE *this*, *that*, *these* and *those*. It is used to refer to things that are more distant than *that* – for example, *yon field used to be full of horses*.

Verbs

Verbs are the most complicated part of a language system, and in non-standard dialects they are frequently different to the standard forms. In the **present tense** many regional dialects standardise the patterns of SE. Eastern dialects tend to drop the third person singular -*s* inflection: *he walk*. Dialects of the North, South-West and Wales, however, tend to add the -*s* inflection throughout: *I walks*, *you walks*, *we walks* and *they walks*.

The simple present tense can be used to refer to events in the past – this is called the HISTORIC PRESENT.

> Well, they'*re* in the room before you know it and he *looks* round and *laughs*.
> They just *turn* and *leave* – he'*s* not sure what to do, so he *carries* on as though it'*s* all fine.

This form of the present tense is not common, although it can be used to make a story more exciting. In Scottish and Irish dialects, the present historic can be recognised by the -*s* inflection used in the first and second persons and the third person plural: *they thinks hard and decides to go*.

Past tense verbs are even more likely to be non-standard in dialects. Many verbs are irregular in SE and dialects often try to standardise the patterns. The verb *to be* in the past tense, for instance, may be conjugated with *was* or *were* for all persons. The regular past tense inflection -*ed* is often added to irregular verbs: *seed*; *doed*. Where verbs have two separate forms for the **simple past tense** and the **past participle**, regional dialects often use only one form.

Base form	Simple past (SE)	Past participle	Dialect form
see	saw	seen	*seen* (simple past)
come	came	come	*come* (simple past)
fall	fell	fallen	*fell* (past participle)
swim	swam	swum	*swam* (past participle)

Sometimes, the vowel change occurring in the past participle of an irregular verb in SE is used alongside the regular past tense suffix in the simple past: *swolled* for *swelled* (past participle *swollen*).

Present participles are often used in an archaic form in which the prefix *a-* is added, particularly in the Midlands and in Eastern dialects: *a-going, a-running, a-sewing*. Where SE uses the **present** and **past progressive**, Northern dialects often replace the present participle with the past participle: *I was sat there like an idiot*. In SE, the verb *to do* can be used as a lexical verb or as a dummy auxiliary in interrogatives, negatives and emphatic utterances. In South-Western and Welsh dialects, it is often used with another verb in wider contexts: *I do go every night* or *we d'see him regularly*.

Negatives

Multiple negatives are used in many dialects. Although now considered non-standard, in older forms of English, multiple negatives were used to create emphasis. The most commonly occurring form is the double negative: *I haven't done nothing* or *you didn't bring no presents*. Forms of the negative vary from dialect to dialect. The negative verb *ain't* however is very common. It can be used for the negative of the first person singular and plural and the third person singular of the verb *to be* and as the negative of the auxiliary *to have*: *I ain't happy* for SE *am not*; *he ain't buying a shirt* for SE *is not*; *you ain't got an apple* for SE *have not*. Another common dialect feature can be seen in the use of *never* to refer to a single occasion, where SE would use *didn't*: *she never came last night*. Other variations are more closely linked to specific regions – for example, *amn't* is the Midlands dialect for *am not*. The use of *no* or *nae* instead of *not* to construct the negative is a distinctive feature of Scottish dialects: *he's no coming*.

ACTIVITY 8.6

Reread the transcripts in Activities 8.1–8.5 and identify any examples of non-standard grammar. Group similar features together and try to categorise the grammatical variations you find.

COMMENTARY

The following non-standard grammatical features are illustrated in the transcripts:

1   non-standard use of **prepositions**: *spuds off the farmer* (l. 19, Activity 8.1) for SE *from*;
2   non-standard use of **pronouns**: *theirselves* (l. 15, Activity 8.3) for SE *themselves*; *them people* (l. 19, Activity 8.5) for SE *those*;
3   non-standard **agreement of subject and verb**: *there was* (l. 43, Activity 8.1) for SE *were*; *there's about . . . ten judges* (ll. 4–5, Activity 8.5) for SE *were*;

4   non-standard **past tense verbs**: *she come* (l. 11, Activity 8.3) for SE *came*; *I see* (l. 11, Activity 8.4) for SE *saw*.

All the examples here are typical dialect features which occur frequently in many regional dialects. The non-standard usage can be classified by focusing on variations from SE in the following areas: prepositions, pronouns and verbs.

ACTIVITY 8.7

Read through the transcript of a Cockney accent below and identify any non-standard usage.

1   I done all that (.) I build it (.) that cost me one hundred and fifty-eight pound
     (.) well when we first come here (.) it was a rock garden come say about six
     foot to the window (.) just all a mass of rocks and rubble so what we done (.)
     I dug it back and (.) we done the plans here (.) we looked out the window
5   and thought do this do that (.) you know (.) and as I dug it it just formed itself
     (.) you know (.) it's er (.) it holds it back (.) and them two beds here are full of
     rocks (.) there's about sort of a foot of earth in there but (.) the rest of it's all
     unbelievable (.) I mean I didn't put no foundations down under them stones
     because it's so solid (.) I just put sand down and put other things down on
10   top of them (.) and it's just stayed there (.) it's been done what four or five
     years (.) hasn't moved

COMMENTARY

Once again the most significantly non-standard forms are the **verbs**. The **simple past tense** forms of the irregular verbs *do* (l. 0), *build* (l. 0) and *come* (l. 0) are simplified.

Infinitive	*Past tense (SE)*	*Past participle (SE)*
do	did	done
build	built	built
come	came	come

In the first and third examples, the speaker uses the irregular past participle form for the simple past tense, thus reducing three verb forms to two. In the second example, he uses the verb in its base form rather than using the irregular SE *built* – the two forms, however, are very close and the speaker is merely replacing the voiceless /t/ with a voiced /d/.

Other typical non-standard grammar can be seen in:

• the use of a **double negative**: *didn't put no foundations* (l. 8);
• the **absence of a plural on a noun following a cardinal number**: *one hundred and fifty-eight pound* (l. 1) and *six foot* (ll. 2–3);
• the use of an **object pronoun** where SE would use a demonstrative determiner *those*: *them two beds* (l. 6) and *them stones* (l. 8);
• the replacement of the **prepositional phrase** *out of* with an adverb: *looked out the window* (l. 4).

8.4 Accent and dialect levelling

A diachronic study of the English language shows its changes over time, but it is also possible to identify changes that are taking place now. As society changes to mirror developments in technology, politics, morals and culture, so language is adapted to meet the new demands placed upon it. Some people dislike the idea of linguistic change – they see new forms of English as lazy and inaccurate. Others, however, see them as part of an inevitable process in which only the useful modifications will survive.

Because people are now far more likely to move around the country, some linguists believe that the traditional regional accents and dialects are dying out. They believe that older forms of English are modified by contact with the language of newcomers – different accents and dialects then emerge within the local speech community. At first, old and new forms will exist alongside each other, but as the young people who use the new forms themselves have children, the more traditional accents and dialects will slowly disappear. Because of contact with other forms of English, regional accents and dialects lose their distinctive features and become more similar. Linguists call this process **LEVELLING**.

Some people change their social class as well as their regional base and this too affects the nature of English. The appearance of 'social' rather than regional accents and dialects is a sign of the way in which people see themselves in terms of their language. By choosing a social rather than a regional form of English, speakers are making a statement about their cultural and political identity rather than their regional background.

The emergence of new or adapted forms of English is linguistically important because of the social changes the process reflects. People are making choices consciously or subconsciously and the results of this are seen in the accents and dialects they use.

An example of the natural evolution of accents and dialects can be seen in the emergence of **Estuary English**, also called the **New London Voice**. It has a high profile because of the number of radio and television personalities who use it – for instance, Ben Elton, Paul Merton and Jonathan Ross. It was first associated with speakers on the banks of the Thames in Essex and in North Kent, but because of the influence of the media it has now spread much further afield. The following characteristic features can be identified:

- /t/ in the medial position is elided: /gæwɪk/ *Gatwick*;
- as in the Southern accent, /l/ is often pronounced as /ʊ/: /bɪʊd/ *build*;
- /p/ and /k/ sounds in the final position are elided: /pɒ/ *pop* and /stɪ/ *stick*;
- it has a distinctive vocabulary with many Americanisms: *cheers*, *basically*, *guesstimate*.

It is sometimes described as **High Cockney**: although both non-standard dialects are similar, many of the traditional 'low prestige' features associated with a Cockney accent have been dropped: the glottal stop for the medial position /t/ is rare; /f/ does not replace /θ/; and /v/ does not replace /ð/.

Estuary English is a social rather than a regional dialect, mirroring the supposed reduction in differences between social classes. It is used by young people who feel that it is a form of English with street credibility. The middle classes use it to avoid being marked out as 'posh'; Southerners who are upwardly mobile adopt it, losing the harshest features of Southern accents in order to move closer to 'prestige' forms of English; and it is used in the City instead of RP which is seen as alienating many people. It is often called a **classless dialect** because its appeal seems to be so wide.

Although some linguists do not believe that Estuary English is a new phenomenon, others see its emergence as an important development in the history of the English language. They believe that this form of the language could replace RP as the dominant accent and dialect for the middle classes around London, changing the language map of Southern England quite dramatically.

8.5 What to look for in British accents and dialects

The following checklist can be used to identify key features in examples of different accents and dialects. There will not be examples of all the features listed in every transcript, but the list can be used as a guide. The points made are general so discussion of specific examples will need to be adapted to take account of the specific context, the participants and the purpose of the communication.

The following are helpful questions to ask.

Register

1   What is the **mode**? – written or spoken?
2   What is the **manner**? – the relationship between participants: formal or informal? socially equal or unequal? familiar or unfamiliar?
3   What is the **field**? – the subject matter, the social standing and the educational background of the participants and the region will govern the kind of language used.

Accent

1   Are any of the **consonants** different from RP? – is the phoneme /h/ **dropped** in the initial position? how is the phoneme /ŋ/ pronounced? is the phoneme /j/ articulated before the pure vowel /uː/? is the **post-vocalic /r/** present or absent? is the **glottal stop** common? is there anything distinctive about the realisation of the phoneme /l/? are any of the consonants **aspirated**? are any consonants **replaced** with other phonemes?
2   Are any of the **vowels** different from RP? – are *-y*, *-ey* and *-ee* realised as /iː/ or /ɪ/? are /æ/ and /ɑː/ distributed as in RP or not? are both /ʌ/ and /ʊ/ used in the phoneme inventory or not? are any of the **pure vowels closer** than in RP? are any **diphthongs narrower** or **wider** than in RP? are there any **distinctive features** which are specifically associated with a particular region?
3   Do the consonant and vowel variants suggest the speaker has a **regional**, **social** or **personal** accent?
4   Is the accent **broad** or **modified**?
5   Is there any evidence of **convergence** or **divergence**?
6   Are there any examples of **hypercorrection**?

Lexis

1   Are there any words that are unique to a **particular region**?
2   Are any of the words **archaic**?
3   Are any words **idiosyncratic**, reflecting an individual view of the world rather than one influenced by a particular region or social group?

4   Are there any examples of **colloquial** words and phrases which cross isogloss boundaries?

Grammar

1   Are any **open class words** other than the verbs non-standard? – are there any **noun plurals** with no *-s* inflection after a cardinal number or with an archaic *-n* suffix? are the **adjectives** marked by archaic **inflections** or double **comparatives** and **superlatives**? are **adverb** inflections dropped?
2   Are the **verbs** non-standard? – the **third person singular** *-s* inflection? **simple past tense** regular and irregular forms? **present** and **past participles**? the **dummy auxiliary** *do*?
3   Are any **closed class words** other than the pronouns non-standard? – **prepositions** or **conjunctions** which are different from RP?
4   Are the **pronouns** non-standard? – archaic forms like *thee* and *thou*? interchangeable **subject** and **object** pronouns? **reflexive** pronouns? **relative** pronouns? **demonstrative** pronouns?
5   Are the **negatives** non-standard? – are **multiple negatives** used? is ***ain't*** used? are there references to a single occasion using ***never***? are there distinctive **regional** forms?

Summary

Accents and dialects reveal something about a speaker's **social, regional** and **personal identity**. They may be consciously or subconsciously modified and most speakers will style-shift in order to meet the requirements of each speech encounter.

Speakers need to make linguistic choices about the most appropriate kind of English for each speech encounter. If they have a **wide repertoire** they will be more able to move between standard and non-standard accents and dialects.

Variations from the norms of SE and RP should not automatically be seen as 'bad' or 'incorrect'. Accents and dialects are not a lazy way of speaking, but are varieties in their own right with **distinctive rules** and **structural systems**.

Few people now remain in one speech community all their lives and we all hear a wide range of accents and dialects on the radio and television. This means that most speech communities show evidence of **dialect contact** – the result of this is **dialect levelling**, and a reduction in the differences between different non-standard and standard forms of English.

9 Child language – learning to talk

9.1 The nature of child language acquisition

Just as children develop physically at more or less the same rate, so all normal children will develop language at about the same time. Because of this parallel between physical and mental growth, it could be suggested that LANGUAGE ACQUISITION is a biologically determined process. This cannot provide the complete explanation, however, because children deprived of normal social contact do not acquire language. This has been seen in cases where children have apparently been reared by wild animals away from a human environment. Equally, where children have been isolated and have received only minimal human contact, their language skills are non-existent. Even when reintroduced to society, children deprived of language during their early years fail to acquire much more than a very basic linguistic knowledge.

If language acquisition was innate (natural to the mind) and linked only to biological factors, then once the appropriate triggers were provided such children should have been able to acquire language in the usual way. Recorded cases of children who have experienced extreme social isolation have therefore led linguists to believe both that language acquisition is dependent on an appropriate linguistic input and that this language experience must be gained before a certain age.

In very general terms, it would seem that language acquisition is linked to:

- **physical growth**: the body has to be mature enough for the child to produce recognisable words by manipulating the speech organs effectively and consciously;
- **social factors**: the environment and culture in which a child grows up will influence the kind of language input experienced – this will, in turn, affect the child's linguistic abilities;
- a **critical age**: if input and language experience occur before a certain point in the child's physical and mental development, learning will be easy, quick, effortless and complete.

Because so many children acquire language effortlessly, it is easy to underestimate the complexity of the process taking place. Research in this field, however, is comparatively new, and linguists still have much to learn about language acquisition.

9.2 The theories of language acquisition

There are four key linguistic approaches that try to explain the ways in which children acquire language.

Behaviourist approach

The **BEHAVIOURISTS** believe that children learn to speak by **imitating** the language structures they hear. Parents automatically **reinforce** and correct children's utterances, and this forms the basis for a child's knowledge of language.

There are, however, significant problems with this theory of language development. Although imitation is obviously important in learning pronunciation and in acquiring new vocabulary, children do not seem to automatically pick up 'correct' forms from imitation. With irregular verbs, for instance, children do not necessarily use the standard form because they hear adults use it. Instead, they over-extend the language patterns they already know.

▓   steal → stealed (stole)   grow → growed (grew)

Equally, children seem unable to imitate adult 'corrections'.

> CHILD: my train is /beə/
> MOTHER: no (.) not 'by there' (.) just 'there'
> CHILD: my train is /beə/
> MOTHER: no just 'there'
> CHILD: oh (.) my train is just /beə/

Such evidence suggests that child language acquisition cannot be based on imitation and reinforcement alone. Although children may add new words to their repertoire by using **LABELS** (words with a naming function) an adult has just introduced, they rarely imitate speech that is not directed at them. Equally, they do not appear to assimilate syntactical structures by imitation. Above all, this approach fails to explain how children are able to produce structures that they have not heard before.

Cognitive approach

The **COGNITIVE** approach links language acquisition directly to intellectual development. The research of Jean Piaget (1896–1980), a Swiss psychologist who did much work on the intellectual development of children, suggested that children can only use a certain linguistic structure when they understand the **concept** involved. For instance, children will only understand the past tense when they understand the concept of past time; they must have learnt to recognise and conceptualise visual and physical differences before they can talk about size and colour. This approach to language acquisition seems to be most effective in describing linguistic progress during the first one and a half years. Even at this stage, however, it is difficult to make precise connections between cognitive and linguistic developmental stages.

Nativist approach

The **NATIVISTS** believe that children are born with an **innate capacity** for language development. When the brain is exposed to speech, it will automatically begin to receive and make sense of utterances because it has been 'programmed' to do so. Noam Chomsky, an American linguist (1928–), suggests that the human brain has a **language acquisition device (LAD)** which enables children to use the language around them to work out what is and what is not linguistically acceptable. This device also provides young children with an innate understanding of the underlying grammatical rules that govern language usage. The programmed patterns are general, and the child then has to learn exact rules through trial and error. The nativists believe the presence of the LAD explains the facts that:

- all normal children acquire language skills in the same kind of order and at the same kind of speed;
- children are able to understand new sentences and constructions without having had any previous experience of them.

The nativists, however, do not appear to pay sufficient attention to the importance of input, the critical age aspect, and the role of imitation and reinforcement.

Interactive approach

Recent studies have shown the importance of **INTERACTION**. Adults alter the way they talk to children, giving them specific opportunities to take part in the discourse. For instance, utterances are simplified; intonation patterns are distinctive; extra information is given for clarification; and questions invite direct participation. Adults will also often expand on a child's speech and research suggests that this can be one of the most positive ways to increase a child's awareness of grammatical structures. This kind of interaction is called **'motherese'** or **'caretaker speech'**, and it differs quite markedly from speech between two adults. Key features can be summarised as follows:

- **Vocabulary** is simplified so that concrete objects are named in broad categories: *dog* rather than *spaniel* or *labrador*; *ball* rather than *football, cricket ball* or *tennis ball*. **'Baby words'** like *doggie* or *moo-cow* do not help a child to learn language more efficiently. The reduplication of sounds in words like *baba* and *dada*, on the other hand, does enable babies to communicate because the words are easy to say.
- **Conversations** tend to be based on concrete things that relate directly to the child's environment.
- **Sentence structures** tend to be short and often use pauses to stress the end of grammatical units. Certain sentence patterns recur regularly: *where is _____?*; *do you want a _____?*; *that's* (pointing) *a _____*.
- **Commands** occur frequently and young children assimilate and use them in their own speech.
- **Tag questions** – questions added to the end of a statement inviting a response from the listener: *isn't it?, aren't we?* – are used to invite direct participation and to encourage a child to ask for clarification if necessary. The high percentage of questions makes 'caretaker speech' distinctive.
- **Repetition** reinforces new words or structures and clarifies meaning.
- Parents often use a higher and wider **pitch range** when talking to small children, possibly because it keeps the child's attention. The singsong intonation and exaggerated stress on key words also make 'caretaker speech' distinctive.
- The **pace** is often slower than in conversations with other adults.

Because the baby or young child receives attention as a direct result of any attempts to communicate, the process is rewarding. 'Caretaker speech' is therefore an important means of creating a positive relationship with the parent which will form the basis for future meaningful communication.

Although the benefits of 'caretaker speech' are clear, it is not possible to identify precisely the links between the language structures parents use and their appearance in the child's language.

Each of the four theoretical approaches highlights a particular element of child language acquisition, but none can provide a complete explanation on its own. More research is needed before linguists can be completely sure about the processes that take place, but it is possible to summarise the basic principles:

- to acquire language, children must be part of a **social and linguistic community**;
- **physical development** plays a part in children's ability to articulate the particular phonemes making up a language;
- children have some kind of **instinctive awareness** of language patterns which enables them to experiment with structures that they have not previously heard;
- in order to use language structures (like the comparative, for example), children must be able to **intellectually conceptualise** the world around them – language acquisition is therefore linked in some way to intellectual development;
- through **imitation**, children can acquire new vocabulary and may be introduced to new grammatical structures;
- **parental reinforcement** highlights non-standard usage and draws attention to 'correct' versions – although children often do not accept adult correction:
- **especially adapted forms of speech** create a positive speech environment in which children are encouraged to participate in a meaningful way.

9.3 The function of communication

Interaction with other language users gives children a purpose – if they too acquire language, they will be able to participate in the communication processes that are taking place around them. They may begin by using different kinds of cries to attract attention to their needs, but as they become more adept at using language, so their range of communication can become more complex. Through their use of language, they can:

- establish relationships with the people around them;
- express their feelings and opinions;
- get others to do as they wish;
- find out new information by asking questions;
- get what they need by explaining exactly what they want;
- communicate their ideas to other people;
- tell stories and use language expressively.

As children acquire language, they become active participants in society. They can suddenly communicate purposefully in a way that others can interpret easily and so can express their own individuality.

9.4 Features of child language

Children acquire language skills rapidly during the first three years of their life. Even before birth, babies have become accustomed to the sound of the human voice; at one day old, they can distinguish their mother's voice from others; and by their second week, they can distinguish between human voices and non-human sounds. This prepares the ground for the communication that will take place before recognisable words are uttered.

Mothers tend to instinctively encourage interaction from very early on by establishing the pattern for conversation. They will:

- leave pauses where responses could be made;
- use question structures frequently;
- include the baby's own 'sounds' in a running dialogue.

This intuitive behaviour prepares babies for language acquisition. It immerses them directly in a simplified version of the linguistic patterns of the adult world by establishing basic turn-taking structures.

The process of language acquisition can be broken down into five main stages and linguists consider certain key areas within each one: **pronunciation**; **prosodic features**; **lexis**; **grammar**; and PRAGMATICS (an understanding of the social factors affecting spoken interaction).

0–12 months

In the first two months, the sounds babies make are linked to their **physical conditions**. They cry if they are hungry or wet; they gulp, burp and cough noisily; and they grizzle if they want to be held. They have to control the flow of air to make these noises and this same control will be used in a more refined way as their ability to communicate becomes more sophisticated.

Between 2 and 5 months, babies begin to experiment more and start to respond directly to parental smiles. At 6–8 weeks, babies will often begin to **coo**. This is a softer sound than crying, made up of velar sounds like [k] and [g] and high vowels like [i] and [uː]. As the baby realises that cooing will elicit a response from the mother, the first interactive dialogues begin. Although cooing sounds like [gæ] and [guː] are sometimes strung together, there are not yet any recognisable patterns. Between 2 and 4 months, the baby will begin to **respond to the 'meaning'** of different tones of voice – anger, pleasure, humour. At around 16 weeks, the first **laugh** will encourage even more varied responses from the mother and this widens the scope of possible interaction.

Physical developments at this stage also prepare the baby for greater communication:

- as the child starts to look around and sit up, the mother will point to things and her intonation will become more exaggerated;
- simple games like peekaboo make interaction fun;
- the tongue starts to move horizontally and vertically, enabling the baby to produce a wider range of sounds;
- the vocal cords are used in conjunction with the movements of the tongue;
- the lips and the tongue play a greater part in sound production, helping the baby to make new sounds – it is possible that babies are beginning to imitate the mouth movements of adult speech at this stage.

The parents will respond instinctively to these physiological developments, and interaction becomes more like a two-way communication.

From 6 months, babies begin to **relate their utterances to specific contexts**. They seem to **recognise some words**, particularly names of family members. By the end of the first year, they will probably be able to **point to things in answer to a question**; to **respond** in some way to situations requiring **predictable feedback** (*say bye-bye; say night-night*); and to **understand several words** even though they cannot yet say any recognisable words. Because the parents will now respond more to utterances that appear to be meaningful rather than random sounds, the baby's communication will begin to be more deliberate. Utterances in the 6–12 month period will become **more varied**. Segments will be longer and will consist of frequently **repeated consonant and vowel-like patterns**. The **pitch level** will usually be high, but will also be marked by **glides** from high to low as the baby experiments.

From the baby's experimentation with a large range of sounds, a smaller, more frequently occurring set will emerge. This stage is known as BABBLING. The sounds are now less randomly selected and begin to adopt rhythms that are closer to that of adult speech. **Reduplication of patterns**, like [bæbæbæ], and sequences in which the consonants and vowels change in each segment, like [dæbæ], are common. As the baby reaches 9 months, **recognisable intonation patterns** will be used for these consonant-vowel combinations. By 10–11 months, when babies can pull themselves into a standing position, they will use **vocalisations to express emotions**. The utterances at this stage are important because they will form the basis for the sounds of early speech.

   Imitations and **sound play** at this point in their linguistic development give babies a much wider experience of the social role of speech. Equally, by **observing adults**, they learn a great deal about conversation even though they cannot yet fully take part. Although many of the sounds of babbling, particularly in the earlier part of this period, do not appear to have meaning, babies do seem to consciously use them to communicate with the people around them. This kind of language use is called JARGON.

12–18 months

Towards the end of the first year, children are able to indicate their intentions more specifically. **Intonation** is used to mark different kinds of purpose: the meaning of particular utterances will probably still be unclear, but intonation patterns will enable parents to interpret them. At this stage, the first real steps towards language acquisition are made as the **first words** are formed, often with the same intonation patterns each time. Language used at this stage will not really resemble adult speech, but parents familiar with the context in which PROTO-WORDS appear will be able to understand many of the utterances. Up to this stage, almost all children develop in the same way and at more or less the same speed, but after this children's language becomes much more individual.

   From 12–18 months, children begin to produce a **variety of recognisable single-word utterances** based on everyday objects. These utterances are HOLOPHRASTIC – they are grammatically unstructured and each consists of a single word. At this stage, pronunciation is often idiosyncratic. In general, children will tend to choose and avoid the same kinds of sounds, but each child will have marked preferences for some sounds rather than others. Equally, the same child might pronounce one word in different ways at different times: *cheese* might be articulated as /giː/, /kiːs/ and /iːs/.

   Children at this stage will be acquiring between ten and twenty new words a month. The vast majority of these words will have a **naming function**, focusing on people, food, body parts, toys, clothing and household things. During the holophrastic stage, children use a **limited vocabulary** to refer to a wide range of unrelated things. OVER-EXTENSION is therefore common – children use the same word to refer to different objects because they see a similarity in size, shape, sound or movement. *Baby*, for instance, may refer to all children; or *flower* to anything with leaves. It is common for the middle term of a set of HYPONYMS (groups of related words in which specific words are seen as sub-categories of a general word) to be used: for instance, *dog* instead of *animal* or *spaniel*. As the child gains linguistic experience, over-extension is replaced by a **narrowing of the field of reference** – more words are learnt so references can be more precise. Other examples of a lack of linguistic sophistication at this stage can be seen in:

* UNDER-EXTENSION, in which words are given a narrower range of reference than is usual – *car*, for instance, may be used to refer only to a family car;
* MISMATCH, in which words are used to label objects with no apparent logic – *doll*, for instance, is used to label a child's trousers.

   Between 12 and 18 months, the first **modifiers** will be used to describe things; **action utterances** (one word accompanied by gestures) like *gosleep* or *allgone* will form the basis for the first verbs; and **social expressions** like *bye-bye* will mark a growing awareness of cultural expectations. Although the utterances are holophrastic, intonation and gesture help the single word to convey the meaning and mood of a sentence. The **conversational skills** of a child at this stage are still limited. Adults continue to do most of the talking and much of the child's communication takes the form of a **monologue**.

18–24 months

By the age of 2, a child's **vocabulary** has probably reached two hundred or more words. **Pronunciation** continues to be erratic, but certain commonly occurring pronunciations can be identified:

- words are often shortened, with unstressed syllables dropped: /teɪtəʊ/ *potato* and /mɑːtəʊ/ *tomato*;
- consonant clusters are avoided: /gaɪ/ *sky* and /deɪ/ *stay*;
- consonants at the end of words are dropped: /be/ *bed* and /je/ *yes*;
- many words are simplified using reduplication of sounds: /dəʊdəʊ/ *Joseph* and /biːbiː/ *baby*;
- vowels often differ from adult pronunciation: /diːdiː/ *daddy* and /nuː/ *no*;
- initial position consonants, particularly velars and fricatives, are often replaced: /dɒp/ *shop* or *stop*, /duːlz/ *tools* and /det/ *get*.

The standardisation of pronunciation takes place over a long period. Some consonants will not be produced accurately until after the age of four. Between the ages of $1\frac{1}{2}$ and 2, for instance, children will begin to pronounce the voiced alveolar nasal [n], but it may take another twelve months for accurate pronunciation of:

- the voiceless labiodental fricative [f];
- the voiced bilabial approximant [w];
- the voiced velar nasal [ŋ].

Between 12 and 18 months, although two words are sometimes used they are spoken as a single unit. From 18 months, words are used as distinct rhythmic units and they can often be analysed as **grammatical sequences**.

S	P	S	A	P	O	S	C
(baby)	(go)	(dummy)	(there)	(eat)	(apple)	(sock)	(red)

These minimal structures mean that the child can describe: a person carrying out an action; the position of something; the effect of a process (verb) on a person or thing (object); and a person's or thing's condition. Adults respond to such utterances even when they are not grammatical or complete, and thus the child becomes a part of real communication. The adult can often determine the meaning from the context and from the child's intonation. For example, an utterance like *Jo-Jo cup* may mean:

- *this is Jo-Jo's cup* (possession);
- *give me my cup* (command);
- *Jo-Jo has got his cup* (statement);
- *where is Jo-Jo's cup?* (question).

During this period, children also begin to use some **inflections**. At 18 months, children will begin to experiment with the present participle although it will not be used correctly for several months. **Questions** will appear at this stage, usually marked by a rising intonation: *eat cheese now?* Sometimes, however, *wh-* question words like *where?* and *what?* will be attached to the beginning of an utterance: *where teddy?*; *what that?*

At the end of this stage, the first **negative words** emerge. *No* and *not* are used as one-word sentences or are tagged onto the beginning of any expression: *no* (in response to a request); *no sit*; *not car*.

The **feedback** children receive during this period of language acquisition is one of the most important elements in the learning process since it establishes them as participants in 'real' communication. Because parents respond to all utterances, even if they do not appear to be meaningful, children are encouraged to experiment and therefore to work out what is and what is not acceptable.

2–3 years

This stage is marked by what is called TELEGRAPHIC TALK. Only the most important lexical words are used to express ideas, and grammatical function words like prepositions, determiners, auxiliary verbs and inflections are often omitted. To understand children's telegraphic speech, it is important to know the **context** – particularly because children tend to talk about the present rather than the past or the future.

Vocabulary expands very quickly; by 2 years 6 months (2;6) children initiate talk rather than just responding to adults. They become inventive, creating new words from patterns they have heard but do not remember accurately.

▪ buffalosaurus (buffalo + dinosaur) tipping bronco (bucking bronco)

Pronunciation becomes closer to the standard adult form too.

tractor: /tæk-tæk/ (2;6) → /tæktə/ (2;8) → /træktə/ (2;9)
badger: /bæbɪdʒ/ (2;5) → /bædʒə/ (2;6)
shirt: /sɜːt/ (1;11) → /ʃɜːt/ (2;6)

Immature pronunciations typical of the previous developmental stage often continue during the 24–36 month period. Some sounds, however, are standardised:

- the bilabial plosives [p] and [b], the alveolar plosives [t] and [d], and the velar plosives [k] and [g];
- the voiced bilabial nasal [m];
- the voiceless glottal fricative [h];
- the voiced palatal approximant [j].

Three further sounds will begin to be pronounced correctly between the ages of 2;8 and 4;0:

- the voiceless alveolar fricative [s];
- the voiced alveolar lateral [l];
- the voiced post-alveolar approximant [r].

The age at which children accurately produce these sounds will vary, but most will be using them correctly by the age of 4.

The pronunciation of many words is still idiosyncratic, but adult correction is not effective in encouraging children to change their pronunciations. Because they do not seem to hear their own mispronunciations, children do not recognise the mispronounced word the parent tries to change. If a child says /æliːæm/ for *animal* she will not recognise the difference between her own and the standard version. Therefore if an adult tries to persuade her to say the word differently, she will be unable to do so.

CHILD: full /diːm ədɜːn/
MOTHER: is your boat going full /diːm ədɜːn/?
CHILD: no

MOTHER: how is your boat going?
CHILD: full /diːm ədɜːn/
MOTHER: oh (.) full steam astern
CHILD: <u>yes</u>

Utterances become longer. Combinations of three and four words are used in a variety of ways, and **clause elements** are less likely to be deleted.

P   O
(Need) (potty) (2;4)

S   P   O
(Mummy) (give) (chair) (2;4)

S   P   A
(I) (going) (to your house). (2;7)

S   P   O   A
(Little pigs) (want) (a ride) (in the boat). (2;7)

S   P   O
(We) ('ve got) (bricks that you can use like heavy boxes to pile up for your
                  SCl–RelCl   SCl–NFCl
presents and things). (2;10)

Utterances are often quite sophisticated because of the embedding of subordinate clauses, and children are often using structures that are far more complicated than the simple sentences of early reading books. **Inflections** are used more frequently and more accurately during this period. Initially suffixes will be overused before standardisation occurs.

-*s* suffix to mark plural nouns: *sheep → sheeps; information → informations*
-*ed* suffix to mark regular past tense: *steal → stealed; go → goed; build → builded*

Auxiliary verbs are still often omitted, but usage becomes more accurate towards the age of 3.

Little pigs always *having* fun. (2;7)   It *be chugging* in the tunnel. (2;10)

Modal auxiliaries are used more frequently to convey variations in attitude.

Frog *might* have a swim. (2;7)   We'*ll* need a ladder. (2;10)

Present participles are more likely to be used with the primary verb *be*, although this will still often have an unmarked form. At the age of 2 **wh- question words** will be tagged on to the beginning of utterances. *What?* and *where?* will be used first, followed by *why?* and later *how?* and *who?*

Where baby? (2;4)
Where's the carriage? (2;10)   *What* the name? (2;10)

Throughout the period, question structures become more complex, although the use of rising intonation to mark a question is still common.

Daddy put it ón.   You need a big bóx.
Why did Daddy put it on? (2;10)   *Do* you need a big box? (2;10)

Negatives are used with more subtlety too. Additional forms like *can't* and *won't* appear alongside *no* and *not*, which are now placed in front of the appropriate verb rather than at the beginning of the utterance.

No books there. (2;4)   I *not* tell story. (2;6)   I *can't* know. (2;8)
I *don't* know.   I *didn't* say anything.   It's *not* Lixie's. (2;10)

Pronouns are used with more variety during this developmental stage, but children are often inaccurate. Because they hear themselves referred to as *you*, they tend to use the second person pronoun to talk about themselves. Equally, the first person singular *I* is used to refer to other people. This shows that imitation does play a part in language acquisition. Although children may copy the pronoun referencing they hear, they seem instinctively to sense that their meaning is unclear – their words are therefore often accompanied by gestures to clarify the reference. A similar confusion occurs with **possessive determiners**.

> CHILD: I mending /maɪs/ chair
> MOTHER: are you mending your chair?
> CHILD: no (.) I mending /maɪs/ chair (*pointing to mother*)
> MOTHER: oh (.) you're mending mummy's chair
> CHILD: yes (.) Mummy's chair (2;5)

As they become more familiar with the different pronouns and determiners, however, children will correct their own mistakes. By the age of 3;0 they will often repair a breakdown in understanding by repeating the utterance with the key word changed.

> this toast is for you (1) toast is for me

Children continue to experiment with language patterns and although they do not always get them right, they clearly begin to initiate and practise new structures.

> willn't   satting   pavementless (no pavements)   sickless (not ill)

Between the ages of 2 and 3, children develop language skills at a remarkable speed. Grammar and pronunciation become steadily more consistent and standard; conversational skills become more sophisticated; and children actively develop their vocabulary by asking for new names and labels.

From 3 years

After the age of 3, telegraphic speech is replaced by more **fluent** and **sophisticated** language use. **Vocabulary** continues to expand and diversify and **pronunciation** continues to become more standard. The last consonantal sounds to be produced accurately are:

- the voiceless palato-alveolar fricative [ʃ];
- the palato-alveolar affricates [tʃ] (voiceless) and [dʒ] (voiced);
- the voiced labiodental fricative [v];
- the voiced alveolar fricative [z];
- the dental fricatives [ð] (voiced) and [θ] (voiceless).

The first sounds listed above may be standard before the age of $3\frac{1}{2}$, but others may not be pronounced in a mature way until after the age of 4.

The **structure of utterances** become more varied. Co-ordination is common by the age of 3, but now subordination is increasingly used. Conjunctions like *because* (/kɒs/), *so*, *if*, *after* and *when* help children to create longer sentences – sentences are often made up of four or five clause elements. The utterances are not always grammatical and are often marked by **normal non-fluency features**. For a time, regular and irregular **past tense verbs** will be confused and a child may use both a standard and a non-standard variant: *broked/breaked* and *broke*; *sitted* and *sat*; *bringed* and *brought*; and *blewed/blowed* and *blew*. By the age of 4, however, most children have worked out the appropriate patterns. It is usually during the early part of this stage that children begin to use the **third person singular inflection -s** more consistently. It appears first with lexical verbs and slightly later with primary auxiliaries: *here it comes*; *the song says she blew*; *he's got a little son*.

Questions are now framed by inverting the subject and verb of a declarative sentence, although in the early part of the period, children do not always use an inversion following a *wh-* word. They have to learn that questions beginning with a *wh-* word must still alter the word order and that where there is no auxiliary verb, the dummy auxiliary *do* must be added: *where is the picture?*; *did I have my milk?* **Other auxiliary forms** like *didn't* and *won't* become part of the repertoire at this stage, and the use of *not* becomes more accurate: *I didn't catch it*; *she won't give it to me.* **Multiple negatives** are used for emphasis: *I didn't get nothing today.* The last negative form to be acquired is usually *isn't.* This means that some inaccurate negative constructions from the previous developmental stage continue to appear alongside standard constructions: *he not going* instead of *he isn't going*; *this not Lixie's* instead of *this isn't Lixie's.* In the early school years, children will begin to understand the difference between more complicated negative structures like *any*.

During this last period of dramatic linguistic change, children learn more about the art of **conversation**. They initiate dialogue and become skilful in controlling turn-taking. They can respond appropriately to other speakers and they start to learn how to alter their register for different contexts and audiences. They are able to anticipate problems and to repair simple breakdowns in communication by repeating things that have not been understood or by asking for clarification.

The 4-year-old will begin to sort out any remaining grammatical inaccuracies and language use will become consistently more adult. By the age of 5, children usually have an operating vocabulary of more than two thousand words and they will be using more complicated grammatical structures. Over the next years (6–11), children will acquire what will probably be their last intuitive grammatical knowledge: **comparative** structures; **comment** and **attitude adverbials**; the ability to recognise the **differences between similar sentences**; and an awareness of the **different ways in which meaning can be conveyed** (active/passive sentences). They will also begin to recognise **implicit meaning** and **metaphorical uses** of language. Although most grammatical structures will have been understood by the ages of 8 or 9, semantics will continue to cause problems.

9.5 Types of child language

Monologues

Children involved in imaginative play will often speak at length about what they are doing. Their actions will be accompanied by a discourse which has no obvious intended audience – they may adopt the role of a character, describe their actions, retell or create stories, issue commands or ask questions. As they become older and more able to play alone, the speech utterances become more like narrative. As their language skills develop, children are able to construct a complete discourse without needing to rely on adult interventions to sustain the speech.

ACTIVITY 9.1a

The following extracts were recorded over a period of three months. In each instance, Joseph is playing and the speech accompanies his activities. His parents are present, but they do not take part in the spoken discourse.

Children acquire new language skills incredibly quickly between the ages of 2 and 3 and the transcriptions here demonstrate linguistic and syntactical features that are typical of the stages of child language acquisition. Within three months, the vocabulary, grammar and the ability to sustain an extended turn change noticeably. By focusing on Joseph's pronunciation, his lexical choices, his grammar and his ability to create a narrative, it is possible to chart key features of his language development.

Read through the extracts and comment on:

1 the lexical and grammatical features;
2 Joseph's ability to sustain an extended turn;
3 the developmental differences revealed by each transcript.

Each transcription is preceded by a standard written version using traditional orthography and punctuation to help you follow Joseph's immature speech patterns. The transcriptions mark prosodic features selectively. A key to the symbols used can be found on page 86.

Joseph, aged 2;4, playing with his ride-along tractor, pretending to be a local beach life guard

Written version

> Fall off. Yes. Dirt on my shirt. Mm. Fall off tractor. Dirt on shirt. Yes. Mm. Think. Mm. Dirt from sand. Fall off tractor. Oh yes dirt on me mm oh oh. Move round chair. Move tractor. Vroom, vroom, vroom, vroom, vroom, vroom, vroom. Cold. Blooming cold. Blooming, blooming cold. Life guard brush off dust. Fell off. Sand. Life guard. Dirt. Little little (*indistinct*). Look out. Tractor in sea.

Spoken version

1 fall off (.) /jeθ/ (.) dirt on my (.) /sɜːt/ (4) mm (5) fall off (.) /træk-træk/ oh dirt on (.) /sɜːt/ /jeθ/ mm /fɪŋk/ (.) mm (.) dirt (1) from sand (.) /fɔːlə/ off (.) /træk-træk/ (1) oh /jeθ/ dirt (.) /æn/ (.) me mm oh oh (.) move /raʊn teə/ (.) move /træk-træk/ (.) /vruːm vruːm vrʌm vrʌm vrʌm vrʌm vrʌm/ (.) /kɒld/ (.) /blʌmɪn kɒld/ (.)
5 /blʌmɪn blʌmɪn kɒld/ (2) life guard (2) /brʌs/ (.) off (.) /dʌs/ (.) fell off (.) sand (.) life guard (.) dirt (.) /lɪlɪ/ (.) /lɪlɪ/ (*indistinct*) (2) look /aʊ/ (.) /træk-træk/ in sea

---

COMMENTARY

The extract here is clearly an example of telegraphic talk. At the age of 2;4, Joseph's utterances are staccato and his intonation is often monotone. Although he is joining words together to form grammatical units, his utterances are incomplete.

The following specific points can be made about Joseph's language at the age of 2;4.

LEXIS
Joseph's vocabulary is growing quickly and the examples here show how children learn from the range of experiences to which they are exposed.

Linguistic features	Examples
Words taken from familiar stories (Raymond Briggs, *Father Christmas*)	/blʌmɪn kɒld/ blooming cold (l. 5)
Words taken from personal experience (limited lexical set of the 'seaside')	life guard (l. 5); sand (l. 2); sea (l. 7)

Words taken from the play context	/træk-træk/ tractor (l. 1); /sɜːt/ shirt (l. 2); /teə/ chair (l. 3)
Onomatopoeic words	/vruːm/ /vrʌm/ (l. 4)
Growing range of verbs	fall (l. 1); move (l. 3); look (l. 6); /brʌs/ brush (l. 5); /fɪŋk/ think (l. 2)
First modifiers used	/blʌmɪn/ (l. 4) – euphemism, slang for 'bloody'; life (l. 5) – noun modifier for *guard*

PRONUNCIATION

Many of the immature pronunciations from the previous developmental stage are still evident in Joseph's speech. Some simplified words continue to be used, although most are now in a recognisable adult form.

Linguistic features	*Examples*
Immature vocabulary (reduplication)	/træk-træk/ (l. 1); /lɪlɪ/ little (l. 6)
Difficult phonemes are avoided:	
• the voiceless palato-alveolar affricate [tʃ] is replaced	/teə/ (l. 3)
Initial position fricatives are replaced:	
• the voiceless palato-alveolar fricative [ʃ]	/sɜːt/ (l. 2)
• the voiceless dental fricative [θ]	/fɪŋk/ (l. 2)
Consonants in the final position are dropped or replaced by another phoneme:	
• the voiceless alveolar fricative [s]	/jeθ/ yes (l. 1)
• the voiceless alveolar plosive [t]	/dʌs/ dust (l. 5)
• the voiced alveolar plosive [d]	/raʊn/ round (l. 3)
• the voiced velar nasal [ŋ]	/blʌmɪn/ bloom*ing* (l. 5)
• the voiceless palato-alveolar fricative [ʃ]	/brʌs/ (l. 5)
Vowels differ from adult pronunciation:	
• [əʊ] → [ɒ]	/kɒld/ (l. 5)
• [uː] → [ʌ]	/blʌmɪn/ bl*oo*ming (l. 4)
• [ɒ] → [æ]	/æn/ (l. 3)
Idiosyncratic pronunciation is used alongside the adult form	fall (l. 1) /fɔːlə/ (l. 2)

GRAMMAR

Utterances are getting longer and combinations of different clause elements make them more varied, but Joseph's clauses are still incomplete. As is typical of telegraphic speech, some clause sites are not filled and determiners are elided. Inflections are not used in this extract and the verb *to be* is omitted. Joseph's meaning is usually clear, but there are points at which an outsider would struggle to understand.

Linguistic features	Examples
Clause elements are now quite varied and are usually in the appropriate position:	
• (S P) (S) A	(S) A (dirt) (on my /sɜːt/) (l. 1)
• (S) P O	P O (fall off) (/træk-træk/) (l. 1)
• (S) P A	P A (move) (/raʊn/) (l. 3)
• (S P) C	C (/blʌmɪn kɒld/) (l. 5)
There is no evidence of co-ordination yet – the utterances are basically simple. There is one grammatically complete simple utterance, although the third person singular inflection is not used	S P O (life guard) (/brʌs/ off) (/dʌs/) (l. 5)
Most of the extract is in the declarative mood, but Joseph uses two imperatives	/fɪŋk/ (l. 2) look (l. 6)
Most verbs are unmarked for tense, but Joseph uses one irregular past tense form accurately	fell off (l. 5)
No subject pronouns are used but a first person object pronoun and a possessive determiner are used accurately	/æn/ (.) me (l. 3) my (.) /sɜːt/ (l. 1)

SUSTAINING AN EXTENDED TURN

Joseph's speech is all directed towards himself – he shows little awareness of his parents although they are present. His monologue, however, becomes almost a running dialogue with himself. His discourse is marked by **normal non-fluency features** like the repeated *mm* which helps him to sustain the extended turn. The **pauses** are all brief and Joseph seems immersed in the story he is creating. The **rhythm** is still very disjointed and the **lexis** and **syntax** are quite repetitive.

ACTIVITY 9.1b

Joseph, aged 2;7, playing with a miniature park, the three bears' house and various characters

Written version

Case little pigs want ride in a boat. In a boat. Going in a boat. Always going in a boat. Always going in a boat. Have fun. Always having fun in girl's house. Oh be. Have tea. Beings, beings, beings, beings under there. Not anybody in the park. No anybody in the park. Nobody in the park. Frog playing in it. Frog might have a swim. Swimming. 'We mi. might visit the park' say Mummy Bear, Daddy Bear and Baby Bear and Baby Bear might see little wee wee frog in the pond. Baby Bear might have a look over there. Look over there. Having a swim. Oh Goldilocks peeping and peeping and peeping.

Goldilocks. Goldilocks ha. hang on. Somebody in the pool. Peace and quiet. Goldilocks go and cook. I coming going to your house little while seeing you in the pond and peered and peered and peered and peered over the fence and Baby Bear and the frog went to went to find the pool. Little little fre. Little animals in in the in the pool. Goldilocks, Goldilocks, Goldilocks saying 'hello all'. Somebody else in the pond. Somebody else in the pond. All the trees. All yellow trees. All yellow trees.

Spoken version

1 case /lɪlɪ/ pigs want ride in a boat (2) in a boat (.) going in a boat (.) all (.) ways going in a boat (.) all (.) ways going in a boat (3) have fun (.) all (.) ways having fun in girl's house (.) oh be (.) have tea (.) /biːʌŋs biːʌŋs biːʌŋs/ (.) /biːɪŋs/ under /eə/ (.) not anybody in /ə/ park (.) no (.) anybody in /ə/ park
5 (.) no (1) body in /ə/ park (.) frog playing /ɪnɪt/ (.) frog might (.) have a /wɪm/ (.) /wɪmɪŋ/ (2) we mi. (.) might visit /ə/ park say Mummy Bear and Daddy Bear and /biːbiː/ Bear and /biːbiː/ Bear mɪ̌ght see /lɪlɪ/ wee wee frog in /ə/ pond (.) /biːbiː/ Bear might (.) have (.) look over /eə/ (.) look over /eə/ (.) having a /wɪm/ (.) oh (.) /gɒlioks piːpɪn/ and /piːpɪn/ and /piːpɪn/ (.) /gɒlioks/ (.)
10 /gɒlɒs/ ha. (.) hang on (1) /sʌmbiː/ in /ə/ pool (.) peace and quiet (1) /gɒlɒks/ go and cook (.) I /kʌmɪn/ (.) going to /ɔːz/ house /lɪlɪ/ while seeing /uː/ in /ə/ pond (.) and peered and peered and peered and peered over fence and /biːbiː/ Bear (.) and and /ə/ frog went to (.) went to find pool (.) /lɪlɪ lɪlɪ fre/ (.) /lɪlɪ æliːæms/ (10) in (2) in /ə/ in /ə/ pool (.) /gɒlɒs/ (.) /gɒlɒs gɒlɒks/ saying
15 hello all (.) somebody else in /ə/ pond (.) somebody else in /ə/ pond (.) all /ə/ trees (.) all /leləʊ/ trees all /leləʊ/ trees

COMMENTARY

The second transcript is longer and Joseph is more able to sustain his discourse. He is becoming more standard in both his pronunciation and grammar, and uses a more varied range of prosodic features. His monologue is now much closer to a recognisable form of narrative which most listeners could understand.

Focusing more closely, it is possible to list the following points about Joseph's developmental stage.

LEXIS

The vocabulary used in this example is far more diverse. Although it is still dominated by concrete nouns like *trees* (l. 16) and *house* (l. 3), abstract nouns like *peace* and *quiet* (l. 10) are beginning to appear. Dynamic verbs like *playing* (l. 5) and *going* (l. 1) occur more frequently, but stative verbs like *want* (l. 1) and *have* (l. 2) are more common than in the earlier extract. Equally, having understood the concept of position, a range of prepositions like *under* (l. 4), *over* (l. 8) and *in* (l. 1) are used to describe 'place' precisely.

Linguistic features	Examples
Words are still often linked to familiar stories	/lɪlɪ/ pigs (l. 1); Mummy Bear and Daddy Bear and /biːbi/ Bear (ll. 6–7); /gɒlɒks/ (l. 10)
As Joseph's vocabulary widens, he begins to use synonyms	pool (l. 10); pond (l. 12) /piːpɪn/ (l. 9); peered (l. 12)
By listening to adults, Joseph is able to identify and later use collocations	peace and quiet (l. 10)
Modifiers are used more often and are more varied	*wee wee* frog – Adj (l. 7) *girl's* house – possessive NP (l. 3) /leləʊ/ trees – Adj (l. 16)
Inevitably much of the vocabulary is still linked to Joseph's own experiences	park (l. 0); trees (l. 16); houses (l. 3)
The verbs are far more varied	want (l. 1); have (l. 2); playing (l. 5); /wɪmɪŋ/ (l. 6)

PRONUNCIATION

In just three months, there is a noticeable difference in Joseph's pronunciation: most words are now pronounced standardly; words that are still pronounced in an immature way are usually close enough to the adult form to be quite easily recognisable.

Linguistic features	Examples
Immature vocabulary (reduplication)	/lɪlɪ/ (l. 1)
Consonant clusters still avoided: • [sw] is simplified	/wɪm/ (l. 9), /wɪmɪŋ/ (l. 6)
Initial position fricatives are absent: • the voiced dental fricative [ð] • the voiceless glottal fricative [h]	/eə/ there (l. 4); /ə/ the (l. 4) /uː/ who (l. 11)
Vowels differ from the 'caretaker speech' (Modified RP), but self-correction eventually results in a standard pronunciation of the vowel: • [iːʌ] instead of [iːɪ] • [iː] instead of [eɪ], adult = /beɪbiː/ The diphthong in the first syllable is simplified and Joseph reduplicates a pure vowel instead • [ɒ] instead of [əʊ], adult = /gəʊdiːlɒks/	/biːʌŋs/, /biːɪŋs/ beings (ll. 3–4) /biːbiː/ baby (l. 7) /gɒlɒs/ (l. 10)
The voiced palatal approximant [j] is absent	/ɔːz/ yours (l. 11)
Some pronunciations are still idiosyncratic. Certain words are pronounced inconsistently – sometimes they will have an adult form and sometimes not	/æliːæms/ animals (l. 14) /gɒlɒs/, /gɒlɒks/, /gɒlɒks/ Goldilocks (ll. 9–10, 14) /sʌmbiː/ somebody (l. 10)

Joseph's language is now more grammatically complete. Determiners are usually included; inflections appear more consistently; and sentences include both co-ordination and subordination. Co-ordination:

> S   P   P
> (/gɒlɒks/) (go) (and) (cook) (ll. 10–11)
>   conj

Subordination:

> S P   A   A   A
> (I) (/kʌmɪn/ going) (to /ɔːz/ house) (/lɪlɪ/ while) (seeing /uː/ in /ə/ pond) (and)
>   SCl–NFCl
>
> P   A   S   P   A
> (peered. . .) (over fence) (and) (/biːbiː/. . .) (went) (to find pool) (ll. 11–13)
>   SCl–NFCl

Linguistic features	Examples
Clause elements are used in a variety of ways to make the narrative interesting. Clause sites are rarely left empty now:	
• S P O	S P O (frog) (might have) (a swim) (l. 5)
• S P A	S P A (/gɒlɒs/) (hang) (on) (l. 10)
• S P O A	S P O A (/biːbiː/ Bear) (might have) (look) (over /eə/) (l. 8)
The narrative uses the declarative mood	frog might have a swim (l. 5)
The verb *to be* is still elided	somebody else in the pond (l. 15) frog playing /ɪnɪt/ (l. 5)
Quoting and quoted clauses are used, adding to the effective creation of a narrative atmosphere	QUOTED QUOTING ('We might visit. . .', (say MB and DB and /biːbiː/) (ll. 6–7)
There are still many unmarked verbs, but some verb forms are marked for tense	hang (l. 10); cook (l. 11) – unmarked verb forms went (l. 13) – irregular simple past tense
Inflections are used more standardly: • present participle inflection -*ing* • regular past tense inflection -*ed* • possessive noun suffix inflection '*s* • plural noun suffix -*s*	having (l. 3), playing (l. 5), going (l. 2) peered (l. 12) girl's house (l. 3) /biːʌŋs/ (l. 3)
There is still no evidence of third person singular -*s* inflection	/gɒlɒks/ go[es] and cook[s] (ll. 10–11)
Modal auxiliaries are used correctly	might visit (l. 6)
Pronouns are now more accurate: • first person subject pronouns • compound indefinite pronouns	I /kʌmɪn/ (l. 11); *we* might visit (l. 6) anybody (l. 4); nobody (l. 5); somebody (l. 10)

second person possessive pronoun used as a possessive determiner	/ɔːz/ house (l. 11)
Negatives are used here – Joseph consciously works through a pattern until he finds the structure he believes is right	not anybody . . . (.) no (.) anybody . . . (.) no (1) body (ll. 4–5)

In this example, telegraphic speech is being replaced by discourse that is closer to the patterns of adult speech. Although Joseph's monologue is still marked by many micro pauses, the overall **rhythm** is far less disjointed than in the transcript made at the age of 2;4. Longer **pauses** reflect Joseph's ability to concentrate for longer on his play activity and this increased concentration results in the creation of a more sophisticated narrative. Utterances are still sometimes **grammatically incomplete** but the meaning of each is now usually clear. For instance, Joseph uses the compound noun phrase *peace and quiet* as a grammatical utterance – although this is grammatically incomplete, a listener can more or less understand the meaning from the context.

Prosodic features are used with more sophistication now. **Stress** is used to highlight important words and the **pitch range** is quite varied. Joseph often adopts the singsong intonation patterns that are common in the speech of young children. **Normal non-fluency features** like repetition of words (*and and*) and false starts (*mi. might; ha. hang*) are typical of all spoken language. Another interesting development can be seen in the way Joseph is starting to **correct himself**. Often he uses repetition to work through a range of alternatives until he finds what he thinks is the correct pronunciation or grammatical form.

The extract here is far more developed than the previous example – Joseph can now **sustain an extended turn** quite successfully. The narrative is linked directly to his play and although it is often repetitive, there is a sense that he is telling a chronological story.

SUMMARY

The extracts clearly show the ways in which Joseph's language has developed within a three-month period. His **lexis** has become more varied; his **grammar** is more accurate; and he uses **prosodic features** more explicitly to highlight key words and to draw attention to important parts of his monologue. At the age of 2;7, he still does not **pronounce** all his words in an adult form and his utterances are still sometimes **grammatically incomplete**. However, it would no longer be difficult for an adult who does not know him to understand what he is saying.

Dialogues

Parents engage children in conversations from very early on. Even before speech acquisition begins, babies are learning about communication from the smiles and sounds which they begin to recognise as responses to their cries and gurgles. After 6 months, mothers tend not to respond to every vocalisation, but pay special attention to utterances that appear to be meaningful. By 8 months, babies will try to attract attention by pointing. It is at this stage that they also become fascinated by adult conversations, watching each speaker and thus learning implicitly about turn-taking.

In the early stages of language acquisition, children rarely initiate dialogue and they cannot easily sustain a conversation. Parents help them by:

- asking direct questions;
- repeating words and phrases spoken by the child;
- basing dialogue on the immediate activities and context.

ACTIVITY 9.2a

The following extracts were recorded over a period of six months: the first was made when Joseph was 2;4 and the second when he was 2;10. Each transcript reveals the same kinds of lexical and grammatical features discussed in Activity 9.1, but the examples are now dialogues rather than monologues. In each case, Joseph is at home talking to his parents. Read through the transcripts and comment on Joseph's ability to sustain a conversation.

Joseph (J), aged 2;4, talking to his father (F)

1	J:	need potty
	F:	okay (8) how many clocks have we got?
	J:	Mummy póint (.) Daddy póint (.) one (.) one (.) one
	F:	so how many clocks have we got, Joseph?
5	J:	two (5) pointing
	F:	point at what (.) what do you want Daddy to point at?
	J:	clock
	F:	clock (.) where's the other clock (2) over there (.) right
	J:	on /self/
10	F:	on <u>shelf</u> (.) yes on the shelf
	J:	by books
	F:	by the books and where's the other clock?
	J:	/eə/ (.) no books
	F:	no books
15	J:	mm
	F:	what's it near?
	J:	/pɪkpɪks/
	F:	the picture and what's underneath the clock?
	J:	/niːf/
20	F:	<u>underneath</u> (.) what's underneath the clock?
	J:	/niːf/ (4) /dɔːdiː/ (.) /dɔːdiː/ (.) Daddy get
	F:	you want Georgie
	J:	woof woof woof woof (.) furry /dɔːdiː/ (.) woof woof /iːiːiːiː/
	F:	what are you doing to Georgie?
25	J:	grab
	F:	you've grabbed ‖ him
	J:	‖ grab him (.) /drəʊk/ him
	F:	where are you putting him?
	J:	/bækɪt/
30	F:	he's in the <u>basket</u>
	J:	give /bækɪt/ (2) pl. (5) Daddy Daddy (2) /dɔːdiː/
	F:	where's Georgie now?
	J:	on (.) /eə/
	F:	where?
35	J:	/teə/
	F:	chair (.) on the chair
	J:	one /eə/ (.) one /teə/
	F:	one chair
	J:	/lɪlɪ teə/ (.) give
40	F:	little chair (.) so that's a little chair (.) what's this chair?
	J:	Mummy's
	F:	Mummy's chair

J:	give
F:	you want Georgie do you?
45 J:	give (.) give (.) give (.)
F:	where is Mummy?
J:	give Mummy give /deə/
F:	Mummy gave you ‖ the chair
J:	‖ /teə/

COMMENTARY

There are signs that Joseph is becoming a more active participant in dialogue. The **turn-taking** is quite smooth, although there is one instance in which he starts his utterance before his father's is grammatically complete: *you've grabbed* ‖ *him* (ll. 26–7). Everything that he says follows on logically from what has gone before, and in each utterance his meaning and intentions are quite clear. The conversation, however, is typical of a child between the ages of 2;0 and 2;6 – Joseph's father **initiates the topics** (ll. 2, 24, 40) and **sustains the dialogue** with a series of questions (ll. 2, 8, 16). Joseph answers the questions appropriately, providing the necessary information: *on* /self/ (l. 9). Sometimes, his answer clearly does not give the information his father expects. In the exchange about the size of the chair, the father takes up the idea of a little chair (l. 40), expecting Joseph to describe the 'big' chair. He instead describes it as *Mummy's* (l. 41) – his response is appropriate although unexpected and shows that he has the **vocabulary** and **necessary grammatical knowledge** to construct a range of meaningful answers. In another instance, Joseph actually completes the utterance simultaneously with his father, showing his **intuitive knowledge of grammar** and his ability to use a word from the appropriate word class: *grab him* (l. 27). There are points at which Joseph changes the direction of the conversation by indicating that he wants something: *Daddy get* (l. 21). He uses imperatives to get things done: *Daddy point* (l. 3).

The father tries to correct Joseph's **pronunciation** by reiterating key words: /self/ – *on shelf (.) yes on the shelf* (ll. 9–10); /niːf/ – *underneath* (ll. 19–20). The father's reiterations also make Joseph's utterances grammatically complete by including the function words that Joseph omits: /pɪkpɪks/ *the picture* (ll. 17–18). Despite the father's attempts to 'educate' him explicitly, Joseph continues to pronounce words idiosyncratically and omit words like determiners. He can, however, recognise when understanding has become a problem and he can **repair the dialogue** in a very basic way. For instance, the father fails to understand that Joseph is saying his mother gave him the chair. To clarify the meaning of his utterance, Joseph stresses the lexical verb *give* (l. 45) and repeats it until his father has understood. He then provides the grammatically standard version to which Joseph adds the noun /teə/ (l. 49) in the object site. In some places, Joseph tries to **correct his own pronunciation** by repeating a word in slightly different forms until it sounds more like the adult version: *one* /eə/ (.) *one* /teə/ (l. 37). The pause marks Joseph's awareness that his first version is not a recognisable word and that there might be problems in communicating his meaning.

ACTIVITY 9.2b

Joseph (J), aged 2;10, talking to his mother (M)

1 J:	/ə/ train is taking /ɪm/ to his ‖ wêdding
M:	‖ watch your knees

	J:	his wedding (.) /ə/ train taking /ɪm/ to his wêdding (3) where's /ə/ cárriages ‖ oh ha.
5	M:	‖ watch your knees Joseph (.) that's a good boy
	J:	/eɪ/ meant to have carriages if /eɪ/ taking Lixie to church
	M:	mm
	J:	/eɪ/ meant to have carriages
	M:	yes they are (.)
10	J:	meant ‖ to
	M:	‖ careful
	J:	/məʊk/ (.) /æt/ be near /ə/ track
	M:	mm (.) smoke
	J:	/æt/ is /ə/ stătion (.) runaway train went over /ə/ hill (.) /ə/ church is /æt/ way
15	M:	the church is <u>that</u> way
	J:	(*indistinct*) /ə/ Lixie's sitting in /ə kəʊwʌl/ carriage
	M:	not /kəʊwʌl/ (.) can you say coal
	J:	in a bit of /kəʊwʌl/
	M:	coal
20	J:	bit of /kəʊwəl/
	M:	can you say coal
	J:	coal (*shouted*)
	M:	that's it
	J:	in a bit of coal (*quiet*)
25	M:	<u>lo</u>vely (.) lovely
	J:	Lixie don't go (.) and he was slowly (1) and he slept in a bêd (2) for ages and ages and he fêll out (.) he fe. (.) wait he says /kɒs/ I not want to have it he says and /ə/ train púffs away (.) and it púffs slowly away to take /ɪm/ home
30	M:	where is he góing
	J:	some people call /ə/ house homes
	M:	some people call them homes (.) a house ‖ or
	J:	‖ a home
	M:	what's Lixie going to call it
35	J:	a <u>cott</u>age (4) /ə/ train is coming out of /ə/ tunnel
	M:	here it comes out of the tunnel
	J:	mm it (.) it coming out soft of a tunnel
	M:	it's coming out sóft (.) what does that mean
	J:	/ə/ <u>track</u> is soft
40	M:	the track is soft?
	J:	mm
	M:	what does that mean (2) what happens if the track is sòft
	J:	one bit is bending in the <u>tunnel</u>
	M:	mm
45	J:	<u>ooo</u> <u>ooo</u> (*train noises*) the runaway train went over the hill (2) and he came onto the track track track (1) he's going into the tunnel now now now (2) where's /ə/ (.) where's /ə/ train (.) it just went into /ə/ tunnel (2) /iː/ it chuffs (*train noises*) out of /ə/ túnnel Lixie (.) out of /ə/ túnnel (.) well (.) Lixie heard it go slow (7) and then /ə/ <u>signal</u> went dòwn (.) and /ə/ <u>signal</u> banged dòwn (.)
50		and /ə/ signal banged down (2) clack (4) look out (*indistinct*) for /ə təʊ/ town (.) /təʊ/ ‖ town
	M:	‖ look out for whát
	J:	[təʊ] town
	M:	what's that?

55	J:	‖ no
	M:	‖ what did you sáy
	J:	I didn't say anything

COMMENTARY

Joseph is clearly more in charge in the second transcript and is far more able to sustain a conversation in his own right. He still drifts between monologue and dialogue, but he is now much more aware of his audience. He is able to **question** (l. 3) as well as **respond** (ll. 34–5) and the **rhythms** of his speech are far less disjointed. Both participants are actively involved and Joseph is clearly listening to the utterances in detail. He **initiates the topics** (ll. 1, 6, 31) and his mother merely helps to develop them with her spoken contributions to the game that he is playing (ll. 35–41). He is more aware of **grammatically complete utterances** and there are few examples of overlapping speech – except where his mother is telling Joseph to be more careful with his toys (ll. 4–5). Everything that Joseph says is recognisable except where he talks about /təʊ/ *town* (l. 50). His mother asks him to reiterate the word in order to clarify what he has said. Joseph, however, refuses to explain, instead opting for an escape – *I didn't say anything* (l. 57). Joseph can now also respond to adult correction. When his mother draws his attention to a mature pronunciation of *coal* (l. 17), he is able to replace /kəʊwʌl/ with *coal* (ll. 18–24).

The second transcript shows the speed at which children acquire linguistic skills. Within six months, Joseph has acquired a much more **diverse vocabulary**; he is able to **recognise** and **use complete grammatical structures** and he is able to **control the conversation** and deal with **turn-taking** effectively.

As well as learning about language structures, children have to understand the patterns that underpin spoken communication. They must learn about turn-taking and repairs; they must recognise when a situation demands an apology or when it is necessary to ask for clarification. Children are never taught these skills, but assimilate them both from participating in and observing spoken interaction in different contexts. The study of the things that influence our choice of language in social contexts is called PRAGMATICS.

Young children often make mistakes as they learn about the 'rules'. A child answering a telephone might be asked 'Is your mother in?' – if she replies 'Yes' and puts the receiver down, she has failed to understand the pragmatics of the interaction. Pragmatic 'mistakes' do not prevent understanding and cannot be classed as 'wrong', but they are seen as 'socially inappropriate'. Children inevitably make such mistakes, but by school age they have acquired a subconscious knowledge of many of society's expectations.

At the age of 2;10, Joseph is well aware of the pragmatics or social rules of conversation. He has already learnt when to speak and how to use language to get the desired result, and he knows the kind of utterance which is expected in a range of contexts. He has assimilated the 'rules' that prevent spoken language exchanges being anarchic and he recognises in an unsophisticated way how to choose the appropriate tone. He can repair simple breakdowns, repeat things when required to do so and respond directly to his mother's utterances.

9.6 What to look for in examples of child language

The following checklist can be used to identify key features in examples of different stages of child language acquisition. There will not be examples of all the features listed in every transcript, but the list can be used as a guide. The points made are general so discussion of specific examples will need to be adapted to take account of the particular context.

The following are helpful questions to ask.

Register

1 What is the **mode**? – spoken.
2 What is the **manner**? – the relationship between the participants: monologue? dialogue? the extent of the interaction? the function of the communication?
3 What is the **field**? – the subject matter will indicate the kind of discourse taking place: usually, it will be directly related to the context and activity going on at the time.

Lexis

0;6–1;0

1 Is the child using **reduplicated sound patterns** to represent meaningful words?
2 Are there any examples of **proto-words**?

1;0–1;6

1 Are there any recognisable **single-word utterances** used to name things directly related to the child (people, food, body parts, toys, etc.)?
2 Are there any examples of **over-extension**? **under-extension**? a **narrowing of the field of reference**? or **mismatch**?
3 Are there any examples of the first **modifiers**?
4 Are there any **action utterances** accompanied by gestures which will form the basis for the first verbs?
5 Are there any examples of **social expressions** that are typical of the child's cultural background?

1;6–2;0

1 Are there any examples of a **wider range of vocabulary** reflecting the child's growing understanding of the world?

2;0–3;0

1 Does any of the lexis relate to **familiar stories** or the child's **personal experience**?

3;0+

1 Is there any evidence of the child's growing **word stock**?

Pronunciation

0;2–1;0

1   Are there any examples of **cooing** using the first recognisable English sounds based on the high vowels [iː] and [uː] or the velar sounds like [k] and [g]?
2   What kinds of **reduplicated sounds** are used in any examples of babbling?

1;0–1;6

1   Is the pronunciation of holophrastic utterances **idiosyncratic**?
2   Are the same words pronounced in a **variety of ways**?

1;6–2;0

1   Are there any examples of words that are shortened by **dropping unstressed syllables**?
2   Are **consonant clusters** avoided?
3   Are **final consonants** dropped?
4   Are there any examples of words that have been simplified? what kinds of **reduplicated sounds** are used?
5   Do any of the **vowels** differ from the 'caretaker' accent?
6   Are any **initial position velars** or **fricatives** replaced?

2;0–3;0

1   Are there still examples of **immature pronunciation** from the previous developmental stage?
2   Has the child standardised:
    *   the plosives [p] and [b], [t] and [d], [k] and [g]?
    *   the voiced bilabial nasal [m]?
    *   the voiceless glottal fricative [h]?
    *   the voiced palatal approximant [j]?
3   Are some of the **consonantal sounds** still immature:
    *   the voiceless alveolar fricative [s] and the voiced alveolar lateral [l]?
    *   the voiced post-alveolar approximant [r]?

3;0+

1   Are pronunciations now **closer to adult forms**?
2   Have the last consonantal sounds to be produced accurately yet become standard:
    *   the voiceless palato-alveolar fricative [ʃ]?
    *   the palato-alveolar affricates [tʃ] (voiceless) and [dʒ] (voiced)?
    *   the voiced labio-dental fricative [v]?
    *   the voiced alveolar fricative [z]?
    *   the dental fricatives [ð] (voiced) and [θ] (voiceless)?

Grammar

1;0–1;6

1   Are **single words** used to represent a grammatically complete utterance?

1;6–2;0

1 Are there any **grammatical sequences** in the rhythmic units?
2 What different kinds of **meaning** do these minimal structures convey?
3 Are any present participle **-ing inflections** used?
4 Are **questions** framed using *wh-* words at the beginning of a sentence (usually *where* or *what*)?
5 Are the **negatives** *no* and *not* used in one-word sentences or at the beginning of a variety of expressions?

2;0–3;0

1 Are there any combinations of three or four words in which different clause elements (usually in standard positions) are used to construct a range of **clause types**?
2 Is the discourse an example of telegraphic talk in which many of the **grammatical function words** are omitted?
3 Are a wider range of **inflections** used? *-s* to mark plural nouns? *-ed* to mark the past tense of regular verbs?
4 Are any of the inflections **overused** as the child experiments?
5 Are any **auxiliary verbs** (primary or modal) used or are they still omitted?
6 Is the **primary verb** *to be* used with present participles: is it marked for person/number or is it still used in the **base form**?
7 Are **question structures** becoming more complex? does the child use *why?* and *how?* as well as *where?* and *when?*
8 Are **negatives** used in a more sophisticated way with *no* and *not* placed before the relevant verb?
9 Are **pronouns** used in a range of contexts, but without a complete understanding of the different forms? are second person pronouns used for first person references?

3;0+

1 Has telegraphic speech been replaced with **more sophisticated sentence structures**?
2 Are there examples of **co-ordination** and **subordination**?
3 Are **inflections** now used standardly? – regular past tense verbs with *-ed*? third person singular present tense with *-s*?
4 Are the subject and verb inverted in **questions** using *wh-* words?
5 Is the **dummy auxiliary** *do* used to frame questions and negatives?
6 Are **contractions** like *don't*, *won't* and *isn't* used?

Prosodic features

0–1;0

1 Is there any evidence that the baby is responding to the meaning of **different tones of voice**?
2 Does the parent use **exaggerated intonation patterns** to attract and hold the child's attention?
3 Does the baby use a **high pitch level** for the repeated consonant and vowel-like segments?
4 Are any **intonation patterns** repeated for consonant-vowel combinations?

1;0–1;6

1 Is there any evidence that the child is using **intonation** to mark different kinds of purpose?
2 Does the **variation of intonation** contribute to the meaning of utterances?

1;6–2;0

1 Are questions marked by a **rising intonation**?
2 Are the **rhythms** of two-word grammatical units distinctive?
3 Are **pauses** used frequently in unusual positions?

2;0–3;0

1 Does the child still use **rising intonation** to mark questions?
2 Are any syllables or key words **stressed**?
3 Are **rising-falling** or **falling-rising intonations** used to make utterances more distinctive?
4 Do **pauses** mark the end of a grammatically complete utterance instead of creating the disjointed rhythms of telegraphic speech?

3;0+

1 Is the child now using **pitch**, **pace**, **pause**, **rhythm** and **stress** in more sophisticated ways to enhance the meaning of utterances?

Conversation skills

0;6–1;0

1 Do the utterances seem to be related directly to **specific contexts**?
2 Are there examples in any of the exchanges in which the child and parent(s) take **recognisable turns**?

1;0–1;6

1 Does the adult take the role of **initiating** and **sustaining** conversation?
2 Does the child produce a **monologue-like string of utterances** with no real sense of audience?

1;6–2;0

1 Is there any evidence that the child is **taking part in real conversations** despite the fact that utterances are still grammatically incomplete?
2 Is the **context** crucial to an understanding of any utterances?
3 Does the child seem to be experimenting with **turn-taking** with an adult who makes all utterances meaningful?

2;0–3;0

1 Is it still important to know the **context** of the talk at this telegraphic stage?
2 Is the child **more actively involved in conversations**? – asking for names of objects,

people and places? relating responses directly to earlier utterances? initiating topics?

3   Are there any examples of **normal non-fluency features**?

3;0+

1   Is the child skilful in controlling **turn-taking**?
2   Are **responses** to other speakers **appropriate**?
3   Is the **register altered** for different contexts, audiences and topics?
4   Is there any evidence that simple breakdowns in communication are **repaired**? – is there repetition of key words or phrases? are there requests for clarification?

Summary

Once children have acquired language, they can become **active participants** in all kinds of communication: they can establish relationships; express their feelings; get others to do things for them; ask for information or explanations; or use language creatively. The more experience they have, the more skilful they will become in adapting their language use to suit their context, audience and purpose.

Apparently effortless **language acquisition** will take place if the child can consciously manipulate the speech organs; if the child lives in a developed social and cultural environment, experiencing an appropriate range of language input; and if the language experience is gained before a critical age. If all these conditions are met language acquisition will usually take place without any formal language teaching.

There are four main **theories** which try to explain the nature of language acquisition: the behaviourists believe that children learn by imitating the language structures that they hear; the cognitive approach suggests that children must have an intellectual understanding of a concept before they can use linguistic structures; the nativists believe that all children have an innate capacity for language acquisition; and more recent studies suggest that interaction is the key. More research needs to be carried out before language acquisition is really understood, but current thinking would suggest that each theory throws some light on the complex processes involved.

PART III

Varieties – English in use

10 Spoken English

10.1 The nature of spoken language

Linguists have become increasingly interested in spoken language, crediting it in recent years with far more significance than did the traditionalists of earlier centuries. The publishing company Longman, for instance, has initiated the Spoken Corpus project (1994) which aims to create a database of ten million words taken directly from everyday situations. It has collected material by taping more than a hundred volunteers over a period of a week. Because of its real sources, the lexicographers will be able to trace the **current development and disappearance** of words and expressions in a very concrete way. Equally, their focus can be on **frequency of usage**, allowing a comparison between words that are spoken and those that are used in writing; on the ways in which **men and women** differ in their use of language: or on **regional differences**. While linguists have been interested in **phatic communication** for a long time, this project will also help them to analyse the non-verbal sounds we make, in a far more detailed way than ever before. There can be no doubt that this research will result in the world's largest database of spoken English and this, in its turn, will also give prestige to the study of spoken language in its own right.

Spoken language is the dominant **mode** in our society because most of us use speech to communicate in a variety of contexts, for a range of purposes and in various registers. We are all experts, able to adapt to the demands of each speech encounter almost subconsciously. This makes a study of the sounds and features of speech central to an understanding of the English language – spoken language is a variety in its own right, with distinctive **lexical, grammatical, stylistic** and **structural characteristics**.

The CULTURAL EXPECTATIONS and SHARED VALUES of a society dictate the roles speakers must fill if they are to be accepted and we begin to learn the necessary skills from a very early age. To enable effective spoken communication to take place, we assimilate ritualistic patterns as the basis for spoken exchanges. Participants are involved in a constant process of evaluation which can be both conscious and subconscious: identifying what is and what is not acceptable; making lexical and grammatical choices which are appropriate for the context; using **paralinguistics** to reinforce and underpin the words spoken; interpreting the meaning of utterances and so on. Although different kinds of speech encounters will display different characteristics, it is possible to establish distinctive features that make spoken and written discourse very different.

10.2 The function of spoken language

For many people, written language is more prestigious than spoken language and yet far more people use speech on a daily basis. **Writing** does have obvious benefits: it is permanent; it makes communication over a physical distance possible; it can be revised and carefully crafted; it can be reread at any time; it can overcome limits of the human memory and therefore encourages intellectual development; and it has made it possible to preserve the canon of literature. SPOKEN LANGUAGE, however, has strengths that cannot be matched by written language: it enables people to take an active role in social groups; responses are often immediate; and the speech of each user is made distinctive by characteristic sound qualities, mannerisms and accompanying gestures – it is far more difficult to establish a personal style of writing.

Even though participants may not be equal, most forms of spoken language are **interactional**: points can be clarified; questions can be asked; topics can be easily changed; and any number of people can take part. Because communication usually takes place in a face-to-face situation, speech does not have to be as explicit as writing. We can rely on **non-verbal signals** like gesture, facial expression and non-verbal sounds as well as the words themselves to understand an exchange. Equally, because the **audience** is more likely to be known, shared knowledge will prevent problems arising from any vagueness.

Just as written varieties can have a whole range of **purposes**, so too can spoken language. It may be informative, in a lecture (**referential**); social, in an informal conversation (**phatic**); it may aim to get something done, as in a telephone call to a plumber (**transactional**); or to reveal a speaker's personal state of mind or attitude at a certain time (**expressive**). In each case, the context, the audience and the speaker's intentions will dictate the linguistic and prosodic choices made.

The key to analysing any spoken discourse is to start by asking yourself the following questions:

- Who are the participants and what are their **roles**?
- Do they have equal **status**?
- What is the **purpose** of the exchange?
- How is the discourse affected by the **context**?

Answers to these questions will provide the basis for a closer focus – having identified the general framework for communication, linguists then consider lexical, grammatical and prosodic choices made by an individual in a specific situation.

10.3 Features of spoken language

Spoken language covers such a wide range of examples that it is difficult to draw up a definitive list of linguistic characteristics. Nevertheless, it is possible to establish a number of distinctive features that mark it out as different from other varieties.

The manner

The MANNER will depend upon the relative status of the participants – the inequality at a job interview between interviewers and interviewee means that the tone will be **formal**; the equality between two students having a chat in the common room means that the tone will be **informal**. Lexical, grammatical and prosodic choices will be dictated by the manner – that is, by the relative formality or informality of the encounter. Because of the cultural and social expectations assimilated from an early age, participants in any spoken discourse will often make the same kinds of decision about what is and what is not acceptable. Thus despite the fact that many speech encounters are informal and spontaneous, spoken language is quite formulaic.

The speakers

The RELATIONSHIP of the speakers or their RELATIVE STATUS is the first area of a transcript to address. Things like the educational, social or economic status of the participants are fixed, but other features are not. Speakers may take it in turns to select topics; turn-taking may be co-operative or one speaker may be more dominant than others; the purpose of the discourse could change, making a different participant the 'expert'.

The topic

The TOPIC and the GOAL of a spoken encounter are also directly related to the manner and the participants. The more clearly defined the purpose, the more formal the exchange is likely to be. A formal **speech** will often first be written in note form or in full, and will have a predetermined content; the subject matter of spontaneous informal **conversation**, on the other hand, is usually random with no clear pattern or evidence of conscious planning. In an informal spoken exchange a speaker can introduce a wide range of material and jump from one topic to another; in a formal context, the topic will be less adaptable. For example, a prearranged **lecture** on 'the nature of religious language' for a group of A-level students will be far more structured and the content will be far less flexible than a conversation taking place in the common room.

TOPIC SHIFTS (the points at which speakers move from one topic to another) mark key points in spoken discourse. The speaker responsible for initiating new topics is clearly in charge of the turn-taking – this role may be taken up by different participants during an exchange, or one particular person may be dominant throughout. Even though topic placement may seem to be random, participants try to introduce them as though they arise naturally. In informal conversation this may mean that the main topic (the reason for the exchange) does not come first.

The **end of a topic** can be identified by linguistic signals: in informal conversation, phrases like *by the way...* and *incidentally...* or clauses like *that reminds me...* and *to change the subject...* may be used to bring one topic to an end and establish a new one; in formal contexts, adverbials like *lastly...* and non-finite clauses like *to conclude...* can be used as indicators that something different will soon be introduced. **New topics** can be found by reintroducing material that cropped up earlier in the exchange but in a **new form**: *as I was saying before...*; by relating a new topic to the old one: *speaking of which...*; or taking a completely new direction: *let's talk about something else...*, and so on. Interruptions may be seen to bring a topic to its end before its natural conclusion. After a digression, an attempt may be made to revive the old topic (*where was I?*), or the new topic may be allowed to replace it because it is seen as more interesting. This kind of **topic management**, however, is unlikely to take place in a formal speech context (lecture or interview) where the topic is usually predefined and particular speakers are dominant.

The structure

The **structure** of spoken exchanges is distinct despite the apparent randomness. Formal discourse, where the words spoken may have been planned on paper before being spoken, will often adopt structural devices typical of written language. Informal speech, however, has its own distinctive structural features. Sequences of utterances called **ADJACENCY PAIRS** create a recognisable structural pattern. They:

- follow each other;
- are produced by different speakers;
- have a logical connection;
- conform to a pattern.

Questions and answers, greetings, and a command followed by a response are all examples of adjacency pairs.

A: Can I come in?	A: Shut that door now.
B: Of course you can.	B: I will any minute, just don't nag.

The order of **TURN-TAKING** also structures spoken discourse. Participants are skilful in manipulating turns: usually only one person will speak at a time; despite the fact that turns vary in length, transitions from one speaker to another occur smoothly, often with no gap; the order of participation is not planned in advance, but speakers seem to instinctively identify where turns are coming to an end; if an overlap does occur, it rarely lasts for long. Speakers have to make decisions about turns throughout an exchange, but the knowledge used to do so has not been learnt explicitly. Research into turn-taking would seem to suggest that participants build up an awareness of general frameworks and then use these as the basis for their decisions. For instance, they 'learn' the pattern of exchanges that will take place in a job interview or a classroom and can therefore contribute effectively to the spoken discourse. Speakers can also rely on their knowledge of structures like adjacency pairs – in a meeting with a new person, participants can confidently introduce themselves using a familiar pattern of statements and questions and answers. Assimilated grammatical knowledge enables smooth turn-taking too since speakers know when an utterance is grammatically complete. Non-verbal clues can work alongside the linguistic ones: changes in eye contact, intonation or volume can indicate that a turn is coming to an end; the final syllable of a turn may be lengthened; or a gesture may imply that a speaker has no more to say.

Openings and closings are marked by distinctive features. Social equals might use a neutral starting point or **OPENING** in a conversation by talking about the weather. This may then lead into a **self-related comment** (focusing on the speaker) or **other-related comment** (focusing on the listener). Vocatives are common as they help to personalise an encounter.

Spoken words	Comment
A: morning (.) oh (.) Richard (.) I must tell you about the holiday = B: = ah (.) I was going to ask about that	The first speaker establishes the topic. He initiates the discourse with a phatic opening, a vocative and a self-related comment. The second speaker adopts a supportive role by creating a link between 'self' and 'other'.
A: come in (.) Peter (.) hang on a sec I've got to turn the oven off (4) do you want a drínk = B: = thought you'd never âsk	The use of the vocative and imperative show that the speaker is focusing on the other participant in the conversation. Speaker B's response is directly related to the last part of the first speaker's utterance, creating an adjacency pair.

Speakers have a wide range of possible openers to draw on: social greetings, hospitality tokens like *have a drink*; neutral topics; or self- or other-related remarks. They can also establish a co-operative atmosphere by selecting a topic that reflects the interests and experiences of all the participants.

CLOSINGS are used to sum up the exchange. Reference is often made to something outside the speech encounter as a reason for ending the discourse. Self- and other-related remarks are common, but neutral tokens like the weather are not. Closings are often repetitive since the speakers use delaying tactics, referring back to earlier topics and adopting frequently occurring formulae.

Spoken words	Comment
A: better be off now (.) I know you're busy (.) enjoy yourself tomorrow (.) B: I'll make sure I do (.) thanks for coming = A: = have a lovely time = B: = I will (.) and thanks again = A: thanks (.) bye (.) B: bye = A: = bye	An other-related remark is used as a reason for ending the speech encounter. This is followed by a return to an earlier topic (reference to an event taking place on the next day). Both of these establish conventional patterns in which Speaker A focuses interest on Speaker B. The exchange is clearly repetitive – social formulae are reiterated.

In the main body of the dialogue, it is possible to classify a number of SPEAKER MOVES:

- FRAMING, in which openings and closings create an overall structure;
- INITIATING, in which a topic is established;
- FOCUSING, in which comments clearly specify the direction of a topic and ensure its development;
- SUPPORTING or FOLLOWING-UP, which encourages continued discussion of a topic;
- CHALLENGING, which interrupts a topic or introduces a new one without mutual agreement.

Prosodic features

PROSODIC FEATURES are a means of dividing spoken utterances into smaller units just as punctuation, capital letters and paragraphing do in a visual way for written language. Whether they are marked or not on a transcript depends upon the purpose of the transcription. A narrow phonetic transcription will contain a lot of information about the quality of sounds used, but most transcriptions you deal with will be broad – that is, less detailed or phonemic. The list below indicates some of the variations that can be identified and the symbols that may be used to highlight them. These are discussed in more detail in Chapter 2. To identify all the prosodic changes in spoken discourse takes great expertise, so you are unlikely to have to use all of them in your own transcriptions. You should, however, be able to recognise the symbols and the sound qualities they represent. The transcripts used here are broad and selective, marking only the most prominent prosodic features.

Intonation

INTONATION PATTERNS can vary dramatically, and each change will usually reinforce the meaning in some way. By varying the intonation, speakers can convey different grammatical moods and attitudes of surprise, excitement, pleasure and so on.

> nŏ   I rĕally mean it   nô   I don't think so
> (indignant)   (certainty)   (doubtful)   (matter-of-fact)

Intonation has functional as well as semantic uses – it marks grammatical boundaries and structures turns.

Pitch

PITCH may be high, low or anywhere in between. Variations (high, mid or low) can be marked on a transcription, but the level, particularly for monosyllabic utterances, will often be quite uniform. Changes in pitch are usually linked to meaning and the speaker's relationship to the topic: a raised pitch often indicates excitement or enthusiasm; a lowered pitch marks a finale or anticlimax of some kind.

> and the most ↑fantastic thing↑ has happened (.) everyone is standing ↑up↑
> (.) the concert is almost over but people are ↑still clapping↑ (.) the soloist is
> ↓smiling↓ (.) the conductor is ↓acknowledging↓ the orchestra (.) and what a
> concert it's ↓been↓ (.) the last night of the Proms is over for another ↓year↓

Stress

The pattern of STRESSED and UNSTRESSED WORDS in English is directly linked to the rhythm of utterances. It also marks words of importance – a change of stress can change meaning.

> I <u>ate</u> an icecream   Focus of sentence: *ate* rather than bought or made
> <u>I</u> ate an icecream   Focus of sentence: *I* rather than someone else
> I ate an <u>icecream</u>   Focus of sentence: *icecream* rather than another kind of food

TONE UNITS help to organise the discourse, directing listener attention to the syntactic structure of an utterance, the relative prominence of the clause elements, and any new information.

Loudness and pace

The LOUDNESS (loud, quiet, or increasing or decreasing in volume) and PACE (fast, slow, or getting faster or slower) of spoken language can also influence the meaning and reveal attitude. Variations in the volume of utterances, for instance, are used to reflect the relative importance of what speakers say.

> 'forte'   it's important (.) 'I <u>need</u> to have it by' ↓tomorrow↓

> 'cresc'   and it's a 'goal (.) Shearer's scored for England again' (.) and ↑what↑ a
> 'dimin'   'goal it ↓was↓'

Pauses

PAUSES are seen to be acceptable in many kinds of spoken discourse, particularly where the manner is informal. This means that the RHYTHM is often uneven. Where the manner is formal, however, although pauses can be used for dramatic effect, the rhythm is usually more regular and stylised. This kind of rhetorical style is commonly found in speeches written to be spoken.

> Never (.) in the field of human conflict (.) was so much owed (.) by so
> many (.) to so few.
>
> Winston Churchill (20 August 1940)

VOICELESS HESITATION, VOICED PAUSES and WORD SEARCHING also create pauses in spoken language. Sometimes they are used intentionally by speakers to encourage equality of status between participants – they prevent speakers giving the impression that they are experts by suggesting that information is not spontaneous, but requires thought. A student, for instance, might hesitate in talking about *Hamlet* so that she did not seem too knowledgeable.

> Hamlet is a (.) complex character who (1) uses his madness to (.) conceal his (1) real intentions

It is important to remember that where written language identifies the end of a sentence with a full stop, spoken language uses a pause. Some pauses therefore have a functional role in spoken discourse – these tend to be micro-pauses rather than timed pauses.

Vocal effects

VOCAL EFFECTS (**giggling**, **coughing**, **throat clearing**) and PARALINGUISTICS (**gestures**, **posture**) can reinforce or contradict the meaning conveyed by the spoken word.

Lexis

The **lexis** of spoken discourse is often less formal than that associated with written language. If a topic does require formal subject-specific language, unless a speaker is specifically assigned the role of expert, participants will often underplay the importance of key words by introducing clauses like *you know* and phrases like *sort of*. An informal atmosphere can be recognised in the use of conversational lexis (*yeah, cos, all right*); colloquial idiom (*in a minute, the thing is, as far as I can see*); clichés (*that's life*); hyperbole (*on and on and on, really stupid, thousands*); and phatic communication and vocalisations. Abbreviations may be used where the speakers are well known enough to have established a code based on familiarity and a shared view of the world. Equally, in-slang or in-jokes will be mutually intelligible among 'insiders'.

Spoken discourse can often be **ambiguous** because speakers use language inexplicitly. Ambiguities, however, usually cause no problems with understanding because participants can rely on the context and non-verbal communication for extra information. Deictic expressions like *this one, over there* or *right now* are common. They are typical of face-to-face interaction where speakers can refer directly to specific characteristics of the context. Their meaning is always relative to the speech situation. Phonologically vague utterances like **mumbling** and **tailing off** can also be overcome because there is a permanent possibility for **recapitulation**.

Grammar

The GRAMMAR of spoken language tends to be looser and more rambling than that of written language, which can be crafted. Typically, spoken discourse in an informal context will be marked by frequent use of minor 'sentences' and co-ordinated clauses; phrasal verbs and informal 'filler' verbs; and contracted forms. In more formal situations, grammar will be less erratic and more likely to conform to standard patterns.

In general terms, phrases tend to be relatively straightforward. Noun phrases are often simple; where they are complex, they tend to consist of one pre-modifier rather than a string. Post-modification occurs less frequently. As the topic becomes more serious and the manner more formal, noun phrases are more likely to be complex. Certain adverbial intensifiers like *very* and *a bit* occur frequently. Verb phrases also tend to have a simple structure: they will often be made up of a lexical verb standing alone or an auxiliary plus a lexical verb. If the manner is formal, a wider range of tense forms and aspects will be used. In many spoken encounters, contracted verbs are common. Colloquial ellipses occur frequently, but use of the passive voice is limited.

Clauses are often quite uncomplicated, made up of S P O/C A.

> S   P   C   A   S   P   A
> (it) (was) (great) (yesterday) – (I) (went) (into town)

>   P   S   P   O
> (can) (you) (bring in) (Mr Jones's letter)
>   aux   lex

Clause structure is often developed by the addition of strings of adverbials which are normally found in the final position.

>   S   P   C   A   A   A   A
> (the train) (was) (late) (in Swansea) (on Platform 2) (last night) (as usual)

If the manner is informal, the relative pronoun introducing the relative clause is often omitted.

>   S   P   C
> (the boys [who go] down the Leisure Centre) (are) (really mad)

The structure of utterances is difficult to establish in spoken discourse because it is hard to say exactly where each one begins and ends. Length is more variable in speech than in any other variety and minor 'sentences' are common as responses to questions or in summary statements. Grammatically incomplete utterances tend to be accepted more readily than in many other varieties. Longer utterances tend to be associated with a developing argument or anecdote. Co-ordination of clauses tends to be loose, often using a clause like *you know* as an introductory link. Internal linkage is created through pronoun referencing, cross-referencing of determiners, and ellipsis. Tag questions and examples of phatic communication maintain the pace of spoken discourse. In most forms of spoken language, interrogatives are more common than the imperative mood. Vocatives in the initial position help to create a personal relationship between speakers and encourage interaction.

Spoken language is very versatile – it can use a range of grammatical modes: reported speech: direct quotations; first-person accounts of events; and so on. Changes in modality are also common.

In most spoken contexts, the relationship created between speakers is sympathetic. Even if the speakers are using different kinds of structures (dialect versus standard English), the discrepancy will not be mentioned. One speaker may, for instance, use the standard form *we were* while someone else will use the dialectal *we was*. Such variations are usually seen as a reflection of the speaker's individuality and background. Even within one conversation, an individual may be inconsistent, using both standard and non-standard grammatical forms alongside each other. The willingness to accept such variation is indicative of the co-operative principles governing most speech exchanges.

Non-fluency features

NORMAL NON-FLUENCY FEATURES are common, clearly distinguishing between written and spoken language. The more formal the manner, the less likely there are to be examples of hesitancy, slips of the tongue, simultaneous speech, and the like. However, even in contexts such as an interview on a news programme or a formal debate, transcripts may reveal evidence of non-fluency. The interesting thing is that such 'errors' are taken for granted and often go unnoticed.

Brief **OVERLAPS**, for instance, are quite common in conversation. They may occur where speakers are having to compete for a turn in a speech encounter where lots of participants are involved (a group of friends chatting in the pub); equally, a speaker may have misjudged the end of a turn (the speaker adding extra information after having used closing formulae to signal the end of a turn); or one speaker who is particularly dominant may insist on interrupting (a heckler at a political meeting).

A: I would like to speak today about our policy on the National ‖ Health Service
B: ‖ you haven't got
one
A: on the National Health Service (.) since we have been in Government
   ‖ we have spent
B: ‖ oh yeah
A: please let me finish =
B: = if you must =
A: = as I was trying to say. . .

The example here is typical of a negative speech interaction in which the overlaps are caused by Speaker B's desire to challenge and disrupt Speaker A's turn. Speech encounters are usually co-operative, however, and most overlaps will therefore be resolved quickly, with one participant ceasing to speak.

Some simultaneous speech is not classed as an interruption because it enhances the collaborative approach of spoken discourse. Where a second speaker utters **MINIMAL RESPONSES** like *mmm* or *yeah*, often the function of the utterances is to support rather than challenge.

A: have you seen the colour of that wall (.) it's horrific (.) it'll have ‖ to be repainted
B: ‖ mmm
A: we'll have to say something (.) ‖ I just can't be expected to put up with that
B: ‖ yeah

VOICED HESITATIONS or **FILLED PAUSES** are also examples of non-fluency which are tolerated in spoken language. Speakers can use these to protect themselves from interruption while they think. In formal contexts, speakers use fillers like *um*, *er* or *ah* to prolong their turns. It would not be acceptable in a co-operative speech encounter to interrupt halfway through a clause, so by pausing in the middle of a clause, a speaker can prevent another speaker taking the turn. Voiced hesitations and false starts can also be used to gain the attention of an audience who have not yet settled. Politicians or public speakers will often repeat the opening of a speech several times during clapping until quiet has again been established – they will only move on when they are sure that everyone is listening.

Normal non-fluency features therefore may be attributed to inaccuracies associated with informal speech encounters, but they can also be used consciously to control turn-taking and to ensure that all participants are listening.

Problems

There can be **problems** in spoken language which the participants must solve if the speech encounter is going to continue. Temporary interruptions can be dealt with in a variety of ways.

Repairs

REPAIRS involve practical approaches to restore conversation. If a speaker chooses a wrong word, for example, she can correct herself or another speaker can correct her; if a listener mishears a word, he can ask for clarification. Even though a side sequence is created running alongside the main topic, the interruption is only temporary.

Spoken words	Comment
A: You know Michelle (.) you know (.) the nurse (.) er (.) no (.) that's it (.) Susan = B: = I know who you mean now (.) yeah she's called Susan	Speaker A starts with a formulaic opener. The number of brief pauses indicates hesitancy and suggests that she is unsure of her information. She corrects herself and Speaker B supports her final choice.
A: I've got English next lecture = B: = English (.) we had English earlier (.) A: sorry (.) yeah (.) you're right (.) it's French actually	Speaker B questions Speaker A's statement by reiterating the key word and introducing information which challenges it. Speaker A accepts the challenge and the repair is complete.

Topic loops

TOPIC LOOPS can offer an alternative method of dealing with a problem. These involve reintroducing an earlier topic in order to move away from the disruption. For instance, a speaker may invite an evaluation from the listener; if the response is minimal or negative, then the first speaker may return to an earlier, safer topic of conversation to repair the damage to the co-operative interaction.

Spoken words	Comment
A: I went to town this morning to get some felt pens and stuff to make a (.) some party invitations (.) B: mmm =	Instead of providing a positive response to Speaker A's opening, Speaker B offers a minimal acknowledgement. This suggests the interaction may not be co-operative.
A: = I couldn't resist getting this too = [holding up a dinosaur magic painting book] B: = why (.) A: well you know he's crazy about them at the moment so ‖ I B: ‖ but we've already got his present (.) A: I know (.) I (.) but he'll like it = B: = yes but you can't keep buying things (.)	Speaker B's question also signals practical trouble since it denies Speaker A the expected positive evaluation. Because of the structure of an adjacency pair, Speaker A is forced to respond. Speaker B is now controlling the turn-taking. The practical trouble is caused by Speaker B's implied criticism of Speaker A's actions. The co-operative nature of the conversation has been lost – the frequency of overlaps and Speaker B's negative evaluations highlight this.
A: I know (1) it <u>was</u> in the sale ‖ so I B: ‖ that's not an excuse for buying everything =	The speakers continue the topic, making no attempt to repair the damage. The disjointed turn-taking suggests that the conversation is still not collaborative.

A: = I (.) well it was only a one off = B: = [*laughs*] fine (.)	Speaker B's laugh is significant because the tone of the conversation has not been humorous. Instead it implies disbelief. The accompanying utterance is also dismissive.
A: I did get all the stuff for the invitations so I can do (.) make those tonight	Speaker A is forced to make a topic loop in order to repair what would otherwise be a complete breakdown in communication.

Listener response

A speaker who is **aware of listener response** can make repairs before communication breaks down. Expressions like *you know*, *you see* or *you understand* are a speaker's way of encouraging the listener to acknowledge that communication is effective. Direct address can also draw listeners into the conversation: *and you know what I said?*, *can you guess what happened?*, *if you ask me...* Such expressions require the listeners to show some kind of approval or encouragement to continue. Questions can have a similar function: *are you with me?*, *do you get what I mean?* or *OK?* If the listener response is negative, the speaker must repair the point of breakdown before moving on. Restating or rephrasing points made can solve the problem: *what I was trying to say was...* or *what I really meant was...* or *in other words...* This kind of monitoring behaviour can prevent spoken discourse breaking down by clarifying structures. It is a form of repair that relies on the speaker being sensitive to listeners.

Silence

SILENCE in a conversation can require repair. Utterances in spoken discourse often come in pairs and if for some reason an answer is not given quickly to a question or if a greeting is not returned, a speaker must decide whether to ignore the breakdown in co-operation or to tackle it. Repeating the utterance may repair the breakdown if the lack of response has been due to mishearing, but it may instead reinforce the conflict.

Pauses can also be responsible for creating a silence so they are usually kept to a minimum in speech. A long pause can cause embarrassment because it is seen as an indicator of failure. Often several people will then begin to speak at once in an attempt to fill the gap. Once a new topic has been established, the collective embarrassment is replaced with relief that the repair has been accomplished.

Silence must always be considered within the spoken context because it can also be used for dramatic effect, particularly in public speaking. Before deciding whether a repair is necessary, participants will have to assess the role of the silence within the discourse. If it enhances the meaning of utterances, it is probably purposeful; if it makes the participants uneasy, it can probably be seen as a breakdown in co-operative behaviour.

10.4 Different kinds of spoken language

A spoken narrative

The following transcript is an extract from a family conversation in which three young girls listen to their great uncle telling stories from his youth. The dominant speaker is the storyteller since his turns are extended, and the extract here focuses specifically on one of the narratives.

ACTIVITY 10.1

The transcription is a broad one: it takes no account of regional accent and only the most prominent examples of intonation and stress are marked.

Read through the transcript and respond to the following. A key to the symbols can be found on page 86.

1 Comment on the opening and closing of the narrative and any other distinctive structural features.
2 Describe the effects of the main prosodic features marked on the transcript.
3 Highlight any significant lexical or grammatical features.
4 List and describe the normal non-fluency features.
5 Identify any points at which the speaker tries to ensure that his audience is still paying attention and comment on the ways in which he does this.

Narrative (1 minute)

```
1     Well (.) you know I was in the band (.) St. Faiths band you know (.) well
      we went a-carol-playing there one (.) just before Christmas (2) we went
      all round St. Faiths and Newton St. Faiths (.) and then we went up to the
      Manor (3) and there was a lot a mud up that old loke and ol' Jack Fisher
5     said (.) i.i.i. ah.h o.o.o. w.wor what about the m.mud (.) he said (.) I g.got
      some w.water boots on b.but they g.got a h.hole in the bottom (1) course
      ol' Jack used to stutter you see (.) anyway, we kept agoing 'n' they called
      at the King's Head and that got on there 'til past ten and so they said (.)
      well we'd better (.) have one more tune before we go home (1) so they
10    played a carol or one or two carols round there (.) 'til someone said (.)
      you know what you are doing altogether don't ya (2) what someone said
      (.) you're playing to an old haystack (.) huh they said (.) that was a wrong
      un (.) so we had to pack that up (.) and of course we had to go home cos
      some of them weren't feeling too good (.) it was dark you know (.) and
15    we didn't know where we were. . .
```

COMMENTARY

Both the **opening** and the **closing** of the narrative provide a framework for the story: the speaker directly addresses his audience using the comment clause *you know* three times (ll. 1, 14). This is typical of storytelling within a conversation because the speaker has to ensure that the audience have accepted his dominant role in the turn-taking. To be effective, a narrative turn needs to be uninterrupted – by **monitoring audience response**, the speaker can prevent a problem occurring in the conversation. If speakers fail to monitor audience response and a breakdown does occur, the necessary repairs interrupt the smooth development of the story, spoiling the atmosphere and destroying the narrative's momentum.

The narrative starts and finishes with a statement that explains something to the audience. First, the speaker describes his own relationship with the story and events using a **self-related comment** – the use of the first person pronoun clearly establishes the tale as autobiographical. The use of the linking adverb *Well* (l. 1) establishes the informal manner and gives the speaker time to think before he starts the story. The concluding statement explains the narrative to the audience in case they have missed the point – it provides a summary which clearly marks the **end of the speaker's turn**.

The speaker uses several **narrative techniques** to dramatise the incident he is recalling. Much of the turn is taken up describing a sequence of events, but there are also key points at which characterisation becomes the focus of the narrative. Direct speech is used to give a sense of the people involved. Old Jack Fisher is distinctive because of the speaker's imitation of his stuttering – to prevent a breakdown of communication at this point, the storyteller again speaks directly to his audience using the comment clause *you see* (l. 7). This enables him to explain the reason for his non-standard speech. Informal utterances like *don't ya* (l. 11) and vocalisations like *huh* (l. 12) are used to animate the story and give it validity.

The **prosodics** help the storyteller to emphasise certain points in the narrative. **Emphatic stress** is used regularly to highlight key words: <u>*band*</u> (l. 1), <u>*Christmas*</u> (l. 2) and <u>*haystack*</u> (l. 12). It ensures that the audience are focused on the central theme. The **intonation patterns** are typical of the speaker's regional accent (Norfolk). Simple rises or falls are often used to mark the end of grammatical utterances or as a lead-in to direct speech. On one occasion a falling-rising tone (l. 12) is used, stressing the response of the players to what they have just been told. It adds variety after the climax of the story has been reached in the stressed noun phrase *an old haystack* (l. 12). **Pauses** are mostly brief and usually correspond to the end of an utterance, helping the listener to divide the speech into meaningful units.

The **lexis** establishes the narrative in **time** – *Christmas* (l. 2) and in **place** – *St. Faiths* (ll. 1, 3), *Newton St. Faiths* (l. 3), *Manor* (l. 4), *King's Head* (l. 8). **Lexical sets** build up a sense of the story's focus: rural – *mud* (l. 4), *haystack* (l. 12), *water boots* (l. 6); musical – *band* (l. 1), *carol playing* (l. 2), *carols* (l. 10), *tune* (l. 9); night – *past ten* (l. 8), *dark* (l. 14). Only one character is named, but **direct speech** helps to create a sense of other participants. Spoken narratives are far less descriptive than written narratives, but the speaker does use a few **complex noun phrases** to build up the atmosphere:

	m	m	h		m	m	h
	that	old	loke		an	old	haystack
	det	Adj	N		det	Adj	N

The noun *loke* (l. 4) is a Norfolk **dialect word** which describes a path leading up to a house – it makes the narrative distinctive because it links the speaker directly to his regional and cultural background. Examples of **abbreviated words** like *'til* (l. 8), *'n'* (l. 7) and *we'd* (l. 9) are typical of all informal speech, not of a particular dialect.

The **grammar** is mostly standard, but it is marked by some dialectal features. While the use of the archaic **present participle** *a-...playing* (l. 2) and *agoing* (l. 7) is typical of dialects in general, the use of the **pronoun** *that* instead of *it* is a variation specifically associated with a Norfolk dialect: *we had to pack that up* (l. 13).

The **sentence structures** are typical of spoken narratives: **co-ordination** is far more common than subordination. It is possible to analyse the clauses using the following model:

CConj	SConj	S	P	O/C/(S)	A
					Well
		you	know		
	(that)	I	was		in the band. . .
		we	went	a-carol-playing	there
					just before Christmas
		we	went		all round. . .
and					then
		we	went		up to the Manor
and		there	was	a lot of mud	up that old loke. . .
					anyway
		we	kept	agoing (NFCl)	
and		they	called		at the K's H
and		that	got		on there
					'til past ten

The columns here indicate clearly the dominance of co-ordinated clauses in the narrative and this is typical of the rambling nature of spoken language. The co-ordination allows the speaker to sustain his turn without interruption. In written language, the structure would seem repetitive, but in speech we accept it. There are examples of **subordinate clauses** like *'til someone said. . .* (l. 10) and *cos some of them* (ll. 13–14), but these are far less common.

Although the **pronouns** begin in the first person (*I* and *we*), the speaker slips into the third person halfway through the narrative: *they* (l. 8). Inconsistencies like these would be eliminated in a first draft in a written narrative, but the audience here would probably barely notice them.

Normal non-fluency features do not significantly affect the fluency of the story. In fact, the speaker is very controlled in his extended turn. There are some examples of restarts like *one (.) just before Christmas* (l. 2) in which the speaker repairs the breakdown himself, and a few longer pauses in which the speaker organises his thoughts before continuing with his tale, but on the whole the narrative seems effortless. Lexis and clause structures are quite repetitive, but that is typical of much spoken discourse.

The speaker uses the same technique on several occasions to ensure that his audience is still responsive. The comment clauses *you know* (l. 1) and *you see* (l. 7) require some kind of response from the listeners which, in a narrative turn, are more likely to be paralinguistic than vocal. Nods of the head, direct eye contact and minimal vocalisations like *mm* will satisfy the speaker that he still has the audience's consent to continue dominating the turn-taking.

A telephone conversation

The next transcript is an extract from a telephone conversation between a husband and wife in which they discuss everyday events. The speakers are involved in a co-operative exchange in which they both take more or less equal turns. Because they cannot rely on clues other than linguistic ones, however, the turns are not so clearly marked as they are in face-to-face informal conversation.

ACTIVITY 10.2

The transcription is a broad one, focusing on only the most significant changes in intonation patterns and stress.

Read through the transcript and respond to the following.

1 Comment on the opening and closing of the conversation and any other distinctive structural features (topic management; turn-taking).
2 Identify and discuss the main prosodic features and their effects.
3 Highlight any significant lexical or grammatical features.
4 List and describe the normal non-fluency features.
5 Comment on the main differences between one speaker telling a story and two speakers contributing to a conversation.

A key to the symbols can be found on page 86.

Telephone conversation (3 minutes)

```
 1  A:  héllo (.)
    B:  Lǔcy =
    A:  = yes (.) hiya (.) work OK̑ =
    B:  = mmm (.) same as ever (.) have you found out when (.) where the
 5      place ‖ is
    A:        ‖ yeah (.) I phoned College (.) and Susan didn't know (.) Mark
        didn't know (.) but then Jane did know (2) that's Jane at work =
    B:  = oh ‖ yes
    A:      ‖ mm (.) it's the big one =
10  B:  = the one on the corner of the road you turn into (.) into for the school =
    A:  = that's it ‖ yeah
    B:          ‖ I don't know where you'll park =
    A:  = well no (.) she said something about parking in the car park d. down
        by the Odeon cinema (.) ôh she means the mǔlti-storey =
15  B:  = mm̂ (.) the Odeon um (.) I don't know whether she means the old (.) I
        think there's an Odeon cinema which is now a Bingo Hall (.) isn't it (.)
    A:  ôh (.) right
    B:  you know ‖ which is just between that ‖ turning
    A:          ‖ I know                   ‖ but I don't know where there's a
20      car park there =
    B:  = mm =
    A:  = anyway (.) she says you probably can park on the road =
    B:  = mm (.) you might (.) should be able to (.) depending on how many
        people are there (.)
25  A:  I'm just wondering whether to go in at half elevenish (.) so I can buy the
        paper first =
    B:  = the paper =
    A:  = er (.) typing paper =
    B:  = oh (.) oh yeah (.) I forgot you were (.) going to do that (.) you've got
30      the card 'n' stuff in (.) it didn't mind (.) matter ‖ if you
    A:                                                      ‖ I think it's er downstairs =
    B:  = oh =
    A:  = the form says (.) do you think it'd be er business ‖ use
    B:                                                      ‖ ehh (.)
35  A:  it's not actually home use really =
```

```
     B:  = mm I'm er not mm convinced ‖ er
     A:                                ‖ one of the bits then later on you know
         (.) it's got what's it for and it's got education ‖ and
     B:                                                    ‖ well put (.) do that ‖ then
40   A:                                                                           ‖ and
         later ‖ on
     B:         ‖ you can put education (.) publishing (1) or something like that (.)
         well I ‖ won't be
     A:         ‖ we won't be playing games or ‖ anything
45   B:                                         ‖ no (.)
     A:  I don't expect it actually makes much difference ‖ I
     B:                                                    ‖ it's probably just for
         their information (.) they might (.) they might (.) ‖ circular (.) circularise
     A:                                                      ‖ yeah
50   B:  things for ‖ businesses
     A:             ‖ is there anything else we need from town =
     B:  = I can't think of anything (.) er I won't be going for a run er now (.) at
         lunch ‖ time
     A:        ‖ you're going ‖ to
55   B:                       ‖ well I won't be ‖ now
     A:                                         ‖ I was thinking you were being a
         bit ‖ brave
     B:      ‖ yeah (.)
     A:  did you go swimming in the end =
60   B:  = yeah (.) I did 60 (.) cos I was doing breaststroke (.) and I interspersed
         with some crawl (1) crawl being the operative word (.) ‖ I think (.)
     A:                                                          ‖ [laughs]
     B:  but ‖ well
     A:      ‖ hang on =
65   B:  = I'd better go ‖ now
     A:                  ‖ right well I'll go and get on with some typing =
     B:  = OK (.) I'll let you get on ‖ so I'll see you later
     A:                               ‖ OK =
     B:  = bye =
70   A:  = bye
```

COMMENTARY

The beginning and end of the conversation are marked by **formulaic utterances**: *hello* (l. 1), *I'd better go then* (l. 65) and *bye* (ll. 69–70). These clearly signal the intentions of the speakers in one of the few spoken contexts where the participants cannot see each other. Because they cannot rely on visual feedback from the exchange, they use patterned linguistic structures to prevent any possible ambiguity.

The **introductory section** includes the formulaic opening (ll. 1–2) and an other-related comment in which Speaker A asks Speaker B a question (l. 3). Having responded to that, Speaker B introduces the first **topic**: finding out about *the place* (ll. 4–5). Because the speakers are familiar, they have a shared knowledge of the topic. This means that they do not make explicit exactly what they are talking about – the participants understand the sequence of exchanges, but for an external listener they are ambiguous. The first **topic shift** occurs when a new topic is introduced by Speaker A: buying *the paper* (ll. 25–6). It leads naturally into a third related topic: the entrance card and the appropriate form for entry to the stationery shop (l. 33). The conversation begins to come towards an end when Speaker B introduces a self-related remark: *I won't be going for a run* (l. 52). The **closing section** is typical of the end of a conversation – it is repetitive; Speaker B shows concern for Speaker A in a statement which becomes the reason for ending the exchange: *I'll let you get on* (l. 67); and traditional formulae are used. The **topic management** is quite equally divided – both speakers introduce and develop the content.

The **turn-taking** is typical of a telephone conversation: speakers tend to avoid long utterances without introducing brief pauses for listeners to mark their continued interest. On the whole, turns are quite short, with neither participant dominating. Because the turns cannot be clearly marked by paralinguistic features, there are many examples of overlaps. Some of these are supportive minimal vocalisations: *yeah* (l. 6), *mm* (l. 9) and *[laughs]* (l. 62), but others mark points at which both speakers talk at once. Because the context is co-operative, usually one speaker will stop to allow the other participant to complete the utterance:

A: I don't expect it actually makes much difference ‖ I

B: ‖ it's probably just for their information (ll. 46–7)

B: I'd better go ‖ now

A: ‖ right well I'll go and get on with some typing (ll. 65–6)

Usually a telephone call will have a **specific purpose** since the conversation does not take place by chance. By dialling a specific phone number, a caller expresses a desire to speak to someone in particular. This means that most topics will not be randomly selected.

The **prosodic features** show the typical variations in **intonation patterns** that mark informal conversation. Because the participants cannot see each other, speakers on the telephone will often compensate by making their intonation more varied. There are many examples in this extract of falling, rising, rising-falling and falling-rising tones. Their function is varied: rising tones can be used to mark a question: *work OḰ* (l. 3); falling tones can be used to show agreement: *do͐ that* (l. 39); rising-falling tones can reflect sudden understanding: *ôh she means the multi-storey* (l. 14); and falling-rising tones can reflect uncertainty: *Lŭcy* (l. 2). Speakers use variations to maintain the listener's interest and to enhance the meaning.

Emphatic stress is used to highlight key lexical items: *work* (l. 7) and *education* (l. 38). It helps to establish a relationship between two participants who cannot see each other. In a telephone conversation, **pauses** will be kept to a minimum. Longer pauses could create a breakdown in communication because participants cannot rely on visual clues to know whether the gap is intentional or not – the listener may think the call has been cut off. Equally, long pauses could leave room for unwanted interruptions. To prevent these kind of breakdowns, participants tend to use pauses only to mark the end of grammatical utterances or while they momentarily order their thoughts. **Voiced hesitations** are common since these allow speakers to pause without communication breaking down: *mm* (l. 21), *er* (l. 31) or repetitions of words.

The **lexis** is linked directly to the topics: directions to *the place* (ll. 4–5), *paper* (l. 26) and *card* (l. 30). There are few examples of descriptive use of language because the purpose here is far more practical than a narrative. Colloquialisms like *hiya* (l. 3), *yeah* (l. 11), *well* (l. 39) and *won't* (l. 43) and imprecise references like *stuff* (l. 30) are common because the manner of the exchange is informal.

The **grammar** has similarities with casual conversation too. There are many grammatically incomplete utterances which function as complete clauses: *the paper* (l. 27) and *same as ever* (l. 4). Because they are in context, the participants can easily understand them. Such **minor 'sentences'** are often used in answer to a question – as part of an adjacency pair, the response is clearly linked directly to the question that precedes it. There are both compound and subordinate clauses, but there are not usually strings of dependent clauses embedded within a main clause. This would place a large load on the memory of the listener and informal conversation is not usually demanding in that way. Compound:

> S P O S P S P
> (I) (phoned) (College) (and) (Susan) (didn't know) (Mark) (didn't know) (but)
>   conj   neg   neg   conj

> A S P
> (then) (Jane) (did know) (ll. 6–7)

Complex:

> S P O
> (I) (was thinking) (you were being a bit brave) (ll. 56–7)
>   SCl–NCl

Although the structure of sentences is still often loose, subordination occurs more frequently than it did in the narrative. The telephone conversation has a quicker pace and the alternation of the two speakers seems to add more variety to the clause patterns.

There are many examples of **normal non-fluency features**. The conversation is spontaneous and this means that both speakers make **false starts** – *have you found out when (.) where the place is* (ll. 4–5); **repeat** words or phrases – *you turn into (.) into...* (l. 10); use **voiced hesitations** – *er* (l. 28), *ehh* (l. 34) and *mm* (l. 36); leave **utterances incomplete** – *I don't know whether she means the old (.)* (l. 15); and **speak over the top** of the other participant. Because the exchange is co-operative, speakers tend to make their own **repairs** – *you might (.) should be able to* (l. 23); *well put (.) do that then* (l. 39). If corrections are made by the other speaker, it can cause tension, but both participants here are at ease because they know each other. No judgements are being made based on the way they speak and this allows them to participate without feeling self-conscious. Equally, all the examples of non-fluency features are typical of informal conversation – when we take part in a conversation, we rarely even notice them. The fact that such inaccuracies are accepted is a distinctive trait of this kind of spoken language.

There are obvious **linguistic differences** between the two transcripts. In the earlier example, the narrative monologue is far less varied both in grammatical structures and prosodic features. The story demands an extended turn which the speaker sustains by repetition of the co-ordinating conjunction *and*; the telephone conversation, on the other hand, specifically involves two participants who share the turns. This automatically makes the grammatical structures of the two types of spoken language quite different: the short bursts of speech in the telephone conversation tend to have a more clearly defined structure in which subordination plays a greater part. Equally, because the storyteller has been granted the right to an extended turn, the prosodic features tended to be less varied; the participants in the telephone conversation cannot see each other and therefore have to use greater variation in intonation patterns and stress in order to keep the conversation alive. Both use formulaic techniques, but the opening and closing of the telephone conversation use conventional formulae far more rigidly because the participants cannot rely on non-linguistic clues. Despite the differences in grammar and prosodic features, in each case the participants are aware of their audience so they use language in a way that will ensure that effective communication is taking place.

An interview

The third transcript is an extract from Classic FM's evening news report on Monday, 17 July 1995. It is an interview between the presenter, Jane Markham (JM) and Classic FM's film critic, Cherie Lloyd (CL). In the interview, they discuss the release of the new Batman movie.

In many interview situations, participants do not have equal status – in a job interview, for example, the interviewee clearly does not have any control over the speech encounter. Here, however, the situation is rather different – Cherie Lloyd is being consulted as an expert and therefore has equal status with the presenter of the hour-long radio programme. The speech encounter takes place within a very precise time allocation and this affects the nature of the linguistic and prosodic features of the discourse.

ACTIVITY 10.3

The transcription is broad and prosodic features are marked selectively. Read through the transcript and make notes on the following areas.

1 Comment on the way in which the speech encounter is structured.
2 Identify the main prosodic features and consider their effects.
3 Highlight any significant lexical or grammatical features.
4 List and describe the normal non-fluency features.
5 Comment on the differences between an informal telephone conversation between two speakers and a radio interview.

A key to the symbols can be found on page 86.

Radio interview (2½ minutes)

1	JM:	there's a new Batman mòvie (.) with a new Bátman and a new director (.) and Cherie Lloyd (.) our film critic (.) has been along to see it (.) Cherie (2) is it vĕry <u>different</u> from the other Batman films that have been ‖ óut
5 'accel'	CL:	‖ yes it is (.) it's 'far more light-<u>hearted</u> um (.) the old director (1) the director' of the <u>old</u> films Tim Burton ha. (.) went for the more <u>Góthic</u> (.) er split personality Bruce Wayne Batman problem (.) where (.) thìs one is just non-stop (.) excitement and action from the first frame (.) um
10		(1) it's (.) it's mu. (.) ↑it's↑ múch more entertaining (.) it's more (.) sort of like an áction fìlm (.) as opposed to a deep psychological dràma =
	JM:	= and a new Bátman of course (.) and that now <u>probably</u> makes quite a difference because you dó <u>identify</u> with the
15		actor who plays Batman =
	CL:	= one of the problems Ì thought with the older films was the fact that (.) Michael Keaton wasn't a very successful Batman
'rall'		for mè (.) um (.) there was just something about him (.) 'super-hero (.) um (.) nò (.) not really' (.) Val Kilmer very much so (.)
20		he's (.) very very good looking and Val Kilmer is far far more convìncing =
	JM:	= ↑they've↑ also brought in the Robin character from the old

<table>
<tr><td></td><td></td><td>television series who didn't appear at all in the other Batman movies (.) um (.) it is nice to have him back =</td></tr>
<tr><td>25</td><td>CL:</td><td>= yes (.) because they've done a really nice <u>parallel</u> between er (.) Bruce Wayne's story in the earlier Batman films and (.) um Robin in this film um (.) Bruce Wayne's parents were killed (.) by a criminal (.) Robin's (.) (indistinct) been killed by a criminal and er it's Batman <u>help</u>ing Robin find himself (.) and that</td></tr>
<tr><td>30</td><td></td><td>sort of <u>thing</u> (.) it's very nice (.) it's very well handled =</td></tr>
<tr><td></td><td>JM:</td><td>= what about the story (.) who's the er arch enemy in this one =</td></tr>
<tr><td></td><td>CL:</td><td>= there's (2) there's um (.) the Riddler (.) <u>brilliantly</u> played by Jim Carrey and Two Face er played by Tommy Lee Jones (.)</td></tr>
<tr><td></td><td>'accel'</td><td>um (1) they're both very (.) Tommy Lee Jones is a little bit (.) 'a</td></tr>
<tr><td>35</td><td></td><td>little bit too similar to the Joker' =</td></tr>
</table>

'accel'

| 35 | | little bit too similar to the Joker' = |

JM: = who did we hear at the beginning of this piece ‖ who was that

CL: ‖ Jim Carrey

as the Riddler =

JM: = uhh =

40   CL: = um (.) Tommy Lee Jones is a little bit too similar to (.) um (.) Jack Nicholson's the Joker (.) for my tastes but (.) Jim Carrey is <u>superb</u> (.) he really is (.) as th. (.) the vill. (.) the villains make a film like this and they've picked a good one with Jim Carrey =

45   JM: = so (.) this (.) looks (.) rather like you haven't actually said anything <u>bad</u> about it at <u>all</u> (.) Cherie (.) which is quite unusual for you when you're doing your film reviews =

CL: = and I've got nothing (.) at <u>all</u> bad to say about this one (.) it's <u>great</u> (.) it's (.) it's <u>great</u> fun (.) it's (.) the script's good (.) it

50   looks brilliant (.) it's entertaining (.) it's a nice (.) <u>slice</u> (.) of escapism (.) in fact I'd go as far as saying it's well worth £7 of <u>any</u>body's money (.) it's just a great film =

JM: = Cherie Lloyd giving it the <u>thumbs</u> up (.) you're listening to Classic Report (.) in a moment a larger than life performance

55   by a larger than life performer. . .

COMMENTARY

The **manner** is formal because the two speakers are participating in a radio broadcast. Despite the formality of the setting, however, they are obviously known to each other and also have equal status. This means that their language mixes both formal and informal registers.

The presenter of *Classic Report*, Jane Markham, **opens** the interview with a clear indication of the content. The opening statement defines the **topic** from the outset: *there's a new Batman movie* (l. 1). An interview does not usually involve a range of topics because it has a clear purpose, and an opening that establishes the theme is typical of this kind of spoken encounter. The whole of the 2½-minute interview then concentrates on the new Batman film. Another topic is not introduced until Jane Markham clearly signals the end of the interview about the film and describes what is to follow the commercial break (ll. 53–5). The **closing** is marked by a summary in which the film critic is again named in full and her comments on the film are generalised in a collo-quial cliché: *giving it the thumbs up* (l. 53).

The **turn-taking** is distinctive. The structure is based on **adjacency pairs** in which the presenter asks a question and the film critic replies. This framework is used throughout the speech encounter. Turns are not short: the presenter tends to make a statement which leads into a question and the reviewer's answers are fully developed. Because the participants are co-operative, giving each other space to develop their views, the radio listener learns a lot about the film within the 2½ minutes. However, it is important to recognise that in this kind of speech encounter, the main body of the interview deals with subjective attitudes rather than objective fact.

In a radio interview, the participants have only a limited amount of time to com-plete their discourse. In most interviews based on a review, the turn-taking will be very carefully organised. In the extract here the participants **latch on** to each other very smoothly: as one speaker finishes, the other picks up the cues and starts to speak. This means that almost every utterance is marked '= =' in the transcription. On only two occasions do the speakers **overlap**. In the first instance, the reviewer, who has been waiting for her turn to start, answers the presenter's question before she has quite fin-ished saying it (ll. 4–5):

> JM: ...is it very <u>different</u> from the other Batman films that have been ‖ out
> CL: ‖ yes it
> is...

An overlap is common in this kind of formal context since the second speaker can only begin to feel at ease once the dialogue has started. It does not cause problems for radio listeners because the main body of the question has already been heard. The second overlap occurs because the presenter rephrases her question just as the reviewer begins to answer the first version (ll. 36–8):

> JM: who did we hear at the beginning of this piece ‖ who was that?
> CL: ‖ Jim Carrey as the
> Riddler...

In both cases the overlap is minimal because the speakers are sensitive to each other and the formal context.

The **prosodic features** seem more prominent than in normal conversation. Because the participants are 'performing' for their radio audience, they exaggerate the prosodics to animate the conversation for listeners who have no visual clues. Key words are **stressed**. Often the stressed words are modifiers revealing the reviewer's attitude: *bril-liantly* (l. 32), *superb* (l. 42) and *great* (l. 49); others are stressed to draw attention to con-trasts: *different* (l. 3) and *old* (l. 6); and some highlight important words in an utterance: *Gothic* (l. 7), *identify* (l. 14) and *slice* (l. 50). **Intonation patterns** enhance the meaning of utterances: questions are marked with a **rising tone**; the listing of the film's positive fea-tures also uses a rising tone: *the scrípt's good (.) it loóks brilliant...* (ll. 49–50); **falling tones** tend to be used when the reviewer refers to herself as though she is emphasising that the viewpoint is personal: *for my tastes* (l. 41); negative responses also have a falling tone: *superhero (.) um (.) no* (ll. 18–19); **falling-rising tones** are used to empha-sise key words prior to a stress: *is it vĕry <u>different</u>...* (l. 3) and *...about this ŏne (.) it's <u>great</u>* (ll. 48–9). **Pitch changes** are used to mark a change of direction: ↑*it's*↑ *much more entertaining* (l. 10) and ↑*they've*↑ *also brought in* (l. 22). Changes in **pace** add interest and are indicative of the limited time allocated within the programme for each feature – the reviewer significantly speeds up on two occasions (ll. 5, 34), and only slows down once when comparing the present and past Batman actors (l. 18). Some of the **pauses** seem to break the long utterances into easily comprehensible units:

(there) ('s) (a new Batman movie PAUSE with a new Batman and a new director)

                       S   P   A   A
PAUSE (and) (CL PAUSE our film critic) PAUSE (has been) (along) (to see it)
        conj   SCl–NFCl

(ll. 1–3)

The pauses in this compound-complex structure help the listener to focus on one section of the utterance at a time.

The **lexis** is all related to the film, but it is not technical. Although there are some subject-specific terms – *frame* (l. 9), *action film* (l. 11) and *psychological drama* (ll. 11–12) – much of the discussion is very informal: *sort of thing* (l. 30), *sort of like* (l. 11). The noun phrases are usually complex because the whole purpose of the discourse is evaluative. Both pre- and post-modification are used:

   m   h   q   m   m   h
the director of the old films (l. 6)   a (really nice) parallel (l. 25)
det   N   PrepP   det   Adv   Adj   N

   m   m   h   m   m   h   q
a (very successful) Batman (l. 17)   a nice slice of escapism (ll. 50–1)
det   Adv   Adj   N   det Adj   N   PrepP

As well as the strings of attributive modifiers, there are also many predicative modifiers functioning as complements.

   S   P   C   S   P   C   S   P   C   S   P   C
(it) ('s) (*great*) . . . (the script) ('s) (*good*) (it) (looks) (*brilliant*) (it) ('s) (*entertaining*)

There are a lot of abstract nouns because the interview is focused on a general analysis of the film: *escapism* (l. 51), *drama* (l. 12) and *reviews* (l. 47).

The **grammar** is quite involved because of the length of the utterances. The relationship between the participants is not formal, but because the context is formal and because there is a clearly defined purpose, grammatical structures are usually complete and utterances are often complex.

                     S   P   C
(one of the problems I thought with the older films) (was) (the fact that MK wasn't
            SCl–ComCl   SCl–NCl
a very successful Batman for me) (ll. 16–18)

There are also several co-ordinated clauses which are more typical of informal spoken language.

      S   P   O   S   P   O   A
(the villains) (make) (a film like this) (and) (they) ('ve picked) (a good one) (with JC)
                                            conj

(ll. 42–4)

The **normal non-fluency features** are typical of any spontaneous speech. Here the speakers are under particular pressure because they are speaking to a large unseen audience and this means that despite their fluency they make some mistakes. **Voiced hesitations** like *um* (l. 6) and *er* (l. 7) are common in the utterances of presenter and reviewer. **Restarts**, however, tend to occur in the reviewer's responses to questions: *it's (.) it's mu. (.) it's much more entertaining* (l. 10); *TLJ is a little bit (.) a little bit too similar. . .* (ll. 34–5). This is to be expected because questions are easier to prepare beforehand than answers. Some of the hesitations are clearly allowing the speaker thinking time while informing the other participant that the turn is not yet complete: *there's (2)* *there's um (.) the Riddler* (l. 32). There is some **repetition** of material (reference to Jack Nicholson's portrayal of the Joker) which is common in spoken discourse where speakers cannot go back and eliminate unnecessary words or phrases as they can in written work. In some places, utterances are **grammatically incomplete**: *they're both very* (l. 34). Even though an utterance is grammatically incomplete, however, intonation patterns ensure that understanding is not affected. When discussing the character of Batman in the old films, for instance, Cherie Lloyd uses the simple noun phrase *superhero* (ll. 18–19) on its own. The accompanying rising intonation, however, ensures that listeners know she is asking a question.

The speech encounter is co-operative and all **repairs** are self-repairs. For example, where the reviewer feels that her words may be misinterpreted, she reorders what she has just said. In discussing the earlier films she talks of *the old director* (l. 6), but realising that the modifier may be misunderstood, she rephrases the nominal group: *the director of the old films* (l. 6). Where time permits, the speakers are **supportive** of each other – turns start with the affirmative *yes* (l. 25) or the minimal vocalisation *uhh* (l. 39).

It is possible to summarise the main differences between a telephone conversation and a radio interview in a table:

Linguistic features	Informal telephone conversation	Radio interview
Audience	One specific person who is known and whose number has been dialled.	On one level the participants are speaking to each other, but they are also speaking to a wider unknown audience listening to the radio programme.
Topic	Although a telephone conversation will normally have a specific purpose, new topics are likely to emerge as the speech encounter develops. To an outsider, topics may seem to arise randomly, but to the participants with their shared knowledge there may well be a logical progression from one to another.	The participants will normally have a clearly defined reason for their discourse. There will often be no more than one topic as the focus for the speech encounter. Tentatively connected topics are unlikely to be a part of the developing discourse.
Turn-taking	Turns tend to be short so that speakers can be sure that the other participant is still listening. Lack of visual clues means that the end of each turn must be clearly marked to avoid confusion. Overlaps are common because speakers do not always interpret linguistic clues properly. Because the context is co-operative, however, the overlaps do not tend to be long.	Turns tend to be quite long and their organisation is very precise. Adjacency pairs are created by the question/answer framework. Because of time limits, latching on makes the turn-taking smooth – each speaker picks up exactly where the last one finishes. Some overlaps occur, but they are rarely long.

Openings and closings	Because speakers cannot see each other, beginnings and endings are marked by formulaic utterances which are easily recognisable.	To ensure that listeners can follow the different parts of a programme, the start and finish of each section must be clear. An interview therefore opens with a statement that focuses attention on the topic and closes with a summary.
Prosodic features	Participants seem to use stress and varied intonation patterns to sustain listener interest. Pauses are usually short so that turn-taking does not become confused. Voiced hesitations are common.	Speakers often exaggerate stress and intonation patterns to add interest to what is being said. Because utterances are often long, pauses divide them into easily understandable units. Pace and pitch also vary quite dramatically. Voiced hesitations give speakers time to order their thoughts.
Lexis and grammar	The words are often informal and grammatical structures are often incomplete. Participants accept inaccuracies because the speech environment is co-operative and supportive. Co-ordination may be more common than subordination.	Lexis can be formal and subject specific, informal or a mixture of the two depending upon the participants, their topic and the context. Utterances are usually grammatically complete and subordination is more common.

Unscripted commentary

The most common forms of unscripted commentary are those which accompany sports events broadcast on television or radio. There are, however, other examples that fall into this category: unscripted commentaries may be used when an event like a royal wedding is televised or when a state occasion like the opening of Parliament is covered on the radio.

Sometimes commentators will speak from a text, but live coverage requires them to describe and comment on events as they happen. This means that the commentators must speak spontaneously. The purpose of a **television** commentary is clearly different from a **radio** version of the same event. Both radio and television commentators comment on and evaluate what is taking place, but because radio listeners cannot see what is happening, a radio commentator must also use language to convey an exact description of the developing action.

ACTIVITY 10.4

The last transcripts in this section are taken from commentaries accompanying the Rugby World Cup England versus Italy match on 30 July 1995. The first is a commentary for the televised match on ITV by Bob Symonds (BS) and Steve Smith (SS); the second is from the Radio 5 live coverage by Ian Robertson (IR) and Mike Burton (MB).

Read through each transcript and make notes on the following.

1 Comment on the turn-taking.
2 Identify the main prosodic features and consider their effects.
3 Highlight any significant lexical or grammatical features.
4 Comment on the normal non-fluency features.
5 List the distinctive features of unscripted commentary and comment on any differences
   between radio and television commentaries.

A key to the symbols can be found on page 86.

Television commentary (3 minutes)

1   BS: and a strânge atmosphere really at the beginning of this
                                 second half (.) Steve (.) it's like (.) a phoney wár (.) isn't
                                 it =
                            SS: = yes a bit of aerial ping-pong at the moment but I'm
5   sure they'll settle down (4)
                            BS: the Italians now (.) calling some variátion at the lineout
     'accel/stacc'   moving Number 8 'Julian Gardner up to the front' but
                                 that's a decoy move for Pedroni (2) Ben Clarke (1)
                                 through quickly through on Cuttitta good rucking too by
10   'rall'   England the Italians 'again up very quickly indeed' (3)
                                 but that's a lovely kick by Rob Andrew (.) forcing them to
     'accel'   turn (5) you saw then (.) the problems that 'Gerosa faced
                                 as Johnson sets it up (indistinct)' (1) just about getting it
                                 away there Dominguez ónly just (1) for a moment it
15   'accel'   looked as if England might 'just get in there' =
                            SS: = it must be that corner Bob it must be jinxed it's where
                                 Mike Catt made his mistake and the Italians were in all
                                 sorts of pressure thère (.) in fact in the end they were
                                 quite lucky to get away with it (1) ball bobbling around
20   needed tídying úp (.) that's a place you don't want to slip
                                 over a yard from your own line (.) and really the Italians
     'accel'   got out of jail in the end Martin Johnson 'really I thought
                                 should have held on here' once again one pass too
                                 mány and intercepted chance gòne (2)
25   BS: Brian Móore (.) a bang in the face for his pâins (4) wait-
                                 ing nòw (.) then to put into the lineout a grèat chance for
                                 Englànd just a few metres out from the Italian line (7)
     'accel'   'Bàyfield in the middle tackles it beâutifully' Rowntree in
                                 to support him now England looking for the drive (7)
30   'accel'   England looking to turn and 'move this rolling maul' (3)
                                 just a couple of metres out then from the Italian line into
                                 Rodber (3) still just held up short (.) Bracken has options
     'accel'   both sides (.) 'Andrew (.) beautiful long pass (.) Catt out
     'rall'   to Rory Underwood' (2) 'beautifully created try' (3) and
35   'leg'/'lento'   it's 'the Underwood brothers who are again' on the 'mark
                                 for England' =

SS: = and that try was a <u>beauty</u> created by England for-
       wards at the lineout terrific forward play (1) in the énd
       they sucked up the Italians and they just ràn out of play-
40   ers.

Radio commentary (3 minutes)

          IR: Underwood takes it rúns úp (.) to his own 22 and right
                 fóoted (.) hámmers it I think is the only phrase I can use
'rall'   there (.) into touch near side of the field (.) 'on the
                 England (.) 10 metre line' (.) that's on the er Italian left =
45   MB: = he had er a much uh better better angle there did
                 Underwood than Mike Catt had from the kick just (.) a
                 few (.) moments earlier Diego Dominguez had put a
'alleg'   'cracking kick into the corner and er even if it hadn't have
                 gone in' then the receiver who was Mike Catt on that
50   occasion had no angle to kick the ball ‖ back
          IR: ‖ and Ben Clarke
                 snaffles the ball from this lineout it comes back to
                 Bracken sends it out to Andrew (.) Andrew puts a kick
                 down towards the corner that's again a <u>very</u> <u>very</u> good
55   kick it's rolling right up to the (.) Italian line Gerosa slips
'accel'   (.) 'he recovers very quickly but can't get his kick in
'cresc'   Johnson picks it up 'all the Italians are offside' the ball's
                 charged down by Brian Moore (.) acŕoss goes Trŏiani (1)
'alleg'   and the scrum half Troncon 'sidefoots it into touch' (.)
60 'dimin'   and that was a sort of 'er <u>pantomime</u> wasn't it (.) a com-
                 edy of èrrors' =
          MB: = yes and the the the main feature of that passage of
                 play was the Rob Andrew kick you see he he he put it
                 down bouncing er behind the the Italian defenders (.)
65   and even if it didn't go into touch then (.) it would have
                 been difficult for (.) the (.) Italian defender to clear
                 because (.) we had no angle in the end Mario Gero.
                 Gerosa (.) the er the left wing er slips on trying to cóllect
                 the ball and even when he got up the thing wouldn't have
70 'accel'   gone any distance and 'it was the same story when Catt
                 took the ball' in a deep position just now (.) clever kick
                 there (.) from Rob Andrew =
          IR: = well Brian Moore's had a bit of treatment thĕre (.) he
                 charged it down with his head which is not a the the best
75   thing to do and he's recovered now so we'll have the
                 lineout after a (.) couple of minutes injury time there (.)
'cresc'   the ball's '<u>won</u> magnificently by Bayfield England are <u>just</u>
                 5 metres' (.) 6 metres short they've got a drive on they're
                 beginning to roll towards the posts and (.) only 5 metres
80   from the line this is where they've <u>got</u> to feed it now
                 Rowntree has it (.) slips it up (.) England now <u>4</u> metres

'accel'   from the line (.) the ball's on the 'ground Bracken pops it
                  up for Rodber <u>he's</u> 2 metres' from the line (.) and this
'rall'   'time perhaps (.) perhaps as it comes out' out to Andrew
85 'accel/cresc' (.) Andrew a long '↑miss pass to Catt out to Rory
'rall/leg'   Underwood↑ for his <u>43rd</u> ↓<u>try</u>' '<u>in</u> international <u>rugby</u> and
                  that <u>made</u> <u>by</u> a <u>touch</u> <u>of</u> génius'↓ from Rob Andrew that
                  he knew where évery one of the 30 players wás was on
'rall'   the pitch sáw 'the yáwning gap on the left' and Rory
90   Underwood doesn't need a second invitation with no one
                  to beát and he shot in for (.) a <u>tremendous</u> trŷ =
         MB: = the long flat er pass obviously gave Rory Underwood
                  the room out wide but the work was done by the for-
                  wards because that's what we've been saying all though
95   the first half England had <u>drawn</u> <u>in</u> all the Italian back
                  row er they weren't er 5 metres out from the Italian line
                  so the Italian midfield men were forced back behind their
                  own line couldn't encroach that at all and (.) it it it created
                  the room out wide for this <u>beautifully</u> long floated flat
100   pass er for Rory Underwood to go in on the left hand
                  side. . .

COMMENTARY

The **function** of a commentary is to describe a sequence of actions, to give the listener or viewer background information and to entertain. The **target audience** will usually be people who are interested in the particular activity taking place and who already have a reasonable knowledge of the subject specific language and structure of the event.

A commentary must be **spontaneous** and **sustained** as it mirrors the process of the activity. This does not mean, however, that the **structure** is random. In fact, unscripted commentary is quite different from the loosely structured nature of informal conversation since the **topic** is predefined and utterances must be orderly. Commentators can use notes to give their utterances structure, but this is really only feasible when they are filling long breaks in the action (half-time, injury time). They must therefore be able to describe ongoing actions fluently and develop a more personal level of comment and interpretation when little is happening.

The **structure** of an unscripted commentary will vary depending upon the kind of activity that is taking place: a cricket match will take place over a longer period of time than a football match, for instance, so the commentary for each will have a different pace. When little is happening, commentators might give **background information** summarising the state of the game so far; when significant activity develops, they will describe **what is happening** and will try to **create an appropriate atmosphere** for people watching or listening; where events follow a recognisable pattern, they may use a **formulaic utterance**; if the outcome of a predictable sequence of moves is exciting, they will choose **emotive language** – if nothing develops from the initial activity, they will choose more **reserved language**. Alongside descriptions of the activity itself, a skilful commentator will provide **interpretative comment** and often **personal asides**. It is this part of a commentary that allows commentators to be idiosyncratic and to develop a personal style.

The **turn-taking** has to be very orderly, just as it is in an interview. Often there will be two people to talk about the activity: one will be in the role of commentator and the other tends to be a sportsman or sportswoman who advises or summarises. The two participants will sometimes directly interact in informal conversation, but usually their turns will be directly related to the event they are watching. In the examples here, the commentators are Bob Symonds (television) and Ian Robertson (radio); the advisers are Steve Smith (television) and Mike Burton (radio). The approach of the commentators and advisers is usually quite different.

In the transcripts of the Rugby World Cup, in almost every example the speakers pick up clues promptly and **latch on** smoothly. In a few places in the television commentary, the end of a turn is marked by a **timed pause** (ll. 5, 12) – the adviser finishes speaking and the commentator waits until the next piece of action develops before starting his turn. On only one occasion in the radio commentary is there an example of an **overlap** (ll. 10–11) – the adviser is finishing his comment as activity develops in the match and the commentator begins his turn. There is no confusion caused by the overlaying of words and the overlap itself is minimal. The dominance of **latched turns** indicates the highly structured nature of unscripted commentary. Although it is a form of spontaneous speech, it is clearly an acquired skill in which certain techniques must be learnt and practised.

Unscripted commentaries are distinctive for the wide range of **prosodic features** on which they draw and even at first sight the marginal notes are obviously more detailed than the other transcripts considered so far. As the activity described changes, so too do the intonation patterns, the pitch, the pace and the volume. Commentators use these to animate the scene they are creating for radio listeners who cannot see what is happening; and to focus the viewer and personalise the event for a television audience. The **timing** of utterances is crucial and this is another reason why spontaneity and sustained speech are so important.

In both transcripts, the commentators use a far wider range of prosodic features than the advisers. This emphasises the fact that unscripted commentary is a variety for which there are techniques to be learnt. The **pace** of utterances is directly linked to the speed of the activity taking place. Where exciting developments occur, commentators frequently increase the pace of their utterances (marked on the transcript as 'accel'). This will usually be followed by a noticeable decrease in pace as the height of activity falls away (marked 'rall'). To signal the end of a dramatic passage of play and the end of a turn, a commentator might use a distinctively slow delivery (marked 'lento'). Changes in **volume** often accompany changes in pace: as excitement builds, the volume will increase (marked 'cresc'); and as a particular period of activity dies away, so too will the volume (marked 'dimin'). Dramatic changes of pitch are also distinctive: a commentator may raise his pitch (marked ↑ ↑) to reflect anticipation and enthusiasm, or lower it (marked ↓ ↓) to indicate a return to less fevered activity.

Emphatic stress is used to highlight key words, just as it is in other forms of spoken language. What can perhaps be seen as a distinctive feature, however, is the emphatic stringing together of stressed words: _his 43rd try in international rugby_ (l. 86). Stress patterns like these are often accompanied by a **rhythmic delivery**: short, abrupt vocalisations (marked 'stacc') may be used to describe players' positions as quickly as possible; drawling, prolonged vocalisations (marked 'leg') may add emphasis to important moments.

Intonation patterns are also noticeably exaggerated in unscripted commentary. **Rising tones** mark excitement: _Underwood takes it rúns úp to his own 22 and right fóoted hámmers it_ (ll. 41–2). They are often used repeatedly as the activity builds to a climax. **Falling tones** tend to mark the end of a turn: _a comedy of érrors_ (ll. 60–1). **Rising-falling** and **falling-rising tones** are used to give emphasis to key words: _tackles it beâutifully_ (l. 28). Intonation patterns are also used to give coherence to utterances where clause elements are often deleted to achieve brevity.

Pauses are used in a distinctive way in commentaries. Because sustained speech is so important there are few examples of the kinds of casual pauses associated with informal conversation. The variety as a whole is noted for its lack of voiced hesitation, so pauses tend to be used consciously: to add emphasis – *but that's a lovely kick by Rob Andrew (.) forcing them to turn* (ll. 11–12); to reflect lack of specific activity – *England looking for the drive (7) England looking to turn* (ll. 29–30); to punctuate a sequence of actions – *Bracken has options both sides (.) Andrew (.) beautiful long pass (.) Catt out to Rory Underwood* (ll. 32–4); and to breathe *and Ben Clarke snaffles the ball from this lineout it comes back to Bracken sends it out to Andrew (.)* (ll. 51–3). It is important to remember that pauses do not always correspond to the end of a grammatical utterance in unscripted commentaries.

The advisers alter the pitch, pace, volume and tone of their utterances less often. Their pace may become fast (marked 'alleg') in order to complete their turn before the next piece of play is described by the commentator, but usually their delivery is far less exaggerated. They imitate the techniques of commentators, but do not always manage to control them as skilfully because they have had less practice. In some stretches of their turns, utterances become very long and it is possible to hear speakers almost running out of breath as they aim for a point at which a pause can be taken for breath: *the long flat er pass. . .encroach that at all and (.). . .* (ll. 92–8).

The basic function of the **language** of unscripted commentaries is to name things and people (nouns) and to describe actions (verbs). The lexis is **subject specific** because the focus of attention is inevitably on one particular kind of activity: *lineout* (l. 76), *try* (l. 34) and *rucking* (l. 9). Many of the technical terms are used in everyday discourse, but in the sporting context have a more specific meaning: *left wing* (l. 68) and *corner* (l. 54). Alongside the technical terms, colloquialisms are common: contractions – *he's* (l. 75) and *we've* (l. 94); phrasal verbs – *get away with* (l. 19) and *ran out of* (l. 39); informal 'trendy' modifiers – *a cracking kick* (l. 48); the use of adverbs like *really* at the front of utterances to indicate disapproval – *really I thought. . .* (l. 22) and *really the Italians. . .* (l. 21); and conversational collocations – *the same story* (l. 70). There tend to be other **collocations** which are directly linked to a particular context: *long pass* (l. 33), *into touch* (l. 43) and *near side of the field* (l. 43). There is a high proportion of **proper nouns** because the commentators have to describe a sequence of actions carried out by a limited number of participants: *Diego Dominguez* (l. 47), *Rory Underwood* (ll. 85–6) and *Rodber* (l. 32). **Modification** is used to add detail – it will often consist of numbers. Strings of modifiers like *beautiful long pass* (l. 33), and adverbial intensifiers like *a very very good kick* (l. 54) are quite common. Often extra detail will be added by placing phrases in apposition: *the receiver/who was Mike Catt on that occasion/had no angle to kick the ball. . .* (ll. 49–50). Both pre- and post-modification are used.

m		m		m	m	h	
this (beautifully long) floated flat pass (ll. 99–100)
det		Adv		Adj	V	adj	N

| m | h | q | |
a bang in the face (l. 25)
| det | N | PrepP | |

Individual commentators develop a **personal approach**. They try to avoid high-frequency clauses like *you see*, *you know* or *I mean* which are common in informal conversation and instead try to make their choice of words striking. Here, *you see* is used as a filler (l. 63). Unusual **descriptive noun phrases** like *phoney war* (l. 2); *a bit of aerial ping-pong* (l. 4) make the account of what is happening more distinctive. Unexpected **verbs** can prevent commentaries describing an event in which similar sequences of action occur from becoming repetitive: *bobbling* (l. 19), *snaffles* (l. 52) and *sidefoots*

(l. 59). The use of **verb modifiers** can dramatise the action, emphasising the ongoing nature of the process: *rolling maul* (l. 30); *yawning gap* (l. 89). In the radio commentary, Ian Robertson uses the verb *hammers* (l. 42), drawing attention to his choice of word by following the clause with a comment clause: *I think is the only phrase I can use there* (ll. 42–3). This is a form of METATALK (a term in linguistics for language used when talking about language) in which the speaker discusses his own lexical selections.

The other way in which a commentator can create a distinctive style is to use **metaphors**. There are many well-known examples of sporting clichés: *sick as a parrot, over the moon, the game's not over until the final whistle's blown* and *it's a game of two halves*. When a commentator uses a new image, however, it can animate the scene he is trying to describe. Metaphorical language is in complete contrast to the factual language used to record what is happening at moments of intense activity – it will most often occur when the speed of the match has slowed down, allowing the commentator to indulge in a more impressionistic kind of comment. In the transcripts here, Ian Robertson develops a theatrical metaphor: *pantomime* and *a comedy of errors* (ll. 60–1) – the title of a play by Shakespeare. This allows him to summarise an uncontrolled passage of play in a vivid and personal way. Steve Smith also uses metaphors in the televised match: *got out of jail* (l. 22) and *sucked up* (l. 39). They are perhaps not as distinctive as the theatrical extended metaphor, but they reflect nevertheless a creative use of language which develops the atmosphere.

The **grammar** of unscripted commentaries has many distinctive features. Because the discourse is spontaneous, **grammatically incomplete utterances** are common. However, in the focused context of a sporting activity these are rarely noticed. Most utterances are in the **declarative**, but **questions** may be asked where two people are involved. These may take the form of tag questions requesting affirmation of a point just made like *isn't it* (ll. 2–3) or may momentarily involve the participants in something more like conversation than commentary. At moments of tension, a commentator may ask rhetorical questions in which he anticipates the outcome without yet knowing what will happen. **Clause elements** will usually appear in a standard order – inversion may be used for dramatic effect, but **marked themes** are not common in unscripted commentary. They are more likely to appear in the turns of the adviser than those of the commentator.

> A   A   S   P   C
> (in fact) (in the end) (they) (were) (quite lucky to get away) (ll. 18–19)
>   SCl–NFCl

The **main verb** usually comes early in the clause and the sentence structures are often **simple**:

> S   P   O   A
> (Ben Clarke) (snaffles) (the ball) (from this lineout) (ll. 51–2)

> S   P   O   A
> (Bracken) (has) (options) (both sides) (ll. 32–3)

Just as informal conversation is marked by loose co-ordination of utterances, so too is spontaneous unscripted commentary. The use of *and* in the initial position is common since it allows speakers to latch onto the end of the previous turn and to sustain the continuous flow of speech.

> S   P   C   A   S   P   O
> (and) (that try) (was) (a beauty) . . . (in the end) (they) (sucked up) (the Italians)
> conj

> S   A   P   O
> (and) (they) (just) (ran out of) (players) (ll. 37–40)
> conj

Subordination is more common in evaluative or summative comment than in description of the action, but long, embedded clauses are not common.

```
      S       P     O    A        A                            A
(he) (charged) (it) (down) (with his head) (which is not the best thing to do)
                                   SCl–RelCl                    SCl–NFCl
```

```
       S        P        A     S    P       O            A
(and) (he) ('s recovered) (now) (so) (we) ('ll have) (the lineout) (after a couple of
conj                            conj
```

minutes of injury time) (ll. 73–6)

One of the most distinctive features of the grammar of unscripted commentary is the number of **deletions**. **Minor 'sentences'** are common – often the subject or predicator or both are omitted, leaving only the essential information. This happens most often when activity is at its height. It is appropriate in this variety since if all the clause elements were included it is likely that the overall structure would be very repetitive. By analysing the clause structure of a particular section of a commentary using a table, it is possible to see which elements are commonly omitted. There is often a marked difference between the deletions in a television and in a radio commentary.

Television (ll. 6–13)

Co conj	Sub conj	S	P	O/C	A
		the Italians	∅	∅	now
		∅	∅ calling	some variation	at the lineout
		∅	∅ moving	Number 8 Julian Gardner	up to the front
but		that	's	a decoy move for Pedroni	
		Ben Clarke	∅		through quickly
		∅	∅		through on Cuttitta
		∅	∅	good rucking	too by England
		the Italians again			up very quickly indeed
but		that	's	a lovely kick by Rob Andrew, forcing them to turn	
		you	saw	the problems	then
	that	Gerosa	faced		
	as	Johnson	sets	it	up

Commonly deleted elements here are the subject of the utterance and verb *to be*. The meaning is still clear despite the number of omissions – it would be quite straightforward to expand the grammatically incomplete utterances by inserting appropriate subjects and predicators. A commentary is describing a series of actions which exist: it would therefore be easy to use the *existential there* + *be* structure repeatedly. The minor 'sentences' help a commentator to avoid a repetitive style and save time.

Radio (ll. 51–8)

Co conj	Sub conj	S	P	O/C	A
and		Ben Clarke	snaffles	the ball	from this lineout
		it	comes		
				back	to Bracken
		Ø	sends	it	out to Andrew
		Andrew	puts	a kick	down towards the corner
		that	's	a very very good kick	again
		it	's rolling		right up to the Italian line
		Gerosa	slips		
		he	recovers		very quickly
but		Ø	can't get	his kick	in
		Johnson	picks	it	up
		all the Italians	are	off-side	
		the ball	's charged		down by Brian Moore

The radio commentary is far more complete than that of the televised version of the match. Perhaps because the radio listener is far more reliant on the commentator for details, a radio commentary needs to be more precise. It is also possible that the number of deletions will vary according to the speed of the action at the time and according to the style of the commentator.

The **verb tenses** in unscripted commentaries are distinctive. The **simple present** is used to describe actions as they are happening: *sets* (l. 13) and *tackles* (l. 28); *puts* (l. 53) and *comes* (l. 52). The **present progressive** is used to create a sense of ongoing movement: *getting* (l. 13); *beginning* (l. 79). The **simple past tense** is used in any reference to events that have just taken place. It is more likely to be found in the summative comments of the advisers: *needed* (l. 20) and *created* (l. 37); *was* (l. 63) and *had* (l. 67). The **present** or **past perfect** may also be used in the reflective sections of the commentary: *have held* (l. 23); *had drawn in* (l. 95).

There are few examples of **normal non-fluency features** in either commentary. **Voiced hesitations** are rarely heard. If they do occur, they are more likely to be in the advisers' summaries: *er* and *uh* (l. 45). Other examples of hesitancy are also rare in the official commentators' utterances, but may appear in the advisers' comments: **repetition** – *much uh better better angle* (l. 45); **false starts** – *and the the the the main feature* (l. 62); and unexpected **pauses** – *it would have been difficult for (.) the (.) Italian defender...* (ll. 65–6). The exceptional fluency of unscripted commentary is one of its distinctive features.

The **distinctive features** of unscripted commentary can be summarised as follows:

- The **audience** have expert knowledge so they are able to fill in the gaps left by the economic nature of the variety as a whole. While television viewers can rely on visual and linguistic clues to decode the event, radio listeners have only language.
- The discourse is **spontaneous** and so it has many of the features of informal conversation. However, there are also marked differences because commentaries have to

be **fluent** and **continuous**, unlike the casual, random nature of conversation.

- The **topic** is predefined and apart from asides in which a commentator may make connections with other things, the focus will be on the actions taking place.
- The **structure** is very precisely ordered. The commentary must: describe the process (particularly on radio where listeners rely on the commentator's linguistic re-creation of actions); create an appropriate background atmosphere; engage the audience's attention; and entertain with interpretation, comment and personal asides.
- **Turn-taking** is co-operative and orderly, as it is in an interview. The professional commentator will provide focused description of who is doing what where and the 'player-expert' will comment and summarise. Most turns end smoothly – each speaker picks up signals marking the end and takes over promptly. Overlaps occur infrequently and are minimal. Some timed pauses occur at the end of an adviser's turn when the commentator waits for the next sequence of events to develop. This is more likely to happen on television where the audience can watch the action; a complete silence on the radio, even for a few seconds, would cause problems for listeners. Radio commentators must therefore be even more fluent and sustained in their commentaries than television presenters.
- **Prosodic features** are used extensively to animate the commentary, particularly by the commentator. Pitch, pace, volume and variations in intonation patterns reflect the dynamics of the event. Stress and rhythm are used to enhance meaning – it is common to find strings of words with emphatic stress that is quite different from most other varieties of spoken language. Pauses tend to be used for emphasis, to punctuate utterances, when nothing of significance is happening, and for breathing. They rarely indicate hesitation. Good timing is very important. Advisers tend to be less fluent and less able to manipulate the range of prosodic features to create dramatic effects.
- The **lexis** is subject specific and technical. However, because unscripted commentaries are spontaneous, examples of informal conversational language are also common. Collocations may be technical or conversational. The variety is marked by its prominent use of proper nouns and its personal and idiosyncratic choice of lexis. Metaphorical language can also make commentaries very characteristic, enabling commentators to develop a recognisable personal style. Modification is common because it adds precise detail – radio commentaries require particularly well-focused descriptions and adverbials of place are common.
- The **grammar** is very distinctive. Grammatically incomplete utterances are common, although these will rarely be noticed in the speed and intensity of the action. The mood is usually declarative, but questions may be addressed to the other participant(s). This kind of interaction can make commentaries resemble informal conversation. Utterances rarely have marked themes – the subject and predicator tend to be placed at the front of the clause so that the actors and processes are clear. Clause structures are often simple or loosely co-ordinated, just as in informal conversation. The co-ordinating conjunction *and* is often used in the initial position as one turn moves smoothly into another – this enhances the audience's sense of a continuous speech turn. Where subordination is used, it rarely involves strings of embedded dependent clauses.

The most noticeable grammatical feature of unscripted commentaries is the number of deletions. Because the focus is on a description of actions which exist, commentators commonly use the *existential there* + *be* structure. To avoid repetition, the subject and predicator are often omitted, resulting in an unusually large number of minor 'sentences'. This is in line with the need to be economic, using as few words as possible to effectively convey the nature of the event. Radio commentaries often have fewer deletions than televised versions because their listeners cannot rely on visual clues to fill in the gaps. Simple present tense and the present progressive are used to describe the facts, creating a sense of immediacy; simple past and the present perfective are used to comment and give opinions.

- The variety can be recognised by an almost complete absence of **normal non-fluency markers**. The commentaries of less experienced speakers may be marked by voiced hesitations, false starts and repetitions, but professional commentators are exceptionally fluent.

10.5   What to look for in spoken language

The following checklist can be used to identify key features in transcripts of spoken language. There will not be examples of all the features listed in every extract, but the list can be used as a guide. The points made are general so discussion of specific examples will need to be adapted to take account of the particular context, participants and function in the discourse.

The following are helpful questions to ask.

Register

1   What is the **mode**? – spoken.
2   What is the **manner**? – the relationship between participants: formal or informal? personal or impersonal? status? dominant speaker? co-operative?
3   What is the **field**? – the lexis will reveal the kind of subject matter that forms the basis for the speech encounter.

Topic management

1   Is there **one clearly focused topic** or are there a number of apparently **random topics**?
2   How are the **topics chosen**? – directly related to the context (job interview, lecture)? related to the interests and experiences of the participants?
3   Are there any **topic shifts**? who introduces the new topics?
4   Do new topics emerge **logically** from previous topics or do they appear to be **unconnected**?
5   Are there any linguistic signals after an interruption where a speaker tries to **return to an earlier topic**?
6   How is the **end of a topic** marked?

Structure

1   Are there any examples of **adjacency pairs**? – questions and answers? greetings? a command and a response?
2   What kind of **opening** is used? – neutral? self-related comment? other-related comment? social greetings? hospitality tokens? vocatives to personalise the discourse?
3. How is the **turn-taking** organised? – dominant speaker? equally shared turns? latching on? overlaps? efficient recognition of linguistic and paralinguistic clues signalling the end of a turn?

4   What kinds of **speaker moves** are used in the main body of the discourse? – framing? initiating? focusing? supporting? challenging?

5   What kind of **closing** is used? – reference to something outside the speech encounter? repetition? delaying tactics? formulaic utterances? self- or other-related remarks?

Prosodic features

1   Do **intonation patterns** vary in order to convey the speaker's attitude? to mark the end of grammatical utterances? to distinguish between new and old information? to indicate the end of a turn?

2   How do the intonation patterns relate to the **semantics** of an utterance? – rising? (question); falling? (statement or completion); rising-falling? (reprimand or denial); falling-rising? (surprise or disbelief).

3   Does the **pitch** change to reflect the speaker's involvement in the discourse? – high? (excitement or enthusiasm); low? (formality or seriousness); midway? (everyday speech encounters).

4   Is **emphatic stress** used to highlight key words?

5   Does the **volume** change significantly to enhance the meaning of utterances? – 'forte'? 'piano'? 'cresc'? 'dimin'?

6   Does the **pace** change? – 'alleg'? 'lento'? 'accel'? 'rall'?

7   Does the **style of delivery** change? – 'stacc'? 'leg'?

8   What are the functions of the **pauses**? – to create emphasis? to dramatise an utterance? to mark hesitation? to allow the speaker to breathe? to make the speech encounter informal? to let the speaker search for a word? to mark the grammatical end of an utterance?

9   Is the transcript marked with any **vocal effects** or **paralinguistics**? how do these relate to the words actually spoken?

Lexis

1   Is the language **formal** or **informal**?

2   Is it **subject specific** or **general**?

3   Are there examples of **high-frequency** conversational clauses – *you know, I see, I mean*, and so on?

4   Are there any **colloquial idioms**? or **collocations**?

5   Is there any evidence of an **abbreviated code** based on shared knowledge or shared expertise?

6   Are there any **ambiguities**?

7   Is **modification** used to create an atmosphere?

Grammar

1   Are the **clause structures** simple? compound? complex? a mixture?

2   Are **loosely co-ordinated** clauses more common than **subordinated** ones?

3   Are there any **minor 'sentences'**? – which clause elements are omitted?

4   Are **phrases** complex or simple? – NPs? AdjPs? VPs? AdvPs? how do they relate to the topic and manner of the speech encounter?

5   Are **different grammatical modes** used to add variety? – direct speech? reported speech? quotations? changes in mood? changes in voice?

6   Are there any **grammatically inaccurate** or **incomplete utterances**? – do other participants show any awareness of these?

7   Are there any **marked themes**?

Normal non-fluency features

1 Are there any **overlaps** in the speech turns? – for how long do they last? what causes them? how do the participants respond? do the overlaps mark an intentional challenge, a supportive minimal vocalisation, or a misreading of linguistic clues?
2 Are there any **voiced hesitations**? – are they preventing interruptions? prolonging a turn? providing thinking time?
3 Are there any **false starts**? or **repetitions**?

Dealing with problems

1 Are there any **repairs**? – self-corrections? other corrections?
2 Are there any **topic loops**? – after a minimal response or a negative evaluation? which topic is reintroduced? why is it considered a safe topic?
3 Is the speaker aware of **listener responses**? – self-monitoring? use of direct address? use of questions requiring some kind of response? restating or rephrasing of points made?
4 Are there any **silences**? – lack of response to a question? failure to introduce new topic? utterances misheard?

Summary

An **analysis of spoken language** is central to any linguistic study because it is speech rather than writing that is dominant in society – it is at the centre of our daily lives and we deal instinctively with the demands of each spoken encounter as it arises. We all have a range of repertoires on which we can draw; and we are all experts, able to make decisions about the kinds of language appropriate for different people and different contexts.

There are many **varieties** of spoken language, all with their own distinctive features. However, it is possible to pinpoint some features that are common to most forms of spoken discourse. Where speech is spontaneous, even if the context is formal, there will be grammatical inaccuracies and incomplete utterances. In written language, these would be unacceptable – in speech, they often remain unnoticed. Because we all assimilate the 'rules' of spoken language from an early age, most speech encounters take place within a co-operative framework – turns are taken in an orderly way; participants find topics that reflect their shared interests; and a wide range of language is accepted as normal.

The **immediacy** of speech makes it an important social tool – it forms the basis for face-to-face interaction in both formal and informal contexts.

11 The language of newspapers

11.1   The nature of newspaper language

In the eighteenth century, newspapers were used by the government as a means of promoting their own interests. The structure and style were therefore formal. By the nineteenth century, however, what can be described as 'modern journalism' began with the appearance of newspapers still popular today: by 1829, *The Times* was very powerful; 1821 marked the first printing of the *Manchester Guardian*; later in the century, this was followed by the *Daily Mail* (1896); and at the beginning of the twentieth century, by the *Daily Express* (1900) and the *Daily Mirror* (1903). Newspaper reporting became more scandalous, and style and form changed to suit the new approaches. The British press became renowned for their distinctive headline styles and their personal and idiosyncratic reporting.

Today, there is much debate about what makes a good news story. Journalists and academics study newspaper reporting and find great variation in what different newspapers will print. Anything **unexpected** or **dramatic** is newsworthy and 'bad news is always good news' for the journalists and editors trying to meet tight deadlines and sell papers. Equally, **élite persons**, whether royalty, pop stars or politicians, make the front pages because many readers like to know about the lifestyles and the scandals of the rich and famous. Editors look for **relevance** in the stories they print, which means that the content must have a direct bearing on the people of Britain in some way: culturally, socially, politically and so on. Certain **élite nations** will receive more coverage too – we are more likely to read about America, for instance, than about a smaller country that has fewer cultural, social and political links with Britain. **Continuity** is important and newspapers like to be able to develop running coverage of an event. To make abstract issues like politics and economics more approachable, journalists try to **personalise** them: John Major is foregrounded, rather than his role as Prime Minister; the Princess of Wales is portrayed as an individual with ordinary emotions, rather than as a distant princess to whom the ordinary public cannot relate. The NEWS VALUES of a newspaper govern the kind of stories which editors print. Choices are ultimately made based on what will sell newspapers, both to readers and advertisers.

Newspapers are often divided into two main categories: **tabloid** and **broadsheet**. This is a very basic distinction and the terms mean different things to different people. In very general terms, a TABLOID paper is printed on A2-size paper, which is folded to A3; this is therefore smaller than the full spread of a BROADSHEET, which is printed on A1 and folded to A2. All the mass-circulation papers are tabloid. The divide between 'big' and 'small' papers goes further, however: broadsheet papers are also known as the **'serious'** or **'quality' press**; tabloid papers are known as the **'popular'** or **'gutter' press**.

The latter definitions go beyond the factual distinction of size and become judgemental and evaluative. Dealing in very general terms, the broadsheets provide information, while the tabloids provide sensation; the former aim for factual representation of the 'truth', while the latter package stories for their entertainment value. Table 11.1 breaks down some of the key linguistic and typographical differences between tabloids and broadsheets.

Table 11.1   Tabloid and broadsheet newspapers

Tabloids	*Broadsheets*
Headlines are typed in bold print and may extend across the whole page. They are often capitalised.	**Headlines** usually only extend over two columns; the print tends to be smaller. Front page headlines, however, are sometimes an exception.
Paragraphs are usually only a few lines long. Superstar Demi Moore's first marriage was illegal, it was revealed last night. *The Sunday Mirror* (3 December 1995)	**Paragraphs** are longer so the reader has to concentrate for longer periods of time. During 1985, a £16.5m project to computerise the Inland Revenue was abandoned. In 1993, the London Stock Exchange abandoned its Taurus automation scheme after spending £50m. The 17-year project to automate the Department of Social Security is likely to overrun its original budget by four times – an overspend equivalent to a penny on basic income tax. And only last Monday, it was reported that the £100m system designed to open the domestic electricity market to competition was unlikely to start on time in April 1998. *The Independent on Sunday* (3 December 1995)
The **typographical features** are very varied: the first paragraph uses larger print and is often bold; the second paragraph is slightly smaller; the third paragraph uses standard print size. Initial letters are usually large.	The **typographical features** are more standard. The same size of print is used throughout except for headlines, straplines and sub-headlines.
Punctuation is used sparingly. • Commas are often omitted after initial adverbials and between strings of adjectives. This avoids breaking up the text and complicating the reading process. Last night Jim 42 said he had always feared redundancy. • Inverted commas are used to mark direct speech and to highlight key words.	**Punctuation** is used traditionally and more formally than in tabloids. Dashes are less frequent. Kenneth Clarke's most curious reform in last week's Budget, the abolition of road tax on old cars, has thrown a spotlight on Parliament's most curious society: the House of Commons Classic Car Club. *The Independent on Sunday* (3 December 1995)

> It's a route more couples will have to follow because 'quickie' divorces are earmarked for abolition.

- Dashes mark parenthesis, which make the style quite informal and chatty.

> MPs are already looking forward to the intriguing possibility of a tussle between Clarke and Michael Heseltine – the driver of a Ford XR3i and a man who is chauffeur driven in his own Daimler – to inherit John Major's crown.
> *The Sunday Mirror* (3 December 1995)

Alliterative patterning is used to make the text more memorable.

> BARNES AND THE BRUNETTE
> Secret trysts with a Cutie from Carlsberg
> *The Sunday Mirror* (3 December 1995)

> Proof that the poor are poorer
> *The People* (3 December 1995)

Rhetorical patterning is more complex. Rhythmical effects are achieved through balanced phrases and antithesis.

> Out of sight, out of mind
> *The Independent on Sunday* (3 December 1995)

Sentence structure is often simple or compound, although one main and one subordinate clause is common.

- Long sentences are kept away from the beginning.

> Eastenders star Michael French has had an amazing bust-up on set.
> *The People* (3 December 1995)

- Paragraphs are usually composed of one or two sentences.
- Word order can be changed.

> Said the TV star, 'It's true.'

Sentence structure is varied to sustain the interest of the reader. Few paragraphs are of only one sentence.

> Whitehall cuts BSE research.
> (Simple sentence: S P O.)
> *The Independent on Sunday* (3 December 1995)

> The jobs of 15 scientists investigating the links between mad cow disease and Creutzfeldt-Jakob disease are to be axed because of a lack of Government funds.
> (A passive voice complex sentence: S P A with two embedded non-finite clause and adverbial clause of reason.)

Paragraphs can, however, be made up of only two or three sentences.

Co-ordinators in the initial position are common. These act as a bridge and sustain the narrative pace. Loosely co-ordinated sentences reflect speech patterns.

> And Lisa, 23, is hoping for success tomorrow. But now one enterprising business is en route for recovery.

Co-ordinators in the initial position are not common. Cohesion is created through referencing and lexical repetition rather than through conjunctions.

Adverbials are used at the start of sentence to change the focus and keep readers interested.

> Instead of walking up the aisle with Susan yesterday, her 28-year-old fiancé was banged-up in a cell.

Adverbials are used in a variety of positions, depending upon the emphasis most appropriate to the meaning.

Modifiers are common and very few nouns stand alone. Pre-modification is more common than post-modification.

- Modifiers are coined.

■ Wacko Jacko
■ sexpert

- Puns are common.

> YULE HATE IT: Joke card
> Outraged clergymen have condemned a joke Christmas card as 'sick and obscene'.
> *The People* (3 December 1995)

- Description is often vivid.

> *Lonely* Diana wrote a *poignant* letter to *love* slug James Hewitt.
> *The People* (3 December 1995)

■ *Chancellor Kenny 'Penny' Clarke*

(after only 1p was deducted from Income Tax in the November 1995 Budget).

Modifiers are used to provide accurate detail. Description is always precise.

■ treasury spokesman
■ quango bosses
■ public-sector statistics

Post-modification is as common as pre-modification.

> a Commons early day motion critical of violent toys the 1970s

> a bitter industrial dispute reminiscent of the 1970s

Lexis is often inventive and emphatic.

- The tone is informal and colloquialisms are common.

■ banged up
■ stitched up

- Compounds are created to attract attention.

■ boozed-up

Lexis is more specific, formal and re-strained. Vivid, dramatic lexis is not used merely to sensationalise.

■ the Bosnian Serb army commanders
■ the US-brokered peace deal

The **angle** adopted is usually human – news stories (political, economic, etc.) are directly linked to people and the ways in which they are affected by an event or issue. The tone is conversational and the approach is often sensational and dramatic. Individual ideas are not always developed and the order of points can seem illogical.

The **angle** adopted tends to be more factual. There is more likely to be evidence of research and a greater concern with accuracy. The tone is often restrained and controlled. Summaries are provided and topic sentences make the approach seem more precise.

Some newspapers can be easily classified in terms of 'tabloid' and 'broadsheet'. However, others, although tabloid in size, would object to being ranked as tabloids because of the wider connotations of this term. A third category, therefore, is useful: the **MIDDLE-MARKET PAPER**. These fall between tabloids and broadsheets: although adopting the A3 format, they would rebut any claims that their content was merely for entertainment or that they were interested only in scandal. It is also important to remember that the stylistic differences between tabloid and broadsheet newspapers are not always clear-cut – broadsheets do sometimes adopt the stylistic features typically associated with the tabloids.

Whether broadsheet, tabloid or middle-market paper, the **IDEOLOGY** of the owner and editor dictates the kinds of stories printed and the political or moral slant transmitted to the reader. The political leanings of a paper, however, may vary in degree according to the kind of story reported.

The style of the tabloid papers is distinctive, with its sensational approach and dominant front page headlines. Its power can be seen in the way it has affected even the broadsheets in small ways: they are now more likely to use puns and emotive language than they were in the past; their style is more like that of ordinary language. Even the regional and evening papers now adopt the style of the popular press for many of their reports.

Linguists are interested in the kinds of language different newspapers choose to attract their intended audience. Tabloids and broadsheets choose different stories to feature on their front pages; they select different angles to present their material; and they use different formats – column lengths vary, the balance of image and text is different, typefaces are different, and so on.

11.2 The function of newspaper language

Originally, newspapers were used by governments to promote certain political views. By the nineteenth century, they were used to convey news; while the twentieth-century newspaper now deals as much with entertainment as it does with information. Many newspapers of the 1990s are closer to magazines in the kinds of features and columns they regularly print. Although their function is **referential**, therefore, **entertainment** has become equally important in the battle to win readers.

Nevertheless, newspapers do convey **information** about everyday events that affect our daily lives. The breadth of the information they cover is very wide: international, national and local news; reviews of film, television, radio, books, music and art; sports events; financial matters; science; personal problems; and so on. Local newspapers act as **community bulletins**, providing information about local events and issues. Their focus is far more specific.

Newspapers can be **influential**: they can affect the way we think about international events and British politics by presenting issues in a certain way. The choice of words, the decisions about which facts to include and which to exclude, and the ranking of events on the front page all influence the reader. The editor of a newspaper will seek to present the world in a certain way so that the intended audience will identify with it.

Different types of people buy different types of papers. Broadsheets tend to be associated with educated professional people, while tabloids are associated with the traditional working class. The middle-market papers fall somewhere between the two. Within these broad categories, people may buy a particular paper because of its ideology, because of a journalist whose style they like, because certain features appear regularly, or because of the front page news, the cover price, or a competition. Although such breakdowns are very general and many readers will not fall neatly into a specific category, it is useful to bear these in mind when analysing a report from a particular paper.

11.3 Features of newspaper language

Analysis of newspapers involves a consideration of both **headlines** and **reporting styles** since these will both reveal much about the ideology and aims of an individual paper.

Headlines

There are three kinds of headlines:

- the main HEADLINE will be larger than the others and may occasionally be in colour to draw attention;
- the STRAPLINE or OVERLINE is the secondary headline that appears above the main one – it is used to provide extra information or to clarify the main headline;
- the SUB-HEADLINE follows the main headline, and qualifies or elaborates it.

Just as the selection of news items and the balance of photographs to text is different in a broadsheet and a tabloid, so are the headlines. While the broadsheets may aim for a **factual** interpretation of an event, the tabloids may look for **sensation**.

MPs rally to Ashdown

The Independent (6 February 1992)

IT'S PADDY PANTSDOWN

The Sun (6 February 1992)

Each of these headlines reports on the same event: the revelation that the politician Paddy Ashdown had had an affair with his secretary. The *Independent* considers the political results of this revelation and the headline reflects this. The *Sun*, on the other hand, approaches the issue from a quite different angle. It focuses on the more sordid side of the event, punning on Ashdown's name and the collocation 'caught with your pants down'. Such a variation in approach for the same story is typical of the difference between headlines of broadsheets and tabloids.

To catch a reader's attention, headlines need to be **simple**, **easily readable** and **appropriate** to the kind of paper in which they are printed. The choice of words for a headline is affected by the **ideas to be expressed**, the **kind of reader** associated with a paper and its HOUSE STYLE. Typographically, broadsheets and tabloids have quite different approaches. Tabloids frequently use capitalisation and colour to draw attention to a front page report: blue or purple print or white printed on a blue or purple background may be used for a royal headline, while the death of a famous person may be headlined in white print on a black background. Broadsheets, on the other hand, are much more conservative. They rarely use capitalisation, and colour is seen only occasionally for front page photographs.

The **lexis** chosen indicates something about the political persuasion of the newspaper and about the intended audience. By analysing **connotations** of the words chosen and the **point of view** conveyed, it is possible to come to conclusions about the aim of a report.

When the Conservative MP Stephen Milligan was found dead, for instance, different newspapers reported the event in different ways on 8 February 1994.

TORY MP FOUND DEAD IN STOCKINGS AND SUSPENDERS

John Kay and Mike Sullivan, *The Sun*

Fears of fresh scandal after senior party sources
talk of 'murder'

MP's death shocks Tories

Patrick Wintour, Duncan Campbell and Louise Jury, *The Guardian*

Nightmare for Major in tragedy of Tory high flier

MP'S MACABRE DEATH SCANDAL

Gordon Greig and Peter Burden, *The Daily Mail*

The *Sun* is interested in the strange circumstances surrounding the death: the sexual connotations of the *STOCKINGS AND SUSPENDERS* is juxtaposed with the formality of the noun phrase *TORY MP*. This creates a sensational tone which is designed to attract typical *Sun* readers. The *Guardian*, on the other hand, has a somewhat different focus. Its headline is not sensational; instead it informs the reader that the death *shocks* the Conservative Party. The strapline uses the abstract noun *scandal* but this only hints that something is strange about the MP's death. This suggestion is developed by the noun *murder* but remains unspecific. The focus is more political than in the *Sun*, as the strapline and headline highlight the response of the Conservative Party and the effect new scandal may have on its political standing. The *Daily Mail* falls between the two extremes: its headline uses both the adjective *MACABRE*, with its connotations of something gruesome, and the noun *SCANDAL*, but its strapline refers to John Major and to Milligan's career with the noun phrase *high flier*. The political issues are juxtaposed with the concept of a strange death, enabling this middle-market paper to provide its readers with both political information and sensation.

The **style** of headlines is important: they need to be **simple**, but must also create IMPACT. Broadsheets and tabloids aim to fulfil these criteria in very different ways. The headlines accompanying a broadsheet report will usually be informative and straightforward.

Three-day week for MPs

Anthony Bevins, *The Observer* (19 March 1995)

Heroin use soars in UK prisons

Ken Hyder, *The Observer* (19 March 1995)

A tabloid, however, will aim for a different kind of simplicity. Puns are common and headlines will often disrupt collocations. This gives the headlines a less formal tone and can suggest that the journalists are not being completely serious about the issue. On the other hand, the tabloids' informal approach and their emphasis on human interest stories can result in a very personal and emotive appeal to the readers.

THE BONK OF ENGLAND

Andrew Golden, *The Sunday Mirror* (19 March 1995)

Clinging to life, clinging to hope

Carole Malone, *The Sunday Express* (19 March 1995)

In the first example, the newspaper alters the well-known noun phrase the 'Bank of England' to discuss the secret affair of a top banker. The colloquial term *BONK* replaces the noun *bank* and thus changes the focus from a serious financial report to a sensational sex scandal. The second headline is typically emotive to match the emotive content of the report: a 4-year-old girl's battle with cancer. It uses parallelism to juxtapose the abstract nouns *life* and *hope*, which immediately attract the reader's attention. The repetition of the present participle *clinging* emphasises both the closeness of death and the power of the little girl and her family to fight it.

The **structure** of headlines is easily recognisable. Many are **noun phrases**.

$$\text{Slim hopes for the fat of the land}$$
$$\text{Adj} \quad \text{N} \quad \text{PrepP} \quad \text{PrepP}$$

with markers: m (Slim), h (hopes), q (for the fat of the land)

Robin McKie, *The Observer* (19 March 1995)

Spending bonus from cash machines
Verbal N — N — PrepP

with markers: m (Spending), h (bonus), q (from cash machines)

The Sunday Express (19 March 1995)

Headlines differ from everyday language because of the **omission** of many of the grammatical function words, copula verbs and auxiliaries. In the examples considered so far, for instance, determiners are deleted from almost all noun phrases. This is one of the characteristic features of headline writing, marking it out as a distinctive variety of English. The structure is often described as 'telegraphic'.

Some headlines are made up of a **simple sentence**.

(Sheen) (goes) (mad) (at orgy)
S — P — C — A

Dan Slater, *The Sunday Mirror* (19 March 1995)

(Part-time boom) (boosts) (jobless figures)
S — P — O

The Observer (19 March 1995)

Some headlines use the **passive voice** to focus the reader's attention on a particular element. By omitting the *by* + *agent*, readers can be left in suspense; and where information is uncertain, newspapers can avoid printing libellous statements.

World Cup matches 'fixed in the Far East'

John Sweeney, *The Observer* (19 March 1995)

Sewage blamed for fungal illness

Polly Ghazi, *The Observer* (19 March 1995)

A telegraphic style is again evident in each example here because the verb *to be* has been omitted. In the first headline, the passive voice is used because nothing has yet been proved and an investigation is under way. The change in word order allows the newspaper to attract attention to the noun phrase *World Cup matches* which would be in the object site of an active sentence. Having omitted the *by* + *agent*, the focus is on the fact that such important games have apparently had their scores fixed, rather than on the people responsible. The second example also uses the passive voice. It brings the noun *sewage*, the object of the active sentence, into the initial position and therefore draws attention to it.

Sometimes a headline can be **ambiguous** – it can have two meanings. Ambiguity can occur when a word could be interpreted differently depending on its word class; when the different connotations of a word alter the meaning; when word order is altered to make the headline concise; or when punctuation is omitted to prevent a headline from being too long. Sometimes the ambiguity created is purposeful, in others it is accidental.

LOCAL MAN FINDS PICASSO DRAWING IN SHED

10-YEAR-OLD SUSPENDED BY HEAD

DO YOU WANT A WOMAN VICAR?

Each of these examples demonstrates a different kind of ambiguity. The first ambiguity occurs in whether the word *DRAWING* is a verbal noun pre-modified by *PICASSO* or whether it is a present participle. The second depends upon the connotations of the verb *SUSPENDED*: it is used here as a subject specific term for a kind of punishment used by schools, but could be seen as denoting *dangling*. The abbreviation of *headmaster* or *headmistress* adds to the ambiguity because *HEAD* can be interpreted as the part of the body by which the child is dangled. In the third example, readers are being asked if they would mind having a female vicar. By changing the function of the nouns *WOMAN* and *VICAR*, however, the sentence means something quite different. If the noun *WOMAN* is seen as the head of the object noun phrase instead of as a noun modifier, and if the noun *VICAR* is described as a vocative instead of the head of the noun phrase, the headline appears to be offering a woman to a vicar.

Typically, tabloids are associated with headlines that are often informal in tone and which are not always serious. The *Sun* is renowned for outrageous headlines like 'FREDDIE STARR ATE MY HAMSTER'. Some examples, however, cause concern because they actively seek to persuade readers to react in a particular way. During the Falklands War, for instance, the informal tone of the front page headline 'GOTCHA' was censured as mindlessly jingoistic and inappropriate since it seemed to make light of the deaths of four hundred Argentinian sailors. Alliteration is common, often adding to the informality of tone. Broadsheets tend to be more conservative in their lexical choices, although they do sometimes use puns.

Reports

The way in which media reports are put together reflects the ideology of the paper as a whole. They give a particular view of events – information that is excluded can be as important as that which is included. In each case journalists and editors are making decisions about what their readers will see. Occasions when a newspaper does not report a certain event while others do, or when it does not report certain features of an event, are examples of **SELECTIVE PERCEPTION**. This is a form of **bias**. Some newspapers claim to be impartial, but by analysing the lexis and syntax it is possible to identify the ways in which a distinctive point of view is conveyed.

The reports in Figures 11.1–11.3 will be used to show how the lexis and syntax of news reporting can

• reflect whether a paper is a broadsheet or a tabloid:
• influence the reader.

Read through the text in each case before considering the points made below. The first two examples are taken from a 'News in Brief' column, while the third is a 'human interest' story.

Figure 11.1 Report 1

> 1 ## 7 kids nicked on school hol
>
> **SEVEN British youngsters accused of theft were arrested during a school trip**
> 5 **to Majorca.**
> **Five boys and two girls aged 13 to 15 were quizzed in Palma after items worth £200 went missing from a shop.**
> **They later rejoined their party from**
> 10 **Breckfield Comprehensive Liverpool. A judge will decide if further action is taken.**

The Sun (22 April 1994)

Figure 11.2 Report 2

> # Shoplifting arrests
>
> Seven teenagers from Breckfield
> 15 Comprehensive School in Liverpool were arrested for alleged shoplifting on a school trip in Majorca. Merseyside Police were waiting for reports from education officials before deciding if any action should
> 20 be taken when they got home.

The Independent (22 April 1994)

Figure 11.3 Report 3

> # *Pool tot is saved by pal Sam, 2*
>
> **By KIERON SAUNDERS**
>
> QUICK thinking two-year-old Sam Hart
> 25 saved his little pal from drowning yesterday.
> He watched in horror when Lee Austin, also two, fell into a murky garden pond.
> Sam ran and grabbed Lee's mum by the
> 30 hand and dragged her to the water, shouting "Lee's dirty, Lee's dirty."
> Caroline Austin, 32, did not realise anything was wrong until her son's coat floated to the top of the 12in-deep pool.
> 35 When she dragged Lee out he was blue and had stopped breathing.
> Sam's mum Helen, 29, a nurse, took over and revived the tot.
> Lee's dad Adrian, 33, of Ipswich,
> 40 Suffolk, said: "Sam's a little hero. My son owes his life to him."

The Sun (22 April 1994)

Lexis

The intended audience dictates the **lexical choices** that journalists make. Vocabulary may be **formal** or **informal**. Usually broadsheets will use formal lexis, while tabloids will use informal. In Report 1, the *Sun* uses the nouns *kids* and *hol* and the verb *nicked* (ll. 1–2), while the *Independent* chooses *teenagers* (l. 14) and the verbal noun *shoplifting* (l. 13). The latter is far more formal and avoids the chatty style of the tabloid. The informal tone of the popular paper's headline helps to create quite a different relationship with readers: while the broadsheet informs its reader of the facts, the tabloid indulges in up-to-date gossip. Despite this, it is important to recognise that Report 1 is not exclusively marked by the informality typically associated with tabloids. Although using a noun like *youngsters* (l. 3) and a verb like *quizzed* (l. 7), it also uses passives: *were arrested* (l. 4).

The way in which **participants** are **named** is an important means of distinguishing between tabloids and broadsheets. Nouns like *kids* (l. 1) and *youngsters* (l. 3) suggest innocent youth and the tone of the *Sun* report perhaps suggests that the event is no more than the result of high spirits. This is juxtaposed with the severe connotations of the noun *judge* (l. 11), which highlights the official response to the alleged shoplifting. In Report 2, the *Independent*, on the other hand, chooses the noun *teenagers* (l. 14), which suggests older and more responsible children who should be aware of the difference between right and wrong. Noun phrases like *Merseyside Police* (l. 17) and *education officials* (ll. 18–19) emphasise the gravity of the accusations. In each case, the report seems to take a particular point of view of the event, and this is conveyed through the lexical choices.

The **connotations** of words chosen are often interesting. In selecting the verb *quizzed* (l. 7) the *Sun* makes the formal questioning by the authorities seem less daunting. The inclusion of the past participle modifier *alleged* (l. 16) in the *Independent* report ensures that the newspaper cannot later be accused of misrepresenting the truth. In Report 1, the *Sun* avoids making libellous accusations by printing actual events: the children were arrested and questioned; items went missing.

Modifiers are used by both styles of paper, but tabloids tend to choose more emotive and sensational ones. The two sample 'News in Brief' stories need to be particularly concise and the modifiers used are therefore restricted. However, the use of modifiers in reports or articles is often distinctive. Tabloids tend to create a narrative style by using multiple modifiers. In Report 3, on the rescue of a little boy who had fallen into a garden pond, the *Sun* journalist aimed to create a narrative scene as the background to a domestic event.

	m	m	h			m	m	m	h
Quick thinking two-year-old Sam Hart (l. 24)					a murky garden pond (l. 28)				
	Adj	V	num	N		det	Adj	N	N

Tabloids regularly include details of age, appearance or location in parenthesis or apposition (separated from the rest of the clause by commas).

Lee's dad, Adrian, 33, of Ipswich, Suffolk (ll. 39–40)

A broadsheet journalist is more likely to select modifiers that provide key information or attitudes.

	m	h	q	
Seven teenagers from Breckfield Comprehensive School in Liverpool (ll. 14–15)				
	num	N	PrepP	PrepP

	m	h			h	q	
alleged shoplifting (l. 16)				reports from education officials (ll. 18–19)			
	V	Verbal N			N	PrepP	

Strings of modifiers seem excessive unless they actually contribute something to the report. Only where they are used to achieve precision are they effective. The broadsheet example in Report 2 provides the reader with factual detail.

Adverbials are used to add extra detail. They can answer questions like *how?*, *when?*, *where?*, *why?*, *what for?* These kinds of details are often used in broadsheets to provide accurate information and in tabloids to develop a sense of narrative. Because Report 3 has a narrative-like structure, it uses many adverbials: *When she dragged Lee out* (l. 35); *in horror* (l. 27); *by pal* (l. 22); *from drowning* (l. 25).

SELECTIVE PERCEPTION means that although reports might cover the same event, the information included may not be the same. Both 'News in Brief' reports here include the fact that seven pupils were involved and other factual details are the same. The *Sun*, however, then develops a more story-like approach by adding details of age and the value of the allegedly stolen items. The *Independent* deals with more factual information like the education reports which will play a part in the judge's decision whether to take the case further.

Grammar

The **grammar** of newspaper reports is said to vary quite markedly in tabloids and broadsheets. The former is said to use simple and compound sentences. Where subordinate clauses are used, they are kept reasonably short so that readers do not have to retain large amounts of information. Broadsheets, on the other hand, are said to use a wider variety of sentence structures. Paragraphs in a tabloid paper are rarely more than three sentences long and can be no more than one sentence in length; broadsheets, however, develop paragraphs more fully. These grammatical differences are not always clear-cut, however, since broadsheets now use features traditionally associated with tabloids. Linguists therefore need to be able to recognise both the distinctive grammatical features of tabloids and broadsheets, and any variations.

S · P · A
(Seven British youngsters accused of theft) (were arrested) (during a school
SCl-NFCl

trip. . .) (ll. 3–4, Report 1)

S · P · O
(Merseyside Police) (were waiting for) (reports from education officials) (before
SCl-NFCl

A
deciding if any action should be taken when they got home.) (ll. 17–20, Report 2)
SCl-ACl · SCl-ACl

The formality of the broadsheet style demands much more concentration on the part of the reader. The use of short simple and compound sentences enables the tabloids to develop a chatty approach, where it is appropriate.

In journalists' training manuals, reporters are advised to avoid cramming too many ideas into one sentence: a sentence should communicate no more than one idea or two connected ideas and should not exceed a maximum of thirty words. A successful report, however, will vary the type of sentence structure to retain readers' interest.

Style

There are several ways in which newspapers can reorder the material in their sentences to draw attention to certain elements. **Marked themes** bring clause elements other than the subject to the front of the sentence and thus gives them prominence. Use of the **passive voice** rather than the active also has this effect. In Report 1 from the *Sun*, the passive (l. 4) is used without the agent. In an active sentence the subject would have been the Majorcan police who arrested the school pupils. By using the passive voice, the children (the object of the active sentence) become the subject and therefore the focus of the sentence.

Newspapers use both **direct** and **indirect speech** – they can quote the exact words spoken by an individual or they can report the words spoken. By interweaving direct quotations, journalists can vividly recreate the personal experiences of ordinary people, and they can allow eminent people to voice their views accurately and directly without intervention. Tabloids often quote eminent people directly, to encourage a feeling that even the rich and famous are ultimately the same as their readers; they quote ordinary people to make their readers feel that they have a voice. Broadsheets tend to use direct quotation to add weight to their arguments, allowing people to prove their points in the words they wish to use. The use of quotation can also vary the pace of an article, making it more interesting for the reader. Formal speeches can be summarised so that the newsworthy points are highlighted. Interviews with ordinary people unaccustomed to speaking in public contexts can be tidied up, eliminating non-fluency markers.

Direct speech is made up of a QUOTING CLAUSE like *said the Prime Minister* or *the Prime Minister said* and a QUOTED CLAUSE which contains the actual words spoken.

> Lee's dad, Adrian, 33, of Ipswich, Suffolk, said: 'Sam's a little hero. . .' (ll. 39–40)
> [quoting clause]   [quoted clause]

Indirect speech can be recognised by the marker *that* which introduces the paraphrase of the actual words spoken. The clause introduced by *that* is called a REPORTED CLAUSE and it takes the form of a noun clause:

> $$ \overset{S}{\text{(Lee's dad, Adrian, 33, of Ipswich, Suffolk,)}} \overset{P}{\text{(said)}} \overset{O}{\text{(that Sam was a hero. . .)}} $$
>   [reported clause]

In most cases, it is possible to delete the marker *that*.

Sources

The **sources** of information are important in newspaper articles and provide another way to distinguish between tabloids and broadsheets. Often, while a quality paper will cite official sources (Parliament, the courts, the police, other emergency services) as the basis for their reports, tabloids will quote ordinary people with no real authority. Variations in sources can affect the credibility of any statements made.

Summary

All the features here help to indicate the point of view or ideology of a newspaper. By contrasting the approach of two or more reports, a linguist can come to conclusions about the intended audience and the house style of a paper.

It is very easy to stereotype broadsheet and tabloid newspapers by assuming that the characteristic features discussed here can always be found in every report. Linguistic analysis, however, has shown that these are generalisations: journalists adapt their approach to suit each report they write. They consider the target audience, the house style of the newspaper, and the effect they wish to create – linguistic analysis has to take account of this. Although the distinctive tabloid and broadsheet styles are useful as a starting point, it is important to remember that broadsheets can use characteristic features of tabloid style and vice versa.

The introductory paragraph of each report must capture the reader's attention. It should concentrate on exactly what has happened, summing it up in no more than twenty words. The rest of the report (the NEWS LEAD) will provide the necessary extra detail.

Action stories

Action stories often package news as entertainment – they create a story from dramatic incidents. Their structure is chronological and they tend to focus on the human results of an event. The introduction will establish what has happened; the news lead will develop the narrative chronologically; and the conclusion will often provide some kind of assessment or evaluation.

ACTIVITY 11.1

Read through the three versions of the action story in Figures 11.4–11.6, and comment on the distinctive linguistic and stylistic features of each report.

Figure 11.4 Report 1 (*DT*)

Girl frozen alive on her own doorstep

A TWO-year-old girl accidentally locked
5 outside her home for almost six hours in
sub-zero temperatures was "like a block of
ice" by the time she was found lying on her
front doorstep, doctors said.

Karlee Kosolofski had no heartbeat and
10 was nearly frozen when she arrived at
Plains Hospital in Regina, Saskatchewan,
on Monday and was still in a serious
condition the following day.

"She was practically dead," said John
15 Burgess, one of the doctors who revived
her. "It is just amazing to get a child of this
age who literally comes in like a block of
ice."

The girl apparently followed her father out
of the house when he left about 2.30 am to 20
begin work at a dairy in Regina, the capital
of the central Canadian province.

He did not notice Karlee following him,
wearing a coat and boots over her pyjamas.

She was trapped outside when the front 25
door swung shut and became locked behind
her. Her mother, Mrs Karrie Kosolofski
found her nearly six hours later in
temperatures of about −8F. An ambulance
took her to the hospital 30 miles away. 30

Dr Burgess said the girl's body
temperature had fallen to 58F. Surgeons
fought for more than three hours to bring
her temperature back up to normal. He
added. "It took nearly an hour and a half 35
for her heart to start beating."

Dr Joy Dobson said Karlee was in
intensive care with extensive frostbite to
her legs, one of which may have to be
amputated, although she was alert and 40
improving.

"She's definitely very strong, very happy
and very determined," her mother, Mrs
Karrie Kosolofski said. "Today we're just
really, really relieved." 45

The Daily Telegraph (3 March 1994)

Figure 11.5 Report 2 *(DM)*

THE ICE GIRL WHO CAME BACK FROM THE DEAD

A GIRL of two has astonished doctors by surviving freezing temperatures which left her 'like a block of ice'.

Karlee Kosolofski, above, was in night-gown, coat and boots when she wandered outside her Canadian prairie home and the door locked behind her.

For six hours, she was subjected to temperatures of −8F (−22C), plunging to −40C in 25mph winds.

When her mother Karrie realised she was missing and found her, Karlee's heart was still beating but her body temperature had fallen to 25 degrees (14C) from the normal 98.6 degrees.

'She was practically dead when she was brought into hospital,' said a doctor. 'Literally like a block of ice.'

Karlee was hooked up to a heart bypass machine for five hours as a medical team of 30 slowly tried to warm her body while avoiding damage to frozen tissues. Twice they had to use shock therapy to keep her heart beating.

Slowly, the girl came back to life. 'We've witnessed a miracle,' said Dr Joy Dobson at the Plains Health Centre in Regina.

It was too early to say how much permanent damage there would be, she said, and Karlee was in danger of losing her left leg to hypothermia. 'But we are hopeful,' she added.

Mrs Kosolofski, who lives in the Saskatchewan town of Rouleau, said: 'She's strong and very determined. We're just really, really relieved.'

The Daily Mail (3 March 1994)

Figure 11.6 Report 3 *(S)*

ICE-BLOCK KID

Karlee, 2, survives six hours locked out of home at −22°C

A GIRL of two who was frozen solid after being shut out of her home for six hours at minus 22°C has been brought back from the dead by doctors.

Tiny Karlee Kosolofski was like "a human ice cube" when she arrived at hospital. She had no heartbeat and her body temperature had fallen to 58°F.

It took medics almost an hour and a half to get her heart beating and three hours to bring her body temperature back to the normal 98.4°F.

Doctors are amazed the toddler is alive. They say no one is known to have survived such a low body temperature.

Karlee, wearing a coat and boots over pyjamas, followed her dad outdoors when he left for work at a dairy in Regina, Canada, at 2.30am.

He failed to spot her — and she was

From CAROLINE GRAHAM in New York

trapped when the front door slammed shut.

Mum Karrio found her lying on the doorstep six hours later. She was taken to hospital 30 miles away in Saskatchewan.

Doctor John Burgess, one of six medics who wrapped Karlee in blankets, said: "She was practically dead.

"It's amazing to get a child this age who literally comes in like a block of ice. She was frozen solid — like a human ice cube."

Karlee, who is in intensive care, has severe frostbite and her left leg may have to be amputated. But dad Robert said: "She's sitting up in bed, grinning away.

"She's no idea what she's been through but she knows from all the attention she's getting that she's a very special little girl."

Caroline Graham, *The Sun* (3 March 1994)

COMMENTARY

Many points can be raised from these three articles both about action stories and the distinctive features of broadsheets and tabloids. The following notes will address only the main issues – there are, however, many other valuable points which could be discussed.

The event has taken place in Canada and is therefore not necessarily of interest to British national dailies and their readers. However, the story is emotive because it involves a young child and it is basically a success story. It has all the elements of drama: life and death issues; extreme weather conditions; teams of doctors working against the odds; and a family having to come to terms with what this tragedy may mean in the long term.

All three articles cover the same basic facts: the age of the child; the temperatures outside; the length of time she spent on the doorstep; the child's clothing; and so on. The difference between the reports emerges in the way they treat their subject matter.

The **headlines** immediately demonstrate the variation in approach of a broadsheet, a middle-market tabloid and a popular tabloid. The *Telegraph* uses a straightforward, factual headline which is simple and yet still dramatic. It is a simple sentence in structure:

> S   P   A   A
> (Girl) (frozen) (alive) (on her own doorstep)

The prepositional phrase functioning as an adverbial highlights the fact that this took place at home, making the story more interesting. The headline is less dominant than those in the other papers and, in line with the paper's house style, it does not use capitalisation.

The *Sun* aims to attract attention and uses both a capitalised headline and an underlined sub-headline. It provides far more information than the *Telegraph*, aiming to catch the reader's interest. The colloquial noun *kid* is typical of the paper's chatty style and the use of parenthesis to give the child's age also contributes to the personal approach. By providing specific details like the age, the number of hours spent outside and the temperature, the paper hopes to arouse the reader's emotions. The headline is a noun phrase made up of a compound modifier and a noun:

> m   h
> ICE-BLOCK KID
> N   N   N

The sub-headline is a complex sentence:

> S   P   A   A
> (Karlee, 2,) (survives) (six hours) (locked out of home at $-22°C$)
>   SCl-NFCl

The use of the present tense creates a sense of immediacy, adding to the dramatic impact.

The *Daily Mail* falls between the styles of the broadsheet and tabloid. It is more emotive than the *Telegraph*, but less informal in tone than the *Sun*. It adapts the well-known noun phrase the 'ice maiden' by replacing the noun 'maiden' with the more appropriate noun *girl*. It is a noun phrase post-modified by a relative clause:

> m   m   h   q
> THE ICE GIRL WHO CAME BACK FROM THE DEAD
> det   N   N   RelCl

By using the resurrection image of coming back from the dead, the paper highlights the dramatic nature of the story.

Ideologically, these three papers are all right-wing. Since this action story is based on human interest, however, different political viewpoints will not substantially alter the way in which the story is told. The **intended audience** in each case is different: the *Telegraph* provides its readers with an informative rather than sensational account; the *Daily Mail* chooses more dramatic lexis, but its style is still quite formal; the *Sun* adopts a chatty, personal tone, encouraging its readers to become involved in the narrative by providing lots of direct quotation.

The broadsheet, the *Daily Telegraph*, uses **modifiers** which give the reader precise information:

    serious condition (ll. 12–13)   six hours (l. 5)   extensive frostbite (l. 38)
    [m] serious [h] condition — Adj N   [m] six [h] hours — num N   [m] extensive [h] frostbite — Adj N

The *Mail* also is quite restrained and many of its noun phrases are part of a medical lexical set:

    heart bypass machine (ll. 21–2)   medical team of 30 (l. 22)   shock therapy (l. 25)
    [m] heart [m] bypass [h] machine — N N N   [m] medical [h] team [q] of 30 — Adj N PrepP   [m] shock [h] therapy — N N

The *Sun* uses noun phrases in which the modifiers give the reader details about the child. They are emotive, but not particularly sensational:

    low body temperature (l. 19)   severe frostbite (ll. 35–6)
    [m] low [m] body [h] temperature — Adj N N   [m] severe [h] frostbite — Adj N

In each case here, the modifiers help to make the action story like a narrative.

The **naming of participants** and **places** tells the reader something about the nature of broadsheets and tabloids. All three papers use proper nouns to give the story a concrete setting: the location is marked by the proper noun *Canada* and the adjective *Canadian* to ensure that readers know where *Regina* and *Saskatchewan* are. The parents are named in different ways by each paper: the *Telegraph* uses the formal *Mrs Karrie Kosolofski* (ll. 43–4); the *Daily Mail* uses the noun phrase *her mother Karrie* (l. 14) and the more formal *Mrs Kosolofski* (l. 33); the *Sun* is more informal using the noun phrases *Mum Karrie* (l. 26) and *dad Robert* (l. 37), trying to draw the reader in by making the family seem familiar. The child is introduced in each report by a general noun phrase, *A two-year-old girl* (l. 4, *DT*) and *A girl of two* (l. 4, *DM* and l. 4, *S*), and is then referred to formally as *Karlee Kosolofski* and familiarly as *Karlee*. The *Sun*, however, aims to make the little girl seem more vulnerable by describing her using the colloquial nouns *kid* (l. 1) and *toddler* (l. 17) and the modifier *tiny* (l. 19). These homely terms are juxtaposed with the drama of the incident. The doctors are the other participants and they are referred to formally using their full names and titles: *Doctor John Burgess* (*S*) and *Dr Joy Dobson* (*DT*, *DM*). This form of address gives the reader a sense of their authority.

The **connotations** of words add to the effects created. The lexis of the *Telegraph* is quite formal and therefore does not rely on wider associations of individual words to create a sense of drama. By choosing a verb like *astonished* (l. 4) in its opening paragraph, the *Daily Mail* emphasises that the story will be about something unusual. The *Sun*'s use of the verb *amazed* (l. 17), typographically highlighted by the use of italics, also suggests an extraordinary event. Both tabloids draw on religious images: the connotations of *witnessed a miracle* (ll. 26–7) link the *Mail*'s report anaphorically with its headline; the *Sun* uses *brought back from the dead* (ll. 7–8) with its implicit references to the story of Jesus and Lazarus (John 11:1–44). The *Mail*'s choices of the phrasal verb *hooked up* (l. 21) and the prepositional verb *subjected to* (l. 11) suggest the young girl's helplessness.

The **adverbials** in the three reports are quite similar, many providing information about the length of time the child spent outside and the place. The *Telegraph* uses many adverbs, however, to create an atmospheric narrative: *accidentally* (l. 4), *nearly* (l. 10), *literally* (l. 17), *apparently* (l. 19).

As a 'narrative' rather than a theoretical political or economical report, the **grammar** of all three reports is reasonably similar. Most paragraphs are short and many are made up of only one sentence.

        S   P   C   A
(Tiny Karlee Kosolofski) (was) (like a 'human ice cube') (when she arrived. . .)
                                                                SCl–ACl

                                                                   (ll. 9–10, *S*)

                              A   A
(When her mother Karrie realised she was missing) (and) (found her)
SCl–ACl   SCl–NCl   conj SCl–ACl
        S   P   A   P   S   P
(Karlee's heart) (was) (still) (beating) (but) (her body temperature) (had fallen) (to
                       aux   lex   conj

  A
25 degrees. . .) (ll. 14–17, *DM*)

           S   P   O   P   C   A
(Karlee Kosolofski) (had) (no heartbeat) (and) (was) (nearly frozen) (when she
                                                  conj   SCl–ACl

                                                               A   P
arrived at Plains Hospital in Regina, Saskatchewan) (on Monday) (and) (was)
                                                                             conj

  A   C   A
(still) (in a serious condition) (on the following day). (ll. 9–13, *DT*)

Each of the examples here places a different demand upon the reader's concentration. Although tabloids are typically associated with simple grammatical structures, there is evidence of subordination in all three reports here. Nevertheless, sentences tend to be longer, with more embedded clauses, in the broadsheet report.

Marked themes are used to dramatise the narrative of the action story: *For six hours* (l. 11) and *slowly* (l. 23) in the *Daily Mail*, for instance. It is usual to see conjunctions in the initial position in tabloids, and the *Sun* uses *But dad Robert said. . .* (l. 37).

The **passive voice** is used to suggest that no one can really be blamed for this accident. The *Telegraph* uses the passive in the opening line although the pronoun *who* and the verb *to be* are elided in the post-modifying relative clause *locked outside her home* (ll. 4–5). Similarly the *Sun* uses the passive voice in the verb phrase *was trapped* (ll. 24–5). The *Daily Mail* uses the passive to refocus some sentences so that *Karlee* can be the subject:

      S   P   S   P   O
(Karlee) (was hooked up) (l. 21)   '(A medical team) (hooked up) (Karlee). . .'
            PASSIVE   ACTIVE

This gives Karlee more prominence and therefore enhances the drama of the story.

Direct speech is important in this kind of story because it adds a personal feeling to the drama. All three reports quote the doctors and their exact words give authority to the statements. The newspapers choose very similar parts of the interviews to quote and adjective phrases like *practically dead* and noun phrases like *block of ice* and *human ice cube* are very dramatic. Quoting clauses are often inverted in tabloids, resulting in *said Dr Joy Dobson* (l. 27, *DM*). All three reports conclude with the words of the parents and this arouses the emotions of the readers, who may be parents themselves.

Action stories have a chronological structure and this is apparent here. Having established the main participant and the dramatic event in the first paragraph, each report then tells the story from beginning to end.

Although broadsheet, middle-market and tabloid newspapers are different in their approaches to reporting, because this is a human interest story differences are not as marked as they would be for a political or economic issue.

Statement and opinion stories

Statement and opinion stories deal with issues rather than just narrative. They attempt to summarise an argument and provide readers with key information. Although a report may be triggered off by a specific event, this will only be the springboard for a wider consideration of related issues. In other words, they give readers more than just a chronological human interest story.

The introductory paragraph usually presents the reader with the most important news points and supporting direct quotation where appropriate. The rest of the report summarises further points and develops the argument, while the conclusion draws all the points together.

Running stories

Journalists make the most of an ongoing story because they hope that once their readers are interested they will continue to buy the newspaper to keep up to date with new findings. Tabloids particularly will sensationalise and dramatise stories to keep old readers and attract new ones.

A running story requires the journalist to report on new information and recap on what has happened so far. This ensures that readers can keep up to date and understand any new developments in context.

ACTIVITY 11.3

Typically, broadsheet readers are loyal and will probably buy the same paper every day; tabloid readers are more likely to choose the paper which attracts them because of its headline and other front page information (advertisements for features inside; competitions; photographs and so on). Tabloids, therefore, often use a dominant headline and photographs, only including part of the report. Readers have to turn to inside pages if they wish to finish reading. This means that the headlines, photographs and opening of a report must capture reader interest, persuading them to continue reading on the inside pages. Broadsheets, on the other hand, have more space and can therefore develop several stories in full. Despite the additional space, however, some reports are continued on the inside pages and readers are directed to the appropriate page and column.

Each of the three reports in Figures 11.7–11.9 was printed on the front page of the relevant paper. They contain new information on the running story of a serial murderer. The newspapers approach the content in different ways.

Read through the reports and comment on the distinctive features of each.

Figure 11.7 Report 1 (*I*)

Gloucester garden yields grisly secrets to police

PETER DUNN and
IAN MACKINNON

CROMWELL STREET in Gloucester is a narrow inner city thoroughfare of slab-fronted Victorian brick terraces which have seen better days and are facing a dismal future. In the long back garden of number 25, lugubrious policemen with shovels have unearthed three bodies.

Yesterday, Frederick West, who lives at number 25, was charged with murdering two women whose bodies were found on Tuesday. He is in custody and has already been charged with the murder of his daughter Heather. Her body was found on Saturday.

One body has yet to be identified, the other was named yesterday as Shirley Robinson, 18, a former lodger. Police said she was heavily pregnant when she died.

Like that other infamous street, Rillington Place (home of John Christie, where four bodies were found in the house and two buried in the garden in the 1950s), Cromwell Street was yesterday heading from mundane obscurity to infamy and notoriety.

Parkers, estate agents of Gloucester, already fear the worst over a basement flat they have on the market for £22,500, two doors up from number 25. "I don't think this is going to help, really," a spokesman said.

Loud hammering could be heard all day at the rear of number 25, three storeys of semi-detached ochre pebble-dash with freshly painted green windows.

Next door neighbour but one, Charlie Keen, a retired gardener who has lived in Cromwell Street for 32 years, has known the West family for two decades. He said: "Fred would do anything for you. If anyone went to him for a tap-washer, a bit of concrete to put down or roofing, anything, he'd do it. About a month ago I was mending my front window and said, 'you haven't got a bit of putty, have you Fred?'. He said, 'give me an hour,' and came back with a bloody great bucket of the stuff.

"His wife's got a bit of a temper, though that's not for me to say. Fred's a happy-go-lucky man, thought the world of his kids. I can't make it out myself. He's the last person in the world ..." and here Mr Keen's voice trailed away.

"I never heard digging or anything over there," he added. "I knew he put a patio in and there's lots of fir trees in the back. He planted them, he said, as a screen for the kids."

The police activity across the street confirmed the worst fears of Helen, 70, and Les, 73, who have lived close to Cromwell Street all their lives.

"It used to be a nice area," Helen said. "Very *sedate*. There'd be people sitting on their doorsteps on warm evenings and they'd never draw their curtains so you could see their rooms looking perfect and the gardens would be full of flowers.

"When we got our house in Berkeley Street all we used to get down there was the pigs and cows and lambs going to the co-op slaughter house. Not any more. You get all types in them houses now. I wouldn't walk round here at night. It's all gone, even the park down the road where the old people walk. A friend of mine had a sovereign on a chain and this chap ripped the whole lot off and fled with it."

Next door to number 25 the little Seventh Day Adventist church — brick-built with kick-proof glass panel windows — expects business as usual on Saturday. Pastor Ian Lorek is trying not to read too much into the constabulary's spadework across the fence. "It's very sad and unfortunate, not just for the church but for the whole of Gloucester, isn't it?" he said.

A notice outside the church says: "Is there hope for our world? Threatened by pollution, disease, war, terrorism ... what next?"

Peter Dunn and Ian MacKinnon, *The Independent* (3 March 1994)

Figure 11.8 Report 2 (*S*)

PREGNANT LESBIAN IS HORROR GARDEN VICTIM

By ANDREW PARKER

ONE of the bodies dug up from Fred West's garden of horror is that of his pregnant lover, it was revealed last night.

Builder West started an affair with lesbian Shirley Robinson, 18, after she moved into a bedsit in his Victorian semi.

Blonde former tenant Liz Brewer said Shirley suddenly vanished days before her baby was due.

One of two other bodies found by police may also be a lodger — a mystery lesbian friend of Shirley.

West, 52, was charged yesterday with murdering Shirley and the other woman. He is already accused of murdering his 16-year-old daughter Heather, whose body was the first dug up behind 25 Cromwell Street, Gloucester.

Police are searching for more bodies in the 40ft by 15ft garden.

Liz, 33, said detectives told her the remains of Shirley and her unborn baby are being studied by forensic experts. She believes bubbly Shirley and her friend died in May 1978, nine years before Heather disappeared.

Mum-of-four Liz said she moved in on the top floor of the three-storey house to find Shirley had been in the pokey room below for a year. Liz said: "She was obviously pregnant and admitted quite openly that Fred

Continued on Page Five

Andrew Parker, *The Sun* (3 March 1994)

Figure 11.9 Report 3 (*DM*)

1 ## Father faces new murder charges

DEATH HOUSE: HORROR GROWS

5

POLICE are urgently trying to trace the first wife of builder Frederick West, the man in the 'Garden of 10 death' case.

They have discovered she has not been in touch with her sister since the marriage broke up more than 20 years ago.

15 The search was stepped up after West was charged yesterday with murdering two women whose bodies were found in the garden of his Gloucester home.

20 He had already been accused of killing his daughter Heather, 16, who was also buried there. West married Catherine Costello in 1962 but by 1970 their marriage had hit trouble. 25 Relatives and neighbours were told

By PETER ROSE

Catherine had run off with another man, leaving West with their two daughters.

Mrs West's sister Isabella Prentice, who lives in Northampton, has been 30 questioned by detectives but told them she has not heard from Catherine for more than 20 years.

Fears for Catherine West grew as police said they believed one of the 35 bodies was 18-year-old Shirley Robinson, who lodged with West and his second wife in the early 1970s.

Though she was a lesbian, Miss Robinson was said to have been keen 40 to have a child and was some seven months pregnant when she died. The second body is that of a woman in her early 20s. She is believed to have been Miss Robinson's lesbian lover, who 45

Turn to Page 15, Col. 1

Peter Rose, *The Daily Mail* (3 March 1994)

COMMENTARY

The three articles here take very different approaches to the same information. The middle-market paper (*Daily Mail*) and the popular tabloid (*Sun*) are quite similar in approach and the styles of reporting adopted are typical of the house style of each. The *Independent* is different from the tabloids here; but also its approach is unusual for the front page of a broadsheet. The tone is noticeably different from the factual accounts readers associate with broadsheet reporting – rather than straight facts, the journalists purposefully adopt a narrative style and tone.

The *Independent*'s **headline** uses phonological patterning in the alliteration of the phoneme /g/. The reader's attention is also drawn by the use of personification: the garden is seen as giving up its secrets to the police. The connotations of the verb *yields* suggest a surrender or submission as the garden is forced to reveal what it has hidden for so long. The impact here is dramatic, reminding the reader of modern horror stories. The headline and report demonstrate how broadsheet newspapers can use approaches typically associated with the tabloids for effect. In **structure**, the headline is a simple sentence:

> $\overset{S}{\text{(Gloucester garden)}} \overset{P}{\text{(yields)}} \overset{Od}{\text{(grisly secrets)}} \overset{Oi}{\text{(to police)}}$

The use of modifiers creates a narrative feel to the report and is quite unlike most broadsheet headlines, which tend to use modifiers only for accuracy or precision.

The **report** continues the narrative style in its very descriptive first paragraph. **Modifiers** are used to create the scene and some of the noun phrases are very long:

> $\underset{\text{det}}{\text{a}} \overset{m}{\underset{\text{Adj}}{\text{narrow}}} \overset{m}{\underset{\text{Adj}}{\text{(inner city)}}} \overset{m}{\underset{\text{N}}{\text{thoroughfare}}} \overset{h}{} \text{of} \overset{q}{\underset{\text{PrepP}}{\text{slab-fronted Victorian brick terraces}}}$ (ll. 4–7)

> $\overset{m}{\underset{\text{num}}{\text{three}}} \overset{h}{\underset{\text{N}}{\text{storeys}}} \overset{q}{\underset{\text{PrepP}}{\text{of}}} \text{semi-detached ochre pebble-dash with} \underset{\text{PrepP}}{\text{freshly painted green}}$
> windows (ll. 52–5)

In each example here the prepositional phrase itself contains a string of pre-modifiers, and in the second example the qualifier is itself also post-modified by another prepositional phrase. This contributes to the literary style developed by the reporters. Tabloid newspapers commonly use strings of modifiers, but the effect created here is quite different because the modifiers chosen are not sensational. An adjective like *lugubrious* (l. 11) denotes a mournful, dismal state of mind and by using this very literary modifier to describe the policemen at work, the journalists succeed in establishing an atmosphere appropriate to a horror story.

Having set the scene, the report then fulfils the criteria of a 'running' story by providing a brief summary of events to date in paragraphs two and three. Factual information, the names and ages of victims and the fact that one of the most recently discovered bodies was pregnant reminds the reader that this is a news report – that it is reality and not fiction. The style in this section is quite different from the almost literary approach in much of the rest of the report. Here it is straightforward and unemotive, merely recording the facts as they stand.

The journalists draw a parallel with another infamous serial murder case of the 1950s and provide an explanation in parenthesis for any readers who do not know about the case. The prepositional phrase *Like that other infamous street* (l. 32–3) functions as an adverbial comparing the present unresolved situation to a past one. This is not a necessary part of the news, but allows the reporters once again to dramatise the present event.

The reader is reminded of the ordinary place in which all this has happened by the introduction of the noun phrase *estate agents* (l. 42). With their reputation for mixing fact and fiction, they seem strangely appropriate in this article which also seems to mix reality and narrative. It forces the reader to remember that this is an ordinary English town, not a Stephen King novel. Proper nouns like *Berkeley Street* (l. 109) and *Cromwell Street* (l. 3) give the report its basis in real life – these are real streets with everyday names which can be found in all kinds of British towns.

This sense of the mundane is further highlighted by the **naming of participants**. The people named are ordinary, and no titles or roles are recorded for most of them: *Shirley Robinson* (ll. 27–8), *Charlie Keen* (l. 57). Some are named almost informally: *Helen* (l. 94) and *Les* (l. 95) – they seem like the local people of any community. The man who has been charged with these murders, however, is named in two different ways: to the journalists writing about his crimes, he is *Frederick West* (ll. 14–15) – he is named formally, but is not credited with the title 'Mr' as though undeserving of it; to his old neighbours, he is *Fred* (ll. 62, 71) – this informal abbreviation marks him not as a monster but as a friend, and is in direct contrast to the nature of the crimes he is alleged to have committed.

The **sentence structure** is indicative of narrative prose – it is very varied. A mixture of simple, compound and complex sentences helps to maintain the readers' interest, drawing them into the world of the report. There are few very complicated sentences, however, and this is not typical of broadsheet reporting.

S   P   A
(Her body) (was found) (on Saturday)   Simple (ll. 22–4)

S   P   O   S   P
(A friend of mine) (had) (a sovereign on a chain) (and) (this chap) (ripped) (the

O   A   P   A
whole lot) (off) (and) (fled) (with it)   Compound (ll. 119–23)

A   S   P   O
(Yesterday,) (FW, who lives at number 25,) (was charged with) (murdering two
               SCl–RelCl   SCl–NFCl

women whose bodies were found on Tuesday)   Complex (ll. 14–19)
      SCl–RelCl

In several places, **marked themes** are used to create a particular focus for the reader. In the third example above, the adverb of time *Yesterday* (l. 14) marks current developments in the investigation. Similarly an adverbial is used in the prepositional phrase *Like that other infamous street* (ll. 32–3) to draw an appropriate dramatic comparison. The **passive voice** is also used to reorder elements where the result will be more dramatic. In the sentence beginning *Yesterday Frederick West...was charged* (ll. 14–16), the use of the passive brings the object of the active sentence, *Frederick West*, to the initial position, thus giving it prominence. A similar effect is achieved in the paragraph beginning *One body...was named* (ll. 25–7).

Perhaps the most unusual feature for a broadsheet is the amount of **direct speech** used. This varies the pace of the report and contributes to the 'real life' atmosphere the journalists aim to create. Neighbours are cited at length, creating quite a different view of Frederick West: he is a friendly local man, not a manic murderer.

Much of the direct speech is very informal. Nouns like *kids* (l. 80) and the abbreviation of *Frederick* to *Fred* (ll. 62, 71) mark the speech as everyday conversation, quite different from the literary style of the article itself. The noun phrases used in the quotations are also quite different to the descriptive approach of the report.

m   m   m   h   q
a bloody great bucket of the stuff (ll. 73–4)
det   Adj   Adj   N   PrepP

Here the colloquial use of the adjective *bloody* as a modifier and the noun *stuff* as a general reference contrast with the formal use of language by the journalists. Many of the linguistic features here are commonly associated with informal conversation: non-agreement of subject and verb (*there was the pigs and cows*, ll. 110–11); phrasal verbs (*make...out*, l. 80); and non-standard use of demonstrative determiners (*them houses*, l. 115). Their use here emphasises that this is real life and that Frederick West was apparently a neighbour like any other.

Clichés like *He's the last person in the world...* (ll. 81–2) and *Fred would do anything for you...* (ll. 62–3) juxtapose the ordinary with the extraordinary. There is also an implicit irony in the fact that neighbours could always get some concrete from Frederick West – from a man who was allegedly burying his victims in the concrete of new floors and a patio.

The journalists end with a reference to the local church and its notice. The rhetorical question *what next?* (l. 143) emphasises the irony of this ordinary town becoming front page news overnight: Frederick West is the most immediate threat to our faith in mankind. The whole report has highlighted how deceptive appearances can be – Cromwell Street, Frederick West, the report itself, all have unexpected depths.

The *Sun* and the *Daily Mail* treat the news in a very different way, both reporting on the running story in a typical tabloid style. The **headlines** immediately mark out the approach of each paper. As a popular tabloid, the *Sun* sensationalises the whole thing. Its headline dominates the page and the juxtaposition of modifier and head word in the noun phrase *PREGNANT LESBIAN* is designed to shock. The noun phrase *HORROR GARDEN VICTIM* is also typical of the dramatic way in which the headline seeks to highlight code words. The use of a simple sentence makes the headline emphatic:

> S P C
> (PREGNANT LESBIAN) (IS) (HORROR GARDEN VICTIM)

The use of the adjective *exclusive* is typical of the drive to attract readers on a day-to-day basis.

The *Daily Mail* uses the same kind of shorthand in its main headline. Because of the need to be concise and dramatic, noun phrases juxtapose unexpected words: *DEATH HOUSE*. The headline is once again a simple sentence – the effect here is striking because the abstract noun *HORROR* is almost personified, while the use of the simple present tense *GROWS* perhaps suggests that the horror is far from over. The *Mail*'s strapline arouses emotions in another way: by describing West using the noun *Father*, the reader is reminded that this man is a parent who should be protecting his children.

In line with a 'running' story, both reports fill in relevant details from previous reports, but then focus in different ways on the current material. The *Sun* is typically informal in its **relationship with its readers**. Noun phrases provide details that may seem more appropriate for gossip over the garden fence:

> m m h h
> Blonde (former tenant) Liz Brewer (ll. 21–2, *S*)
> Adj Adj N N

> m h
> Mum-of-four Liz (l. 49, *S*)
> N num N

> m h
> bubbly Shirley (ll. 45–6, *S*)
> Adj N

> m m m h q
> a mystery lesbian friend of Shirley (ll. 27–8, *S*)
> det N Adj N PrepP

The first two examples use two noun phrases in apposition, allowing journalists to convey a lot of information concisely.

There are many examples of lexis that is quite informal: adjectives like *pokey*

(l. 53) and abbreviations like *semi* (l. 20). The *Daily Mail* on the other hand, is far more restrained in its reporting style. Few modifiers are used except where they provide precise detail like age or length of pregnancy. This is typical of a middle-market newspaper which does not aim to be as sensational as the popular press.

Sentence structure is also different in each: the *Sun* uses complex sentences, but they are not long and do not have sequences of dependent clauses; the *Mail*, although not as varied as a broadsheet, does demand more of the reader.

     S   P   O   A
(Builder West) (started) (an affair with lesbian SR, 18,) (after she moved into a
                                            SCl–ACl
bedsit. . .) (ll. 15–19, *S*)

     S   P   O
(They) (have discovered) (she has not been in touch with her sister since the
                          SCl–NCl   SCl–ACl
marriage broke up more than twenty years ago). (ll. 11–14, *DM*)

Each report only uses one **marked theme**: the *Sun* aims for dramatic impact in its first sentence by foregrounding the object of the sentence *One of the bodies...* (ll. 7–8, *S*); the *Daily Mail* also creates impact by foregrounding the subordinate adverbial clause *Though she was a lesbian...* (l. 39, *DM*). It is significant that the middle-market paper waits until the last front page paragraph to include this information, while the popular newspaper uses it in a dominating headline.

The *Mail* does not use any **direct speech** and the resulting report is very much like a summary of events so far. The *Sun*, however, concludes its front page with a quotation from a former tenant of Frederick West. This is itself dramatic since she has 'lived to tell the tale...'.

The **style** of the *Mail* is far more formal than the *Sun*, but is quite different from the narrative approach of the *Independent*. The three accounts here take the same information and treat it in very different ways. The broadsheet aims to emphasise the irony of the 'ordinary man who is a monster' and uses a narrative, literary style to subtly remind the reader that life can be as strange and horrific as the popular horror stories which are consumed by so many. The *Mail* adopts a factual approach, focusing on fears for West's missing first wife – thus emphasising that the horror is not yet over. The *Sun* aims for sensationalism by concentrating on the fact that one of the dead was a pregnant lesbian. The report bases much of its content on the words of a former tenant – its source is therefore an ordinary woman and the overall tone is gossipy.

11.5 What to look for in newspapers

The following checklist can be used to identify key features in examples of different kinds of newspaper reporting. There will not be examples of all the features listed in every report, but the list can be used as a guide. The points made are general so discussion of specific examples will need to be adapted to take account of the specific context, intended audience and purpose in the given discourse.

The following are helpful questions to ask.

Register

1   What is the **mode**? – written.
2   What is the **manner**? – the relationship between the participants (journalist and

reader): formal or informal? ideology? function (to inform, persuade, entertain, and so on)?

3   What is the **field**? – the subject matter and the journalist's approach to it will govern the particular kind of newspaper language used.

Lexis

Headlines

1   What is noticeable about the **style**? – simple? easily readable? appropriate? impact created?
2   What are the **connotations** of words chosen?
3   What kinds of **modifiers** are used?
4   What **point of view** or **ideology** is conveyed?

Reports

1   Are the words chosen **formal** or **informal**?
2   Are the **modifiers** used to express precise detail or for making the report emotive or sensational?
3   How are the **participants named**? – use of titles? use of Christian names or surnames? use of abbreviated, familiar names?
4   What are the **connotations** of words? – nouns: description of people and things and the associations that will be picked up by readers? verbs: description of actions and processes and the associations that will be picked up by readers?
5   What kinds of **adverbials** are used? – time? place? manner?

Grammar

Headlines

1   What is the **structure**? – NP? simple/compound/complex sentence?
2   Do the **straplines** and **subheadings** explain or qualify the main headline?
3   Is the **passive voice** used?
4   Is there any **ambiguity**? – intentional to create humorous tone? accidental?

Reports

1   Is the **sentence structure** varied? – simple/compound/complex? variety?
2   Is the **passive voice** used with or without an agent?
3   Is there any **direct speech**? – ordinary or authoritative speaker? formal or informal tone? adding weight to argument or giving ordinary people's views? variation in pace?
4   Is there any **indirect speech**? – summary of formal speech? paraphrase to make speaker's response more fluent?

Metaphorical language

1   Do any **metaphors/images** help to establish a narrative atmosphere? make the report more dramatic? make abstract issues more concrete?
2   Is there any **repetition**? – emphasis on key words/phrases/clauses, making headlines and reports more dramatic or notable?

3 Are there any **puns**? – used to attract attention to a report? humorous? clever? informal/colloquial?
4 Is the **focus** of any sentence altered by using **marked themes** to highlight a clause element other than the subject in the initial position?
5 Is the **passive voice** used to alter the position of the object? is the *by* + *agent* included or omitted?

Sources

1 Are there any **official** sources giving authority to evidence? – police? emergency services? courts? investigating bodies? the government?
2 Are there any **unofficial** sources allowing ordinary people to have a voice?

Typographical features

1 Does **capitalisation** attract readers?
2 Is there any **variation in print size** to draw readers into the report?
3 Is **colour** used, drawing on wider symbolic associations to enhance meaning?
4 Do the **images** dramatise or support the story?

Summary

The **function** of newspaper language is to inform and entertain people; to present them with a particular ideology and interpretation of events.

The **impartiality** of the press is often questioned. By considering the language, grammar and sources of headlines and reports it is possible to assess the extent of any media bias.

An editor or a newspaper owner can dictate which stories or facts are to be included or excluded. This **selective perception** can influence the view a reader has of the world and of particular events.

The **relationship between a newspaper and its intended audience** dictates the kind of reporting in its pages. Content, style, typographical features and the use of images are distinctive to each paper, whether tabloid or broadsheet.

12 The language of advertising

12.1 The nature of advertising

We are surrounded by ADVERTISING in everyday life: **advertisements** directed at general groups of consumers appear on commercial television and radio, at the cinema, on billboard posters and in newspapers and magazines; subject specific advertisements appear in subject specific contexts focused on individuals and groups with certain interests; and **direct mail** (often known as **junk mail**) arrives through the letterbox sent straight to named individuals. The aim of all these advertisements is to draw attention to particular products or services through announcements paid for by an individual or a group wishing to inform or influence a particular audience.

In the eighteenth and nineteenth century, most advertising was straightforward and informative. Its language and style were formal and respectful; its tone was often ceremonious. In the late twentieth century, however, the power of the mass market has changed this. Since advertisers aim to **persuade** people to 'buy', 'give' or 'vote for' their own particular product or service, their approach is biased. In a competitive market, advertisers have to be better or more persuasive than their rivals if they are to succeed. Their **marketing campaigns** seek to encourage 'customer loyalty' by establishing a clear and distinctive image and identity which will make their products or services stand out from equivalent brands from other companies.

Advertisers focus their advertising on particular groups of people. They may divide people by age, gender, race or social class. Traditional CLASSIFICATIONS are used. **Age groupings** often fall into these categories:

- 0–15
- 16–24
- 25–35
- 36–55
- 56+

Social class groupings are equally common:

- A   higher managerial, administrative and professional;
- B   intermediate managerial, administrative and professional;
- C1   supervisory or clerical and junior managerial, administrative and professional;
- C2   skilled manual;
- D   semi-skilled and unskilled manual;
- E   casual labourers, state pensioners and the unemployed.

Such groupings help advertisers to **target** the people most likely to buy their products. On commercial television, programming schedules try to 'package' audiences by running certain kinds of programmes at certain times: this encourages advertisers to buy time, because it is easier to focus on a specific audience than on a very general one. For instance, advertisements on television usually promote particular types of household cleaning products, food and drink, toothpaste and cars at times when adults may be watching, and toys at times when children may make up the main part of the audience. In newspapers and magazines, the target audience is clearer because publishers and advertisers are more aware of the kind of people who buy each publication. Certain newspapers attract an affluent middle-class audience: because of these readers' spending power, advertisers will be prepared to buy advertising space. This means that although the broadsheets may not have large circulation figures, they can survive because they can sell advertising space easily. Popular newspapers, on the other hand, have to rely on high circulation figures because advertising revenue is relatively low. Their target audience do not have the same amounts of disposable income and therefore advertising space is a less saleable commodity.

Advertisements work by raising interest in a product or service. Once a potential customer has the **desire** to 'buy' or 'give', the 'sale' or 'donation' is more likely to happen. The strategies used in each case must be appropriate both to the target audience and to the kind of product or service offered. Some advertisements try to modify the attitudes of the audience: slogans like *Fairy Lasts Longer*, for example, aim to persuade the consumer to buy one particular brand rather than another by convincing them that the product is more successful, more stylish, or better value even if more expensive. Other advertisements have to convince consumers that they need an item that is not essential to everyday living: cars and perfume manufacturers therefore use a 'reason why' approach to their advertisements.

Research has shown that people remember particular advertisements if the product is different; if the advertisement itself is unusual; or if it has some personal relevance. Often the initial impact will be caused by the visual content and the overall design. But it is the **use of language** that will ensure that the product or service identity and the brand name are remembered. Typically, the language of advertising is **positive**, **unreserved** and **colloquial**. Advertisers choose **vivid concrete words** and make their COPY (the words attached to an advert) memorable by using **metaphorical language** and **non-standard spellings**. Because advertisements are designed to appeal to 'typical' members of certain groups, they use **stereotypes**. Women are often portrayed in the house, and advertisements like the ones for Oxo stock cubes draw on the image of the happy family. Black actors are not commonly used in mainstream advertising campaigns, with the exception of famous athletes and models. Naomi Campbell, for instance, is seen by advertisers to have popular appeal and has been used to promote Müller yoghurt and milk.

In Britain there are stringent controls on what is acceptable in advertising. Regulations like the British Code of Advertising Practice and the British Code of Sales Promotion try to ensure that all advertisements are **legal**, **decent**, **honest** and **truthful**. They state that advertisers must show responsibility both to consumers and to society as a whole. They must also conform to the principles of fair trading.

Despite detailed codes of conduct, however, there are still campaigns that people object to. The Advertising Standards Authority acts on complaints made by the general public and can, if necessary, insist that a certain campaign is stopped. Complaints might be based on various features of the campaign.

'Hard sell' tactics or fraudulent claims

Health campaigners have made many complaints about supposedly 'sugar-free' products, for instance, and the ASA ruled that Ribena was misleading consumers in advertising its 'sugar-free' blackcurrant drink.

The effect on children

Advertisements for 'Tango' orange drink, in which an orange man gave someone waiting at a bus stop a nasty shock by slapping him round the ears, were taken off the television because their images and slogan, *You'll know when you've been Tango'd*, were resulting in copycat behaviour.

The morals apparently promoted

When a famous person like Gary Lineker is used to promote a certain product, complaints can focus on the way in which the celebrity is portrayed. His advertisements for Walkers' crisps caused a stir because the football hero was seen taking crisps from a young boy and from a nun. Viewers objected that a positive role model for young children was behaving in a morally unacceptable way, since Gary Lineker could be seen to be endorsing such behaviour. Equally, in 1995 the advertising campaign for 'Club 18–30 Holidays' was widely criticised. Complaints were made about slogans like *Discover your erogenous zones* because they were seen to promote the sexual promiscuity often associated with such holidays.

Shock tactics

Benetton, with its slogan 'The United Colors of Benetton', are renowned for their provocative campaigns. They aim to market goods worldwide and their campaigns are meant to reflect this. Their official policy states that their advertisements will raise awareness of key social issues on a global level, thus 'uniting' nations. Many people, however, have complained about Benetton's poster campaigns which they believe to be immoral and distasteful. Billboard posters of a new born baby still covered with blood, of a man dying of AIDS with his family around him, and of the bloodstained clothes of a dead Croatian soldier – all these have been described as 'shock' advertising.

12.2 The function of advertising

The main function of advertising is to **persuade** (CONATIVE FUNCTION); its subordinate function is to **provide information** (REFERENTIAL FUNCTION). Different kinds of advertising use different techniques to persuade and inform. Some will use the copy to provide information like the size, the brand name, the price, and the address and telephone number of the shop or company, relying on the product itself to promote sales. Other advertisements will **highlight a particular background** as more important than the product, so that the **image** of the product is the selling point. Others will rely on the **associations between the product and a particular context** – dream-like fantasies, for instance, will suggest the potential a product has for changing an individual's life.

Advertisers appeal to our desire to be a 'successful career man or woman', a 'wonderful lover' or part of a 'happy family'; they exploit our wish to be 'beautiful', 'powerful', 'responsible' and 'knowledgeable'. To persuade viewers or readers to buy a car, an advertisement will try to convince us that we will be stylish, prestigious and exciting if we own that particular model. Advertisements can suggest that buying a certain brand of baby food because it is supposedly purer or more natural than its rivals will make you into a 'better' parent; that wearing certain clothes will make you more desirable or more powerful; that eating certain ice cream will make you more attractive or more alluring. In each case, the **function** of the advertisement is to get you to buy. Although information may be provided, it will not be neutral because there is an implicit purpose: the advertiser has primarily chosen the content and the language of the advertisement to influence rather than to inform.

Advertisements, however, do more than just sell products – different advertisers have different purposes. Table 12.1 summarises the main kinds of advertiser and their main functions.

Table 12.1 Advertisers and their functions

Advertiser	Function
Charities	Collecting funds; attracting support and voluntary helpers.
Commercial companies	Selling goods and services; attracting investment; changing attitudes; creating new desires in a target audience; giving information about a product or service.
Government	Giving information; publicising planning proposals and health and safety issues.
Media	Attracting a target audience; selling advertising space.
Event organisers	Promoting events and demonstrations.
Political parties	Winning votes; attracting members or financial support.
Private individuals	Selling and purchasing goods and services; announcing personal events and occasions.
Schools, colleges, universities	Informing prospective students of courses facilities, and future career possibilities.

12.3 Features of advertising language

Inevitably, advertisements designed for a visual medium like television or the cinema screen will be dominated by images, and usually these will be more important than any accompanying spoken or written words. However, prosodic features like intonation, pace and rhythm will influence the viewer and the use of a written slogan can make the product more memorable. In print forms like newspapers and magazines, advertisements rely on a combination of copy and image – it is the balance of the two that is important. Because print is not transient, as an image on the screen is, it can be reconsidered: the written language accompanying the image can therefore be more extensive.

Advertisements for different media use different techniques, but there are a number of features that are common to both spoken and written examples. First, it is always important to establish:

- the **advertiser** (logo, slogan, brand name, distinctive colour or image);
- the **target audience** (age, gender, social grade);
- the **function** of the advertisement or its message ('buy this', 'give generously', 'join us' and so on);

- the **selling techniques**:
  - a **product-based approach** will praise the features of a product or service, hoping to win customers on the strength of the product or service itself;
  - an **audience-based approach** will try to convince the target audience that they need a particular product or service: by concentrating on practical needs like saving time, or psychological needs like the desire to look better or younger, advertisers will try to persuade consumers that their lives will be better if they use a certain product or service;
  - an **impact-based approach** will aim to attract attention visually or linguistically.

Having considered these general motivations, it is important to look more closely at the design of each advertisement. By focusing on the language and images, it is possible to analyse the way in which an advertisement is meant to influence its target audience.

Design

Often the first thing to influence a viewer or reader will be the overall **design** of an advertisement. Juxtapositions of **slogan**, **image**, **copy** and **logo** contribute to the overall effect. They all work together to create a certain view of a particular product or service.

The **images** will also attract the attention of the intended audience. The people, the settings, the props (objects used in a particular context to create a sense of reality) and the product which together make up the image can be described as **non-verbal communication**. These can all work in a literal and a symbolic way. In an advertisement for perfume, for instance, the clothes the actors wear, the kind of background used, and props like a diamond necklace and a waiting Rolls Royce car, will symbolise that this perfume is associated with wealth, luxury and status. A reader or viewer will automatically recognise the implicit meaning of the non-verbal signals and will therefore make certain assumptions about the perfume.

Stereotypes

Advertisers use **cultural stereotypes** in their images so that they can be sure that their target audience will associate good things with a product or service. Women are invariably beautiful; children are angelic; men are strong and rugged; and young people are up to date with current trends. Props help to create these stereotypes – glasses symbolise cleverness; books symbolise education; beer has connotations of masculinity; and so on. By breaking down the codes that are used in the images, it is possible to learn something about the advertisers' intentions even before reading the copy.

Language and tone

The **language** of advertising is quite often associated with the language of everyday conversation: the **tone** is often informal and chatty, and colloquial expressions are common. Verbal **contractions** like *we've* and *you'll* are easily recognisable features of informal spoken language which would be inappropriate in a more formal variety. Advertising language, however, is distinct from conversation and other linguistic features make this field a variety in its own right.

Slogans

SLOGANS are crucial if an advertising campaign is to succeed, because it is the slogan that will stick in people's minds. The structure varies, and may use a noun phrase, a simple sentence or a complex sentence. Advertisers can use puns, they can disrupt collocations, or they can work on our emotions, but whatever approach a particular campaign uses, the slogan is always made eye-catching. A British Telecom campaign in 1994 used a sequence of slogans based on well-known sayings that were cleverly altered: the common cliché *Chatterbox* was used alongside the picture of a telephone box; the imperative clause 'pause for thought' became *Pause for Talk*; the successful advertising slogan *Have a Break, Have a Kit-Kat* was adapted so that a similar parallel structure was retained but the brand name was replaced with something appropriate for a telephone advertisement:

>   P   O   P   O
> (Have) (a Break), (Have) (a Chit-Chat)

and the cliché 'sizzling sausage' was adapted in a complex noun phrase:

>   m   m   h   q
> (10 Minutes') Sizzling Conversation for the Price of a Sausage
> num   N   V   N   PrepP

The success of the campaign was in using sayings that were already well known so that people reading the billboards were struck simultaneously by the familiarity and the novelty of each slogan.

Lexical choice

Lexical choice is crucial to the effect an advertisement will have since it helps to create a relationship with the audience. The copy of an advertisement can have two functions: modifiers can be used to emphasise the positive attributes of a product in order to **persuade** a consumer to buy it (conative function); or the written text can provide technical facts about the product to **inform** the consumer, of size, power, range of features, price and so on (referential function).

The language of advertising can also **influence the contemporary word stock**. Slogans and phrases can become part of everyday usage during the period of a campaign.

- **Colloquial expressions** can now be heard in everyday conversation, like the *pinta* which is used in milk advertisements.
- **Adjective phrases** can become catchphrases, like the phrase *naughty but nice* from advertisements promoting real cream, which suggests that something is pleasant even if not really a good thing to do.
- **Sentences** can be applied to new contexts, like the complex sentence

>   S   P   O
> (Heineken) (refreshes) (the parts that other beers can't reach)
>   SCl–RelCl

which is often adapted so that it can apply to the power of other things to revitalise the body. Because advertising language changes so fast, however, coined words and phrases soon become stale and are then replaced with new expressions.

The **structure of noun phrases** is often complex, with strings of pre-modifiers being used. Post-modifiers are also common. The use of both kinds of modification provides precise information in a concise way, but the complex noun phrases of advertising can be a substitute for clear and honest description. The information may be technical, but more often it is emotive and based on opinion rather than fact.

>   m   m   h   q
> Another legendary service from Lloyds Bank
>   det   Adj   N   PrepP

Sainsbury's, where good food costs less
  N   RelCl (= 'at which')

Adjective phrases are also often subjective.

The new dessert from ____ is (dangerously deep) and (devilishly delicious)
                                Adv   Adj   Adv   Adj

The **possessive** form of nouns is often used with inanimate objects in advertising language and this is not common in any other variety.

the *car's* outstanding performance...   the *food's* aromatic aroma...

Modifiers are a distinctive feature of advertising language because they are powerful words used to attract attention. By using them in strings, advertisers can arouse emotions, stimulate desires and so on. They are described as TRIGGER WORDS because they allow advertisers to evoke the kind of image they want to associate with a particular product or service. Some modifiers, like *big*, *long* or *double*, indicate physical qualities and these can to some extent be proved; others, like *wonderful*, *elegant* or *incredible*, are intangible and cannot therefore be measured. Advertisers often use these quality words precisely because they are vague. The most common adjectives are: *good*, *better*, *best*, *free*, *special*, *great*, *real*, *new* and *big*. These all create a positive image but without really telling the consumer anything about the product or service. Other modifiers relate directly to price: the verb *reduced*, the adjective *cheap* and the noun *bargain* can all modify the noun *prices*. Compound phrases suggest that their products have special features. By combining adjectives, noun, adverb and verb modifiers, advertisers can convey a sense of a product's uniqueness.

Do you want *radiantly-glowing naturally-coloured full-styled* hair? Then try our new hair-care range.

Because each new campaign must attract attention, advertising language is often **innovative**. Advertisers **coin new words** to make a brand more memorable.

Cookability – that's the beauty of gas
Gordon's and Tonic – *innervigoration*
Technobeer – Get Real!

New words are also coined by using the brand name of an item as the basis for a word. Often **non-standard spelling** will be used to attract attention.

Beanz Meanz Heinz

Advertisers use the copy to enhance the associations an image has evoked, with the language working alongside the picture to reinforce the intended message. Each lexical choice must make a particular product or service more memorable because space in print advertisements and time for television advertisements cost money. The lexis must therefore convey the essential points in a concise and dramatic way. This makes the language of advertising almost like a shorthand code – every word included has a specific function.

Grammar

The **grammar** of advertisements is also similar to **informal spoken language**. It can be disjointed and abbreviated. Slogans will often omit verbs to make a catchphrase more concise and striking.

■ Hydra-star (∅) the first moisturising range with a choice of textures.

Imperatives are used frequently because consumers are being urged to 'buy', 'give' or 'join'.

Free your potential . . . *Join* the search for a brighter future.
The Department of Employment, television advertisement (March 1995)

Through variations in **mood**, the advertisers appeal to their target audience to take notice, to act.

Verb tenses allow the advertisers to implicitly convey differences in the semantics. Simple present tense emphasises features of a product; simple past tense and the perfect aspect allow advertisers to draw comparisons; and future time, often constructed using the modal verb *will*, makes assumptions about what is possible if the consumer uses a particular product or service.

Pronouns help advertisers create a personal relationship with consumers. By using the second person pronoun *you*, advertisements can appeal directly to the reader or viewer, aiming to make them feel special. Other **interactive features**, like coupons to save money on a particular product or forms to complete and return, also encourage the consumer's direct participation. Some advertisements use a checklist system of boxes to tick or questionnaires to fill in in order to make the customer more active.

Sentence structures are unusual because elements are often left out in order to keep sentences short. **Verbless clauses** are common and sentences are often divided in unexpected ways to keep the copy simple for the reader. This means that often sentences are literally ungrammatical, although they do convey meaning.

Sentences are often **simple** and **co-ordination** is more common than subordination. **Co-ordinating conjunctions** are often used in the initial position, as is typical of informal spoken language.

> A S P O S P
> (Every year) (we) (deal with) (thousands of sad cases like this). (But) (we) (receive)
> conj
> O
> (no funding from the Government) . . .
> RSPCA (April 1994)

This kind of structure gives a separate emphasis to each clause and is therefore useful since it allows advertisers to highlight a number of key points. **Adverbials** are also placed at the beginning of sentences to emphasise key information.

> A S P A
> (In parts of Russia), (dogs) (are killed) (for their skins).
> Pet Respect (March 1994)

> A S P O
> (But) (to help pets just like yours all over the world) (we) (need) (your help).
> SCl–NFCl
> Pet Respect (March 1994)

Metaphorical language

Advertisements use **metaphorical language** to attract attention to the product, often 'breaking the rules' of conventional language. Advertisers can construct different layers of meaning: **metaphors** link emotive associations to a product, building up an impression that will influence potential consumers; **symbolism** likewise encourages viewers or readers to make certain connections that will colour their view; **personification** or **animation** of inanimate objects can create a mysterious or comic atmosphere;

puns can be clever or humorous in their manipulation of language; and **ambiguity** can both create humour and provoke interest through the double meanings it promotes.

Rhetorical devices

Advertisers also play with language using certain **rhetorical techniques** to draw attention to products: **repetition** highlights key points or a particular brand name; **parallelism** allows advertisers to use structured patterns to contrast or emphasise points; **rhythmic beats** make copy more memorable; and phonological patterning like **alliteration** and **rhyme** make slogans and copy stand out.

Typography

The **typographical features** of advertising are also important because they can help consumers to identify certain brands or products. **Print size** and **shape**, **colour** and **layout** are often used consistently throughout a campaign, and these therefore become as significant as the language in persuading readers and viewers to act in the way the advertisers intend.

12.4 Types of advertising

There are many different types of advertising, all using the same techniques but requiring different responses from the intended audience. Advertisements can be **persuasive**, using the 'hard sell' approach, aiming to make consumers go out and buy a product. They can be **informative**, relying on the influence of technical data to help the consumer make an informed choice. Or they can be **competitive**, attempting to gain a new share of the market at the expense of their rivals. Advertisements may be product-, audience- or impact-based; or they may use variations in type face, juxtapositions of striking images, or emotive appeals to make them eye-catching. But besides distinguishing between advertisements by their approach, it is also possible to classify them according to the **content**.

Product advertising

On a very basic level, CLASSIFIED ADVERTISEMENTS try to sell products or services to people who already know what they are looking for. They are described as 'unintrusive advertising' because readers seek them. For this reason, they tend to be straightforward. They use the minimum number of words and convey the most relevant information in as concise a way as possible. Because they are so short, abbreviations are commonly used. Although they are more likely to be informative than persuasive, some value words may be used.

> Thatched, detached converted barn. 4 beds, c/h, small garden. Beautiful moorland-edged village, school, pub, shop/PO 5 mins. Owners moving abroad. Low price for quick sale. £89,000. Tel. 01234 123456.

> 25YR OLD SINGLE MALE, 6ft, good build, reasonably goodlooking, GSOH seeks female 23–28 for nights in and out. Love? Friendship? Maybe more? Who knows? Are you the lady for me? ALA. Box No. 123456.

> THREE PIECE BEDROOM SUITE consisting of a mirrored teak dressing table and two single wardrobes one of which is mirrored. All VGC. £50 ono. Tel. 01234 1234.

To the reader looking for a partner, a particular piece of furniture or a certain kind of property, the codes are straightforward: *ono – or near offer*; *VGC – very good condition*; *ALA – all letters answered*; *GSOH – good sense of humour*; and *c/h – central heating*. Sometimes there will be 'sales talk', particularly in property small ads, but usually this type of advertisement will be marked by its factual approach. Classified advertisements can be local in community newspapers or national in many daily and Sunday newspapers; the contents of publications like *Exchange and Mart* and *freeADS* are exclusively made up of classified advertisements.

POINT-OF-SALE ADVERTISING is very much the same. Local people will write out a card and place it where other local people shop: on a supermarket display board, in a shop window and so on. This kind of advertising is directed specifically at the local community and therefore its target audience is quite limited.

DIRECT MAIL comes straight to people's homes, addressed to individuals whose names have been taken from sources like the electoral register. The form of such advertising is usually a letter which tries to persuade the addressee to buy a particular product. A sample or a 'money off' coupon will often be enclosed. The tone is informal and direct address is used to try and create a personal relationship between sender and reader. Famous people are sometimes used to endorse the product advertised.

ACTIVITY 12.1

Read through the letter in Figure 12.1 and comment on the linguistic and stylistic features which make it typical of the field of advertising.

Try to establish whether direct mail is different from other kinds of advertising.

COMMENTARY

The **advertiser** is Crest and mothers with young children are the **intended audience**. The **function** of the letter is to convince mothers that this particular brand is better at caring for children's teeth than other equivalent products – and, as a result of this, to persuade them to buy *Crest Milkteeth*.

The letter format is used to shape the **overall design** – it is addressed to a particular person and ends with *Yours sincerely* (l. 25). Because it is sent by an individual rather than a company, the advertising seems less explicit. The use of the sender's full name, *Kathy Graham* (l. 27) reinforces this sense of a one-to-one address; the use of her role title, *Consumer Health Advisor for Crest* (l. 28) suggests that she is an authoritative person, with objective knowledge of the product. The decoration of the letter with a cartoon character draws attention to the indirect target audience – children. The beaver is appealing and appears in active poses – the fact that beavers are known for their strong and prominent front teeth is also appropriate for the promotion of a toothpaste. The repeated use of the illustration aims to attract the children's attention as well as the mother's. More explicit visual references to the product are found in the illustration of a toothbrush and a photograph of the product itself. This ensures that the product is easy to recognise on the supermarket shelf.

The **tone** is personal because it is addressed to one named individual from another. It mixes an informal, friendly tone with a more formal offer of dental health advice. The chatty tone is marked by **contractions** like *That's* (l. 9); by direct address using **second person pronouns**; and by **colloquial language** like *Hi* and *kids* (l. 6).

Figure 12.1 Direct mailshot

PG676 32392486

Mrs J Markham
379 Deer Street
New Town
NT16 OCD

Dear Mrs Markham

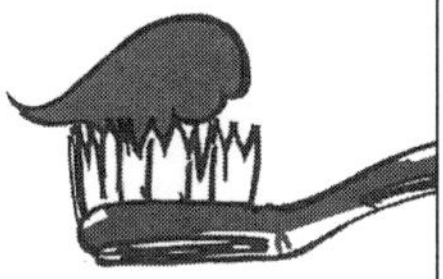

You know how hard it is to get kids to brush their teeth. But did you know that healthy milkteeth are also an important start to having healthy adult teeth?

That's why we have sent you a sample of a new toothpaste specially designed for your child's milkteeth. Introducing new Crest Milkteeth.

Crest Milkteeth contains a special low level of fluoride – as recommended by many dentists – which helps protect your child's teeth against tooth decay.

Its great raspberry taste can encourage children to brush, and what's more, it is sugar free. On the front of each tube is the friendly McEaver Beaver character, and your children will look forward to brushing with him.

We have also enclosed a leaflet which we hope will be helpful to you in looking after your children's teeth.

Crest Milkteeth has an easy twist cap and a less-mess nozzle. It comes in a handy 50ml tube, and is available from all good grocery stores and pharmacies.

We hope that your child will enjoy brushing with the new Crest Milkteeth, helping you to give them healthy teeth for life.

Yours sincerely

Kathy Graham

Kathy Graham
CONSUMER HEALTH ADVISOR FOR CREST

"AND THEY LOVE THE TASTE!"

Crest Milkteeth is a trademark . Crest is a registered trademark
McEaver Beaver is a trademark.

The **lexis** mirrors the mixture of informal and formal, creating a personal relationship between addresser and addressee. The **subject specific lexis** reflects the field of dental health: *milkteeth* (l. 7) and *fluoride* (l. 11). The **modifiers** are typical of advertising: *new* (l. 9), *great* (l. 14) and *good* (l. 21) – most are subjective rather than factual since they are difficult to quantify or prove. Modifiers like *helpful* (l. 18) and *easy* (l. 20) appeal to overworked mothers, suggesting that this product will encourage children to clean their teeth willingly. Many **noun phrases** are long, providing information concisely.

> $\overset{m}{~~~~~}$ $\overset{h}{~~}$ $\overset{q}{~~}$ $\overset{q}{~~~~~~}$
> a sample of a new toothpaste specially designed for your child's milkteeth
> $\underset{det}{~~~~~}$ $\underset{N}{~~}$ $\underset{PrepP}{~~~~~}$ $\underset{NFCl}{~~~~~~}$

(ll. 9–10)

Repetition of the brand name is typical of advertising since it ensures that the target audience will remember it. The **connotations** of certain words build up a positive image: verbs like *recommended* (l. 12) and nouns like *dentists* (l. 12) suggest that the information offered in the letter has an authoritative source; the modifier *healthy* (l. 7) is influential because mothers want to give their children the best. Equally, a verb like *hope* (l. 23) offers the company's tentative view that the product will be successful, while the verb *know* (l. 6) implies that the mother is an expert. The letter therefore persuades implicitly: it does not suggest that Crest can teach the target audience about being parents, but it does offer some technical knowledge of toothpaste which will add to their success as mothers.

The **grammar** is more varied than in many advertisements because of the letter format. **Sentences** are not long, but few are simple in structure. The sentence below is basically simple with a co-ordinated object.

> $\overset{S}{~~~~~~~~~~~~~~~}$ $\overset{P}{~~~~~~}$ $\overset{O}{~~~~~~~~~~~~~~~~~~~~~~~~~~~~~~~~~~~~~}$
> (Crest Milkteeth) (has) (an easy twist cap and less-mess nozzle). (l. 20)

Most sentences are complex.

> $\overset{S}{~~~~}$ $\overset{P}{~~~~~~~}$ $\overset{O}{~~~~~~}$
> (We) (hope) (that your child will enjoy brushing with the new Crest Milkteeth),
> $\underset{SCl–NCl}{~~~~~~~~~~~~~~~~~~~~~~~~~~~~~~~~~~~~~}$ $\underset{SCl–NFCl}{~~~~~~~~~~~~~~~~~~~~~~~~~~~}$
>
> $\overset{A}{~~~~~~~~~~~~~~~~~~~~~~~~}$
> (helping you to give them healthy teeth for life). (ll. 23–4)
> $\underset{SCl–NFCl}{~~~~~~~}$ $\underset{SCl–NFCl}{~~~~~~~~~~~~~~~~~~}$

One sentence is minor in its structure, which is typical of the field of advertising: a non-finite clause, *Introducing new Crest Milkteeth* (l. 10) is used to draw attention to the product. The **mood** is mostly declarative, but the first paragraph uses the interrogative mood to involve the reader: *But did you know. . .* (ll. 6–7). Direct mail is different from other forms of advertising in that there are no imperatives telling the reader or viewer to 'buy', 'give' or 'support' and so on. The use of the **second person pronoun**, *you* (l. 6), suggests that the mother is an expert, knowing her own children and caring for them in the most appropriate way; the use of the **first person plural pronoun**, *we* (l. 9), gives a caring face to the company. **Modal verbs** are used to state the company's certainty about the success of their product without making unrealistic claims: the verb phrase *can encourage* (l. 14) is tentative, avoiding a factual statement that could be proved wrong; the verb phrases *will enjoy. . .* (l. 23) and *will look forward to. . .* (l. 16) are more certain because Crest are confident in their product. **Tenses** are more varied than in other advertising: the present tense provides the immediate context of the mother, *it is. . .* (l. 6), and factual information about the product, *it is sugar free* (l. 15); the perfect aspect describes completed acts, *have sent* (l. 9) and *have enclosed* (l. 18); and future time is conveyed using the modal *will* (l. 23).

The absence of **metaphorical language** is to be expected in this kind of letter because the target audience is wide and the purpose is referential rather than poetic. Other **rhetorical techniques** are used, however: **parallelism** encourages the reader to think about the future – *healthy milkteeth. . .healthy adult teeth* (ll. 7–8); and **phonological patterning** like rhyme makes the text more memorable – *less-mess* (l. 20) and *McEaver Beaver* (l. 16).

The **typographical features** are typical of advertising: **bold print**, for instance, is used in the first and last paragraphs to draw the reader in and to highlight the final statement of the company. Some features, however, are associated specifically with the letter format: the handwritten signature encourages the reader to see this as a personal letter rather than a form of advertising; the handwritten *Hi* introduces the beaver character to children in an informal way. The **direct quotation** marked by inverted commas suggests that the beaver is talking – the print catches the reader's attention because it does not follow the traditional straight lines of the letter.

The main differences between direct mail and other forms of explicit advertising are linked to the letter format: the address to a named individual; the use of a named sender; the more varied grammatical structures associated with prose in letters; and the absence of metaphorical language. In place of implicit imperatives, letters of this kind often enclose a sample or a 'money-off' coupon to encourage the target audience to purchase the product being promoted.

The most far-reaching mainstream source of product advertising can be found in **magazines** and **newspapers**, on **billboards** and on **television**. These kinds of advertisements are an everyday part of our lives and we take them for granted. They use typical rhetorical techniques to influence their intended audience, and juxtapose slogans, copy and images to evoke an appropriate response.

Television product advertisements rely far more heavily on **images** and because these are often animated by actors, the images are far more powerful. The words and actions together aim to reveal new ways of visualising people, places and events. By producing a certain view of the world in this way, advertisers can then suggest that their target audience could also be a part of this world if only they bought the right product. The **logo** and **slogan** have exactly the same form as they would in a magazine or newspaper advertisement and this allows advertisers to create a consistent brand identity across a range of media. The copy of a written advertisement might be delivered by a **voiceover** in which an unseen speaker draws attention to certain features of a product. Typical prosodic features of intonation, pace, pitch and so on affect the way the product is received. These can be marked on a commercial script just as they would be on a transcription, enabling the actor to evoke a certain mood or atmosphere.

Print advertisements cover a wide range of forms and products, so advertisers design different kinds of campaigns depending upon the kind of intended audience they wish to attract. The images, tone and language chosen will all reflect the target group, but in each case the variety will be distinctive.

ACTIVITY 12.2

The advertisements in Figures 12.2 and 12.3 are examples of product advertising found in broadsheet newspapers. Consider each advertisement in turn:

1   Identify the advertiser and comment on the possible target audience in each case.

2   Identify the function and the main selling technique for each advertisement.

3   Jot down some general points about the design of each advertisement. Consider the juxtaposition of any slogans, images, copy or logos.

4   Comment on the tone and its effect on the relationship between advertiser and reader.

5   Reread each example and identify any distinctive lexical choices. Think about:
     a   the slogan;
     b   the noun phrases and any modifiers used;
     c   the overall effect of the copy.

6   Reread each example and note any interesting grammatical usage. Think about:
     a   verbless clauses;
     b   different moods;
     c   changes in tense;
     d   the use of direct address and any interactive features;
     e   sentence structure;
     f   the techniques used to focus attention on key elements.

7   Identify and evaluate the effects of any metaphorical or rhetorical language used.

8   Comment on the typographical features. Think about:
     a   variations in print size or shape;
     b   the overall layout.

COMMENTARY

Although each advertisement is promoting a product, they appeal to their **intended audiences** in different ways. In Figure 12.2, the advertiser is the Government of India Tourist Office. Because the advertisement is promoting a country as a whole rather than a particular holiday company's package deals, the tone is quite formal. The aim is to make the audience see the cultural and historical aspects of India as important rather than the advantages of a particular hotel in a particular resort. Persuading people to respond to this advertisement will not benefit one company, but the country as a whole. 'India' is the product and the approach in this example is focused on the power of the product itself to charm and inspire people.

The car advertisement in Figure 12.3 is more typical of product advertising: the product-based approach is clear in the number of positive details listed in the copy. A car is a 'luxury' purchase and therefore a manufacturer has to persuade people to spend money – the target audience here is a middle-market group who have money to spare for a car associated with a *Speed Endurance Record* and rallies.

The **design** of the advertisements is different and this reflects the overall aim of each advertiser. The Government of India Tourist Office choose to let the image of the palace dominate the page – as well as the amount of space the photograph takes up on the page, the darkness of the background further highlights the brightness of the palace itself. The new moon at the left could symbolise the romance and potential for new beginnings which the advertisement seems to suggest can be found in India. In contrast to the power of the image, the copy is restricted to the bottom left-hand corner of the page. Subaru, on the other hand, use a balance of image and text, suggesting that the company is selling more than a car that looks good. The image at the top of the advertisement is dramatic because of the car's sleek appearance, but it is straightforward – the style suggests that there is no need to glamorise this car. The overall layout is made easier for the reader's eye with the use of symbols to break up the text: the logo for Subaru makes the advertisement's brand immediately recognisable and the symbolic laurels make the car's records stand out.

The **relationship with potential customers** created by both Subaru and the Government of India Tourist Office is respectful. The **tone** in each case is quite formal.

Figure 12.2 Product advertisement (in *The Independent*, 15 March 1994)

East of the Sun, West of the Moon.

This fairy tale water-palace, nestling beneath Rajasthan's rugged Nahargarh hills, was in real life an extravagant hunting lodge for the Maharajahs of Jaipur.

India is studded with such jewels, in settings that will take your breath away.

Beyond words, such images live on in the imagination. It could be the exquisite beauty of the Taj Mahal by moonlight, tiny prayer leaf vessels spangling the velvety Ganges at Varanasi, iridescent tropical fish among coral atolls in the Andamans, or dawn stealthily bringing a blush to the cheeks of the snowy Himalaya.

India. The finest holiday under the sun (and moon).

Our free colour brochure line is 081 812 0929. Call us today for your copy or fill in the coupon.

To: The Government of India Tourist Office, 7 Cork Street, London W1X 1PB. Fax 071 494 1048

Please send me your free 32 page colour brochure about holidays in India.

Name_____

Address_____

_____

_____ PALACE

The Subaru advertisers provide a lot of factual information and seem to be aiming the copy at purchasers who are interested in precise technical data, not just the status or image of a car. The advertisement for India adopts a tone that is very literary and quite different from the conversational approach of some campaigns. Reading the advertisement becomes a parallel to reading a novel – the consumer is drawn into the unknown, almost fictional world.

The **slogan** immediately draws attention to any advertisement and in product

Figure 12.3 Product advertisement (in *The Independent* on Sunday, 19 June 1994)

1

The new Subaru Legacy. *The next generation.*

"What their engineers don't know about all-wheel propulsion isn't worth knowing."

CARWEEK

5

Applauded for its surefooted command of the road, the 4WD Legacy has earned universal

Holders of the World Land Speed Endurance Record

acclaim as a driver's car. But not resting on their laurels, Subaru now

reshape and refine the world beating Legacy saloon. Uprating torque

British Rally Champions 1991 · 1992 · 1993

in the famed horizontally opposed 2.0/2.2 litre 16 valve engines.

Optimising traction with legendary Subaru full-time 4WD. Engineering

Asia Pacific Rally Champions 1993

10

new advances in ride and road holding. Reinforcing safety with ABS*.

twin front air bags* and impact protection beams. Creating more space, luxury and security.

(An anti-theft immobiliser is standard.) And, as you'd expect with build strength and reliability

proven on the toughest roads and roughest rallies on Earth, a 3 year/60,000 mile warranty.

The new Subaru Legacy saloon. The next generation.

15

CALL 0753 696200 OR WRITE TO SUBARU (UK) LTD., RYDER STREET, WEST BROMWICH, WEST MIDLANDS, B70 0EL. A SUBSIDIARY OF I.M. GROUP LIMITED. SALOON PRICES FROM £13,649 (FOR THE 2.0 GL). ESTATE PRICES FROM £14,999 (FOR THE 2.0GL). PRICES CORRECT AT TIME OF GOING TO PRESS. EXCLUDE DELIVERY CHARGE TO DEALER PREMISES OF £330.00 (INC. VAT) (UK MAINLAND ONLY). NUMBER PLATES AND ROAD FUND LICENCE. *ABS AND AIR BAGS ON GLS AND GX MODELS ONLY.

advertising it is common to find the brand name embedded somewhere in the slogan. Subaru uses two complex noun phrases in juxtaposition:

m	m	m	h		m	m	h
The	new	Subaru	Legacy (l. 1)		The	next	generation (l. 1)
det	Adj	N	N		det	Adj	N

The noun *Legacy*, the brand name for this new car, has connotations of a gift left in a will, and this idea of something left from the past for the present is developed in the noun *generation* with its connotations of family descendants. Both of these nouns are associated with people and their use in the slogan suggests that each new Subaru car is maturing and becoming more refined as the company becomes older and more experienced, just as a person does. The modifiers *new* and *next*, however, emphasise that this car is designed for the future with only the best of the past surviving. To contrast with the non-specific approach of the noun phrases, the quotation from *Carweek* uses a subject specific noun phrase, *all-wheel propulsion* (l. 3). This, along with the repetition of the verb *know* (l. 3) and the verbal noun *knowing* (l. 4), emphasises the expertise of the Subaru engineers.

The India advertisement uses a phonological technique to draw attention to the product. Traditional orthography is used to mimic /ɑː/ (where __ denotes a 'held' phoneme), the sighing sound made when people are contented or amazed. The fact that the phoneme /ɑː/ is literally joined to the final *a* of *India* highlights the fact that it is India itself that will evoke this mood. The typographical features actually force the reader to take a second look. The subheading *East of the Sun*, *West of the Moon*, has its origins in the title of a fairy tale. It therefore builds upon the romantic image of India: a land only reached by magic; a land that will fire your imagination. The connotations are of something romantic and yet almost impossible.

The **lexis** of each advertisement is quite different. The **noun phrases** describing the car are quite technical:

m	m	h		m	m	m	h
(2.0/2.2 litre)	(16 valve)	engines (l. 8)		a	(3 year)/	(60,000 mile)	warranty (l. 13)
num N	num N	N		det num N	num N	N

Small print at the bottom of the advertisement includes details of price and the company address – information that may be important if a reader is to be persuaded to buy a 'luxury' item. **Subject specific lexis** provides the technical background which ensures that the reader knows that Subaru are experts: *torque* (l. 7), *traction* (l. 9), *ABS* (l. 10). But alongside these are **modifiers** which cannot be proved, expressing evaluative judgements instead: *famed* (l. 8), *legendary* (l. 9), *universal* (l. 5). **Superlatives** like *toughest* and *roughest* (l. 13) are equally difficult to qualify, but they reinforce the idea that this car is superior to others in the same category. The India advertisement is quite different: the Tourist Office are not selling something concrete like a car, so there is no technical data and price is not mentioned; the language is more poetic and extravagant because they are portraying India as a country quite out of the ordinary. **Noun phrases** can be very long:

m	m	h	q
This	(fairy tale)	water-palace,	nestling beneath Rajasthan's rugged Nahargarh hills
det	N N	N	NFCl

(ll. 3–4)

Abstract nouns like *beauty* (l. 9) and *imagination* (l. 9) are typical of the mysterious image of India which is built up. **Modifiers** like *extravagant* (l. 5) and *exquisite* (l. 9) reinforce the sense of something unique, while the adjectives *velvety* and *iridescent* (l. 11) are more usual in a poetic genre than in an advertisement. The noun modifiers *fairy tale* (l. 3) are used in the opening paragraph and are typical of the mood the advertisers wish to create. Nouns like *moonlight* (l. 10) and *dawn* (l. 13) have romantic **connotations** and the **superlative adjective** *finest* (l. 15) suggests that no other holiday could equal one in India. The use of **proper nouns** like *Rajasthan* (l. 4), *Nahargarh hills* (l. 4) and *Taj Mahal* (l. 10) give a concrete basis to what appears to be a fairy tale world, reminding the reader that this is not just a vision, but reality.

The **grammar** of the advertisements is quite different. The narrative or descriptive approach of the India advertisement means that the **sentences** are quite long.

> S   P   C   C
> (It) (could be) (the exquisite beauty of the TM by moonlight), (tiny prayer leaf
>
>   C
> vessels spangling the velvety Ganges at Varanasi) (iridescent tropical fish among
>   SCl–NFCl
>
>   C
> coral atolls in the Andamans), (or) (dawn stealthily bringing a blush to the cheeks
>   SCl–NFCl
>
> of the snowy Himalaya). (ll. 9–14)

Where the sentences are simple, the effect can be dramatic. A change of **mood** from declarative to imperative highlights the response required of the reader:

>   S   P   C   P   O   A
> (Our free colour brochure line) (is) (081 812 0929). (Call) (us) (today). . .
>   (ll. 17–18)

Tense changes are also significant. The use of the simple past tense verbs *was* (l. 4) suggests that India is a land of historical interest, but the main body of the copy uses simple present tense verbs like *is* (l. 6) and *live* (l. 8) because the advertisers want people to visit **now**.

The use of the **perfect aspect** *has earned* (l. 5) in the car advertisement implies that the quality of Subaru cars has already been recognised in the past. By using the co-ordinating conjunction *But* (l. 6) in the initial position in the second sentence, a contrast is developed – Subaru cars are now even better. **Initial position conjunctions** are used twice and this makes the copy of this advertisement more like spoken conversation than is the Government of India Tourist Office advertisement. In addition, many sentences are very short, made up of non-finite clauses which function as adverbials:

>   A   S   A   P
> (But) (not resting on their laurels) (Subaru) (now) (reshape and refine) (the world
> conj   SCl–NFCl
>
>   O   A   A
> beating Legacy saloon). (Uprating torque. . .). (Optimising traction. . .).
>   SCl–NFCl   SCl–NFCl
>
>   A   A   A
> (Engineering new advances. . .). (Reinforcing safety. . .). (Creating more
> SCl–NFCl   SCl–NFCl   SCl–NFCl
>
> space. . .) (ll. 6–11)

This kind of division of sentences places fewer demands on the reader than the longer, more complicated sentences in the India advertisement. Although these are not sentences, the reader understands the points being made. The disjointed style is typical of many advertisements and the list-like effect highlights the advances made by the Subaru engineers. The **mood** is declarative until the small print advises readers to *Call 0753 696200. . .* (l. 15).

Both advertisements try to draw their reader in through their use of **pronouns**, but in slightly different ways. The India advertisement does use the possessive determiner *your*

(l. 18), but this is the only example of direct address. By using the possessive determiner *our* (l. 17), however, the advertisers give the reader a sense of the people behind the institution, and this makes the concept of a holiday in India more appealing. The advertisers' main technique for involving the reader, however, is through their creation of what seems to be a mysterious and almost fictional world. The Subaru advertisement uses the typical second person pronoun *you* (l. 12), which more explicitly draws the reader in. The adverbial clause *as you'd expect* (l. 12) also encourages the reader to identify with Subaru's product – it suggests that the company knows that their customers are wise consumers. **Interactive features** encourage the same kind of response: write or telephone. The India advertisement provides a form to make this easier. By printing *PALACES* at the bottom of the form, it becomes possible for a post-campaign evaluation to be carried out: the number of returns will to some extent indicate the success of the advertisement.

Metaphorical and **rhetorical techniques** help to make both examples persuasive. **Marked themes** are used on several occasions: *Applauded for its surefooted command of the road...* (l. 5, Subaru); *And, as you'd expect...* (l. 12, Subaru); *Beyond words...* (l. 8, India). In each case, the focus changes and the advertisers are able to draw attention to an important concept. The copy of the India advertisement uses metaphorical language more extensively to build up the fairy tale world of India. The present participle *nestling* (l. 3) has connotations of something alive, but also suggests a secure and comfortable environment. The **metaphor** of the *jewel* (l. 6) is developed through the verb past participle *studded* (l. 6) – by describing India's historic buildings in this way, the copy implicitly reveals their value and beauty. The description of *dawn stealthily bringing a blush to the cheeks of the snowy Himalaya* (ll. 13–14) uses **personification** to animate the environment, once again adding a sense of mystery to the reader's view of India. The metaphorical language humanises the unknown country, making it appealing to the traveller who is unfamiliar with it.

Subaru use a **metaphor** in their description of the car as *surefooted* (l. 5), but beyond this, the advertisers rely on rhetorical patterning to persuade their audience. **Tripling** is used in describing the qualities of the car: *space, luxury and security* (l. 11). The **repetition** of the non-finite clause structure highlights the improvements made, and the extensive **listing** suggests that the car's design has been carefully considered.

The **typographical features** of each advertisement draw attention to the respective products. The **print size** used for the copy in the Subaru advertisement makes the amount of writing seem less daunting; the small print for the India advertisement suggests that they are sure that their intended audience will be interested enough to read the copy whatever the print size. **Colours** can be dramatic and here light and dark shades are used to advantage: the reader is automatically drawn to the illuminated palace – this is the image that does what the words cannot; and the car seems to have prestige without being overtly flashy. The Subaru advertisement includes the Subaru **logo** which helps consumers identify the brand. The advertisers have also used **symbols**: the laurel represents victory and is a quick way to indicate the connection between the Subaru car and certain awards. The symbols are linked directly to the copy with the use of the cliché *resting on their laurels* (l. 6). Because it is used in the negative here, the reader knows that this company is actively seeking improvements all the time. Perhaps the most dramatic use of symbol, however, can be found in the top right-hand corner, where the *Childline* logo and telephone number are included. This implies that Subaru not only actively aims to produce high-quality cars, but is also a caring company which tries to use its money and advertising space for good causes.

Both advertisements are successful in their use of design and language since they manage to draw the reader into the world the advertisement creates. They are promoting quite different products and therefore use different techniques. Nevertheless, in each case distinctive features of the language of advertising can be identified.

Service advertising

This kind of advertising is very similar to product advertising except that instead of a concrete product, a service is offered. It may be a banking service or a mortgage, a personal service like massage or reflexology, or a range of educational or leisure evening classes at a local school or college. Classified advertisements, point-of-sale advertisements and direct mail can all offer a 'service' to a target audience.

Charity advertising

This kind of advertising is distinctive because it is non-profit making. Although it uses the mass-marketing approach of mainstream product and service advertising, the persuasive techniques are used for a quite different purpose: rather than 'buy', the message is now 'give'. Charities depend upon reminding the public that there is a continuing need for donations, and advertising fulfils this purpose, particularly when the campaigns are emotive or sensational in some way.

In a competitive market, charities have to win their prospective donors and then persuade them to be loyal. They have to find effective ways of encouraging people to give voluntarily. Instead of standing in shopping centres with collecting tins, more and more charities are now opting for a 'brand identity'. By using the same kind of advertising techniques as commercial companies, they are able to create a distinctive image, encouraging donors to identify with a particular 'brand' of charity. Their distinctive advertising campaigns allow them to say something about the people who give, as well as about their own work and aims.

Charities therefore employ advertising agencies just as commercial companies do, and their campaigns are carefully crafted to influence the public. Advertisements like those in the Multiple Sclerosis Society's ongoing campaign recognisable by the 'torn edge' damaging the image, and the RSPCA's mountain of dead dogs, have a powerful effect on their audiences. This kind of dramatic approach allows charities to get more public attention because it generates more media coverage than a charity could afford to pay for.

ACTIVITY 12.3

Consider the advertisement in Figure 12.4, and comment on the features that make it successful.

COMMENTARY

The **function** of a charity advertisement is clearly to encourage donations so that the work of a particular group can be continued, and at first glance the image and slogan here immediately create interest. The **advertiser** can be identified by the **logo** in the bottom right-hand corner and this helps the reader to understand the context. As with many charity advertisements, the **target audience** is wide. 'Animal' charities are often supported by children who, even though they may have only limited financial means to support the work of a group, have commitment and enthusiasm for the cause. Supporters can therefore contribute in different ways and this advertisement offers alternatives: different sizes of donation; different credit cards for payment; and membership. The **selling technique** is impact-centred and draws attention to the campaign by choosing an emotive image.

Figure 12.4 Charity advertisement (in *The Independent*, 14 April 1994)

Some of our Inspectors can't tell one end of a dog from the other.

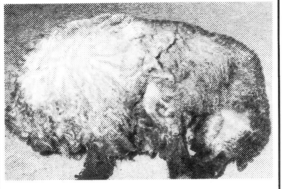

This poodle (yes, poodle) was found starving and miserable in the pouring rain.

His coat was so filthy and overgrown, our Inspector couldn't immediately tell which end his head was.

(If you're wondering, it's to the left.)

Every year, we deal with thousands of sad cases like this.

But we receive no funding from the Government, so we need your help to continue our good work.

Please give generously. Your donation will save us having to cut our coat.

Please tick the box if you are already a supporter. ☐ 1

Please tick the box if you would like information on becoming an RSPCA member. ☐ 2

Please use my donation to fight animal cruelty.

£60 ☐ £30 ☐ £12 ☐ £8 ☐ I prefer to give £ ☐

I wish to give via Visa/Access/RSPCA Mastercard no:

Signature _____ Expiry _____

Name _____

Address _____

_____ Postcode _____ **RSPCA**

To: RSPCA, Dept. TG1D, Freepost, Bristol BS3 3YY.   REG. CHARITY 219099

The **overall design** is dramatic because the dog in the photograph is almost unrecognisable. Although the image only takes up about a quarter of the whole advertisement, it influences the **tone**: the approach is quite formal, but very emotive. **Contractions** like *it's* (l. 10) and *couldn't* (l. 8) and **conjunctions in the initial position** like *But...* (l. 13) link the copy to informal spoken language. The use of **direct address** with the second person pronoun *you* (l. 18) creates a personal relationship between reader and advertiser. This mix of formal and informal is appropriate because although the advertisement seeks to establish a rapport between reader and advertiser, the subject matter is serious and disturbing.

The **lexis** is used to arouse the emotions. By using the common **collocation** *couldn't tell one end of it from the other* in an unusual context, the **slogan** disturbs the reader. The noun *Inspectors* has **connotations** of authority and this is ironically juxtaposed with their confusion. When read in conjunction with the photograph, however, the reader understands that the condition of some of the dogs they find is so bad that the animals are literally no longer recognisable. The fact that this mistreated dog is a poodle makes its condition even more emotive. Poodles are often associated with 'Poodle Parlours' and are thought of as precious pets whose coats are often unnaturally styled. Here the tangle of fur is more like a bundle of sheepskin than a dog. The parenthesis *(yes, poodle)* (l. 5) directly involves the reader – it takes account of the initial impact of the image and the shock at reading the opening noun phrase. The anaphoric reference *This poodle* (l. 5) forces the reader to understand that the photograph is not just a bundle of rags.

Modifiers are used to enhance the effect created by the photograph. The verb modifier *starving* (l. 5) and the adjective *miserable* (l. 6) change the tone – the reader understands that the lightheartedness of the slogan is ambiguous. Examples like *filthy* and *overgrown* (l. 7) use language to build on the visual image created, and because they are complements rather than pre-modifiers they are given more emphasis. The RSPCA avoids being overbearing in its approach and pre-modifiers like *sad* (l. 11) understate the situation, leaving room for the reader to feel indignant. Adverbials like *Every year* (l. 11) and the numeral *thousands* (l. 11) which is functioning as a noun emphasise the need for a charity like the RSPCA, reminding readers of the importance of any donations they can make.

Sentences are not long and several are simple. This serves to emphasise the sincerity of the advertisers.

       S   P   O
▌ (Some of our Inspectors) (can't tell) (one end of a dog from the other). (ll. 1–4)

     A   S   P   O
▌ (Every year), (we) (deal with) (thousands of sad cases like this). (ll. 11–12)

There are, however, also complex sentences. These are carefully balanced and add weight to the argument put forward. The subordinate clause *so we need your help...* (l. 14) is a result clause – it uses a balanced pattern: main clause + *so [that]* + result clause. This provides the reader with a strong reason for making a donation.

The **mood** is mostly declarative, but imperatives are used to urge the reader to respond. The commands are made more polite by the addition of the adverb *Please* (l. 16) in the initial position. Changes in the **tenses** guide the reader's responses. The simple past tense is used in the first two paragraphs creating a story-like atmosphere: *was found* (l. 5) and *was* (l. 7). However, the change to present tense in the fourth paragraph reminds the reader that this is happening now, not in the past: *deal* (l. 11) and *receive* (l. 13). The use of the **passive voice** in the verb phrase *was found* allows the sentence elements to be refocused. In an active sentence, a noun such as *Inspectors* would have filled the subject site. By using the passive, the object of the active sentence *This* *poodle* (l. 5) moves to the front of the sentence and thus gains more weight. Equally, **marked themes** like the foregrounded adverbial *Every year* (l. 11) draw attention to the extent of the problem, making sure that readers do not think this is an unusual case.

As well as the **direct address** and the **coupon** at the bottom, which are typical of many examples of advertising, the RSPCA tries to involve the reader in other ways. Through the **parenthesis**, the advertiser aims to anticipate the responses of the reader. Having established that even an RSPCA Inspector could not immediately tell where the dog's head was, the copy assumes that the reader will have the same problem. The sentence in parenthesis provides the answer to the confusion the reader is expected to feel:

> A S P A
> (If you're wondering) (it) ('s) (to the left) (l. 10)
> SCl–ACl

This creates a feeling of empathy between reader and advertiser. It encourages a feeling of outrage from the reader, akin to that felt by the RSPCA Inspectors who have to deal directly with such cases.

Most of the language in this advertisement is used literally. However, the final sentence uses a **metaphor** based on a common cliché: 'to cut your coat according to your cloth'. This traditional saying implies that you should not live beyond your means, but it works here on two levels. If the charity receives donations, it will have more money and will therefore be able to work more effectively without worrying about overspending; the noun *coat* (l. 17) also reminds the reader, however, of the poodle and the condition in which it was found. The advertisement has therefore drawn on a saying which will be familiar to most readers, while also managing to implicitly remind readers of the emotive image that initially caught their attention.

The **typographical features** are effective because they prevent a reader from passing over this advertisement as they read through a newspaper. **Bold print** is used for the copy, ensuring that the reader will focus on the text after having been interested by the image. The RSPCA is a respected charity, so readers will not doubt the claims made; and 'brand' identification is made easy because the **logo** uses white print on a black background and this stands out against the predominantly white form.

Information advertising

Most non-profit-making information advertising campaigns are associated with the Government and its various departments. The Government may wish to inform the population in general of some changes in its services. In the 1990s, the Conservative Government introduced the idea of 'charters' which established the rights of ordinary people. To promote knowledge of these charters, the Government used billboard advertisements and explanatory leaflets were sent to each house. Equally, to make sure that people understood the nature of AIDS and the ways in which it can be transmitted, television campaigns emphasised the need for 'safe sex'. Every Christmas, the Government and the police promote a campaign to encourage people not to drink and drive. In recent years, the approach has been hard-hitting, emphasising the horrors both for the victims and their families and for the driver.

Sometimes a commercial company will use advertising to inform its customers of a change in policy or a problem. Toy manufacturers may discover that a certain product has a fault, and advertisements will be placed in the national newspapers to alert parents of the potential danger, with refunds or replacements offered. To advise British Telecom customers of a change to all national dialling codes in April 1995, a year-long campaign was designed to promote awareness. Initially the advertisements just gave brief detail and a 'freephone' number for customers who wanted more information. As the April deadline came closer, the advertising campaign became more intense. The slogan *It's an 01 day* was used against a range of images: the first man on the moon; the first showing of the Daleks on the children's television programme *Doctor Who*, and so on.

Non-profit-making bodies like the Government and commercial companies use the same kinds of mass-marketing techniques for disseminating important information. The only difference between this kind of advertising and product/service or charity advertising is that the function is different. People are no longer asked to 'buy' or 'give', but to 'know'.

12.5 What to look for in the language of advertising

The following checklist can be used to identify key features in examples of advertising. There will not be examples of all the features listed in every example, but the list can be used as a guide. The points made are general so discussion of specific examples will need to be adapted to take account of the specific context, target audience and function in the given advertisement.

The following are helpful questions to ask.

Register

1   What is the **mode**? – spoken or written? newspaper, magazine, billboard, radio or television?
2   What is the **manner**? – the relationship between the advertiser and the reader or viewer: formal or informal? persuasive or informative? personal or impersonal?
3   What is the **field**? – the advertiser, the target audience and the subject matter will reflect the kind of advertising in question.

Overall design

1   What kinds of **images** are used? – people? settings? props? literal or symbolic? cultural stereotypes?
2   What effect does the **juxtaposition** of **slogan**, **logo** and **copy** have?

Lexis

1   What is noticeable about the **slogan**? – structure? puns? disrupted collocations?
2   Is anything significant about the **lexical choice**? – positive descriptions of a product? information about an issue? formal or colloquial language?
3   Are the **noun phrases** simple or complex? – pre- or post-modification? technical or emotive words?
4   Is anything significant about the **modifiers**? – strings? trigger words? physical or emotive qualities? compound words? link to price?
5   Are there any examples of language which has influenced the **contemporary word stock**? – colloquial expressions? coinages? clichés?
6   Are there any **possessive form of nouns** used for inanimate objects?
7   Are there any **innovations**? – words or phrases which make a brand memorable because the advertising campaign manipulates language?

Grammar

1   Are there any links to **spoken language**? – contractions or colloquial language? abbreviated or disjointed sentences?
2   Does the **mood** change? – declarative to make statements about a product or service? interrogative to involve the reader or viewer in decision making? imperative to reinforce the function of the advertisement?
3   Are there any **tense** changes? – simple present establishing the key features of a product, or the present state of affairs? simple past tense and perfect aspect developing comparisons? future time proposing potential changes? modal verbs implying certainty or possibility?
4   Is there anything noticeable about the **sentence structure**? – verbless clauses reflecting the disjointed and abbreviated grammatical forms of spoken language and breaking the copy up into easily readable chunks? short sentences avoiding alienation of the readers or viewers? longer sentences reflecting the nature of the subject matter and the message conveyed?
5   Are there any **marked themes**? – reordering of sentence elements to allow advertisers to refocus attention on key points? foregrounding of adverbials to provide extra information which the advertiser believes is important in making the target audience act in certain way? repositioning of the object of an active sentence in the initial position of a passive sentence for emphasis?

Metaphorical and rhetorical language

1   Is there any **phonological patterning**? – alliteration? rhythm and rhyme making a memorable slogan or phrase?
2   Is there any **lexical** and **syntactic patterning**? – repetition of words, clauses or sentences highlighting key points or a particular brand name? parallelism emphasising important attributes or contrasting two products or services?
3   Is there any **semantic patterning**? – metaphors and similes evoking emotive associations in the mind of the reader or viewer? symbolism forcing the reader or viewer to make connections that will colour the way an advertisement is interpreted? personification or animation creating a mysterious or humorous atmosphere? clever or comic puns? ambiguity adding interest or amusing the reader or viewer?

Typographical features

1   Is there anything significant about the **print size**, **shape** and **style**? – drawing attention to certain elements of an advertisement at the expense of others? encouraging the reader to concentrate on longer pieces of text? breaking up the text into easily manageable sections?
2   Is **colour** used effectively? – encouraging symbolic associations? catching the reader's or viewer's interest? creating clear contrasts?
3   Is the **layout** successful? – size of advertisement? balance of copy and images? techniques used to attract attention?

Summary

The **function** of advertising language and style is to persuade people to act in a certain way; to make them believe in certain claims; to inform them of key information.

Advertising uses many features of **informal spoken language** to develop a personal relationship between advertiser and 'consumer'. However, the purpose of the advertisement can affect the extent of the informality used – the more serious the issues, the more formal the approach will be.

Advertising **manipulates language**, **images** and **layout** to achieve the best possible results, but most people will be aware to some extent of the ways in which they are being manipulated. In the 1960s, it was commonly believed that the mass media 'injected' their message into passive unsuspecting consumers who were unable to form their own opinions. Now, however, the audience is recognised as being more active – they do not passively accept the mass media messages that they are fed, but make informed decisions based on information taken from a range of sources.

13 The language of literature – narrative prose

13.1 The nature of narrative prose

It is difficult to categorise narrative **PROSE** because prose is so wide-ranging. Above all, it offers opportunities for authors to experiment, to manipulate language in order to create the best possible effects. At the heart of a novelist's work is the desire to create a fictional world which exists alongside the real one. It may be a representation of the past, the present or of an unknown future; the characters may be realistic or caricatures; the physical and social backgrounds may be familiar or unfamiliar – ultimately, the author must decide whether to draw readers into this created world or to alienate them.

13.2 The function of narrative prose

The words on the page are the novelist's raw material: it is by manipulating language and style that the author can influence the reader. The dominant function of language is therefore **poetic**. Because literature deals with human emotions and states of mind, the **expressive** use of language is also important.

One of the main functions of fiction is to **entertain**, but authors can do much more than this through their creation of an imaginary world. Narrative prose can implicitly raise the reader's awareness about an issue or about the world in general, and can thus educate and inform (**referential** function).

Each short story or novel is different and each author will make decisions about the purpose and style of the prose. Most fiction will not fall neatly into categories, but will have a mixture of functions. It is important to establish what an author is trying to achieve in order to understand the approach adopted and the effects created.

13.3 Features of narrative prose

Novels and short stories can use language in such a wide variety of ways that it is difficult to be specific about linguistic and stylistic features. There are, however, certain features that are worth looking out for.

Manner

The **manner** can be formal or informal, depending upon the relationship the author wants to create with the reader. Often the modern novel will try to re-create the language of everyday, particularly in FIRST PERSON NARRATIVES (stories told from the point of view of one individual, using the first person singular personal pronoun *I*). Older novels tend to be more formal in their address to the reader. It is also important to decide what the author's attitude to characters and events is: **irony**, for instance, allows the author to write in a contradictory way – what is actually meant is contrary to what the words on the page appear to say. An author may use irony to show the difference between how things are and how they might be; to mock certain characters; to highlight a discrepancy between how characters see a situation and its true nature; or to emphasise that a reader knows more than the characters themselves.

Point of view

The POINT OF VIEW is central to narrative prose because the reader needs to know who is telling the story. In a **first person narrative**, the *I* narrator relates the events she or he experiences. This allows the reader a direct insight into the character's mind. Often the experiences are viewed retrospectively so that there is a difference between the character's mature and immature personalities (for instance, *Jane Eyre*, by Charlotte Brontë; *Great Expectations*, by Charles Dickens; *A Clockwork Orange*, by Anthony Burgess). The choice of a first person narrator produces a personal relationship which tends to encourage the reader to empathise with the main character. Because this approach gives only one person's view of the story, however, it can be biased, showing a limited understanding of the events and other characters.

In a THIRD PERSON NARRATIVE the narrator is often omniscient – all-seeing and all-knowing. Such narrators tend to give an overview of the story. Because there is no *I*, the narration is presented to the reader directly without an intermediary. There are two kinds of omniscient narrator: the unintrusive and the intrusive. The **unintrusive narrator** allows the author to tell the story from a distance, without the reader being aware of a persona telling the story or making judgements. The action is presented without many explicit comments or judgements. Writers like Graham Greene and E. M. Forster are known for their invisible narrators. The **intrusive narrator**, on the other hand, explicitly comments on events and characters, often pointing to the significance of what they are presenting and providing a moral interpretation. Authors like Jane Austen and George Eliot intervene in their novels, explicitly guiding and influencing the reader's judgements.

Normally, third person narrators relate events and make descriptions using the declarative mood. The interrogative or imperative moods can be used to make direct addresses to the reader, inviting judgements or opinions on events and characters. Such addresses will often be marked by a change from simple past tense to simple present.

Writers can choose to make their narrators **reliable** or **unreliable**. A reliable narrator is used in realistic novels, in which the writer aims to offer the reader a true picture of life. He or she will provide an accurate picture or interpretation of events. Sometimes characters interpreting the events are limited in their understanding because they are aware only of their own beliefs and values. By failing to recognise other viewpoints or possible interpretations, the characters fail to understand what is happening and so the reader is offered an unreliable interpretation. Writers who choose to use an unreliable narrator can draw attention to the complexity of experience by suggesting that there is always a gap between life itself and the way individuals interpret it.

Novelists are interested in more than just events. The thoughts and opinions of characters are central to the creation of a fictional world. In the nineteenth century, many novelists used INTERIOR MONOLOGUES to build up the thought patterns of their characters. Although supposedly reflecting a character's thoughts, the author would order and pattern these so that they were fluent and logical. In the twentieth century, writers like James Joyce and Virginia Woolf were some of the first to experiment with STREAM OF CONSCIOUSNESS writing, in which thought patterns appear on the page randomly. To show how chaotic and jumbled thoughts often are, writers can manipulate syntax and layout. This approach attempts to convey on the page the complexity of the human mind.

Lexis

The **lexis** can be simple or complicated, formal or colloquial, descriptive or evaluative. The choices made depend upon the author's intentions. Words may be subject specific, belonging to a particular field; they may be archaic; they may be idiosyncratic, clearly linked to a particular character; or they may be linked to a real or imaginary dialect appropriate to the setting of the novel. The connotations of the words chosen will build up a particular viewpoint of the fictional world.

Nouns may be abstract or concrete, depending upon whether the prose focuses on events or states of mind. **Proper nouns** may be used to give the fictional world and its inhabitants a concrete basis. The intentional omission of names may create a mysterious atmosphere.

Modifiers may provide physical, psychological, emotive or visual detail. They may focus on colour, sound or noise to create the fictional world. It is through the modifiers that authors can influence the reader – they can describe or evaluate using words with positive or negative connotations which direct the reader to respond in chosen ways. Modifiers are crucial in forming a parallel world; in helping the reader to make decisions about events, characters and places; and in adding depth to any underlying message.

Verbs tell the reader about the kinds of actions and processes occurring. The use of stative verbs suggests that the author's interest lies in description, whether it be of setting or states of mind; dynamic verbs place an emphasis on what is happening, implying that an author is more interested in action than in contemplation.

All consideration of the lexis of fictional prose must take account of the time and place in which the novel is set. Authors' lexical choices will vary depending upon the kinds of worlds and the people they are creating.

Speech

Writers can adopt a variety of approaches to convey the **speech** of their characters on the page. DIRECT SPEECH is an exact copy of the precise words spoken, allowing characters to speak for themselves. This approach gives prominence to the speaker's point of view. If writers vary spelling, vocabulary, word order and so on, it is possible to produce an accurate phonological, lexical and syntactical written version of characters' accents and dialects. INDIRECT SPEECH reports what someone has said, using a subordinate *that* clause. The person who is reporting the conversation intervenes as an interpreter by selecting the reported words. This submerges the original speaker's point of view.

FREE INDIRECT SPEECH is a form of indirect speech in which the main reporting clause (for instance, *he said that...*) is omitted. This merges the approach of both direct and indirect speech. It uses the same third person pronouns and past tense as indirect speech, but reproduces the actual words spoken more accurately. It can be used to create irony because it gives the reader the flavour of characters' words, while keeping the narrator in a position where he or she can intervene. Free indirect speech can also be used to direct readers' sympathy away from certain characters or to indicate changes in the role of a character. Writers can present a character's thoughts in a similar range of ways.

Grammar

The **grammar** of narrative prose will reflect the kind of world created and the kind of viewpoint offered. In many ways, novelists are freer in their potential choices than writers are in other varieties – in fiction, non-standard grammar and lexis are acceptable because they are part of a created world and are an integral part of the characters who inhabit that world.

Most fiction is written in the **simple past tense** – extensive use of other tenses or timescales is worth commenting on. The effects created by writing completely in the present tense, for instance, can be quite dramatic. **Mood** will vary depending upon the requirements of the author. Declarative mood is most common, but interrogatives and imperatives are used to vary the pace and change the focus. In fiction, **sentence structures** are often complex. When simple sentences are used, they are often emphatic or striking. Because writers can experiment, there can also be sentences that do not appear to conform to standard grammatical patterns. Writers vary the kind of sentence structure they use, to maintain readers' interest and to make their fictional world seem alive.

Metaphorical language

Metaphorical language is a writer's way of personalising the world created. **Metaphors**, **symbolism** and so on tell the reader something about an author's relationship with the fictional world. Such language usage makes the imaginary world real and guides the reader in judging the characters, setting and events.

Rhetorical techniques

The **rhetorical techniques** a writer chooses persuade readers to involve themselves or distance themselves from the fictional world. **Juxtapositions**, **listing**, **parallelism** and so on can be used to influence the reader's perception of characters, settings and events. **Patterning** may be stylistic or phonological, but the end results all guide readers' responses. **Marked themes**, the **passive voice** and **end focus** all throw emphasis on certain elements of the text, highlighting things that the author considers to be important.

13.4 Different kinds of authorial intention

To characterise

Writers can allow characters to reveal themselves to the reader by using a first person narrative or they can mediate using a third person narrator who comments and makes explicit judgements. In both methods other linguistic and stylistic techniques inevitably play a part in the effects created overall.

Physical description is the most obvious way in which a character can be given a concrete presence. Such detail may be provided by the author or by other characters. It is important to decide whose view is being given so that the reliability of the description can be assessed.

> 1 Aleph, the 'beauty', was pale in complexion, her skin (of course innocent of make-up) faintly glowing, her face from a large brow tapering into an oval form, her eyes, beneath long, almost straight dark eyebrows, large and dark brown, thoughtful, expressive of sympathy, also of judgment, her hair, a dark
> 5 shining chestnut colour, a lively complex of curls which framed her face and cascaded in orderly disorder to her long slim pale neck.
>
> Iris Murdoch (1919–), *The Green Knight*

Murdoch provides a lot of detail about the character, distinguishing between the narrator's viewpoint and that of other characters by using inverted commas to highlight the **abstract noun** in parenthesis, *beauty* (l. 1). Certain **modifiers**, like *large*, *long* and *dark* (ll. 2–6), are repeated to emphasise key qualities of Aleph. These physical qualities give a visual image of the girl, but abstract nouns like *sympathy* and *judgment* (l. 4) build up a more complex portrait. Other modifiers like *lively* (l. 5) and the present participle *shining* (l. 5) and the paradox of *orderly disorder* (l. 6), although actually describing the girl's hair, also suggest something about her character. The parenthesis emphasises that this girl is a natural beauty and the adverbial expressing certainty, *of course* (l. 1), suggests that readers should have guessed this for themselves.

In the one long **sentence** here, Murdoch manages to convey precisely many physical and personal details about Aleph. It is made up from a sequence of S P C clauses in which the stative verb *to be* is omitted. No explicit metaphorical language is used because the portrait relies on literal description, but Murdoch makes sure that readers realise the **symbolic** value of the physical details. The positive **connotations** of the lexis chosen and the asyndetic **listing** of the details about Aleph's *skin* (l. 1), *eyes* (l. 3), *hair* (l. 5) and *face* (l. 6) persuade the reader to like the character just as the narrator clearly does.

Apart from information provided by the author, what characters **say**, **do** and **think** is also an important means of characterisation. **Direct speech** and **thought** (interior monologue and stream of consciousness) reflect the characters as they really are, without apparent intervention by the writer or other characters.

> 1 'It is over! it is over!' she [Anne] repeated to herself again, and again, in nervous gratitude. 'The worst is over!'
> Mary talked, but she could not attend. She had seen him. They had met. They had been once more in the same room!
> 5 Soon, however, she began to reason with herself, and try to be feeling less. Eight years, almost eight years had passed, since all had been given up. How absurd to be resuming the agitation which such an interval had banished into distance and indistinctness! What might not eight years do? Events of every description, changes, alienations, removals, – all, all must be
> 10 compromised in it; and oblivion of the past – how natural, how certain too! It included nearly a third part of her own life.
>
> Jane Austen, *Persuasion*

The subject matter here focuses on the main character's response to meeting an old lover. Austen uses an **interior monologue** to convey Anne's emotions – the rhetorical techniques and disjointed style also reflect on her state of mind. The event – the meeting – is insignificant, but Anne's response is an important stage in Austen's characterisation. There are many **abstract nouns** to stress internal rather than external reactions: *agitation* (l. 7), *changes*, *alienations* (l. 9) and *gratitude* (l. 2). By contrast, there are no descriptions of actions other than Mary's talking (from which Anne feels distanced) and Anne's summary of the meeting. The sequence of **simple sentences** used to represent the visit emphasises the minor event that has occurred in comparison to the great emotions it has stirred.

> S   P   O   S   P   S   P   A
> (She) (had seen) (him). (They) (had met). (They) (had been) (once more) (in the
> A
> same room)! (ll. 3–4)

Verbs like *banished* (ll. 7–8) and abstract nouns like *oblivion* (l. 10) are dramatic and seem ironic when juxtaposed with such an insignificant occasion.

The **mood** varies frequently to mirror Anne's state of mind. As is usual, declaratives are used to tell the story, but Anne is questioning her own reactions and emotions and therefore interrogatives are common: *What might not...* (l. 8). There are also a number of exclamations to mark Anne's feelings: *How natural, how certain...* (l. 10). By changing from one mood to another, Austen is able to reflect Anne's disturbed emotional state in the style as well as the lexis.

Direct speech is used at the opening of the extract. The simple sentences are emphatic:

> S   P   C   S   P   C
> '(It) (is) (over)! (it) (is) (over)!' (l. 1)

The **repetition** of the S P C structure marks Anne's attempts to regain control. The repetition of the third person plural pronoun *they* (ll. 3–4) suggests some kind of unity between Anne and the unnamed man, yet the rest of the extract emphasises that they have been separated for eight years. This contradiction underlines the effect the meeting has had on her. As she tries to rationalise what has happened, the **sentences** tend to be complex because they are conveying Anne's confusion. Austen mirrors the complexity of Anne's thoughts in the style she chooses – this is typical of interior monologue, in which the author orders a character's thoughts on the page.

> A   S   P   O   O
> (Soon), (however), (she) (began) (to reason with herself), (and) (try to be feeling less).
> conj   SCl–NFCl   SCl–NFCl
>
> (ll. 5–6)

Some **verb phrases** differ from Late Modern English usage: Austen uses expanded verb phrases like *try to be feeling* (l. 5) and *to be resuming* (l. 7). The use of the **progressive aspects** expresses the depth of Anne's feelings and suggests that there is an ongoing process as she struggles to resume control of her emotions.

The style is very rhetorical. Austen **repeats** the noun phrase *eight years* (ll. 6, 8) to draw attention to the length of time since Anne and the man last saw each other. She uses **tripling** to show Anne's thought processes as she tries to sort out her unexpected emotions: *changes, alienations, removals* (l. 9). **Antithesis** juxtaposes Anne's actual responses with the ones she feels to be more appropriate: verb phrases like *to reason* and *try to be feeling less* (ll. 5–6); noun phrases like *agitation* (l. 7) and *oblivion* (l. 10).

The author's main interest is in conveying Anne's inner experience after a brief meeting. She is more concerned with Anne than the event itself. The **point of view** varies in the extract: Austen allows Anne to present her own thoughts and feelings directly in the form of an interior monologue, but she also provides an authorial overview, *Soon, however, she began...* (l. 5). By using **free indirect thought**, Anne's feelings are given strength: *She had seen him...* (l. 3). Her inner feelings are given a 'voice', allowing the narrator to stand back and imply that the character is directly revealing herself to the reader.

Twentieth-century authors often use **stream of consciousness** to convey a character's thoughts to the reader in a more realistic way. James Joyce was one of the first to experiment with style in this way.

> 1 Once upon a time and a very good time it was there was a moocow coming down along the road and this moocow that was down along the road met a nicens little boy named baby tuckoo . . .
>   His father told him that story: his father looked at him through glass: he
> 5 had a hairy face.
>   He was baby tuckoo. The moocow came down the road where Betty Byrne lived . . .

James Joyce, Portrait of the Artist as a Young Man

In this extract, Joyce is trying to re-create a child's eye view of the world in both the words and the style he chooses. The child's perspective is captured in the focus on senses: the sight of his father's face seen through *glass* (l. 4) – his glasses; the feel of his *hairy* (l. 5) face. Childlike lexis such as *moocow* (l. 1) and *tuckoo* (l. 3) mark the register. Equally, the **syntax** resembles child language: sentences are long and the co-ordinating conjunction *and* is common. The opening sentence uses a traditional adverbial associated with narrative: *Once upon a time* (l. 1). Here the child retells himself the story his father tells. **Repetition** of phrases is also a typical feature of children's stories because it creates a memorable pattern.

The reader's knowledge of the child here seems to come directly from the child himself with no narrator intervention. In the Austen extract, the narrator orders Anne's thoughts so that although the lexis and syntax convey her sense of confusion, the grammatical structures are standard. Joyce, on the other hand, uses lexis and syntax that specifically reflect a child's character – the words and sentence structures have been chosen to suggest the child's actual pattern of thought.

ACTIVITY 13.1

Read this extract from George Eliot's The Mill on the Floss and comment on the techniques used to characterise Maggie.

> 1 You may see her now, as she walks down the favourite turning, and enters the Deeps by a narrow path through a group of Scotch firs – her tall figure and old lavender-gown visible through an hereditary black-silk shawl of some wide-meshed net-like material; and now she is sure of being unseen, she
> 5 takes off her bonnet and ties it over her arm. One would certainly suppose her to be farther on in life than her seventeenth year – perhaps because of the slow resigned sadness of the glance, from which all search and unrest seem to have departed, perhaps because her broad-chested figure has the mould of early womanhood. Youth and health have withstood well the invol-
> 10 untary and voluntary hardships of her lot, and the nights in which she has lain on the hard floor for a penance have left no obvious trace; the eyes are liquid, the brown cheek is firm and rounded, the full lips are red. With her dark colouring and jet crown surmounting her tall figure, she seems to have a sort of kinship with the grand Scotch firs, at which she is looking up as if
> 15 she loved them well. Yet one has a sense of uneasiness in looking at her – a sense of opposing elements, of which a fierce collision is imminent: surely there is a hushed expression, such as one often sees in older faces under borderless caps, out of keeping with the resistant youth, which one expects to flash out in a sudden, passionate glance, that will dissipate all the qui-
> 20 etude, like a damped fire leaping out again when all seemed safe.

But Maggie herself was not uneasy at this moment. She was calmly enjoying the free air, while she looked up at the old fir-trees, and thought that those broken ends of branches were the records of past storms, which had only made the red stems soar higher.

George Eliot (Mary Ann Evans, 1819–80), <u>The Mill on the Floss</u>

COMMENTARY

The **third person narrator** directly addresses the reader here using the second person pronoun *you*. This kind of narrator is described as **intrusive** because the reader is made explicitly aware of her presence. By revealing her thoughts and speculations on Maggie, the narrator creates a personal relationship with the reader – the **tone** is almost conspiratorial as they observe Maggie unseen. In the first paragraph, the focus is on Maggie's external features and on what can be deduced from these. The narrator is tentative, using verbs like *suppose* (l. 5), *seems* (l. 13) and *may* (l. 1); adverbs like *perhaps* (l. 6); and noun phrases like *a sense of...* (l. 15). The second paragraph changes the focus and approach: the narrator is no longer so obvious; Maggie's actions and thoughts are described. Verbs are now stative, describing Maggie as she is, not as she seems to be: *was* (l. 21); they also describe processes: *looked* (l. 22) and *thought* (l. 22).

Initially, **physical description** characterises Maggie. The narrator draws the reader's attention to literal features using complex noun phrases:

> ^{m   m   h}   ^m   ^h   ^{m   m}   ^m   ^{h   q}
> her tall figure . . . old lavender-gown . . . an hereditary black-silk shawl of some
> _{det Adj N}   _{Adj Adj}   _N   _{det Adj}   _{Adj N}   _{N PrepP}
>
> wide-meshed net-like material (ll. 2–4)

The **modifiers** suggest conformity of dress. Her clothes are not bright or extravagant, but practical and old. **Compound modifiers** allow the writer to provide detailed information in a concise way. Other modifiers describe her face: her eyes are *liquid* (l. 12); her cheeks *brown...firm...rounded* (l. 12); her lips *full* and *red* (l. 12). The author creates a very visual picture of Maggie, but also hints at her mood using noun phrases like *slow resigned sadness* (l. 7) and *hushed expression* (l. 17). A contradiction is built up between the physical details of dress and facial features and Maggie's mood.

Metaphorical language creates another layer to Maggie's character. The post-modified noun phrase *a sense of opposing elements* (ll. 15–16) summarises the knowledge the reader has gained from the description of Maggie in the first paragraph. The pre-modifier *fierce* (l. 16) and the complement *imminent* (l. 16) used to modify the abstract noun *collision* imply that Maggie's apparent external calm does not reflect her inner state of mind. Such lexical choices prepare the reader for conflict. The **metaphor** of the *damped fire* (l. 20) and the verbs *flash* (l. 19) and *leaping* (l. 20) develop this sense of Maggie's inner strength – she has an inner spark that cannot be quelled by external circumstances like poverty and hardship. By comparing her to the fir trees, Eliot suggests that Maggie has an inner grandeur that will enable her to rise above everyday problems. The modifier *grand* (l. 14) used to describe the trees can equally be applied to Maggie's ability to cope with a life that does not fulfil her dreams.

The **syntax** reflects the kind of character described. The **present tense** is used in the first paragraph where Maggie is portrayed through her physical characteristics. It unites the reader and writer, while separating them from Maggie. The second paragraph uses the **simple past tense** which is traditional for narratives. It allows the narrator to return to unintrusive narrative comment. The reader is aware of the narrator's omniscience since although judgements are apparently made on the basis of observations, some of the details describing Maggie's internal state of mind could not be known.

The **sentences** are mostly complex, which is appropriate for the detailed nature of the characterisation. A relationship is created between external details and internal feelings – because the narrator's thoughts are not simple, the sentences are invariably complex.

> S   P   A   O
> (Youth and health) (have withstood) (well) (the involuntary and voluntary
>
>   S
> hardships of her lot), (and) (the nights in which she has lain on the hard floor for
>   conj   SCl–RelCl
>
>   P   O   S   P   C   S
> a penance) (have left) (no obvious trace); (the eyes) (are) (liquid), (the brown
>
>   P   C   S   P   C
> cheek) (is) (firm and rounded), (the full lips) (are) (red). (ll. 9–12)

The style is **rhetorical** because the author is trying to persuade the reader to react to Maggie in a certain way. The **repetition** of the adverb *now* (ll. 1, 4) suggests that readers are being given a chance to observe Maggie for themselves – allowing them to make their own decisions about the nature of her character. By using **compound phrases**, Eliot gives her style a balance which encourages the reader to accept the conclusions reached: the co-ordinated noun phrase *search and unrest* (l. 7) suggests that Maggie has been forced to accept her life rather than to challenge events; the abstract nouns *Youth and health* (l. 9) are almost personified, implying that despite the hardships of her life, Maggie's physical and psychological nature is strong. **Tripling** is used to list the physical features of Maggie's face so that the writer seems to be scrutinising her. Most importantly, the **antithesis** reminds the reader of the apparent contradictions within Maggie: *hushed...resistant* (ll. 17–18); *involuntary...voluntary* (ll. 9–10); *uneasy...calmly* (l. 21) and so on. These **juxtapositions** imply that although externally Maggie seems to accept her fate, she is repressing her true nature.

Eliot uses several techniques to characterise Maggie. She presents her in a positive light, encouraging readers to empathise with her through the lexis and stylistic features. The contradictions in her character are emphasised – Maggie seems old before her time, yet she has an inner strength and dignity.

To set the scene

Setting the scene is important if the writer wishes readers to immerse themselves in the fictional world created. By providing physical details of time and place, the author can enable the reader to visualise the background. It may just provide a context for characters to interrelate and events to take place, but often it is symbolic. Even literal descriptions can tell the reader something about the characters who are seen in a particular location.

By providing **literal details**, a writer can build up a sense of place. In particular, rooms can tell us something about the characters who inhabit them.

> 1 The room had scarcely altered since their father had furnished it, hastily but not cheaply ... The desk was handsome and huge, with an almost military look, its dark green leather glowing, its brass fitments gleaming. Lucas, who scarcely tolerated other people in the house, cleaned the place himself ...
> 5 Bookshelves covered the entire wall behind the desk, and also the opposite wall by the door. A large dark brown leather sofa, rarely sat upon, shiny as on the day of its purchase, stretched out beside the door to the garden,

above it hung a watercolour of Lake Geneva showing the Château de Chillon. There were several powerful strong upright chairs with leather seats
10 and ladderbacks ... There was a huge dark Persian carpet now pleasantly worn ...

Iris Murdoch, The Green Knight

The details here not only create a background for the events that are about to occur, but also tell the reader something about Lucas, who has deliberately left the room as it was in his father's time. The **concrete nouns** *desk* (l. 2), *bookshelves* (l. 5) and *watercolour* (l. 8) all suggest that the owner is an educated person; while the reference to the *leather sofa* (l. 6) and the *Persian carpet* (l. 10) suggest that he is affluent. Although the verb **modifiers** *glowing* and *gleaming* (l. 3) and the adjective modifier *shiny* (l. 6) imply that the owner takes a pride in his environment, the repetition of the modifier *dark* (ll. 3, 6 and 10) gives the room a mysterious atmosphere, suggesting that perhaps he has something to hide. Developing this sense of a possibly mysterious side to Lucas, the modifiers *large* (l. 6), *powerful* and *strong* (l. 9) seem to imply that his personality can daunt and dominate the people around him. The military **metaphor** used to describe his desk reinforces the reader's awareness of his power. The description of the furniture thus becomes **symbolic** of the character who inhabits the room.

Some descriptions are more explicitly symbolic: by using metaphorical language to create a sense of place, an author can develop a theme.

1 It is the long vacation in the regions of Chancery Lane. The good ships Law and Equity, those teak-built, copper-bottomed, iron-fastened, brazen-faced, and not by any means fast-sailing Clippers, are laid up in ordinary. The Flying Dutchman, with a crew of ghostly clients imploring all whom they may
5 encounter to peruse their papers, has drifted, for the time being, Heaven knows where. The Courts are all shut up, the public offices lie in a hot sleep, Westminster Hall itself is a shady solitude where nightingales might sing, and a tenderer class of suitors than is usually found there, walk.
    The Temple, Chancery Lane, Sergeants' Inn and Lincoln's Inn even unto
10 the Fields, are like tidal harbours at low water; where stranded proceedings, offices at anchor, idle clerks lounging on lop-sided stools that will not recover their perpendicular until the current of Term sets in, lie high and dry upon the ooze of the long vacation. Outer doors of chambers are shut up by the score, messages and parcels are to be left at the Porter's Lodge by the bushel. A
15 crop of grass would grow in the chinks of the stone pavement outside Lincoln's Inn Hall, but that the ticket-porters, who have nothing to do beyond sitting in the shade there, with their white aprons over their heads to keep the flies off, grub it up and eat it thoughtfully.

Charles Dickens, Bleak House

This is a vivid picture of the deserted Inns of Court when the lawyers have left London during the holiday period. The **tone** is formal because the theme is serious: the nature of justice. Even though the lawyers are absent, there is still a sense of the rituals which are linked to the Courts – it is a public world and Dickens's prose reflects this.

He uses a simple sentence in the declarative **mood** to make the time clear:

S   P   C   A
(It) (is) (the long vacation) (in the regions of Chancery Lane). (l. 1)

To discuss his theme implicitly, he takes a metaphor and develops it, giving a concrete presence to the inactivity he describes in the Inns of Court. His metaphorical language is used to indirectly criticise what he sees: *Law and Equity* become *good ships* (ll. 1–2) and an **extended metaphor** of the sea is used to make the reader aware of Dickens' view of these institutions. Because it is the vacation, the *good ships...are laid up* (ll. 1–3), allowing the reader to come close and inspect them. The string of **compound modifiers** suggests something about the nature of the law: *teak-built*, *copper-bottomed* and *iron-fastened* (l. 2) all imply that the Law is solid and long-lasting, that it has been lovingly created for the safety of those who come into contact with it. The compound modifier *brazen-faced* (l. 2) and the prepositional phrase *not by any means* (l. 3) which pre-modifies the final compound modifier *fast-sailing* (l. 3) create a different kind of response from the reader. Both these examples have negative connotations: the lawyers, the text implies, are shameless – interested only in prolonging legal action rather than in bringing cases to an end. To mirror the inactivity during the vacation, Dickens continues his sea metaphor by referring to the *Flying Dutchman* (l. 4) which has *drifted* (l. 5). The **connotations** of an unmanned ghost ship are appropriate here to describe the aimlessness of Chancery Lane now that the lawyers have gone. The **simile** *like tidal harbours at low water* (l. 10) suggests that the other law courts are equally unable to do anything constructive. The **lexical set** of the sea continues with verbs like *stranded* (l. 10) and nouns like *anchor* (l. 11), *current* (l. 12) and *ooze* (l. 13).

Having established his metaphor, Dickens can describe the location more literally: the *Outer doors of chambers are shut up* (l. 13); the ticket-porters *have nothing to do* (l. 16); and so on. The description of small details like the *lopsided stools* (l. 11) and the *stone pavement* (l. 15) help the reader to build up a visual image running parallel to the metaphorical image of ships moored in a harbour when the tide is out. The present participle *lounging* (l. 11) and the use of the modal verb to describe the grass that *would grow* (l. 15) emphasise the idleness of all who are left behind.

At one level, this extract is no more than a description of a place during the summer: Dickens uses the **present tense** and **stative verbs** to create a strong sense of the Inns of Court. However, the underlying meaning makes this more than just a picture created from words. The theme is the law and its public and private faces: Dickens indirectly suggests that the lawyers are more interested in their fees than in their clients and that the Law is not as efficient as it might be. To convey this message, he uses metaphorical language that forces the reader to make connections and recognise that there is a purpose to the description.

In autobiographical fiction, writers may recall a place of personal significance. Such description will often be distinctive either in its content or in its style because it is based on an individual's memory of a particular place. Authors may pick out small details that seemed important to them at the time, or they may use non-standard lexical and grammatical forms in order to recreate the power of the place.

> 1 August Bank Holiday. A tune on an ice-cream cornet. A slap of sea and a
>   tickle of sand. A fanfare of sunshades opening. A wince and whinny of
>   bathers dancing into deceptive waters. A tuck of dresses. A rolling of
>   trousers. A compromise of paddlers. A sunburn of girls and a lark of boys. A
> 5 silent hullabaloo of balloons.
>
> Dylan Thomas, 'Holiday Memory'

Each **sentence** in this opening paragraph of Thomas's short story is a complex noun phrase:

m	h	q
A fanfare	of sunshades opening. (l. 2)	
det	N	PrepP

m	m	h	q
A	silent	hullabaloo	of balloons. (ll. 4–5)
det	Adj	N	PrepP

The effect is almost cinematic as the eye sweeps across the sands and sees each group doing something different. Thomas experiments with words as well as sentence structures. He disrupts **collocations**: the 'slap and tickle' of bawdy seaside postcards is linked to the sea and the sand (ll. 1–2). He creates a powerful sense of the sounds of the beach as well as the sights: the *slap* (l. 1) of the sea; the *wince and whinny* (l. 2) of bathers. However, he also gives sounds to things that are essentially visual: the ice-cream *cornet* (l. 1) becomes a trumpet playing a tune – possibly the jingle of the ice-cream van itself; developing the musical image, the sunshades open in a *fanfare* (l. 2) – the association with royal occasions and the arrival of someone significant makes every-one on the beach seem important. Even the jostling of balloons is portrayed in the **oxymoron** *silent hullabaloo* (l. 5).

Thomas's opening description immediately creates an active beach holiday scene in the reader's mind. His individual approach to conveying the sounds and sights is effective because even though his style is not familiar, the scene he offers readers is. The verbless sentences capture life as it is happening – the effect is photographic.

ACTIVITY 13.2

Read the extract below and consider both the techniques used to set the scene and the authorial intention in creating it.

1   The house was left; the house was deserted. It was left like a shell on a
sandhill to fill with dry salt grains now that life had left it. The long night
seemed to have set in; the trifling airs, nibbling, the clammy breaths, fum-
bling, seemed to have triumphed. The saucepan had rusted and the mat
5   decayed. Toads had nosed their way in. Idly, aimlessly, the swaying shawl
swung to and fro. A thistle thrust itself between the tiles in the larder. The
swallows nested in the drawing-room; the floor was strewn with straw; the
plaster fell in shovelfuls; rafters were laid bare; rats carried off this and that to
gnaw behind the wainscots. Tortoise-shell butterflies burst from the chrysalis
10   and pattered their life out on the window-pane. Poppies sowed themselves
among the dahlias; the lawn waved with long grass; giant artichokes towered
among roses; a fringed carnation flowered among the cabbages; while the
gentle tapping of a weed at the window had become, on winters' nights, a
drumming from sturdy trees and thorned briars which made the whole room
15   green in summer.

Virginia Woolf (1882–1941), <u>To the Lighthouse</u>

COMMENTARY

The **lexical repetition** of the first two sentences emphasises a sense of abandonment. The past participles *left* and *deserted* (l. 1) stress the absence of any human life, while the stative verb *was* (l. 1) reinforces the apparent stasis. To make this image more concrete the author uses the **simile** of the shell: just as the snail has left an empty shell, so people have left this house. The comparison links the house to its environment – the sea – and makes it seem fragile. Equally, the abandoned building, like the empty shell, is open for others to take control. The complex noun phrase *The long night* (l. 2) is possibly **symbolic** of death, reminiscent of the phrase 'the dark night of the soul' which describes a time of mental and spiritual suffering before some kind of change takes place. The writer uses the **verb phrases** to mark both the present stasis and the potential for change. Although the perfect aspect in the verb phrase *had left* (l. 2) suggests a finality, the stative verb *seemed* (l. 3) prepares the reader for change.

The scene starts to become more active with the introduction of present participles which imply ongoing movement:

m	m	h	q
the	trifling	airs,	nibbling (l. 3)
det	V	N	V
	(pres pa)		(pres pa)

m	m	h	q
the	clammy	breaths,	fumbling (ll. 3–4)
det	Adj	N	V
			(pres pa)

Even though the movement is tentative and is apparently linked to the death-like atmosphere of the house, it begins to replace a sense of stasis with a sense of life. The life here, however, is not linked to people – the end of their time in the house is symbolised by the saucepan and mat. The perfect aspect used in the verb phrases *had rusted* and *decayed* (ll. 4–5) indicates that the process is complete – people and their domestic possessions no longer have a place in the house. This mood is reinforced by the adverbs describing the movement of the shawl: *Idly, aimlessly* (l. 5). Even the verb modifier *swaying* (l. 5) suggests only insignificant movement.

The house now becomes a source of new life as the natural world takes over. The verb used to describe the appearance of the toads, *nosed* (l. 5), is tentative, but dynamic verbs like *thrust* (l. 6) and *burst* (l. 9) change the atmosphere dramatically. The use of the **simple past tense** rather than the perfect aspect reinforces the sense of immediacy. The **juxtaposition** of the natural and the domestic highlights the changes occurring. Nouns like *thistle* (l. 6), *swallows* (l. 7) and *rats* (l. 8) are juxtaposed with *the tiles* (l. 6), *the larder* (l. 6), *the drawing-room* (l. 7) and *the wainscots* (l. 9). The house begins to take on a new form – the plaster is crumbling, the floor is covered with straw, but verbs like *nested* (l. 7) have **connotations** of new life rather than destruction.

However, the writer reminds the reader that this will always be a human environment and will never be perfectly adapted for the natural life. The connotations of energy in the verb *burst* (l. 9), for instance, are juxtaposed with the verb *pattered* (l. 10). Ultimately the butterflies are trapped by the windows – although apparently offering a way out, these ultimately destroy them.

The changes in the garden also reflect the end of one kind of order and the beginning of another. The reflexive verb phrase *sowed themselves* (l. 10) reminds the reader that the natural world is now in control. This knowledge is reinforced by the **juxtaposition** of plants in unexpected contexts: *poppies* and *dahlias* (ll. 10, 11); *artichokes* and *roses* (ll. 11, 12); *carnation* and *cabbages* (l. 12). The timescale of these changes is highlighted by the description of the *weed* (l. 13). The verbal nouns *tapping* and *drumming* (ll. 13, 14) mark the transition from something weak to something strong and this change becomes symbolic of the growing power of the natural world and the diminishing power of the human world. The concluding noun phrase emphasises this by using a predicative modifier normally associated with the natural world to describe the room. The use of the adjective *green* (l. 15), with its connotations of new life and growth, contrasts with the earlier descriptions of the house.

The description of the house appeals to the senses. Its attention to detail makes it easy for the reader to visualise. **Noun phrases** are often complex, providing detailed information in a concise way.

m	m	h
a	fringed	carnation (l. 12)
det	V	N

m	h
Tortoise-shell	butterflies (l. 9)
N N	N

m	m	h	q
the	gentle	tapping	of a weed (ll. 12–13)
det	Adj	V/N	PrepP

The focus of the description is the house and yet it is possible to say that the unnamed people who have left the house are also important. The way in which the opening **sentence structure** is grammatically described dictates whether the house itself or the unnamed people should be the focus of the reader's attention. The verb phrase *was left* (l. 1) could be the simple past tense of the verb phrase *to be left*; it could, however, be the passive form of the verb *to leave* with the agent omitted. The first interpretation allows the house itself to gain prominence; the use of the passive voice, however, suggests that the underlying mystery should be considered. Whichever interpretation is chosen, the extract certainly builds up a clear visual picture of the abandoned house, drawing the reader into the fictional world created.

To evoke a powerful atmosphere

The creation of a range of different atmospheres is essential to the success of fiction. If readers are to believe in the world of the novel or short story, the writer must be able to arouse their emotions. By creating a dramatic, poignant or euphoric atmosphere, writers can persuade their readers to feel as the characters do.

Often a striking atmosphere is created through description mirroring a character's state of mind or a theme.

> 1 Fog everywhere, fog up the river, where it flows among green aits and meadows; fog down the river, where it rolls defiled among the tiers of shipping, and the waterside pollution of a great (and dirty) city. Fog on the Essex Marshes, fog on the Kentish heights. Fog creeping into the cabooses of
> 5 collier-brigs; fog lying out on the yards, and hovering in the rigging of great ships; fog drooping on the gunwales of barges and small boats. Fog in the eyes and throats of ancient Greenwich pensioners, wheezing by the firesides of their wards; fog in the stem and bowl of the afternoon pipe of the wrathful skipper, down in his close cabin; fog cruelly pinching the toes and fingers of
> 10 his shivering little 'prentice boy on deck. Chance people on the bridges peeping over the parapets into a nether sky of fog, with fog all round them, as if they were up in a balloon, and hanging in the misty clouds. . . .
>   The raw afternoon is rawest, and the dense fog is densest, and the muddy streets are muddiest, near that leaden-headed old obstruction, appro-
> 15 priate ornament for the threshold of a leaden-headed old corporation: Temple Bar. And hard by Temple Bar, in Lincoln's Inn Hall, at the very heart of the fog, sits the Lord High Chancellor in his High Court of Chancery.
>
> Charles Dickens, *Bleak House*

By opening the extract with a **verbless sentence**, Dickens is able to attract attention to the noun *fog* (ll. 1–3). He further emphasises its importance by **repeating** it throughout the paragraph and by using the basic pattern of subject and adverbial several times. Although **proper nouns** like *Essex Marshes* (ll. 3–4), *Greenwich* (l. 7) and *Temple Bar* (l. 16) give the places described a sense of reality, the fog in fact destroys all individuality and the repetitive grammatical structures seem to mirror the way it makes everywhere look the same.

To emphasise the all-pervading nature of the fog, Dickens uses a range of contrasts: the adverbs *up* (l. 1) and *down* (l. 2); a sequence of sentences starting *Fog on. . .* and *Fog in. . .*; and present participles like *Fog creeping. . .* (l. 4), *fog lying. . .* (l. 5) and *fog. . .pinching. . .* (l. 9). This very patterned approach forces the reader to recognise the power of the fog. **Lexical sets** create a sense of the environment: nouns like *river* (l. 1) and *waterside* (l. 3); nautical nouns like *cabooses* (ships' kitchens, l. 4), *collier-brigs* (l. 5), *rigging* (l. 5) and *barges* (l. 6); legal nouns like *Lincoln's Inn Hall* (l. 16) and *Lord High Chancellor* (l. 17). **Modifiers** like *great* (l. 3) and *small* (l. 6) remind the reader that nothing can escape the fog. Although its effect on the landscape dominates the extract, people are also at its mercy. The noun phrases referring to the people who inhabit these scenes are as wide-ranging as the kinds of landscapes affected: *ancient Greenwich pensioners* (l. 7), *the wrathful skipper* (ll. 8–9), the *shivering little 'prentice boy* (l. 10) and *Chance people* (l. 10). Through the breadth of his references, Dickens creates a microcosm – the fictional world becomes a miniature version of reality.

A verb modifier like *defiled* (l. 2), an adjective modifier like *dirty* (l. 3) and the abstract noun *pollution* (l. 3) all have negative **connotations**. They evoke an atmosphere that is unpleasant, reinforced by verbs like *wheezing* (l. 7), adverbs like *cruelly* (l. 9) and adjectives like *wrathful* (l. 8). Everyone becomes detached, as though suspended in a balloon – all sense of community has gone. The second paragraph then uses **superlatives** like *rawest* (l. 13), *densest* (l. 13) and *muddiest* (l. 14) to stress that the worst of all conditions are to be found at *Temple Bar* (l. 16). By using the prepositional phrase *at the very heart of* (ll. 16–17) Dickens indicates that the fog has more than just a descriptive purpose: it actually becomes **symbolic** of the legal process as a whole.

In evoking this atmosphere, Dickens aims to create a parallel between the landscape and people obscured by literal fog and the legal system. The Law has its own symbolic 'fog' – its impenetrable processes confuse and bewilder the people caught up in its impersonal and uncaring systems.

The extract from Dickens's *Bleak House* uses **repetition** as the main technique for creating an evocative atmosphere. Recurring lexis and syntactical patterns draw attention to the central theme: the deceptive nature of the Law. Writers can also exploit less explicit ways of evoking a mood, such as using modifiers. The choice of words with positive or negative connotations can influence readers, persuading them to immerse themselves in, or distance themselves from, the scene and the events occurring there.

The interaction of characters in a certain context can also create an evocative scene. By focusing on a particular environment, the characters in it and the way it affects them, it is possible to arouse the reader's emotions.

> 1 They worked together, coming and going, in a rhythm, which carried their feet and their bodies in tune. She stooped, she lifted the burden of sheaves, she turned her face to the dimness where he was, and went with her burden over the stubble. She hesitated, set down her sheaves, there was a swish
> 5 and hiss of mingling oats, he was drawing near, and she must turn again. And there was the flaring moon laying bare her bosom again, making her drift and ebb like a wave.
>
> He worked steadily, engrossed, threading backwards and forwards like a shuttle across the strip of cleared stubble, weaving the long line of riding
> 10 shocks, nearer and nearer to the shadowy trees, threading his sheaves with hers.
>
> And always, she was gone before he came. As he came, she drew away, as he drew away, she came. Were they never to meet? Gradually a low, deep-sounding will in him vibrated to her, tried to set her in accord, tried
> 15 to bring her gradually to him, to a meeting, till they should be together, till they should meet as the sheaves that swished together.

D. H. Lawrence, *The Rainbow*

The atmosphere is created here because of the relationship between the characters, their environment and their task. Harvesting has **connotations** of abundance and fertility, yet the two characters cannot meet – the very pattern of their task keeps them separate. Although they are in harmony physically, they are distanced emotionally. The fact that the characters are unnamed in the extract reinforces this sense of their detachment – they become secondary to the task they must complete.

The natural world is given a concrete presence by the **lexical set** that is developed:

nouns like *sheaves* (l. 2), *shocks* (l. 10), *stubble* (l. 4) and *oats* (l. 5) all create the background against which the reader sees the man and the woman. The **symbolic** fruitfulness of the harvest mirrors the sexual urges of the man and woman – their inability to relate to each other is therefore ironic. The noun phrase *the flaring moon* (l. 6) makes the irony more explicit: traditionally, the moon represents passion, but here, ironically, it makes the woman indistinct. By using the verbs *drift* and *ebb* (l. 7), Lawrence is able to contrast the solidity and reality of their task with the ephemeral nature of their relationship.

The **lexis** is chosen to portray the ritual nature of their work: prepositional phrases like *in a rhythm* (l. 1) and *in tune* (l. 2) indicate the harmony they achieve. A sense of balance is also developed through the **antithesis** of verbs like *stooped* and *lifted* (l. 2) and adverbs like *backwards* and *forwards* (l. 8). References to light and dark enhance the idea of opposition: nouns like *dimness* (l. 3) and *moon* (l. 6), and modifiers like *flaring* (l. 6) and *shadowy* (l. 10). The contrast becomes symbolic of the desire to meet which is not fulfilled.

The **rhetorical patterning** of the sentences helps to create the atmosphere. The verbs are dynamic: *worked* (l. 1), *threading* (l. 8) and *weaving* (l. 9). The **repetition** of these and of the sentence structures mimics the repetitive nature of their task:

S　　P　　　S　　P　　　　　　　　O　　　　　S　　　P　　　　O
(She) (stooped), (she) (lifted) (the burden of sheaves), (she) (turned) (her face)

　　　　　A
(to the dimness) (ll. 2–3)

　　　A　　　　S　　P　　　　　　A　　　　　　　　S　　　P
(As he came), (she) (drew away), (as he drew away), (she) (came). (ll. 12–13)
SCl–ACl　　　　　　　　　　　　　SCl–ACl

In contrast to their actions, the author uses **free indirect thought** in the man's question: *Were they never to meet?* (l. 13). The move from declarative to interrogative **mood** changes the pace and makes the atmosphere more dramatic because the reader knows that the man is not happy at the distance which remains between himself and the woman. The **repetition** of the tentative verb *tried* (l. 14) marks his attempts to alter the pattern. The use of the subordinating conjunction *till* (l. 15) and the modal *should* (l. 16), however, remind the reader that any disruption to the pattern is hypothetical.

The **metaphorical language** intensifies the atmosphere because it is poetic. Lawrence uses natural imagery which is appropriate to the context: the woman is compared to a wave; the man thinks of meeting the woman just as the sheaves meet. Juxtaposed with these is the image of the *shuttle* (l. 9). By choosing an industrial comparison, the writer creates a conflict within the metaphorical language which is a parallel to the conflict between the man and woman. They are divided by their work and this is symbolically represented by the *shuttle* of a loom threading backwards and forwards creating a patterned material.

The power of this writing lies in its intensity. Lawrence uses language poetically and thus creates a scene that is out of the ordinary. The reader is drawn into the pattern of the work, into the inability of the man and the woman to approach each other, by the lexical choices and syntactical patterns.

To experiment with language

By using non-standard language, writers can intensify the effect of the fictional world on the reader. Using variations in language for different characters makes them more authentic and places them more specifically in a time and a place.

Traditionally, non-standard language was confined to dialogue in novels. It was used to reflect the accent and dialect of characters.

> 1 'I'm a goin' to leave you, Samivel my boy, and there's no telling ven I shall
> see you again. Your mother-in-law may ha' been too much for me, or a thou-
> sand things may have happened by the time you next hears any news o' the
> celebrated Mr Veller o' the Bell Savage. The family name depends wery
> 5 much upon you, Samivel, and I hope you'll do wot's right by it . . . If ever you
> gets to up'ards o' fifty, and feels disposed to go a marryin' anybody – no mat-
> ter who – jist you shut yourself up in your own room, if you've got one, and
> pison yourself off hand . . .'

Charles Dickens, The Pickwick Papers

In this example, Dickens is interested in conveying the 'sound' or accent of Samuel Weller's father. There is no unrecognisable lexis, the spellings are merely manipulated in order to reflect the pronunciation. The phoneme /w/ is pronounced /v/: *ven* (l. 1); and the phoneme /v/ is pronounced /w/: *wery* (l. 4). Other features mirror the contracted nature of spoken language: *o'* (l. 4) = *of*; *goin'* (l. 1) = *going*; *up'ards* (l. 6) = *upwards*; and *ha'* (l. 2) = *have*. The spelling of *jist* (l. 7) and *pison* (l. 8) aim to indicate the way in which the RP vowel sounds /ʌ/ and /ɔɪ/ have been altered. The spelling of *wot* (l. 5) tries to mirror the traditional pronunciation in a phonetic-like simplification. Dialect features can be seen in the use of the third person singular verb inflection *-s* with a sec-ond person pronoun, *you...hears* (l. 3), *you...feels* (ll. 5–6) and *you gets* (ll. 5–6), and in the use of the archaic present participle *a goin'* (l. 1) and *a marryin'* (l. 6).

Where Dickens deviates from the standard English of his own narrative, the effect is often intentionally comic. The characters who speak using non-standard language are invariably of a lower social class and the features chosen reflect this status. Here the character speaking is a working-class father giving homely advice to his son – the con-tent itself is comic, but when delivered in the non-standard form that Dickens chooses, the comedy is intensified.

Hardy uses non-standard language in more serious contexts: his aim is to create an authentic regional and social background for his characters.

> 'Bring on that water, will ye, you idle young harlican!'

Thomas Hardy (1840–1928), Jude the Obscure

The use of the archaic second person pronoun *ye* is representative of the tone here – the address is informal and the speaker is in a position of superiority. The noun *harli-can* is a dialect term of abuse, reinforcing the idea that the addressee is being treated as an inferior.

The movement in the twentieth century towards more realistic novels meant that it was important to write in a style appropriate to the characters and settings. Traditionally, minor characters used dialect, but as writers experimented, non-standard language became an important means of characterisation. Some writers chose to write whole novels in non-standard English. Although the effects still could be comic, more often writers had serious intentions.

The choice of a particular form of language can make the fictional world more credible, helping the reader to identify and empathise with the characters. In first per-son narratives, the use of non-standard language appropriate to the *I* character clearly marks the viewpoint. It reminds readers that they are being presented with a subjective interpretation of events.

In *The Color Purple*, Alice Walker's main character is Celie, a young Black American girl living in the South in the 1920s and 1930s. The novel is a first person nar-rative, using a sequence of Celie's letters as a record of her life. Walker chooses to use non-standard English throughout the novel because it is a form of language more appropriate to Celie than standard English.

1 Dear God,
   Shug Avery is coming to town! She coming with her orkestra. She going
to sing in the Lucky Star out on Coalman road. Mr. _____ going to hear her.
He dress all up in front the glass, look at himself, then undress and dress all
5 over again. He slick back his hair with pomade, then wash it out again. He
been spitting on his shoes and hitting it with a quick rag.
   He tell me, Wash this. Iron that. Look for this. Look for that. Find this.
Find that. . .
   I move round darning and ironing, find hanskers. Anything happening? I
10 ast.
   What you mean? he say, like he mad. Just trying to git some of the hick
farmer off myself. Any other woman be glad.
   I'm is glad, I say.
   What you mean? he ast.
15   You looks nice, I say. Any woman be proud.
   You think so? he say. . .

Alice Walker (1944–), The Color Purple

Alice Walker chooses to write in Black American English since this is a form of English appropriate for Celie. The list below summarises the main non-standard linguistic features.

- Some non-standard spellings reflect pronunciation: *git* (l. 11), *ast* (l. 10). For others, while pronunciation remains the same, traditional orthography is simplified: *orkestra* (l. 2).
- Some words are part of the Black English dialect and are therefore unfamiliar: *hanskers* (l. 9).
- Some words are representative of American English rather than British English: *glass* (l. 4) for *mirror*.
- The noun phrase *a quick rag* (l. 6) is unusual – in Standard English the adverb 'quickly' would have been used following the pronoun *it*, describing the movement rather than the rag itself.
- Although in narrative the simple past tense is usual, most third person singular verbs here use the base form – since Black English dialects often omit verb suffixes, it is not possible to be certain which tense is intended: *He dress* (l. 4), *He slick* (l. 5), *He tell me* (l. 7).
- Auxiliaries are often used non-standardly or omitted: *She coming* (l. 2), *He been spitting* (l. 6), *I'm is glad* (l. 13). When the auxiliary 'to be' is included, it seems to be used to give emphasis.
- Modal auxiliaries are also omitted: *Any other woman be glad* (l. 12).
- Interrogatives are formed without the dummy auxiliary *do*: *What you mean?* (l. 11), *You think so?* (l. 16).
- Some prepositions are used non-standardly: *in front the glass* (l. 4).

A first person narrative always offers a limited point of view and here the reader is immediately aware of this both because of the dialect and because of the choice of a letter format. However, by using this particular form and structure of English, Walker gives Celie an appropriate means of self-expression. The short sentences, the reports of what has been said and the literal nature of the content make the novel immediate and dramatic. Although Celie is uneducated, the way she records her observations and experiences is distinctive. Walker has created a 'real' character and the reader can believe in Celie because she is so obviously a product of the society in which she lives.

   Other writers aim to alienate their reader through their choice of language and style. By writing in an unfamiliar form of English, authors can distance readers, forcing them to learn something both about the fictional and real world.

Anthony Burgess's novel *A Clockwork Orange* uses a partially made-up language to convey the kind of society he visualised for the future.

> 1 'What's it going to be then, eh?'
>   There was me, that is Alex, and my three droogs, that is Pete, Georgie, and Dim, Dim being really dim, and we sat in the Korova Milkbar making our rassoodocks what to do with the evening, a flip dark chill winter bastard
> 5 though dry . . .
>   Our pockets were full of deng, so there was no real need from the point of view of crasting any more pretty polly to tolchock some old veck in an alley and viddy him swim in his blood while we counted the takings and divided by four, nor to do the ultra-violent on some shivering starry grey-haired ptitsa in
> 10 a shop and go smecking off with the till's guts. But, as they say, money isn't everything.
>   The four of us were dressed in the height of fashion, which in those days was a pair of black very tight tights with the old jelly mould, as we called it, fitting on the crotch underneath the tights, this being to protect and also a
> 15 sort of design you could viddy clear enough in a certain light . . . We wore our hair not too long and we had flip horrorshow boots for kicking.
>
> Anthony Burgess (John Burgess Wilson, 1917–), *A Clockwork Orange*

Much of the text is in Standard English, but certain nouns, adjectives, verbs and adverbs are created specifically for the novel. Many of the non-standard words are of Russian origin. Readers can use their instinctive knowledge of English linguistic structures to guess at the word class of words and to some extent the context can hint at the meaning, but the glossary provided at the back of the novel is an essential part of the decoding process. The list that follows suggests some of the ways in which a reader can begin to decipher Burgess's code:

- A noun can be preceded by a determiner and can take an *-s* inflection to mark the plural: *droogs* (l. 2) for *friends*; *rassoodocks* (l. 4) for *minds*; *ptitsa* (l. 9) for *chick*; *deng* (l. 6) for *money*; *veck* (l. 7) for *man*.
- Verbs can take an *-ing* inflection: *crasting* (l. 7) for *stealing*; *smecking* (l. 10) for *laughing*.
- A verb infinitive is preceded by the preposition *to*: *to tolchock* (l. 7) for *to hit* or *to beat*.
- A lexical verb follows a modal auxiliary: *could viddy* (l. 15) for *could see*.
- Adjectives can pre-modify nouns in a noun phrase: *flip* (l. 4) for *wild*; *starry* (l. 9) for *ancient*; *horrorshow* (l. 16) for *good*.

Burgess uses these unusual words in familiar linguistic patterns and therefore the reader can begin to recognise and understand them. Other linguistic games are played too: rhyming slang is used – *pretty polly* (l. 7) for *lolly* or *money*; and the Standard English associations of a word are inverted – *horrorshow* (l. 16) will probably have negative connotations for the reader, but in this society 'bad' has become 'good'.

The language here is the language of youth. It is a coded form of communication which clearly marks out insiders and outsiders. The novel is about a violent drug-orientated society and Burgess wants to show the reader the way in which language can conceal the truth about what is happening. By using a unique form of English, Burgess forces the reader to remain outside the fictional world he has created – it is very difficult for readers to immerse themselves in the society and its violence because they have to concentrate so hard on the language. Screening of the film version was banned because people were concerned that viewers would do no more than relish the violence. Once the barrier of the created language was removed so that audiences could understand what was going on, the process of alienation itself was removed. Instead of conveying a warning about the potential violence of society, the film actually seemed to promote violence. This shows that the Nadsat (teenage) language is absolutely central to the novel – it creates a distinct group within society which lives by its own rules and has its own cultural and social customs.

ACTIVITY 13.3

Debra Chase is a second-rate model, appearing in second-rate beauty contests, but she is unaware of her own limitations. Her purpose in Keith Waterhouse's novel, <u>Bimbo</u>, is to correct the untruths told about her in a tabloid paper, the <u>Sunday Shocker</u>, but her own version of events appears to be equally sensational.

Read through the extract below and comment on the non-standard language used and the writer's purpose in choosing it.

Chap One
MY EARLY LIVELIHOOD

1

Now it can be told. The biggest majority of the Debra Chase By Herself series in the *Sunday Shocker* which I am sposed to of written was a load of
5 rubbish, a virago of lies from start to finish.

Frinstance it is just not true that I had one-night stands with half the Seathorpe Wanderers team before I was seventeen. If it is of any concedable interest I did not even meet most of the lads until I had been selected Miss South-east Coast and that was when I was eighteen at least as I can
10 prove.

Not true that after sex romps with playboy MP Sir Monty Pratt – The Sir as I always called him – I threatenised I would swallow a whole bottle of aspirin to stop him bringing our sizzling romance to an end. I do not even like aspirin, it just so happens it always gives me a headache. All right, so at the
15 death The Sir was pressured into choosing between I and his wife Pussy as all the world now knows – but Debra Chase is still alive and kicking, thank you very much.

And it is defnitely not true that me and rival model Suzie Dawn, reel name Norma Borridge, fought like alley cats over super soap stud Den
20 Dobbs, two-timing mini-cab driver Terry of the chart-topping series *The Brummies*, whose reel-life scorching romance with barmaid Sally – raven-haired sexpot Donna Matthews – was the cause of a love-tug punch-up with burly boy friend Bruce Bridges, ex-welterweight boxer who is now a top DJ.

Keith Waterhouse (1929–), <u>Bimbo</u>

COMMENTARY

Keith Waterhouse uses a form of English that closely resembles spoken language in order to characterise his first person narrator appropriately. **Colloquial noun phrases** like *a load of rubbish* (ll. 4–5), *one-night stands* (l. 6) and *lads* (l. 8) are typical of informal spoken discourse. Waterhouse also uses **non-standard spellings** to reflect the way in which Debra pronounces words: *sposed* (l. 4), *Frinstance* (l. 6) and *defnitely* (l. 18) show the way in which informal speech elides certain sounds. This elision has an effect on the grammar of Debra's speech when the auxiliary verb *have*, used to construct the perfect aspect in the verb phrase *have written*, becomes *of* (l. 4). In speech, the auxiliary *have* is pronounced as the phonemes /əv/ and many people mistake it for the preposition *of*.

The language is clearly influenced by the **tabloid newspapers** – Debra dramatises events by using the language of the tabloids. The first chapter opens with a **marked theme**:

>   A   S   P
> (Now) (it) (can be told). (l. 3)

This immediately sets the **tone** and prepares the reader for what is to follow. The stories about the Seathorpe Wanderers, Sir Monty Pratt and the actors in the soap, however, are an anticlimax – the writer wants readers to recognise Debra's limitations even if she cannot see them herself. She sometimes writes in the telegraphic style of headlines: *Not true that...* (l. 11). The **noun phrases** are often complex with sequences of modifiers:

>   m   h   m   m   h   q
> raven-haired sexpot (ll. 21–2)   a whole bottle of aspirin (ll. 12–13)
> Adj   V   N   det Adj   N   PrepP

>   m   m   h
> reel-life scorching romance (l. 21)
> Adj   N   V   N

Words typical of tabloids are chosen: modifiers like the present participles *sizzling* (l. 13) and *scorching* (l. 21) describing the head noun *romance* develop the cliché of passion as a fire; the noun phrase *sex romps* (l. 11) uses tabloid 'code' words which are used as a shorthand to signify immediately to the reader a certain kind of affair. The juxtaposition of the nouns *playboy* and *MP* (l. 11) are also typical of tabloidese since they imply something sensational: the authority of a politician is undermined when placed in the sexual context associated with a *playboy*. Other common tabloid linguistic features are seen in the frequent use of compound words like *love-tug punch-up* (l. 22) and *two-timing mini-cab driver* (l. 20) and in the alliteration of *super soap star Den Dobbs* (ll. 19–20) and *burly boy friend Bruce Bridges* (l. 23).

The **grammar** is similarly influenced by the tabloids. Sentences are loosely structured – conjunctions are used in the initial position and parenthesis is common:

>   dumS P   C   (S)
> (And) (it) (is) (defnitely not true) (that me and rival model . . . fought like alley cats
> conj   neg   SCl–NCl
>
> over super soap stud Den Dobbs . . . whose reel-life scorching romance . . . was
>   SCl–RelCl
>
> the cause of a love-tug punch-up with burly boy friend Bruce Bridges . . .
>
> who is now . . .) (ll. 18–23)
> SCl–RelCl

Finally, the language is often **idiosyncratic** – it is specifically marked by features that are typical of Debra as an individual. She tries to make herself seem educated by using long words, but often she uses them inappropriately. MALAPROPISMS (similar words used mistakenly in the wrong contexts) like *virago* (l. 5) for *farrago* and *concedable* (ll. 7–8) for *conceivable* and PLEONASMS (words used unnecessarily to convey meaning) like *biggest majority* (l. 3) suggest that Debra is not well read. She lengthens words by adding the inflection *-ised* when it is not needed: *threatenised* (l. 12) for *threatened*. She uses common clichés like *alive and kicking* (l. 16), *fought like alley cats* (l. 19) and *at the death* (ll. 14–15). Grammatically, Debra confuses her subject and object pronouns, using *I and his wife* (l. 15) instead of the object pronoun *me*; and *me and rival model Suzie Dawn* (l. 18) instead of the subject pronoun *I*. All these features suggest that Debra is more familiar with spoken rather then written forms of language, but that she is trying to write in a formal way.

Waterhouse makes Debra seem a somewhat comic character, but the reader is not meant to dislike her. She is sincere in what she writes and is trying to find an appropriate formal style for her memoirs. Although she fails, the reader is aware that society has made her what she is – reading the tabloids, living in a society where informal spoken language takes precedence over written language, it is inevitable that she writes as she does. Above all, the reader is aware of her liveliness and her basic honesty and these are more important characteristics than any linguistic inaccuracies.

The form of English Waterhouse has chosen for this first person narrative makes Debra Chase a more realistic character, helping the reader to empathise with her. It makes the fictional world of the novel more credible and allows Waterhouse to suggest something about the nature of Late Modern English itself.

13.5 What to look for in the language of narrative prose

The following checklist can be used to identify key features in examples of prose. There will not be examples of all the features in every extract, but the list can be used as a guide. The points made are general so discussion of specific examples will need to be adapted to take account of the specific context and authorial purpose.

The following are helpful questions to ask.

Register

1   What is the **mode**? – written.
2   What is the **manner**? – the relationship between writer and reader: formal or informal? personal or impersonal? authorial intention (to characterise, describe a place or time, create an atmosphere, convey a message, and so on)?
3   What is the **field**? – the lexis will suggest something about the nature of the subject matter.

Point of view

1   Is it a **first person narrative**, giving a direct insight into a character's mind? – limitations of understanding? signs of bias?
2   Is it a **third person narrative**, providing an omniscient view of events and characters? – intrusive or unintrusive? informing or evaluating?
3   Is the narrator **reliable** or **unreliable**? – can readers rely on the version of events provided by the narrator? or should they mistrust the narrator?
4   Are there any examples of **interior monologue** or **stream of consciousness**? – are the characters' thoughts ordered or random?

Lexis

1   Are **words** simple or complicated? formal or colloquial? descriptive or evaluative? modern or archaic?

2   Are there any examples of **subject specific words** or specific **lexical sets**?

3   Has the writer chosen to use **non-standard language**? – dialect? idiosyncratic linguistic choices? code language identifying insiders and outsiders?

4   Are the **nouns concrete** (to do with the physical environment) or **abstract** (linked to thought or spiritual matters)?

5   Is the **naming of characters** important? are any names omitted on purpose?

6   Do any words have significant **connotations**?

7   What function do the **modifiers** have? what effects do they create?

8   What kinds of actions and processes do the **verbs** describe?

Speech and thought

1   Does the writer use **direct speech** or **thought** to let the characters speak for themselves?

2   Does the writer use **indirect speech** or **thought** to interpret or comment on the things that characters say?

3   Does the writer use **free indirect speech** or **thought** to both intervene and give the true sense of a character's words?

Grammar

1   Is the grammar **standard** or **non-standard**? **formal** or **informal**? **modern** or **archaic**?

2   Are there any occasions when the **tense** changes from the simple past? what effect does this have?

3   Do changes of **mood** create any interesting effects?

4   Is the **sentence structure** varied? – simple? compound? complex? what effect do the changes have?

Metaphorical language

1   Does the writer use **images** to give the fictional world a concrete visual quality? to which senses does the description appeal?

2   Are there any **metaphors** or **symbols**? what effect do these have?

3   Are there any other examples of **poetic** use of language?

Rhetorical techniques

1   How does the writer persuade the reader to believe in the fictional world created?

2   Are contrasts created through the use of **patterning**? **juxtapositions**? **listing**? **parallelism**? what effects do these have?

3   Does the writer emphasise certain elements by using **marked themes**? the **passive voice**? **end focus**? what effect do these have?

Summary

The **function** of prose is to entertain, but writers can also implicitly or explicitly convey a message about society or life.

The language of fictional prose is very **varied** because writers can manipulate language in order to make their fictional worlds more powerful and credible. Non-standard language can be used to add depth to a characterisation, word class boundaries can be broken to create dramatic effects, and poetic techniques can be used to build up the atmosphere.

Authorial intention dictates the kinds of linguistic and stylistic choices made and the kind of relationship created with the reader.

14 The language of literature – poetry

14.1 The nature of poetry

Like prose, POETRY cannot be neatly categorised. Poets can choose a range of structures and techniques; they can manipulate language; and can, at times, almost seem to invent a special language to express their ideas and individuality. It is a very disciplined genre because of the restrictions poetic form places on poets. Because thoughts are often compressed into a short space, it can be difficult for readers to understand the message conveyed by a particular poem. Equally, because poets are creating something unique, the language of poetry can deviate from generally observed rules. Poetic licence allows poets to experiment: parts of words may be omitted; word order can be altered; archaisms and dialect can be used; the word classes of words can be changed; and lexical and syntactical patterns can be used to reinforce the meaning.

14.2 The function of poetry

The language of poetry is both **poetic** and **expressive**. It has a wide range of functions: it can **entertain**, **arouse emotions** and **provoke thought**; it can **describe**, **evaluate** or **inform**. The lexis can be poetic and intense, or ordinary and conversational.

By considering the linguistic and stylistic features of a poem it is possible to come to conclusions about the poet's intentions. The content, form and style will give the reader clues to the meaning and often there will be an underlying message or theme which is only revealed on close reading.

14.3 Features of poetry

Each poem is distinctive and it is important to identify what the poet is trying to convey to the reader and the linguistic and stylistic techniques used to do this. It is not possible to be prescriptive about the kinds of features to comment on, but there are certain devices and forms that it is worth looking out for.

Manner

The **manner** can be formal or informal, depending upon the relationship the poet wants to create with the reader. Because poets often convey their message in a concise way, the language of poetry tends to be far more intense than that of everyday conversation. The language of traditional poetry tends to be concentrated and heightened, but there are many examples of poems that aim to mirror the language of speech to create a very different tone.

Form and structure

The **form** and **structure** tell the reader something about the poet's intentions. Stanza and line length, for instance, are chosen to best convey a poem's message. By choosing a particular format, poets can reinforce their messages through the structure. It is therefore useful to be able to identify some of the main poetic structures.

Ballads

BALLADS date back to the oral tradition of the late Middle Ages. They are poems in which an impersonal narrator tells a story – the focus is on action and dialogue rather than on interpretative comment. They usually begin abruptly at a point where a tragic event of some kind is about to take place. This single episode is the focus for the whole poem, with only minimal background detail provided. They are usually very dramatic and the poet creates a sense of intensity and immediacy both through the content and the style.

The structure is usually straightforward: the story is told in rhyming QUATRAINS (four-lined stanzas); the language is simple; the poets draw on stock phrases; and ballads are often written in dialect. **Repetition** is used to make the poems memorable – this is typical of poems written in the oral tradition.

Sonnets

SONNETS are fourteen-line poems which have a very structured rhyme scheme and rhythm (usually **iambic pentameter**). Because the form is so disciplined poets are forced to craft their ideas. Often the subject matter deals with love, the problems of life or with questions of disorder – poets then use the patterned structure to create an ordered response to complex issues. There are two main kinds of sonnet: the **Petrarchan** (Italian) and the **Shakespearean** (English).

The PETRARCHAN SONNET divides the fourteen lines into an **octave** (eight lines) and a **sestet** (six lines), using the rhyme scheme abbaabba cdecde or abbaabba cdcdcd. The octave sets out the problem and the sestet is used to resolve it. The turning point acts as a pivot on which the two sections are balanced – the pause is called the VOLTA. The two stanzas allow the poet to explore an issue and reflect or change direction.

The SHAKESPEAREAN SONNET divides the lines into three **quatrains** and a **couplet**, using the rhyme scheme abab cdcd efef gg. The quatrains present the ideas or themes to be developed and the final couplet summarises the central theme, rounding off the argument and resolving the tension created.

Odes

ODES are elaborate lyrical poems addressed to a person, a thing or an abstraction able to transcend the problems of life. They can consist of straightforward praise of their subject or they can be more hesitant and philosophical; they can focus on positive celebration or negative feelings. Because they deal with difficult ideas and involved arguments, odes tend to be complex, drawing on many images in a single stanza. The poet often tries to convey an awareness of being trapped in everyday difficulties and of the difference between the ideal and the real. Elevated lexis is used to create a sense of things that transcend the mundane and images are juxtaposed to create a sense of the harsher realities of life.

Blank verse

BLANK VERSE is often used for long narrative poems or lyric poems in which a poet is thinking in a discursive way. It does not have an obvious overall pattern or structure as other poetic forms do, but despite the fact that it does not rhyme, blank verse is a very disciplined form in which each line has ten syllables with five stresses (an **iambic** pattern). Its rhythms are closer to speech than other poetic forms, but it is recognisably more stylised than speech or prose. Although it appears to be less formally contrived than a poem that rhymes, the regularity of the verse implies a search for order. The sentence structure is often complex and the imagery is fully developed.

> We love the things we love for what they are.
>> Robert Frost (1874–1963), extract from 'Hyla Brook'

Free verse

FREE VERSE is often chosen by modern poets to confront a disorganised world because it acknowledges the untidiness of life and the mind. It is written in irregular lines and has no regular metre (the pattern of stressed and unstressed syllables). Rhyme is used infrequently, but repetition of words or phrases is often significant in providing an internal pattern.

Poetic devices

Poets will use the same kinds of metaphorical and rhetorical techniques common in other varieties of English, but they also use some distinctive **POETIC DEVICES** which are particular to poetry.

End stop

An **END STOP** describes a line of verse in which a grammatical break coincides with the end of a line. It is often marked by punctuation.

> Some say the world will end in fire,
> Some say in ice.
>> Robert Frost, extract from 'Fire and Ice'

Enjambement

ENJAMBEMENT describes a line of verse in which the grammatical structures run on from line to line. This allows the poet to defeat the reader's expectations – the meaning is not complete at the end of the line; punctuation is not used to make the reader pause. This technique can be used to reinforce a poem's meaning.

> My heart leaps up when I behold
> A rainbow in the sky;
>> William Wordsworth (1770–1850), extract from 'My Heart Leaps Up'

Metre

Poetic **METRE** is the pattern of stressed and unstressed syllables in a line of poetry. It is one way in which a poet can order language to make it more meaningful. By analysing the metre, a reader can appreciate how the poet is using stress patterns to convey meaning. Variations in the pattern may mark changes in the mood or the poet's attitude.

There are five basic patterns of stress. Stressed syllables are marked ´ while unstressed syllables are marked ˘ .

- **IAMBIC**: one unstressed syllable is followed by one stressed syllable (dĕ|líght, ă|bóut).

> Sweet day, sŏ cóol, sŏ cálm, sŏ bríght
>> George Herbert (1593–1633), extract from 'Virtue'

- **TROCHAIC**: one stressed syllable is followed by one unstressed syllable (gá|thĕr, féel|ĭng).

> Sóft ănd éasў ĭs thў crádlĕ
> Coárse ănd hárd thў Sáviouŕ láy.

- **DACTYLIC**: one stressed syllable is followed by two unstressed syllables (há|ppĭ|nĕss, sén|tĭ|mĕnt).

> Síng ĭt áll mérrilў

- **ANAPAESTIC**: two unstressed syllables are followed by one stressed syllable (ĭn|tĕr|rúpt, dĭs|ă|ppéar).

> Wĕ ărĕ théy whŏ rĭdĕ éarlў oŕ láte
>> J. E. Flecker (1884–1915)

- **SPONDEE**: two stressed syllables (heárt|bréak, wíne|gláss).

> Óne twó
> Búckle my shoe
> Thrée fóur
> Knóck at the door

Having identified the stress pattern, each line of poetry can then be divided into metrical **FEET** (groups of syllables forming metrical units). Each foot consists of a stressed syllable and any unstressed syllables that accompany it. The foot will therefore be iambic, trochaic or whatever.

- 1 foot = **monometer**;
- 2 feet = **dimeter**;
- 3 feet = **trimeter**;
- 4 feet = **tetrameter**;
- 5 feet = **pentameter**;
- 6 feet = **hexameter**;
- 7 feet = **heptameter**;
- 8 feet = **octameter**;

To **SCAN** a line of poetry it is necessary first to decide the pattern of the stress, then to count the number of stressed syllables to determine the number of feet, and finally to combine the two.

> Shĕ líved | ĭn stórm | ănd strífe,
> Hĕr sóul | hăd súch | dĕsíre
> Foŕ whăt | próud déath | măy bríng

That it | could not | endure
The com|mon good | of life
> William Butler Yeats (1865–1939), extract from 'That the Night Come'

- stress pattern: ˘ ´;
- number of stresses per line: three;
- metre: iambic trimeter.

Learn to | speak first, | then to | woo; to | wooing | much per|taineth;
He that | courts us, | wanting | art, soon | falters | when he | feigneth
> Thomas Campion (1567–1620), extract from 'Think'st Thou to Seduce Me Then'

- stress pattern: ´ ˘;
- number of stresses per line: seven;
- metre: trochaic heptameter.

This kind of patterning makes poetry very different from speech. If poets want to mimic the rhythms of informal conversation, they choose iambic pentameter because the pattern it creates is closer to the spontaneity of speech.

Pause

The CAESURA (a break or pause in a line of verse) is very important in poetry. It is used to achieve a degree of variety in the metre and rhythm: it can make verse formal and stylised; or it can relax rigid metrical patterns and mimic the rhythms of speech. The position of a caesura is often marked by punctuation, but the natural rhythms of language can also dictate a pause.

> To be or not to be: [caesura] that is the question.
> William Shakespeare (1564–1616), *Hamlet*

Rhythm

The RHYTHM of a poem is governed by the language and the way we speak it. It is closely linked to semantics since meaning dictates the way lines are read. In everyday speech, lexical words bear the **stress** and grammatical or function words are **unstressed**. In poetry, stress patterns are directly linked to metre as well as to the natural stress of words.

Lexical choice

The **lexical choice** (DICTION) depends upon the context and the content. Inevitably, it will reflect the relationship created between reader and poet: formal or informal; familiar or polite; personal or impersonal. **Abstract** or **concrete nouns** may be chosen, depending upon the subject matter. **Modifiers** can be used to describe places or people in detail; to arouse the reader's emotions; or to evaluate and judge. The kinds of actions or processes the **verbs** describe and the form they take can also tell the reader something about the message the poet wishes to convey.

Dialect words can be used to create a certain social or regional atmosphere. ARCHAISMS can heighten the dignity and solemnity of the language – such lexical choices can remind the reader of the poetic and cultural traditions on which poetry draws. Poets can equally make their lexis very modern by using NEOLOGISMS (invented words) which give their writing a sense of individuality. Sometimes words can seem **incongruous** – poets borrow words from non-poetic registers in order to disrupt readers' expectations. **Collocations** can be disrupted as poets experiment, throwing new light on familiar things and forcing readers to reconsider things previously taken for granted.

Grammar

The **grammar** of poetry is sometimes complicated, particularly when poets manipulate language to conform to the restrictions of traditional poetic forms. Poetic licence equally allows poets to manipulate language structures to achieve distinctive end results. **Sentence structures** are therefore often complex and the omission of clause elements can make a poem difficult to understand. By changing the **focus**, poets can emphasise important parts of a poem – the **position of clause elements** can help the reader to interpret the poem by drawing attention to key words, phrases and clauses. Changes in **tense** or **mood** also indicate that the poet is highlighting something significant. **Cohesion** is used to establish exact connections because the compression of thought can make the syntax seem disjointed. **Pronoun referencing**, **ellipsis** and the use of **synonyms**, however, can make the imagery and message stand out more clearly.

Metaphorical devices

Metaphorical devices make the language of poetry intense since poets use them to add layers of meaning beyond what the words on the page literally say. They clarify the poet's message and enhance the emotive impact. Metaphorical language can sometimes be difficult to interpret because poets can invent their own systems of references which readers may not immediately understand. **Images** are used to appeal to the senses, evoking atmosphere in a very tangible way. They can suggest meanings without the poet having to make them explicit. **Metaphors** and **similes** make the abstract concrete or the concrete abstract by referring to one thing either directly or indirectly in terms of another. **Symbols** help poets to widen the range of their references, whether they draw on commonly recognised symbols or create their own.

Rhetorical techniques

Rhetorical techniques also provide extra layers of meaning. Phonological patterning like **alliteration**, **onomatopoeia** and **rhyme**, and structural patterning like **parallelism**, **repetition**, **antithesis** and **listing**, can be used to reinforce the meaning.

Typography and layout

Typographical and structural features can also be important in poetry. Variations in **type face** or **layout** are significant in terms of the poet's intentions.

14.4 Different kinds of poetic intention

To characterise

Poets, like prose writers, can present characters directly to readers or they can allow characters to present themselves; they can intervene and comment on characters or allow readers to make their own judgements from the information provided.

Physical description usually focuses on the external features of a character, but inevitably it also tells the reader something about the inner person too.

The Face in the Mirror

1 Grey haunted eyes, absent-mindedly glaring
   From wide, uneven orbits; one brow drooping
   Somewhat over the eye
   Because of a missile fragment still inhering,
5 Skin deep, as a foolish record of old-world fighting.

   Crookedly broken nose – low tackling caused it;
   Cheeks, furrowed; coarse grey hair, flying frenetic;
   Forehead, wrinkled and high;
   Jowls, prominent; ears, large; jaw, pugilistic;
10 Teeth, few; lips, full and ruddy; mouth, ascetic.

   I pause with razor poised, scowling derision
   At the mirrored man whose beard needs my attention,
   And once more ask him why
   He still stands ready, with a boy's presumption,
15 To court the queen in her high silk pavilion.

Robert Graves (1895–1985)

In this poem, the poet observes himself in the mirror and the physical features of his face become reminders of past experiences as a World War I soldier and as a sports-man. The **enjambement** (ll. 1–2, 2–3, etc.) seems to parallel the poet's gaze as he moves from eyes to brow to nose, assessing all the features he sees in the mirror. The **lexis** is concrete: *cheeks* (l. 7), *forehead* (l. 8) and *lips* (l. 10). **Modifiers** indicate the way in which the poet sees himself. Some are descriptive – adjectives like *grey* (l. 1), *large* (l. 9) and *high* (l. 8); others are evaluative – the verb modifier *haunted* (l. 1), the adjectives *pugilistic* (l. 9) meaning 'boxer-like' and *ascetic* (l. 10) meaning 'austere'. Together these provide a factual description of the poet and a sense of his character.

The **sentence structure** is disjointed and this reinforces the sense that the poet is immersed in an analysis of his reflection. The first two stanzas are made up of a sequence of head words which are usually both pre- and post-modified.

      m   h
(Crookedly broken) nose (l. 6)
    Adv   V   N

  m   m   h   q
Grey haunted eyes, absent-mindedly glaring/From wide, uneven orbits (ll. 1–2)
  Adj   V   N   NFCl   PrepP

Verbs are omitted and this draws attention to the things that Graves sees – the lan-guage has been reduced to the bare minimum, leaving only the words crucial to our understanding of the poet's external and internal nature.

    S   C   S   C
(Cheeks), (furrowed); (coarse grey hair), (flying frenetic);

      S   C
(Forehead), (wrinkled and high); (ll. 7–8)

The omission of the stative verb *to be* intensifies the observations, and the use of pred-icative modifiers like *furrowed* and *frenetic* (l. 7) instead of attributive modifiers is more dramatic. As complements, they have more emphasis. A grammatically complete sen-tence is used in the second stanza:

      S   P   O
(low tackling) (caused) (it) (l. 6)

Only in the third stanza does the context of the poem establish itself clearly. The use of the grammatically complete sentence here implies that the reader can now pause with the poet to reconsider the disjointed sequence of observations presented so far:

S   P   A   A
(I) (pause) (with razor poised), (scowling derision
                                SCl–NFCl

At the mirrored man whose beard needs my attention) (ll. 11–12)
                  SCl–RelCl

The poet does not draw on **metaphorical language** to describe his face but the physical features do become **symbolic** of the life he has led and the effect it has had on him. **Rhetorical techniques** are used to enhance the things that the poet sees in his face: **listing** forces the reader to follow the sequence of observations; **repetition** of the S and C clause elements gives a balanced and logical atmosphere to the self-examination. Both these rhetorical techniques suggest that the descriptions are honest and that the poet's self-evaluation can be trusted. Although the poet basically uses **free verse**, the **rhyme pattern** is very structured: within each five-line stanza the four longer lines rhyme; the shorter third line rhymes from stanza to stanza.

Stanza 1: the phonemes /ɪŋ/ are used to rhyme *glaring, drooping, inhering* and *fighting.*
Stanzas 1–3: the phoneme /aɪ/ is used to rhyme *eye, high* and *why.*

The poem appears to be a straightforward physical description of what the poet sees in the mirror, but the reader is aware that it represents more than this. The compression of language and the patterned structure of the poem force the reader to contemplate more than just the appearance of the poet.

Poets can create imaginary characters or use real people as the basis for their poems. Rather than describing and interpreting these characters, poets can allow them to present **themselves** to the reader. The **dramatic monologue** gives life to characters because it allows a direct insight into their minds without using physical description. Often the character created will have some significance to the poet and in some ways the poem will be as much about the poet as about the character.

To set the scene

The language of a poem may provide concrete detail of a particular place, but beyond this the setting will often be symbolic, telling the reader something about the poet's mood, about a character's state of mind, or about the place itself. Changes in the description are significant because they indicate a change in mood or attitude.

The natural world can be a backdrop for the poet's experiences and by focusing on key details of place, a poet can recapture important moments. Recollecting a particular place therefore becomes a means of understanding oneself.

1 And in the frosty season, when the sun
  Was set, and visible for many a mile
  The cottage windows blazed through twilight gloom,
  I heeded not their summons: happy time
5 It was indeed for all of us – for me
  It was a time of rapture! Clear and loud
  The village clock tolled six, – I wheeled about,

Proud and exulting like an untired horse
That cares not for his home. All shod with steel,
10 We hissed along the polished ice in games
Confederate, imitative of the chase
And woodland pleasures, – the resounding horn,
The pack loud chiming, and the hunted hare.
So through the darkness and the cold we flew,
15 And not a voice was idle. . .

William Wordsworth, extract from 'The Prelude'

The **manner** is formal here, but because the poet is recalling a personal experience which in retrospect he considers to be important, a kind of intimacy is developed between the reader and the poet. The poem captures the exhilaration and excitement of the boy, but the lexical choices reflect the adult's understanding of the event.

The **lexis** appeals directly to the senses of sight and sound, re-creating the time, place and weather vividly. **Concrete nouns** make the physical environment seem real. References to the *cottage windows* (l. 3) and the *clock* (l. 7) remind the reader that the skating takes place not far from the boys' homes. Some **abstract nouns** like *season* (l. 1) and *darkness* (l. 14) build up a picture of the time and weather, but others like *summons* (l. 4) and *rapture* (l. 6) reflect the mature poet interpreting the experience. **Modifiers** are used to create the mood: for instance, adjectives like *happy* (l. 4), *Clear and loud* (l. 6) and *Proud* (l. 8); and present participles like *exulting* (l. 8), *resounding* (l. 12) and *chiming* (l. 13). The verb modifiers convey a sense of the children's activity and perpetual movement. The **connotations** of certain verbs develop this: the simple past tense verbs *wheeled* (l. 7) and *flew* (l. 14) suggest the children's freedom. However, juxtaposed with these are the verbs *tolled* (l. 7), with its connotations of a bell ringing to mark someone's death, and *blazed* (l. 3), with its connotations of security and comfort. Both these verbs are linked to the adult world which the children ignore during their games.

The **grammar** is formal, but Wordsworth does manipulate **word order** to draw attention to key words and phrases. In clauses like *I heeded not. . .* (l. 4) and *That cares not. . .* (l. 9), Wordsworth forms the negative without using the dummy auxiliary *do*. By choosing what may have already been an archaic structure, Wordsworth places emphasis on the negative *not*, making the children's refusal to respond to their parents' calls seem more purposeful. The **simple past tense** is used to retell the experience. The **pronouns** show that Wordsworth sees himself both as a member of the group and as an individual who experiences things more intensely than others. He juxtaposes the first person plural pronouns *we* (l. 10) and *us* (l. 5) with the first person singular pronouns *I* (l. 4) and *me* (l. 5) to mark his own difference. The **sentences** are mostly complex, although there are some simple structures. Simple:

> A   S   P   A   A
> (All shod with steel)/(We) (hissed) (along the polished ice) (in games/. . .pleasures)
> (ll. 9–12)

Complex:

> A   A   A
> (And) (in the frosty season) (when the sun/Was set) (and) (visible for many a mile/
> conj   SCl–ACl   conj   SCl–ACl
>
>   S   P   O
> The cottage windows blazed through twilight gloom)/(I) (heeded not) (their summons)
> (ll. 1–4)

The many **adverbials** provide detail of the environment, and the use of a **conjunction** in the **initial position** makes the extract seem as though the poet is addressing the reader directly.

The **metaphorical language** in the extract helps Wordsworth to reveal the importance of the moment. The **simile** *like an untired horse* (l. 8) becomes a **metaphor** as the young Wordsworth is described as *Proud and exulting* (l. 8). It is developed in the reference to the children being *All shod with steel* (l. 9) and to their games as a hunt in which their voices are like the *resounding horn* (l. 12). They become a pack of hounds *loud chiming* (l. 13) chasing their prey the *hunted hare* (l. 13). The *cottage windows* (l. 3) are **symbolic** of the adult world which calls the children to come in for bed. The use of the **possessive determiner** *their* (l. 4) and the abstract noun *summons* (l. 4) with its legal **connotations** clearly divide the children from their parents.

Rhetorical patterning gives the extract its ordered structure. **Marked themes** reorganise clause elements to draw attention to important words or phrases:

> A   S   P   C
> (for me)/(It) (was) (a time of rapture) (ll. 5–6)

In this example, Wordsworth emphasises that the experience is different for him by placing the adverbial in the initial position. This structure also throws emphasis on the abstract noun *rapture* since it is given end focus. **Repetition** of key words like *time* reinforces the importance of the recaptured moment. **Phonological patterning** contributes to the sounds of the experience: *sibilance* mimics the sound of the skates on ice: *all shod with steel,/We hissed along the polished ice* (ll. 9–10); the **onomatopoeia** of *hissed* reinforces this; **alliteration** of the phoneme /h/ in *hunted hare* (l. 13) adds to the range of sounds.

Semantic patterning builds up the contrasts. **Antithesis** of the verb *blazed* (l. 3) and the noun *gloom* (l. 3) juxtaposes the security of the cottages compared with the growing darkness outside. The two noun phrases

> m   h   m   h   q
> happy time (l. 4)   a time of rapture (l. 6)
> Adj   N   det   N PrepP

juxtapose Wordsworth's intensified experience of the moment with the ordinary enjoyment of the other children.

The **form** and **structure** of the poem enable Wordsworth to give order to his memory. He chooses **blank verse** in which the **line lengths** are very regular, with ten syllables in each. The **metre** is **iambic pentameter** (one unstressed and one stressed syllable; five stresses or feet per line).

> The cott|age wind|ows blazed | through twi|light gloom
> I heed|ed not | their sum|mons: ha|ppy time. . .

ACTIVITY 14.1

Read the poem and comment on the techniques the poet uses to create a sense of time and place, and on the features that make this typical of the language of poetry.

1 The winter evening settles down
   With smell of steaks in passageways.
   Six o'clock.
   The burnt-out ends of smoky days.
5 And now a gusty shower wraps
   The grimy scraps
   Of withered leaves about your feet

And newspapers from vacant lots;
The showers beat
10   On broken blinds and chimney-pots,
And at the corner of the street
A lonely cab-horse steams and stamps.

And then the lighting of the lamps.

T. S. Eliot, extract from 'Preludes', I

COMMENTARY

The **manner** is formal in the poem, but the poet wants the reader to feel the same as he does himself about the place he describes. By using the possessive pronoun *your* (l. 7), he therefore places the reader directly into the landscape he creates. The reader is forced to experience the desolation at first hand.

The **lexis** creates a very vivid picture of the place by appealing to the senses of sight, sound and smell. The **concrete nouns** build up the town environment – *passage-ways* (l. 2), *street* (l. 11), *cab-horse* (l. 12) and *lamps* (l. 13); there is a reference to a *gusty shower* (l. 5); the sounds of the town are developed by the dynamic verb *stamps* (l. 12) which describes the cab-horse and by the minor sentence *Six o'clock* (l. 3) which draws attention to the time, implying that the clock is chiming; while descriptions of the *smell of steaks* (l. 2), the *smoky days* (l. 4) and the cab-horse who *steams* (l. 12) conjure up the smells of the winter evening. The **modifiers** emphasise the mood. Lexical sets of adjective modifiers like *lonely* (l. 12) and *vacant* (l. 8) and verb modifiers like *burnt-out* (l. 4) and *withered* (l. 7) highlight the desolation; others like the adjectives *grimy* (l. 6) and *smoky* (l. 4) draw attention to the darkness and gloominess of the scene. The **con-notations** of these words make the reader aware that the poet is describing a decaying and lifeless place.

The **grammar** is straightforward, but some sentences are minor because they are made up of noun phrases standing alone:

>   h q   m   m   h   q
> Six o'clock (l. 3)   The burnt-out ends of smoky days (l. 4)
> num PrepP   det   V   N   PrepP

The other sentences are simple or compound:

>   S   P   A   A
> (The winter evening) (settles down)/(With smell of steaks) (in passageways).
>   (ll. 1–2)

>   S   P   A   A
> (The showers) (beat)/(On broken blinds and chimney-pots)/(And) (at the corner
>   conj
>   S   P
> of the street)/(A lonely cab-horse) (steams and stamps). (ll. 9–12)

The **tense** is present throughout and this reinforces the sense that this is happening now. There are only two **marked themes** and both occur at the end of the poem: the adverbial of place *at the corner of the street* (l. 11) draws attention to the cab-horse, which other than the reference to the *feet* (l. 7), is the only living thing in the poem; the adverbial of time *then* (l. 13) marks a change in atmosphere as the lamps are lit and everything is illuminated.

The lexis and syntax of the poem are much closer to the language of everyday speech and so the **metaphorical language** is far less complicated than in the

Wordsworth extract. This reflects the bleakness of the scene. The evening is **personified** as it *settles down* (l. 1) and the noun modifier *winter* (l. 1) **symbolises** the lack of life that is typical of the scene Eliot portrays. The title serves as an introduction to the poem as a whole, symbolising the possibility of something developing from the desolation here. A 'prelude' is an event leading up to or preceding another event of greater importance and here the lighting of the lamps implies that the darkness will be replaced by the light of day, that morning will follow night. **Structurally**, this suggestion is reinforced by the blank line left between lines 1–12 and line 13. The lighting of the lamps is the first definite human action and it seems to lighten the mood of despair.

The main **rhetorical features** used are **phonological**. The **alliteration** of the phoneme /b/ in *beat...broken blinds* (ll. 9–10), /g/ in *gusty* (l. 5) and *grimy* (l. 6), and /l/ in *the lighting of the lamps* (l. 13) contribute to the resonance of the poem. **Sibilance** is used to mimic the cooking of the steaks: ...*settles.../...smell of steaks in passageways./Six...* (ll. 1–3).

The **distinctive features** of poetry can be seen:

- the longer lines all have eight syllables, while the shorter ones have three or four;
- the metre is quite regular, with four stresses in each of the longer lines (tetrameter) and two in each of the short lines (dimeter); most lines are iambic (one unstressed and one stressed syllable);
- the rhymes are clear, but the pattern does not follow any recognisable form – the phonemes /eɪz/ in *passageways* and *days*; the phonemes /æps/ in *wraps* and *scraps*; the phonemes /iːt/ in *feet* and *beat*; the phonemes /ɒts/ in *pots* and *lots*; and the phonemes /æmps/ in *stamps* and *lamps*;
- the language, tone and structure are typical of much modern poetry which aims to move away from romantic considerations of nature, finding the harsh reality of everyday life a more rewarding subject.

To evoke atmosphere

Because of the intensity and compression of the language of poetry, poets can create very powerful atmospheres which will influence the reader. The charged atmospheres they create can then be used to convey a message.

> *Dulce et Decorum Est*
>
> 1 Bent double, like old beggars under sacks,
>   Knock-kneed, coughing like hags, we cursed through sludge,
>   Till on the haunting flares we turned our backs
>   And towards our distant rest began to trudge.
> 5 Men marched asleep. Many had lost their boots
>   But limped on, blood-shod. All went lame; all blind;
>   Drunk with fatigue; deaf even to the hoots
>   Of gas shells dropping softly behind . . .
>
> Wilfred Owen, extract

The **manner** is formal – the poet is revealing the reality of war through a description of soldiers returning from the front line for a rest period. The context is serious and in creating an emotive atmosphere, the poet aims to convey a message to the reader. The title is Latin and translates as 'it is sweet and glorious to die for one's country' – Owen uses this ironically since his poem proves that war is far from heroic.

The **lexis** is emotive and it is through his choice of words that Owen creates a dramatic atmosphere. **Subject specific nouns** like *flares* (l. 3) and *gas shells* (l. 8) identify the military context. The poet uses the noun *men* (l. 5) instead of *soldiers* and this reinforces the sense that they are ordinary people. The **modifiers** are emotive and build up a disturbing picture of the men: adjectives *lame, blind* (l. 6) and *deaf* (l. 7) suggest that the men are isolated from reality – all their senses have been overwhelmed by the horrific experiences of war; verb modifiers like *bent double* (l. 1), *knock-kneed* and *coughing* (l. 2) develop the reader's awareness of the men's physical condition – their state of health does not reflect the stereotypical strength of soldiers. The verb modifier *haunting* (l. 3) becomes symbolic of the whole experience from which the men are now retreating but from which they cannot escape in their minds. The **connotations** of the verbs are also disturbing. Although the dynamic verb *marched* (l. 5) is used to describe the soldiers, it is used in conjunction with the adverbial *asleep*. Other verbs describing their movements are more emotive and less expected: *trudge* (l. 4) and *limped* (l. 6) imply the physical and emotional weariness of the men; *cursed* (l. 2) is used to convey literally the oaths they utter and almost metaphorically the way movements are hindered by the mud.

The **grammar** is marked by the compression and omission of grammatical function words that is typical of poetry. It contributes to the intensity of the atmosphere created. The poem uses the **past tense** throughout and is clearly made up of the recollections of one of the soldiers. By using the first person plural **pronoun** *we* (l. 2), the poet reveals that he was one of the men described. While he has shared the experience, however, the reader is excluded from the reference. This intensifies the atmosphere in two ways:

- the use of the inclusive pronoun reference links the poet directly to the descriptions, thus making them more horrific;
- because readers have been excluded, they will recognise that they can never fully understand the nature of what these men have experienced, and will therefore feel personally involved in ensuring that such appalling conflicts do not happen again.

The **sentence structures** are varied: the poet uses a mixture of simple, compound and complex sentences. This is appropriate because he is both recounting personal experience using a descriptive narrative style and conveying a message about the horrors of war. Simple and compound sentences are emphatic, stating facts in an unemotional way which makes the horror of what is being described all the more brutal. Simple:

> S   P   A
> (Men) (marched) (asleep). (l. 5)

Compound:

> S   P   O   P   A
> (Many) (had lost) (their boots)/(But) (limped on), (blood-shod). (ll. 5–6)
>   conj

The complex sentences use many adverbials in order to provide the reader with precise details. The omission of grammatical function words intensifies the effect, leaving the reader with only the emotive lexical words:

>   A   A   A
> (Bent double, like old beggars under sacks),/(Knock-kneed), (coughing like hags),
>   SCl–NFCl

> S   P   A   A
> (we) (cursed) (through sludge)/(Till on the haunting flares we turned our backs)/
>   SCl–ACl

>   A
> (And) (towards our distant rest began to trudge). (ll. 1–4)
> conj   SCl–NFCl

The poem uses **metaphorical language** to intensify the atmosphere created. **Similes** like the references to *old beggars* (l. 1) and *hags* (l. 2) disturb the reader because they are unexpected comparisons – the soldiers are far from being glorious and heroic, but are instead physically and emotionally broken. The **neologism** *blood-shod* (l. 6) is equally disturbing: the soldiers have no shoes, but their feet are so covered with blood that they appear to be wearing shoes. The compound noun expresses this graphically in a very concise way.

The **rhetorical patterning** helps to make the poem effective: the juxtaposition between the horror of the content and the order of the poetic structure is dramatic. **Marked themes** like *Bent double...* (l. 1) and **listing** like *All...lame; all blind;/Drunk...deaf* (ll. 6–7) focus attention on the condition of the soldiers. They appear to be oblivious to everything around them, cut off from normal life by the inescapable reality of life at the front. **Antithesis** is used to reinforce this sense of two different worlds: *turned our backs* (l. 3) and *distant* (l. 4) are juxtaposed with the verb modifier *haunting* (l. 3) to emphasise that the men cannot forget what they have seen and experienced just by walking away towards *rest* (l. 4). The **phonological patterning** is what gives the poem its sense of order. The **rhyme scheme** links alternate lines: the phonemes /æks/ in *sacks* and *backs*; /ʌdʒ/ in *sludge* and *trudge*; /uːts/ in *boots* and *hoots*; and /aɪnd/ in *blind* and *behind*.

The poem is written mainly in iambic pentameter. Most lines have ten syllables; the pattern of stressed and unstressed syllables is not always the same but each line has either five or six stresses. The variation in the stress pattern draws attention to the key elements used to build up the atmosphere.

ACTIVITY 14.2

Read the following short poem by D. H. Lawrence and comment on the way content and form help to create the atmosphere.

Discord in Childhood

1   Outside the house an ash-tree hung its terrible whips,
    And at night when the wind rose, the lash of the tree
    Shrieked and slashed the wind, as a ship's
    Weird rigging in a storm shrieks hideously.

5   Within the house two voices arose, a slender lash
    Whistling she-delirious rage, and the dreadful sound
    Of a male thong booming and bruising, until it had drowned
    The other voice in a silence of blood, 'neath the noise of the ash.

D. H. Lawrence

COMMENTARY

The atmosphere created in the poem is one of violence and disruption. It is made more effective because of the juxtaposition of the child's and the adult's perspectives. Although the focus of the poem is on the tree that the child sees and the sounds heard, the adult poet explicitly reveals the connection between the two through his choice of lexis and structure.

The **language** creates a physical background for the conflict between the parents. **Concrete nouns** like *ash-tree* (l. 1) and *house* (l. 1) directly link the two elements of the poet's memory. The poem implies that the child is upstairs in bed, able to see only the tree outside while listening to the parents arguing downstairs. By **naming the partici-**

pants using the noun phrase *two voices* (l. 5), the poet dehumanises them, reducing them to what the child hears. The **modifiers** develop the dramatic atmosphere of the poem. The adjective *terrible* (l. 1) describes the tree, but becomes symbolic of the child's feelings about what is happening downstairs. Other modifiers clearly divide the mother and father: *slender* (l. 5) is juxtaposed with *dreadful* (l. 6) to suggest the respective parts played by the parents in the battle the child can only hear. **Noun phrases** are complex, conveying a lot of information and emphasising the effect of the parents' conflict on the child:

> ^m   ^m   ^h ^q
> a slender lash/Whistling she-delirious rage (ll. 5–6)
> det   Adj   N   NFCl

> ^m   ^m   ^h ^q   ^q
> the dreadful sound/Of a male thong booming and bruising (ll. 6–7)
> det   Adj   N   PrepP   NFCl

Throughout, the **connotations** of words are negative: verbs like *shrieked* and *slashed* (l. 3); nouns like *lash* (l. 2) and *thong* (l. 7); abstract nouns like *discord* (in the title); and modifiers like the adverb *hideously* (l. 4) and the adjective *weird* (l. 4). All these make the atmosphere of the poem disturbing.

The **grammar** intensifies the atmosphere by concentrating the descriptions. Each stanza is made up of a complex sentence:

> A   S   P   O   A
> (Outside the house) (an ash-tree) (hung) (its terrible whips)/(And) (at night)
>   conj

> A   S   P   P   O
> (when the wind rose) (the lash of the tree)/(Shrieked) (and) (slashed) (the wind)
> SCl–ACl   conj

> A
> (as a ship's/Weird rigging in a storm shrieks hideously). (ll. 1–4)
> SCl–ACl

The **metaphorical language** is central to the child's impression of what is happening. The child cannot see the parents, but the tree is visible as it lashes in storms and this becomes symbolic of the sounds coming from below. The concrete nouns *lash* and *whips* describe the tree in the first stanza but become linked to the voices the child can hear in the second stanza. The description of the mother's voice as a *lash* and the father's as a *thong* builds up the connotations of violence and punishment. The conclusion of the argument is made dramatic as noise is replaced by *silence* (l. 8). The effect is intensified by the juxtaposition of this abstract noun with *blood* (l. 8) and the use of the verb *drowned* (l. 7), which suddenly make the violence real rather than metaphorical. The simile *as a ship's/Weird rigging...* (ll. 3–4) contributes to the child's sense that something unearthly is happening.

The most obvious **rhetorical patterning** is the use of **antithesis**: the roles of the mother and father are contrasted; the tree in a storm is juxtaposed with the parents' discord; and the noise of the argument is contrasted with the silence that follows its violent end. **Marked themes** are used to contrast the content of each stanza: *Outside...* (l. 1) and *Within...* (l. 5). The **phonological patterning** helps to create the cacophony of sounds: **alliteration** of the phoneme /b/ and **sibilance** mimic the noise of the father and mother respectively. The **rhyme** scheme is different in each stanza and this draws a distinction between the description of the tree and of the parents: in lines 1 and 3, the phonemes /ɪps/ rhyme in the words *whips* and *ships*; in lines 2 and 4, the phoneme /iː/ rhymes in *tree* and *hideously*; in lines 5 and 8, the phonemes /æʃ/ rhyme in *lash* and *ash*; in lines 6 and 7, the phonemes /aʊnd/ rhyme in *sound* and *drowned*.

The poet chooses **free verse** and the number of syllables and stresses per line varies, making this poem closer to the patterns of ordinary speech than older, more structured poetic forms. The end result, however, is still more intense than everyday conversation. The atmosphere is heightened in two ways: the violence is made more shocking by the almost matter-of-fact way in which it is revealed; and the metaphorical language is emotive because it is the child's way of understanding what he or she cannot see or be a part of.

To experiment with language and structure

As a variety, poetry is very flexible: by adapting language and form, poets can convey their messages in very personal ways. Traditional ballads often used **dialect**, and this makes them more immediate and dramatic.

The Twa Corbies

1 As I was walking all alane,
    I heard twa corbies making a mane;
The tane unto the t'other say,
    'Where sall we gang and dine to-day?'

5 'In behint yon auld fail dyke,
    I wot there lies a new-slain knight;
And naebody kens that he lies there,
    But his hawk, his hound, and lady fair . . .

Anonymous, extract

In this extract from a Scottish ballad, it is immediately possible to pick out **dialect words** which mark its origin: *twa* (l. 2) for 'two'; *corbies* (l. 2) for 'ravens'; *tane* (l. 3) for 'one'; *gang* (l. 4) for 'go'; *auld* (l. 5) for 'old'; *fail* (l. 5) for 'turf'; *wot* (l. 6) for 'know'; *naebody* (l. 7) for 'nobody'; and *kens* (l. 7) for 'knows'. Since the poem is basically a record of the conversation between two birds about their next meal, the dialect is appropriate, giving the poem an authentic and unsentimental tone.

The poem opens abruptly with no time spent building up a background. Only salient details like the *auld fail dyke* (l. 5) are included, to emphasise the isolation of the newly dead knight. The **lexis** is simple and direct and the **sound pattern** is distinctive: the quatrains are rhymed in couplets; the feet are iambic:

▓ Aš Í | wǎs wál|kiňg áll | aǐané (l. 1)

▓ Ǐ wót | thěre líes | ǎ néw|-slaín kníght (l. 6)

Ballads are a traditional form of oral poetry and it is common for them to be written in dialect. Few of the poets are known, but the dialect forms used tell the reader something about their origins. Modern poets can choose to write in dialect and this makes their approach more distinctive.

Other poets choose to manipulate **structure**, not selecting a traditional form but devising one that suits their particular purpose.

Prayer Before Birth

1 I am not yet born; O hear me.
Let not the bloodsucking bat or the rat or the stoat or the
    club-footed ghoul near me.

I am not yet born; console me.
5 I fear that the human race may with tall walls wall me,
with strong drugs dope me, with wise lies lure me,
on black racks rack me, in blood-baths roll me.

I am not yet born; provide me
With water to dandle me, grass to grow for me, trees to talk
10 to me, sky to sing to me, birds and a white light
in the back of my mind to guide me . . .

Louis MacNeice (1907–63), extract

These three stanzas are taken from the beginning of a poem whose form draws on the liturgical prayer. **Repetition of grammatical structures** and of **sounds** makes the poem's appeal more powerful. The opening of each stanza reinforces the context. The poem is a plea that people create an appropriate environment in which the child may live and therefore after the declarative **mood** of the first clause, an imperative is used.

$$\overset{\text{S}}{(I)} \overset{\text{P}}{\underset{\text{neg}}{(am\ not)}} \overset{\text{A}}{(yet)} \overset{\text{C}}{(born)} \ldots \overset{\text{P}}{hear} \ldots \overset{\text{P}}{console} \ldots \overset{\text{P}}{provide} \ldots (ll.\ 1\text{–}8)$$

The poem also uses the sonorous tones of **prayer** – it is clearly a poem to be read aloud. Although there are no end rhymes, **internal rhyme** is used. The phonemes /ɔːl/ are repeated in *tall walls wall me* (l. 5) and the phonemes /æk/ in *black racks rack me* (l. 7). **Alliteration** is frequent: the phoneme /b/ in *bloodsucking bat* (l. 2) and *blood-baths* (l. 7); /l/ in *lies lure me* (l. 6); /g/ in *grass. . .grow* (l. 9); /s/ in *sky. . .sing* (l. 10). All of these poetic devices contribute to the rhythmical chant of the poem.

Structurally, the poem is distinctive on the page. The third and any subsequent lines are inset, giving the poem a disjointed and jagged appearance. Stanzas also differ in length – as the appeals of the unborn child become more urgent, so the stanzas become longer.

Both the layout and the structure make the poem distinctive, allowing the poet to draw attention to his plea to make a better world – because the unborn child actually makes the appeal, the poem is very poignant. The repetitions make the poem seem like a never-ending list which must be addressed if the world is to be made into a more humane place. The liturgical qualities give the appeal a very formal tone.

Whichever structure or style a poet chooses will tell the reader something about the kind of relationship the poet wishes to create with the reader and about the kind of message to be conveyed. If a poet chooses a form or layout that is unusual in any way, it makes the message more distinctive and personal.

14.5 What to look for in the language of poetry

The following checklist can be used to identify key features in examples of poetry. There will not be examples of all the features in every poem, but the list can be used as a guide. The points made are general so discussion of specific examples will need to be adapted to take account of the specific context and authorial purpose.

The following are helpful questions to ask.

Register

1   What is the **mode**? – written.
2   What is the **manner**? – the relationship between poet and reader, or poet and

subject: formal or informal? personal or impersonal? poet's intention (to characterise, describe a place or time, create an atmosphere, convey a message)?

3   What is the **field**? – the lexis will suggest something about the nature of the subject
matter.

Poetic form and structure

1   Has the poet used a recognisable **poetic form**? – sonnet? ballad? ode?
2   Has the poet used **blank verse** (ten syllables and five stresses) or **free verse**
(irregular lines with no regular metre)?
3   Are the lines **end stopped** or are there examples of **enjambement**?
4   Is there a noticeable **metre**? – pattern of stressed and unstressed syllables? number
of stressed syllables per line?
5   Are there any significant **pauses**?
6   Is the **rhythm** striking in any way? – very patterned and regular? similar to the
irregular patterns of speech?
7   Is anything unusual about the **layout**?
8   Are **stanza lengths** regular or irregular? – what effect does the division into stanzas
have?
9   Is the **structure** used to draw attention to key elements? – what effect does this
have?

Lexis

1   Are **words** simple or complex? formal or colloquial? descriptive or evaluative?
modern or archaic?
2   Are there any examples of **subject specific words** or specific **lexical sets**?
3   Has the poet chosen to use **non-standard language**? – dialect? idiosyncratic
linguistic choices? code language identifying insiders and outsiders? archaisms?
neologisms?
4   Are the **nouns concrete** or **abstract**?
5   Is the **naming of participants** important? – are any names omitted intentionally?
6   Do any words have significant **connotations**?
7   What function do the **modifiers** have? – what effects do they create?
8   What kinds of actions and processes do the **verbs** describe?
9   Are any **collocations** used? – are they changed in any way? what effect does this
have?

Grammar

1   Is the grammar **standard** or not? – **formal** or **informal**? **modern** or **archaic**? **minor
sentences**?
2   Are there any significant changes of **tense** or **mood**?
3   Is the **sentence structure** varied? – what effect do changes in the sentence type
have?
4   Are there any examples of **ellipsis**? – what effect does the compression of language
have?

Metaphorical language

1   Does the poet use **images** to add depth to the description or message of the poem?
2   Does the poem appeal to the **senses**? – sight, sound, touch?

3   Are there any **metaphors** or **symbols**? – what effect do these have?
4   Are there any other examples of **poetic devices**?

Rhetorical techniques

1   How does the poet try to influence the reader?
2   Are structural contrasts created through the use of **patterning**? **juxtapositions**? **listing**? **parallelism**? **repetition**? – what effects do these have?
3   Does the poet emphasise certain elements using **marked themes**? the **passive voice**? **end focus**? – what effect do these have?
4   What kinds of **phonological patterning** are used? – **alliteration**? **sibilance**? **onomatopoeia**? **end rhyme**? **internal rhyme**?

Summary

The **function** of poetry is to entertain, but poets can also implicitly or explicitly convey a message about society or life.

The language of poetry is very **varied** because poets can manipulate language in order to make their work striking. Unusual and archaic language can be used to add depth to a characterisation or authenticity to a message; word class boundaries can be broken to create unusual effects; grammatical words can be omitted to intensify the mood of the poem; and rhythm and metre can be used to mark poetry as different from ordinary speech.

The **poet's intention** will dictate the kinds of linguistic, stylistic and structural choices made: poets can use heightened and elevated language or ordinary conversational language; they can use predefined strict forms or freer more personal forms; they can compress language until it no longer seems to conform to standard grammatical patterns or they can use the irregular patterns of speech.

15 The language of the law

15.1 The nature of legal language

The language of law is very distinctive and its lexical and syntactical patterns owe much to traditional forms of English. Its conservatism is linked directly to the need for unambiguous language that has already been tried and tested in the courts. By retaining traditional lexis and syntax, lawyers can be confident that the language of the law is consistent and precise. Campaigners for **plain English** (English that is straightforward and easy to understand) argue that legal language could be simplified so that it is both more comprehensible to ordinary people and more practical for lawyers themselves. Many lawyers fear, however, that if changes were made, new simplified language structures could create legal loopholes.

Legal language is used in a range of legal contexts in both written and spoken forms. It is marked by complex grammatical structures, technical lexis, archaic expressions and limited punctuation, which together make it quite different from other varieties. Nothing is left implicit and there is perhaps no other variety in which anything not stated explicitly is disregarded. Such linguistic features make it easily recognisable even to people who are not part of the profession.

I swear by Almighty God to tell the truth, the whole truth and nothing but the truth . . .

You may approach the bench . . .

Legal language is the domain of a specialist occupation and the intended audience are experts in the field. Because the same kinds of legal transactions occur regularly, linguistic formulae have been developed. This means that legal language is not spontaneous – it is quite unlike informal speech with its irregular patterns, and quite unlike the language of literature with its personal, often idiosyncratic approach. Instead, it draws on structures that have been predefined and pretested, and uses jargon that is familiar only to the experts and grammatical structures that are difficult to decode.

The **lexis** and **syntax** can make it difficult for an ordinary reader to understand a legal document, as can the **layout**. Traditionally, the contents were often written as a solid block with no paragraphs or spacing to mark out sections of the text. To avoid any ambiguity in the interpretation of written documents, punctuation was used sparingly. Examples of blocked layout and minimal punctuation can still be found, but more recently legal documents have tended to use typographical devices to make the variety less obscure. Capitalisation, underlining, different print styles, numbered lists and paragraphs are now often used to highlight the development of key points.

15.2 The function of legal language

The language of the law is used to regulate society by establishing obligations that must be fulfilled and by ensuring that rights are granted. Although legal language can be difficult to understand, we all come into contact with it on a regular basis. Statutes dictate what is and what is not acceptable behaviour in society; contracts are made with insurance companies and mortgage lenders; property conveyancing is completed; and wills are drawn up. The spoken language of the courts is portrayed on television in the numerous courtroom dramas and in live trial coverage like that in 1995 of the O. J. Simpson murder trial in America, which was broadcast on British television.

The main function of legal language is **referential** (to convey information). Its subordinate functions are **conative** (persuasive) and **metalinguistic** (discussing language itself). It is always formal, whether it is written or spoken, although a meeting between solicitor and client will be less formal than a cross-questioning in court.

15.3 Features of written legal language

Modern printing techniques and attempts to simplify legal language have had some effect on the nature of written documents, but for the main part the legal variety has changed little over the centuries. In analysing legal texts, linguists must be aware of both the customary approaches and the ways in which these are being changed in order to make the variety less obscure. For instance, whereas traditional documents used no paragraphing and often used Gothic script for the opening letter, modern documents will usually divide the text into distinct units and will avoid decorative printing. Such changes are linked to the desire for plain English in all public official language. Despite this, the basic language structures remain unchanged.

Manner

The **manner** is always formal and the language of the law has little similarity with the language of conversation. There are, for instance, no contractions for negatives or auxiliary verbs in written documents. Because it is a traditional form of language, it retains archaic features. These and the many formulaic utterances like 'signed in the joint presence of…' contribute to the ceremonial tone. It is a public form of language, but its intended audience is legal experts rather than the general public.

Typography and layout

The **typographical features** are designed to draw attention to key elements of the text. The overall **layout** is often distinctive. Traditional documents are printed in a solid block with no indentation, but more modern examples tend to be indented and subdivided. Although the traditional style gives an overall visual coherence to legal documents, modern layouts are more acceptable to the non-specialist. Variations in **typeface** are used to reveal the structure of the content. Capitalisation, underlining and variations in typeface can emphasise important lexical items. References to people, companies or parts of a document may be highlighted by using such techniques.

Punctuation is used sparingly in legal documents because it can cause ambiguity. Commas are often omitted in lists and for clauses in parenthesis; colons and dashes can mark the beginning of a list of subsections, but are also often omitted; brackets are sometimes used to identify parenthesis. Sentences in legal documents tend to be very long and full stops are only used at the end of key sections or at the very end of the document.

> 1 There is reserved for the benefit of any adjoining property of the Vendors or their predecessors or successors in title the free and uninterrupted passage and running of water and soil and gas and electricity from and to other buildings . . .

A comma following the past participle *reserved* (l. 1) and following the post-modified noun phrase *successors in title* (l. 2) would make this sentence easier to read. By isolating the adverbial, the relationship between the dummy subject *there* (l. 1) and the delayed subject *the free and uninterrupted passage. . .* (l. 2) would be clearer.

Lexis

The **lexis** of legal language is very distinctive. There is a mixture of **subject specific jargon** or 'terms of art' like *tort*, *alibi* and *bail* which all lawyers will interpret in the same way, and other **ordinary words** like *damage*, *malice* and *valid* which will be interpreted differently depending upon the context. The **specialist terminology** can be divided into two categories: ordinary language used in a specialist way, like *proposal* and *life*, and specialist language used in everyday contexts, like *liable*. The subject specific lexis contributes to the formal tone of legal language.

Archaic lexis like *hereafter* and **collocations** like *it shall be deemed* also make the variety formal. **Synonyms** are common, reflecting the influence of both French and Latin on legal language and the need to be all-inclusive.

> made and signed: make (OE *macian*); sign (Fr *signe*, L *signum*)
> able and willing: able (OFr *ableté*, Fr *habileté*, L *habilitās*); will (OE *willa*)

As would be expected, words marking grammatical relationships are mainly descended from Old English, but there is evidence of many French and Latin **loan words** which have since been assimilated into the language.

> proposal: Fr *proposer*   conveyance: OFr *conveier*
> contract: L *contractus*   evidence: L *evidens*

Other borrowings are not used in ordinary discourse but have been retained as specialist terms.

> estoppel: a conclusive admission which cannot be denied by the person(s) it affects
> estop: to hinder or prevent (OFr *estoper*)
> res gestae: facts relevant to the case and admissible in evidence (L)
> caveat emptor: let the buyer beware or 'it's the buyer's lookout' (L)

Many nouns are **abstract**: *valuation*, *bonus*, *evidence* and *policy*. Legal language is not concerned with the creation of mood, nor with description or evaluation, so **pre-modifiers** are used infrequently except where they can provide exact information: *the first premium*, *the current monthly payment* and *the freehold land*. The determiner site in a noun phrase is nearly always filled: *the Valuer*, *a Mortgagee*, *the Lease* and *the Life Insured*. If the determiner is omitted, it is usually because the phrase is part of a formula: *details of proposed occupiers* and *interest accruing*. The use of *said* and *aforesaid* (meaning *mentioned before*) as pre-modifiers allows legal documents to be very precise in any anaphoric references that are made: *the sum of £5000. . .the said sum*; *the period of 28 days. . .the said period*. **Post-modification** is common, however, since it provides factual information like names, addresses and legal conditions. Long sequences of post-modifying subordinate clauses can mean that the head noun of the subject and predicator are separated, making the text difficult to decipher.

> (h)   S
> (A *conveyance* of the land in this title dated 23 May 1946 made between
>   SCl–NFCl   SCl–NFCl
>
> 1. Mark Stephens and Brian Morris [Vendors] and 2. Julie Mary Ryan and others
>
>   P   O
> [Purchasers]) (contains) (the exceptions and reservations as set out below) . . .
>   SCl–ACl

The **verbs** are distinctive in legal language because few other varieties have as many non-finite and modal auxiliary verbs. The auxiliary and lexical verbs are often separated by sequences of phrases and clauses, making the documents difficult to read. The lexical verbs found in written legal documents tend to be limited and the same ones are used regularly: *indemnify, accept, be conveyed, be deemed*. **Adverbials** are used frequently and tend to cluster at the beginning of sentences. They are often linked to the archaic prepositional words like *hereto, hereafter* and *thereof*. The use of adverbials is one of the distinctive features of legal language.

>   A
> (If the loss of or damage to the Insured Vehicle is caused by theft or attempted
> SCl–ACl
>
>   A
> theft) (where the Insured Vehicle has been fitted with an immobilising system or
> SCl–ACl
>
> an alarm system recognised by the Company) (and) (where the Insured is in
>   SCl–NFCl   conj   SCl–ACl
>   A
> possession of all the keys and/or activating accessories and the Certificate of
>
> Installation as provided by the manufacturer of the immobilising system or alarm
> SCl–ACl
>
>   S   P
> system) (the excess as specified in Section 2 of the Policy) (will not apply).
> SCl–ACl   neg

Pronoun referencing is not often used in legal documents, so that any ambiguity can be avoided. Instead, nouns are repeated throughout, as in the previous example where noun phrases like *the Insured Vehicle* and the compound noun phrase *immobilising system or alarm system* are repeated in full. So that references can be all-inclusive, neuter words focusing on function like *the Insured Party* or *the Life Insured* are chosen. This avoids words that are marked by gender. Where a pronoun is used, however, it will usually be the third person singular *he* or the third person plural *they*.

Grammar

The **grammar** of legal language is complicated by the length of the sentences. Strings of dependent clauses are used to provide precise information about the legal conditions attached to each transaction, whether it is a life assurance or car insurance policy, a will or a property sale. The embedded clauses make the legal terms of reference clear, but the reader has to retain a lot of information to decode the meaning. The **mood** is almost always declarative, but imperatives are used occasionally. Interrogatives are used in the spoken legal language of the courts, but not in written documents. The **passive voice** is often used.

> If the Insured Vehicle <u>has been owned</u> by one owner only since the date of
> its first registration as new . . .

As an active sentence the noun phrase *one owner only* would fill the subject site of the adverbial clause. The passive voice is more appropriate in this example since it brings the noun phrase *the Insured Vehicle* to the front of the sentence. The focus of this insurance policy is the car and it is logical to bring that lexical item forward. It does, however, make the sentence more difficult to read. Campaigners for plain English believe that the use of the passive voice is one of the linguistic and stylistic features of legal language that unnecessarily complicates meaning.

Sentences in legal documents are long because they have to include all relevant points in a single statement. Although the high number of co-ordinated phrases and clauses make the variety seem list-like, they insure that it is inclusive. The **sentence structure** is usually complex, compound or compound-complex. Few sentences are simple and none are minor sentences.

> (If the Life Insured shall pay or cause to be paid to the Society or to the duly
> SCl–ACl   SCl–NFCl
>
> authorised Agent thereof every subsequent premium at the date due thereof) (on
>
> the expiration of the term of years specified in the Schedule hereto or on the
> SCl–NFCl
>
> previous death of the Life Insured) (the funds of the Society) (shall) (in
> S   P
>
> accordance with the terms and conditions of the said Table) (become and be)
> A   P
>
> (liable to pay to him/her or to his/her personal representative or next-of-kin the
> SCl–NFCl
>
> sum due).

As can be seen in this example, the word order is distinctive: adverbials are often clustered at the beginning; almost all clauses contain adverbials to clarify the meaning; and there are many co-ordinated phrases. Such chain-like constructions make legal language distinctive. **Cohesion** is created through **repetition** of **lexical sets**. Because of the interrelated sequences of clauses, sentences in legal language tend to be like self-contained units – they do not need to be linked closely to what has gone before or what follows. This makes anaphoric and cataphoric referencing less important between sentences and avoids any possible ambiguity which might constitute a loophole in the law.

15.4 Types of legal language

Statutes

A STATUTE is a formal set of rules or rules of conduct which have to be observed. The Government makes policies that establish general principles for guidance and then legislation makes them into law: *Offences Against the Person Act 1861* and *Theft Act 1968*. The **tone** is formal and each word is important because a statute has to convey its meaning precisely so that it can be upheld in law. **Words used loosely in ordinary conversation** take on special significance. **Modal auxiliaries**, for instance, each have a specific meaning which will dictate the way in which a statute is interpreted and enforced: *may* denotes that you can do something, while *shall* denotes that you must do something.

Statutes have a distinctive structure. They are named formally.

> ### Race Relations Act 1968
> ### ELIZABETH II
> ### 1968 CHAPTER 71
> An Act to make fresh provision with respect to discrimination on racial grounds and to make provision with respect to relations between people of different racial origins. [25th October 1968]

Complex prepositions like *with respect to* and the number of abstract nouns like *provision, discrimination* and *origins* make the tone public and official. The statute name is made up of the noun phrase *An Act* which is post-modified by two non-finite clauses beginning with *to make...* The parallelism of the structure and the formality of the lexis are typical of this kind of legal language. The title is then followed by an **enacting formula**.

> Be it enacted by the Queen's most Excellent Majesty, by and with the advice and consent of the Lords Spiritual and Temporal, and Commons, in the present Parliament assembled, and by the authority of the same as follows:– ...

There is a clear pattern to the structure: an imperative in the passive voice, *Be...enacted*, is followed by a sequence of adverbials: *by the Queen's most Excellent Majesty, by...the Lords Spiritual and Temporal, and Commons, in the present* and *by the authority*. The use of the passive voice allows the sentence to be refocused: the long subject of an active sentence becomes the sequence of *by + agent* adverbials, allowing greater emphasis to be placed on the past participle *enacted*. The style of the formula introducing the Act adds to the ceremonial tone. It is followed by numbered sections which categorise the different elements of the law.

> 1   **PART I**
> ### DISCRIMINATION
> *General*
> **1.**–(1) For the purposes of this Act a person discriminates against another if
> 5 on the ground of colour, race or ethnic or national origins he treats that other, in any situation to which section 2, 3, 4 or 5 below applies, less favourably than he treats or would treat other persons, and in this Act references to discrimination are references to discrimination on any of those grounds.

After the official naming of the Act, it opens with a formula. The prepositional phrase *For the purpose of this Act...* (l. 4) establishes the legal definition of discrimination. Repetition highlights key words and avoids ambiguity: for instance, the abstract noun *discrimination* (l. 2) and the verb *discriminates* (l. 4), the abstract noun *references* (l.7) and the verb *treat* (l. 5). The example is typical of legal language in a number of ways: third person pronoun references to *he* (ll. 5, 7) are seen to be inclusive of 'she'; lists of alternatives like *colour, race, or ethnic or national origins* (l. 5) ensure that all possibilities are legally covered; there are many abstract nouns; and the sentence structure is complex with adverbials in each part of the compound sentence.

>   A   S   P   O   A
> (For the purpose of. . .) (a person) (discriminates against) (another) (if. . .) (and)
>   SCl–ACl conj
>
>   A   S   P   C   A
> (in this Act) (references. . .) (are) (references. . .) (on any. . .)

ACTIVITY 15.1

Read through this example of a statute taken from the Income and Corporation Taxes Act 1988 and comment on the distinctive features of legal language.

1

PART I

THE CHARGE TO TAX

Income Tax

4.–(1) Any provision of the Income Tax Acts requiring, permitting or assum-
5   ing the deduction of income tax from any amount (otherwise than in pur-
suance of section 203) or treating income tax as having been deducted from
or paid on any amount, shall, subject to any provision to the contrary, be
construed as referring to deduction or payment of income tax at the basic
rate in force for the relevant year of assessment.
10   (2) For the purposes of subsection (1) above, the relevant year of
assessment shall be taken to be (except where otherwise provided) –
  (a) if the amount is an amount payable wholly out of profits or gains
brought into charge to tax, the year in which the amount becomes
due;
15   (b) in any other case, the year in which the amount is paid.

The Taxes Acts, 'Income tax, Corporation tax and Capital gains tax'

COMMENTARY

The **manner** is formal: there are no contractions, and formulaic utterances like the prepositional phrase *For the purposes of. . .* (l. 10) are typical in this kind of legal language. The book from which this extract is taken is clearly written for experts rather than the general public and this also contributes to the formality of the tone.

The **typographical features** show that this is a modern document since the layout has been divided for easier reading. **Paragraphs** are marked numerically and **subdivisions** make each point clear. **Punctuation** is used more extensively than in more traditional documents. Lists of verbs are divided with commas – *requiring, permitting or assuming* (l. 4); parenthesis is marked by commas and brackets; and a dash marks the beginning of a list of subsections. These typographical marks help the reader by dividing the text into semantic units that are more easily readable.

The **lexis** is **subject specific. Abstract nouns** like *deduction* (l. 5) and *profits or gains* (l. 12) and **collocations** like *the relevant year of assessment* (l. 10) indicate that the field is financial. Nouns like *assessment* (l. 9) are ordinary words used in a specialist context in tax law. The origins of many words can be traced to Latin and French sources:

> deduction (l. 8): L *dēdŭcĕre*   tax (l. 2): Fr *taxe*, L *taxāre*
> assessment (l. 9): L *assidēre*   *payment* (l. 8): *Fr payer*, L *pacāre*

The only **pre-modifiers** make the information provided more precise:

> | m   h | m   m   h | m   m   h   q |
> | income tax (l. 4) | the basic rate (ll. 8–9) | the relevant year of assessment (l. 9) |
> | N   N | det   Adj   N | det   Adj   N   PrepP |

Post-modifying prepositional phrases and non-finite clauses are common:

> | m   h   q | q |
> | Any provision of the Income Tax Acts requiring, permitting or assuming . . . (l. 4) |
> | det   N   PrepP | NFCl |

By placing adverbial clauses in listed subsections after the predicator, this example avoids the clusters of adverbials at the beginnings of sentences associated with traditional legal documents. Each semantic unit still begins with an adverbial, however.

> A   S   P
> (For the purposes of. . .) (the relevant year. . .) (shall be taken to be). . . –
>
> A   C
> (a) (if the amount is. . .) (the year in which the amount becomes due);
>   SCl–ACl   SCl–RelCl
>
> A   C
> (b) (in any other case), (the year in which the amount is paid). (ll. 10–15)
>   SCl–RelCl

The **verbs** are typical of legal language: the modal auxiliary *shall* (l. 7) is repeated; there are many non-finite verbs where other varieties would use a finite clause: *requiring, permitting or assuming* (ll. 4–5); and the verbs are part of a limited lexical set that is linked to the field: *deducted* (l. 6) and *paid* (l. 7).

The **grammar** is complicated despite the fact that modern visual features divide the long sentences into discrete units.

> S
> (Any provision of the Income Tax Acts requiring, permitting or assuming the
>   SCl–NFCl
>
> deduction of income tax from any amount. . .or treating income tax as having
>   SCl–NFCl   SCl–ACl
>
>   P   A
> been deducted from or paid on any amount), (shall), (subject to any provision to
>   aux
>
>   P   A
> the contrary), (be construed) (as referring to deduction or payment of income tax
>   aux   lex   SCl–ACl
>
>   A
> at the basic rate in force) (for the relevant year of assessment). (ll. 4–9)

The **mood** throughout is declarative and all sentences are major. The **passive voice** is used in verb phrases like *having been deducted from* (l. 6), *(having been) paid on* (ll. 6–7) and *be construed* (ll. 7–8). No agent is used, but the implication is that the unnamed agents are the legal or accounting profession and the Civil Service who establish and uphold the rules. In this context, it is not important to include the subject of the active sentence because the document is merely providing the regulations that tax inspectors must follow. **Marked themes** draw attention to information that is important in interpreting the legal conditions: *For the purposes of subsection (1) above. . .* (l. 10). **Cohesion** is created through the repetition of key words like *income tax* (l. 3), *deduction* (l. 5) and *amount* (l. 5). Pronoun referencing is avoided so that there can be no doubt about the intended interpretation.

Campaigners for plain English have argued that it is unnecessary to use archaic language, to eliminate punctuation and to conform to traditional block layouts. The example of statute law here is still complicated but modern approaches to the presentation of legal language have made it more accessible than traditional documents. The extract is clearly typical of the legal variety with its complex sentence structures, lexical repetition and French and Latin loan words. It is less daunting, however, because it attempts to guide inexperienced readers by dividing the document into smaller semantic units.

Contracts

A legal **CONTRACT** is a written document in which a legal agreement of some kind is undertaken between two or more parties. Contracts determine when a promise or set of promises is legally enforceable. Transactions like selling houses, leasing property or insuring lives and possessions are covered by legal contracts.

In signing a contract, the participants are agreeing to carry out a series of acts or to fulfil a series of conditions. Because these can be enforced by the law, the language is formal and the syntax complicated.

> A   S
> (Where agreed with the Applicant) (the insurance of the property to be mortgaged)
> SCl–ACl   SCl–NFCl
>
> P   A   A
> (will be arranged) (by the Society) (unless the property is leasehold and
>   SCl–ACl
>
> the lease contains a covenant to insure through a specified agency).
> SCl–ACl   SCl–NFCl

There are a number of linguistic and stylistic features making this extract from a mortgage contract typical of legal language.

- **Subject specific words** define the nature of the contract: the verb *mortgaged* and the abstract nouns *insurance* and *covenant*.
- The noun *property*, which is used in ordinary discourse in a loose way, is used here in a **specific way** to refer to the building to be insured.
- **Collocations** like *where agreed...* and *will be arranged...* are formulaic.
- **Determiners** are used to pre-modify every noun except one where other pre-modification is used to provide precise information:

> m   m   h
> the specified agency
> det   V   N

- **Post-modification** is used on several occasions:

> m   h   q   m   h   q
> the insurance of the property to be mortgaged   a covenant to insure. . .
> det   N   PrepP   NFCl   det   N   NFCl

- The **adverbials** provide exact information about the conditions to be met: insurance arranged *by the Society...*, *Unless....*
- The **passive voice** is used to place the object of the active sentence, *the insurance of the property...*, in the subject site of the passive sentence to give it more emphasis.
- Nouns like *property* are **repeated** instead of being substituted by pronouns, to avoid ambiguity.

Despite the fact that contracts like this are now divided into subsections to make reading easier, the typical features of legal language are still clear. Contracts are legally enforceable, so the language must ensure that there are no loopholes and this inevitably makes the text complicated.

Wills

A **WILL** is a declaration of a person's intentions concerning the allocation of property after death. It can be altered at any point up to death. It must be a written document and it must be signed *at the foot or end*. Two or more witnesses must authenticate the signature of the **TESTATOR** (the person making the will).

A will is a formal document and the language is formulaic. Much of the lexis is subject specific:

> devise (N): the arrangements for disposing of freehold land
> legacy/bequest (N): the arrangements for disposing of any other possessions
> grant of probate (N): an official acceptance that a will is genuine

The structure follows certain patterns, although an official will can be no more than a letter.

ACTIVITY 15.2

Read through the following example of a will and comment on the linguistic and stylistic features making it typical of the legal variety.

1 I, JONATHAN MOORES, of 123 Wood Lane, Newtown, HEREBY REVOKE all Wills and testamentary documents heretofore made by me AND DECLARE this to be my LAST WILL and TESTAMENT.

   1. I DESIRE my body to be donated to medical science.

5 2. I APPOINT my wife *Alice Moores* (hereinafter called 'my wife') to be my sole executrix of this my will but if the foregoing appointment shall fail for any reason then I appoint my children *Edward Moores* of 456 Smithfield Road, Newtown and *Louise Moores* of 789 Church Street, Newtown (hereinafter together called 'my trustees' which expression where the context admits

10 shall include the trustees or trustee hereof for the time being) to be the executors and trustees of this my will.

   3. I BEQUEATH to my wife all my real and personal property whatsoever and wheresoever for her own use and benefit absolutely if she shall survive me by thirty days but if she does not survive me by the thirty days then

15 4. I DIVIDE and BEQUEATH all my real and personal property whatsoever and wheresoever unto my trustees UPON TRUST that my trustees shall sell call in and convert into money the same and shall therefore pay my funeral and testamentary expenses and debts and inheritance tax due and shall stand possessed of the residue of such moneys (hereinafter called 'my resid-

20 uary estate') UPON TRUST for my children *Edward Moores* and *Louise Moores* in equal shares absolutely PROVIDED ALWAYS that if any shall have predeceased me leaving a child or children who attain the age of 18 years such child or children shall stand in place of such deceased and shall take by substitution and equally between them if more than one the share of

25 my residuary estate which such a deceased child of mine would have taken if he or she had survived me.

   IN WITNESS whereof I the said *Jonathon Moores* the Testator have to this my LAST WILL set my hand this twenty-first day of May One Thousand Nine Hundred and Ninety-Five.

30 SIGNED AND ACKNOWLEDGED by the above-
named *Jonathon Moores* the Testator as and for
his LAST WILL in the presence of us both present
at the same time who at his request in his presence and in the presence of each other have here-

35 unto subscribed our names as witnesses:

COMMENTARY

The **manner** is formal and the relationship between writer and addressees is official despite the fact that the participants are well known to each other. There are no contractions, and formulaic utterances like *IN WITNESS whereof* (l. 27) and *last will and testament* (l. 3) add to the formal tone. The document is legally binding and the language and style are therefore typical of the legal variety.

The **typographical features** are typical of a modern will: each point is clearly **numbered**; **capitalisation** is used to highlight key lexical items; **italic print** is used to draw attention to the names of the trustees; and **block paragraphs** are used to indicate different sections of the document. **Punctuation** is closer to standard written usage than in traditional legal documents, but commas are still omitted in lists like *sell call in and convert* (ll. 16–17) and for much of the parenthesis.

The **lexis** is typical of legal language. **Subject specific words**, like the verb *REVOKE* (l. 1), the plural noun *trustees* (l. 9) and the prepositional phrase *UPON TRUST* (l. 16), reflect the exact nature of the legal language. Because a will deals with the theoretical division of property at a time in the future, there are many abstract nouns like *substitution* (l. 24), *presence* (l. 32) and *shares* (l. 21). **Ordinary words** like the nouns *appointment* (l. 6) and *estate* (l. 25) take on a specific legal meaning in this context. **Archaisms** are typical of the legal variety as a whole: for instance, prepositional words like *hereinafter* (l. 5), *hereof* (l. 10) and *heretofore* (l. 2); and the collocation *set my hand* (l. 28). **Collocations** like *real and personal property* (l. 15) and *SIGNED AND ACKNOWLEDGED* (l. 30), however, are characteristic of wills in particular. Some collocations are made up of **synonyms** – an Old English and a Latin word are used together to ensure that the meaning is all-inclusive.

> will and testament (l. 3): OE *willa*, L *testāmentum*
> divide and bequeath (l. 15): L *dividĕre*, OE *becwethan*

Because Latin and French were for a long time the languages of the legal system and the courts, there are many examples of **loan words** that have now been assimilated.

> executor/executrix (l. 6): L *exsequī*   appoint (l. 5): OFr *apointer*
> revoke (l. 1): L *revocāre*   estate (l. 25): OFr *estat*
> residuary (ll. 19–20): L *residuum*   deceased (l. 23): OFr *deces*

Modification provides precise information. Where pre-modification is used it is always factual and never descriptive:

>   m   m   h   m   h
> the foregoing appointment (l. 6)   medical science (l. 4)
> det   V   N   Adj   N

>   m   m   m   h
> my real and personal property (l. 12)
> det Adj   Adj   N

Post-modification is more common:

>   m   h   q   h   q
> the residue of such moneys (l. 19)   *Edward Moores* of 456 Smithfield Road (l. 7)
> det N   PrepP   N   PrepP

>   m   h   q   q
> the share of my residuary estate which such a deceased child of mine (ll. 24–5)
> det N PrepP   RelCl

The **verbs** are distinctive and make up a limited lexical set which is typical of any will: *REVOKE* (l. 1), *appoint* (l. 5), *divide and bequeath* (l. 15) and *declare* (l. 3). **Modal**

auxiliaries like *shall* (l. 6) denote actions that have to be undertaken in the future and **adverbials** like the prepositional phrases *UPON TRUST* (l. 16), *by thirty days* (l. 14) and *for her own use* (l. 13) define the exact conditions that must be met.

The **grammar** is less complicated than older legal documents because the text is broken up into smaller units in numbered sections. The **mood** is declarative. The present **tense** is used because the document will be read as a current declaration of intent at the death of the testator. The will does not construct sentences with the **passive voice** because the actor (subject) and affected (object) must be clear if the declared intentions are to be carried out appropriately. Although there are many adverbials, there are not many **marked themes**. Most sentences have the subject in the initial position because if the testator's wishes are to be fulfilled after death, the declaration needs to be as clear as possible. Clause elements, therefore, are not often rearranged. Examples like *IN WITNESS whereof...* (l. 27), however, draw attention to the final act of signing the will and therefore officially authorise the declarations it contains.

Sentence structures are often complex:

    S   A   P   O
(I, JM of. . .) (HEREBY) (REVOKE) (all Wills and testamentary documents. . .

                    P   O
made. . .) (and) (declare) (this to be my. . .) (ll. 1–3)
SCl–NFCl   conj   SCl–NFCl

  S   P   Od   Oi
(I) (divide and bequeath) (all my real and personal property. . .) (unto my trustees)

                                      A
(upon trust that my trustees shall sell. . .and shall therefore pay. . .and shall stand
        SCl–NCl   SCl–NCl   SCl–NCl

                                       A
possessed of. . .) (provided always that if any shall have predeceased me leaving
         SCl–ACl   SCl–ACl   SCl–NFCl

a child or children who attain. . .such child or children shall stand. . .and shall
          SCl–RelCl   SCl–ACl

take. . .the share. . .which such a deceased child. . .would have taken. . .if he or
          SCl–RelCl   SCl–ACl

she had survived me). (ll. 15–26)

The need to include detailed conditions that must be met after the death of the testator means that the sentence is complicated by numerous adverbials. Many of the clauses are co-ordinated and ellipsis makes it even more difficult to identify the clause structure. The **cohesion** is typical of legal language in using repetition of key lexical items like *trustees* (l. 9) and *property* (l. 12) to avoid pronoun referencing which might cause ambiguity. The use of the first person singular pronoun *I* is appropriate here, however, since the document is a written statement from the testator who is clearly named in the post-modification of *I* in the opening sentence of the will. Object pronouns are used where the reference is clear: *them* (l. 24) is used as an anaphoric reference to the possible future children of one of the testator's own children; and the object pronoun *us* (l. 32) is used as a cataphoric reference to the signatures of the witnesses.

The will has a distinctive format which will only vary slightly from example to example. The language and syntax are typical of the legal variety as a whole, but are also marked by characteristics of this particular kind of legally binding contract.

The language of the courts

The spoken legal language of the courts is governed by complex rules: witnesses are not allowed to say what other people have said (hearsay); they are not allowed to evaluate (opinion); and they are not allowed to show emotions. Instead all contributors must do no more than respond directly to the questions.

Lawyers are advised to vary the way in which they ask questions in order to draw more from the witnesses and to use different questioning approaches for different kinds of people. For example, a good lawyer will choose different styles for expert witnesses, for the elderly and for the very young. Repetition can be used as a rhetorical device, but overuse can bore the jury. Prosodic features like rhythm, pitch and pace are also important variants if the jury are to be persuaded to agree with the particular interpretation of events put forward.

Different kinds of courts deal with different kinds of offences and the manner of a particular hearing is therefore dependent on the legal context. Civil offences are tried in both county courts and the High Court. The county courts are less formal since they deal with local affairs in which small sums of money are involved, social matters like housing and the welfare of children, and undefended matrimonial cases. The High Court deals with problems on a larger scale, like mortgages, bankruptcy and divorce appeals, so hearings are far more formal. Criminal cases are heard in the magistrates' courts and the crown court. In magistrates' courts, there is no jury; people can choose to defend themselves or to be represented by a barrister or solicitor; the justices decide whether the defendant is innocent or guilty and fix a sentence where appropriate. The tone here is less formal than in the crown court, where all serious indictable crimes are dealt with.

The spoken language of the courts is often similar to that of written legal documents, but because it is spoken rather than written it tends to be less complicated. Its formal **manner**, nevertheless, is marked by **formulaic utterances** which are immediately recognisable from the courtroom dramas that appear on television: *You may approach the Bench*, *If your Lordship pleases*, *leading counsel for defence*. The **naming of participants** also contributes to the formality of the setting: the judge is called *My Lord* and *Your Lordship*; lawyers address each other as *my learned friend*; and witnesses are addressed by their full names and title – for example, *Mr Philip White*.

The structure of a court case is patterned and the proceedings of any trial will be opened and closed formally. In a crown court, the clerk of the court will probably begin the hearing by saying:

> Members of the Jury, the Prisoner at the Bar is charged that on _____ s/he
> _____. To this indictment s/he has pleaded not guilty and it is your charge to
> say, having heard the evidence, whether s/he be guilty or not.

The official tone and the subject specific lexis immediately mark this as an example of the legal variety. Although not as complicated as a legal contract, the sentence structure is still noticeably complex:

> S   P   O   A   O   A   S
> (Members. . .) (the Prisoner. . .) (is charged) (that (on. . .) s/he. . .). (To. . .) (s/he)
> voc   SCl–NCl
>
> P   C   dumS P   C   A
> (has pleaded) (not guilty) (and) (it) (is) (your charge to say), (having heard the
>   conj   SCl–NFCl   SCl–NFCl
>
> (S)
> evidence), (whether. . .)
> SCl–NCl

The number of subordinate clauses makes the sentence structure elaborate and clearly marks spoken legal language as more similar to a written register than to an informal spoken one. The use of the subjunctive *s/he be* is also more common in formal written discourse.

Many lexical items are **subject specific**, like the nouns *witness-box*, *Common Law* and *jury*, and the verbs *adjourn*, *cross-examine* and *prosecute*. In a spoken as in a written register, legal language uses many **loan words** of French and Latin origin.

defendant: L *dēfendĕre*   adjourn: OFr *ajorner*
prosecution: L *prōsequī*   verdict: OFr *verdit*
evidence: L *ēvidēns*   counsel: Fr *conseil*

Archaisms are less common in court because the language has to be appropriate for the general public as well as the experts. **Questions** often require closed *yes/no* responses, but equally lawyers may force witnesses to develop their answers by framing questions using *wh-* question words.

In a spoken context, there is no time for lengthy reconsiderations of unfamiliar words and complex sentence structures, so although the language is always formal, it is not usually marked by the convoluted style of legal written language.

ACTIVITY 15.3

In October 1960 at the Old Bailey in London, Penguin Books Ltd was charged under the 1959 Obscene Publications Act with publishing an obscene article – D. H. Lawrence's book Lady Chatterley's Lover. The court case revolved around the issue of whether the novel would 'deprave' and 'corrupt' its readers. After a trial lasting six days, the jury decided that Penguin Books was not guilty of publishing obscene material.

The following extract taken from the court hearing is part of the fifth day's proceedings, in which Mr Justice Byrne began his summing up for the jury. Read through the court transcript and comment on:

1   linguistic features that are typical of the legal variety;
2   ways in which spoken and written legal language are different.

SUMMING UP BY MR JUSTICE BYRNE

1   MR JUSTICE BYRNE: Members of the jury, you have listened with the greatest care and attention to this case, and you have read this book. Now the time is rapidly approaching when you will have to return a verdict . . .
    You will recollect that publication has to be proved: the offence is pub-
5   lishing an obscene article. All that is meant by 'publishing' for the purposes of this case is handing a copy of this book to somebody . . .
    . . . And you, of course, will not exercise questions of taste or the functions of a censor, but you will decide whether it has been proved beyond reasonable doubt that this book is obscene. That is the first question. How the
10   Statute puts the matter is this: it provides that an article shall be deemed to be obscene if its effect is, if taken as a whole, such as to tend to deprave and corrupt persons who are likely having regard to all relevant circumstances, to read the matter contained in it.
    Of course, the first thing you would want to know is, what is meant by
15   the words to 'deprave and corrupt', and you have had those words defined from dictionaries, one was the Oxford Dictionary, and I think it would be quite fair to put it in this way, that to deprave means to make morally bad. To pervert. To debase or corrupt morally.
    The words 'to corrupt' mean to render morally unsound or rotten. To
20   destroy the moral purity or chastity of, to pervert or ruin a good quality, to debase, to defile . . . Having read the book the question is, does it tend to deprave or corrupt?

The next matter you have to consider is this, that you have to decide whether there is in this book a tendency to deprave and corrupt persons who
25 are likely, having regard to all relevant circumstances, to read the matter contained in it.

Now what are the relevant circumstances? Who are the people having regard to the relevant circumstances, who are likely to read the book? . . .

If you have any reasonable doubt as to whether it has been proved to
30 your satisfaction that the tendency of the book is to deprave and corrupt morals, of course you will acquit, and that would be an end of this case. But, on the other hand, if with your knowledge of the world and with your knowledge now of the book, having read it for yourselves, you are satisfied beyond reasonable doubt that the book has a tendency to deprave and corrupt those
35 who might, in the circumstances, be expected to read it, you, of course, will not hesitate to say so.

And that really is the first limb of this case, and, as I said to you, before 1959, before the passing of the Obscene Publications Act of that year, the defendant company felt, although they wished to do so, that they could not
40 publish that book because, prior to the passing of the Statute under which this charge is made, defendants were not allowed by law to call any evidence with regard to the literary or other merits of the book . . .

But in 1959 a change in the law was made, and by virtue of Section 4 of the Statute the defendants are enabled to call evidence.
45 That section . . . provides that a person shall not be convicted, that is to say, of publishing an obscene publication, if it is proved that publication of the article in question is justified as being for the public good on the ground that it is in the interests of science, literature, art or learning or other objects of general concern . . .
50 I am going to break off now, members of the jury, because I want to refer you to some of the evidence given by the witnesses who were called on behalf of the defendant company with regard to this second limb about which I have been telling you, that is the question whether the probability is that the merits of the book are so high that they out-balance the obscenity so that its
55 publication is for the public good.

Members of the jury, rather than begin that and then break off again I think we will adjourn now until to-morrow morning. Then I shall not take so very long to complete my observations, and you will then be able to retire to consider your verdict. Will you kindly be in your places again at half-past-ten
60 to-morrow morning, and in the meantime, forgive me once again if I remind you of the warning which I gave you, keep your own counsel.

Before Mr Justice Byrne – Regina v Penguin Books Limited:
Central Criminal Court, Old Bailey, London (Thursday, 20 October 1960)

COMMENTARY

The **manner** is inevitably formal because the trial is taking place in the Central Criminal Court at the Old Bailey. The relationship between the participants is official and the presence of 'experts' makes the context very specific. The language is a mixture of both legal and ordinary words since the spoken register used in court is less convoluted and more familiar than the written legal register. **Formulaic utterances** like the formal opening of the judge's summing up, *Members of the jury* (l. 1) mark the gravity of the occasion.

Since this is a transcript of spoken language, there are no distinctive **typographical features**. Written legal language relies on its layout and typographical features to avoid legal loopholes and to guide the reader through complicated legal conditions. The language of the courtroom, however, is primarily a spoken register which is written down only for official records. Jurors, for instance, do not reach their verdict by reading what has been said in court, but by listening. This means that prosodic features like pitch, pace and rhythm replace changes in typeface, underlining and capitalisation. Transcripts of a trial do not mark the prosodic features because when such records are consulted, **what** is said is more important than **how** it was said.

The **lexis** is still recognisably part of the legal variety, but there are more ordinary words too. **Subject specific words** like the nouns *jury* (l. 1), *offence* (l. 4) and *verdict* (l. 59) mark the variety, but there are also far more everyday words like the nouns *book* (l. 2) and *knowledge* (l. 32) and colloquial phrases like *in the meantime* (l. 60) and *of course* (l. 7). Some **ordinary words**, however, are used in a specialist way: *publication* (l. 4) now has a specific legal meaning which is defined by the judge; the meaning of the verbs *deprave* and *corrupt* (l. 15) is also established so that the jury are in a position to interpret the legal test for obscene publications. This is an example of the metalinguistic function of legal language. There are no **archaisms** because these would sound awkward in speech and might unnecessarily complicate the legal judgements being made. **Loan words** from French and Latin are still apparent, but technical legal jargon is used less frequently: *statute* (l. 10) from L *statūtum*; *adjourn* (l. 57) from OFr *ajorner*; *doubt* (l. 9) from OFr *douter* and L *dubitāre*. While the verb *proved* (l. 4) has its origins in OE *prōfian*, OF *prover* and L *probāre*, other words like the verb *deemed* (l. 10) and the noun *law* (l. 43) have their origins in OE *dēman* and *lagu*.

The legal **collocations** are often familiar because they commonly appear in the media: for instance, jurors have listened with *the greatest care and attention* (ll. 1–2); they will have to *return a verdict* (l. 3); and they must decide whether they have *any reasonable doubt* (l. 29). Other collocations are associated with contexts that are not legal: for instance, *on the other hand* (l. 32), *of course* (l. 7) and *as I said to you* (l. 37). This kind of almost informal language use clearly marks one of the key differences between written and spoken legal language. Another difference can be seen in the absence of any **synonyms**. Where written legal documents use these throughout to ensure that all options have been covered, courtroom language has a different purpose. There are still patterns and formulae that must be adhered to, but rather than being a watertight legal document which must guarantee an individual's or a group's rights, spoken legal language uses the law to make judgements. Even though the language is still used by experts, non-experts are also involved as jurors, witnesses, prosecutors and defendants – the spoken language of the courts must therefore be approachable for the general public too.

Abstract nouns are common because the trial is about concepts of taste and decency: *doubt* (l. 9), *quality* (l. 20) and *tendency* (l. 24), for instance. **Modification** is still restrained, providing factual information rather than emotive or descriptive detail.

m	m	h	
all	relevant	circumstances	(l. 25)
det	Adj	N	

m	h	q	
the	passing	of the	Obscene Publications Act (l. 38)
det	V/N	PrepP	

Verbs seem to be of a less restrictive lexical set because the discourse is spoken and therefore uses verbs that are appropriate for face-to-face exchanges. **Modal verbs** are used to convey attitude, just as they are in written legal language: for instance, *will* (l. 3) marks a time in the future; *shall* (l. 10) denotes the legal conditions under which an article can be deemed 'obscene'; and *could* (l. 39) marks possibility. While the first two have connotations of certainty, the latter is conditional. The use of the auxiliary *will* to frame questions is both polite and formal: *Will you kindly be in your places...* (l. 59). **Adverbials** defining specific conditions which must be met are not used in the same way and this makes the sentence structures seem less elaborate.

The **grammar** is still formal and standard, but there are features that link it to spoken language. Sentences are still long, but this tends to be because spoken language is less purposefully crafted; direct address makes the manner seem more personal; and adverbs like *now* (l. 2) and prepositional phrases like *of course* (l. 14) in the initial position (**marked themes**) give the discourse a less ceremonious tone. The **mood** is a mixture of declarative, imperatives like *keep your own counsel* (l. 61) and interrogatives like *Who are the people...?* (l. 27). This variation in mood is typical of the different kinds of exchanges that take place in a trial and is quite different from the declarative mood of most written legal documents. The **passive voice** tends to be used in direct references to the Statute: *shall be deemed* (l. 10); *was made* (l. 43); and *were not allowed by law* (l. 41). This adds to the overall formality and links the language of the court to written rather than spoken language.

The **sentence structure** is quite different from that of written legal language. Simple and compound sentences are more frequent:

> S   P   A
> (Members of the jury) (you) (have listened) (with the greatest care and attention)
> voc
>
> A   S   P   O   A   C   P
> (to this case) (and) (you) (have read) (this book). .... (Now) (what) (are) (the
> conj
>
> S
> relevant circumstances?) (ll. 1–2, 27)

Some sentences are grammatically incomplete, which is less likely in written legal language: *To pervert* (ll. 17–18) and *To debase or corrupt morally* (l. 18). Complex and compound-complex sentence structures are common, but they tend to contain fewer dependent subordinate clauses.

> (If you have any reasonable doubt as to whether it has been proved to your
> SCl–ACl   SCl–ACl   A
>
> satisfaction that the tendency of the book is to deprave and corrupt morals)
> SCl–NCl   SCl–NFCls
>
> A   S   P   S   P   O
> (of course) (you) (will acquit) (and) (that) (would be) (an end of this case).
> conj

(ll. 29–31)

Repetition is again used as a form of **cohesion**. Key legal lexical items like the noun phrases *reasonable doubt* (ll. 8–9) and *relevant circumstances* (l. 27) are reiterated to ensure that the jury understand the legal implications of the trial. Other repetitions like *first limb* (l. 37) and *second limb* (l. 52) show how the judge is dividing his summing up into discrete sections to clarify the facts that the jurors must consider to reach their verdict.

The extract from the transcript clearly bears many similarities to written legal language, but also differs in marked ways. The following list summarises the key similarities and differences between spoken and written legal language.

MANNER
- The manner is formal in both instances, but in a courtroom context, some informal collocations and speech patterns may be used.

TYPOGRAPHICAL FEATURES
- The typographical features of written legal language are an integral part of the document since they ensure that interpretation is unambiguous – such features are unimportant in spoken legal language because what is said is more important than how it is said.

LEXIS
- In both instances, subject specific language identifies the legal variety.
- It is common in both written and spoken legal language to find ordinary words used in specialist ways and also specialist words that have become a part of everyday discourse.
- Archaisms are rarely found in spoken legal language whereas they are common in written documentation.
- The all-inclusive synonyms of written legal language are less common in courtroom language.
- French and Latin loan words form the basis of both written and spoken technical legal language.
- Abstract nouns are common in both kinds of discourse because both are dealing with abstract issues of justice and law.
- Modification is similar in both contexts since it provides factual information rather than descriptive or evaluative detail.
- Clusters of adverbials tend to be more frequent in written documents, but when judges are summing up they may also list various conditions that must be considered before reaching a verdict.

GRAMMAR
- Modal verbs are common in both legal registers.
- Spoken legal language is less likely to use limited lexical sets of verbs than are written documents, in which the context is far more specific.
- Pronouns are more likely to be used in spoken language because the immediacy of the context will prevent the possibility of ambiguous interpretation.
- The grammatical mood of sentences is more varied in a courtroom because the kind of exchanges are more diverse.
- The passive voice is less common in the courtroom – rearranging the word order of an active sentence could make interpretation more difficult in a spoken context as it is not immediately possible to reread a complicated sentence.
- In spoken legal language, informal phrases are sometimes used in the initial position. Although inappropriate for written legal language, these marked themes are accepted alongside the formal legal language of the courtroom.
- Repetition is used in both cases to give cohesion to the discourse.
- Simple sentences are more common in spoken legal language.
- Both types of legal language use complex and compound-complex sentences, but the sentences of spoken language tend to be less convoluted.

15.5 What to look for in the language of the law

The following checklist can be used to identify key features in examples of legal language. There will not be examples of all the features listed in every text or transcription, but the list can be used as a guide. The points made are general so discussion of specific examples will need to be adapted to take account of the specific context, audience and purpose of the given discourse.

The following are helpful questions to ask.

Register

1 What is the **mode**? – written? spoken?
2 What is the **manner**? – formal? traditional? modernised? relationship between participants?
3 What is the **field**? – the subject matter will reflect specific uses or kinds of legal language.

Typographical features

1 Is the written text in a **block** or divided into **paragraphs** and **subsections**?
2 Are any **typographical features** used to guide readers? – **capitalisation**? **underlining**? changes in **typeface**?
3 Is the **punctuation** used standardly? – are any commas omitted? are colons or dashes used to mark the beginning of sections? are brackets used for parenthesis?

Lexis

1 Is there any **subject specific vocabulary**? – general technical terms? words typical of a particular branch of the law?
2 Are any **ordinary words** used with a specific legal meaning?
3 Is there any **specialist language** which is now a part of everyday conversation?
4 Are there any **archaisms** that mark out the traditional nature of written legal language?
5 Are there **collocations** or **synonyms** that are typical of the formulaic patterns of legal language?
6 Are there examples of French and Latin **loan words** that go back to the establishment of the legal structures in society when English was not considered to be suitable for such formal contexts?
7 Are there any examples of **abstract nouns** that link to the abstract nature of law and justice?
8 Are there any examples of **pre-** and **post-modification** used to provide factual information?
9 Do **adverbials** cluster together, defining the legal conditions that must be met or considered?
10 Are there any **limited lexical sets** of **verbs** that indicate the kind of legal context of the example?
11 Are there lots of **non-finite verbs** and **modal auxiliaries**, making the legal variety distinctive from other varieties?

Grammar

1 Are there any examples of the **passive voice** used to refocus the reader on key lexical items by rearranging the word order?
2 Is the **mood** mainly declarative (written) or does it vary (spoken)?
3 Are **marked themes** used to draw attention to key legal conditions?
4 Are the **sentences** long and complicated? – are there sequences of **dependent clauses**? are there any **simple** or **compound** sentences? is there any difference between the structures of spoken and written legal language?
5 Is repetition used to create **cohesion**? – are pronoun references used anaphorically? cataphorically? is any ambiguity created with pronoun referencing?

Summary

The **function** of legal language is to enforce obligations and to confer rights. It must therefore say exactly what is intended. Clear interpretation is crucial, so documents are constructed extremely precisely.

The **audience** for written legal documents is not expected to be ordinary language users – instead they are written by one expert for another. The style reflects this: its complexity can alienate the ordinary reader. The spoken legal language of a courtroom context, however, must be accessible since the jury is made up of ordinary people and the witnesses called up are not always experts. The differentiation in intended audience is one of the key elements, making spoken and written legal language different.

Tradition plays a large part in making legal language distinctive. The variety is marked by its conservatism. It has preserved forms which, though abandoned in other varieties, have proved successful in legal practice. The ceremonial element of legal language is linked to its use of archaisms.

Legal language is often accused of being **obscure** and **lacking clarity**. Because all its intentions must be externalised to avoid ambiguity, legal language often appears to be unnecessarily convoluted. Paradoxically, while the complexity of the language makes legal documents obscure to the lay person, its precision gives clarity to the expert.

16 The language of the Church

16.1 The nature of the language of the Church

The language of Christianity in Britain is very distinctive and its lexical and syntactical patterns have influenced the development of English in all kinds of ways. Traditionally, religious language was at the heart of a community, since literacy was often spread through religion. In contemporary society, although it is far removed from the language of everyday conversation, it is still a variety that most people can recognise because of its widespread use beyond the specific context of the Church. It is a part of everyday life both for believers and non-believers: writers use biblical quotations in their work; the origin of some common clichés can be traced back to the **Authorised Version** of the BIBLE (**AV**) and the BOOK OF COMMON PRAYER (**BCP**); and other formal varieties draw on some of the archaisms associated with religious language. We talk about *the blind leading the blind* (Matthew 15:14, 'They be blind leaders of the blind. And if the blind lead the blind, both shall fall into the ditch') and *the powers that be* (Romans 13:1, 'There is no power but of God: the powers that be are ordained by God'); we use *Jesus wept* (John 11:35, from the story of the raising of Lazarus) as an expletive; and expressions like *Till Death Us Do Part* and *In Sickness and in Health* from the marriage service have been used as the titles of BBC television comedies. Despite the varied uses of religious language, it can be recognised by the distinctive features that mark it.

The language of religion generally can be found in many contexts: religious newspapers and magazines, Radio 4's 'Thought for the Day', and local publicity material promoting church events. The specific language of the Church, however, is a very distinctive form of religious language, to a large extent preserved free from the influences of other varieties of English such as the language of newspapers or broadcasting.

Religious language in the context of the Church has both written and spoken forms. In all religions, written SACRED TEXTS provide the central focus for worship: for Christians, the Bible; for Buddhists, the PALI CANON; for Muslims, the KORAN; and so on. These texts have a historical significance since they are the basis for the spiritual tradition of each religion. Alterations to a given translation are often considered controversial because they change the revered norms with which people are familiar. Both religious leaders and the worshippers expect translations to be historically accurate and faithful to the meaning of the source. Contemporary versions must therefore both preserve the linguistic features of the original as far as possible, and take account of current social and linguistic trends. Up-to-date translations of the traditional texts try to avoid changes that may evoke strong reactions, but seek to bridge the gap between sometimes unintelligible archaisms and the language of everyday speech.

Spoken religious language is also distinctive. It is marked by special pronunciation, and prosodic features such as intonation patterns play a crucial part in ensuring that the worshippers relate to and understand the spiritual message.

16.2 The function of the language of the Church

The sacred texts of different religions have always been a means of **upholding spiritual belief**. Equally, because their written forms do not substantially change, these traditional documents have protected the sacred knowledge central to each religion. Each type of religious language has a slightly different function, but basically the variety as a whole seeks to **persuade** people to believe and to act in a certain moral way (conative function). Religious texts like the Bible also have an **expressive** function since they are partly concerned with an expression of feelings.

Both in public and in private contexts, the function of religious language is to develop a more moral and spiritual outlook. Whether in a church congregation or worshipping in a private individual way, religious language **prescribes** a specific attitude to life.

16.3 Features of the language of the Church

Each religion has a body of sacred texts and written **doctrine** which sustain and promote its particular spiritual wisdom. Because Christianity is the religion of the English-speaking Church, however, the examples discussed here will focus on material drawn from Christian sources. In the Christian religion, **prayers** are a special form of polite command or request addressed to God; **liturgies** are chants, thanksgivings, hymns and psalms; **sermons** are moral statements which aim to dictate a certain kind of behaviour through stories or examples; and **theological texts** are discursive documents with a moral purpose written by biblical scholars, theologians or the clergy – they may contain justifications for certain beliefs and lifestyles, spiritual guidelines or explanations of religious teachings.

The distinctive linguistic features of Christian writings discussed in this section will often find parallels in texts promoting the spiritual values of other religions and the methods of analysis used can also be applied to other world religions.

Many of the examples considered here are taken from traditional sources (AV and BCP) because these are marked by the most distinctive linguistic features of the variety as a whole. Although modern versions reduce the number of archaisms, provide a paraphrase for any subject specific terms and avoid unnecessarily complicated sentence structures, many of the characteristic features of the traditional versions still remain. In its contemporary forms, therefore, the language of the Church is still formal and distinctive, but less likely to alienate the intended modern audience.

The traditional language of the Church as exemplified by the AV and the BCP can be summarised as follows.

Manner

The **manner** is usually formal and has little similarity with informal spoken or written language despite the fact that examples of religious language are scattered throughout our everyday usage. In written texts, for instance, there are no contractions for auxiliaries or negatives and spoken religious language is not marked by the hesitancy and normal non-fluency features associated with informal speech. Because it is a traditional form of language, the language of the Church often retains archaic linguistic features which add to the formality of the medium. Its main use is in public group contexts, however, so although some features are archaic, it must still be accessible to the intended audience. Formulaic utterances like *Glory be to God* are common, and these too create a formal tone.

Lexis

The **lexis** is **subject specific**, with nouns like *disciples* and *parables* and verbs like *pray* and *forgive*. In the narrative of the AV, the vocabulary is often **archaic**: some words no longer have a contemporary equivalent; others have been replaced with a modern synonym; many are linked directly to a specific person, place or action and take their meaning from the historical situation.

Because of its traditional nature, there are many **formal phrases** and **idioms**: *In the beginning* and *Let there be light* are taken from the written language of the Bible, while *Dearly beloved brethren, we are gathered here together* and *Let us pray* are spoken directly to the congregation. The language is often **formulaic**, with openings like *we beseech thee* and closings like *Amen* to mark the beginning and end of a prayer. **Antithesis** is common: *heaven* and *hell*, *sin* and *forgiveness*, and *death* and *resurrection*.

Nominal groups in religious language, particularly in prayers, tend to be quite long. Most nouns are modified by at least one modifier and post-modification and noun phrases in apposition are common. Adjectives are often modified by adverbs.

m	m	h		m	m	h
thine	only	son	Jesus Christ	dearly	beloved	brethren
det	Adj	N	NP in apposition	Adv	V	N

In prayers, post-modification is usually in the form of a relative clause following a vocative or personal pronoun in the subject site. It can also take the form of prepositional phrases or non-finite clauses.

m	h	q		m	h	q
Our	Father	who art in heaven		the	kingdom	of heaven
det	N	RelCl		det	N	PrepP

h	q
we	worthily lamenting our sins
pron	SCl–NFCl

The **naming of the godhead** is important since it is the central concept of any religion (though in some other religious contexts, the name of God is seen as being too holy to pronounce and is replaced by a symbolic term). The theological terms which represent God in the Christian religion form a clear focus point, helping to make religious language distinctive from other varieties. Post-modifying phrases or clauses often take a human concept like being a father or a king and use it as an analogy for God: *Almighty God, most merciful Father; O Lord our heavenly Father, high and mighty, king of kings.* A link between the known human world and the unknown theological world is also created through **modifiers** that define divine attributes. Adjectives like *Almighty* denote God's omnipotence, while *merciful* emphasises that God's power is not tyrannical. God is the central cohesive concept in Christianity and therefore many references are made to God and to theological concepts or figures linked to God. This means that more than half of the **determiners** used are possessive. Because of the abstract spiritual nature of religion, many of the **nouns** are non-count: *heaven, compassion, salvation* and so on.

Grammar

The **grammar** of traditional Church language often resembles older forms of English, particularly in the AV and the BCP. In the AV, for instance, third person singular verbs are inflected with the **suffixes** *-(e)th* and *-(e)st*: *creepeth, mayest* and *doth*; and some verbs still have the older **strong forms**: *sware* for *swore, shewed* for *showed* and *spake* for *spoke*. The use of the **unstressed auxiliary** *do* to indicate past time is also archaic: *I did eat*. In modernised versions of traditional religious language, many of these features will have been replaced with Late Modern English equivalent forms.

The **present tense** is often used in the BCP, while the **simple past** is most common in the AV. The **mood** is rarely interrogative, but frequently declarative: *A false balance is abomination to the Lord; but a just weight is his delight* (AV, Proverbs 11:1). Imperatives are also common: *Give heed unto reading, exhortation, and doctrine. Think upon the things contained in this Book* (BCP, The Consecration of Bishops). The **subjunctive** is more common in the written language of the Church than in Late Modern English and this marks the variety as formal since the subjunctive is not commonly used in speech. It can be used to express an intention or a proposal about the future or to convey that something which is supposed to happen is not yet happening. In the subjunctive, verbs that would normally take an *-s* inflection are used in the base form: *For if the first fruit <u>be</u> holy, the lump is also holy* (AV, Romans 11:16); *If any man <u>think</u> himself to be a prophet* (AV, Corinthians 15:37).

Modal verbs are also common, implying contrasts in speaker attitudes. They are often used to convey a certainty in future time or to mark a spiritual command which should be followed: *And the woman said unto the serpent, We <u>may</u> eat of the fruit...* (AV, Genesis 3:2); *So <u>will</u> I send upon you a famine and evil beasts, and they <u>shall</u> bereave thee* (AV, Ezekiel 5:17).

In traditional versions, **pronouns** are distinctive because of their archaic forms: *ye* and *thee* are widely used. In many updated versions, these have been revised and replaced with the contemporary form of direct address, *you*. Pronouns in prayers are often post-modified.

>   h   q
> Thou who takest away the sins of the world
>   pron   SCl–RelCl

The first person singular is rarely used in formal prayer, but the first person plural is common. This reflects the public, group nature of worship.

Sentences in the AV are often basically simple, but because of the accumulated strings of co-ordinated finite and non-finite clauses, the structure is ultimately complex.

>   A   S   P   O
> (In the beginning) (God) (created) (the heaven and the earth)   Genesis 1:1
>
>   S   P   O   Co   S
> (And) (God) (called) (the firmament) (Heaven). (And) (the evening and the
>
>   P   C
> morning) (were) (the second day).   Genesis 1:8

Such use of **co-ordinators in the initial position** is common in the Authorised Version of the Bible and it is not unusual to see an **inversion of the subject and verb**.

> And Micaiah said, As the Lord liveth, even what my God saith, that *will* I speak
> The Second Book of Chronicles 18:13

▍ Then *answered the Lord* unto Job out of the whirlwind . . .   Job 40:6

Modernised versions, however, avoid such inversions, making religious language more like that of everyday speech.

▍ But Micaiah said, 'As the Lord lives, what my God says, that *I will* speak.'
  Then *the Lord answered* Job out of the whirlwind . . .
                                        Revised Standard Version (1971)

Sometimes, the **subject can be separated from the verb** by a sequence of subordinate clauses.

▍   S
  (God, who at sundry times and in divers manners spake in time past unto the
        SCl–RelCl

                  P   A   P   Oi
  fathers by the prophets), (Hath) (in these last days) (spoken) (unto us) . . .
                                        Hebrews 1:1–2

Structures like this are also simplified in modern versions.

▍   A   S   P   A   Oi   A
  (In many and various ways) (God) (spoke) (of old) (to our fathers) (by the prophets);
         A   S   P   Oi
  (but) (in these last days) (he) (has spoken) (to us) . . .

By contrast, in **litanies**, which are chanted by the congregation after the priest, sentences can be very short.

▍ S   P   Oi   Od
  (We) (beseech) (thee) (to hear us), (good Lord).
                SCl–NFCl   voc

▍ P   Oi   Od
  (Grant) (to us) (thy peace).

Prayers too have a distinctive sentence structure:

• they being with a vocative (a single proper noun which may be preceded by *O* + *adjective* or which may be followed by a post-modifying relative clause);
• they contain an imperative verb which is followed by an object and its dependent clauses;
• they conclude with the formulaic *Amen*.

Other optional vocatives and dependent clauses can be used, but this pattern establishes the most common structure.

▍ (O God, who hast prepared for them that love thee such good things as pass
   voc   SCl–RelCl   SCl–RelCl

                  P   A   O
  man's understanding; (Pour) (into our hearts) (such love toward thee), (that we,
                                         SCl–ACl

                            A
  loving thee above all things, may obtain thy promises, which exceed all that we
  SCl–NFCl   SCl–RelCl   SCl–RelCl

  can desire); through Jesus Christ our Lord. Amen.

Imperatives of this length and complexity are rarely found in other varieties of English.

The AV clearly has a different type of sentence structure from that used in prayers and ritual ceremonies in the BCP. The former is more likely to use archaic features such as inversion of the subject and verb or the direct and indirect objects, while prayers are more likely to have long sequences of dependent clauses. Rites are usually more straightforward, often using simple and compound sentences. In each case, the structure is distinctive, helping to classify examples as representative of religious language.

Metaphorical language

The use of **metaphorical language** is central to the field of religion. Both the AV and modern versions of the Bible use a range of techniques to make it more than just narrative. **Metaphor** adds an extra layer of meaning to the stories that provide the spiritual philosophy of Christianity. In Genesis 3:8, the description of Adam and Eve hearing *the voice of the Lord God walking in the garden* conveys effectively God's omnipresent power. The **personification** here enables the reader to understand Adam and Eve's fear at having disobeyed God's wishes because it gives a concrete presence to even God's voice. The description of God's anger as fire also portrays the power of God to punish those who do not follow the spiritual path:

> and the fire of the Lord burnt among them and consumed them that were in
> the uttermost parts of the camp. Numbers 11:1

Symbolism is central to the interpretation of the language of the Church. Although service books like the BCP and its modern equivalents are more literal, rarely using metaphors, all religious language requires believers to look beyond the words to a spiritual framework. Thus in Genesis, Adam and Eve represent humanity; the serpent represents evil; and the apple represents temptation. The symbolism makes the Adam and Eve story more than just a narrative – it becomes a moral lesson exemplifying the spiritual and religious message.

The function of religious texts is perhaps to persuade people to believe and act in a way that is appropriate for a particular religion. **Rhetoric**, the art of persuasion, therefore, is very important. Techniques like **antithesis** are central since the nature of religion itself juxtaposes good and evil. Concepts like *heaven* and *earth*, *death* and *life* and *crucifixion* and *resurrection* form part of the fundamental belief structure. Terms like these are then reiterated throughout the texts in order to emphasise their significance. **Marked themes** are also used to draw attention to key elements. In the Bible, many adverbs of time like *now* and *then* are used to establish key moments; other adverbial clauses convey a condition or reason:

> A
> (If any man among you seem to be religious, and brideth not his tongue, but
> SCl–ACl   SCl–NFCl   SCl–ACl
>
> S   P   C
> deceiveth his own heart), (this man's religion) (is) (vain).   AV, James 1:26
> SCl–ACl

> A   A   S   P
> (Therefore seeing we have this ministry), (as we have received mercy), (we) (faint) (not).
> SCl–NFCl   SCl–ACl   neg

AV, The Second Epistle to the Corinthians 4:1

In twentieth-century versions, although the archaic features of the AV are modernised, the fronted adverbials remain.

> A
> (If any one thinks he is religious and does not bridle his tongue but deceives his
> SCl–ACl   SCl–NCl   SCl–ACl   SCl–ACl
>
> S   P   C
> own heart) (this man's religion) (is) (vain).

	A		A	S	P	O

(Therefore having this ministry) (by the mercy of God) (we) (do not lose) (heart).
SCl–NFCl   neg

Revised Standard Version (1971)

All these techniques help to make the language of the Church persuasive and emotive, but the **phonological patterning** is just as important. The Bible has a controlled framework of balanced structures and the division of the text into verses makes it easy to read aloud. **Co-ordination** and the frequent use of **pauses** marked by commas give it a sonorous and resonant tone. The Book of Common Prayer and other service books are actually written to be read aloud – part of the text is to be read by clergy who are experienced, while other sections are to be read by the inexperienced congregation speaking in unison. The tone variations are often predictable and the sentences are rhythmically balanced.

Typographical features

Typographical features are often used to help the congregation read the relevant parts of the service successfully. **Paragraphing** and **spacing** split text into units which guide the reader. **Capitalisation** marks proper nouns, personal titles and pronouns referring to the deity. In some texts, **punctuation** has a phonetic value. Full stops are not always used to mark the grammatical end of a sentence, but sometimes imply a major phonological pause; commas can reflect a brief pause; and colons can be equivalent to either.

This variety is quite unlike the language of everyday conversation because even in modernised versions many distinctive features can be traced directly to the traditional religious language of the AV and the BCP. Although both of the traditional texts are marked by archaic language and structures, the 1662 BCP is more innovative in its use of language than the 1611 AV – it was the first systematic attempt to adapt the language of the Church's public liturgy, to

> keep the mean between two extremes, of too much stiffness in refusing, and of too much easiness in admitting, any variation from [the original]
> Preface, The Book of Common Prayer

Because people are familiar with these traditional forms and are unwilling to see them change dramatically, religious language alters very little. However, much of the language of the Church is to be spoken aloud and it must therefore be appropriate for the worshippers. Although the traditional framework is relatively fixed, there are some variations that aim to approximate everyday English in an attempt to engage contemporary worshippers.

16.4 Types of Church language

Sacred texts

The sacred texts of each religion provide a focus for believers. They aim to preserve both the essential characteristics of a particular faith and the linguistic features associated with its earliest written forms.

Christianity has the Bible as its core: the Old Testament was originally written in Hebrew and the New Testament in Greek and Aramaic. The English Church used the fourth-century Latin translation of the Bible, the Vulgate, for centuries. A few hand-written English copies were produced in the 1380s by John Wycliffe and his followers, but reading the Bible in English was still prohibited in the 1430s. The first Bible printed in English was translated by William Tyndale in the 1520s and 1530s, straight from the original Hebrew and Greek. Tyndale tried to use everyday words, aiming for clarity rather than for literal translation. He wrote as ordinary people spoke rather than as the scholars wrote and in many ways his version is therefore distinctively English. Because of his work, Tyndale was tried for heresy in Antwerp and in 1536 was garrotted.

The 1611 Authorised Version borrowed freely from Tyndale's work and about four-fifths of the New Testament and much of the Old actually use his words. The AV Bible, however, returned to a more formal style, replacing Tyndale's homely rhythms with a more scholarly tone.

ACTIVITY 16.1

Read the extract taken from The Gospel According to Saint John (AV) and list any features that are distinctive of religious language. Consider the tone, lexis, grammar and metaphorical language.

At the Last Supper, Jesus spoke to his disciples after washing their feet to show that a master is no better than his servant in the eyes of God. In Chapter 15, verses 1–12, having already said that one of the disciples will betray him, he asks that they keep the commandments and love one another.

1   1 I am the true vine, and my Father is the husbandman.
  2 Every branch in me that beareth not fruit he taketh away: and every branch that beareth fruit, he purgeth it, that it may bring forth more fruit.
  3 Now ye are clean through the word which I have spoken unto you.
5   4 Abide in me, and I in you. As the branch cannot bear fruit of itself, except it abide in the vine; no more can ye, except ye abide in me.
  5 I am the vine, ye are the branches: He that abideth in me, and I in him, the same bringeth forth much fruit: for without me ye can do nothing.
  6 If a man abide not in me, he is cast forth as a branch, and is withered; and
10   men gather them, and cast them into the fire, and they are burned.
  7 If ye abide in me, and my words abide in you, ye shall ask what ye will, and it shall be done unto you.
  8 Herein is my Father glorified, that ye bear much fruit; so shall ye be my disciples.
15   9 As the Father hath loved me, so have I loved you: continue ye in my love.
  10 If ye keep my commandments, ye shall abide in my love; even as I have kept my Father's commandments, and abide in his love.
  11 These things I have spoken unto you, that my joy might remain in you, and that your joy might be full.
20   12 This is my commandment, That ye love one another, as I have loved you.

COMMENTARY

The table here summarises the key points that make this text typical of religious language. It lists linguistic features that are commonly found in traditional sacred texts like the AV.

Examples	Comment
beareth not (l. 2), cannot (l. 5)	There are no **contractions** for negative verb forms and the **dummy auxiliary** *do* is not used to make a negative. These make the tone formal.
disciples (l. 14), commandments (l. 16)	**Subject specific lexis** clearly marks the field as religious.
spoken unto (l. 18), herein (l. 13)	**Archaisms** give traditional religious language its distinctive tone. Late Modern English simplifies these: the preposition *unto* becomes *to*; the adverb *herein* is replaced by *here*.
abide in me (l. 5)	The verb *abide* has an archaic ring, but still exists in some phrases like *abide by the law* in a legal context. Here it is almost a **collocation**.
_m _h the Father (l. 15) the vine (1.1) _{det} _N _{det} _N _m _m _h my Father's commandments (l. 17) _{det} _N _N	The **nominal groups** are mostly simple. Although in the Book of Common Prayer the noun phrases tend to be complex, here Jesus is speaking to the disciples and the style to some extent resembles spoken language.
Father (l. 1)	The **godhead** is here named exclusively in relation to Jesus. The use of *Father* instead of 'God' emphasises that Jesus is a man like any other. It draws attention to his human rather than his spiritual side and therefore makes it seem easier for the disciples to do as he does.

GRAMMAR

Examples	Comment
taketh (l. 2), purgeth (l. 3), abideth (l. 7)	The **archaic form** of the third person singular is used. This gives traditional religious language its distinctive tone.
it *shall* be done (l. 12), my joy *might* remain in you (l. 18)	**Modal verbs** are used to reflect a range of meanings: *shall* – certainty; *might* – possibility or potential.
ye (l. 4), you (l. 12)	The **pronouns** almost all reflect Late Modern English usage, but the use of *ye* in the subject site is archaic. In the object site, the standard Late Modern English *you* is used.

Compound:

S   P   C   S
(I) (am) (the true vine) (and) (my Father)
                              conj

P   C
(is) (the husbandman) (l. 1)

Complex:

A   S   P   C
(Now) (ye) (are) (clean) (through the word
                                          A
which I have spoken unto you) (l. 4)
SCl–RelCl

Compound-complex:

                                    A
(If ye abide in me, and my words abide
SCl–ACl

          S   P   O
in you), (ye) (shall ask) (what ye will)
                              SCl–NCl

          S   P   Oi
(and) (it) (shall be done) (unto you).
conj

                              (ll. 11–12)

          P   S
So (shall) (ye) be my disciples (ll. 13–14)
    Od   P   S   P
(These things) (have (I) spoken)
    Oi
(unto you). (l. 18)

The **sentence structure** is rarely simple
because of the literary tone of the AV,
unlike the earlier and more homely style
of Tyndale.

Often **subjects and verb are inverted**,
making the word order seem quite
different from Late Modern English.
Objects can also be moved from their
standard position after the verb. The
marked theme in the second example
foregrounds the object of the active
sentence. The **anaphoric reference**
draws attention to the alternatives
offered by Jesus to his hearers.

METAPHORICAL LANGUAGE

Examples	*Comment*
husbandman (l. 1), fruit (l. 2), vine (l. 1)	The extended **metaphor** here is based on a natural image of growth and good husbandry. It is used to represent the idea that someone who follows the Christian teachings of God will lead a productive life. It makes a very abstract spiritual concept concrete.
bringeth forth much fruit (l. 8), withered. . . cast. . .into the fire. . .burned. . . (ll. 9–10)	The **juxtaposition of negative and positive** here emphasises the alternatives offered to people. It underlines that they can choose the right way by following the advice Jesus offers, but by ignoring it they risk falling from God's favour. The

	emphasis throughout is on the positive rewards of faith rather than on the punishment for lack of faith.
abideth (l. 7), abide (l. 6); loved (l. 15), love (l. 15)	**Repetition** helps to establish the central message: belief in Jesus and love for one another.
I am the true vine. . . (l. 1), I am the vine. . . (l. 7); As the Father hath loved me, so have I loved you. . . (l. 15)	**Parallelism** is used to link Jesus and God with Jesus and the disciples. Throughout, he asks them to do as he has done. This again reinforces our sense of Jesus as an ordinary man whom we can imitate despite his divine status.

Rituals

Different societies have different cultural practices and religion formalises these in different ways. In most cultures, birth, marriage and death, for instance, are seen as significant moments in life and religion draws attention to these occasions by performing some kind of ceremony or rite.

The Christian Church has specific ceremonies to mark baptisms and funerals; it can give blessings, exorcise spirits and so on. Each time a given ceremony is performed, the ritual will be almost identical. Although expressions may be modernised, or versions may vary slightly depending upon the specific church or clergyman, the Church of England takes the basic structure from recognised service books like the BCP.

Liturgies

Liturgical forms are written to be read or sung. They can be invocations, petitions, rosaries, hymns or psalms. They are a distinctive form of religious language, and prayers in particular are recognisable because they are a special form of polite plea addressed to the deity.

ACTIVITY 16.2

Read the communion prayer from the BCP below, and identify the distinctive linguistic and stylistic features.

1   ALMIGHTY God, the fountain of all wisdom, who knowest our necessities
before we ask, and our ignorance in asking; We beseech thee to have compassion upon our infirmities; and those things, which for our unworthiness we
dare not, and for our blindness we cannot ask, vouchsafe to give us, for the
5   worthiness of thy Son Jesus Christ our Lord. *Amen.*

COMMENTARY

Here the prayer is read by the minister and is addressed to God. The **lexis** is typically religious, focusing on God and Jesus. There are many **abstract nouns** like *wisdom* (l. 1), *ignorance* (l. 2) and *compassion* (ll. 2–3) and these reflect the spiritual nature of the request being made. Most **noun phrases** are simple, but the vocative consists of a complex noun phrase:

> ALMIGHTY God, (the fountain of all wisdom), who knowest . . .
> m h q
> Adj N NP in apposition SCl–RelCl

Archaisms like *knowest* (l. 1) identify this as a traditional variety and the opening and closing **formulae** *Almighty God* (l. 1) and *Amen* (l. 5) are typical of religious utterances. The verb *vouchsafe* (l. 4) is now only used in formal contexts and has an archaic ring to it. It means 'to be graciously willing' or, in older contexts, 'to condescend to grant'. Its use here reinforces the sense of the unworthy congregation asking for a wise and merciful God's help.

The **sentence structure** is typical of a prayer: vocative + S P O. It appears much more complicated than this, however, because of the sequences of dependent clauses.

> (ALMIGHTY God), (the fountain. . .) (who knowest. . .before we ask. . .); (We)
> voc NP in apposition SCl–RelCl S
>
> (beseech) (thee) (to have compassion. . .); (and) (those things, which. . ., and
> P Oi Od Od
> SCl–NFCl conj SCl–RelCl conj
>
> for our blindness we cannot. . .), (vouchsafe to give) (us), (for the worthiness. . .)
> SCl–RelCl P Oi A

Ellipsis in several places makes relative clauses difficult to recognise: the direct object *those things* has two post-modifying clauses, only one of which is actually introduced by *which*. The clause beginning with the noun phrase *those things* **inverts the word order**, placing the direct object first, thus giving it greater emphasis. In common with other examples of religious language, the **pronoun** *thee* (l. 2) is used for the second person in the object site, identifying this variety with archaic forms of the English language.

The **symbol** of the *fountain* (l. 1) is used to portray God as a natural source of wisdom. Traditionally, water is linked with purity and this image implicitly reinforces our sense of God's purity. There are several **co-ordinated phrases and clauses**: co-ordinated noun phrases – *our necessities. . .and our ignorance* (ll. 1–2); co-ordinated prepositional phrases – *for our unworthiness. . .for our blindness. . .* (ll. 3–4); and co-ordinated clauses – *we dare not, and. . .we cannot ask* (ll. 3–4). These all contribute to the **rhetorical** effects, adding a sense of balance and reason to the plea.

The initial vocative is **capitalised** and **italic print** is used to mark the point at which the congregation join in and say *Amen* after the priest has finished the prayer. The structure throughout is traditional and to a large extent predictable.

Sermons

Sermons are religious statements based on a particular moral and spiritual view of the world. Ministers may write them as speeches to be delivered to their congregation or they may speak spontaneously on an appropriate topic. Many will craft their sermons carefully, but will then learn them in order to speak in a more immediate and dramatic way. Sermons are varied in their content since they can draw on the whole range of religious writing. They may contain modern or biblical stories, examples, parables, psalms, poetry, and so on. Statements within the discourse will often implicitly be understood as instructions since their purpose is to promote a certain way of life.

Individual ministers are required by the Roman Catholic Church to deliver the same pastoral letter at a particular time. This is a sermon, usually from the Archbishop to every person in his diocese. These pastoral letters are read out exactly from the

Archbishop's script and no comments are made on its contents. Personal sermons, or homilies, will reflect a priest's individuality, but all sermons in the Roman Catholic tradition are based on specified readings of the day. Current events may be introduced as long as they relate to the day's message. Individual ministers may vary the degree of formality of their approach, some adopting more modern references and forms of speech than others.

ACTIVITY 16.3

The sermon that follows was written for Passion Sunday, the fifth Sunday in Lent (in 1995, the date for this particular service was 2 April) by the Reverend W. Barlow, a minister in the Anglican Church of Wales. It is clearly an example of religious language and yet it is very different from the traditional language of the Bible and the Book of Common Prayer. In order to involve a modern congregation, the rector chooses language and examples appropriate for the 1990s. Read through the text of the sermon and jot down notes:

1 Comment on the register used.
2 Identify lexis which shows this to be an example of religious language.
3 Identify language use that is modern, and comment on its function.
4 Make notes on the grammar of the sermon, including the use of modal verbs and pronouns, the sentence structure and the mood.
5 Identify any metaphorical language and comment on its function.
6 Make notes on the use of rhetorical techniques, including the use of repetition, juxtaposition, antithesis, parallelism and marked themes.
7 Comment on the ways in which the linguistic, grammatical and stylistic features help to transmit the message effectively to the congregation.

CHRIST CHURCH RADYR, CARDIFF   PASSION SUNDAY, APRIL 1995

'From that time Jesus began to show his disciples that he MUST go. . .and suffer. . .'   (Matthew 16:21)

1 The danger of war has receded; the doom-laden propaganda of Hollywood spy thrillers has lost its power to scare. Yet rarely does civilisation die through sword or conquest. The historian Collingwood claimed that civilisations die not with the rattle of machine guns, but quietly, imperceptibly. Only
5 after many years did men, looking back, see what had happened – happened because of the accumulation of unrepented wrong moral choices; because of the slow erosion of moral standards, public and private, so that immorality was excused . . .
        Our society, too, may be terminally ill. Our homes are daily invaded by
10 images that play seductively on every base imagination of the human heart. Avarice, gluttony, envy, lust are seen, not in their true light, but as harmless or even enlightened attitudes. Boccaccio, Chaucer and Shakespeare spared nobody's blushes, but they never pretended that bad behaviour was anything but bad . . . Othello, Hamlet, Antony and Cleopatra had to die . . . modern
15 entertainment is no longer sure if right or wrong matters. In the simplistic Westerns of my childhood, the 'goodies' wore white hats while the 'baddies' wore black, but at least we knew when to cheer and when to boo . . . Now everyone wears grey, even the behaviour of the hero leaves much to be desired, and we are left morally bewildered.
20   Why be surprised? Society has effectively rejected God, and without Him all we have left is public opinion or social convention. No individual or

group has the right to dictate behaviour ... and democracy in the realm of ethics [leaves] ... the media as the final arbiter of right and wrong, manipulating the crowd to justify both state crime and public sin.

25　　　Men may prefer the moral twilight of compromise, but our Lord had no such uncertainty. He is totally identified with good; he alone has gazed into the unsullied light of the divine. There he saw the absolute. He knew what was eternal. From this flowed a moral law that is not negotiable. Certain deeds are not wrong because they are forbidden; they are forbidden

30　because they are inherently wrong – wrong for Moses, wrong for me, wrong for my great-grandchildren ...
　　　Our text announces what is to be obeyed, not debated. It is the divine MUST. It proclaims an OUGHT in the full sense of the word; not human coercion, 'You will be punished when you disobey, if you are caught!', but an

35　OUGHT because this is the moral law at the root of the universe. It must be obeyed though you lose money, position, even life itself.
　　　Our Lord recognised that the future of the world depended upon maintaining this difference between right and wrong for it is as wide as the difference between heaven and hell. To maintain that difference he was

40　prepared to die, even the death on the Cross ... all that mattered to him was that God's integrity should be honoured on earth, and so his destiny was sealed.
　　　Holy love would not come to terms with hate; selflessness would not accommodate itself to selfishness; truth could not live with falsehood, nor

45　beauty with ugliness. There was only one place these mortal enemies could meet – on the battlefield of the heart of God's obedient son. It was a battle to the death and on its outcome hung the destiny of the world. In his determination to create one place on earth where God's attitude to sin could be seen, God's will be done, God's holy love established in the process of history,

50　Christ was harder than the nails that drove into his hands, stronger than the Cross on which he was raised.
　　　If our society, our civilisation, is to be rebuilt, it will only be through a return to that holy moral integrity which led our Lord to Calvary.

COMMENTARY

The **mode** of the sermon bridges both written and spoken language: it is written, carefully crafted on the page, before being delivered orally to a congregation. The text displays many features of formal written language, but by practising 'speaking' a written text, a minister can make the language seem spontaneous. In its spoken form intonation, pitch, pace and emphasis would help the congregation to focus on key elements of the sermon even if they were unaccustomed to listening to complex language structures. The **manner** is inevitably formal and this reflects the relationship between the minister and his congregation. In essence, a minister is God's representative on earth and in preaching his sermon can be seen in the role of mentor, educator and advisor. With a rector who is known to his congregation, however, there is a personal relationship beyond the formality of the Sunday services. The **field** is clearly religious even though the traditional archaic language and verb inflections have been replaced by modern English. The sermon becomes almost a literary text with a religious and spiritual message. It adopts a traditional prose format, using paragraphs rather than the verses of the Bible, and conveys its message using traditional literary and rhetorical techniques.

The sermon opens with a quotation from the Bible in which the concept of 'suffering' is introduced. This direct link provides the congregation with a traditional religious context for the lesson they are about to hear. The **moral message** that follows is quite complicated because it is embedded in a philosophical discussion of the present nature of the society. The sermon suggests that our society is now so tolerant that it no longer recognises the difference between right and wrong.

The **subject specific lexis** immediately identifies this as a religious variety: **proper nouns** like *Moses* (l. 30) and *Calvary* (l. 53); **modifiers** like *holy* (l. 49), *eternal* (l. 28) and *moral* (l. 28); **abstract nouns** like *immorality* (l. 8), *heaven and hell* (l. 39); and **biblical names** like *our Lord* (l. 37), *Christ* (l. 50) and *God* (l. 20) are all found in the Bible. Using traditional religious **collocations** like *God's will be done* (l. 49) also helps the congregation to make direct links with traditional religious teachings. The **noun phrases** are often complex and these make the variety distinctive even though the sermon is modern:

>   m   h   q
> the battlefield of the heart of God's obedient son (l. 46)
> det   N   PrepP   PrepP

>   m   m   h q
> the unsullied light of the divine (l. 27)
> det   V   N PrepP

The adjective modifier *obedient* (l. 46) and the past participle modifier *unsullied* (l. 27) are both linked to the central moral lesson of the sermon: society must now learn to be **obedient** to God's wishes and must again learn to recognise what is good and pure.

To ensure that members of the congregation are not alienated and to ensure that the sermon relates directly to their lives, many **modern references** are introduced. Everybody is familiar with the media: we are exposed to advertising, television, cinema and newspapers every day of our lives. The sermon draws on these everyday experiences in order to make the spiritual message meaningful in a modern context. To convey the idea of *right* and *wrong* (l. 15) the rector talks **symbolically** of *Westerns* and *goodies* and *baddies* (l. 16). **Proper nouns** like *Hollywood* (l. 1) and **abstract nouns** like the *media* (l. 23) all indicate that this is a contemporary text. Because a sermon contains a spiritual message reminding the congregation of the way in which life should be lived according to God's will, it uses many **abstract nouns**. Examples like *ethics* (l. 23), *convention* (l. 21), *standards* (l. 7) and *behaviour* (l. 13) all build up the central theme of the sermon. In contrast to the abstract nouns promoting a spiritual approach to life are those that reflect the worldly path: *money* (l. 36), *position* (l. 36) and *lust* (l. 11). The central juxtaposition of the worldly and the spiritual forms the basis for this Lent sermon: Christ was crucified because he was not prepared to accept a world in which right and wrong were no longer distinct. The suggestion is that in the 1990s, the congregation should also think about their priorities and ensure that they too have Christ's *integrity* (l. 53).

The **grammar** is no longer archaic – verbs do not use *-eth* **inflections**; **word order** is standard. However, there are some examples of very formal usage that is not commonly found in informal spoken language.

>   A   P   S   P
> (Yet) (rarely) (does) (civilisation) (die) . . . (l. 2)
>   aux   lex

>   A   P   S   P
> (Only after many years) (did) (men). . .(see) . . . (ll. 4–5)
>   aux   lex

In both examples, the **dummy auxiliary** *do* is used for emphasis and this means that the order of subject and verb is inverted. The **sentence structure** is often complex: in the first paragraph, the final sentence uses a sequence of dependent subordinate clauses in the object site. The many complex sentences are appropriate for the formal and literary approach.

> A S P A P
> (If our society, our civilisation is to be rebuilt), (it) (will) (only) (be) (through a
> SCl–ACl   SCl–NFCl   aux   lex
>
> A
> return to that holy moral integrity which led our Lord to Calvary) (ll. 52–3)
>   SCl–RelCl

However, when the sentences are simple, they are emphatic and persuasive.

> S A P C
> (Our society) (too) (may be) (terminally ill). (l. 9)

> A S P O
> (There) (he) (saw) (the absolute). (l. 27)

The **mood** is almost exclusively declarative since the sermon takes the form of a sequence of statements. One interrogative is used: *Why be surprised?* (l. 20) – the first three paragraphs establish the current state of affairs and the rhetorical question is used to suggest that a confusion between right and wrong is inevitable because society has forsaken God. There are no explicit imperatives, but the whole of the sermon is an implied command since it is suggesting that our lifestyle needs to be refocused and that Christ is the model to be followed.

Modal verbs occur frequently. The capitalisation of *MUST* and *OUGHT* (l. 33) draw attention to words that will have been stressed when spoken. The sermon suggests that society has raised *democracy* (l. 22) as its new God – debate and discussion have become more important than faith. The focus on the modal verbs, however, suggests that we have no choice: we **have to** do what is morally right. Although the use of the modal *may* (ll. 9 and 25) suggests that there may be alternatives, the repetition of *OUGHT* (ll. 33–5) reminds us of an obligation to behave in the right way. The stress reminds the congregation of the quotation from Matthew 16:21 at the opening of the sermon, since Christ told the disciples that suffering was a necessary part of his moral life.

Pronouns help to create a personal relationship between minister and congregation. By using the first person plural personal pronoun *we* (l. 17) and the possessive determiner *our* (l. 9), the minister implies that he is the same as his congregation. He does not take the moral high ground and suggest that the congregation alone are sinners. This makes everybody responsible both for the present state of the world and for changing it.

The **metaphorical language** is a central part of the emotive appeal to the congregation to lead better lives. The **symbolic value** of the reference to *goodies* and *baddies* (l. 16) gives a concrete basis to an abstract concept. Equally, the traditional colour symbolism of the *white*, *black* and *grey* (ll. 16–18) allows the rector to distinguish between a range of moral judgements. The **metaphor** of the *battlefield* and the *mortal enemies* (ll. 45–6) gives a visual quality to the spiritual conflicts which Christ could not accept.

The sermon is very **rhetorical** because it is trying to persuade people to act in a certain way. **Repetition** of key words like the adjective *moral* (l. 6) and the abstract nouns *law* (l. 28) and *integrity* (l. 41) establish the theme. The central contrast between Christ's way of life and the way society lives now forms the basis for a range of **juxtapositions**: *right* and *wrong* (l. 15), *heaven* and *hell* (l. 39), *selflessness* (l. 43) and *selfishness* (l. 44), *truth* and *falsehood* (l. 44), and *love* and *hate* (l. 43). All these abstract nouns offer people a choice, but the sermon emphasises that there is only one real option.

The verbs *obeyed* and *debated* (l. 32) are juxtaposed to summarise the heart of the debate: Christ had a selfless faith which enabled him to sacrifice everything worldly in order to worship God; people now allow a false idea of democracy to lead them away from God's moral law. The sermon is persuasive, balancing opposites to show the congregation the 'right' way forward. The use of **parallelism** adds weight to the argument: *wrong...forbidden...wrong*; *wrong for...* (ll. 29–30). The circular structure of these sentences leads the congregation to contemplate the nature of what is right and wrong. Perhaps the most striking example of parallelism can be seen in the direct references to Christ's crucifixion. The comparative clauses *was harder than nails* and *stronger than the Cross* (ll. 50–1) remind the congregation both of the events that are celebrated at Easter and the symbolic power of Christ himself. The **listing** of the traditional sins (l. 11) reminds the present congregation of the sinners of the past – because the abstract nouns are linked asyndetically without any use of the conjunction 'and', there is a sense that the list is not complete and that these qualities are now almost uncontrollable.

The sermon is effective because it draws on things the congregation will be familiar with. Literary references to Shakespeare and the well-known characters from his plays, to spy thrillers and media images serve to illustrate the religious theme. The linguistic patterning makes the lesson more memorable, leaving the congregation to reconsider the choices offered to them.

ACTIVITY 16.4

The following extract is taken from a pastoral letter which was issued under the name of five Archbishops on 29 September 1993, having first been verified by the Conference of Bishops of England and Wales. It was written in response to the appearance in the Press of inaccurate comments about Pope John Paul II's Encyclical Letter (a letter addressed by the Pope to all his bishops), <u>Veritatis Splendor</u>, which was to be published on 5 October 1993.

Read through the extract and make notes on:

1 any distinctive linguistic features making this typical of a religious variety;
2 the ways in which this differs from a sermon written by an individual minister for his local congregation.

1   Dear Brothers and Sister in Christ,

. . . Taking as his starting-point the question which the rich young man in the gospel addressed to Jesus, 'What good must I do to possess eternal life?' (Matt. 19:16), Pope John Paul sets out answers which are relevant to all 5   those who today seek a right way of living . . .
As Christians we are called to witness to the gospel in our world which seems increasingly doubtful about the permanence and truth of moral values. The complexities of life today frequently add to our difficulty in making decisions about right and wrong. It is here that the teaching authority of the 10   Church comes to our help. In our search for what is true and good, we make use of both the light of reason and the truths of faith. The Encyclical asks all of us to reflect on how we should decide on what is right or wrong, both for ourselves as individuals and in society at large. It deals with the whole of human life, social and political as well as personal.
15   This is timely because there is widespread concern today about the loss of moral values. It indicates the need to be able to recognise that there *are* some situations and actions which are right and some which are wrong. The

Pope reminds us then that there are actions which objectively are good or
evil in themselves. He also tells us that 'the power to decide what is good
20 and what is evil does not belong to man, but to God alone'. But whilst with
some situations, like genocide and child-abuse, it is easy to judge their
wrongness, with many others, both personal and social, it is much more difficult to make a proper judgement.

How then are we to judge what is right and what is wrong? For
25 Christians, the source of moral truths is the Ten Commandments and the
Gospel law of love. There are also principles, such as the dignity of the
human person and the sanctity of life, which are held by many people, from
moral or religious conviction. But where particular actions and situations are
concerned, the Pope reaffirms traditional Catholic teaching that, in determin-
30 ing guilt, intentions and circumstances must be kept in mind. . . . It is the task
of the Church, as Mother and Teacher, to help its members to grow constantly in moral understanding . . . Pope John Paul stresses that 'we must
carefully inquire into the meaning of the young man in the gospel, and even
more the meaning of Jesus' reply, allowing ourselves to be guided by him.
35 Jesus, as a patient and sensitive teacher, answers the young man by taking
him, as it were, by the hand, and leading him step by step to the full truth.'
He is showing *us* the way.

> Signed in the name of the Bishops' Conference of England and Wales
> George Basil Cardinal Hume, Archbishop of Westminster (President)
40 Derek Worlock, Archbishop of Liverpool (Vice-President)
> Michael Bowen, Archbishop of Southark
> Maurice Couve de Murville, Archbishop of Birmingham
> John Aloysius Ward, Archbishop of Cardiff

COMMENTARY

The **mode** mixes written and spoken registers, but the pastoral letter is primarily a written form even though it is delivered orally. The **manner** is formal because the sermon is
addressed from archbishops to a congregation that is not known personally. The **field** is
clearly religious, but there are fewer obvious markers here because this sermon adopts
the form of an official letter. It begins with a typical collocation *Dear. . .* (l. 1) and concludes with the signatures of the senders (ll. 38–43).

The quotation from the Bible immediately marks the variety as religious. It establishes the moral message by introducing the idea of 'the right way to live' and the
importance of distinguishing between right and wrong.

Subject specific lexis reinforces the field here: proper nouns like *Christians* (l. 6)
and *Pope* (l. 4); abstract nouns like *values* (ll. 7–8), *faith* (l. 11) and *truths* (l. 11); modifiers like *moral* (l. 7) and *religious* (l. 28); and biblical names like *God* (l. 20) and
Jesus (l. 3). **Collocations** like *the sanctity of life* (l. 27) and *Ten Commandments* (l. 25)
also build up the specifically religious lexis. Unlike the Bible and prayers, this pastoral letter does not often use strings of modifiers except in the quotations from the
Bible.

    m   m   m   h   m   h   q
the rich young man (l. 2)   the dignity of the human person (ll. 26–7)
  det Adj   Adj   N   det   N   PrepP

     m   h
eternal life (l. 3)
  Adj   N

Modern references in the noun phrases *genocide* and *child-abuse* (l. 21) place the discussion of good and evil in a contemporary context.

The **grammar** is no longer archaic and the word order throughout is standard. The use of the **subjunctive** *as it were...* (l. 36), however, reminds us that this is a formal field with a tendency to use language in its more traditional forms. Because this is a theoretical discussion, the **sentence structure** is complex.

> A   A   P   S   P   O   O
> (How) (then) (are) (we) (to judge) (what is right) (and) (what is wrong) (l. 24)
> *wh-* question word   SCl–NCl   SCl–NCl

There are few simple or compound sentences, although when they are used, they are emphatic.

> S   P   Oi   Od
> (He) (is showing) (*us*) (the way). (l. 37)

The **mood** is mostly declarative, but there are some interrogatives: *What good...?* (l. 3) and *How then...?* (l. 24). These create a parallel between the biblical story which introduces the sermon and the current situation in contemporary society. Because it is not a prayer, there are no imperatives, but the sermon as a whole promotes a certain kind of lifestyle which is dictated by the Church. The use of the **modal verbs** *must* (l. 32) and *should* (l. 12) is in line with this since they both denote an obligation to do something. By using first person plural **pronouns** *we* (l. 6) and *us* (l. 19), the pastoral letter suggests that the Archbishops as well as their congregations must ask themselves questions about the nature of right and wrong.

The pastoral letter uses almost no **metaphorical language** – in many ways, it is far more like a formal public letter than the poetic prose of the Bible. The only example here is in the **personification** of the Church as a *Mother and Teacher* (l. 31). This gives the institution a caring face, casting it in the role of advisor and protector.

Because the sermon aims to promote a certain way of life, it uses **rhetorical techniques** to persuade the congregation to follow Catholic teachings. **Repetition** establishes the central themes: nouns like *situations* and *actions* (l. 17); modifiers like *moral* (l. 7); words like the adjective *true* (l. 10) and the noun *truth* (l. 7), and the noun *judgement* (l. 23) and the verb *judge* (l. 24). **Juxtapositions** remind the congregation of the opposing choices offered to them: *good* (l. 18) or *evil* (l. 19), *right* or *wrong* (l. 9). **Parallelism** creates a sense of balance and the many compound phrases reinforce the logic behind what the Church is offering worshippers: *the light of reason and the truths of faith* (l. 11); *the dignity of the human person and the sanctity of life* (ll. 26–7). **Marked themes** draw attention to key elements. The non-finite clause introducing the biblical quotation (l. 2) foregrounds the question that Jesus is asked and therefore draws it to the attention of the congregation. The prepositional phrases *As Christians...* (l. 6) and *For Christians...* (ll. 24–5) are each used in the initial position, encouraging the congregation to remember that they have a duty to follow the teachings of Jesus.

The pastoral letter here focuses on the nature of good and evil and our society's ability to recognise each quality. This is very similar to the lesson of the personal sermon considered earlier (Activity 16.5), which was written by an individual minister. However, there are marked differences in approach between the two:

- The **tone** is more formal here: the minister has written his own sermon and is preaching to a congregation he knows; the pastoral letter is written by a group of archbishops to be read out in all churches before congregations not known personally to the writers.
- The **style** is less poetic here: the minister can develop a personal approach, drawing on references that are meaningful to him personally; in the pastoral letter, the approach is far more objective, using less literary and more practical terms of reference.
- The **function** is different in each case: the minister's sermon is written in response to a key date in the religious calendar – Lent; the pastoral letter is written as an introduction to the Pope's Encyclical Letter which will be published soon, and to dispel any misconceptions that the Press may have aroused. Both, however, aim to give people guidance about the kind of life the Church believes they should be leading.

16.5 What to look for in the language of the Church

The following checklist can be used to identify key features in examples of religious language. There will not be examples of all the features listed in every text or transcription, but the list can be used as a guide. The points made are general, so discussion of specific examples will need to be adapted to take account of the specific context, audience and purpose of the given discourse.

The following are helpful questions to ask.

Register

1   What is the **mode**? – written? spoken by congregation or minister?
2   What is the **manner**? – formal or traditional? relationship between participants?
3   What is the **field**? – the subject matter will reflect specific uses or kinds of religious language.

Lexis

1   Is there any **subject specific vocabulary**? – general? typical of a certain ceremony or particular religion?
2   Is lexis **archaic** or has it been modernised? – words with no contemporary equivalent? words with modern synonyms? words linked to specific people, places or events?
3   Are there any **abstract nouns** that convey spiritual and theological concepts?
4   Are there any **formulaic phrases and collocations** that contribute to the traditional and formal tone of religious texts?
5   Are there any **sequences of post-modified relative clauses** in prayers which make the nominal groups particularly long?
6   How is the **godhead named**? – variations? use of human qualities to describe the divine?

Grammar

1 Is the grammar **archaic** or has it been modernised?
2 Are there any examples of the **archaic third person singular inflection** *-eth/-est*?
3 Are there any examples of non-standard **past participle strong forms**?
4 Is the **dummy auxiliary** *do* used to indicate past time?
5 Which **moods** are used? – declaratives for stories from a sacred text? imperatives for prayers? interrogatives to make a congregation question?
6 Is the **subjunctive** used to express possible or potential processes?
7 Are **modal verbs** used to express certainty? possibility? and so on?
8 Are any of the **pronouns archaic**? – second person forms *thou* and *thee*?
9 Are the **sentence structures** varied? – basically simple, but sequences of dependent clauses to make the structure more elaborate? simple sentences to make points emphatically? compound sentences to create a balanced argument? complex to deal with spiritual concepts?
10 Are there any **initial position co-ordinators** to help simplify compound and compound-complex sentences for the congregation, by dividing these logically into smaller, more easily visible units?
11 Are **vocatives** used in prayers to address the godhead?
12 Is the **word order** archaic? – inversion of subject and predicator? use of the object as a marked theme?

Metaphorical and rhetorical language

1 Are there any **metaphors** to help symbolise abstract, spiritual matters in a concrete way?
2 Is **repetition** used? – key words, phrases or clauses reiterated to highlight a moral point?
3 Are there any examples of **juxtaposition/antithesis**? – creating contrasts between good and evil? believers and non-believers?
4 Is there any **parallelism**? – creating a sense of balance in religious texts? adding weight to their message?
5 Do **marked themes** bring key elements to the front of the sentence, thereby giving them added stress?

Typographical features

1 Are any words **capitalised**? – proper nouns? other key words? vocatives?
2 Is the text **divided into verses** to help make reading and understanding easier for the congregation?

Summary

The **function** of religious language is to preserve and promote a particular spiritual belief system; to persuade the congregation or individual worshippers to live their lives in a certain way.

To a large extent, **traditional texts** like the AV and the BCP play an important role in defining the nature of religious language: archaic features provide links with the past; well-known phrases and clauses from the Bible embedded in everyday conversation mean that religious language is recognised even by non-believers.

Semantically, the language of the Church must be accessible, so although it changes very little, it must adapt in some ways to the expectations of a modern congregation. Religious utterances can be statements of belief, prayers of supplication, narratives with spiritual or moral messages, or celebrations of important days or occasions.

17 The language of politics

17.1 The nature of political language

In 1946, George Orwell wrote 'Politics and the English language', an essay in which he discussed the nature of political language. He criticised politicians for failing to use *a fresh, vivid home-made turn of speech* and instead choosing *ready-made phrases*. Through a metaphor of mechanisation, he suggested that speakers had turned themselves into machines and were no longer aware of the importance of what they were saying. He believed that political language had become mechanical instead of reflecting individual speakers and that meaning was often concealed by the *lifeless, imitative style* which, in his view, was common. Fifty years later, it may seem that little has changed.

Political language is often accused of attempting to conceal the truth and euphemism is a common way of making a harsh reality more palatable. EUPHEMISMS are words or phrases that substitute mild or vague language to soften the harsh reality of an event – for example, *pushing up the daisies* or *passing away* for *dying*; *letting someone go* for *sacking*. In the Bosnian conflict of the 1990s, there was talk of *ethnic cleansing* – the positive connotations of the verb *cleanse* conceal the bitter reality of killing people because of their ethnic origin. *Conflict* replaces *war*, and when bombing raids hit civilian rather than military targets it is described as *collateral damage*; no longer are the *dead* brought home, but the *body bags* are returned. All these examples conceal the horror of war: they make the whole issue less unpalatable. Government reports replace phrases like *health and inequality of the elderly* with *differential ageing among social sub-groups*. In an example like this, the focus changes – instead of being drawn to the key word *inequality*, readers are faced with far more objective terms like *differential* and *social sub-groups*. These kinds of changes make the political reality of the noun phrases less human and therefore make financial restrictions easier to impose.

Many people believe that language influences thought: therefore if language is manipulated, so are the very processes of thought. In other words, politicians can influence the way we think about the events happening around us, and the words they choose are a crucial part of that process.

Each politician has a particular way of seeing the world, a particular IDEOLOGY. The concept of ideology refers to a body of ideas or a belief system which is organised from a specific point of view – for instance, Conservative and Labour politicians think about society in different ways. Because they have different ideologies, they approach political issues from different angles and often find contrasting solutions to the same political problems. Through their use of language they encourage the voters to identify with their own particular ideology or world view.

17.2 The function of political language

Linguists are interested in the words and structures politicians use to create a certain view of the world. This world view will be directly linked to their purpose and audience and will affect the language they choose in order to achieve a set goal. Lexical and syntactical choices can affect the voters, persuading them to vote for certain policies or personalities. By analysing these, it is possible to identify occasions when politicians try to subvert or obscure issues, evade questions or arouse audience emotions.

As well as the actual words and structures used, however, linguists are also interested in the PRAGMATICS of political language. Pragmatics considers the meaning beyond what has actually been said and concentrates on the way meaning is constructed in different contexts. The focus here is therefore wider than just the lexis and syntax itself since the factors influencing a speaker or writer's choices are analysed.

Political language can be recognised in a variety of forms but in each case lexical and syntactical choices are directly linked to the audience, purpose and context of the discourse. Speeches are scripted as part of an election campaign or a fund-raising event; unscripted responses are made in reply to questions in the House of Commons or in a media interview; manifestos are circulated as part of information campaigns; motions are drafted for debate; a written record (Hansard) is made of everything that occurs in Parliament and so on.

Political language can be informative (**referential function**) or persuasive (**conative function**) and is often rhetorical. It is always useful to consider the **speaker** or **writer**, the **audience**, the **purpose** and the **context** of any example since each of these factors can change the nature of the language used.

17.3 Features of political language

There are many examples of political language in everyday life and it is possible to categorise some linguistic features that are common to most of these.

Manner

The **manner** is usually formal, and there tend to be **formulaic utterances** which add to the formality. In the House of Commons, for instance, phrases like *I beg to move...* and *the honourable Lady* are common.

Sometimes **informal language** is used and the change in tone is obvious. In March 1994, Dale Campbell-Savours, the MP for Workington, was asked to leave the House of Commons because he used the phrase *ripped off*.

> It has been two months since it was exposed that a Conservative Back Bencher, The hon. Member for Rutland and Melton (Mr Duncan) made £50,000 on buying the council house next door to his house in Westminster. Cannot we have a debate on the whole question of the right to buy, especially as that hon. Gentleman still refuses to pay back to the ratepayers of Westminster the £50,000 that he ripped off them?
>
> Business of the House, Hansard (3 March 1994)

The Speaker of the House asked the MP to withdraw the statement, saying 'I cannot accept those words.' He refused because he said that the phrase had been used before and had not then been questioned. Betty Boothroyd, the Speaker, replied:

> I think that the hon. Gentleman has not heard that phrase in respect of one hon. Member. It may have been used in a corporate context, but not in that way . . .

Because Campbell-Savours refused to rephrase *ripped off*, he had to leave the House. Hansard recorded the conclusion of the incident as follows:

> The hon. Member, having used a grossly disorderly expression, was ordered by MADAM SPEAKER to withdraw the same, but he declined to comply with that direction; whereupon MADAM SPEAKER, pursuant to Standing Order No. 42 (Disorderly Conduct), ordered him to withdraw immediately from the House for the remainder of this day's Sitting, and he withdrew accordingly.

There are other occasions when informal language is used and the Press report on the unexpected tone. On 7 February 1995, the Prime Minister, John Major, called the Leader of the Opposition, Tony Blair, a *dimwit* after Blair had suggested that his leadership of the Conservative Party was weak. This colloquial use of language marked the conclusion of a noisy 'Prime Minister's Questions' during which Major had upset convention by asking the Labour leader a question. The choice of word caused interest because it did not reflect the tone normally associated with Parliament.

John Major's insult was followed on 8 February 1995 by two more linguistic offences: Nigel Griffiths, a Labour spokesman, called Charles Wardle, an Under-Secretary, a *nitwit*; and Tony Banks, Labour MP for Newham NW, told Steven Norris, the minister with responsibility for public transport:

> We know you are the most proficient bullshitter that the Government has got . . .

Betty Boothroyd intervened after this sequence of insults saying that some MPs seemed to think it was 'rather smart or clever to manipulate the English language in making references to other members.' She then made a statement drawing attention to the expected tenor of parliamentary language:

> Good temper and moderation are the characteristics of parliamentary language.
>   I do hope that in future interventions, all members will bear that in mind and we shall make use of the richness of the English language to select elegant phrases that express their meaning without causing offence to others.
>   I have to tell this House that I know only too well from my postbag that some of the exchanges across the floor of this House do not enhance it in the eyes of our electorate.
>
> Hansard (8 February 1995)

The public expect politicians to choose language that reflects the formal parliamentary context. When the manner is changed, inevitably some people complain because informal language is seen to be inappropriate in the formal and public field of politics.

Lexis

The **lexis** is usually **subject specific** and **abstract nouns** are quite common since discussions are often theoretical even though they may be directly linked to a proposed plan of action. Politicians aim to represent society as it really is, but as has already been seen, they can use language to adapt reality to suit their purposes. It is therefore useful to identify any use of **implication** or secondary meaning. This allows politicians to state the truth while using words that can be interpreted in more than one way. For example, if someone were to say that a room was too warm, the intention could in fact be to imply that the fire should be turned off. In a social context, it might be considered more polite not to make the request more directly; in a political context, the implication might represent an attempt by a politician to evade a direct answer.

The **naming of politicians** is often significant: sometimes their **role title** is used rather than their **name**. This can be appropriate when their individual identity is irrelevant because the actions associated with the role would be the same whichever individual was involved. However, the use of the role title instead of an individual name can also be used to direct people away from a focus on the person. In redirecting the audience's attention, a politician can sometimes deflect personal responsibilities.

▓ Tony Blair, the leader of the Labour Party, will take the party in a new direction

▓ The leader of the Labour Party, Tony Blair, opposed the Government's standpoint

In the first example, the fact that the leader is now Tony Blair is important because *he* personally will affect the nature of the Labour Party; in the second, it would not matter which individual filled the role, since all Opposition leaders would do the same.

In December 1994, there was great concern about the veal calf trade. Much activity centred around the seaports from which the calves were sent to European farms where they would be kept in veal crates which have been banned in this country. When it was revealed that the Minister for Agriculture, William Waldegrave, exported his own calves to European farms, the newspapers exploited the apparent conflict of interest. As a Government minister, his main concern was to ensure that British animals were treated properly and that British farmers were not put at a disadvantage because their more humane methods of rearing the calves were more expensive. As an individual, however, newspaper coverage suggested that he was more interested in the sale of his animals than in their destination and welfare. In this case, the role and individual name of the politician were apparently at odds and the newspapers emphasised this, juxtaposing Waldegrave's official title role and his personal name.

Grammar

The **grammar** of political discourse varies, depending upon whether the utterances are spoken or written – inevitably, written statements tend to be more complex than speeches that have been written to be spoken or oral replies to questions. However, the use of **pronouns** is significant in that pronominal choices often reflect the ideology of individual politicians by conveying their personal negative and positive attitudes. The connotations of the pronouns selected are not always predictable, but politicians with the same world view will probably choose the same kinds of pronouns.

> Thatcher and *her* followers have divided *our* society and widened inequality. . .
> *We* want to build a society that is united.
> Robin Cook MP, *Labour Party News* (January 1995)

Here Robin Cook clearly distances Margaret Thatcher and her supporters by using the third person singular pronoun *her*. It also robs the individual politicians of their identity since they are seen only as an extension of Thatcher herself. The use of the possessive determiner *our* and the first person plural *we*, however, unites the Labour Party politicians. This choice reinforces the underlying message since Cook implies that Thatcherism has *divided* society, while Labour policies will *unite* it.

The choice of pronouns in the next example illustrates a more subtle divide than that of Conservatives versus Labour.

> The attack on Clause IV is a distraction and *we* must tell *our* leaders to get
> on with the job for which *they* were elected.
> Tony Benn MP, *Labour Party News* (January 1995)

Although the first person plural *we* and the possessive determiner *our* unite the speaker with other Labour Party members who identify with his own viewpoint, Tony Benn and his supporters remain distanced from the leadership of the party. By using the third person plural *they*, he suggests that the leadership and those campaigning for change within the party have lost sight of Labour's real goals.

Linguists need to think about the formality or informality of the pronouns used; the personal involvement of the speaker or writer; and whether their status, class or sex makes any difference. Pronouns enable politicians to accept, deny or distance themselves from their responsibilities; to encourage their supporters; to distance the opposition; and to give a personal touch to their discourse.

The **framing of questions** is also important. In a democracy, the very nature of alternative parties, and therefore alternative ways of tackling issues, is central to the whole process of government. The right to ask questions, whether it be in Parliament or in the domain of the media, is an obvious way in which a real democracy can be created. Questions are rarely straightforward and use techniques to allow the speaker to clearly establish the context and to manipulate the addressee: sentences in declarative mood precede the question and convey the speaker's own attitudes; the adverb *so* is commonly used to suggest that the proposition following is a logical consequence and should be automatically accepted; and negative forms that are sometimes contracted like *don't* allow the questioner to lead by suggesting that the truth of the proposition is already taken for granted.

> Should not she [Clare Short] pay tribute to the achievement of those women, who now have new opportunities? Does not it show that what the Government say is right?
>> Oliver Heald, Orders of the Day – debate on Sexual Discrimination, Hansard
>> (10 March 1994)

Interrogative *wh-* words are often used to frame questions.

> *What* about the case of the sale of arms to Iraq where it appears that the guidelines had been changed and MPs have been giving answers which suggest that the theory and practice is different from what is going on?
>> Minutes of Evidence, Treasury and Civil Service Sub-Committee (8 March 1994)

Questions demanding a *yes/no* reply are more common. These are less open and presuppose a particular answer to the question as more acceptable than any other possible ones. The use of these *yes/no* questions is an attempt to force politicians to accept or deny the allegations made.

> Does the Prime Minister think it right that those who can afford to pay fuel bills in advance can avoid paying the new VAT charges on gas and electricity?
>> John Smith, leader of the Labour Party, Questions in the House, Hansard
>> (22 March 1994)

When questions start with the **modal** *will*, they imply that because of the added politeness associated with the verb any rejection of the request made will seem unnecessarily rude. By using it, politicians try to get the addressees to commit themselves to action.

> Bearing in mind that it was the Prime Minister's predecessor, when she was Education Secretary nearly a quarter of a century ago, who first formulated that policy, *will* the Prime Minister tell us when he thinks that that promise [the provision of nursery education for all] might be delivered – this year, next year, sometime or never?
>> Paddy Ashdown, Questions in the House, Hansard (22 March 1994)

Metaphorical language

Metaphorical language is a significant part of the rhetoric used by politicians to persuade their audience, and the more original the image created, the more effectively the idea will be conveyed. **Metaphors** help explain complex arguments since one element is used to develop understanding of another element. Politicians use metaphor to prove a point, to provide light relief, and so on. The repetition or development of a single metaphor can be a powerful means of reinforcing a message.

> The *tide* is *turning* in our favour and for the first time for years people are asking for socialist policies.
>
> Tony Benn, *Labour Party News* (January 1995)

> . . . I think any sensible market person understands this issue because any body who is buying or selling is negotiating over the price of something and is not going to lay out his bottom line in the first negotiation and much of Government activity is much more like negotiation, much more like *playing poker* than it is like *playing chess*. You do not *put all the cards up* all the time in the interests of the country.
>
> William Waldegrave, Minutes of Evidence, Treasury and Civil Sub-Committee
> (8 March 1994)

Individual politicians have their own ways of speaking and writing and analysis should focus on the choices made in each case. Discussion of linguistic features should be linked closely to pragmatics because it is these wider factors that often dictate the lexical and syntactical choices made. By considering the distinctive linguistic and pragmatic features, it is then possible to come to conclusions not only about the individual in question but about political language in general.

17.4 Types of political language

Manifestos and campaign statements

Voting is central to our political system and therefore politicians are accustomed to producing statements that enable the electorate to make informed decisions at the ballot box. Candidates for general elections produce material presenting the views of their party, but also convey their own personal stance in order to give their campaign a distinctive identity. Such documentation will be read by people who oppose the viewpoint put forward, by those who support it, and by those who may be persuaded to agree with it. The main function is therefore **conative**. The **referential** function is subordinate, but it is often the information included in the statement which may persuade 'floating' voters to support the party in question. Most of the documentation will be written for campaign leaflets which will be delivered to the local constituents in their homes.

ACTIVITY 17.1

Read the following extracts from a manifesto written by a candidate for the Ecology Party (now known as the Green Party) and printed in the Pontypridd Observer in June 1983. Think about:

1 the intended audience, the purpose and the context (pragmatics);
2 the lexis;
3 the grammar;
4 the rhetorical features.

1 Ecology: The Green Alternative.

I am standing as the candidate for the Ecology Party in the Pontypridd Constituency because I believe that the 5 major political parties do not face the real underlying problem which confronts us in industrial societies today: the obsession with economic growth.

This, I believe, is the key difference 10 between ecology and the other parties, whose aim is to further growth at all costs. But it is these very costs which, if not recognised for what they are, can take us along the path of social disinte- 15 gration and possible annihilation of all forms of life on this planet. I will exam- ine these costs under three headings: (1) Environmental; (2) Personal and (3) Social.

20 Environmental costs.

The obsession with growth places enormous demands on the resources of the earth upon which we depend for our livelihood. No prudent business person 25 would run a business by steadily deplet- ing its capital; yet that is precisely what we are doing to feed the voracious appetite of industry.

Fossil fuels such as coal and oil 30 took millions of years to form in the earth's crust; we are using them up within the space of a few hundred years. Much the same can be said about other essential minerals such as copper, tin 35 and zinc. It is no good arguing, as many do, that it is just a population problem; the whole way of life in industrial soci- eties must be called into question. For instance, the world's most materially 40 rich country, the USA, has only about six per cent of the world's population, yet its present level of consumption is about 50–60 per cent of the world's total consumption of resources in any one 45 year . . .

People in the Pontypridd Constituency should be well aware of the problems of pollution: indeed, the defilement of the countryside through 50 mining activities over many generations, the River Taff, quarrying and noise bear witness to the intensity of industrial activity in the area . . .

Personal costs.

The environmental issue is not going to 55 be resolved until we begin to question the need for industrial expansion as a basis for living. Such questioning is diffi- cult in a society in which its inhabitants 60 are turned into passive consumers of industrial products. The profitability of industry depends upon high levels of production and consumption.

Needs must therefore be artificially 65 created through advertising and other ploys to lure consumers into a false belief that their needs are being met.

In such circumstances what are needs become associated in the minds 70 of the public with the material products of industry i.e. we accept, virtually with- out question, that the standard of living is enhanced by increasing our con- sumption of goods and services. But 75 does such material consumption necessarily enhance the quality of our lives?

Does not our dependence on drugs for health, on the replacement of home 80 cooking by packaged foods, or on the TV for entertainment, to give only a few examples, tear at the very core of our human capacity to do things for our- selves within the context of meaningful 85 human relationships? Is this not the very denial of the human spirit?

Social costs.

But are meaningful human relationships possible in an industrial society? A soci- 90 ety which attaches so much importance to material growth encourages competi- tion not co-operation, is subject to rapid technological change and is not, there- fore, conducive to the development of 95 integrated and stable community living in which caring and sharing are para- mount and lasting human values.

Alwyn Jones

COMMENTARY

Since this was published in a local newspaper, the **intended audience** is clearly the constituents who will be taking part in the election. The **purpose** of the statement is therefore to persuade the voters to choose the Ecology Party candidate rather than other party representatives. The **context** is formal and the manifesto has been written to be read. The lexical and syntactical choices reflect this.

The **lexis** is **subject specific** – often linked to the environmental concerns of the Ecology Party. Nouns like *pollution* (l. 48), *minerals* (l. 34) and *planet* (l. 16) are juxtaposed with *business* (l. 25), *consumption* (l. 44) and *advertising* (l. 65) to imply that other political parties have misplaced interests. Because the debate is theoretical, there are many **abstract nouns** like *production* (l. 63), *quality* (l. 76) and *obsession* (l. 8). Statistics are also used, however, to substantiate the argument put forward:

> the USA has only about *six per cent* of the world's population, yet its present level of consumption is about *50–60 per cent* of the world's total consumption (ll. 40–4)

Abstract nouns like *disintegration* (ll. 14–15) and *annihilation* (l. 15) are emotive and suggest that immediate action is necessary – implicitly emphasising the importance of placing a vote in the coming election. The noun phrases also use emotive **modifiers** in order to persuade the voters of the ethical strength of the Ecology Party's moral position. Phrases like *enormous demands* (ll. 21–2) and *passive consumers* (l. 60) aim to encourage the reader to question the current governmental approaches. The **connotations** of nouns like *defilement* (l. 49) and *ploys* (l. 66) and verbs like *lure* (l. 66) suggest that we as citizens are being tricked, and that the Ecology Party is offering a new kind of politics. To give the statement an appropriate local feel, **proper nouns** like *Pontypridd Constituency* (ll. 46–7) and the *River Taff* (l. 51) encourage voters to feel that the candidate has a knowledge of the area and its particular problems.

As a written text, the **sentence structure** is quite complicated. Sentences tend to be compound and complex rather than simple. Simple sentence:

> S   P   O   A
> (I) (will examine) (these costs) (under three headings. . .) (ll. 16–17)

Compound sentence:

>   A   S   P
> (For instance), (the world's most materially rich country, the USA,) (has) (only
>   O   S
> about six per cent of the world's population), (yet) (its present level of
>   conj
>   P   C
> consumption) (is) (about 50–60 per cent of the world's total consumption of
>   A
> resources) (in any one year). (ll. 38–45)

Complex sentence:

> S   P   C   A
> (I) (am standing as) (the candidate for the Ecology Party) (in the Pontypridd
>   A
> Constituency) (because I believe that the major political parties do not face the
>   SCl–ACl   SCl–NCl
> real underlying problem which confronts us in industrial societies today).
>   SCl–RelCl
>   (ll. 2–7)

The **passive voice** is chosen on several occasions without the agent: *the whole way of life must <u>be called</u> into question* (ll. 37–8); *Such questioning is difficult in a society in* *which its inhabitants <u>are turned</u> into passive consumers* (ll. 58–60); *Needs must therefore <u>be</u> artificially <u>created</u> through advertising...needs <u>are being met</u>* (ll. 64–7). The second and third examples here suggest that we are being manipulated by nameless people in control. The fact that *by* + *agent* is omitted reinforces the sense that an inhuman government has created this supposedly destructive industrial society for their own ends. The use of the **progressive** *being met* (l. 67) emphasises the idea of an ongoing apparently inescapable cycle. The first example, however, implicitly suggests that there is an alternative for those who recognise the importance of the Ecology Party.

The many **interrogatives** highlight the alternative offered. The questions are often rhetorical – although no answers are supplied, it is implied that the Ecology Party can find solutions.

> P   S   C
> (Is) (this) (not) (the very denial of the human spirit)? (ll. 85–6)
>   neg

This emphasis on **questioning** the lifestyle we take for granted is underlined by **repetition** of noun phrases like *without question* (ll. 71–2) and *Such questioning* (l. 58) and verb phrases like *must be...called into question* (l. 38) and *to question* (l. 56).

The **pronouns** in the manifesto define both the individual standing as a representative of the Ecology Party and the party itself. The repetition of the first person singular pronoun *I* in the first two paragraphs draws attention to the individual standpoint being taken. The use of the verb *believe* (l. 9) reinforces a sense of personal commitment. The first person plural pronoun *we* is often selected by politicians to refer to their party, but here the reference is wider. Since the Ecology Party stands for environmental issues and believes conservation is the responsibility of us all, the use of *we* is representative of society as a whole. The referencing attempts to unite readers of all political persuasions, suggesting that the issues here are beyond party politics.

> The obsession with growth places enormous demands on the resources of the earth upon which *we* depend (ll. 21–3)

> The environmental issue is not going to be resolved until *we* begin to question the need for industrial expansion as a basis for living. (ll. 55–8)

The use of *we* implies that everybody is guilty of accepting a way of life that is destroying the planet, and that we can all do something about it by voting appropriately. By using *we* inclusively, the candidate identifies himself with the voters – however, although he is equally responsible for the kind of society we live in, he has now done something about changing it by standing for a party that has environmental concerns at its heart.

Many **rhetorical features** can be identified here, all of which add to the persuasive nature of the text. To make the abstract issue of the destruction of the planet concrete, the candidate chooses a **metaphor** which is typical of the business-orientated society he sees us living in:

> No prudent *business person* would run a *business* by steadily depleting its *capital*
> (ll. 24–6)

The politically correct noun phrase *business person* (l. 24) replaces the traditional noun *businessman* and this is typical of the party's stance on equality. The metaphor explains the illogicality of our treatment of the earth through a **symbolic** figure who could be seen to represent self-interest. If such a person would not waste resources, surely, the manifesto suggests, we too are foolish not to look after our own best interests – the conservation of the earth's resources and the way to a more meaningful life.

Repetition of key words emphasises important issues: nouns like *consumption*

(l. 42) and *human* (l. 86); modifiers like *material* (l. 75) and *materially rich* (ll. 39–40); and verbs like *believe* (l. 9) and *question* (l. 56). **Antithesis** is used to reinforce the underlying message – that the Ecology Party is offering an alternative to the other major parties. The juxtapositions of noun phrases like *drugs* and *health* (ll. 78–9) and *home cooking* and *packaged foods* (ll. 79–80) draw attention to the present reality and to a potentially better way of life. Equally, the last paragraph uses antithesis to draw the argument to a conclusion. By contrasting abstract nouns like *competition* and *co-operation* (ll. 91–2), the prospective MP offers us a positive view of life to replace the negative view of society with which he started. The negative **connotations** of nouns like *annihilation* (l. 15) and *defilement* (l. 49) are exchanged for the positive connotations of the verbal nouns *caring and sharing* (l. 96). This means that the political message ends on a high note, offering us hope after the despair of the beginning.

The lexical, grammatical and rhetorical features of this written political statement make it a typical example of political language. The overall structure is clearly defined using subheadings to guide the reader through the key points of the argument. The prospective MP uses pathos, working on readers' emotions, to win their votes; the logical development of the argument and the use of facts to substantiate points made suggests the use of logos. Both these types of persuasion underpin the message: 'vote for me'.

ACTIVITY 17.2

Read the following statements made by two of the candidates for the Labour Leadership and Deputy Leadership contest. Use the questions that follow to identify any differences or similarities in the approaches of Margaret Beckett and John Prescott.

1   Jot down the audience, purpose and context for these written campaign statements.
2   Comment on the tone.
3   Identify any subject specific lexis. Is there anything that could be considered typical of the Labour Party?
4   Identify any abstract nouns and comment on their significance.
5   Comment on the use of proper nouns and on the ways in which people or parties are named.
6   Discuss the use of first person singular and plural pronouns and the possessive determiners <u>my</u> and <u>our</u> in each statement.
7   Find examples of a range of sentence types and comment on your findings.
8   Find examples of the following rhetorical techniques and comment on their effects:
     a   listing;
     b   repetition;
     c   marked theme.
9   Jot down any other interesting features of each written statement and try to decide which you consider to be more effective overall.

Margaret Beckett (MB)

1   Under John Smith's leadership we all recognised that we could play to his personal strengths.
         Now we need the same resonance in our new leadership team. We need to show people that we are honest politicians. We need to tell the truth
5   and to be seen to be telling the truth, even if it's hard. We must combine practical common sense and compassion.
         I have proved that I can exercise leadership, take tough decisions, hold

the party together and run a team that draws on the talents of all shades of party opinion. This has been my record for over two years, during which I
10 have been in charge of the party's election campaigns.

In those years we have rebuilt our morale. More importantly, we have won elections – in the counties, the cities and most recently across the nation.

To achieve further success, we must continue to take on not only the
15 Conservatives, but the Liberals as well. Ours is the politics of conviction, not of opportunism.

We must defeat the Tories' policies of despair. There is a better way. A better way to run our health service, our schools and our railways! We must rebuild our welfare state, based on full employment, but reflecting the family
20 and work patterns of the next century.

We must show that we share the ambition of ordinary British families.

Our fate lies in our own hands. Those newspapers which attack John Major today will support him, however grudgingly, at the next election. We know our country needs a Labour Government. We alone can take that mes-
25 sage to the people.

To succeed we must draw on the strengths of the broad church of the Labour movement. I believe I can unite the party, and that the party can unite the country.

John Prescott (JP)

1 I am standing for both leader and deputy leader to give you a real choice in this election. The principles at the heart of my campaign are those that John Smith had already set in train: full employment and social justice.

It is easy to say we believe in these goals. It is not so easy to achieve
5 them. But I am prepared to put my ideas to the test, and campaign for them with passion and conviction.

We cannot take the millions off the dole overnight, but we can make a start right away with an emergency jobs recovery programme in housing, manufacturing, transport, schools and hospitals. Then we can build sustain-
10 able employment through investment, through training and through partner-ship between public and private, employee and employer.

Britain needs full employment to go hand in hand with a welfare state that provides security and dignity for all our people. And we need social jus-tice to bind us all together in a contented community and a safe environment,
15 free from misery, pollution and crime.

We must create quality jobs, with effective employment protection, real job security and lifetime training opportunities. These must be underpinned by rights to union recognition and a statutory minimum wage.

Women and men should be treated equally, and paid equally for jobs of
20 equal worth. Discrimination on the grounds of gender, race, age or disability is unacceptable.

Nothing is more important than winning the next General Election. If we fail again, we cannot create jobs for the jobless, homes for the homeless or provide care for the sick and the elderly.

25 But to win power, Labour must give Britain a real choice, combining straight-talking with practical policies that will work. That is why I ask for your support in this election.

COMMENTARY

In response to the questions raised above, you may have picked up on some of the following points.

PURPOSE

The **purpose** here is very specific: a new leader and deputy leader had to be elected after the sudden death of John Smith in May 1994. This context made the **tone** of the election campaign very restrained since MPs did not want to appear to be insensitive. The campaign statements are addressed to Labour Party members who are entitled to vote in the leadership election. The candidates therefore need to appeal to ordinary people as well as their fellow politicians and union members. Because their statements have to convince both laymen and experts, they must achieve a balance between technical arguments and issues of concern to the general public.

TONE

The **tone** is inevitably formal, particularly because of the sad circumstances surrounding the need for election. However, John Prescott uses direct address, drawing his audience in by using the second person pronoun *you*. This makes his statement seem more personal and the manner slightly less formal.

SUBJECT SPECIFIC NOUNS

There are many **subject specific nouns** which are commonly associated with politics in both statements: Margaret Beckett talks of *politicians* (l. 4), *Government* (l. 24) and *party* (l. 8); John Prescott refers to *policies* (l. 26), *election* (l. 2) and *campaign* (l. 2). There are also many nouns that can be more specifically associated with Labour Party policy: the *welfare state* (ll. 19, MB, and 12, JP) is mentioned by both candidates, as is *employment* (ll. 19, MB; 3, JP). Prescott is known to be a supporter of the trades unions and his statement clearly addresses issues which are traditionally associated with Labour in noun phrases like:

m	h		m	m	h
union	recognition (l. 18)		statutory	minimum	wage (l. 18)
N	N		Adj	Adj	N

He also uses the adverb *equally* (l. 19) and the adjective *equal* (l. 20), emphasising Labour's interest in equality for everyone. Beckett raises the concept of the *health service* (l. 18), which is also a central part of Labour Party policy.

These examples of political language clearly mark out the field, but also relate it specifically to the Labour Party rather than any other political party.

ABSTRACT NOUNS

There are numerous examples of **abstract nouns** which could be selected here. They are used so extensively because these statements are meant to convey the philosophical as well as practical standpoint of the candidates. Once again, many of them are typical of Labour Party ethics. Nouns like *misery* (l. 15, JP) and *despair* (l. 17, MB) represent the Labour Party view that the Conservative Government has misplaced values. Instead, the Labour politicians suggest that **they** offer the *truth* (l. 4, MB). The negative **connotations** of abstract nouns like *pollution* and *crime* (l. 15, JP) are replaced with the positive connotations of *security* and *dignity* (l. 13, JP) and *common sense and compassion* (l. 6, MB).

PROPER NOUNS

The **proper nouns** used in each campaign statement are similar. John Smith is mentioned in the first paragraph of each text. This not only sets the context but also allows the candidates to commend what he had already achieved as an individual leader of the Labour Party. Both also mention the country as a whole: *ordinary British families* (l. 21, MB) and *Britain* (l. 25, JP). In doing so, they move beyond the individual who will lead the Party and beyond the Party itself to the electorate who are made to feel a part of the whole process of government. Beckett refers to the *Conservatives* and *Liberals* (l. 15) and by using the plural noun, she makes each party seem like a faceless institution. She later uses the abbreviation *Tories* (l. 17), which in this context has negative connotations.

PRONOUNS

Both candidates use the singular and plural first person **pronouns** but in different ways. Margaret Beckett begins using *we* (l. 1) to refer to the Labour Party as a whole, seeing herself as just one part of the overall structure. This immediately sets the tone of her statement since she seems to be most interested in the Party and its future – her own campaign seems only to be important in the sense that she believes she will be able to lead an effective **team**. She uses the first person singular *I* and the possessive determiner *my* in the third paragraph when she draws attention to her own personal qualities:

> *I* have proved that *I* can exercise leadership. . .This has been *my* record. . .during which *I* have been in charge of the party's election campaigns. (ll. 7–10)

The pronouns *we* (l. 3) and *ours* (l. 15) and the possessive determiner *our* (l. 3) all create a sense of unity. Beckett seems to stress the importance of the Party rather than an individual, replacing what has been described as 'personality politics' with issues and policies. In the final paragraph, however, she reminds the reader of the individual whom she believes can effectively carry out the role of co-ordination for the Labour Party by using the first person singular pronoun again:

> *I* believe that *I* can unite the party . . . (l. 27)

John Prescott's use of pronoun referencing creates a slightly different effect. He too uses *we* in an inclusive way, referring to both the Party and himself, but he opens his statement with the first person singular pronoun *I* and the possessive determiner *my* (ll. 1–2). This immediately draws more attention to him and his aims. Since he also uses the direct address, the approach here is far more personal, perhaps appealing more to the ordinary voter or union member. In paragraph four, his use of the pronouns *we* and *us* (ll. 12–14) widens the field of reference – he now includes everyone in Britain. The shifting meaning of these pronouns enables him to move beyond the Labour Party itself to the voters, including them directly in his appeal. Such an appeal is implicit in Beckett's statement, but Prescott seems to electioneer more explicitly. This is emphasised in his final sentence where he once more uses the first person singular pronoun and a possessive determiner:

> That is why *I* ask for *your* support in this election. (ll. 26–7)

SENTENCE STRUCTURE

Because these are written statements of intent, the **sentence structure** is mostly quite complicated. Interestingly, although it would seem that John Prescott's text appeals more directly to the ordinary reader in the referencing, Margaret Beckett's sentence structure is far less complicated. While Prescott uses few simple sentences, Beckett uses many, often with a marked theme:

> ^{A}(Now) ^{S}(we) ^{P}(need) ^{O}(the same resonance) ^{A}(in our new leadership). (l. 3, MB)

	A		S		P		O	

▌ (In those years) (we) (have rebuilt) (our morale). (l. 11, MB)

    S   P   A

▌ (Our fate) (lies) (in our own hands). (l. 22, MB)

                                      S   P   C

▌ (Discrimination on the grounds of gender, race, age or disability) (is) (unacceptable.)
                                                                                    (ll. 20–1, JP)

Both candidates use a range of compound and compound-complex sentences. These kinds of sentences enable them to link significant issues together in the mind of the reader.

    S   P   A   P   A   A

▌ (Women and men) (should be treated) (equally) (and) (paid) (equally) (for jobs of
                                          conj

equal worth). (ll. 19–20, JP)

  S   P   O   O   A

▌ (We) (need) (to tell the truth) (and) (to be seen to be telling the truth) (even if it's
          SCl–NFCl   conj   SCl–NFCl   NFCl   NFCl   SCl–ACl

hard) (ll. 4–5, MB)

The complex and compound-complex sentences reflect the nature of the writing – political language, focusing on both philosophical and practical issues, which is intended to persuade readers to act in a certain way.

          A   S   P   O

▌ (Under John Smith's leadership) (we all) (recognised) (that we could play to his
                                                                 SCl–NCl

personal strengths). (ll. 1–2, MB)

    A   S   P   O   O

▌ (If we fail again), (we) (cannot create) (jobs for the jobless), (homes for the homeless)
  SCl–ACl

    P   O

▌ (or) (provide) (care for the sick and the elderly). (ll. 22–4, JP)
  conj

RHETORICAL TECHNIQUES

The texts use a range of **rhetorical techniques** to underpin their message. Both Prescott and Beckett use **listing** to emphasise things that they think are important. Examples like the listing of the abstract nouns *gender, race, age or disability* (l. 20, JP) and the listing of clauses *I can exercise leadership, take tough decisions, hold the party together and run a team. . .* (ll. 7–8, MB) provide the reader with evidence supporting the argument being put forward.

Repetition is used by both candidates. Both politicians repeat modal verbs: Beckett's repetition of *must* (l. 14) emphasises her view of the obligation the Labour Party has to carry out its promises; Prescott also implies the necessity of doing certain things with his repetition of *must* (l. 16), while using *can* (l. 7) and the negative form *cannot* (l. 23) to develop a sense of the key things the Labour Party needs to tackle. Other examples of repetition reflect the central issues of the candidates: nouns like *employment* (ll. 19, MB; 16, JP) and *welfare state* (ll. 19, MB; 12, JP). Beckett's use of the **comparative noun phrase** *a better way* (l. 17) emphasises her apparent belief that the leadership election is about more than just a new leader. The use of the comparative adjective suggests that it is about making sure that at the next general election Britain elects a Labour rather than a Conservative government. The choice of leader is merely a part of this overall aim.

Marked themes are used to draw attention to an element of the sentence which is not the subject. Beckett begins her statement with the adverbial *Under John Smith's leadership* (l. 1) which reminds the reader of the reason for the election and pays tribute to Smith's achievements. The second paragraph then uses another marked theme – the adverb *now* (l. 3) marks a change in timescale and prepares the reader for the argument which will try to convince them that Beckett is the most appropriate leader at this point. Two non-finite clauses, *To achieve further success* (l. 14) and *To succeed* (l. 26), also function as marked themes. They emphasise the importance of the Labour Party's success as a whole rather than just suggesting that Beckett's personal success is significant. Prescott's sentence structure usually follows the traditional pattern, with the subject coming first. He does, however, use the adverb *Then* (l. 9) to mark a transition period of immediate action before the long-term goals of the Labour Party can be achieved.

COMPARISON

Both written statements are interesting for different reasons and will have appealed to different voters for different reasons. While John Prescott seems to speak directly to the reader in a personal way, Margaret Beckett uses more simple sentences which make easier reading. Her use of marked themes also draws attention to key elements of her argument. Their respective use of pronouns also means that they present themselves for the role in very different ways. While both emphasise the role of the Labour Party overall through their use of the inclusive first person pronoun *we*, Beckett seems to offer herself as a 'team' leader. She waits until the third paragraph to use the first person pronoun and her use of the modal verb *could* (l. 1) demonstrates that the Party has already shown that it is able to work **together** to achieve things. The suggestion that **she** would be the one to lead is implicit until she uses the perfect form of the verb phrase to convey concrete achievement in *have proved* (l. 7). In opening his statement with the first person pronoun. Prescott's intention seems more explicit – his approach seems to suggest more directly that he personally is the candidate to choose.

Beckett makes more of the political divide between the major parties by juxtaposing the politics of *opportunism* and *policies of despair* (ll. 16–17) with the *politics of conviction* (l. 15). This refocuses the reader's immediate interest in the Labour Party leadership contest by considering the ultimate aim of the party as a whole – displacing the Conservative Government. The abstract nouns lead away from the importance of one individual leader to the Labour Party itself.

This basic difference in approach is reinforced in the final paragraphs of each candidate. Prescott concludes with a marked theme similar to Beckett's: the adverbial clause of purpose, *But to win power* (l. 25). The compound verbal noun *straight-talking* (l. 26) and the modifier *practical* (l. 26) could be seen as implicit references to Prescott himself since these are both attributes that are commonly associated with him. They then lead to the emphatic final sentence which takes the form of an indirect question:

>   S   P   C   A
> (That) (is) (why I ask for your support) (in this election). (ll. 26–7)
>   SCl–NCl

Indirect questions are noun clauses – that is, subordinate clauses that fill the position of noun phrases. A noun clause can be introduced by a *wh-* word and the following elements of the clause will have the same basic structure as a main clause. Its function here is to allow Prescott to reintroduce the first person singular pronoun, stressing the personal appeal behind the campaign statement. Beckett's emphasis is slightly different since she seems to continue to refer to *the party* (l. 8) and the *Labour Government* (l. 24) as more significant than herself. Her use of the metaphor *the broad church* (l. 26) reinforces the importance of the 'team' approach since it suggests that a wide range of talents and views can be drawn upon. She begins her final sentence with the first person pronoun *I* (l. 27), but its use with the verb *believe* makes her appeal seem more tentative. The modal verb *can* implies her potential as a leader, but the repetition of the noun *party* and the verb *unite* seem to underline her role as a team figurehead. The structure of the compound sentence itself reflects the subtlety of Beckett's approach:

S   P   O   O

(I) (believe) (I can unite the party) (and) (that the party can unite the country).
              SCl–NCl   conj   SCl–NCl

(ll. 26–7)

Both Margaret Beckett and John Prescott employ typical features of political language here. Although there are many differences in their approaches, the end result is effective in each case. The most important thing to recognise is that the individual focus in each will attract different voters.

Pre-scripted speeches

Any speech which has been prepared ahead of delivery has been consciously planned – the politician is involved in the selection of lexical, syntactical and metaphorical features and in the overall organisation. Like a campaign statement, choices are made in advance to achieve the maximum possible effect on the audience. It is likely, however, that a politician will attempt to use some techniques that reflect formal spoken language. The first person pronoun is often used more frequently and spontaneity markers like *I know* or *you know* may be chosen to make the manner seem less formal than it actually is. The overall effect will inevitably depend upon the audience and context, but in analysis of a scripted speech it is important to first identify the features of 'speeches written to be read' and then to consider any features that seem to resemble spoken language.

ACTIVITY 17.3

The following speeches were both written to be read aloud in a formal context. The first was delivered by the Prime Minister, John Major, to the European Policy Forum in London on 27 July 1994; the second was a conference speech by the President of Plaid Cymru, Dafydd Wigley, on 28 November 1994. In both cases, the speeches contain many examples of formal written language, but there are also features which can be linked to formal spoken language. Only the introduction is printed in each case, and these do not include examples of all the features that can be adopted by politicians to make their speeches seem more spontaneous than written statements.

Read through the two examples and list:

1   lexical, syntactical and rhetorical features;
2   techniques used to make the speech seem like spoken language.

John Major (JM)

THE ROLE AND LIMITS OF THE STATE

1   The party I lead has always been a party of change and reform. But we're a conservative party. Our instincts are for stability. We are wary of schemes to uproot what is familiar. So in discussing the role and limits of the state I am not going to unveil some new constitutional blueprint. I don't think this coun-
5   try needs politicians throwing the British constitution up in the air to see how the broken pieces fall.

Today, we are opening up the map of how Britain is governed. It's a big agenda, dwarfing any changes we've seen since the modern pattern of government was established. Times change; needs change. But change
10 must come against a stable background.

So you will find me wary of change in the basis of our constitutional settlement – the Union between England, Scotland, Wales and Northern Ireland; wary of new voting systems. You will find me opposed to those who think that national identity must be suppressed in the interests of political
15 progress. I strongly reject that view. The nation state is the greatest fixed point in our political firmament. You cannot suppress the individualism of an island race. We are content to build on consensus and co-operation, unwilling to accept centralism and direction.

In my first speeches as Prime Minister I placed wider personal owner-
20 ship and higher quality in public service at the heart of our objectives for the 1990s. In 1991, I called for a revolution in ownership. I said then:
'I want to give individuals greater control over their own lives. For every family, the right to have and to hold their own private corner of life; their own home, their own savings, their own security for the future. Building the
25 self-respect that comes from ownership, and showing the responsibility that follows from self-respect: that is our programme for 1990s. I will put it in a single phrase; the power to choose – and the right to own.'
Conservatives have always stood for ownership. As well as ownership of property we need ownership of the important decisions in our own life. Which
30 school for our children? What skill training for ourselves? What pension provision for our retirement? These are decisions for individual adults. To deliver these choices, I believed we needed a second revolution – in the way public services are delivered.

As a councillor in Lambeth 25 years ago, I saw the alienation between
35 bureaucracy and people, and I didn't like what I saw. So in 1991, with the Citizen's Charter, I launched a long-term programme to make services much more responsive to the people who use them.

In the past four years much has been achieved in making government more accountable and in raising the quality of service. We are pursuing
40 change not for the sake of change, but for the sake of people. And today, as a result, when people want to learn something about reinventing government, they come to Britain to do so.

Dafydd Wigley (DW)

PRESIDENTIAL ADDRESS

1 This year has been an historic one in the political field. Nelson Mandela was elected President of South Africa; Israel and the Palestinians have made peace; and the new chapter has opened in the history of Ireland. Here we see a new period of radical politics opening – as happens about once each
5 generation. We saw it before in the sixties – a period of new politics. That was when Gwynfor Evans was first elected to Parliament and we saw the significant growth of Plaid Cymru and the SNP. It was a period of hope. The argument for a Parliament of Wales was high on the political agenda then, as in many previous radical periods of history. In each one, however, the objec-
10 tive of a Parliament was not achieved and as we face a new radical period, let us ensure that we learn the lessons from the past and this time succeed to establish those constitutional changes that are so essential for the well-

being of our country.

During the past year we have seen success coming to Plaid Cymru's
15 efforts in the European context. There is no doubt that it was Plaid Cymru's
work that secured three seats for Wales on the European Committee of the
Regions, and subsequently a place for Councillor Eurig Wyn on the Cabinet
of the Regions. The Labour Party and Tories alike were forced to accept the
principle of a European National Forum for Wales. We succeeded in getting
20 a fifth seat for Wales in the European Parliament, to get Interreg Funds for
Gwynedd and Dyfed for the first time and to open the possibility of electrify-
ing our rail connections.

The year was also one of electoral success for Plaid Cymru. We won
local elections and by now as a Party we have more seats on local authori-
25 ties in Wales than either the Tories or the Liberals. And in the elections to the
European Parliament in June, we were confirmed as the second Party on the
all-Wales level, with over 17% of the vote – the highest proportion ever.

In Clwyd we won 25,000 brand new votes – a large proportion of them
from amongst the non-Welsh-speaking population of the county. On the
30 basis of the European Election, Plaid Cymru would have won not only the
Conwy seat from the Tories, but also the new constituency – Clwyd West,
and thereby releasing Rod Richards to return to his television duties!

In contemplating this very successful record, I want to get one point over
to you with all the force I can muster. Political success this year has not been
35 a fluke – it has been the result of very hard work and careful organisation by
a team of dedicated workers. We need to break through in other areas – particularly in the industrial valleys – and we have more new blood, willing to
give up well-paid jobs, to work full-time for Plaid Cymru, as did Karl Davies
last year. But we will not be able to make these essential appointments
40 unless we have the finance to support them . . .

COMMENTARY

There are numerous features here that are typical of political language. Some of the
main examples are included in the table below.

LEXIS

Examples	Comment
politics (l. 4, DW), Parliament (l. 6, DW), party (l. 1, JM), government (l. 9, JM)	This **subject specific language** is typical of all kinds of political discourse. It marks no specific political ideology, but is used by all politicians.
Gwynfor Evans (l. 6, DW), Clwyd (l. 28, DW)	The use of these **proper nouns** identifies the regional interests of a Welsh national party.
Tories (l. 18, DW), Conservatives (l. 28, JM)	The use of the abbreviated **name** of the Conservative Party by Dafydd Wigley reflects his lack of sympathy with the party, while John Major's use of the full name is a mark of respect.

| Union (l. 12, JM) | Major makes this a **proper noun** with the use of a capital letter in the written script – he probably used stress to mark its importance in the oral presentation. It reflects Conservative policy to maintain a unified Britain despite calls for devolution. |

GRAMMAR

Pronouns

Examples	Comment
The party *I* lead. . . (l. 1, JM)	Major foregrounds the Conservative Party, referring to himself in a **post-modifying relative clause**, i.e. 'the party that I lead'.
In *my* first speeches as Prime Minister *I* placed. . . (l. 19, JM)	The use of the **possessive determiner** and the **first person singular pronoun** give this section of the speech a very clear personal tone. Major balances his use of *I* with his use of *we* to give a sense that he has an individual role as Prime Minister as well as being a team member.
But *we*'re a conservative party. *Our* instincts are for stability. *We* are wary. . . (ll. 1–2, JM)	The emphasis here is on unity. Having established that he, as an individual, is responsible for leading the party, he develops a sense of the Party's strength through his repetition of the **first person plural pronoun** and the **possessive determiner**.
So *you* will find me wary of change. . . (l. 11, JM)	Throughout, Major addresses his audience **directly**, thus creating a more personal relationship with them.
We saw it before. . . (l. 5, DW)	The predominant pronoun form used in this speech is the **first person plural**. This creates a feeling of unity which is commonly found in party conference speeches. The speaker is addressing an audience of like-minded people and therefore wants to arouse their emotions and to make them feel included.
I want to get one point over to *you* with all the force *I* can. . . (ll. 33–4, DW)	The use of the **first person singular pronoun** allows the President to draw attention to this point after the previous repetition of *we*. The repetition of *I* and

the use of **direct address** (second person pronoun) makes the point seem like a personal view of the President. It is thus given emphasis and the audience are made aware of the importance of committed hard work for the cause.

Verbs

Examples	Comment
much *has been achieved*. . . (l. 38, JM)	The **passive** form of the verb is used to imply a general sense of responsibility.
The Labour Party and Tories alike *were forced to accept*. . . (l. 18, DW)	The **passive voice** reinforces the sense that the two major political parties had no choice. It makes the supposedly dominant parties seem helpless in the face of an increasingly popular and powerful Plaid Cymru.
we *were confirmed* as the second Party on the all-Wales level. . . (ll. 26–7, DW)	No **agent** is included here and it suggests that the recognition of Plaid Cymru's success was universal – it could not be denied by anyone.

General

Examples	Comment
Which school. . . ? *What* skill. . . (ll. 29–30, JM)	**Wh- questions** are listed to show how the Conservatives' target of personal choice will affect everyday life. Such questions are open rather than closed and the framing therefore reinforces the idea of choice.
let us ensure. . . (l. 11, DW)	The use of the **imperative** encourages the audience to identify with the President and aims to persuade them to believe as he does.
On the basis of the European Election, Plaid Cymru *would* have won not only. . . (ll. 29–30, DW)	The use of the **modal verb** here implies a **hypothetical** situation and encourages the audience to envisage a political future in which the Welsh national party could influence British politics as a whole.

Sentence structure

Sentence structure is very varied in each speech, as would be expected since such variety guarantees that the audience will be kept interested. However, John Major's speech contains far more simple sentences than Dafydd Wigley's and this adds to the rhetorical effect.

> S P C A
> (This year) (has been) (an historic one) (in the political field). (l. 1, DW)

> S P A P O
> (Conservatives) (have) (always) (stood for) (ownership). (l. 28, JM)
>   aux   lex

John Major's use of numerous simple sentences makes his speech seem emphatic; it adds a sense of certainty to his statements:

> S P S P S P A
> (Times) (change); (needs) (change). (But) (change) (must come) (against a stable
>   conj
> background). (ll. 9–10, JM)

Both speakers also use compound and compound-complex sentences in which elements from the first main clause are omitted in the second. This allows the speakers to link ideas together for their audiences. Many of the sentence structures are compound-complex because they combine co-ordination and subordination. This reflects both the formality of the contexts and the reflective nature of the content of each speech.

> A A S P O
> (As a councillor in Lambeth) (25 years ago), (I) (saw) (the alienation between
>
> S P O
> bureaucracy and people) (and) (I) (didn't like) (what I saw). (ll. 34–5, JM)
>   conj   SCl–NCl

> S P A P A S
> (That was when Gwynfor Evans) (was) (first) (elected) (to Parliament) (and) (we)
> SCl–NCl   aux   lex   conj
>
> P O
> (saw) (the significant growth of Plaid Cymru and the SNP). (ll. 5–7, DW)

Complex sentences place a greater demand upon the listener because they need to remember the key elements and are unable to look back as a reader can.

> A A S P O
> (So in 1991), (with the Citizen's Charter) (I) (launched) (a long-term programme)
>
> A
> (to make services much more responsive to the people who use them) (ll. 35–7, JM).
> SCl–NFCl   SCl–RelCl

> S P O A A A
> (We) (need) (to break through) (in other areas) – (particularly) (in the industrial
>   SCl–NFCl
>
> S P O
> valleys) – (and) (we) (have) (more new blood, willing to give up well-paid jobs),
>   conj   SCl–NFCl
>
> O A A
> (to work full-time for Plaid Cymru), (as did Karl Davies) (last year). (ll. 36–9, DW)
> SCl–NFCl   SCl–ACl

Both these examples provide a lot of information for the listener and try to prove the worth of the ideological standpoint of the speaker. They use logos to persuade the audience that they too should believe in the party that does such things. Complex sentences like these were appropriate because the context was formal. In each case, the purpose was to convey an ideological standpoint and to encourage the listeners to agree. It is also important that the audience will have had knowledge of and an interest in the issues to be discussed.

RHETORIC

Examples	Comment
We are content to build on *consensus and co-operation*, unwilling to accept *centralism and direction*. . . (ll. 17–18, JM)	These examples of **listing** enable the speaker in each case to emphasise a point. John Major juxtaposes a positive and a negative in order to stress the Conservative view of the best way to govern Britain as a whole.
Nelson Mandela was elected. . .; Israel and the Palestinians have made peace; and the new chapter has opened. . . (ll. 1–3, DW)	Wigley lists a sequence of international examples showing how 1994 has been a politically important year. By starting from this point, he is able to link Plaid Cymru's achievements to events that everyone will have known about. This adds status to Plaid Cymru's own success in 1994.
During the past year. . . (l. 14, DW) Today, we are opening. . . (l. 7, JM)	There are many **marked themes**. Often these are used to mark out a specific time, drawing a distinction between past and present. This shows how far each party has come in terms of its achievements or success.
As well as ownership of property. . . (ll. 28–9, JM) In contemplating this very successful record. . . (l. 33, DW)	Other **marked themes** highlight key points to be considered alongside the one being made at the time. Major wishes to remind the audience of his earlier speech and to move on to another linked point. Wigley wants to stress that success has to be worked for.
succeed (l. 11), success (l. 23), successful (l. 33, DW) ownership (ll. 19–20), change (l. 9, JM)	Each speaker has a central theme or themes and **repetition** of a word or linked words enables him to emphasise this.

SPOKEN LANGUAGE

Inevitably when a speech is delivered before an audience, the listener has the benefit of intonation patterns, stress patterns and other such prosodic features to help them understand what is being said. Unless actually transcribed for linguistic analysis, a written record of a speech does not mark these variations. Nevertheless, it is possible to identify certain features in the written language that are included in order to make the speech seem more like the spoken than the written word.

Examples	Comment
I want. . . (l. 33, DW) *I* called for. . . (l. 21, JM)	Use of the **first person singular pronoun** is more frequent in spoken language and gives a speech a more personal feel.
You will find me. . . (l. 13, JM) . . .get one point over to *you*. . . (ll. 33–4, DW)	The direct address of the **second person pronoun** is personal because it makes the audience feel that they are being individually involved by the speaker.
we're (l. 1), *don't* (l. 4), *It's* (l. 7, JM)	**Contractions** are commonly associated with the spoken word and are seen to be quite informal.
So you will find me. . . (l. 11, JM) a fluke (l. 35, DW)	Some words or phrases may seem quite **conversational** compared with the formality of the context.
But change. . . (l. 9), *And* today. . . (l. 40, JM) *And* in the elections. . . (l. 25), *But* we will not. . . (l. 39, DW)	**Conjunctions** used in the **initial position** are associated with informal spoken language. Their use in a formal context creates a more relaxed manner.
. . . – particularly in the industrial valleys. . . (ll. 36–7, DW) . . . – the Union between England, Scotland. . . (l. 12, JM)	**Parenthesis** is used to add extra information. It gives the sentence in which it is included a looser structure, which is again reminiscent of conversation.

Both of the texts reproduced here are extracts from written copies of speeches composed to be spoken. In fact, their style remains very similar to that of the manifestos and campaign statements in the previous section. The main differences lie in features which can be linked to informal spoken language. Because of the formal context and informed audience in each case, however, these informal features are less dominant than those associated with the more formal register of the written word.

The Houses of Parliament

Although pre-scripted speeches and debates are a central part of Parliament, many of the exchanges are not scripted. Everything which is spoken is recorded in Hansard and this provides language students with interesting examples of political language in use.

Much of the language is **formulaic** and traditional patterns are used time and time again. This can be seen in the framing of a **motion for debate**. Hansard records the motion on 10 March 1994 from Clare Short MP which was to introduce a debate on sex discrimination:

> 1 I beg to move,
> That this House, in the week of International Women's Day, notes that women in Britain face discrimination in all aspects of their lives; deplores the Government's failure to fully implement European equality legislation
> 5 or the recommendations of the Equal Opportunities Commission; and calls on the Government to introduce legislation to simplify, strengthen and extend the Sex Discrimination and Equal Pay Acts.

The formulaic *I beg to move* (l. 1) is the traditional opening to a debate. The verb phrase *beg to move* allows the speaker to provide a number of objects in the form of a noun clause introduced by *that* which is often omitted after the first clause:

```
   S        P             O                      O                       O
(I) (beg to move) (that this House. . .notes. . .); (deplores. . .); (and) (calls. . .)
                       SCl-NCl                       SCl-NCl          conj   SCl-NCl
```

(ll. 1–5)

Abstract nouns like *legislation* (l. 6) and *Acts* (l. 7) mark this as political language and **subject specific proper nouns** like *International Women's Day* (l. 2) and *Equal Opportunities Commission* (l. 5) define the content.

A later intervention by the Secretary of State for Employment, David Hunt MP, after thirty-eight minutes of debate, replaces Clare Short's motion with the following version:

> 1 I beg to move, to leave out from 'House' to the end of the Question, and to add
>   thereof:
>   'notes, in the week of International Women's Day, that women in Britain
>   now enjoy exceptionally wide and increasing opportunities underpinned by
> 5   comprehensive and effective legislation; and calls on the Government to
>   continue to pursue the policies which have made this possible.'

This motion provides a complete contradiction in terms of ideology, but the basic structure remains exactly the same. Interestingly, the opposing stance of Labour and Conservative politicians can be seen in the clause structure: while Clare Short, Labour MP, uses a **marked theme**, the adverbial *In the week of International Women's Day* (l. 2, CS), the Secretary of State draws less attention to the particular week by placing the prepositional phrase after the verb (l. 3, DH). Equally, the **modifiers** chosen by David Hunt obviously praise the Government's action:

```
            m                    m          h
(exceptionally wide) and increasing opportunities (l. 4, DH)
   Adv        Adj         V            N
```

```
     m                  m           h
comprehensive and effective legislation (l. 5, DH)
   Adj              Adj          N
```

This is in direct contrast to the **connotations** of verbs like *deplores* (l. 3, CS) and nouns like *failure* (l. 4, CS) in the first motion.

These examples of political language are pre-scripted and they follow a very precise pattern. They bear little resemblance to spoken language because of their formulaic structure. The speech turns are not equal because the speaker introducing the motion dominates, allowing interventions when considered appropriate. The verb phrase *to give way* is used to mark the points in the debate when the speaker allows another politician to make a statement or ask a question. The speech following the introductory motion is scripted, but interventions from the floor are unlikely to have been prepared. Although they are still formal because of the nature of the context in which they take place, sometimes interventions can be introduced by phrases that seem rather informal. Phrases like *just one second* or clauses like *you know* are described as SPONTANEITY MARKERS because they reflect the unscripted nature of the language.

One of the most important features of parliamentary language is the **framing of questions**. The first question asked in the House of Commons was in 1721, and since then questioning has become a central part of parliamentary procedure. Each week there are now two timetabled sessions in which questions are addressed to the Prime Minister. Because of the nature of these sessions, questions are structured in a particular way. They are doing more than just requesting information – often they are used to make statements, and can equally criticise or praise the speakers to whom they are addressed. Politicians will usually only have one chance to ask a question, so questions are carefully constructed for maximum effect.

Questions are rarely straightforward: they must include appropriate facts; establish the nature of the question; address a minister's knowledge about a view on the issue in question; and provide a conclusion linked to the speaker's own viewpoint. Such complexity forces the politician being questioned to provide a more detailed answer. If ministers give a straightforward answer to a complicated question, they may find that they have committed themselves to a sequence of propositions with which they do not actually agree.

All the exchanges take place orally, but they are recorded exactly in Hansard. However, because the questions are often pre-scripted, their structure is closer to written rather than spoken language. Responses are not prepared, but because of the complexity of the questions addressed and the necessity of a detailed reply, the answers also resemble written language. Although parliamentary questions closely resemble formal written speeches in both structure and style, some features can reflect spoken discourse.

ACTIVITY 17.4

Questions and answers will usually convey a certain ideology and will follow party lines. MPs of the party in government will ask questions that enable ministers to respond in a positive way, showing their knowledge of a subject, the strength of Government policy and so on. Opposition MPs, however, will try to test ministers, revealing any weakness in their approaches or gaps in their knowledge, and so forth.

Read the two exchanges below, which took place in March 1994 when the Conservative Party was in government and the Labour Party was in opposition. Giles Brandreth spoke as a Conservative backbencher; John Smith as the Leader of the Labour Party. Comment on:

1   the attitude towards the Prime Minister in each case;
2   the structure of the questions;
3   any features that are typical of political language.

Extract 1

1   **Mr Brandreth**: Will my right hon. Friend consider adding to his list of engagements a visit to the uniquely beautiful city of Chester, where he will find inward investment at record levels, and unemployment 6 per cent lower than a year ago and 26 per cent lower than six years ago? Does he agree
5   that, in terms of inward investment to the European Community, the United Kingdom in general, and the city of Chester in particular, are now leading the way?

The Prime Minister: I am certainly pleased to hear of the particular inward investment to Chester. There has been a dramatic amount of inward invest-
10   ment into every part of the United Kingdom over the last few years – Wales and Scotland have certainly received a great degree of inward investment. That is very largely connected with the fact that we have a very flexible economy and a very effective business tax system, we do not have too many social on-costs, and investment here is welcome.

Extract 2

1 **Mr John Smith**: Does the Prime Minister think it right that those who can afford to pay fuel bills in advance can avoid paying the new VAT charges on gas and electricity?

The Prime Minister: As the right hon. and learned Gentleman knows, it has
5 long been the case that customers for a wide range of services can pay for them in advance. [*Interruption.*] There is nothing unusual about that. It has happened before every Budget that the right hon. and learned Gentleman can remember since he entered the House.

Mr John Smith: The Prime Minister does not even begin to understand the
10 problem here. Does he not understand that it is deeply unfair that those who are better off can avoid a tax obligation which millions of others have to shoulder because they do not have the money to exploit the loophole that the Government have permitted?

The Prime Minister: It is not a loophole, as the right hon. and learned
15 Gentleman says; it is a position that has applied for very many years. As far as people who are less well off are concerned, as the right hon. and learned Gentleman knows, we have provided help for them worth £2.5 billion over three years – more to pensioners, more to disabled people and more to single parents. The right hon. and learned Gentleman did not mention that all
20 those people will get the money before the bills arrive. That is a prepayment that the right hon. and learned Gentleman forgot to mention.

Mr John Smith: Does the Prime Minister not understand that in those replies he has revealed the Tory attitude to tax in a nutshell – loopholes for the bet-ter off, and everyone else has to pay in full?

25 **The Prime Minister**: What has been revealed is that the right hon. and learned Gentleman is up to his old tricks, yet again, telling other people how to spend their own money. It boils down to the fact that the right hon. and learned Gentleman is a meddler in everything – in private sector pay, in com-pany decisions and in how people pay their own bills. What he does not
30 mention is the fact that electricity companies, for example, have announced next year's prices and all of them have frozen the price or cut it. When did that ever happen under Labour Administrations?

Oral Answers, Prime Minister's Question Time, Hansard (22 March 1994)

COMMENTARY

Giles Brandreth's question is aimed to show how Conservative economic policies are working: levels of investment are up and unemployment is down. It offers John Major an opportunity to comment generally on the party's success. **Noun phrases** like

m	m	h
a	(very flexible)	economy (ll. 12–13)
det	Adv Adj	N

m	m	m	m	h
a	(very effective)	business	tax	system (l. 13)
det	Adv Adj	N	N	N

are used to promote the present state of economic affairs in a positive light. The ques-tion requires a *yes/no* answer, but since it is not addressed merely to acquire informa-tion, a more detailed reply is offered.

By using the **modal verb** *Will* (l. 1), the speaker suggests that he expects his request to be fulfilled. This immediately marks the question as one that will be acceptable to the Prime Minister. The request to visit Chester, however, is never answered since it is really only an excuse for introducing the second question which enables John Major to discuss investment and economic policy for the whole country.

John Smith's questions, on the other hand, are clearly more demanding. They constitute an attack on Conservative policy rather than offering an opportunity to show it in a positive light. The questions are not as simple as they would appear – although they apparently demand only a *yes/no* answer, to give a simple reply would compromise the Prime Minister. If his response to Smith's first question was 'yes', Major would be favouring people who have more money at the expense of people who are less well off. If he were to answer 'no', then he would be contradicting Conservative Party policy.

In each case, Major evades a direct answer by avoiding the key words in the question. The first asks him to question whether the Government's decision to allow the gas and electricity companies to collect payment *in advance* without the new VAT charges is *right* (l. 1). By using the clause

	dumS	P	A	P	C	(S)
	(it)	(has)	(long)	(been)	(the case)	(that customers. . .) (ll. 4–5)
		aux		lex		

Major is able to sidestep the central part of the question and therefore avoids making a moral judgement. In the second question the key word is the adjective *unfair* (l. 10), but Major focuses on the idea of *loophole* (l. 14); while in the third, Smith's focus on the Conservative *attitude to tax* (l. 23) is replaced by an attack on Labour Party policy in his sequence of prepositional phrases which function as adverbials: *in private sector pay, in company decisions. . .* (ll. 28–9).

John Smith's use of the negative linked to the verb *understand* (l. 9) suggests that the Prime Minister is in some way failing to recognise the obvious. The formal nature of the exchange means that a contraction is inappropriate, but equally by using the full form of *Does he not. . .* (l. 10) emphasis is placed upon the negative.

The formality of the context is reflected in the **traditional titles** used to address people. A politician who is also a Privy Counsellor will be referred to using the phrase *my right hon. Friend*, while one who is a barrister will be called *the learned Gentleman* (l. 7), and so on.

Subject specific lexis like the nouns *Administrations* (l. 32), *tax* (l. 11) and *VAT* (l. 2) indicate that this is a political field, but the **connotations** of certain words suggest something about the political persuasion of the speaker. Smith's use of the noun *loophole* (l. 14) reflects his belief that the Conservative Party has given **some** people a means to **avoid** taxation. This belief of a division between rich and poor is developed through verbs like *exploit* (l. 12), with its connotations of gain at the expense of someone else, and the infinitive *to shoulder* (ll. 11–12), suggesting that a burden is being borne – but not by all. In choosing the verb *permitted* (l. 13), Smith implies that the Government is responsible for the division between rich and poor. They have accepted that it is legal for customers to make pre-payments for gas and electricity which will be exempt from the new VAT charges and are therefore enabling those with more money to avoid taxation. Major describes Smith as a *meddler* (l. 28), implying that he is interfering unnecessarily in other people's business. Such lexis clearly marks out the ideological stance of the two party leaders.

The register here is primarily influenced by the written word, but there are examples of **colloquial language** which would probably not have appeared in pre-scripted speeches. Clichés like *it boils down to. . .* (l. 27) and *up to his old tricks. . .* (l. 26) are more commonly associated with spoken language. Their presence here reminds the reader that this is a written version of an oral exchange. Smith's metaphor of *the nut-shell* (l. 23) can be described as a **dead metaphor**: it is no longer a vivid use of language to convey an abstract meaning concisely; instead, it is a well-worn cliché which has lost its originality. In a pre-scripted speech, it is likely that a speaker would have used a more original metaphor since the writer would have had time to consider and select the most powerful language to influence the audience.

Grammatically, the structure of the speech utterances here resembles written language more closely than spoken language because of its complexity. **Sentence structures** are rarely simple and usually complex.

$$\begin{array}{ccccc}S & P & A & P & O\end{array}$$

(The Prime Minister) (does) (not) (even) (begin) (to understand the problem here).
                  aux   neg   lex   SCl–NFCl

$$\begin{array}{cccc}P & S & P & O\end{array}$$

(Does) (he) (not) (understand) (that it is deeply unfair that those who are better off
  aux   neg   lex   SCl–NCl   SCl–NCl   SCl–RelCl

can avoid a tax obligation which millions of others have to shoulder because they do
              SCl–RelCl   SCl–NFCl   SCl–ACl

not have the money to exploit the loophole that the Government have permitted?)
    SCl–NFCl   SCl–RelCl

(ll. 9–13, JS)

$$\begin{array}{ccc}S & P & C\end{array}$$

(What has been revealed) (is) (that the right hon. and learned Gentleman is up to
  SCl–NCl   SCl–NCl

his old tricks yet again, telling other people how to spend their own money.)
              SCl–NFCl   SCl–NCl

(ll. 25–7, JM)

Such complexity is not usually associated with spoken language. The sentence structure here is complex because each speaker wishes to provide a lot of qualifying information and this makes both the questions and the answers complicated.

The **pronoun referencing** is typical of political language. John Major uses the first person singular when asked to visit Chester. Despite the fact that this request is addressed to him in the role of Prime Minister, he responds personally and this makes his pleasure at the high levels of investment seem sincere. When he later uses the first person plural, however, he is able to stress the caring nature of the Government as a whole.

17.5 What to look for in the language of politics

The following checklist can be used to identify key features in examples of political language. There will not be examples of all the features listed in every text or transcription, but the list can be used as a guide. The points made are general so discussion of specific examples will need to be adapted to take account of the specific context, audience and purpose in the given discourse.

The following are helpful questions to ask.

Register

1   What is the **mode**? – spoken or written? written to be read? written to be spoken? spontaneous spoken answers?

2   What is the **manner** – the relationship between the participants: formal or informal? the same or different ideology? supporters or opposers?

3   What is the **field**? – the subject matter will reflect the political variety.

Lexis

1   Are there any examples of **subject specific vocabulary**? – general? typical of a certain ideological stance?

2   Are there any **abstract nouns** reflecting beliefs or political policy?

3   How are the participants **named**? – use of titles? use of forenames or surnames? focus on the role or the individual? the relationship between speaker, topic and audience?

4   Is there anything significant about the **connotations** of words? – positive? negative?

Grammar

1   Are there any **pronouns** creating a sense of **distance**? – dividing the speaker and audience by using *those*? dehumanising the reference and making it seem faceless and threatening by using *it* and *they*? conveying a sense of opposition by using *they*? creating a very formal tone often associated with high social class by using *one* as a first person or second person personal reference? distancing the speaker from an action or conveying a sense of authority by using *one*?

2   Are there any **pronouns** bringing the speaker and audience **together**? – giving an individual tone and suggesting a sincere attitude by repeating or 'blocking' the *I*, particularly with mental process verbs (*think, feel* or *believe*)? establishing a rapport with the audience by using the *I*? linking issues and policies to a particular person by using *his, hers* and *theirs*, thus placing an emphasis on people rather than policies? focusing on the institution as well as the individual by using *we*, thus including the speaker and suggesting support for actions or policies? drawing the audience in by using *you*?

3   Are there any **pronouns** conveying degrees of **responsibility**? – marking the speaker as the instigator of an action or process by using *I*? showing an acceptance of responsibility by using *I*? making the degree of responsibility less clear by using *we*? allowing speakers to subtly alter their personal responsibility for certain acts by using *we* exclusively rather than inclusively? placing responsibility at a distance, explicitly excluding the speaker by using *they*?

4   How are the questions **framed**? – **negatives** allowing questioners to lead an addressee to a particular answer by suggesting that their propositions are undeniable? **modal verbs** like *will*, suggesting that any rejection will seem unacceptably rude? structures aiming to make the addressees commit themselves to action? closed *yes/no* **questions** attempting to force the addressee to accept or deny any proposition directly? *wh-* **words** requiring a more focused answer? **embedded statements** within the question, enabling the speaker to establish a context or viewpoint?

5   Are there any examples of the **passive voice**? – refocusing the audience's attention on certain elements? concealing the person(s) responsible for an action by omitting *by + agent*?

6   Is the **sentence structure** varied? – simple sentences making direct and emphatic statements? compound sentences balancing arguments? complex sentences exploring abstract concepts?

Metaphorical and rhetorical language

1　Are there any **metaphors**? – establishing a direct link between abstract theories and concrete examples? helping the listener to understand? extended metaphors emphasising a particular message?
2　What is the **focus** or **theme** of key sentences? – reordering of sentences to bring key elements to the attention of the audience?
3　Are there any examples of **repeated words**, **phrases** or **clauses**? – emphasising important concepts? helping to establish a core topic or attitude?

Summary

The **function** of political language is to make people believe in a certain world view; to persuade them to a certain course of action.

To a large extent, **tradition** plays an important role in defining the nature of political language: in the Houses of Parliament, certain formulaic utterances add to the formality of the field; in speeches, traditional rhetorical techniques are used to manipulate audience response.

Semantically, written and spoken words often have **underlying meaning(s)**: answers to direct questions are often non-committal, even evasive; by using **implications**, politicians can avoid direct answers and statements of belief and make an implicit point, quite different from what is apparently being said.

18 The language of broadcasting

18.1 The nature of broadcasting language

BROADCASTING can be defined as the sending of messages via **television** or **radio** with no technical control over who receives them. These messages are sent to a **mass audience**, the unknown individuals and groups who watch and listen to the transmissions. Broadcasters use codes to organise and convey meaning and the audience interpret these in order to understand the programmes.

There are three main CODES: **image**, **language** and **symbol**. Different kinds of broadcasting use these three in different proportions – for television, visual codes are often more important than linguistic ones, since the images provide messages which are not transmitted by the words; radio, on the other hand, can use no visual codes and relies exclusively on linguistic ones. Both television and radio use symbolic codes since this allows broadcasters to provide extra layers of meaning – on television, body language, the use of colour and props can be symbolic; on the radio, sound effects and prosodic features fulfil the same function.

The **form of communication** between participants is distinctive: communication is direct from the media source to the target audience, but there is no visual contact. The process is one-way because the watcher or listener has no means of questioning or redirecting the messages that are being conveyed. Although in the age of cassette and video recordings playbacks can be arranged to suit the listener or viewer, no real intervention can be made by the audience. Some programmes, however, now encourage audience responses and provide a telephone number for advice, information, casting votes or asking questions. Nevertheless, this is quite unlike the informal interaction that takes place in ordinary conversation because the context is quite different. Even where the relationship between participants seems informal, because the context is public, the tone is often formal.

Public broadcasting began in the 1920s and since then has developed significantly, becoming a national institution with which most people are familiar. The overall variety of 'broadcasting' can be subdivided into a number of distinctive categories, each with its own characteristic features. Newsreaders, sports commentators, continuity announcers, weather readers and DJs all have distinctive styles which viewers and listeners can recognise. Typical codes and conventions in each category allow broadcasters to organise and transmit messages for viewers and listeners to interpret.

In the early period of broadcasting it was possible to describe **BBC English** as the medium of communication. The BBC originally adopted RP for its announcers because it was thought to be the form of English most likely to be understood universally and least likely to be criticised. In the 1990s, however, both television and radio use a wide range of **regional** and **social accents**. Because mass communication transmits its programmes to a vast audience, this means that people are now familiar with accents and dialects which would otherwise not be heard locally. The growth of regional accents and the increase in informal and colloquial language has inevitably brought complaints from people who believe that this is just another example of the way in which the standards of spoken English are slipping. The result is that the language of broadcasting is now as diverse as its programme schedule and it is impossible to define one recognisable kind of language use. In each case, the purpose and style of the communication dictate the nature of the language used.

Because most viewers and listeners will listen to the linguistic codes only once as a programme is transmitted, the language of broadcasting needs to be **easily understandable**. Utterances must be **carefully organised** because the audience cannot ask for clarification, and they are often made up of short, uncomplicated units. Much of the language of broadcasting is **not spontaneous**, despite the fact that it is sometimes presented as such. People who work regularly in the medium of television or radio learn to speak in a way that emulates the spontaneous spoken word even if they are reading aloud. Where ordinary people appear in programmes, editing will often have eliminated all the false starts, hesitations and repetitions which are characteristic of spontaneous informal conversation. In drama, the writers and actors will actually 'write' these into the script in order to emulate the structures of normal interaction.

The language of broadcasting is an unusual mix of **spoken and written language**: like written language, it can be polished and edited, yet it is usually delivered as though it is spontaneous speech. Because it is written to be 'read' aloud to a very diverse audience, the language must be **easy to articulate**, **fluent** and **approachable**. Although each kind of programme has its own distinctive lexical, grammatical and prosodic features, certain characteristics can be identified as typical of broadcasting as a whole.

18.2 The function of broadcasting

Just as broadcasting covers a wide range of programme types, adopting different kinds of language to meet the requirements of each, so it has a number of **functions**. Documentaries and discussion programmes can **inform** the audience; schools' services and Open University schedules can **educate**; situation comedies and soaps can **entertain**; and advertising can **persuade**.

Language choice, grammatical structures and prosodic features will depend upon the kind of programme, its purpose, the intended audience and the time of transmission. An informative feature for children shown at teatime on a programme like *Blue Peter*, for instance, will be quite different from a documentary for adults such as *QED*, shown after the nine o'clock watershed; the content and language of a drama shown during 'family' viewing hours will be very different from those of a mini-series broadcast late at night; the six o'clock news may contain the same material as the nine o'clock news, but there will always be a warning before any disturbing images are shown.

In order to analyse the language of broadcasting effectively, it is important to establish some background information first. Linguists need to start by asking themselves the following questions:

- Is the **medium** television or radio?
- What **type** of programme is it?
- What is its **purpose**?

- Who is the **intended audience**, and what kind of **relationship** is established with them?
- What **time** is the programme broadcast?
- Is the **tone** serious, comic or somewhere in between?

Answers to these questions will provide the basis for a closer focus – having identified the broadcasting framework, linguists can then consider how these affect the lexical, grammatical and prosodic choices made by writers, actors and programmers.

18.3 Features of broadcasting language

The language of broadcasting covers such a wide range of linguistic forms that it is difficult to draw up a definitive list of language features. Nevertheless, it is possible to establish a number of distinctive features which mark it out as different from other varieties.

Mode

The **mode** will often be both written and spoken. There will, however, be examples of truly spontaneous speech (unprepared answers in a debate; live commentaries) and of language that is written with no attempt to mimic spontaneous speech (short stories read on the radio; written statements read out when the people concerned are unable or unwilling to attend). The language and structure of a programme will display features associated with speech or writing depending upon the balance the broadcasters aim to create between the two modes.

Manner

The **manner** will also vary depending upon the kind of programme transmitted. Although there is rarely any direct interaction between writers or programmers and actors or presenters, broadcasters do create a relationship with their unknown audience. Just as in face-to-face communication, this may be formal or informal depending upon the content, purpose and time-slot of the programme. News programmes, documentaries and serious drama establish a formal relationship with their audience, while situation comedies, game shows and soaps establish an informal relationship.

Status

The relative **status** of a programme and its audience is directly linked to the relationship created between them. The broadcasters may use 'experts' who are in the role of advisers or educators (*Floyd on Fish*, *Moneybox*, *Law in Action*). They may imply that the people on television or radio are no different from the viewers and listeners, using ordinary people as an integral part of the programme (*Challenge Anneka*, *Beadle's About*, *Barrymore*). In other forms of programming, the audience become the 'flies on the wall' overhearing and overlooking everyday life as it goes on (soaps, video diaries). The relative status assigned to the audience will inevitably affect the linguistic and prosodic choices made.

Topics

A programme may have one or more **topics**. A documentary will focus on a particular issue, for instance, while a soap will cover a different story for each set of characters. The kind of topic and the depth of coverage it is given will depend upon the **goal** of the programme. An informative documentary on the financial, emotional and physical difficulties of being a single parent would provide a wide range of information and sources; a drama would address the topic in a more individual way by describing the problems encountered by a particular character and the views of other characters; while the news would perhaps focus on a newly released report or new government legislation.

Topic shifts will be clearly marked where more than one issue is addressed. On programmes like the news or *Tomorrow's World*, linguistic and prosodic clues will indicate that one topic is coming to an end and that another is about to start. Speakers on these programmes will use the same approaches as speakers in formal situations would use to mark the end of a topic. Because the links are pre-written, most topic shifts will be smooth. They will rarely be challenged as they might in informal conversation because the structure is predefined.

The **end of a topic** is equally carefully organised. Timing is crucial because of the pre-published programming schedules which are available in national daily newspapers, free local papers and television and radio listings magazines like *The Radio Times*. If time is running out, presenters may have to break off a discussion by explicitly reminding participants that the programme is about to end; they can use stock phrases like *and I'm afraid I'll have to stop you there...* or *and we'll have to leave it there...*; or technicians can literally 'fade out' the sound. Pre-recorded programmes do not have the same problems because scriptwriters and editors have already established the cut-off point. They will nevertheless ensure that each episode or section concludes at an appropriate point – the audience may be left with a cliffhanger for continuation in the next programme or a neat summary which finalises the issues covered.

Structure

The **structure** of a programme will depend upon its type – if it is part of an ongoing series, characters, storylines and locations will run from episode to episode; if it is a one-off programme, its structure must be self-contained. In either case, the overall structure will be very carefully planned so that maximum use can be made of the time-slot allocated in the programming schedule.

Some programmes are marked by distinctive structural features. The **opening** and **closing** of the news or a documentary, for instance, will always follow a predefined pattern. For instance, the news will start with a formal greeting, an indication of the specific programme being broadcast and the newsreader's name; it will end with a summary of the main news and a formal closing: *and that's all we have time for... (.) from _____, goodnight.* A documentary is less likely to address its audience directly. Instead, it will start with a general introduction to the topic on which the programme will focus and conclude with a summary of the key issues. Intonation patterns will also indicate to the audience that the programme is coming to an end.

Other programmes will be structured around a very organised form of **turn-taking**. Programmes like *Mastermind* and game shows based on asking the contestants questions will require participants to behave according to certain 'rules' which enable communication to take place effectively. Although there may be interruptions, overlaps or digressions, **adjacency pairs** will establish the basic structure of such programmes.

Prosodic features

Because broadcasting relies on the spoken word to communicate effectively with its audience, **prosodic features** play an important part in conveying meaning. Although most of the programmes will first exist in a written form, actors, presenters and other kinds of speakers use their voices to bring the words to life. **Intonation patterns** reinforce the meaning of the words spoken. Changes in intonation can indicate different attitudes and moods; mark grammatical structures like questions or commands; and help to establish a rhythm by drawing attention to grammatical boundaries in utterances. **Pitch variations** underpin intonation changes, allowing speakers to reinforce their attitudes and responses. **Loudness** and **pace** also contribute to the meaning system, allowing speakers to reflect the relative importance of what they are saying in a dramatic way. Information programmes are more likely to adopt an average sound level and pace, but any programme which attempts to re-create real speech or which involves ordinary people in an informal context will use variations in the prosodic features to enhance meaning. **Vocal effects** will play a similar role. They are more likely to be found in less formal contexts, but even in pre-scripted, pre-recorded programmes there may be some evidence of throat-clearing or coughing which has not been edited out.

Stress patterns and pauses allow speakers to draw attention to certain lexical items. Viewers and listeners sometimes complain about the way in which stress is used by the people involved in television and radio broadcasting. Newsreaders in particular are sometimes accused of stressing inappropriate syllables and words and of pausing after grammatical function words. Many people think that television and radio are very influential and they see such 'inaccuracies' as eroding the standards of English. They would argue that because prestigious people are heard eliding final consonants, pronouncing words with the emphasis on the 'wrong' syllable and stressing words that are insignificant in terms of the meaning, the individuals who make up the audience will do the same. In the eyes of the prescriptivists, the 'error' is perpetuated, slowly changing the 'correct' form.

Lexis

The **lexis** will be directly linked to the content of the programme. Some will be subject specific and the language will reflect this; others will be based on ordinary informal interaction and the language will therefore be far more wide-ranging. In order to assess the nature of the language used, it is important to come to some conclusions about:

- the kind of programme;
- the intended audience (age, gender, educational or cultural background);
- the subject matter;
- the approach (formal or informal? serious or comic? detailed or general? one-off or a series?).

From this starting point, analysis can focus specifically on the kind of words used and the effects created.

Grammar

The **grammar** will also be linked to the kind of broadcast, the target audience, the topic and the approach. The more serious the context, the more likely the grammar is to be both formal and complex. Equally, where a broadcast is imitating the structures of informal conversation, the utterances are more likely to be incomplete and the grammatical structures more likely to be straightforward.

Accents and dialects

Accents and **dialects** will vary according to the kind of programme, the participants and the regional and social background. Newsreaders are more likely to speak SE with an RP accent – although it is now quite common to hear reporters and correspondents with regional accents. Certain programmes will be geographically located and will therefore use an appropriate regional accent for many characters: most characters in *Coronation Street* have Northern accents; in *Brookside*, they have Liverpudlian accents; in *Eastenders*, they have London accents; and in *Neighbours*, they have Australian accents. Because individuals all speak in different ways, however, the variation from character to character is quite significant. The accents and dialects of characters vary according to their age, gender, social class and their occupational and educational background.

Normal non-fluency features

Normal non-fluency features will only be apparent in certain kinds of programmes because in many cases, editing will have eliminated evidence of hesitancy, repetition and lack of fluency. Live broadcasts are more likely to contain such features, but even in these many speakers will be polished and articulate. While politicians are accustomed to speaking spontaneously about a range of subjects in a formal context, ordinary people have usually had less experience. Where inexperienced speakers take part in a broadcast, therefore, their speech will often be marked by non-fluency features. Programmes that aim to mirror reality (drama, situation comedy, soaps) can use non-fluency features to make characters seem more real or to create comedy.

As in informal conversation, **repairs** can take a number of forms in television and radio broadcasts. Editing will sort out many of the problems in pre-recorded programmes, but in live contexts, participants have to assess the cause of any breakdown in communication and then act accordingly. In live contexts, there is considerable pressure on participants to communicate effectively within a limited amount of time and this can lead to problems which require immediate repairs (misunderstood questions in an interview; participants talking simultaneously in a debate; unexpected silences in a discussion). On the whole, however, because the structure of spoken interaction in any broadcast is quite tightly defined and because most participants follow the expected patterns of behaviour, most examples of interaction will not show any evidence of breakdown.

In order to analyse the 'language of broadcasting', linguists use the key features of spoken language covered in Chapter 10. By identifying and commenting on the way in which language use is both similar and dissimilar to that of spoken language, it is possible to assess the way in which broadcasting language draws on both spoken and written registers.

18.4 Different kinds of broadcasting language

The news

The news will vary in form and structure depending upon the time of its transmission, its intended audience and whether it is broadcast on radio or television. Each individual news programme, however, will be recognisable by its format and length, its presenter and its distinctive approach to presenting news stories.

The dominant **function** is to inform, although there will often be some stories which entertain. The **tone** will be directly linked to the function – the lighthearted topics may be marked by more varied prosodic features, while the serious ones will tend to be delivered in a level or neutral tone and pitch, with few volume or pace changes.

The **structure** is distinctive. After an opening social greeting addressed directly to the audience, a summary of the programme's main features will draw the viewer or listener's attention to the subject matter that will be covered. On television news, these news 'headlines' will be accompanied by film footage which will encourage continued viewing. The main body of the news programme is made up of more detailed coverage of the headline events. Each topic will be introduced by the news reporter and then interviews, on-the-spot reports or comment by 'expert' correspondents will develop the coverage. On television, voiceovers may accompany images to provide the audience with important information.

Stories will be **selected** depending upon the range of possible stories for a particular broadcast, the relative impact of available film images, and the need to balance serious and light items. Stories selected will have cultural, social and geographical relevance to the intended audience; they will usually focus on celebrities or current issues; and their content will usually be negative. The order of broadcasting will affect the way the audience interprets events: by juxtaposing certain stories, it is possible to create implicit links which influence the way the audience responds.

Many people would say that the news is objective, presenting information in a neutral and unbiased form. However, because news stories are selected and presented in a certain way, there will always be evidence of subjectivity. There are many ways in which it is possible to recognise **bias** in news broadcasts: certain stories are included at the expense of others; priority is given to some stories by placing them first in the running order; words are chosen to convey the intended message in a way that suits the particular media institution; and the images which accompany television news can be chosen to influence the audience emotively rather than intellectually.

It is important to realise that the news does not present us with reality, but with a view of events which has been **ordered** and **constructed**. Words, prosodic features and the images accompanying television news are used to influence the target audience. While the content may disturb the viewer or listener, the continuity of the programme structure, the fluency of the programme as a whole and the stability and order of the studio are all designed to reassure.

ACTIVITY 18.1

The following extracts are taken from three different kinds of news programmes: the Nine O'Clock News (BBC Television), Good Evening Wales (Radio Wales) and Newsbeat (BBC Radio 1). Each programme is transmitted at a different time, is aimed at a different audience and has either national or regional interest. As a national programme broadcast in the evening, the Nine O'Clock News will appeal to a wide range of people. It is transmitted after the nine o'clock watershed which means that its images and reporting may be more disturbing than earlier news programmes. Good Evening Wales, on the other hand, can only be received in Wales and therefore focuses on stories of regional interest. National stories are still covered, but regional links will often be developed. Its transmission time means that families may be listening and reports will take account of this. Because it is a radio programme, words are the only means of communication and often prosodic features will be slightly exaggerated to engage listeners. Newsbeat will appeal mainly to the younger listeners at whom the station as a whole is directed. It is transmitted at 12.30 p.m. sandwiched between popular music programmes which attract a distinctive audience. The news coverage is fitted into just fifteen minutes and this means that the treatment of each story is very brief. Radio 1 is often treated as 'background' noise and in some workplaces, it is played permanently. This means that <u>Newsbeat</u> must adopt a dynamic form of presentation to attract the attention of listeners.

The transcripts below record the opening and closing sequences for each of the three news programmes broadcast on 12 April 1995. Read through the text and comment on the following:

1   any structures used to mark the opening and closing of each programme;
2   the relationship created with the intended audience;
3   the topics summarised in the headlines;
4   the prosodic features used to attract audience attention.

Only the most prominent prosodic features are marked on the transcripts. A key to the symbols can be found on page 86.

Transcript 1: <u>The Nine O'Clock News</u>, BBC Television [9N], read by Michael Buerk [MB]

1   MB the High <u>Court</u> has <u>bácked</u> live animal exports against what it calls the
     <u>mob</u> rule of demónstrators (.) official <u>báns</u> on the trade at some ports
     have been ruled <u>unlàwful</u> (.) as security barriers come down in Belfàst (.)
     a new stage in the peace pròcess (.) and how <u>Japan</u>'s latest export is
5   jóbs and these are <u>not</u> coming to Britàin
                                          *   *   *

     MB tonight's main news agàin (.) <u>bans</u> on the export of <u>live</u> animals from
     some ports and airports have been ruled <u>unlàwful</u> by the High Court (.)
     from the Nine O'Clock Néws (.) good nìght

Transcript 2: <u>Good Evening Wales</u>, Radio Wales [GEW], read by Patrick Hannan [PH]

1   PH it's five o'clock this is Patrick Hánnan (.) Good Evening Wàles (5) the
     headlines this évening (.) there are <u>fears</u> of renewed <u>clashes</u> as port
     authorities are tóld they've got no <u>right</u> to ban the export of livestòck (1)
     unemployment continues to fáll in Wales but there's bad news for ↑one↑
5   firm (.) new figures show that Wales is ahéad of England in providing
     education for the under fìves (5) also in the programme (.) we'll be
     reporting on the High Court victory for the so-called exiled Welsh soccer
     clùbs (.) we'll be looking at President Mandela's surpríse décision to
     restore his estranged wife Winnie to the South African cábinet (.) on
10   <u>legal</u> gróunds (1) and we'll find out why house prices in Wales are con-
     tinuing to fáll (.) we'll also have spórt (.) weàther and tràvel between now
     and six o'clock (.) but first the latest news (.) from Charlotte Èvans
                                          *   *   *

     PH finally (.) don't fórget that Annlee Roberts will be here at half-past nine
     with Wales Tónight (.) and after the High Court ruling on livestock
15   exports the programme talks to the owners of Swansea Airpòrt (.) the
     scene of angry protésts earlier in the yéar (.) that's Wales Tonight at half-
     past nìne but that's it from ùs (.) this is Patrick Hánnan (.) I'll be back at
     five o'clock tomòrrow (.) for nòw (1) Good Evèning Wales

Transcript 3: <u>Newsbeat</u>, BBC Radio 1 [NB], read by Rod McKenzie [RM]

1   Jingle   97 to 99 FM (.) Radio 1 (.) Newsbeat (2)

RM	trouble for the tunnel as the Eurostar train gets <u>tangled</u> (.) a judge says <u>nó</u> to mob rule in the veal wars (.) and the ↑plan↑ to <u>pepper</u> the <u>planets</u> with ↓<u>pound</u>↓ coins (1)
5 Jingle	Newsbeat

*　*　*

Jingle	1 FM the <u>gréatest</u> music (.) the latest nèws (.)
RM	the <u>top</u> stories this lunch-time (.) the High Court's ruled ports and councils can't <u>ban</u> the export of livestock (.) the judge says they shouldn't surrender to <u>mob</u> rùle (.) and the <u>main</u> story this lunch-time
10	(.) hundreds of Channel Tunnel passengers <u>wère</u> stranded after a Eurostar train was <u>tangled</u> in <u>power</u> <u>lines</u> in Kènt (.) we hear they're now on their way ↑<u>back</u>↑ to London Wàterloo (.) at <u>1.15</u> the <u>Net</u> gives <u>its</u> <u>verdict</u> on the first <u>Menswear</u> gíg (.) and an exclúsive on Pato Banton's new record with <u>Sting</u> (.) Radio 1 Newsbéat (.) I'm
15	Rod McKenzie =
Jingle	= Radio 1 (.) more music

COMMENTARY

Both the radio news programmes **open** with a direct reference to their respective titles: *Good Evening Wales* and *Newsbeat*. Because the television broadcast can rely on images as well as words to identify itself, there is no spoken reference to the title. While the opening of the television news focuses on the headlines, Radio 1 uses an instantly recognisable jingle to provide a framework for the news summary. Radio Wales, on the other hand, introduces its programme in a far more structured way. The listeners are given details of the time and newsreader in two consecutive simple utterances followed by a reference to *this evening* (l. 2, GEW) which reinforces the sense that the headlines have been updated specifically for this broadcast. The BBC1 (25 minutes) and Radio 1 (15 minutes) news slots are both considerably shorter than the hour-long Radio Wales programme, and this difference in time allocation is reflected in the overall approach of each broadcast.

All three programmes use linguistic signals to mark the end of the broadcast: *finally* (l. 13, GEW); *tonight's main news again* (l. 6, 9N); and *the top stories this lunch-time* (l. 7, NB). A summary of the main features follows, drawing attention to stories that have been given the most prominence. Both radio broadcasts also tell listeners what they can hear later. Radio Wales reminds listeners of the next news programme, linking the two broadcasts with a reference to one of the key stories on the five o'clock news (animal livestock exports). Radio 1, on the other hand, promotes music and features which will appear in the programme following *Newsbeat*. The two different approaches here indicate something about the kinds of audience each programme attracts: *Good Evening Wales* listeners are likely to be specifically interested in the news and therefore may wish to follow up any developments which occur later in the evening; Radio 1 listeners are likely to be more interested in music and popular culture, so rather than referring them to another news programme, the newsreader informs them of forthcoming features.

Social tokens often precede the closing title music. Both BBC1 and Radio Wales adopt formal phrases: *good night* (l. 8, 9N) and *good evening* (l. 18, GEW). The conclusion to the Radio Wales news actually brings the programme full circle since the phrase is used both as a social greeting and as a reiteration of the title at both the beginning and the end. Radio 1 has no social greeting, but reiterates the title of the programme. The newsreaders name themselves in both the radio broadcasts: *this is Patrick Hannan* (ll. 1, 17, GEW); *I'm Rod McKenzie* (ll. 14–15, NB). The television news can rely on the viewers recognising the presenter instead – written credit titles can also be used to label people where appropriate.

The **relationship** created between the target audience and the newsreader in each case is quite different. The use of first person plural pronouns and the informal contraction of *will* in Radio Wales' repetition of *we'll* (ll. 6–11) makes the institution less impersonal – the broadcasting company are given a human face and this makes the tone of the news as a whole more approachable. A similar effect is created in the *Newsbeat* bulletin: *we hear* (l. 11, NB). Radio Wales' negative command *don't forget* (l. 13, GEW) also contributes to the more personal relationship created between listener and broadcaster. The BBC1 news, however, remains more impersonal because it avoids all first person pronominal references – it provides a summary of the main stories and no more.

All three news programmes cover the **topic** of live animal exports – BBC1 and Radio Wales give it priority, while Radio 1 uses it as the second story. Both BBC1 and Radio Wales cover jobs and unemployment: the regional station relates it directly to Wales, while the national station focuses on Britain as a whole. Beyond this, the headlines summarise quite different news stories. The shorter news programmes inevitably carry fewer items. BBC1 ranks the Irish peace process as a main story and this is a reflection of the target audience who are interested in national political issues. Radio 1, on the other hand, takes a story that neither of the other programmes cover at all – the accident which brings the Eurostar train to a halt. By the news summary which concludes *Newsbeat*, the problem has in fact already been resolved – by the five o'clock and nine o'clock news bulletins therefore, it is no longer newsworthy. Radio Wales deals with the largest range of stories. Its headlines provide a detailed list of what is to come and the issues covered are very varied: politics; education; sport; economics. Equally, information is given about weather and travel, as appropriate to Wales.

The **prosodic features** are distinctive. The beginning and end of each utterance is usually marked by rising and falling intonation patterns. This ensures that the meaning is clear for viewers and listeners. Stress is far more frequent than it would be in informal conversation and it allows newsreaders to draw attention to key words. The Radio 1 bulletin is particularly marked by its stress patterns: the newsreader often stresses several consecutive words and this makes his delivery very emphatic and rhythmic. There are occasional pitch changes, but these are less frequent than in other spoken varieties. The tone adopted throughout is formal and serious, although news programmes will often end with a trivial or lighthearted story where time permits: *pepper the planets with pound coins* (ll. 3–4, NB). Because of this consistency of tone, changes in pitch, pace and volume are not common. Equally, headlines are usually prewritten, so although newsreaders may alter word order or adapt the script so that it sounds more spontaneous, ultimately they are delivering material which is quite inflexible. This also contributes to the even quality of the utterances.

Documentaries

Documentaries try to present real life in as **objective** a way as possible without fictionalising an issue or using professional actors. They focus on **facts** and attempt to provide useful information on a chosen subject. The **field** may be political, social, educational or cultural and the documentary makers will try to draw on as many sources of information as they can. **Contributors** may be ordinary members of the public or experts who can discuss an issue from an academic or practical point of view.

It is important to remember, however, that although a documentary may seem to be an objective presentation of the facts, the material has been **selected** and **presented** in order to promote a certain view of the subject. By omitting certain details or examples, by juxtaposing certain scenes or by inviting particular people to contribute, programmes can provide a subjective rather than an objective interpretation. Equally, **editing** of contributors' utterances or the framing of an image in a certain way can alter audience response. Voiceovers can add authority to the words spoken, encouraging viewers or listeners to agree; music can be used to engage the audience's emotions rather than their intellect; 'leading' questions can be asked, forcing interviewees to say things they did not really mean or did not wish to deal with; and speakers with non-standard accents and dialects may be presented as having a less valid viewpoint.

In order to identify any **bias** or underlying viewpoint, it is important to look closely at the lexical and grammatical choices and at the overall structure of a documentary. This kind of linguistic analysis will reveal the angle adopted by the programme, providing evidence to show whether the presentation of a particular topic is positive or negative. While the news aims to cover regional, national and international events in an objective way, documentaries aim to provide an interpretation of events which is inevitably subjective.

ACTIVITY 18.2

Read the following extract from a BBC2 documentary called 'Sex Acts' in the QED series, shown on 28 March 1994. The programme focuses on people who cross gender barriers either by undergoing operations which change or remove their sexual identity or by cross-dressing. Rachel O'Connor who appears in the extract below describes herself later in the programme as 'a biological man' who works as a man and lives as a woman. She discusses gender roles alongside Dr Gerda Siann, Reader in Psychology at Glasgow Caledonian University and Diane Torr, a performance artist who runs a 'Drag King for a Day' workshop in which women take on the persona of a man.

The production script from which this extract is taken shows how an apparently seamless programme is put together from lots of smaller units of language and image. Annotations mark new speakers, the kind of images selected and the way in which the spoken word is used. The following key explains the technical annotations marked on the extract.

Key

SYNC	the synchronisation of image and spoken word
V/O	the superimposition of a voice over an image when the actual speaker is not seen
WS	wide-range shot
MS	medium-range shot
CU	close-up
MCU	medium close-up
Freeze frame/aston CAPTION	printed title appearing at the bottom of the screen
ARCHIVE: BW video	pre-filmed footage inserted into documentary

Because this is an extract from a production script it uses the normal conventions of written language rather than those associated with transcripts of the spoken word.

As you read, jot down notes on the following:

1 the register;
2 the kind of people who contribute to the discussion;
3 the grammatical structures used by different speakers;

4   the overall structure of the extract;
5   the viewpoint(s) presented;
6   any distinctive features of formal or informal speech.

Extract from <u>QED</u> production script (Series Editor: Lorraine Heggessey)

1 MCU Rachel O'Connor in shopping mall Freeze 5 frame/aston CAPTION: Rachel O'Connor, Physicist 10	SYNC RACHEL O'CONNOR: Well I think most people go through a kind of schizo- phrenic situation where in the workplace they're one per- son and at home they're another person, you know. And it seems like when they go to work, because they've got this, this uniform that they're wearing for the workplace, they perform a certain ritual with other people that are wearing this uniform in the workplace. And so you get a whole kind of system set up whereby, you know, you're acting out a certain role, just because of that particular type of uniform that you're wearing, you know.
HA WS Hospital lobby in time lapse, tilt up and 15 pan L to MS 'Labour Ward' doors	V/O RACHEL O'CONNOR: I think gender is a sort of act that we have to live out. A sort of script that we have to perform and this sort of per- formance starts from a very early age. Even at the very start of our lives.
CU Dr Siann Freeze frame/aston 20 CAPTION: Dr Gerda Siann, Reader in Psychology, Glasgow Caledonian 25 University	V/O DR SIANN: . . . is it a boy or a girl. And often we start imputing things to them. So, for example, when a boy baby cries it can often be seen as anger and when a girl baby cries it seems distressed. And there's lots of evidence that even people who think that they're not doing things about gen- der and they're trying – and I'm not gonna have a, to make a little boy to be a little girl – they do actually treat boys and girls very differently in all sorts of ways.
ARCHIVE: BW video WS maternity ward 30	V/O DR SIANN: For example, one of the most interesting investigations was done in an American maternity home where they just simply taped what people said when they looked at newborn babies.
CU Dr Siann 35	SYNC DR SIANN: And if it was a boy people said, you know, oh you know he looks like a fighter or with girls they say things like lovely eyelashes. And I mean they drew attention to dif- ferent aspects of the baby's behaviour.
ARCHIVE: BW video, CU mother feeding newborn baby	V/O MOTHER: Oh what a beautiful little girl. Going to be a real heart- breaker when you grow up.

<table>
<tr><td>40</td><td>MS Diane Torr in dressing room</td><td>**SYNC DIANE TORR:**
Have you ever heard a baby who's 8 pounds yelling for its dinner, you know, starving? Their mouths are their stomachs. Their stomachs are their mouths, you know. And that baby who's 8 pounds has no comprehension of its gender. It doesn't know whether it's male or female.</td></tr>
</table>

	MS Diane Torr in dressing room	**SYNC DIANE TORR:**
40		Have you ever heard a baby who's 8 pounds yelling for its dinner, you know, starving? Their mouths are their stomachs. Their stomachs are their mouths, you know. And that baby who's 8 pounds has no comprehension of
45		its gender. It doesn't know whether it's male or female. All it knows is it's hungry and it wants food. Now how come that 8 pound baby gets to be 25 or 30 or whatever, and talks in a meek little voice like this? . . .
	MCU Naomi	**V/O DIANE TORR:**
50	2/S Sophie & Anna	We're talking about learned behaviour. Because that 8 pound baby . . .
	MS Diane in dressing room	. . . knows how to use voice with volume, you know. And gradually over the period of a lifetime, that female loses that capacity, or tones herself down. Repeatedly told at school, shut up, you know. A girl is uppity in the class, be
55		quiet. If a boy is uppity in class, he's the class clown and everybody applauds him. A girl is uppity, how dare she interfere, you know, you bossy bitch, sit down.

COMMENTARY

The **register** of this extract is typical of many documentaries. The **field**, of course, will be directly linked to the subject of each individual broadcast – in this extract the focus is on the roles of men and women in society and the ways in which gender affects their behaviour. Key lexical items are repeated to provide lexical cohesion: *gender* (l. 13), *boy* (l. 18), *girl* (l. 18), *male* (l. 44) and *female* (l. 44). The **mode** is clearly spoken and although contributors may have planned what they were going to say beforehand, their utterances are marked by the normal non-fluency features that are typical of informal conversation. The format of the documentary pre-defines the structure of turn-taking: each turn latches smoothly to the next and there are no adjacency pairs because the programme is not made up of the question-and-answer pattern of an interview. The **manner** is formal because the programme is targeted at a public audience who will be unknown to the participants. The range of contributors will provide an appropriate breadth of information on the topic of discussion – their relationship with the subject matter may be personal, academic or practical. By ensuring that a documentary is made up of speakers who develop the discussion in quite different ways, producers can target their programme at a mass audience. If an issue like 'gender roles' was approached exclusively from an academic standpoint, for instance, the programme would appeal to a more limited audience. The repetitions of *you know* (ll. 4, 9, 11) hesitations like *this, this uniform* (l. 6) and other features of informal conversation like *Well* (l. 2) and *And* (l. 4) in the initial position help to make the information conveyed more approachable. Viewers are encouraged to see the utterances as spontaneous and 'real' rather than theoretical and pre-planned.

The **speakers** are identified by name and professional role on a caption which is printed at the bottom of the screen on their first appearance. Rachel O'Connor is first seen in an ordinary background – a shopping centre. The caption which follows describes her as a physicist, thus identifying her professional scientific role. The juxtaposition of context and caption reinforces the programme's interest in challenging stereotypes: a stereotypically male environment (science) is placed in opposition with what many would call a stereotypically female environment (a shopping centre). This becomes symbolic of Rachel O'Connor's own dual role in which she is able to take the benefits of both male and female identities. Her contributions to the debate are personal because she talks from her own experiences.

This personal perspective is developed by the academic contributions of the university reader, Gerda Siann. Where O'Connor has discussed the issue from a personal standpoint, Siann talks theoretically about the concepts of male and female identity. He refers to investigations that have been undertaken to prove how we treat individuals differently from birth according to their gender. The debate is widened further by the fourth speaker, who runs day courses for women who want to experience what life is like for men. She therefore adds a practical dimension – showing women how men speak, move and relate to other people.

The four speakers in this extract are not engaged in a dialogue with each other, but their contributions are all linked thematically. Although there is no linguistic interaction between them, their comments have been edited so that these follow on logically. The contributors' different experiences and their different relationships with the issue of 'gender identity' provide the audience with a wide range of responses from which to establish their own standpoint.

The **structure** of the extract engages the audience on many layers. The juxtaposition of images and the spoken word, the organisation of speech turns and the distinctive grammatical patterns of each speaker all contribute to the overall effect of the documentary. Images are used to reinforce and develop the words that accompany them: shots of a mother feeding a newborn baby and a Labour Ward door run alongside Siann's discussion of the ways in which we behave differently towards male and female babies. The editing process ensures that each new speaker latches smoothly onto the end of the previous turn: Rachel O'Connor ends her turn by talking about the 'performance' society expects males and females to act out from birth and Gerda Siann immediately begins his discussion about society's gender expectations of babies.

The **grammatical structures** of the speakers are typical of spoken language. Despite the fact that the manner is formal their speech is marked by the features of informal conversation. Clauses are often long and complex with several embedded subordinate clauses – spoken language tends to be loosely structured unlike the tighter structures associated with the written word, which can be redrafted and polished.

A
(And) (it seems like) (when they go to work), (because they've got this, this
conj   ComCl   SCl–ACl   SCl–ACl

A   S   P
uniform that they're wearing for the workplace), (they) (perform) (a certain ritual
     SCl–RelCl

O
with other people that are wearing this uniform in the workplace). (ll. 4–8)
                SCl–RelCl

An utterance like this is typical of spoken language: it starts with the co-ordinating conjunction *And*; it uses *it seems like* as a comment clause which is typical of informal speech; it is marked by repetitions like *this, this*; it has contractions like *they're* (l. 4); and the structure is looser than a written sentence. Where there are simple sentences, they tend to be used rhetorically to create dramatic effect.

S   P   C   S   P   C
(Their mouths) (are) (their stomachs). (Their stomachs) (are) (their mouths) . . .
                                                                    (ll. 41–2)

Many utterances are grammatically incomplete, but this does not affect understanding – we are accustomed to hearing disjointed structures in spontaneous speech.

           A
(Even at the very start of our lives). (ll. 15–16)

This utterance relates directly to the previous one in which O'Connor talks about the stage at which a 'gender act' begins. It adds new information to the earlier adverbial: *from a very early age* (l. 15). Although it is spoken as if it is a distinct grammatical utterance, listeners recognise it as a development of the more general noun phrase:

  m   m   h
a (very early) age
det Adv   Adj   N

At other times, speakers actually imitate informal conversation to prove a point and inevitably, grammatical structures then tend to be incomplete.

  S   P   C   A
($\varnothing$) ($\varnothing$ Going to be) (a real heartbreaker) (when you grow up). (ll. 37–8)
                                                        SCl-ACl

The omission of a subject pronoun and the verb auxiliary *are* here does not create comprehension problems because listeners are accustomed to shortened forms like this occurring in spoken discourse.

The **viewpoints** presented in this extract persuade viewers to recognise the way in which society influences both males and females from a very early age. Rachel O'Connor speaks from her own personal experiences both in an occupational and social context. By working as a man, she believes that she can earn more money than a woman can because of society's prejudices; by living as a woman outside the work environment, she believes that she can enjoy closer relationships with others. She sees the 'gender training' which distinguishes men and women in this way as starting from birth. A similar view is developed in the academic perspective of Dr Siann. He quotes from research that proves on a larger scale what O'Connor has found in her own life – that boys and girls are treated differently from birth. Diane Torr as a performance artist deals with the issue in a more physical way. Her observations of men show women the ways in which society has taught them to be different – to speak mildly, to act submissively and to accept that men are dominant. She believes that male and female babies are the same until society has taught them the gender role that they are expected to fill.

Each viewpoint here adopts a different perspective on the issue of gender roles. The speakers do not address the issue in the same way, nor do they explicitly develop each other's arguments. Nevertheless, they all have one thing in common – each argument places babies and society's gender expectations at the centre of the debate. This enables the broadcasters to convey a convincing argument because viewers are presented with a range of perspectives which ultimately converge. The end result is therefore persuasive.

Documentaries combine the features of **formal** and **informal spoken language** interestingly. The context is formal because of the public nature of the transmission, and in many ways the extract resembles a kind of public lecture. Abstract nouns like *gender* (l. 13), *investigations* (l. 27) and *comprehension* (l. 43) are typical of a theoretical consideration of an issue. Equally, the persuasive approach of the documentary is reinforced by rhetorical features like parallelism: *if it was a boy...with girls* (ll. 32–3) and *Their mouths are their stomachs. Their stomachs are their mouths* (ll. 41–2); and juxtaposition: *male* and *female* (l. 44), *workplace* (l. 3) and *home* (l. 4). The use of metaphorical language is also typical of formal spoken language, where concrete images are used to make abstract issues more accessible. In this extract, the metaphor of *uniform* (l. 6) is used to explain the idea that we all adopt different roles depending upon our context. This is pushed further by the metaphor of acting, which literally describes the process of adopting roles: *acting out* (l. 10), *script* (l. 14), *perform* (l. 7) and *performance* (ll. 14–15).

Alongside these characteristics of formal speech, however, there are many features that are more typical of informal spoken language. Features commonly associated with spontaneous spoken language occur in the utterances of all the speakers: the adverb *Well* (l. 2) is often used to provide thinking time at the beginning of an utterance; comment clauses like *you know* (l. 4) occur frequently; *And* (l. 4) occurs in the initial position; and there are false starts. Interestingly, however, there are no voiced hesitations, although these occur frequently in speech. Because a documentary is created from edited statements and images, the producers can polish the end product even when particular contributors are unaccustomed to speaking in public. This means that although the speech may seem spontaneous, it is very different from everyday interaction in which the spoken words cannot be recalled and redrafted.

The **function** of a documentary is to educate, inform or enlighten. Because the information is conveyed through a medium that is commonly associated with entertainment, however, documentaries are quite unlike academic lectures. Rather than targeting an expert audience, they aim to appeal to a wide range of people. The mix of expert and ordinary viewpoints means that they do not alienate viewers. By balancing facts and theories with the experiences of ordinary people, programme makers engage their audiences and make abstract issues more approachable.

Drama

While documentaries aim to discuss the 'truth' of real issues, radio and television dramas **dramatise** life, considering the possible consequences of real events in a fictional context. Some dramas aim to be realistic, portraying life as it really is; others create an obviously fictional version of reality in which characters, places and events are sanitised.

The use of **sets** and **locations** gives a concrete background to the fictional world created, helping to establish both the characters and the audience as part of a reality which runs parallel to real life. In television drama, characters rarely address the camera or the audience directly and this reinforces our sense that the fiction is real rather than something created. Dramas, just like documentaries, are presented to their audiences as a seamless whole in which there is no evidence of the way the end result has been achieved. The world created, however, is **manipulated** – in both television and radio drama, volume levels are adjusted so that audiences never really hear sounds or speech in the distance; shots and scenes are edited smoothly so that the audience is unaware of the movement from one to another; cameras and microphones move so that the audience becomes omniscient, seeing and hearing things that would be impossible to see or hear in a real context.

A general knowledge of the ways in which television and radio drama manipulate their audiences is useful in assessing the 'reality' of an extract. As well as the **spoken language**, it is important to consider the kinds of **shots** or **sound effects** that accompany the spoken word and the ways in which the end product is created from a wide range of **visual** and **aural source material**.

The kind of **speech** used will depend directly upon the geographical location, the historical period, the cultural and social background of individual characters and the function of the communication. Like speakers in real life, fictional characters will have a range of repertoires and they will vary their speech according to their audience, purpose and context. Where characters do not, the results will often be comic. **Prosodic features** are often exaggerated so that audiences recognise the mood and attitude of speakers.

There are three main types of television and radio drama: single plays, series, and serials.

Single plays

These often have transmission times of more than an hour and are self-contained. They tend to be associated with serious art: *Play for Today* (BBC1); Radio 3 presentations of traditional and modern classic plays.

Series

These have a recurring set of characters and are usually set in the same location over a number of episodes, but each episode is based on a different story: *A Touch of Frost* (ITV); *Cracker* (ITV).

Serials

These have continuity of action, characters and location, with stories that run from episode to episode. Episodes often end with a cliffhanger to encourage viewers to watch the next transmission. Both dramatisations of classic novels and soap operas fall into this category. *Martin Chuzzlewit* (BBC1); *Coronation Street* (ITV); *The Archers* (BBC Radio 4).

ACTIVITY 18.3

A transmission script records camera shots, sound effects and facial expressions, as well as the actual words to be spoken. The extract that follows is taken from the transmission script for Episode 9 of <u>Peak Practice</u> (ITV), 'A Normal Life', broadcast on 4 April 1995.

Read through the text and jot down notes in response to the following questions:

1   What technical information does the transmission script provide?
2   Will an audience be aware of the technical processes in the polished end product?
3   How will the written descriptions of character and setting be conveyed to the audience in the televised version?
4   Does the written description have any advantages over the sequence of images it will become on television? Which is more effective?
5   How realistic is the dialogue?
6   What will the dialogue gain by being spoken aloud rather than read?

Key
EXT   exterior shot.   INT   interior shot

Extract from the opening of Episode 9 of <u>Peak Practice</u> (Scriptwriter: Michael Jenner; Producer: Ted Childs)

1   <u>SCENE 1: EXT. SHEARER'S HOUSE (GARDEN) / NIGHT 1</u>
    Night. The house is in darkness. The only light is from a cloudless, star infested sky. Under the opening credits we are focused on a small garden. We become aware of movement. A figure, ROY SHEARER (40s), dressed
5   solely in pyjama bottoms, passes. He stops. For a few moments nothing

happens. We move to focus on ROY's face. He's now at that blurred moment of waking after sleepwalking. There's no great reaction, just a flicker of confusion, of trying to find his bearings. After a moment he lets out the very faintest of anguished groans.

10   CUT TO:

SCENE 2: EXT. HILL (OVERLOOKING CARDALE SEC SCHOOL) / DAY 2
A view overlooking Cardale Secondary School.

                                                CUT TO:

SCENE 3: INT. CARDALE SECONDARY SCHOOL (CLASSROOM) / DAY 2

15   Within a classroom an English Language lesson is in progress for a class of fourteen year olds. The teacher is ROY SHEARER. He listens as one of the pupils, FIONA CRAMPTON, reads from Shakespeare's 'Romeo and Juliet'. FIONA is making a mockery of the language.

                                                FIONA
20   *'Come, night! Come, Romeo! Come, thou day in night!'*
                                               SHEARER
        Fiona, Juliet is a fourteen year old girl. This is her first experience of love. Of boys. Surely that's something you can relate to?
Another girl, MANDY STEWART, pipes up.
25   MANDY
        Fiona did all her 'relating' last summer hols. Sir. Down the Rec. With Kevin Armfield.
The class roar with laughter.
                                               SHEARER
30   What I'm suggesting, Fiona, is that Juliet would infuse her words with a mite more feeling. She's not reading out the ingredients from a bottle of brown sauce.
                                                FIONA
        If she's fourteen, how old's Romeo then?
35   SHEARER
        Convention has it that Romeo is in his early to mid-twenties.
                                                MANDY
        What. . . ? And he's going out with a girl our age?
                                                FIONA
40   Round here we'd call 'im a cradle-snatcher.
The class spots a chance for sport and goad the girls on.
                                                MANDY
        My dad'd kill me if I came home with a bloke that age. He'd say he were only after one thing.
45   SHEARER
        Okay, okay, you've had your fun.
                                                FIONA
        No wonder the Capulets are pissed off, Sir. Romeo's a right perv.
The class roar. SHEARER is struggling to regain control.
50   SHEARER
        That's enough. Quieten down.
The class reluctantly subsides.
                                               SHEARER
        Josie Davies. Carry on reading. Top of the page, please.
55   For the first time we see JOSIE DAVIES. She's the same age as her class-

mates but diminutive, less mature. She reads perfectly, albeit quietly, without display.

JOSIE

'Give me my Romeo: and, when I shall die,
60 *Take him and cut him out in little stars,*
And he will make the face of heaven
so fine that all the world will be in love
with night and pay no worship to the
garnish sun. Oh, I have brought the
65 *mansion of a love. . .'*

SHEARER's regained control. He closes his eyes. FIONA clocks the evidence of SHEARER's favouritism.

CUT TO:

SCENE 3A: INT. SCHOOL (LOCKER ROOM) / DAY 2
70 Lunch time. JOSIE's by her locker collecting her possessions together into her satchel. FIONA and MANDY arrive looking for trouble.

MANDY

Hey, swot. Got enough room in yer bag for all yer homework?

FIONA

75 Still got room for these though.
FIONA deposits a pack of three condoms into JOSIE's bag.

FIONA (CONT)

Never know when they're going to come in handy.

JOSIE

80 One track mind, you.
JOSIE takes the condoms, she hurls them across the floor.

MANDY

Ooh, temper, temper.

FIONA

85 They were a present. You don't go chucking pressies away.
FIONA throws JOSIE up against the locker. JOSIE's hurt and falls to the floor; she's close to tears.

FIONA

Ooh, did that hurt?

90 MANDY

Need somebody to kiss it better?

FIONA

Romeo, Romeo, where for art thou, Romeo? Where's yer boyfriend now, eh?
FIONA kicks JOSIE's satchel out of her reach. JOSIE curls herself up into a ball anti-
95 cipating further attacks.

COMMENTARY

The script clearly marks **technical information** by capitalising the scene number, the location and the chronological time sequence for each section. It uses subject specific phrases like *CUT TO* (l. 10) as an indication of the points at which editing will take place. A production script, annotated with far more technical information about camera angles, the focus and range of shots and sound effects, would be used alongside this transmission script.

Because the film footage is **edited**, viewers see no evidence of the units in which it will have been filmed. Individual scenes fade into each other in a polished and seamless whole and this reinforces the sense that television drama is 'real'. The audience are presented with a community, its local inhabitants and a sequence of events as though these are authentic. During transmission, viewers immerse themselves in the fictional world, forgetting that the camera is allowing them to be 'all-seeing' and 'all-knowing' in a way that would be impossible in real life.

The **written descriptions** of character and place at the beginning of the transmission script are very detailed. They create a dramatic atmosphere through their attention to detail. The noun phrases are complex, using language emotively to engage the reader. Descriptions of the environment give the setting a concrete background.

> m   m   m   h   m   m   h
> a cloudless, (star infested) sky (ll. 2–3)   a small garden (l. 3)
> det   Adj   N   V   N   det   Adj   N

The character of Roy Shearer is also portrayed in detail. Post-modification is used to convey both his physical appearance and his state of mind.

> m   h   q
> a figure. . .dressed solely in pyjama bottoms (ll. 4–5)
> det N   NFCl

> m   h   q   q
> a flicker of confusion, of trying to find his bearings (ll. 7–8)
> det N   PrepP   PrepP   NFCl

Other descriptions are more factual, giving a background to the scene that is about to take place: prepositional phrases like *within a classroom* (l. 15) and *by her locker* (l. 70); noun phrases like *lunch time* (l. 70). When the camera focuses on another key character, Josie Davies, further details are provided.

> S   P   C   C   C
> (She) ('s) (the same age as her classmates) (but) (diminutive), (less mature).
>   conj
>
> (ll. 55–6)

In the televised version, all this information is conveyed through **images**. Camera angles and the physical appearance of actors replace the verbal descriptions seen in the transmission script. In order to notice all the details provided in the written directions, viewers would have to be very observant – descriptions of Roy's face, for instance, would be translated into the focus of a camera shot.

Images and the written word demand different things of their intended audience and are therefore **effective** in different ways. Images are immediately accessible and the eye can interpret them very quickly; the printed word, on the other hand, has to be read and this can take time. While a written description can draw attention to many things, a viewer may not notice a particular facial expression or an important item in a room embedded within a sequence of images. Descriptive or metaphorical use of language can be matched by technical codes like the camera angle, the depth of focus or a symbolic use of colour. Viewers, however, will not necessarily recognise these as part of the way that meaning is conveyed. Above all, the written word can be reread whereas an image may be gone before the viewer has recognised its significance.

The **dialogue** aims to imitate real classroom interaction by adopting the features of spoken language. Verbal contractions are common in both formal and informal spoken language and are therefore appropriate in this context: *that's* (l. 23); *old's* (l. 34); *dad'd* (l. 43). Minor sentences like *Of boys* (l. 23) and *One track mind, you* (l. 80) reflect the looser structure of spoken language. The teacher's language is more formal than that of his pupils. While they use slang like *bloke* (l. 43), *pissed off* (l. 48), *a right perv* (l. 48) and *swot* (l. 73) and abbreviations like *hols* (l. 26), *Rec* (l. 26) and *pressies* (l. 85), the teacher uses verbs like *infuse* (l. 30) and collocations like *Convention has it...* (l. 36). Non-standard dialect is seen only once when a subject and verb do not agree – *he were* (l. 43). In a classroom context, many pupils will modify their language, using structures associated with SE rather than the local dialect.

In a real classroom situation, **interaction** would probably be far less orderly with pupils talking at once and interrupting each other. In order to make communication clear, however, televised drama structures speech acts so that latching on is smooth. This prevents the meaning of utterances being lost. Although there may be background noise like the class goading the girls on (l. 41), meaningful utterances that further the development of the story are always clear. This is not really realistic and emphasises the fact that drama is basically an orderly written form of spoken language.

The transmission script has been written to be **read aloud**. Actors animate the words and their accompanying actions add extra layers of meaning to the written text. Prosodic features also enhance the meaning conveyed by the words – changes in volume, pitch, pace and intonation bring characters and events to life. In places, the written script attempts to mirror pronunciation by using non-standard spelling of words like *'im* (l. 40) and *yer* (l. 93), but most of the variations will be introduced as individual actors develop their particular roles. Accents will reflect the local pronunciations and idiosyncratic features will make characters distinctive in a way that the words on the page cannot.

ACTIVITY 18.4

The following transcript is an extract from the Radio 4 soap The Archers, broadcast on 17 April 1995. It records a conversation between Jennifer Aldridge (JA) and Richard Locke (RL), the local doctor, about Jennifer's daughter Kate.

Read the transcript and jot down notes on the following:

1   the relationship between the speakers;
2   the way in which the two speakers interact;
3   the prosodic features;
4   the difference between a transmission script and a transcription.

A key to the symbols used can be found on page 86.

Transcript from an episode of The Archers (Scriptwriter: Mary Cutler; Programme Editor: Vanessa Whitburn)

1	JA	everyone in this house seems to be having a <u>wild</u> social life at the moment except mè =
	RL	= h° (.) Kate out is she =
	JA	= well she was last night °h consequently she's still in ‖ bèd
5	RL	‖ ahh I don't know (.) what ↑it is to be young↑ and have no responsìbilities =
	JA	= yes (2) Richard (2) I know you suggested I made an appointment to see you but h° er but now you're hére (.) if if you've got five minutes er er I mean h° i. it was advice about Kate that I
10		wanted (2)
	RL	go on thèn (.) <u>spit</u> it out (.) I can see something's worrying yòu =
	JA	= the thing is (.) you see h° er well (1) she's been smoking cannabis (2)
	RL	àh =

15	JA	= you're not surprised =
	RL	= h° (.) I'm afraid it is fairly <u>common</u> for her age group =
	JA	= you don't think I should be worried about it (1)
	RL	well (1) I don't think it's a <u>good</u> idea for her to take <u>drugs</u> (.)
		Jennifer (.) no (.) n. it's <u>illegal</u> after all (.) oh she's not doing it all
20		the time =
	JA	= no (.) I was very ↑angry↑ with her and I I told her not to smoke it
		in the house =
'accel'	RL	= mm (.) is she 'mixing it with alcohol' =
	JA	= h° she doesn't really drink at all =
25	RL	= well that's good (.) mixing it can be dangerous (2)
'piano'	JA	'oh God' h° =
	RL	= look (.) I'll have a word with her if you like =
	JA	= <u>no</u> (.) <u>no</u> Richard (.) no thank you I don't want a fuss (1) I'm
		afraid she'll <u>go</u> again you see if we say too much =
30 'accel'	RL	= you '<u>must</u> ↑talk to her <u>again</u>↑ Jennifer' (2) or let me have a word
		(1) it some times <u>helps</u> you see (.) because I can talk from a health
		point of view and not be appearing to take the moral <u>high ground</u> =
	JA	= I know Richard it's just m. h° =
	RL	= what (1)
35	JA	I don't want her to <u>leave</u> again

COMMENTARY

The transcript records an informal conversation between two people who are known to each other. Their **relationship** is established in the way that they refer to each other. Rather than using formal titles like *Mrs* or *Doctor*, they use forenames: *Jennifer* (l. 19) and *Richard* (l. 7). There are several examples of informal language too: utterances starting with *well* (l. 4); colloquial phrases like *the thing is...* (l. 12); high frequency clauses like *you see* (l. 12); and the collocation *spit it out* (l. 11).

Although Richard is the local doctor, he is visiting as a friend of the family rather than in his professional role – the topics of conversation are therefore personal. They first talk about the family in general, but then about Kate in particular. In the latter part of the conversation, however, Richard's roles as friend and doctor are not distinct. He offers advice both on a professional and personal level.

Neither speaker seems dominant in the **interaction**. They are talking in an informal environment (Jennifer's home) and take it in turns to lead the turn-taking. The tone at the beginning is light-hearted: the topic is introduced by Jennifer and Richard develops it by adopting a tongue-in-cheek tone. It is Jennifer who then changes the topic and mood of the conversation (l. 7). Although she has answered Richard's indirect question (l. 6), her pause suggests that she is about to introduce a more serious topic. This is prefaced by the vocative *Richard*, which also marks an imminent change in direction. The contrastive conjunction *but* (l. 8) and the loose structure of the utterance reinforces the audience's sense that Jennifer is trying to introduce a new topic.

	S	P		O	
(Richard)	(I)	(know)	(you suggested I made an appointment to see you)	(but)
vocative		SCl–NCl	SCl–NCl	SCl–NFCl	conj

A	S	P	A	A	S	P	dumS	P	O
(now)	(you)	('re)	(here)	(if you've got five minutes)	(I)	(mean)	(it)	(was)	(advice
				SCl–ACl					

about Kate) (that) (I) (wanted) (ll. 7–10)
(S) (P)
rel pron

The informal structure of the beginning is replaced by the more formal organisation of question and answer associated with adjacency pairs when the topic changes. Jennifer's first questions (ll. 15, 17) are marked by a rising intonation rather than by inversion of the word order – they reflect her need for reassurance from Richard. Richard's question (l. 23), on the other hand, reflects his medical knowledge of cannabis – he is trying to establish the facts.

Unlike real informal conversation, there is only one example of speaker turns overlapping: Richard makes a humorous comment based on a clichéd view of young people (ll. 5–6). Other than this, most turns latch smoothly onto the end of the previous speaker's words. At the end of some turns, there is a pause. Many of the pauses occur because Jennifer hesitates at the end of her turn and Richard waits for her to continue (ll. 10–11, 13–14). Others occur as Richard takes stock of the situation before replying (ll. 17–18) and as Richard's warning about the dangers of mixing cannabis and alcohol sinks in (ll. 25–6).

The turns reflect their equality in the situation. Even though Jennifer is asking for Richard's advice as a doctor, the register is informal because the discourse takes place in an informal context and because Richard is offering advice as a friend.

The **prosodic features** quite closely resemble those found in informal spoken language. Changes in intonation mark questions (ll. 15, 17); the grammatical end of utterances (ll. 4, 22); and add emphasis to key words. Stress is used to draw attention to lexical items that are important semantically: _common_ (l. 16); _must_ (l. 30); _drugs_ (l. 18). Richard uses changes in pitch to make sure that his comment about the young is seen as stereotypical: _what ↑it is to be young↑_ (l. 6); and to convey a sense of urgency to Jennifer: _you must ↑talk to her again↑_ (l. 30). He also changes his pace to emphasise what is serious: 'accel' (ll. 23, 30). Jennifer speaks quietly to reflect her horror at the thought of the dangers Kate could be facing: 'piano' (l. 26).

Normal non-fluency features appear in all kinds of spoken language. Few speakers can sustain a turn without hesitation of some kind. In this transcription, however, only Jennifer's speech is marked by non-fluency. On several occasions she uses voiced hesitations like _er_ (ll. 8, 12) and this reflects her tentative approach to introducing Kate as a topic of conversation. Her concern for her daughter is seen in repetitions of words like _I I_ (l. 21) and _if if_ (l. 8) and in incomplete words like _i._ (l. 9) and _m._ (l. 33). The number of sighs marked _h°_ is also indicative of her worry. Richard's lack of normal non-fluency features reminds the listener that this is not real conversation, but something that has been scripted and spoken aloud.

All of the prosodic features are linked to the meaning speakers wish to communicate: they reinforce and highlight the attitudes and moods of the speakers. The techniques used by the actors in this extract bring the written text to life. By adding personal touches to the written word, they make the interaction more real.

While a **transmission script** records the written text and the scene cuts, a **transcription** aims to record the way in which the words are delivered. It adds the extra information which shows how the written script is made into a spoken interaction. The addition of the prosodic features to the text marks how individual actors interpret their roles – normal non-fluency features and changes in pitch, pace, volume and intonation reinforce the meaning of the words spoken and bring the fictional world to life.

Comedy

Both television and radio broadcasting schedules contain many comedy programmes because these are popular: they often appear at peak transmission times, and attract large audiences. There are four main types of comedy.

Situation comedies

Situation comedies aim to mirror real life in a way that reveals something about the context. They attempt to explore and shed light on specific kinds of experience through humour. The characters are supposed to have their roots in reality, even if they are larger than life in some way. Many situation comedies, however, do little more than present the viewer with tightly constructed plots, predictable twists and neat endings. The main focus is no longer to reveal something of significance about real life, but to develop a parallel world in which character and plot are more important than social insight.

Situation comedies take stock situations and stock characters and build an appropriate environment around them. Recent examples can be seen in:

- men living alone in a 'bachelor' flat: *Men Behaving Badly*;
- young woman marries older man: *May to December*;
- old people shown to be vivacious, sexually active and adventurous: *Waiting for God*;
- an inversion of mother/child roles and a send-up of the PR and fashion worlds: *Absolutely Fabulous*.

In each of these, stereotypical characters interact with one another in one or two core settings. Such programmes entertain their viewers – they develop characters who are likeable despite their flaws. They do not usually reveal anything significant about the context in which they are set (bachelor flat; family home and legal office; old people's home; domestic and social environments). Some situation comedies, however, do still manage to make characters and settings amusing and simultaneously suggest something about the nature of life in a particular context. The four series of *Blackadder*, for instance, have been researched by the writers so that key period details and references are embedded in the fictional world that is created. In the series, *Blackadder Goes Forth*, the focus is on World War I. Despite the fact that it treats life in the trenches and the absurdity of many of the commands given humorously, it also reveals something about the nature of war itself. The series works on two levels: it both entertains and provides social insight.

Surrealistic comedies

Surrealistic comedy uses the traditions of absurd humour. It challenges social conformity by ridiculing things that society values. Programmes like *Monty Python* and parts of the *All New Alexei Sayle Show* on television and the *Goon Show* and *I'm Sorry I'll Read That Again* on the radio use language in ways that defy audience expectations. This kind of comedy is interested in chance happenings and the power of the unconscious. Some situation comedies, like *Fawlty Towers* and *The Rise and Fall of Reginald Perrin*, contain strands of surrealist humour.

Stand-up comedy

Stand-up comedians rely on a sequence of narrated anecdotes and jokes to entertain their audience. Their stories will often be based on close observations of things which will be familiar to many people. A comedian like Ben Elton describes overflowing kitchen bins with great attention to detail; he mocks the stereotyping on which advertising is based; and reveals the realities of sex which society prefers to gloss over. Lenny Henry creates characters like Theophilus P. Wildebeest and Delbert Wilkins who are based in reality even if features of their personality are exaggerated for comic effect. Jo Brand discusses issues of femininity, challenging society's preconceptions of male and female gender roles. The comedy lies in the fact that everybody can identify with the observations made – the comedians speak what otherwise remains unspoken. The content is comic not so much because it is outrageous as because it is taboo or so ordinary that it is taken for granted.

When stand-up comedians have television shows, their stand-up routine is often interspersed with sketches. These may develop the roles of characters created for stand-up comedy or may dramatise the kinds of social observations made in a stand-up routine. Comedians on television will often work in pairs so that the contrast in personalities creates comedy as well as the material and delivery: *French and Saunders, A Bit of Fry and Laurie* and *Alas Smith and Jones*.

Star turns and variety

Star turns and **variety acts** tend to appeal to a wider audience. Traditional jokes about 'mothers-in-law' and 'her indoors' constitute safe material because they have been tried and tested. Unlike the 'alternative' stand-up comedians, this kind of comedy will often use music and dance as well as spoken language to entertain the audience. Where stand-up comics often provide social insight alongside their comic observations, star turns and variety acts tend to offer pure entertainment.

ACTIVITY 18.5

The following transcription records part of an episode in the third series of <u>Blackadder</u> (BBC) which focuses on Dr Samuel Johnson's dictionary. In the extract, Dr Johnson asks the Prince Regent to be the patron of his book – the interaction between Prince George, Dr Johnson and the butler Edmund Blackadder results in both visual and linguistic comedy.

Read through the following selective transcription and discuss the techniques used to create comedy. A key to the symbols can be found on page 86.

Key to participants

PG   Prince George   EB   Edmund Blackadder   DJ   Dr Samuel Johnson

Transcription from 'Ink and Incapability', an episode of <u>Blackadder</u> (Scriptwriters: Richard Curtis and Ben Elton; Producer John Lloyd)

1	PG:	énter (2)
	EB:	Dr Jóhnson (.) Your Highness =
	PG:	= ah (.) Dr Johnson (.) damned cold dày =
	DJ:	= indeed it is sir but a very fine òne (.) for I celebrated last night (.)
5		the encyclopaedic implementation (.) of my pre<u>medi</u>tated orches-
'rall'		<u>tra</u>tion (.) of demotic 'Anglo-↑<u>Saxon</u>↑' (3)
	PG:	nope (.) didn't catch àny of that (1)
'accel'	DJ:	well I just simply observed 'that I am felicitous' (1) since during the
		course of the penultimate solar <u>so</u>journ (.) I terminated my uninter-

10 'rall' rupted <u>categori</u>sation (.) of the vocabulary of our 'Po<u>st</u>-Nor̀man (.) ↓tongue↓' (2)

'accel' PG: I don't know 'what you're talking about' (.) but it sounds damn ↑<u>saucy</u>↑ (.) you lucky thing (.) I know some <u>fairly</u> <u>lib</u>erally minded girls but I've never <u>penultimated</u> any of them in the <u>so</u>lar sòjourn

15 (1) or for that matter been given any <u>Nor</u>man tóngue (4)

'rall' EB: I bèlieve sir (.) that the Doctor 'is trying to tell you that he is happy' because he has ↑<u>finished</u>↑ his book (.) it has ↑apparently↑ taken him (.) ten ↓<u>years</u>↓ =

PG: = yes well I'm a slow reader mysèlf (3)

20 'accel' DJ: here it is sir (.) 'the very <u>cor</u>nerstone of English scholarship' (.) this
'rall' book sir (.) contains '<u>every</u> <u>word</u> (.) in our be<u>lov</u>ed lànguage' =

PG: = mm =

EB: = every single one ↑sír↑ =

DJ: = every single ↑one↑ ↓sìr↓ =

25 EB: = òh in that case sir (.) I hope you will not object if I <u>al</u>so offer the Doctor my most ↑enthusiastic↑ (.) ↓contrafibulàrities↓ (4)

DJ: what =

EB: = contrafibulárities ↑sir↑ it is a common word (.) down our wày =

DJ: = dàmn (3)

30 'stacc' EB: oh I'm sorry sir (.) I'm 'anaspèptic (.) frasmòtic (1) even ↑compúnctuous↑' to have caused you such ↓pericombobulàtion↓ (1)

DJ: what what ↑whát↑ =

PG: = what <u>are</u> you on about Blackadder (.) this is all beginning to

35 sound a bit like dàgo talk to me (2)

EB: I'm sòrry sir (.) I merely wished to cong<u>ra</u>tulate the Doctor on not
'rall' having left out 'a ↑<u>single</u>↑ ↓word↓' (2) shall I fetch the tea Your Highness =

PG: = er yes (.) yes and and get that <u>damned</u> <u>fire</u> up here wíll you =

40 EB: = certainly sir (.) I shall return (1) interfràstically (3)

'accel' PG: 'so Doctor Johnson' (1) sit you down (.) <u>now</u> this book of yours (.) <u>tell</u> me (.) what's it all about =

DJ: = it is a book (.) about the English lànguage sir =

PG: = I <u>see</u> and the hero's name is whát (2)

45 DJ: there's no hèro sir =

PG: = no ↑hérò↑ (1) well lucky I reminded you (.) better put one in pronto (.) um call him Geòrge (.) George is a good name for a hèro (.) um now what about hèroines =

DJ: = there is <u>no</u> heroine sir (.) unless it is our <u>mo</u>ther tòngue =

50 PG: = er the <u>mo</u>ther's the heroine (.) nice t<u>wist</u> (.) so how far have we got thèn (.) old Mother Tongue (.) is in love with <u>Geòrge</u> the hero (.) now what about mùrders (.) Mother Tongue doesn't get mur-dered does she ́ =

DJ: = no she <u>does</u>n't (.) no one gets múrdered <u>or</u> maìmed <u>or</u> in a tricky

55 situation over over a <u>pound</u> ↑nòte↑ (2)

PG: well <u>now</u> look Doctor Jóhnson (.) I may be as <u>thick</u> as a <u>whale</u>

		ọmelette (.) but even Í know (.) a book's got to have a plòt =
	DJ:	= not this one sir (.) it is a book that tells you what English words mèan (1)
60	PG:	I knòw what English words mèan (.) I speak English (.) you must be a bit of a thìcko (2)
	DJ:	perhaps you would rather not ↑be↑ patron of my book if you can see no value in it whàtsoever ‖ sir
	PG:	‖ well perhaps so sìr (.) as it sounds
65		to me as if my being patron of this complete ↑cowpat↑ of a book (.) will set the seàl once and for àll on my reputàtion as an utter tùrnip-head =
	DJ:	= well well it is a reputation well desèrved sir (.) fare wèll (4)
	EB:	leaving already Dóctor (.) not staying for your (.) pendagestatory
70		interlùdicure (3)
	DJ:	no sir (.) show me out =
	EB:	= certainly sir (.) anything I can do to (.) facilìtate your velocitous excommuniarisàtion (1)
	DJ:	you will regret this doùbly sir (.) huh not only have you impecu-
75		liarated huh my díctionary (.) but you have also lost the chance to act as patron (.) to the only book in the world that is evèn bètter =
'rall'	EB:	= óh (.) and what is that sir (.) 'Díctionary twó (.) the Return (.) of the Killer Dictìonary' (2)
'accel'	DJ:	no sir (.) it is (.) 'Edmund: a Butler's Tàle' (.) (*indistinct*) a huge
80 'rall'		roller-coaster of a novel crammed with sizzling ↓gypsies↓ (.) 'had you sùpported it sir' (.) it would have made you and me and Gertrude míllionaires =
	EB:	= ↑míllionaires↑ =
	DJ:	= but it was not to bé sir (.) fare yóu wèll I shall not return

COMMENTARY

Because *Blackadder* is broadcast on television, much of the comedy results from visual images: facial expressions; gestures; actions. Nevertheless, the extract here is concerned with the nature of language and defining language, and this means that much of the comedy is based on the words used by the characters.

Some words and phrases are used to create a **sense of period**, but they result in a stereotypical rather than a real representation of the language of the time. Comedy arises from the repetition of the words *damn* or *damned* used as a modifier which inten- sifies meaning in phrases like *damn saucy* (ll. 12–13), *damned cold day* (l. 3) and *damned fire* (l. 39). The writers are not suggesting that its usage here is historically accurate, but because it is often associated with stereotypical presentations of aristo- crats, the result is humorous. Similarly, inverted word orders like *fare you well* (l. 84) and *sit you down* (l. 41) create a form of language that is recognisably different to con- temporary English. They are humorous because they are not typical of the speech in the extract as a whole – the usage is self-conscious, drawing attention to the nature of the language in a comic way.

In some places, **contemporary lexis** is used to create comedy in a similar way. References to nouns like *roller-coaster* (l. 80) and *millionaires* (l. 82) are clearly anachronistic since they refer to things that would not have existed in the period covered by 'Ink and Incapability'. An adjective like *thick* (l. 56) and a noun like *thicko* (l. 61) with their connotations of stupidity are also more relevant to language use today than in the reign of George III. Other examples are humorous because they are associated with informal usage – adverbs like *pronto* (l. 47) and *nope* (l. 7) seem inappropriate in a mid-eighteenth-century setting. Some noun phrases are marked by structures and lexis which viewers would immediately recognise as contemporary. Edmund's satiric references to the possibility of a second volume of the dictionary clearly mimic film titles of the 1990s:

>   h   q   h   q
> Dictionary two (l. 77)   Return of the Killer Dictionary (ll. 77–8)
>   N   num   N   PrepP

Similarly, the description of Edmund's novel imitates the sensational style often associated with tabloid newspapers:

> m   m   h   m   m   h   q
> a Butler's Tale, a huge roller-coaster of a novel crammed with sizzling gypsies
> det   N   N   det Adj   N   PrepP   NFCl
>
> (ll. 79–80)

The comedy lies in the fact that the language of the eighteenth and the late twentieth centuries has been juxtaposed.

Comedy is also created where **informal** and **formal tones** are used in unexpected places. A noun like *turnip-head* (l. 67) and certain noun phrases are unlikely to be heard in a formal context. Such references immediately strike the viewer as both inappropriate and anachronistic and therefore funny:

> m   m   h   m   m   h   q
> a tricky situation (ll. 54–5)   this complete cowpat of a book (l. 65)
> det Adj   N   det   Adj   N   PrepP

At the other end of the scale, some references are very formal. Verbs like *terminated* (l. 9) and *facilitate* (l. 72) replace *finished* and *help*, while the noun phrase *our Post-Norman tongue* (ll. 10–11) replaces *English*. The writers enhance the visual comedy of Johnson's character by giving him long noun phrases which are made up of formal lexis:

> m   m   h   q
> the encyclopaedic implementation of my premeditated orchestration of demotic
> det   Adj   N   PrepP   PrepP
> Anglo-Saxon (ll. 5–6)

By using the *-ation* suffix twice alongside the noun phrase *demotic Anglo-Saxon* instead of the less formal phrase *popular English*, Johnson is presented as pompous and ludicrous. This interpretation of his character is reinforced by other unnecessarily formal noun phrases:

> m   m   m   h
> the penultimate solar sojourn (l. 9)
> det   Adj   N   N

The presentation of Johnson in this extract provides the context for comedy since it allows the writers to exploit the way in which language can be used by different people in different situations. When lexical choices are inappropriate, the results are often amusing.

Johnson's dictionary is supposed to include every single word and the most obvious form of humour in this extract can be found in Blackadder's **made-up words**. In his attempts to undermine Johnson, he uses words that seem real because they are derived using common English prefixes and suffixes. Table 18.1 summarises the morphological structure of the invented words.

Table 18.1 The morphological derivation of made-up words

l.	Nonsense word	Word class	Prefix	Suffix	Real words with the same affixes
26	contrafibularities	N	*contra-* (against)		*contra*band (smuggled goods)
				-ity	popular*ity*
30	anaspeptic	Adj		*-ic*	dramat*ic*
30	frasmotic				
31	pericombobulation	N	*peri-* (around)		*peri*phrasis (round-about expression)
				-ation	jubil*ation*
40	interfrastically	Adv	*inter-* (between)		*inter*national
				-ly	theatrical*ly*
69	pendagestatory	Adj		*-ory*	hallucinat*ory*
70	interludicure	N		*-cure*	epi*cure*, pedi*cure*
72	velocitous	Adj		*-ous*	contemptu*ous*
73	excommuniarisation	N	*ex-* (from/out of)		*ex*communicate (act of expelling from the Church)
				-isation	familiar*isation*
74–5	impeculiarated	V	*im-* (negative)		*im*mobile
				-ate	stagn*ate*

The **prosodic features** are also a source of the comedy in this extract. Changes in pitch exaggerate reactions: ↑*apparently*↑ (l. 17); stress draws attention to key lexical items which are often humorous in their own right: *I may be as <u>thick</u> as a <u>whale</u> <u>omelette</u>* (ll. 56–7); pace variations reinforce changes in tone and emphasise comic juxtapositions of the characters (ll. 4–21). Rising and falling tones are used more consciously and more frequently than in ordinary informal conversation – this adds to the comic effect by exaggerating the intonation patterns associated with everyday speech. Pauses are usually minimal in order to ensure that interaction between characters is fast-moving. Where they are longer, they mark either time allowed for audience laughs or points at which visual images rather than words convey meaning. Unlike normal conversation, there is little evidence here of normal non-fluency features. Hesitations, repetitions and minimal vocalisations appear infrequently – this is indicative of the edited and polished nature of the programme.

The comedy works on many levels in this extract. In most cases, the juxtaposition of the expected and the unexpected is the source of the humour: the language of the eighteenth century versus the language of the 1990s; informal versus formal tones; slang versus technical words; invented words versus their real equivalents; and exaggerated prosodic features versus the more balanced characteristics of everyday conversation.

18.5 What to look for in the language of broadcasting

The following checklist can be used to identify key features in examples taken from different kinds of broadcasts. There will not be examples of all the features in every extract or transcript, but the list can be used as a guide. The points made are general, so discussion of specific examples will need to be adapted to take account of the specific programme, its purpose and target audience.

The following are helpful questions to ask.

Programme type

1 Is the transmission on **television** or **radio**?
2 What **kind of programme** is it?
3 What is the **purpose** of the broadcast?
4 Who is the **intended audience**?
5 What **time** is the programme transmitted?
6 Is the **tone** serious, comic, or somewhere in between?

Register

1 What is the **mode**? – spoken? written to be read aloud?
2 What is the **manner**? – the relationship between participants? the relative status of the participants? direct or indirect address? formal or informal? personal or impersonal?
3 What is the **field**? – the lexis will reveal the kind of subject matter that forms the basis for the speech encounter.

Structure

1 Is the programme part of an **ongoing series** with a running story? a **one-off broadcast** which is self-contained?
2 How is the **opening** marked? – formal greeting? a summary of the topic(s) to be considered? a general introduction? distinctive intonation patterns?
3 How is the **closing** marked? – a summary? a formal closing phrase? a cliffhanger? distinctive intonation patterns?
4 Is there anything distinctive about the **turn-taking**? – adjacency pairs? interruptions? overlaps? latchings? digressions?

Topic management

1 What is the **goal** of the programme? – to convey information? to question? to entertain?
2 Is the **topic range** broad or narrow?
3 Are there any **topic shifts**? – how are they marked? are the changes smooth?
4 How is the **end of a topic** marked? – stock phrases? fade-out? a cliffhanger? a summary?

Prosodic features

1 Do **intonation patterns** reinforce the meaning of the words spoken? – indicate

different attitudes? mark grammatical structures? draw attention to grammatical boundaries?

2 Does the **pitch** change to reinforce speakers' attitudes and responses? – are the effects emphatic or comic?

3 Is **stress** used to draw attention to certain lexical items? – is there anything about the pattern of stress that is unusual?

4 Does the **volume** change significantly to enhance the meaning of utterances?

5 Does the **pace** change to draw attention to key parts of utterances?

6 How are **pauses** used? – emphasis? drama? hesitation? breathing? grammatical break?

7 Is the transcript or transmission script marked with any **vocal effects** or **paralinguistics**? – how do these relate to the words actually spoken?

Lexis

1 Is the language **formal** or **informal**? – **subject specific** or **general**? **serious** or **comic**?

2 Are there any examples of **high-frequency conversational clauses**? **colloquial idioms**? **collocations**?

Grammar

1 Is the **function** of utterances simple? compound? complex? a mixture?

2 Are **loosely co-ordinated** or **subordinate clauses** more common?

3 Are there any **minor sentences**?

4 Are **phrases** complex or simple? – how do they relate to the topic and manner of the programme?

5 Are **different grammatical modes** used to add variety? – direct speech? reported speech? changes in mood and voice?

6 Are there any **grammatically non-standard** or **incomplete utterances**? do other participants show any awareness of them?

7 Are there any **marked themes**?

Normal non-fluency features

1 Are there any **overlaps** in the speech turns? – for how long do they last? what causes them? how do the participants respond? do the overlaps mark an intentional challenge, supportive minimal vocalisation, or a mishearing of linguistic clues?

2 Are there any **voiced hesitations**? – preventing interruptions? prolonging a turn? thinking time?

3 Are there any **false starts** or **repetitions**?

Repairs

1 Has the **editing** produced a seamless, polished programme?

2 Are there any **repairs**? – self-correction? other corrections?

3 Are there any **topic loops**?

4 Are speakers aware of **listener responses**? – self-monitoring? direct address? questions? rephrasing or restating points?

5 Are there any **silences**? – lack of responses? failure to introduce a new topic? utterances misheard?

Summary

Because all utterances from a written text, whether live or pre-recorded, are marked by prosodic features, the language of broadcasting ultimately has more in common with **spoken** than written language. Although it is primarily spoken rather than written, it is important to recognise the difference between spontaneous and scripted language. Scripted language will often be written in such a way that it mimics many of the characteristics of speech; spontaneous commentaries, on the other hand, will automatically be less formally organised and more random.

Accents and **dialects** will vary according to the kind of programme, the participants and their regional and social backgrounds. Other variants will also affect the kind of language used: age, gender, occupational background and status; time of broadcast; target audience; and so on.

Having recognised the features that the language of broadcasting has in common with spoken language, it is important to identify characteristics dictated by the **genre**. Documentaries, dramas, comedies and news programmes, for instance, all have distinctive features marking the overall structure, the topic management, and the lexical and grammatical choices.

Other varieties

19.1 How to classify other varieties

There are so many distinct varieties of English that it would be impossible to cover every kind. It is, however, possible to establish a framework so that unfamiliar varieties can be analysed in the same way that newspapers, legal language or advertising have been tackled in earlier sections.

Different linguists classify texts in different ways. For instance, texts can be **chronological** or **non-chronological**. The structure of a chronological text is based on a sequence of events which occur in a certain order and follow a logical timescale; the verbs will often describe actions and events; and time adverbs like *then*, *next* and *after* are common. A non-chronological text is not structured by time, but by a logical relationship between its parts – comparison, contrast or logical development of an argument. Another method of classifying texts uses the categories established by James Britton and colleagues in *The Development of Writing Abilities (11–18)* (Macmillan, 1975). **Expressive writing** deals with thinking processes in a very general way – jottings are personal and really represent no more than 'thinking aloud on paper'; **transactional writing** gets things done – it aims to inform, persuade, instruct; and **poetic writing** is text produced for its own sake.

Although such categories are a useful starting point, they are difficult to apply because they have few distinctive linguistic or stylistic features. The examples covered in this section are therefore divided into categories based on **content** since this allows a range of similar text types to be studied together. The notes that accompany each section aim to provide at least a general idea of the linguistic and stylistic features for which it is worth looking.

19.2 Instruction texts

Instruction texts have the following characteristics.

- They have a **practical purpose**. They tell the reader how to do something – how to change a spark plug, make a cake, hang wallpaper, fill in an application form, or whatever.
- They are **written** texts (mode), but they are interactive because they require the reader to perform a sequence of activities. The **relationship created between reader and writer** (manner) is formal. The writer is distant and assumes the dominant role

as an expert in the discourse. Despite the interactive response to the instructions, the communication is one-way since the reader obeys and cannot directly question the writer. The **field** will dictate the kind of language used – the lexis will relate directly to the activity being carried out.

- The **tone** is impersonal because there is seldom any mention of the reader or the writer. Instruction texts do not often provide encouragement or develop a relationship between writer and reader – there is no need to employ persuasive techniques because the reader has already decided to carry out a particular activity independently.
- Instruction texts are **chronological** – the sequence of the instructions is dictated by the order of the process and this cannot usually be altered. Each part of the process must be clear and unambiguous if it is to be completed successfully.
- The **lexis** and **grammar** are often repetitive because the focus of an instruction text is always narrow – the completion of a particular task or activity. The mood is usually imperative, so there is no need for a grammatical subject. Because the second person pronoun references *you* are omitted, the process is seen to be more important than the creation of a relationship between writer and reader.
- Because reading will be interspersed with action, the **layout** is often distinctive, with numbered paragraphs dividing the text clearly into a sequence of actions. This makes it easy for readers to re-find their place in the text quickly. The instructions are brief and illustrations may be provided to clarify instructions.
- The process is designed to produce the same **end result** each time the instructions are followed.
- An **expert writer** is writing for an audience who may not be experts but who share some subject specific knowledge (an appropriate vocabulary; relevant equipment; some understanding of the processes involved).

Some examples of instruction texts

Recipes

The **layout** is distinctive: the title will often use bold print to draw attention to the particular dish to be made. A list of ingredients and relevant quantities (often in parenthesis) will precede the instructions. Abbreviations will be used as a shorthand recognisable to the reader: *tsp* for *teaspoon*; *tbsp* for *tablespoon*. Paragraphs will often be numbered. Drawings or photographs will show the end product. Diagrams may be used to explain any complex processes.

The **lexis** will be subject specific: *heat, boil, mix*. Often words will be used with a narrower reference than is usual in everyday speech: *rub in* specifically refers to the process of mixing butter and flour, for instance. Many nouns will be concrete, based on the ingredients and the equipment: *flour, butter, spoon, bowl, whisk*. Nominal groups tend to be long so that references are very precise:

m	m	m	h		m	m	m	m	h
2 oz	sieved	wholemeal	flour		9 in	(20 cm)	round	cake	tin
num	V	Adj	N		num	num	Adj	N	N

Modifiers are used to give the reader clear guidance, ensuring that earlier processes have been carried out:

P	O		m	m	m	h
(grease)	(the baking tray)	→	the	greased	baking	tray
			det	V	V	N

P	O	A		m	m	h
(place)	(half the sugar)	(in the bowl)	→	the	remaining	sugar
				det	V	N

Usually modifiers are attributive: *the beaten yolks*. Predicative modifiers, however, are also used:

P   O   A

(cream) (the butter and sugar) (until the mixture is *smooth*)
                     SCl–ACl

Determiners are used distinctively: the indefinite article is used to refer to equipment, since any bowl or implement will be appropriate: *a bowl, a skewer*; definite articles are used to refer specifically to the ingredients listed at the beginning of the recipe: *the cornflour, the grated rind and juice of the lemon*. However, determiners are often omitted.

The **grammar** is also distinctive. Verbs tend to be dynamic and the mood is almost always imperative. There are lots of non-finite verbs functioning as modifiers and adverbial non-finite clauses: *when cooked...*, *by folding*. Clause structures are often repetitive (PO, POA, APO):

P   O   P   O   A

(Grease) (the tin) (and) (line) (it) (with greaseproof paper)
                  conj

P   A   A

(Bake) (until the cake is firm to the touch) (and) (∅ a skewer inserted into its
   SCl–ACl   conj   SCl–ACl   SCl–NFCl

centre comes out clean).

Verbs are usually transitive because the process requires an action done to something, and phrases or clauses are often compound because a recipe involves combining ingredients. Cohesion is created by repetition of nouns and anaphoric references to the list of ingredients and processes already completed. Adverbials make the instructions precise by focusing on details of time, place and manner.

P   O   A = place   P   A = time   A = time

(place) (the dough) (on a floured surface)   (leave) (for one hour) (or) (until risen)
                                                 conj   SCl–ACl

P   O   A = manner   P   O   A = manner

(fold in) (the flour) (gently)   (shape) (the pasties) (by pinching the edges)
                                               SCl–NFCl

The adverbials give details of length of time, speed, place.

Word-processing user's manual

The **layout** is made distinctive by the combination of text and diagrams. Bold print may be used to highlight the particular process explained: **Printing blocks**; and definitions succinctly describe its nature: *This function allows you to print a marked block of text*. Numbered paragraphs enable readers to carry out the prescribed sequence of actions without losing their place as they move from reading to carrying out appropriate instructions. Cross-references ensure that readers can easily pinpoint instructions in other parts of the manual which may be a necessary part of the process they are currently carrying out: *Define a block as described on page 70*. Graphics underpin and clarify textual explanations – marginal symbols show the reader exactly which key or combination of keys needs to be pressed:

> RETURN CODE * UNDO

Capitalisation and bold print also draw attention to the keys to be selected.

The **lexis** is subject specific: *cut sheet feeder, printer, keyboard*; and some nouns are used with a narrow field of reference that makes them semantically quite different from everyday usage: *menu*, *window*. Modifiers make references very precise, and post- as well as pre-modification is used:

	m	m	h	q
	a	marked	block	of text
	det	V	N	PrepP

	m	m	h
	letter-	quality	print
	N	N	N

	m	h
	draft	setting
	N	N

The verbs tend to be part of a limited set: *press*, *select*, *cancel*, *return*.

The **grammar** is less disjointed than that found in a recipe or knitting pattern. Because the reader might not be an expert, each grammatical utterance must be complete with no abbreviations and no ellipsis since these may cause confusion. Equally, a user's manual is long and contains information which will be used over a period of time. Rather than a sequence of actions that will produce one complete product, it has to cover a whole range of possible processes. The verbs are usually dynamic and the mood is imperative: *insert*, *check*, *print*. Because there are explanations as well as commands, however, the declarative is also used frequently. A more personal relationship is created between reader and writer in this kind of text with the use of second person pronoun references: *you can shade text to make it stand out*. This makes the whole process seem less daunting to a beginner. The use of contractions like the negative *won't* and the imperative *let's* contribute to the friendly approach. Adverbials are common:

> *as described on page 275*
> SCl–ACl

A = cross-reference to another instruction

> press any key *to enter the program*
> SCl–NFCl

A = reason

> *If you want to print a page*, press _____
> SCl–ACl

A = condition

Sentences in the imperative mood tend to have a P O A clause structure:

> P   O   A
> (Insert) (a sheet of paper) (into the printer).

> P   O   A
> (Follow) (this procedure) (to shade text).
> SCl–NFCl

Explanations in the declarative mood also tend to have at least one adverbial:

> S   P   A
> (The cursor) (will be displayed) (at the word).

> S   P   A   A
> (All shading directions) (are displayed) (on the screen) (as the same pattern).

Modal verbs like *will* conveying certainty and *can* conveying ability occur in many declarative sentences. Marked themes are common, particularly in the form of adverbial clauses:

> A
> (If you don't move the cursor to the beginning of the text), (scanning) (will start)
> SCl–ACl   S   P

> A
> (from the current cursor position).

Sentence structures are far more varied in this kind of guide than in recipes and knitting patterns. Cohesion is created by the numbered step-by-step processes described; by the typographical features like diagrams, symbols and bold print; and by the use of the definite article which makes reference specific.

19.3 Information texts

Information texts have the following characteristics.

- They may have a **physical purpose** – encouraging you to visit a historic site; persuading you to go and see a particular film at the cinema – but often the result will be more closely associated with **education**. An information text can help you to gain knowledge or to change your attitudes.
- The **mode** can be written or spoken depending upon the context. Communication is usually one-way, with the information conveyed from an expert writer or speaker to a specific audience. However, developments in computer technology and CD-Rom can now make reading an encyclopaedia an interactive process.
- The **manner** is usually formal: a distant writer is linked to readers only by the text; a speaker in a large lecture hall cannot form a close relationship with individuals. Nevertheless, a writer can choose to use techniques that make the text seem less impersonal (using second person pronoun references and contractions), and a speaker in a smaller room may establish direct links with individuals by inviting questions. The manner of some leaflets is also informal. Although they would describe themselves as 'informative', they are in fact covert advertisements. They are more concerned with persuasion than education and use many of the features of advertising language (direct address, grammatically incomplete utterances and informal language).
- The **tone** will usually be impersonal and formal in a textbook or a large-scale lecture, but may be more personal and informal in promotion material or seminars and tutorials.
- Where the discourse is primarily interested in **conveying information objectively** for academic and intellectual purposes, there is less need to use persuasive techniques. In examples like Tourist Board leaflets or entertainment news sheets, however, the information is used in order to **persuade** readers to visit certain places or do certain things.
- Some information texts will be **chronological** (explaining chemical processes, recording historical events, or lecturing on the structure of a play); others may be **non-chronological** (describing places of interest in a certain area).
- Information texts must be **clear** and **unambiguous** if the facts are to be conveyed effectively.
- The **lexis** and **grammar** will usually be subject specific, linked directly to the field. Modifiers in formal information texts will be technical, numerical and factual. In less formal examples which are really covert advertisements, modifiers will be descriptive and evaluative to convince readers of the value of a particular place or event. Sentence structures in texts with an academic purpose are more likely to be complex; in a leaflet, they are likely to be short and often grammatically incomplete.
- The **mood** will usually be declarative, although in advertisements framed as information texts, imperatives may be used to urge the reader to *visit* _____ or *see* _____ .
- The **layout** will vary. Textbooks will have chapters, subheadings, numbered sections and subsections and a content lists to guide the reader. They may have photographs, diagrams or tables to reinforce the information provided in the text. Leaflets are more likely to use visual effects such as colour and montage (pictures made up by superimposing images) and to keep the written text brief.
- Usually the writer or speaker will be an **expert**, but the way information is conveyed will depend upon the target audience. The approach needed to present a scientific

theory to other experts will be different from the simplified approach needed for a first-year A-level group; a lecturer on a university degree course talking about legal precedents and a policeman talking about bicycles and road safety to junior-school children will use different lexis and sentence structure. In analysing an information text, it is therefore important to establish the function and the intended audience.

Some examples of information texts

Science textbooks

The **mode** is written and the **manner** is usually formal. The writer is dominant because the text is a one-way communication and often the writer will have more expertise in the field than the intended audience. The **field** will depend upon the specific area of physics, chemistry, biology and so on.

The **layout** will use a mixture of written, symbolic and diagrammatic codes. Paragraphs are likely to be long and may be numbered in subsections for clarity: *1.1, 1.2*. Symbols like H_2O and equations like

$$CuO \quad + \quad H_2 \quad = \quad Cu \quad + \quad H_2O$$
(copper (hydrogen) (copper) (water)
oxide)

are used as a technical shorthand understood by an audience with shared knowledge. Diagrams may clarify processes or the arrangement of equipment. Bold print may highlight key words. Italic print may be used for special purposes: *Erithacus rubecula*, the robin; the radius *r*.

The **lexis** will be subject specific and technical: *electrolysis, concentrated sodium chloride solution*. Some general words are used in a subject specific way: *interference, light, waves, reflection*. Modifiers are technical rather than evaluative or descriptive and both pre- and post-modification are common:

$$\overset{\text{m}}{\text{bimetallic}} \overset{\text{h}}{\text{strip}} \quad \overset{\text{m}}{\text{potassium}} \overset{\text{h}}{\text{permanganate}}$$
Adj   N   N   N

m h q   m   h q   m h q
the rate of diffusion   the molecules of liquid   the gas dispersed in the flask
det N PrepP   det   N   PrepP   det N SCl–NFCl

The **grammar** is standard, in line with the formality of the tone. There are many stative verbs: *found, involves, notice*; dynamic verbs describe processes: *heat, melt, test*. Modal verbs like *will* describe certainties: *sound will travel through liquid*; and *may* describes possibilities: *a catalyst may be used to increase the rate of the reaction*. The passive voice is common and is typical of the impersonal nature of scientific texts. By refocusing the elements of a sentence, the object of an active sentence can be foregrounded – this is appropriate in scientific writing because the person carrying out the procedure is less important than the objects being tested.

Passive: Substrate concentration can *be increased* if necessary.
Active: *The chemist* can increase the substrate concentration if necessary.

Modern textbooks, however, may choose a less formal approach, using the active voice and direct address.

Many passive constructions are formulaic.

It is found. . .   It has been suggested. . .
It can be seen that. . .   It would be expected that. . .

Many adverbials are conditional: *If iron and steam are heated...* Others, however, supply information about time: *when heating, within a few minutes*; or place: *in a Petri dish, in secondary cells*. The mood is usually declarative since scientists are dealing with explanations and records of processes carried out. Sentence structures are usually complex or compound complex.

> dumS   P   (S)
> (It) (is found) (that the potential difference across the terminals of a cell decreases)
>   SCl–NCl
>
>   A
> (as larger values of current are taken from it).
> SCl–ACl

>   A   S   P
> (If only one coil is used and the motor is not self-starting), (the coil) (may come)
> SCl–ACl   SCl–ACl
>
>   A   S
> (to rest with the brushes across the break of the split ring) (and) (the armature)
> SCl–NFCl
>
>   P   A
> (will have to be moved) (to start it).
>   SCl–NFCl

Many sentences have long sequences of dependent clauses. Cohesion is created by the repetition of subject specific lexis, by the chronological order of events described, and by the sequence of conditions that must be fulfilled.

Science writing for **children** is distinctive in quite different ways. The tone is usually personal and direct address is used. Writers are also likely to include themselves in references by using the first person plural: *Let's start...* Imperatives are common because writers tend to try and make the text interactive. Sentences are often shorter with fewer dependent clauses: Simple:

>   S   P   C
> (Every plant) (is) (a chemical factory).

Complex:

>   S   P   C   A
> (The unexposed parts of the leaf) (turn) (brown) (when sunlight does not reach them).
>   SCl–ACl

Publicity leaflets

The **mode** is written and the **manner** is often quite informal. Although the writer is in a position of authority, recommending and advising the reader, the text does try to establish a relationship between the participants. Because leaflets are often covert advertisements, the tone often has more similarities with the field of advertising than with other more formal information texts. The **field** may be subject specific, relating to new cinema releases, classical concerts or particular geographic areas, but the lexis will probably not be technical.

The **layout** is often striking. Colour adds interest and variations in print size will attract a reader's attention. Leaflets are often produced on A4 size paper, but are folded in half or thirds to divide information into units which can be easily manipulated. Images are often dominant and logos and symbols are used as a shorthand to make the message or promoter clear. More details can usually be obtained by contacting the promoter or the venue – telephone numbers and addresses are a crucial part of the information provided. Dates, times, admission prices and other factual information are commonly included as part of the promotion.

The **lexis** will be marked by the use of lexical sets linked to the subject matter: *exhibition, gallery, artist in residence; cinema, screening, film*. Long nominal groups are a distinctive feature of this kind of information text because the language must persuade the reader to do certain things. The modifiers therefore tend to be evaluative and descriptive:

> m   m   m   h   m   m   m   h
> the top tourist attraction   a superb adventure playground
> det Adj   N   N   det Adj   N   N

> m   m   h   m   m   m   h
> The controversial novelist _____ a powerful and (bitingly humorous) film
> det   Adj   N   det   Adj   Adv   Adj   N

Both pre- and post-modification are common:

> m   h   q   q
> a night of music and performance with outstanding performance poets and writers
> det N   PrepP   PrepP

The **grammar** is also similar to the field of advertising: most sentences are in the active rather than the passive voice; declarative mood is common although some imperatives are used: *Visit _____ and enjoy _____*; sentences are often not grammatically complete; non-finite clauses are common: *Controversial playwright and novelist _____ reading a selection of her most outrageous offerings*. The modal auxiliary *will* conveys a writer's sense of certainty: *You will experience the ride of a lifetime*. Determiners are often omitted: *Workshops by local artist*; and verbal nouns are common: *opening, screening, reading*. Adverbials give details of time: *tonight, on January 4*; and place: *in the park, at your local cinema*. They are often used in strings. Sentence structures are varied, but publicity leaflets do not tend to have the strings of dependent clauses that are typical of scientific textbooks. Simple:

> S   P   C
> (The local church) (is) (a building of great interest).

Complex:

>   A   S
> (Originally built by the Normans in the 12th century) (the motte and bailey castle)
> SCl–NFCl

> P   A   A
> (was rebuilt) (in stone) (in 1275).

Marked themes are used to draw attention to information that is considered important:

>   A   S   P   O
> (Over the centuries) (this old town) (has seen) (a number of famous faces

> including _____ who have all left their mark).
> SCl–NFCl   SCl–RelCl

Lectures

The **mode** is spoken and the **manner** will vary depending upon the size of the event. In a large lecture hall, the relationship between speaker and audience will be impersonal. The lecturer is dominant as an expert in a particular field and the communication will usually be one-way. On a smaller scale, however, in a seminar or tutorial, a more personal relationship can be created between the lecturer and individuals; communication can become a two-way process because the lecturer is more likely to encourage questions from the audience. The **field** will be directly linked to the subject matter: physics, literature, history and so on.

The **presentation** will be marked by prosodic features. Intonation, pitch, pace and rhythm will add variety to the lecture, attracting and holding audience attention. Written hand-outs may be used to reinforce the content of the lecture. Equally, slides and overhead projector transparencies can use images, tables or diagrams to clarify points made. Sometimes a lecturer will deliver a pre-written essay orally, while others may speak more spontaneously from notes. The first approach will result in a form which more closely resembles a formal speech; the second approach will have similarities to spoken language – there may be false starts, normal non-fluency features, repetitions or repairs.

The **lexis** will be subject specific: *Shakespeare, revenge tragedy, ghost.* If the context is more personal, the language is more likely to be similar to everyday formal spoken usage. The language of the lecture will then be made up of subject specific jargon and examples of ordinary language. Modifiers will be related to the topic:

> m   m   h   m   m   h   q
> Austen's distinctive style   a descriptive approach to language
> N   Adj   N   det   Adj   N   PrepP

The **grammar** will be formal whether the lecture is delivered in an impersonal lecture hall or a smaller-scale seminar. The most common mood will be the declarative, although imperatives may be used to direct the audience's attention to the hand-outs and the like. Most sentences will be active and the sentence structures will often be long. In a lecture that is read from a written essay, the sentences are more likely to be complex with many embedded clauses: in one delivered from notes, they will tend to be looser in construction.

Spontaneous:

> P   A   S   P   O   A
> (Look) (at Chapter 1). (Austen) (uses) (irony) (to characterise Sir Walter) (and)
>   SCl–NFCl   conj
>
> S   P   O   A
> (her approach) (portrays) (him) (as an unpleasant person who thinks only of
>   SCl–RelCl
>
> himself and his position).

Scripted:

> A   S   P
> (By using metaphorical language), (an author) (can ensure) (that readers
> SCl–ACl   SCl–NCl
>
>   O
> appreciate the sub-textual meaning of a novel), (that they understand both the
>   SCl–NCl
>
>   O
> literal and symbolic implications of plot and character) (and) (make appropriate
>   conj   SCl–NCl
>
>   O
> structural connections).

Both examples here are compound-complex sentences, but the rhetorical patterning of the second clearly marks it as closer to written than spoken language.

19.4 Personal texts

Personal texts have the following characteristics.

* This kind of writing is concerned with the expression of personal ideas, aims, attitudes, and so forth. The **purpose** will depend on the writer and his or her relation-

ship with the text. Some personal texts, such as letters, are written for a wider audience; others, such as diaries and journals, are intended only for the eyes of the author.

- The **mode** is usually written, although 'video diaries' are now a popular source of personal material on the television. At the time they are written, diaries are usually a form of one-way communication: the content is not intended for a wide audience and there is little interaction once each entry is complete. It is important to remember, however, that the diaries of famous people are often published. These reveal the private side of public figures. Samuel Pepys' diary has become well known as a historical document since it recounts key events like the Fire of London from an individual's point of view. In more recent years, politicians have published their diaries. Tony Benn's commentaries, for example, are interesting because they are spoken diaries, taped recordings of his years in politics: as well as having been broadcast on BBC Radio 4, they have been made publicly available by the BBC as cassettes in their 'Radio Collection'.

  Letters are a one-way communication, but they allow the recipient to respond at a later time. The writer is not always dominant – informal letters, for instance, will usually be written to equals.

- The **manner** can be formal or informal depending upon the relationship between participants and the purpose of the communication. An official diary of appointments or a job application will be formal and impersonal; correspondence between friends or a personal record of events and the writer's feelings will often be informal and personal.

- Personal writing can be **informative**: factual details on a curriculum vitae will be formal, whereas details about a holiday and the places visited will be informal. It can also be **descriptive** or **evaluative**: a letter to a friend comparing two different social occasions will be informal, while an artist's account of a place which later formed the basis of a painting will tend to be formal.

- Personal writing may be **chronological** (focusing on dates and times) or it may treat events **non-chronologically** (focusing on arguments and comparisons).

- Texts that are written for a formal context like a job application must be **unambiguous**. Personal letters and diaries, however, may adopt the same spontaneous approach as everyday conversation and may therefore be **ambiguous** at times. Such texts may contain non-fluency markers like repetition, grammatical inaccuracies and spelling mistakes: these are a parallel to the kinds of non-fluency associated with informal spoken language.

- The **lexis** will vary depending upon the purpose and the intended audience. The language used in a job application will be formal and subject specific. It will be marked by distinctive uses of language: collocations like *I enclose a CV as requested...* and *In response to the advertisement in* _____; terms of address like *Dear Sir/Madam*, *Yours faithfully*, *Yours sincerely*; and subject specific lexis like *book-keeping, accounts, cashing-up*. A letter to a friend, on the other hand, will be marked by informalities: colloquialisms like *well, you'll never guess what...*; terms of address like *Dear Sue, Hi!, Love Mike*.

- The **grammar** of personal writing will be directly linked to the purpose and intended audience – the more formal the context, the more complicated the grammar is likely to be. The mood of sentences will vary: in informal personal writing, declaratives, interrogatives and imperatives will be common; in formal personal writing, declaratives will be the usual choice. Sentence structures will tend to have a looser construction in informal examples: co-ordination will be more common and sentences will resemble the more rambling structure of spoken utterances. In formal writing, subordination will be more common.

- The **layout** for personal writing is dictated by convention. In formal writing, traditions will be followed carefully in order to make a good impression; in informal texts, however, each individual writer can make decisions about the way the text will appear on the page.
- The **context**, **audience** and **purpose** will dictate the role of the writer in each case.

Some examples of personal writing

Letters

The **mode** is written. The **manner** can be at any point on a sliding scale between formal and informal. Choices will be made depending upon the intended audience and the purpose of the communication: a job application or a letter to an MP will be formal; a holiday postcard or a letter to a friend will be informal. The **field** may be subject specific in formal examples, but will often be everyday or conversational in informal examples.

The **layout** is more likely to be individualistic in an informal letter because writers are free to alter traditional structures to suit themselves. The patterns of spoken language can be mirrored because recipients are more likely to accept inaccuracies (spelling, punctuation, grammar) without making judgements about the sender. A formal letter needs to make an immediate impression, however, so the conventions of written language will often be adhered to far more strictly. Recipients expect paragraph structures to be logically developed, sentences to be controlled, and spelling to be accurate. The use of headed notepaper or logos help the reader to identify the sender immediately and add to the formality.

Such letters should have a traditional layout, with the sender's address and telephone number and the date in the top right-hand corner, the recipient's name and address below on the left, a formal greeting, *Dear Sir/Madam*, and a formal closing, *Yours faithfully*. Traditionally, if a formal letter is addressed to a named person, *Mr John Brown*, it must conclude with *Yours sincerely*. Informal letters do not have to include the recipient's address and will start less impersonally with *Dear Susy* or *Dear all*. They will also conclude with more personal phrases like *Love from Jo* or *See you soon, Chris*.

The **lexis** is dependent on purpose. Some types of letter will be subject specific, but many will not.

The **grammar** will reflect the manner. If letters are formal and impersonal, the grammar is more likely to be complicated and the sentences complex. The following example is taken from the letter of resignation from Peter Brooke, Secretary of State for National Heritage, to the Prime Minister, John Major, dated 20 July 1994:

> A
> (When you called me back to the Government, like in one of our mutual passions
> SCl–ACl
>
>   S   P   Oi   Od
> a retired cricketer to the Test team), (you) (gave) (me) (an Indian summer which
>   SCl–RelCl
>
> ensured an exception to the rule that all political careers end in tears).
>   SCl–NCl

An informal letter is more likely to use simple and compound sentences. Where subordination is used, strings of embedded clauses are less common.

>   A   P   S   S   S
> (Here) (is) (a belated birthday present) (and) (something for Joseph's room). (I)
>
>   P   O
> (hope) (you like it).
>   SCl–NCl

Letters can mix a formal and informal manner. An artist writing to a friend, for example, may discuss his work, creating a theoretical discourse on the nature of art and the artist in a personal context. Although the relationship between the participants can be described as informal, the content will be subject specific and formal. The following extract is taken from a letter from Vincent van Gogh to his brother Theo in the 1880s in which he discusses his painting *Potato Eaters*:

> S   P   O
> (I) (have tried) (to emphasise that these people eating their potatoes in the lamplight,
>   SCl–NFCl   SCl–NCl   SCl–NFCl
>
>   S
> have dug the earth with those very hands they put into the dish) (and so) (it)
>   SCl–RelCl   conj
>
> P   O   O
> (speaks of) (manual labour) (and) (how they have honestly earned their food).
>   conj   SCl–NCl

The complexity of the clause structure here is typical of a formal rather than informal letter. Although Van Gogh is writing to his brother, he treats his correspondence as an integral part of his art so the content and style are formal.

Metaphorical language can be used to personalise both formal and informal letters. In examples where the style closely resembles spoken language, however, metaphorical language will be less common. When used in formal correspondence, it can make a letter distinctive and personal without it becoming informal. The following extract is taken from the letter of resignation from the post of Secretary of State for Transport sent by John MacGregor to the Prime Minister, John Major, dated 20 July 1994:

> I have had a *long innings*. It has been a great privilege to serve since 1979
> under outstanding Prime Ministers . . .

Although the letter had a formal purpose, MacGregor was able to draw on his own and Major's love of cricket in the metaphor: *long innings*. This enabled him to establish a more personal relationship with the recipient while still adopting all the formal conventions associated with a letter of resignation from public office.

Diaries and journals

The **mode** is usually written and the **manner** may be formal (work appointments), informal (a personal record of ideas) or anywhere on the scale between the two extremes. The **field** will depend upon the writer and his or her purpose – a diary may contain a record of homework due or interview times or may be a description of day-to-day activities, thoughts and feelings. Usually they are private and not for publication, but historians can use diaries of both ordinary and famous people to get an impression of what life was like at a particular time. Novelists can use diaries as a means of characterising people: the Adrian Mole novels by Sue Townsend use a diary format to allow the reader to see directly into Adrian's private thoughts – the reader almost seems to be invading his privacy.

The **layout** will vary. At one extreme, a diary will be made up of no more than lists of times, dates and events; at the other end of the scale, it may be written in detailed prose. Divisions into days, weeks and months are common. Private, secret diaries may be written in a shorthand or code which is understandable only to the reader. The length of entries can vary considerably.

The **lexis** may be subject specific or very personal. It will often be distinctive.

The **grammar** will reflect the nature of the writer and the content. Since diarists often use a personal shorthand, ellipsis of determiners and verbless clauses are common. Grammatical words are omitted, leaving the focus on lexical items.

> (Day of rest)! (In garden) (later). (Evening) (tranquil). (Remarkably clear view of
>   NP   PrepP   AdvP   NP   AdjP   NP
>
> coast).

Verbs will usually be in the past tense since a diary records events, feelings and attitudes after they have occurred. First person pronouns will be dominant because the text is specifically related to the writer. The mood will vary depending upon the writer's intentions: declaratives will be most common, but imperatives and interrogatives can also be used.

Diaries or journals can be kept for practical reasons (listing birthdays) or for more artistic purposes. Factual diaries will vary very little from person to person in terms of their content and structure, but a personal diary will often be idiosyncratic, revealing much about the person who is keeping it. Dorothy Wordsworth, sister of the Romantic poet William Wordsworth, kept a diary in which she recorded details about the weather, domestic tasks, natural observations and the people who surrounded her. Sometimes the entries are written in a shorthand and the sentences are often made up of noun phrases or verbless clauses. Where sentences are composed of grammatically complete clauses, they are all simple sentences. Even at these times, however, the style is clearly poetic.

> *Friday, [31st] October 1800*
>
>   S   P   A   S   C   S   P
> (W. and S.) (did not rise) (till 1 o'clock). (W.) (very sick and very ill). (S.) (drank)
>   neg
>
>   O   A   P   A   A   C
> (tea) (at Lloyds) (and) (came) (home) (immediately after). (∅) (∅) (A very fine
>
>   S   P   A
> moonlight night). (The moon) (shone) (like herrings in the water).

At other times, the sentence structure is complex to match the content. Where Dorothy Wordsworth's style becomes more expressive and literary, the grammatical utterances are more likely to be complete and the prose is therefore more fluent.

> *Friday 23rd April, 1802*
>
>   S   P   O
> (William) (observed) (that the umbrella Yew tree that breasts the wind had lost its
>   SCl–NCl   SCl–RelCl
>
>   O   S
> character as a tree) (and) (∅ had become something like to solid wood). .... (We)
>   conj   SCl–NCl
>
> P   O   A   A   S
> (left) (William) (sitting on the stones) (feasting with silence) – (and) (C. and I)
>   SCl–NFCl   SCl–NFCl
>
> P   A   A   C   S   P   A
> (sate) (down) (upon a rocky seat) – (a Couch) (it) (might be) (under the Bower of
>
> William's Eglantine, Andrew's Broom).

The style here is quite different: subordination is common; strings of adverbials give details of the environment; and a marked theme throws emphasis on the object of the sentence.

19.5 Narrative texts

Narrative texts have the following characteristics.

- **Expression** will usually be personal in narrative texts. Although the content will reflect the writer's interests, experiences and attitudes, there is a greater sense of audience than in other personal writing. Unlike diaries and journals, which are written for the writer's eyes only, and letters, which are written for a clearly defined audience, narrative texts will have a wider and more diverse audience. The style will often be poetic, although authors can choose to mirror the language of everyday conversation too.
- The **mode** is usually written, although stories can also be recorded and we all tell narratives in our everyday speech encounters. The **manner** will depend upon the intended audience and on the author's purpose – a narrative written for an examiner may adopt a more formal approach than a controversial script written for the Edinburgh Fringe Festival. The audience will not usually be directly engaged in an active way, although implicitly the authors draw the reader into the fictional worlds they create. The **field** will be linked to the subject matter: science fiction; a particular historical period or country; people of different social classes.
- The **function** of a narrative text is to entertain, but it can also educate and inform. Plays can focus on topical issues such as AIDS, the environment, or war; a comic strip format can be used for educational purposes. In the _____ *for Beginners* series (*Feminism for Beginners*, *Freud for Beginners*), for instance, a comic format is used to introduce complex issues and key historical figures.
- Narratives are **chronological**, but authors do not have to relate events in order. They can use flashbacks, retrospective reflection, parallel timescales, and so on. Children's first narratives will tend to be chronological, moving from the beginning to the end in a straightforward linear development.
- **Ambiguity** can be used intentionally to create suspense: some novels, like B. S. Johnson's *House Mother Normal*, have to be read to the end before everything makes sense.
- The **lexis** will link to the kinds of character speaking, the locations and the different relationships established. Choices will be dictated by authorial intention.
- The **grammar** of narrative texts will be varied since authors use a wide range of techniques to influence readers. However, most prose narratives will be in the past tense while comics and playscripts will use the present tense.
- The **layout** is distinctive for comic strips and playscripts. Most prose narratives will use the traditional conventions of written language. However, since authors are creating something personal, they can alter conventions to make their end product more distinctive.
- The writers of narratives are **creative**: they therefore manipulate lexis and language structures to achieve the effects that will most influence their audiences.

Some examples of narrative texts

Playscripts

The **mode** is written, but a play is essentially made up of language to be spoken. The **manner** is formal, but some playwrights or particular kinds of performance may aim to create a more informal relationship with the audience. Pantomimes, for instance, make the audience less passive by encouraging participation: *He's behind you!* Because there is no omniscient narrator as there is in a novel, the audience must also actively make connections, interpret the sub-plot and deduce things about the characters. The **field** is linked directly to the topic of the play: issue-related, profession-related, everyday usage.

The **layout** is distinctive. Often the names of speakers are in capital letters, the text running on but with second and subsequent lines indented.

> HELEN: Well! This is the place.
> JO: And I don't like it.
> Shelagh Delaney (1939–), *A Taste of Honey* (Act 1, scene 1)

Italic print may be used to mark stage directions:

> Scene one. *A hotel lounge. Crumbling grandeur. Cane chairs. A great expanse of black-and-white checked floor stretching back into the distance. Porticos. Windows at the back and, to one side, oak doors. But the scene must only be sketched in, not realistically complete.*
> David Hare (1947–), *A Map of the World* (Act 1, scene 1)

Parenthesis is used to show any specific instructions about the way characters should deliver their lines or move:

> THIRD WORKER (*coming on*). I shouted to him to run.
> FOREMAN (*coming downstage*). Go back, go back! Work!
> FOURTH WORKER *goes off again.*
> THIRD WORKER. You heard me shout!
> FIRST WORKER. He says he's dead.
> FOREMAN. Work!
> SOLDIER (*to* FIRST WORKER). You! – make yerself responsible for 'andin' in 'is pick t' stores. (*Suddenly he sees something off stage and runs down to the others.*) Cover 'im! Quick!
> FOREMAN (*points to tarpaulin*). Take that!
> Edward Bond (1934–), *Lear* (Act 1, scene 1)

The **lexis** will reflect the content, the characters and the particular time and location of the play. It is the language accompanied by action that is the dominant means of characterisation. Equally important, a dramatist's choice of words will indicate the tone and atmosphere: comic, tragic, elevated or colloquial. Descriptions in the stage directions give the director or reader a concrete sense of the physical and social context and modifiers provide detailed references. Because scripts do not usually have an omniscient narrator to make implicit points explicit, the audience must interpret language and gesture themselves in order to understand characters and their relationships. Subjective thoughts and feelings may be revealed in a monologue, but more often paralinguistics and prosodics guide audience response. Metaphorical language and rhetorical techniques can also tell the audience something about a character.

The **dialogue** is initially written rather than spoken, but in most modern plays, dramatists want it to sound like spontaneous speech rather than formal prose. Despite this, most scripts will be more formally structured than everyday conversation.

The **prosodic features** are an important means of making the written text seem spontaneous. Characters will express their feelings in a more exaggerated way on stage – each response will be heightened so that the audience can appreciate subtle changes. Variations in pace may be linked to emotions and actions; silence and pause can be used to create dramatic effects; and intonation patterns will be different for each character and context. Through the prosodic techniques, actors will bring the words on the page to life.

The **grammar** may be formal or informal depending upon the character speaking. If the script mimics the looser patterns of speech, grammatical structures may be incomplete; if the script is in verse, word orders may be manipulated in order to conform to a particular rhythmic pattern. Lines imitating everyday speech may use minor sentences and utterances may overlap, but a verse play will have a heightened style, adopting poetic rather than spoken conventions. If the character speaking is idiosyncratic, then the grammar will be distinctive; if the character comes from a particular historical period or geographical context, then the grammar may be marked by archaisms or dialect features.

If considering an extract from a script, watch out also for: **changes in scene**; the **centre of interest**; the **location** in **time** and **place**; the **relationship** created between the **characters** and **audience**; any **dramatic use of language** to create **atmosphere**; any references to **costume**, **sound effects** and **music**.

Comic strips

The **mode** is written. The **manner** is often informal. A personal relationship is created between the reader, writer and artist – the tone may be colloquial, satirical or informative. The **field** is subject specific – traditional girls' comics focus on make-up, boyfriends, dieting; traditional boys' comics focus on futuristic societies, superheroes, sport and practical activities. Where comic strip is used as an educative medium, the lexis will reflect the topic: drugs, politics, sexism.

The **layout** combines text and image. Each page is divided into strips or unequal sections, making the reading process less demanding than it would be for a page of dense prose. The words are usually clearly marked out: narrative comment or description which sets the scene is placed in a box; direct speech is placed in a bubble; onomatopoeic words such as *BANG* or *HISS* are capitalised and have a larger print size. Equally, stories in a particular comic may use a distinctive print style which is immediately recognisable to regular readers. Comics are often dominated by bright colours, and photo stories are common. Although words are an important part of the storyline, the main means of communication is visual.

The **lexis** is directly related to the content. Photo stories in girls' comics aim to re-create the language of their intended audience, thus 'cult' words and colloquialisms are common. Science-fiction comics like *Judge Dredd* create a new language which is appropriate for the fictional world of a particular story (see Figure 19.1). The language in these publications is idiosyncratic – writers do not aim to mirror reality and their lexical choices are therefore distinctive. The world created in futuristic stories is often male-dominated, and the language tends to be linked directly to violence and male superheroes. Text is used to build up atmosphere, provide comment, set the scene or develop characters. Direct speech attempts to reflect the spontaneity of informal conversation. These kinds of comics are often accused of having ugly, crude and vulgar language.

On the other hand, comics can be subject specific, linked directly to a particular topic (see Figure 19.2). Although comic strips are traditionally associated with non-serious material, they can be used to communicate sophisticated ideas to a wide audience. In educative comic strip, the tone will still usually be informal, but images will be accompanied by text that uses technical or factual language as an integral part of the communication.

The **grammar** will vary depending upon the kind of publication. Direct speech will often be made up of grammatically incomplete utterances, particularly in comics creating fictional worlds. Informative comic strip is more likely to use grammatical

Figure 19.1   Extract from *Judge Dredd*

Figure 19.2 Extract from *Marx for Beginners*

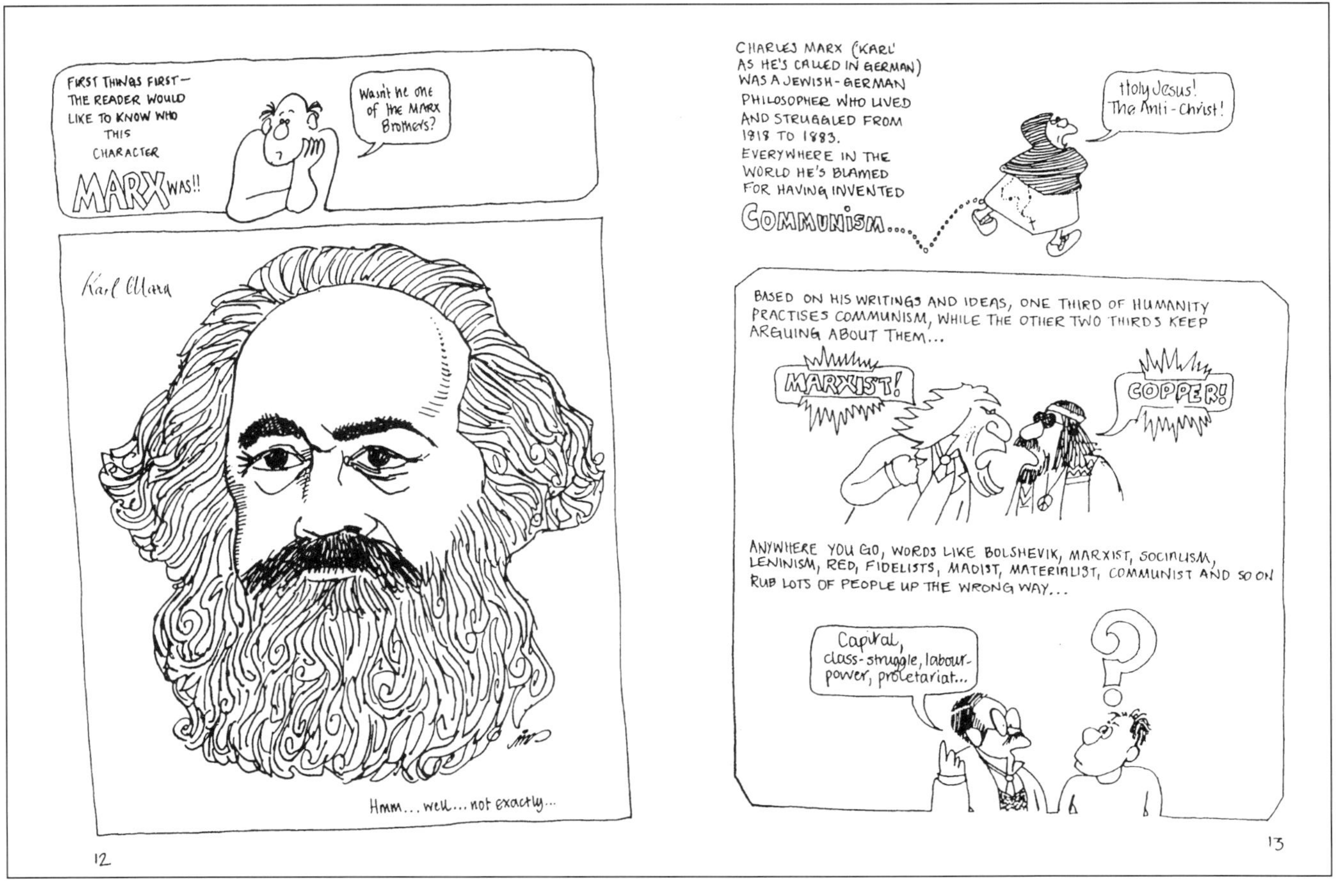

utterances, but verbless clauses and noun phrases are still common. The sentence structures are more likely to be complex in educative comic strip texts:

> A   S   P
> (Based on his writings and ideas), (one third of humanity) (practises)
> SCl–NFCl
>
>   O   A
> (Communism) (while the other two thirds keep arguing about them) . . .
>   SCl–ACl   SCl–NFCl

(Figure 19.2)

In comic strip that is basically narrative, sentences tend to be simple, often marked by
typical non-standard usage:

>   S   P   C   P   O
> (The M.I.A.S.) (are) (in the open)! (Go) (chain guns)! (Figure 19.1)

Comics aim to create a personal relationship with their readers. They are often
described as 'alternative' because they do not conform to expectations of traditional
narrative.

19.6 What to look for in an unfamiliar variety of English

The following checklist can be used to identify key features in an unfamiliar variety.
There will not be examples of all the features listed in every text, but the list can be
used as a guide.

   The following are helpful questions to ask.

Register

1   What is the **mode**? – spoken or written?
2   What is the **manner**? – the relationship between the participants: personal or
    impersonal? formal or informal? one-way or two-way communication? the
    purpose of the communication? the relative status of the participants?
3   What is the **field**? – the subject matter will indicate the kind of discourse taking
    place.

Lexis

1   Is the language **formal** or **informal**? **subject specific** or **colloquial**?
2   Are the **nouns** concrete or abstract?
3   Are the **verbs** dynamic or stative?
4   Are the **modifiers** descriptive/evaluative or factual/technical? is pre- or post-
    modification used?
5   Are the **nominal groups** long or short?
6   Are there any recognisable **collocations**?
7   What kinds of **adverbials** are used? – time? place? manner?
8   Are any **abbreviations** or **codes** used?
9   Does the language reflect a specific **person, place** or **historical period**?

Prosodics

1   Do variations in **tone, pitch** or **pace** indicate a speaker's attitude? thoughts?
    feelings?

2 Do rising, falling, rising-falling or falling-rising **intonation patterns** mark a speaker's intentions? make utterances distinctive?
3 Is **stress** used for effect? to draw attention to key lexical items?
4 Do **pauses** mark the end of a grammatically complete utterance? enhance meaning?

Grammar

1 Are **grammatical utterances** complete? incomplete?
2 Are there any links with **spoken language**? – contractions? colloquialisms? abbreviated or disjointed sentences?
3 Does the **mood** change? – declarative to make statements? interrogatives to question? imperatives to instruct?
4 Is anything noticeable about the **tense of verbs**? – simple present for playscripts, comics or information texts? simple past for narratives, letters or diaries?
5 Is the **sentence structure** varied? – simple, compound, complex, or compound-complex? verbless clauses? minor sentences?
6 What kinds of **subordinate clauses** are used? – NCl? ACl? NFCl? RelCl?
7 Are any **modal verbs** used?
8 Are the sentences **active** or **passive**?
9 Are **marked themes** used to draw attention to key elements of the clause?
10 What kinds of **cohesion** are used? – repetition of lexis? pronominal references? chronological sequences?

Metaphorical and rhetorical language

1 Is there any **phonological patterning**? – alliteration? rhythm? rhyme?
2 Is there any **lexical and syntactical patterning**? – repetition of words, clauses or sentence structures? parallelism? antithesis? listing?
3 Is there any **semantic patterning**? – metaphors? similes? symbolism? personification or animation? puns? ambiguity?

Graphological/typographical features

1 Is the text handwritten or typed?
2 Is there anything distinctive about the **style of the handwriting** (graphology)? – child? adult? abbreviations? capitalisation?
3 Is there anything significant about the **print size**? **shape**? **style**? (typography)
4 Is **colour** used?
5 Is the **layout** distinctive?

Summary

Comment on the **function** of the discourse.

Consider the **effect** of the linguistic and stylistic features, and the ways in which they aim to influence the target audience.

Concentrate on what makes the discourse **distinctive** – that is, different from other varieties.

Be open-minded and avoid approaching texts with rigid expectations. The material in this section establishes general expectations, but writers can draw upon a range of techniques, mixing formats and styles to communicate effectively with their intended audience.

(20) How to use your knowledge

The information covered in Parts II and III can be used in a variety of ways and you should be prepared to be versatile in your approach. Initially, you need to be confident about the reference material in Part I so that you can respond to questions using the appropriate terminology. When you feel able to recognise and discuss lexical, grammatical, phonological and stylistic features, you are ready to focus on the specific demands of coursework projects and examination questions. If you intend to sit a language examination, check the requirements of the syllabus and look at past papers so that you know exactly what kind of tasks you will be expected to tackle.

20.1 Analysis

Whatever the task that faces you, there are certain processes you can follow in order to become familiar with unseen material. Always start by asking yourself some general questions about the **register** – assess the possible **audience**, **purpose** and **context**; note the **mode**, **manner** and **field**. Always mark out or jot down appropriate examples so that you have **evidence** for the conclusions you reach. Having established some general parameters, consider the **variety** of English and the **distinctive features** with which it is associated. Read the material again, marking any examples of the distinctive features you have remembered. Your study of the text(s) should cover the following key areas:

1 **Written texts** Lexis, grammar, cohesion, stylistic features, point of view and layout.
2 **Spoken transcripts** Pronunciation, lexis, grammar, cohesion, stylistic features, prosodic features and discourse features.

Not all the areas will be appropriate for each example, but they will give you a way into the material with which you are presented.

Having worked through the key areas methodically, you will be quite familiar with the material. At this stage, it is absolutely essential to work out exactly what the question requires you to do.

20.2 Original writing

As well as analysing texts produced by other people, language courses will often encourage students to develop their own writing skills. A knowledge of the ways in which audience, purpose and context affect speech and writing, an understanding of lexical and grammatical patterns, a sensitivity to rhetorical and metaphorical language and an ability to recognise different formats should help you to 'craft' your own writing. By manipulating linguistic structures, you will be able to create effective examples of a range of different varieties of English.

Some questions may require you to use language poetically to entertain your intended audience – to write a **poem** or a **short story** effectively, you need to be confident about the linguistic features of literary language. If you can recognise key techniques used by other writers, you can adapt them to make your own work more individual. Other questions may need you to adopt a factual rather than a fictional approach – **information** and **instruction** texts need to be approached logically. Make sure that you think about an appropriate layout as well as the lexis and grammar that will suit the intended audience. If you tackle a **letter**, make sure that you use the correct format – the address layout, date, opening and closing greetings and paragraph structure must follow accepted conventions. In other cases, you may have to write a **newspaper article** to cover a particular story – the layout, tone, lexis and grammar will have to be appropriate. You need to be familiar with the features of newspaper language so that you can indicate through the lexis, grammar and style whether you are writing in tabloid or broadsheet form.

Often you will have to provide an **evaluation** of the work you have carried out. In your **introduction**, it is useful to establish what you have learnt from your wider study of similar text types – identify the distinctive features of the form you have chosen. The middle section of your evaluation should then focus on three key areas of your work:

1 **Content** The selection of appropriate material; your approach to making it suitable for your chosen format and audience; any omissions or additions.
2 **Linguistic and stylistic choices** The reasons behind lexical and grammatical choices; the points at which the tone changes; and the effects created by any rhetorical or metaphorical language.
3 **Difficulties and successes** An assessment of areas of the writing that caused problems and a description of any areas that seem to have worked particularly well.

The **conclusion** should then tackle your overall aims and try to assess how far you feel you have met them.

In your original writing you will be expected to:

• engage your audience;
• show a clear sense of purpose;
• manipulate language and style to create appropriate effects;
• use redrafting strategies to develop your material effectively.

20.3 Tackling a coursework project

This part of your course will offer you the chance to undertake a practical and investigative study of an area of personal interest. You will be expected to show a good understanding of the area you have chosen and your project will have to show your ability to apply linguistic knowledge to the spoken data or written material you have collected.

The first stage of your investigation will be to establish an appropriate **topic** or **area of study**. Having decided on this, you need to define a **field of reference** – outline some key questions which pinpoint the aim of your project. Try to establish a **hypothesis** so that your work can either prove or disprove your initial standpoint. You will then need to collect the kind of material your examination board requires. If you are going to carry out a study of spoken language, it is important to spend time getting the **transcript** as accurate as possible before beginning work on your commentary. Remember to provide a key if you use symbols to mark significant prosodic features.

The next stage is to tackle the **commentary** which will provide an objective assessment of the material you have collected. The **introduction** should give a brief outline of your field of reference, clearly establishing your interests and aims. The three middle sections should focus on:

1 **Description** Some overall comment needs to be provided on: the content of your material; where you found it; and any other background material that is necessary for an examiner to understand your investigation.
2 **Transcription/presentation of written material** An accessible format needs to be adopted so that an examiner can easily link your discussion to the original material.
3 **Analysis** The focus should be linked both to the kind of material you have selected and to the hypothesis with which you started. In order to reach appropriate conclusions about your hypothesis, your commentary should address relevant areas of lexis, grammar and style – for spoken language, prosodic features, pronunciation and discourse features should also be considered.

The **conclusion** should try to summarise your findings, returning to your original hypothesis and assessing whether or not your expectations have been met. You should try to explain what you have learnt from your investigation and show an awareness of the inevitable limitations of your study.

In your project work, you will be expected to:

- establish a context for your analysis;
- present your findings in an accessible way, using diagrams, tables and graphs where appropriate;
- focus your discussion clearly, so that an examiner can see whether your investigation has borne out your original assumption or not;
- balance linguistic analysis with appropriate theoretical knowledge of the topic you are studying.

20.4 Tackling examination questions

Questions can take a variety of forms. **Desk studies** will test your ability to read closely and to produce writing for specific purposes and audiences. You will be presented with a range of textual material about forty-eight hours before your examination, and it is important to spend time annotating the text. It is worth using the following process to become familiar with the material:

1 Identify the **variety** and jot down a list of the **distinctive features** usually associated with the text type.
2 Make notes on the **intended audience**, the **purpose** and the **context**.
3 Establish the **register**: field, mode and manner.
4 Text mark the material so that you can easily identify the **key points** made in the content.
5 Highlight **lexical**, **grammatical** and **stylistic features** which are typical of the variety. Be prepared to look at words, phrases, clauses and sentences as well as at the overall structure and layout.

In the examination you will be given questions which require you to **re-present the material** you have studied. The task may be to produce a report, to write a letter, to design a leaflet or hand-out, to create a radio or television script for transmission, or to write an article. To tackle the written task successfully, you need to identify the **intended audience**, the purpose and the **format** of the end product you have to create. You **lexical**, **grammatical** and **stylistic choices** must also be appropriate.

Your knowledge of grammar and the characteristics of different varieties will help you to establish your approach to the task set. If you are familiar with the typical features of the written form you have to produce, you will be more likely to adapt the source material appropriately.

Other **editorial questions** may require you to rewrite a tabloid newspaper article as a broadsheet, or to simplify an extract so that it is appropriate for a young child or a foreign student learning English as a second language. You may be asked to re-present a poetic description as a factual document or to adapt an extract from a novel as a radio script. The key to doing these kinds of tasks well lies in your ability to:

- identify the relevant subject matter in the source material;
- use the appropriate layout and structure for the rewritten version;
- adapt the lexis, grammar and style for the given audience and purpose.

On some occasions, you may be asked to **evaluate** the differences between your rewritten version and the source material. Efficient text marking will help you to establish the characteristic features of the **source material**: identify the variety and look for any relevant lexical, grammatical and stylistic evidence to support your decision. You then need to follow a similar approach with **your own writing**: decide which features are typical of the form you have been asked to use and select appropriate examples to show that you have adopted the main characteristics. Finally, you will need to **compare** the two versions, thinking about what has been gained or lost in the rewrite.

In some areas of the examination, you will also have to write traditional **essays**. Because of the pressure of time, planning is essential – you need to ensure that you cover the key areas and organise your ideas appropriately. Before starting to write the essay, you should prepare in this way:

1 Underline the key words in the title so that you can work out exactly what the question is asking you to do.
2 Establish a starting point – jot down 'Introduction' and list some key points that will provide you with a general framework for your essay.
3 Define **three** key areas to make up the main body of your essay – give each area a title so that you can make sure that you focus on only one thing at a time. Use these headings for your notes only.
4 Under each heading, jot down the key points you wish to make. Try to group together similar points, and find links between different areas.
5 Choose appropriate examples to substantiate the points you make – evidence is crucial, so draw on knowledge from other areas of your course.
6 Round off your discussion with a strong conclusion. List some related new points, rather than just repeating earlier ones.

You should be prepared to provide **relevant information**, **examples** and your **own viewpoint**. Successful essays will also show your ability to **cross-reference**. Language topics are not discrete units, and you should be able to draw on your knowledge of:

- social, cultural, geographical and historical aspects of English;
- lexical, grammatical and stylistic features of written and spoken English;
- key issues and current debates.

It is important to remember that your essay will not only be assessed for the relevance and organisation of its content. The **accuracy** and **fluency** of your own writing style are also crucial – many examination boards now draw attention on the front page of the examination paper to the importance of a good style and a well-organised structure. Always try to reread your work so that you can pinpoint any minor inaccuracies which might otherwise spoil the overall effect of your essay.

20.5 Preparing for an examination

Revision is a crucial part of any examination preparation. You need time to look back at work covered in order to establish what you feel confident about and what causes you problems. If you do this in plenty of time, you can immediately begin to fill any gaps in your understanding, avoiding last-minute panics. Plan ahead and organise your time effectively, remembering that few people can sit for hours on end learning topic after topic.

In the course of your study, you will have covered all kinds of **linguistic terminology**. You need to be able to use this as a shorthand to describe the linguistic patterns and processes you encounter. Use the Glossary (page 466) to establish what you know, and then work logically through the terms which still seem difficult. Your starting point should be Part I, as this defines and explains the grammatical, phonetic, phonological and stylistic terms which have been used in the rest of the book.

The next stage in your preparation should focus on the key areas of **linguistic debate**. Reread Part II and draw up lists of key points and appropriate evidence for each topic covered. Add examples and any other relevant information from your own study of language. These checklists should form the framework for your revision – read around the key points you have listed in order to broaden your basic knowledge.

Alongside your knowledge of language topics, you need to develop a bank of information about the different **varieties of English**. Again develop lists of key points which will help you to identify the characteristic features of different kinds of spoken and written English. Be prepared to have a general approach which can be applied to unfamiliar varieties. Remember that you may have to use these lists to analyse examples or to help you tackle editorial-type questions.

When you are actually sitting with the examination paper in front of you, read the whole of the **rubric** before you start. Make sure you know how many questions you have to answer, which sections they should come from, and the time you should allocate to each. Then work out the times at which you should start each question.

Choose questions carefully, making sure before you start that you know exactly what they require you to do. Always underline the key information in a question, to draw your attention to its precise requirements. Spend time planning: good organisation will always be rewarded. It is better to focus closely on three key areas than to cover everything in such a general way that your answer is rambling and vague. If you do feel you have tackled the wrong question, think very carefully before abandoning a half-finished answer – you are more likely to be able to redeem what you have started than to begin again from scratch.

Although thorough revision will help you to succeed in your examinations, the ability to **apply your knowledge** in new contexts is crucial. You must be versatile in your approach, able to:

* discuss language topics knowledgeably;
* analyse examples of spoken and written English;

- summarise the key points in source material and re-present them for a new audience;
- write in a variety of formats, tones and styles;
- describe and evaluate the differences between your rewrite and the source material;
- make cross-references and develop links between different areas of language study;
- cope with unfamiliar topics and examples, applying knowledge and analytical processes in new contexts.

Above all, a study of English reveals the complexity and versatility of the language. It is impossible to cover all areas of interest in one book, but the information and suggested approaches here should help you to embark on your study of English with confidence.

PART IV

Appendices

A Answers to activities

Activity 1.1 (page 6)

1 Nouns: *December, Monday, Christmas Eve, kid, fact, trauma, parents, existence, Santa Claus, age, bit, God, things, earthquakes, famines, motorway crashes, bed, blankets, word, Tog rating, quilts, heart, palms, anticipation, Beano album.*

2 Proper nouns: *Christmas, Santa Claus, Beano.*
Common nouns: *parents, existence, quilt, heart, trauma, bed, anticipation.*
Concrete nouns: *parents, quilt, heart, bed.*
Abstract nouns: *existence, trauma, anticipation.*

Activity 1.2 (page 8)

1 Modifiers: *gloomy, glorious, ancient, crimson, far, lower, redder, calm, calmest, long, tiny, seaweed-edged, glowing, flying, careless, young, old, harsh, rotting, solemn, lonely, sad, despairing, customary, large, golden, little.*

2 a Descriptive adjectives: *gloomy, glorious, calm, careless, harsh, solemn, lonely, sad, customary.*
  b Size or distance adjectives: *far, long, tiny, large, little.*
  c Age adjectives: *ancient, young, old.*
  d Colour adjectives: *crimson, redder, golden.*
  e Comparative and superlative adjectives: *lower, redder, calmest.*
  f Noun or verb modifiers: *seaweed-edged, glowing, flying, rotting, despairing.*

Activity 1.3 (page 13)

1 a *had* (aux) *gone* (lex)
  b *had* (lex)
  c *can* (aux) *do* (lex)
  d *did* (aux) *like* (lex)

2 a *flapped*: finite; past tense; third person; plural.
  b *laughs*: finite; present tense; third person; singular.
  c *have*: finite; present tense; second person; singular.
    gone: non-finite; past participle.
  d *carried*: finite; past tense; first person; singular.
  e *was*: finite; past tense; third person; singular.
    croaking: non-finite; present participle.
  f *chased*: finite; past tense; first person; plural.
  g *have*: finite; present tense; second person; singular.
    been: non-finite; past participle.

h *has*: finite; present tense; third person; singular.
   been: non-finite; past participle.
   happening: non-finite; present participle.
i *does*: finite; present tense; third person; singular.
   know: non-finite; base form.
3 a The boat *was lifted* above the dangerous sandbank *by the strong waves*.
   b The bells *were rung by the monks* to warn the surrounding villagers of the
      impending danger.
   c After the disturbance, the pub *was shut by the police*.
4 a The Black South African prisoners *were beaten*.
   b The child *was left* face down in the playground.
   c The way to split the atom *was discovered* and the first atom bomb *was created*.
   In each case the person or persons responsible for the action of the verb is omitted.
   In the passive sentences, therefore, the reader no longer knows who is
   accountable.

Activity 1.4 (page 14)

1 Verbs: *was woken, refusing to start, know, should have gone, helped to push,
   seemed to be doing, must be, flinging, were. . .pretending to be, went. . .to sleep,
   licked, took, was(n't), must. . .be staying, passed, was kicking, seemed, stopped to
   talk, asked, (I)'d had.*
2 a Two lexical verbs: *ask, licked.*
   b Two stative verbs: *be, seemed.*
   c Two dynamic verbs: *kicking, passed.*
   d Two primary auxiliary verbs: *was* woken, *'d* [had] *had.*
   e Two modal auxiliary verbs: *should, must.*
3 Passive voice: *I was woken at dawn by the sound of Grandad Sugden's rusty Ford
   Escort refusing to start.*
   Active version: *The sound of Grandad Sugden's rusty Ford Escort refusing to start
   woke me at dawn.*
4 Progressive aspect: *were. . .pretending.*
   Perfect aspect: *I'd had.*
5 Present tense: *I know.*
   Past tense: *I stopped.*
6 Two finite verbs: *I was, He seemed.*
   Two non-finite verbs: *refusing, woken.*

Activity 1.5 (page 16)

1 Circumstance adverbs: *brightly, well, again, anxiously, generally, recently, warily,
   often, sometimes, desperately, properly.*
2 Degree adverbs: *completely, really, very.*
3 Sentence adverbs: *nevertheless, however, perhaps, actually.*

Activity 1.6 (pages 18–19)

1 Personal pronouns: *we, it, I, me, he, she, her.*
2 Possessive pronouns: *ours, mine, hers.*
3 Reflexive pronoun: *myself.*
4 Demonstrative pronouns: *this, that.*
5 Interrogative pronouns: *who, what.*
6 Relative pronoun: *which.*
7 Indefinite pronouns: *everyone, some, everything, something.*

Activity 1.7 (page 20)

1 Articles: definite-*the*; indefinite-*a*, *an*.
2 Possessive determiner: *her*.
3 Demonstrative determiners: *this*, *that*.
4 Indefinite determiners: *any*, *either*, *many*, *both*, *every*, *some*, *more*.
5 Numbers: *one*, *two*, *second*.

Activity 1.8 (pages 20–1)

1 *out*: particle.
2 *into*: preposition.
3 *out of*: prepositions.
4 *on*: particle.
5 *in*: particle.
6 *towards*: preposition.
7 *down*: particle.
8 *above*: preposition.
9 *up*: particle.
10 *down to*: prepositions.
11 *out*: particle.

Activity 1.9 (page 22)

1 *While*: subordinating conjunction (time).
2 *and*: co-ordinating conjunction (addition).
3 *but*: co-ordinating conjunction (contrast).
4 *Because*: subordinating conjunction (reason).
5 *Unless*: subordinating conjunction (condition).
6 *and*: co-ordinating conjunction (addition).
7 *if*: subordinating conjunction (condition).
8 *Wherever*: subordinating conjunction (place).
9 *Because*: subordinating conjunction (reason).
10 *since*: subordinating conjunction (reason).
11 *than*: subordinating conjunction (comparison).

Activity 1.10 (page 23)

1 *un-* (bound) + *justify* (free) + *-able* (bound).
2 *summa(ry)* (free) + *-ative* (bound).
3 *mid-* (bound) + *night* (free).
4 *day* (free) + *-ly* (bound).
5 *negative* (free) + *-ity* (bound).
6 *un-* (bound) + *like* (free) + *-ly* (bound).
7 *pity* (free) + *-ful* (bound).

Activity 1.11 (page 24)

(The answers here are single possibilities only – many other words could be cited as valid examples.)

1 *re-* + *present*.
2 *hospital* + *-ise*.
3 *calm* + *-ly*.
4 *child* + *-less*.
5 *glorifi* + *-cation*; *audit* + *-or*; *act* + *-or*.

Activity 1.12 (page 26)

1 *s*: plural noun inflection.

2 *ed*: past tense inflection.
3 *s'*: plural noun inflection and possessive inflection.
4 *ing*: present participle inflection.
5 *'s*: possessive inflection.
6 *s*: present tense third person singular inflection.

Activity 1.13 (page 26)

1 *greatness* (N): free = *great* (Adj); bound = *-ness* (derivational).
2 *multigym* (N): free = *gym* (N); bound = *multi-* (derivational).
3 *declaration* (N): free = *declare* (V); bound = *-ation* (derivational).
4 *delimited* (V): free = *limit* (V); bound = *de-* (derivational); bound = *-ed* (inflectional).
5 *inter-rivalry* (N): free = *rival* (N); bound = *inter-* (derivational); bound = *-ry* (derivational).
6 *illogical* (Adj): free = *logic* (N); bound = *il-* (derivational); bound = *-al* (derivational).
7 *predetermination* (N): free = *determine* (V); bound = *pre-* (derivational); bound = *-ation* (derivational).
8 *horrifying* (V): free = *horrify* (V); bound = *-ing* (inflectional).
9 *institutionalise* (V): free = *institute* (V); bound = *-ion* (derivational); bound = *-al* (derivational); bound = *-ise* (derivational).
10 *reassesses* (V): free = *assess* (V); bound = *re-* (derivational); *-es* (inflectional).

Activity 1.14 (pages 28–9)

    pre-mod   pre-mod   pre-mod   pre-mod   post-mod
(The first summer's) *day*; (my) *curtains*; (the new dawn's) *sunlight*; (the) *paths* (of dust)
     post-mod   pre-mod   post-mod
(which lay on the ancient sea chest); (the) *scratches*; *tribute* (to a life of hardship); *I*;
    pre-mod   post-mod
(the interesting) *stories* (which were linked to the marks);
    pre-mod   post-mod   pre-mod   post-mod
(the drowned) *men* (who had owned this chest); (their own) *versions* (of events);
    pre-mod   pre-mod   post-mod pre-mod
them; (the) *wall*; (another withered) *mark* (of the past); (this) *time*;
    pre-mod   pre-mod   post-mod   pre-mod
(the faded rose) *wallpaper*; (The) *memory* (of another place); (my hazy) *mind*; *me*;
      pre-mod   post-mod   pre-mod
connections; (that first disturbing) *visit* (to the ruined cottage); (it's ongoing) *effects*;
    pre-mod   post-mod
(this second historical) *link* (waiting for me); *me*.

Activity 1.15 (page 29)

  m   m   h   q
1 the interesting stories which were linked to the marks
  det   V   N   RelCl

  m   m   h   q
2 their own versions of events
  det   Adj   N   PrepP

  m   h
3 the wall
  det N

    m   m   m   h

4   the faded rose wallpaper
   det   V   N   N

    m   m   m   h   q

5   This second historical link waiting for me
   det   num   Adj   N   NFCl

Activity 1.16 (page 30)

 h   h   m   h   m   h   q

deep and white; rather sad; quite sure of his need for company;
Adj   Adj   Adv   Adj   Adv   Adj PrepP

 m   h   q   h   m   h

very sincere about the purpose of his journey; isolated and very bleak;
Adv   Adj   PrepP   V   Adv   Adj

    m   h   m   h   q

surprisingly fierce; quite certain that he had made the right decision;
   Adv   Adj   Adv   Adj   NCl

m   m   h   q

so unbelievably withdrawn that I could not agree with his interpretation of events;
Adv   Adv   Adj   NCl

   h   m   h   h   q

unsure and rather quiet; certain   he wished he had not come.
Adj   Adv   Adj   Adj   ∅   NCl

Activity 1.17 (pages 36–7)

  S   P   C   S   P   Od

(He) (was) (a very strong and good-looking man), (but) (he) (had) (a red face and
                                                       conj

              S   P   C   P   C

rather reddish hair). (He) (was) (not) (a good man) (and) (was) (cruel to his people).
                          neg   conj

     A   S   P   Od   A   S

(Like his father), (he) (enjoyed) (hunting animals). (One day) (the Red King's arrow)
  A   P   Od   S   P   C   P

(just) (missed) (a big deer). (William) (was) (very excited) (and) (called out to)
                                                    conj

        O   S   P   Od   A   S   P

(his friend, Walter). (Walter) (fired) (an arrow), (but) (by accident) (it) (stuck)
                                          conj

    A   S   P   C   S   P   C   S

(in the King's eye) (and) (he) (fell) (dead). (Walter) (was) (very frightened) (and) (he)
           conj   conj

P   A   S   P   A   A   A   S

(rode) (away). (The King's body) (lay) (in the forest) (all day). (In the evening) (it)
 P   A   A   P   A

(was carried) (away) (in a workman's cart) (and) (buried) (in the big church)
                                          conj

         A

(at a town called Winchester).

Activity 1.18 (page 42)

when we arrived; *because* things were not quite *what* they seemed; *Looking* back; the
  ACl   ACl   NCl   NFCl

key *which* did not fit; *leaving* us stranded; nothing for us *to do*; The fact *that* we were
    RelCl   NFCl   NFCl   NCl

helpless; *since* we were stuck outside; *Although* we could do nothing for the moment;
          ACl   ACl

obliged to act; *rushing* around like a headless chicken *while* the rain fell steadily; *so that*
NFCl   NFCl   NFCl   ACl   ACl

we could go into the house and (∅) wait for the removal van in the dry; *that* it was on
                                  ACl   NCl

its way at last; *as* we settled into a bare and disorganised house *what* was *to come* next
                 ACl   NCl   NFCl

Activity 2.2 (pages 56–7)

1	a	[f]: labiodental.		d	*th* [θ]: dental.	
	b	[n]: alveolar.		e	*sh* [ʃ]: palato-alveolar.	
	c	[m]: bilabial.		f	[k]: velar.	
2	a	[p]: voiceless.		d	*ng* [ŋ]: voiced.	
	b	*ch* [tʃ]: voiceless.		e	[l]: voiced.	
	c	[d]: voiced.		f	*dge* [dʒ]: voiced.	
3	a	[g]: voiced velar plosive.		d	[p]: voiceless bilabial plosive.	
	b	[ʃ]: voiceless palato-alveolar fricative.		e	[m]: voiced bilabial nasal.	
	c	[v]: voiced labiodental fricative.		f	[h]: voiceless glottal fricative.	

Activity 2.3 (page 59)

1 [i]: close front spread.
2 [ɔ]: half-open back moderate rounding.
3 [a]: open front neutral.
4 [o]: half-close back slightly rounded.
5 [u]: close back rounded.

Activity 2.4 (page 60)

1 [ʌ]: The centre of the tongue is just below half-open position with the lips in a neutral position.
2 [iː]: The front of the tongue is in a close position with the lips spread.
3 [uː]: The back of the tongue is in a close position with the lips closely rounded.
4 [æ]: The front of the tongue is just above open position with the lips in a neutral position.

Activity 2.5 (page 61)

1 [eɪ]: The front of the tongue moves from between half-open and half-close to just above half-close position with the lips moving from neutral to loosely spread; it is a closing diphthong.
2 [əʊ]: The centre and then the back of the tongue move from between half-open and half-close to just above half-close position with the lips moving from neutral to rounded; it is a closing diphthong.
3 [ʊə]: The back and then the centre of the tongue move from just above half-close

to between half-open and half-close position with the lips moving from rounded to neutral; it is a centring diphthong.
4 [aʊ]: The back of the tongue moves from open to just above half-close position with the lips moving from neutral to rounded; it is a closing diphthong.

Activity 2.6 (page 64)

1 *cot* /kɒt/, *got* /gɒt/; *hackle* /hækəl/, *haggle* /hægəl/; *back* /bæk/, *bag* /bæg/.
2 *more* /mɔː/, *nor* /nɔː/; *limit* /lɪmɪt/, *linnet* /lɪnɪt/; *comb* /kəʊm/, *cone* /kəʊn/.
3 *sot* /sɒt/, *shot* /ʃɒt/; *massing* /mæsɪŋ/, *mashing* /mæʃɪŋ/; *puss* /pʊs/, *push* /pʊʃ/.
4 *bat* /bæt/, *vat* /væt/; *rebel* /rebəl/, *revel* /revəl/; *Job* /dʒəʊb/, *Jove* /dʒəʊv/.

Activity 2.7 (page 65)

1 *is the train coming?* [ɪs ðə treɪŋ kʌmɪŋ]: alveolar nasal /n/ in *train* becomes velar nasal /ŋ/ before velar plosive /k/ in *coming*.
2 *what do you want?* [wɒt dʒ uː wɒnt]: alveolar plosive /d/ in *do* becomes palato-alveolar affricate /dʒ/ before palatal-approximant /j/ in *you*.
3 *he sails ships* [hɪ seɪlʃ ʃɪps]: alveolar fricative /s/ in *sails* becomes palato-alveolar fricative /ʃ/ before palato-alveolar fricative /ʃ/ in *ships*.

Activity 2.8 (pages 66–7)

1 *she should **have** gone home*: /hæv/ → /əv/.
   Elision: Word-initial /h/ frequently undergoes elision in informal conversation.
   Reduction: Vowels in unstressed syllables are often reduced to /ə/.
2 *she'll be here in **an** hour **or** two*: /æn/ → /ən/ [aʊərɔ tuː].
   Reduction: Vowels in unstressed syllables are often reduced to /ə/.
   Liaison: Word-final unstressed vowel /ə/ followed by initial vowel /ɔː/ is often linked by insertion of /r/ in speech.
3 *the train came in late*: [treɪŋ keɪm].
   Assimilation: Word-final alveolar nasal /n/ becomes velar before velar plosive /k/.

B Glossary

This glossary contains a brief definition of the key words used in this book. Examples are printed in *italics*, with **bold type** to highlight the key item.

abstract A term used in grammar to denote nouns that have no physical qualities (*courage, idea*).

accelererando A term used to describe speech that is getting faster.

accent A set of distinctive pronunciations that mark regional or social identity.

acceptable A term that denotes any usage that native speakers feel is allowed.

accusative case In an inflected language, (cf. an inflection) which marks the object of a verb.

active voice A grammatical structure in which the subject is the actor of a sentence.

adjective A word that defines attributes of a noun (*The **blue** flower*) and that can also express contrasts of degree (*The **smallest** boy was the **fastest***).

adjunct An adverb that relates directly to the meaning of the verb, giving details of time, manner and place.

adverb A word that describes the action of the verb (*The girl laughed **loudly***); that can act as an intensifier (***very** fierce*); and that can function as a sentence connector (***Somehow**, I did not believe him*).

adverbial A term to denote words, phrases or clauses that function as adverbs.

affix A morpheme which is attached to other words to create new words (***un-** + child + **-like***), or to mark a grammatical relationship (*go + **-ing***).

affricate A term used to denote consonants in which a complete closure of the vocal tract is followed by a slow release characteristic of a fricative (***church***).

agent A linguistic form describing who or what is responsible for the action of a verb (***The little dog** laughed. . .and **the dish** ran away with the spoon*).

agreement A grammatical relationship between words in which the choice of one element determines the form of another (*The girl **runs**; he talked to **himself** regularly*). Also called **concord**.

allegro A term used to describe speech that is articulated quickly.

alliteration The repetition of the same sound in the initial position in a sequence of words.

alveolar A term used to denote consonants produced by raising the tongue to the alveolar ridge (*[t]*).

ambiguous The term used to describe a word, phrase, clause or sentence with multiple meanings.

anapest A unit of poetic metre made up of two unstressed syllables followed by a stressed syllable (*ŭn·ă·líke*).

anaphoric A form of referencing in which a pronoun or noun phrase points backwards to something mentioned earlier in a discourse (*The film was breathtaking and the audience watched **it** in silence*).

antonyms Words that are opposite in meaning (*hot/cold; fast/slow*).

apposition A sequence of nouns or noun phrases that have the same meaning (*my neighbour, the builder, came to see me yesterday*).

appropriate A term used to describe any language use that is seen as suitable for the context in which it occurs.

approximant A term used to denote consonants in which the organs of speech approach each other but do not get sufficiently close to produce a plosive, nasal or fricative ([l]; [j]). Also called a **frictionless continuant**.

archaism A word or phrase no longer in current use.

article A word that indicates whether a noun is definite (*the*) or indefinite (*a/an*).

articulation The movements of the speech organs modifying the air flow in order to produce speech sounds.

aspect The timescale of the action expressed by a verb, which may be complete or in progress. There are two forms: **progressive** and **perfect**.

aspiration The term used to denote audible breath accompanying a sound (*pʰeople*).

assimilation 1. In phonology, the way in which the sounds of one word can change the sounds in neighbouring words. 2. The process by which native inflections are added to loan words as they become part of the general word stock.

assonance A repetition of the same or similar vowel sounds.

asyndetic The linking of linguistic units without a conjunction (*The girl sang quickly, hesitantly, fearfully*).

attributive A term used to denote adjectives or other modifiers that precede the noun in a noun phrase (*the red apple*).

auxiliary verb A verb that precedes the lexical verb in a verb phrase (*I can go; I have gone*).

baby talk A simplified form of speech used by adults to children, or the immature language forms used by children.

base The minimal form of a word to which affixes can be added.

bilabial A term used to denote consonants formed with both lips ([b], [m]).

blank verse Unrhymed poetry with a very disciplined verse form (iambic pentameter) in which each line will usually have ten syllables and five stresses.

blend A word composed of the parts of more than one word (*guess + estimate → guesstimate*).

borrow To introduce a loan word from one language into another.

bound morpheme A morpheme that can only occur in words attached to other morphemes (*un-, -ing*).

broad A term used to denote a phonetic or phonemic transcription of spoken language that shows only the functionally important features.

caesura The natural pause in a line of verse, which often follows the strongest stress.

cardinal number The basic form of a number (*one, two, three*).

cardinal vowels A set of reference vowels which are used as a means of describing, classifying and comparing vowel sounds.

caretaker speech The distinctive speech of adults when they talk to children; also called **motherese**.

cataphoric A form of referencing in which a pronoun or noun phrase points forwards to something mentioned later in a discourse (*It was lovely, a day to remember*).

centring diphthong A diphthong where the second element moves towards the unstressed (schwa) vowel [ə].

clause A group of words, usually with a finite verb which is structurally larger than a phrase. Clauses may be described as **independent** (main) or **dependent** (subordinate).

clear *l* A lateral consonant which resembles the vowel [i] with the front of the tongue raised (*leg*); a dark *l*, however, resembles the vowel [u] with the back of the tongue raised (*deal*).

cliché An image that has become meaningless because of overuse (*we'll **leave no stone unturned***).

close A term used to denote a vowel sound made with the tongue in the highest position ([i], [u]). Vowels may also be described as **half-close**.

closed class words Grammatical function words like prepositions, determiners and conjunctions: new words are seldom added to the existing stock.

closing diphthong A diphthong where the second element moves towards a closer vowel like [ɪ] or [ʊ].

cohesion Links and connections which unite the elements of a discourse or text.

coinage The construction and addition of new words to the word stock.

collective noun A noun that refers to a group of people, animals or things (*family, government*).

collocation Two or more words that frequently occur together as part of a set phrase.

command An utterance intended to get other people to do something.

comment clause A commonly occurring clause which adds a remark to another clause in parenthesis (*I can come, **you know**, but I'm not sure I want to*).

common noun A noun that refers to a general group of objects or concepts (*table, happiness*).

complement A clause element that adds extra information about the subject or object of the clause after a copula verb (*The girl was **beautiful***).

complex sentence A sentence made up of one main and one or more subordinate or dependent clauses.

compound A word made up of at least two free morphemes (*database, skateboard*).

compound-complex sentence A sentence that contains both co-ordination and subordination.

compound sentence A sentence made up of at least two main clauses joined together by a co-ordinating conjunction.

concrete noun A noun that refers to physical things like people, objects, places, or substances.

conjunct A sentence adverb with a linking function (*however, otherwise*).

connotations The associations attached to a word in addition to its dictionary definition.

consonance A repetition of consonant sounds in the same position in a sequence of words.

consonant A speech sound produced when the vocal tract is either completely blocked or sufficiently blocked to cause noticeable friction ([p], [d]).

consonant cluster A series of consonants occurring at the beginning or end of a syllable.

contact language A marginal language created by people with no common language who need to communicate.

context The social circumstances in which speech and writing take place.

continuant A sound that can be made without interruption until the air in the lungs is exhausted ([l], [s], [θ]).

contraction A shortened word (*can't, you're*).

contrastive stress An emphatic stress placed on a particular linguistic item to draw attention to its significance (*The boy has **gone**; **the boy** has gone*).

convergence A process in which accents and dialects move closer to each other, reducing the difference between them.

conversation analysis A study of the key features of informal spoken interaction.

co-ordinating conjunction A word that joins elements of equal rank (*and, or, but*).

co-ordination The linking of lexical items which have the same grammatical status (*The girls and the boys; ran and jumped; slowly and proudly*).

copula A linking verb used to connect other clause elements (*The sky **became** overcast*).

corpus A collection of spoken and written material gathered for linguistic analysis.

count noun A noun that refers to things that can be counted and that has a plural form (*cats, lorries*).

creole A pidgin language that has become the native tongue of a speech community and is learned by children as their first language.

crescendo A term used to describe speech that is getting louder.

critical age The period between early childhood and puberty during which children can acquire language without instruction.

dactyl A unit of poetic metre made up of one stressed syllable followed by two unstressed syllables (*rápǐd·lў*).

dative case In an inflected language, an inflection which marks the indirect object of a verb.

declarative A grammatical mood used to express a statement (*I live in a flat*).

decreolisation The process of modification by which creole languages are made more like the standard language of an area.

degree A comparison of adjectives or adverbs: **comparative** (*louder, more intelligent*) and **superlative** (*loudest, most intelligent*).

deictic, deixis Terms used to denote words or expressions that rely on the context to convey meaning (*now, over there, you*).

demonstrative A term used to describe determiners or pronouns that distinguish one item from other similar ones (*this/that, these/those*).

denotation The dictionary definition of a word.

dental A term used to describe consonants made when the tongue touches the inside of the teeth ([ð] or [θ]).

derivation A morphological process of word formation in which affixes are added to create new words.

descriptive A term used to denote an approach to language based on observation of language in use, focusing on appropriateness and acceptability rather than on concepts of 'right' and 'wrong'.

determiner A lexical item which specifies the number and definiteness of a noun (*the, a, some*).

diachronic A term used to describe the study of language change over time.

diacritics Marks added to phonetic symbols to specify various sound qualities, such as length, tone, stress, and nasalisation.

dialect A language variety marked by distinctive grammar and vocabulary, which is used by a group of speakers with common regional or social backgrounds.

dialect levelling A decrease in dialect differences caused by language contact and possibly by the mass media use of one dialect.

dialogue Language interaction with two or more participants.

diminuendo A term used to describe speech that is getting quieter.

diphthong A vowel sound in which there is a change of quality during its articulation.

direct object A clause element directly affected by the action of the verb (*The dog ate a bone*).

direct speech The actual words spoken by a person which are recorded in a written form enclosed in quotation marks (*'You know I love books,' he said*).

discourse Any spoken or written language that is longer than a sentence.

disjunct A sentence adverb giving the speaker or writer a chance to comment on the content or style of a sentence as a whole (***Regrettably***, *he died last night*).

disyllabic Having two syllables.

divergence A process in which accents and dialects move further apart, thus increasing the difference between them.

double negative A structure in which more than one negative is used in one verb phrase (*I haven't done **nothing***).

dummy word A word that has no specific meaning but has a grammatical function (***Do** you like reading?*; ***It** was the train on Platform 1 that I was meant to catch*).

dynamic A verb that expresses an action rather than a state and that can be used in the progressive (*run/run**ning**; fly/fly**ing***).

elision The omission of sounds in connected speech.

ellipsis The omission of a part of a sentence which can be understood from the context.

embedded clause A subordinate clause which functions as a subject, object, complement or adverbial within a sentence (*The man **who lives next door** is very friendly*).

end-stopped A term used to describe a line of verse in which there is a natural pause in the meaning or phrasing at the end of a line.

enjambement The overlapping of meaning from one line of verse to the next.

etymology A study of the origins and history of words.

euphemism A word that replaces a term seen by society as taboo, socially unacceptable or unpleasant.

existential *there* A sentence in which *there* is a dummy subject followed by a delayed subject after the verb *to be* (***There** were **people** everywhere*).

exophoric A form of referencing in which a lexical item points directly to the wider linguistic context (*That man **there***).

field An area of meaning (for example, *medicine*) which is characterised by common lexical items (*GP, surgeon, nurse, injection, clinic*).

filled pause A voiced hesitation.

finite A term used to denote verbs marked for tense, person and number (*the boy sings, they sing, he sang*).

first language The language acquired by children as a native tongue and used as a main language in writing and speech.

focus The arrangement of clause elements so that attention is focused on a particular linguistic item (*it was **the red car** that broke down, **the house** was sold*).

foot A poetic unit of measure containing one or two stressed syllables and a variable number of unstressed syllables.

foregrounding A change in the sequence of clause elements in order to draw attention to a particular linguistic item.

form The word class and structure of a word (*living* – a present participle verb).

formulaic A term used to denote language that is patterned and that always occurs in the same form (*Yours sincerely, Wish you were here!*).

forte A term used to describe speech that is articulated loudly.

free morpheme The smallest meaningful unit of written language that can occur on its own.

fricative A term used to describe consonants where air escapes through a small passage, making a hissing noise ([v] or [f]).

fronting The movement of a clause element other than the subject to the beginning of a sentence.

full stop A punctuation mark signalling the end of a sentence in written language.

function The role of words or phrases within a clause (*subject, object, complement*).

function word Grammatical words like conjunctions, prepositions and determiners which express grammatical relationships.

genitive case In an inflected language, an inflection which marks possession.

glottal stop A sound produced when air stopped completely at the glottis by tightly closed vocal cords is released.

glottis The opening between the vocal cords.

gradable An adjective or adverb that can be compared (*happier, happiest*) or intensified (***so** happy*).

graphology A study of the writing system.

half-close/half-open The terms used to describe vowel sounds that are articulated with the tongue between close and open positions.

head word The main element in a phrase.

hexameter A line of verse containing six feet.

historic present The use of the present tense to narrate events which took place in the past.

holophrastic The stage of child language acquisition at which children produce grammatically unstructured single-word utterances.

homonyms Words with the same form but different meanings.

homophones Words that are pronounced the same but that have different meanings.

hyperbole Exaggeration used to heighten feeling and intensity.

hypercorrection A process of overcompensation whereby speakers who are trying to modify their accent or dialect produce a linguistic form that does not occur in the standard variety.

hypercreolisation The use of pure creole forms as a challenge to standard language.

hyponymy The relationship between words where the meaning of one form is included in the meaning of another (*tree – oak, ash, beech*; *drink – wine, coffee, water*). The inclusive term (*tree, drink*) is called the **superordinate**.

iambic A unit of poetic metre containing one unstressed syllable followed by a stressed syllable (*a̅·gó*).

idiolect An individual's own distinctive way of speaking.

idiom An expression in which the meaning of the whole conveys more than the meaning of the parts (*put your foot in it*).

imagery A descriptive or metaphorical use of language which creates a vivid picture.

imitation The adoption of linguistic features from copying the language of other users.

imperative A grammatical mood expressing a directive (commanding, warning, requesting, inviting, pleading, etc.): usually there is no subject and the verb is in the base form.

inclusive A term used to describe a first person plural reference which includes the speaker as well as the addressee(s).

indirect object An animate being that receives the action of a verb (*he gave **her** a present*; *the woman told the story **to her neighbour***).

indirect speech The words of a speaker reported in the form of a subordinate clause introduced by *that* (*He replied **that everyone was well***), instead of being quoted directly.

infinitive A non-finite verb which is in the base form and often preceded by the preposition *to* (*to live, to sleep*).

inflection The marking of a grammatical relationship with an affix (*-ing, -ed, 's*).

intensifier A word of phrase adding emphasis (*so, very, incredibly*).

internal rhyme The repetition of rhymes within a line of a verse.

interrogative A grammatical mood expressing a question in which the subject and verb are inverted.

interrogative word A question word used at the beginning of a clause to mark a question. Also known as a *wh- word*.

intonation The quality or tone of the voice in speech.

intransitive A term used to denote a verb that does not take a direct object.

intuition Instinctive knowledge about the acceptability or appropriateness of language use.

inversion Reversing the order of clause elements (*he laughed*; *did he laugh?*).

irony A way of writing in which what is meant is the opposite of what the words appear to say.

irregular A term used to denote language forms that do not conform to the standard pattern.

isogloss The boundary line separating one regional accent and dialect area from another.

labial A term used to describe consonants articulated with the lips ([m], [p]).

labiodental A term used to describe consonants produced by touching the bottom lip to the upper teeth ([v] or [f]).

language acquisition The process of learning a first language as a child, or learning a second or foreign language.

language change The process of change in a language over a period of time.

lateral A term used to describe consonants made by the flow of air around one or both sides of a closure made in the mouth (*clear l; dark l*).

legato A term used to describe speech that is marked by drawled or elongated pronunciation.

lento A term used to describe speech that is articulated slowly.

lexical diffusion The gradual spread of linguistic change.

lexical verb A verb conveying an action, an event or a state. Also called a **main verb**.

lexis The term used to describe the vocabulary of a language. Also called **lexicon**.

liaison A process that changes the pronunciation of words at boundary points.

lingua franca The main language used in an area in which speakers of more than one language live.

linking The introduction of a sound between two syllables to make pronunciation easier (**linking r** in *here and now*).

litotes A deliberate understatement.

loan word A word borrowed from another language.

main clause A clause that is not dependent and makes sense on its own.

malapropism A misuse of words that sound similar (*description* for *prescription*).

manner The relationship between participants in a language interaction.

metalanguage Language used to talk about language.

metaphor A descriptive use of language in which one thing is directly seen in terms of another (*a sea of troubles*).

metaphorical language The term used to describe any language use that is non-literal, using devices like metaphor, simile and oxymoron to create poetic and descriptive effects.

metonymy The use of an attribute for the thing meant (*the Crown* for *royalty*).

metre The pattern of stressed and unstressed syllables in a line of verse.

minimal pair/set A pair or set of words that are identical except for one phoneme occurring in the same place which alters meaning (*sit, bit, kit, lit, fit*).

minor sentence A sentence or utterance that lacks one or more of the clause elements and that often occurs as an unchanging formulaic structure (*Thanks. Great party!*).

modal Auxiliary verbs that mark contrasts in attitude such as obligation, possibility and prediction (*must, can, will*).

modification The use of one linguistic item to specify the nature of another (*the **blue** sea; the lion roared **loudly***).

monologue Speech or writing produced by a single person.

monometer A line of verse containing only one foot.

monophthong A simple or pure vowel sound.

monosyllabic Having one syllable.

mood Main clauses can have one of three moods: the **declarative** mood is used to make statements; the **imperative** mood is used to give orders and make requests; and the **interrogative** mood is used to ask questions.

morpheme The smallest unit of meaning.

morphology The study of the structure of words in terms of free and bound morphemes.

narrow A term used to denote a transcription that records the phonetic properties of spoken language in great detail.

nasal A term used to describe consonants produced with an open nasal passage, which allows air to escape through the nose as well as the mouth ([m] or [n]).

native speaker A speaker who uses a first language or mother tongue.

negation The use of negative forms to convey disagreement or to contradict (*not, never, nothing*).

neologism The creation of a word from existing lexical items (*bodified, zeroised*). Also called **coinage**.

nominative case In an inflected language, an inflection which marks the subject of a sentence.

non-count noun A noun that refers to things which cannot be counted and usually have no plural form (*heaven, happiness, spring*).

non-finite Verbs which are not marked for tense, person or number such as present and past participles and infinitives.

non-segmental phonology The analysis of prosodic and paralinguistic features in connected utterances of speech.

non-standard Any variety that does not conform to the standard prestige form used as a norm by society.

noun A word class with a naming function which can be used as a subject or object in a clause.

noun phrase A phrase which usually has a noun as the head word and that can function as subject or object in a clause.

nucleus The main syllable in a tone unit, which is stressed and carries a tone. Also called the **tonic syllable**.

number A grammatical classification marking singular and plural (*I/we, book/books*).

octameter A line of verse containing eight feet.

onomatopoeia The term used to denote words that imitate sounds.

open A term used to describe a vowel sound made with the tongue in the lowest position ([a], [ɒ]); vowels may also be described as **half-open**.

open class words Lexical words (adjectives, nouns, verbs and adverbs), new examples of which can be added to the existing stock.

ordinal number Numbers that indicate the order of a sequence (*first, second, third*).

orthography A study of spelling and the ways in which letters are used in a language.

over-generalisation The process used by children and learners to extend the meaning of a word (*dada* as a reference to all men). Also called **over-extension**.

oxymoron The use of apparently contradictory words in a phrase (*delicious poison*).

palatal A term used to denote consonants made by raising the front part of the tongue to the palate ([j]).

palato-alveolar A term used to denote consonants made by placing the tongue at the front of the hard palate near the alveolar ridge ([ʒ] or [ʃ]).

paradox A statement which although apparently ridiculous or self-contradictory contains a truth.

paragraph A unit of written discourse made up of sentences, which is marked either by indentation or by a blank line before and after it.

paralinguistics Non-verbal communication using gestures, posture and facial expressions.

parallelism The patterning of pairs of sounds, words or structures to create a sense of balance and logic in spoken and written discourse.

paraphrase The expression of the same thing in other words.

parenthesis In written language, the use of brackets, dashes or commas to mark out an optional element of a sentence.

participle The non-finite form of verbs which can occur after an auxiliary verb (*was **running*** – present participle; *had **run*** – past participle), or before a head noun in a noun phrase (*the **running** boy*; *the **completed** essay*). Present participles end in *-ing* and past participles usually end in *-ed* or *-en*.

particle A grammatical function word which never changes its form, like an adverb in a phrasal verb (*cleared **up**, kicked **down***) or a preposition in a prepositional verb (*look **after**, believe **in***).

passive voice A grammatical structure in which the subject and object can change places in order to alter the focus of a sentence. In the passive voice, the object of an active sentence occurs in the subject site followed by *to be + past participle* (*the bone **was eaten***). The subject of the active sentence can be included following *by* (*the bone was eaten **by the dog***).

pentameter A line of verse containing five feet in which a caesura can occur between the two halves.

perfect/perfective The perfect aspect is made up of *to have + past participle* and has two forms: present perfect, describing a past action with present relevance (*the girl **has finished** her dinner*); and past perfect, describing an action completed before a specific time (*the girl **had finished** her dinner*).

person A grammatical term used to describe the number and kind of participants involved in a situation: first person references relate directly to the speaker or writer or to a group of people including the speaker or writer (*I, we*); second person references relate to the person or people addressed by the speaker or writer (*you*); and third person references relate to other people, animals or objects (*he, she, it, they*).

personal pronouns Subject pronouns (*I, you, he, she, it, we, they*) replace a noun phrase in the subject site, and object pronouns (*me, you, him, her, it, us, them*) replace a noun phrase in the object site of a sentence.

personification A device in which the non-human is given personality and human qualities.

phatic A term used to denote language used to create social contact.

phonemes The smallest distinctive sound segments in a language.

phonemics The analysis of phonemes.

phonemic transcription A broad transcription recording phonemes, concentrating on meaning in language rather than on details of articulation.

phonetic alphabet Symbols and diacritics designed to represent exactly the sounds of spoken language. Also known as the **International Phonetic Alphabet** or **IPA**.

phonetics The study of spoken sounds and the way in which they are produced, transmitted and received.

phonetic transcription A detailed transcription using IPA symbols, concentrating on the physical details of pronunciation.

phonology The study of sounds in a particular language and the way in which they are combined to create meaning.

phrasal verb A verb made up of a lexical verb and a particle (an adverb).

phrase A group of words that has no finite verb (except for a verb phrase): noun phrase (*the green tree*); adjective phrase (*very blue*); verb phrase (*has gone*); adverb phrase (*quite slowly*).

piano A term used to describe speech that is articulated quietly.

pidgin A simple but rule-governed language which emerges as the basis for communication between speakers with no common language.

pitch The level of a sound: **low, medium, high**.

place of articulation The point at which the airstream is stopped in the mouth to produce consonantal sounds (bilabial, labiodental, dental, alveolar, palato-alveolar, palatal, velar, glottal).

pleonasm The use of unnecessary words or ineffective repetition in an expression (*safe haven, cheap bargain, hear with your ears*). Also called **tautology**.

plosive A term used to denote consonants made by a complete closure of the air passage followed by a sudden release of air ([p] or [t]).

plural A grammatical expression of more than one in number (*cars*, *they*).

polysyllabic Having more than one syllable.

possessive A word or inflection signalling possession (*Julie's*, *hers*).

post-alveolar A term used to denote the consonant [r], made by moving the tongue towards the alveolar ridge without touching it.

post-creole continuum The range of creole forms existing when creole speakers adapt their native language to conform to the standard.

post-modification Lexical items that follow the head in a phrase (*the path **down the mountain***).

pragmatics The study of how context influences a speaker's or writer's lexical choices.

predicative The term used to denote adjectives or other modifiers that follow a copula verb in a noun phrase (*the girl appeared **sad**, the children seem **happy**, the plants grew **tall***).

predicator The verb phrase that fills the verb site in a clause.

prefix A bound morpheme that occurs before a free morpheme (*un-*, *re-*, *dis-*).

pre-modification Lexical items that precede the head in a phrase (***the serious** incident, **very** fast*).

preposition A closed class word like *in*, *on* or *by* which precedes a noun phrase, pronoun or other lexical item to express a relationship between it and the rest of a clause.

prepositional phrase A grammatical structure made up of a preposition and a noun phrase (*in the car*).

prescriptive A term used to denote an approach to language that dictates rules of usage, focusing on concepts of 'right' and 'wrong' rather than 'appropriateness' and 'acceptability'.

primary verb A verb that can function as a lexical or an auxiliary verb (*be*, *have*, *do*).

progressive An aspect used to describe an event which is in progress. It is made up of *to be* + *present participle* (*the girl **is eating**, the girl **was eating***).

pronoun A closed class word that can replace a noun phrase.

pronunciation The mode of articulating sounds, syllables or words.

proper noun A name of a distinctive person, place or other unique reference. It is marked by a capital letter in written language.

prosodic features The use of pitch, volume, pace and rhythm to draw attention to key elements of spoken language.

pun Word play which uses the different meanings of a word or two words with similar forms and different meanings for comic effect.

punctuation The use of graphic marks in written language to signal different sections of a sentence.

pure vowel A vowel made up of only one sound.

qualifier A word or phrase that post-modifies a head word (*the tree **in the orchard**, the baby **crawling in the garden***).

question A sentence or utterance that requests information or some kind of response.

quotation marks Punctuation marks in written language which indicate direct speech or an extract cited from another text.

raising The pronunciation of a vowel in which the tongue is raised higher than in RP.

rallentando A term used to describe speech that is getting slower.

rank The hierarchical arrangement of words, phrases, clauses and sentences whereby phrases are made up of words, clauses are made up of sentences, and sentences are made up of clauses.

Received Pronunciation An English accent which has a high social status and is not connected to a specific region. Also known as **RP**.

reduction The process in which front and back vowels are replaced by weak central vowels in monosyllabic function words or unstressed syllables of polysyllabic words.

reduplication A structural repetition within a word (*baba, dada, pell-mell*).

reflexive pronoun A grammatical function word ending in *-self* or *-selves* in which the subject and object are directly related (*I cut **myself***).

register A variety of language defined according to use. It can be described in terms of **mode** (speech or writing; format); **manner** (participants; levels of formality); and **field** (content).

regular A term used to denote linguistic forms that conform to the rules of a language.

relative pronoun A grammatical function word which marks the beginning of a relative clause post-modifying a noun phrase (*the weather **which** was unpredictable*; *the man **who** was red with anger*).

repair The correction of a mistake or misunderstanding in conversation.

repertoire A speaker's range of spoken and written language forms.

repetition A device which emphasises an idea through reiteration.

rhetoric The use of dramatic or persuasive words and structures in spoken and written language to manipulate the intended audience.

rhetorical question A question that does not require an answer.

rhotic Accents that pronounce /r/ after vowels. If /r/ is not articulated, the accents are described as **non-rhotic**.

rhyme The arrangement of word endings which agree in vowel and consonant sounds.

rhythm The pattern of stressed and unstressed syllables in language.

rounded The shape of the lips where the corners come together and the lips are pushed forward to make vowel sounds like [u].

rule A principle of language structure which prescriptivists use to dictate 'correct' and 'incorrect' usage.

schwa The unstressed centre vowel [ə] which occurs at the end of words (*actor* [æktə]) or as the vowel in unstressed syllables (*can* [kən]).

segmental phonology The analysis of speech into distinctive units or phonemes.

semantics The study of the meaning of language.

semi-vowel A consonant such as [w] and [j] which, although it sounds like a vowel, has many of the characteristics of a consonant. Semi-vowels are also known as **approximants** or **frictionless continuants**.

sentence A grammatical structure made up of one or more clauses. In written language the beginning is signalled by a capital letter and the end by a full stop; in conversation analysis, linguists usually refer to **utterances** rather than sentences.

sibilant Consonantal sounds like affricates and alveolar and palatal fricatives which are articulated with a hissing sound.

simile A device which makes a direct comparison between two things using *like* or *as* (*the boy was fierce **like a lion***).

slang Distinctive words and phrases associated with informal speech. It tends to be used within clearly defined social or age groups and is often short-lived.

sonnet A traditional fourteen-line verse form in which rhyme and stanza divisions are usually observed strictly according to two distinct patterns: the **Italian** or **Petrarchan** sonnet or the **English** or **Shakespearean** sonnet. It was originally a medium for expression of love, but its scope has widened considerably.

source language The language from which loan words have been borrowed.

speech community A regionally or socially defined group of people who have a language or variety in common.

split infinitive The separation of the preposition *to* from the base form of a verb (*to **loudly** ring*).

spondee A unit of poetic metre containing two stressed syllables (*chíld·líke*).

spread The shape of the lips where the corners move away from each other to make vowel sounds like [iː].

staccato A term used to describe speech that is marked by an irregular delivery.

standard The form of a language considered to be the norm and used as the medium of education, government and the law. Varieties which differ from this are said to be **non-standard**.

standardisation The process of making non-standard usage conform to the standard, prestige form of a language.

stative verbs Verbs that express states of being or processes in which there is no obvious action (*know, believe*).

stops Sounds like [p] and [m] in which the air flow is briefly stopped in the mouth.

stress The comparative force, length, loudness and pitch with which a syllable is pronounced. Syllables may be **stressed** or **unstressed**.

strong verb A verb that does not follow the regular pattern, but instead changes a vowel to mark the past tense (*hang → hung; swim → swam*).

stylistics The study of lexical and structural variations in language according to use, user and purpose.

subject A noun phrase or pronoun which is usually the actor of the verb in a clause.

subjunctive A grammatical mood which expresses something hypothetical or tentative. It is no longer used widely, but occurs in formulaic expressions like *Heaven forbid* and following *if* in structures like *If I were to come*.

subordinate clause A clause that cannot stand as a sentence on its own, but needs another clause to complete its meaning. Also known as a **dependent clause**.

subordinating conjunction A conjunction used to introduce a subordinate clause (*because, while, until*).

substitution The replacement of one lexical item, such as a noun phrase, with another, such as a pronoun (*the unhappy girl → she*).

suffix A bound morpheme that occurs after a free morpheme (*-like, -wise*).

syllabic A term used to denote a consonant that can stand alone as a syllable.

syllable A word or part of a word that can be uttered by a single effort of the voice. Patterns of stressed and unstressed syllables constitute the rhythm of a language.

symbol A device in which a word or phrase represents something else (*dove* for *peace*).

synchronic The study of language at a particular point in time.

synecdoche A device in which a part is used to represent the whole (*There were several new faces at the meeting tonight* for *There were several new people at the meeting tonight*).

synonyms Different words with the same or nearly the same meaning (*valiant* and *brave*).

syntax The study of the grammatical relationships between words in sentences.

tag question An interrogative structure attached to the end of a sentence which expects a reply (*It's nice today, isn't it?*).

telegraphic speech Spoken or written language that omits function words (*Boy go school*).

tense A change in the structure of a verb to signal changes in the timescale. There are two tenses in English: **present** and **past**. The present tense uses the base form of the verb except for the third person singular which is inflected with an *-s*; it refers to actions in the present time and describes habitual actions. The past tense is formed by adding an *-ed* inflection to regular verbs; it refers to actions or states that have taken place in the past.

tetrameter A line of verse containing four feet.

tone The distinctive pitch level of a syllable. Tones can be **rising**, **falling**, **rising-falling** or **falling-rising**.

tone units A segment of spoken language consisting of one or more syllables with a series of rises or falls in tone where there is one particularly marked syllable.

topic The thing or person about which something is said in a sentence; the focus of a written or spoken text.

transcription A written record of spoken language, which can use symbols and markings to illustrate the distinctive nature of speech.

transitive A term used to describe verbs that have to be followed by an object.

trimeter A unit of poetic metre containing three feet.

trochee A unit of poetic metre containing a stressed followed by an unstressed syllable (*tém·pĕr*).

turn-taking The organisation of speakers' contributions in a conversation. Turns may be equal, or one of the participants may dominate.

typography The study of features of the printed page.

under-extension The use of a word in a limited way which does not recognise its full meaning – young children may use *dog* to refer only to the family pet.

utterance A stretch of spoken language which is often preceded by silence and followed by silence or a change of speaker. It is often used as an alternative to 'sentence' in conversation analysis since it is difficult to apply the traditional characteristics of a written sentence to spoken language.

variety Language use which has distinctive features because of its context, intended audience and purpose (*religious language, legal language*).

velar A term used to denote consonants produced by raising the back of the tongue to the soft palate or velum ([g] or [k]).

verbal noun A noun derived from a verb (*The **driving** is hard work*).

verbless clause A clause that contains no verb (*wherever possible; what about a drink?*).

verb phrase A group of verbs consisting of a lexical verb and up to four auxiliaries.

verbs Open class words that express states, actions or processes. They can be marked for tense, aspect, voice and mood.

vernacular The native language of a speech community.

vocabulary The words of a language: in linguistics, synonymous with **lexis**.

vocal organs The organs of speech used to articulate sound.

vocative The words used to name or refer to people when talking to them.

voiced sounds Sounds made when the vocal cords are drawn together and the air from the lungs has to push them apart, creating a vibration.

voiceless sounds Sounds made when the vocal cords are spread apart so that the air can pass between them without obstruction.

volume Contrasting levels of loudness in speech, which may be described as **loud**, **quiet**, **getting louder** or **getting quieter**.

vowel A sound produced by the free flow of air through the mouth. In written language, a letter that can be used alone or in combination to represent a vowel sound (*a, e, i, o, u*).

wh- questions Questions introduced by *wh-* words, which can be used alone or in a sentence. They expect new information in the reply (***Where** did you go?*).

word The smallest grammatical unit that can stand alone. Words can be divided into two groups: **lexical** and **function words**.

word class Groups of words with characteristic features (*nouns, adjectives, verbs, determiners*).

word formation The process of creating words from bound and free morphemes (*dis-* + *order* + *-ly*).

word order The arrangement of words in a sentence.

yes/no questions Questions marked by the inversion of the subject and the first verb in a verb phrase. They expect *yes* or *no* for an answer.

C Wider reading

Grammar

D. Crystal (1988), *Rediscover English Grammar* (Penguin).
D. Freeborn (1987), *A Course Book in English Grammar* (Macmillan).
D. Graddol, J. Cheshire and J. Swann (1987), *Describing Language* (The Open University Press).
M. A. K. Halliday and R. Hasan (1969), *Cohesion in English* (Longman).
G. Leech (1989), *An A–Z of English Grammar and Usage* (Edward Arnold).
G. Leech, M. Deuchar and R. Hoogenraad (1982), *English Grammar for Today* (Macmillan).
R. Quirk, S. Greenbaum, G. Leech and J. Svartvik (1985), *A Comprehensive Grammar of the English Language* (Longman).

Phonetics and phonology

A. C. Gimson (1980), *An Introduction to the Pronunciation of English* (Edward Arnold).
C. W. Kriedler (1989), *The Pronunciation of English: A Course Book in Phonology* (Blackwell).
J. D. O'Connor (1973), *Phonetics* (Penguin).
P. Roach (1983), *English Phonetics and Phonology* (CUP).
J. C. Wells and G. Colson (1971), *Practical Phonetics* (Pitman).

Style

R. F. Bailey (1984), *A Survival Kit for Writing English* (Longman).
R. Quirk (1968), *The Use of English* (Longman).
G. W. Turner (1973), *Stylistics* (Pelican).

General

J. Aitchinson (1990), *Teach Yourself Linguistics* (Hodder & Stoughton).
N. F. Blake and J. Moorhead (1993), *Introduction to English Language* (Macmillan).
B. Bryson (1990), *Mother Tongue* (Penguin).
D. Crystal (1987), *The Cambridge Encyclopedia of Language* (CUP).
D. Crystal (1988), *The English Language* (Penguin).
D. Crystal (1991), *A Dictionary of Linguistics and Phonetics* (Blackwell).

D. Crystal (1995), *The Cambridge Encyclopedia of the English Language* (CUP).
V. Fromkin and R. Rodman (1993), *An Introduction to Language* (Harcourt & Brace).
P. Howard (1990), *A Word in Time* (Sinclair-Stevenson).
G. Yule (1985), *The Study of Language* (CUP).

Aspects of English

Language and society

J. Aitchinson (1981), *Language Change: Progress or Decay?* (Fontana).
D. Crystal (1984), *Who Cares about English Usage?* (Penguin).
D. Leith (1983), *A Social History of English* (RKP).
J. Milroy and L. Milroy (1989), *Authority in Language: Investigating Language Prescription and Standardisation* (RKP).
L. Milroy (1987), *Language and Social Networks* (Blackwell).
M. Montgomery (1986), *An Introduction to Language and Society* (Methuen).
L. Todd (1984), *Modern Englishes: Pidgins and Creoles* (Blackwell).
P. Trudgill (1974), *Sociolinguistics: An Introduction* (Penguin).

The history of English

C. L. Barber (1964), *The Story of Language* (OUP).
A. C. Baugh and T. Cable (1978), *A History of the English Language* (RKP).
R. Burchfield (1987), *The English Language* (OUP).
R. Claiborne (1990), *The Life and Times of the English Language* (Bloomsbury).
D. Freeborn (1992), *From Old English to Standard English* (Macmillan).

Accent and dialect

J. Honey (1989), *Does Accent Matter?* (Faber).
A. Hughes and P. Trudgill (1976), *English Accents and Dialects* (Longman).
P. Trudgill (1975), *Accent, Dialect and the School* (Arnold).
J. C. Wells (1982), *Accents of English* (CUP).

Child language acquisition

J. Bruner (1983), *Child's Talk: Learning to Use Language* (OUP).
D. Crystal (1986), *Listen to your Child: a Parent's Guide to Children's Language* (Penguin).
P. de Villiers and J. de Villiers (1979), *Early Language* (Fontana).
K. Perera (1984), *Children's Writing and Reading* (Blackwell).

Varieties of English

N. F. Blake (1990), *An Introduction to the Language of Literature* (Macmillan).
D. Crystal and D. Davy (1969), *Investigating English Style* (Longman).
D. Freeborn (1986), *Varieties of English* (Macmillan).
G. Leech and M. Short (1981), *Style in Fiction* (Longman).
W. R. O'Donnell and L. Todd (1988), *Variety in Contemporary English* (Allen & Unwin).
M. Stubbs (1983), *Discourse Analysis* (Blackwell).
R. Wardhaugh (1985), *How Conversation Works* (Blackwell).
K. Waterhouse (1989), *Waterhouse on Newspaper Style* (Viking).

Index

abstract nouns   5
accents   139–55, 403
  broad   139, 140, 154
  modified   54, 92
  personal   140
  regional   139, 141–55
  social   139, 140–1
acceptability   93–5, 101
active voice   11
adjacency pairs   196
adjectives   7–8, 156–7
  nouns as   8
  phrases   29–30
adverbials   32
adverbs   14–46, 157
  conjunct   15
  degree   15
  disjunct   15
  phrases   32
advertising   257–80
  charity   276
  classified   265
  complaints   258–9
  design   261, 270, 278
  direct mail   257, 266
  grammar   263–4, 273–5, 278–9
  'hard sell' tactics   258
  information   279–80
  lexis   262–3, 278
  metaphorical language   264–5, 275, 279
  products   265–75
  rhetorical devices   265, 275
  services   276
  slogans   261, 271–3
  typography   265, 275, 279
affixes   22
affricates   55
alliteration   75
alveolars   53

ambiguity   237, 326, 345, 439, 443
American English   109, 115
anaphoric references   46
Anglo-Saxon Chronicle   118–20
anti-climax   79
anti-language   111
antithesis   78
appropriateness   93–5, 101
approximants   56
articles   19
articulation   50–6
  manner   54–6
  organs of speech   50–2
  place   52–4
aspect   11
aspiration   154
assimilation   64, 69, 140
assonance   75
attributive adjectives   7
audience   93–5
Australian English   115
Authorised Version of the Bible (AV)
  346, 353–6, 366
auxiliary verbs   9–10

babbling   168
'baby words'   166
base forms   9, 10, 43
BBC English   91, 398–9
'Beowulf'   118
bias   238, 404, 408
Bible   346, 353–6, 366
bilabials   53
Birmingham accent   146–7
Black English   108–14
Black English Vernacular (BEV)   109
book hand   125
Book of Common Prayer (BCP)   346,
  356–7, 366

borrowing   121, 125, 127, 128, 132
branching   82
broadcasting   398–429
  accents and dialects   403, 418, 429
  comedy   421–6
  documentaries   407–13
  drama   413–20
  formal *vs* informal   412–13
  grammar   402, 411
  lexis   402, 424–6
  manner   400, 410
  mode   400, 410
  news   403–7
  normal non-fluency features   403, 420
  prosodic features   402, 407, 418, 420, 426
  status   400, 407
  structure   401, 404, 406, 411
  topics   401, 407

Canterbury Tales   118, 125
'caretaker speech'   166
case (grammar)   121
cataphoric references   146
CD-Rom   434
centring diphthong   60–1
child language   164–90
  behaviourist approach   165
  cognitive approach   165
  conversation skills   170, 171, 173, 174, 181, 183, 185
  dialogue   181–5
  grammar   170–1, 172–3, 173–4, 176–7, 180–1
  monologue   170, 174–81
  nativist approach   165–6
  pronunciation   170, 171, 176, 179, 183
  stages of acquisition   167–74
  vocabulary   169, 171, 173, 176–6, 178–9
chronological texts   430, 431, 434, 49, 443
Church language   346–67
  grammar   349–51, 354–5, 357, 360–1, 364
  lexis   348–9, 354, 356–7, 360, 363–4
  liturgies   356–7
  manner   347–8, 359, 363
  metaphorical language   351, 355, 361, 364
  rhetorical language   351–2, 355–6, 361–2, 364
  rituals   356
  sacred texts   346–7, 352–6
  sermons   357–65

typographical features   352
clauses   33–6, 84
  adverbial   39
  comparative   39
  elements   33–5
  non-finite   40
  noun clause   39
  relative   39–40
  structure   35–6
  verbless   40
clear *l*   55
clichés   253
closed class words   4
close vowels   57
closing diphthongs   60–1
Cockney accent   150–2
collective nouns   5
collocations   44
comic strips   445–8
commands   43
comment clauses   99, 206, 214
common nouns   4
complements   34–5
complex sentences   39–40, 81
compound-complex sentences   40–1
compound sentences   37–8
concrete nouns   4
conjunctions   21, 157
consonance   76
consonants   56–7
contact languages   109
continuants   54
convergence   140, 154
cooing   168
cookery
co-ordinating conjunctions   21
copula verbs   7
Corpus project   193
correctness   92
countability   5
courtroom language   337–43
creoles   109–10

dark *l*   55–6
declaratives   42
decreolisation   110
definite articles   19
deictic expressions   17, 199
demonstrative pronouns   17, 19
dentals   53
descriptive approach   92, 101, 102
determiners   19

diachronic approach   102, 103, 117
diacritics   50
dialects   155–62, 403
  grammar   156
  in literature   298–301
  lexis   156
  regional   155
  social   155–6
diaries   441–2
dimeter   310
diphthongs   60–1
direct speech   241, 246, 252, 254, 285
direct *vs* indirect objects   34
divergence   140
drama   413–20
dynamic verbs   8

Early Modern English   117, 126–9
  grammar   127
  graphology   128
  phonology   128
  spelling   127
  typographical features   128–9
  vocabulary   127, 128
elision   65–6, 140
ellipsis   38, 45, 69
end focus   73
English
  future of   102, 114–6
  in France   116
  see also American English; Australian
    English; Black English; Received
    Pronunciation
English as a world language   114–16
Estuary English   92, 161–2
euphemisms   368
exaggeration   79
existential *there*   73
exophoric references   46
extension   169

falling tones   67
falling-rising tones   68
feet *see* foot
fiction *see* narrative prose
field   95
finite verbs   12
first words   169
focus   72–4
  end focus   73
  existential *there*   73–4
  marked theme   72–3

passive voice   74
foot, metrical   310–11
foregrounding   72
free direct or indirect speech   285–6
free verse   309
French
  borrowing from   123, 124–5, 127–8
fricatives   55
frictionless continuants   56
fronting (grammatical)   72, 115
function *vs* form   26–7
future time   10–1

Gawain and the Green Knight   118, 125
gender   104–8, 137
gestures   71
glides   56
glottals   54
glottal stops   54, 142
grammar
  child   170–1, 172–3, 173–4
  creole   110
  in advertising   263–4
  in commentary   222–4, 225–6
  in religion   349–51
  Middle English   125
  Old English   121
  reasons for study   3
  regional   156–9
  spoken *vs* written   99
grammatical words   4
graphology   121, 125

half-close vowels   57
half-open vowels   57
Hansard   369, 370, 372, 390–1, 392–5
headlines   234–8
heptameter   310
hesitation   71
hexameter   310
historic present   158
holophrastic phase   169
homonyms   80
homophones   80
house style   234
hyperbole   79
hypercorrection   141, 146
hypercreolisation   110
hyponyms   44, 169

iambic pentameter   310
identity   138–9

ideology 233, 368
imperatives 43
indefinite articles *see* articles
indefinite pronouns 18
Indian English 116
indirect objects 34
indirect speech 241, 285
  free 285–6
infinitives 9
inflection 120, 121, 123, 125, 127, 128
information texts 434–8
  lectures 437–8
  publicity leaflets 436–7
  textbooks 435–6
inkhorn terms 128
instruction texts 430–3
  manuals 432–3
  recipes 431–2
International Phonetic Alphabet 49, 62
interrogatives *see* questions
interviews 211–15
  vs telephone conversation 215–16
intonation 67–8, 197–8
intransitive verbs 9
irony 76–7
irregular verbs 9

Japanese English 116
jargon 169
Jewish English 115
jingles 406

labiodentals 53
language
  attitudes 92, 138–9
  change 92, 95, 102–16, 137–9
  contact 155, 161
Late Modern English 117
laterals 55–6
Latin
  borrowing from 121, 127, 128
lectures 437–8
legal language 326–45
  contracts 334–7
  grammar 329–30, 333, 337, 342
  language of the courts 337–43
  lexis 328–9, 332, 336–7, 338–9, 341–2
  manner 327
  spoken *vs* written 343
  statutes 330–3
  typography and layout 327–8, 332, 336, 341

levelling 161–2
level tone 67–8
lexical diffusion 135
liaison 66, 69, 140, 142
lingua franca 109
lip-rounding 58
listing 79
litotes 79
liturgy 356–7
  see also Church language

main clauses 37
major sentences 41
malapropisms 303
manner 95
manner of articulation 54–6
marked themes 72–3
metalinguists 327, 341
metaphors 77
metonymy 77
metre 310–11
Middle English 117, 121–5
  dialects 125
  grammar 124, 125
  graphology 125
  phonology 125
  poetry 118
  spelling 123
  vocabulary 123, 124, 125
minimal pairs 64
minor sentences 41
mismatches 169
modal verbs 10
mode 95
Modern English 117, 129–32
  grammar 131
  graphology 132
  phonology 132
  vocabulary 130–1, 132
modification 8
monometer 310
mood 42–3
morphemes 22
morphology 3, 22–5
  in humour 425–6
'motherese' 166
multiple negatives 94, 128, 159

naming of participants 239, 245, 252
narratives
  characterisation 286–91
  evoking an atmosphere 296–8

experimenting with language 298–304
first person 284
grammar 286, 288
interior monologues 285, 287
lexis 285
manner 284
metaphorical language 286, 290
rhetorical language 286, 288, 291
setting the scene 291–6
stream of consciousness 285, 288
third person 284, 290
narrative texts 443–8
nasals 55
National Curriculum 138–9
negatives 159, 171, 172, 174
multiple 94, 128, 159
neologisms 300–2, 425–6
neutral (lips) 58
news 400, 401, 402, 403–7
newspapers 229–56
action stories 242–7
broadsheets *vs* tabloids 229–33
grammar 240
lexis 239–40
reports 238–41
running stories 247–54
sources 241
statement and opinion stories 247
style 240–1
see also headlines
news values 229
non-chronological texts 430, 434, 439
non-count nouns 5
non-finite verbs 12
non-rhotic accents 56
nonsense words 425–6
non-sexist language 104–8
non-standard English 91
Norfolk accent 148–9
normal non-fluency features 71, 173, 199, 200–1, 403
Norse, Old 121
nouns 4–6
abstract *vs* concrete 4–5
collective 5
count *vs* non-count 5
plural 5, 156
possessive 5
proper *vs* common 4
nucleus (of syllable) 70–1
number 13, 28
numerals 19

objects (grammatical)
clauses 34
direct *vs* indirect 34
octameter 310
Old English 117, 118–21
closed class words 120
grammar 121
graphology 121
inflections 121
open class words 120
phonology 121
poetry 118
word order 120
Old Norse 121
onomatopoeia 76
open class words 4
open vowels 57
over-extension 169
overstatement 79
oxymorons 77

pace 71, 198
palatals 53
palato-alveolars 53
paradox 77
paralinguistic features 71, 193
parallelism 81
parental speech style 166, 168, 171–2
parent-child dialogue 181–5
parliamentary language 369–70, 390–5
particles 20
passive voice 11–12, 74
Paston Letters 122–4, 126–8
past participles 9, 11, 12
past perfect 11
past tense 10
pauses 71, 198
pentameter 310
perfect aspect 11
personal pronouns 16–17
personal texts 438–42
comics 445–8
diaries and journals 441–2
letters 440–1
playscripts 443–5
personification 77
phoneme inventory 143
phonemic transcription 63, 85–6
phonetics 48–62, 85
phonetic transcription 63, 85–6
phonology 62–71, 85
non-segmental 67–71

phonology, *continued*
  segmental   64–7, 140
phrasal verbs   31
phrases   27–32, 83–4
  adjective   29–30
  adverb   32
  noun   27–8
  prepositional   31–2
  verb   30–1
pidgin   109
pitch   68, 198
place of articulation   52–4
Plain English   326, 327, 333
pleonasms   303
plosives   54
plurals   5
poetry   307–25
  characterising   312–14
  evoking atmosphere   318–22
  experimenting with language and
      structure   322–3
  form and structure   308–9
  grammar   312
  layout   312
  lexis   311–12
  metre   310–11
  Middle English   118
  Old English   118
  poetic devices   309, 311, 312
  setting the scene   314–18
point of view   284–5
political correctness   104, 107
political language
  grammar   371–3, 375–6, 380–1, 386–9,
      395
  Houses of Parliament   390–5
  informality   369–70
  lexis   370–1, 375, 379–80, 385–6, 390–1,
      393–5
  manifestos and campaign
      statements   373–83
  manner   369
  metaphorical language   373
  pre-scripted speeches   383–90
  rhetorical devices   376–7, 381–3, 389
  spoken features   389–90, 391
'Politics and the English Language'   368
possessive pronouns   5–6
post-alveolars   53–6
post-creole continuum   110
post-modification   27, 28, 29–30, 32
post-vocalic /r/   142

pragmatics   168, 185, 369
prayers   356–7
predeterminers   28
predicative adjectives   7
predicators   36
prefixes   22, 23
pre-modification   27–8, 29
prepositional verbs   31
prepositions   20, 157
  at end of sentence   94
prescriptive approach to language   92,
      101, 102, 132
present participle   9, 11, 12
present perfect aspect   11
present tense   10
prestige   91, 98, 100
primary verbs   9
printing   123, 128–9
progressive aspect   11
pronouns   16–18, 157–8
  demonstrative   17
  indefinite   18
  interrogative   18
  personal   16–17
  possessive   17
  reflexive   17
  relative   18
proper nouns   4
publicity leaflets   436–7
puns   80

qualifiers   27, 28
quality *vs* tabloid press   229–33
Queen's English   91
questions   9–10, 42–3
  intonation   43, 68, 170, 172
  political   372, 391–5
Question Time (parliamentary)   372,
      391–5
question words   18, 170, 172, 174
quoted *vs* quoting clause   241

Received Pronunciation (RP)   91, 138–9,
      154
  modified   92, 140
recipes   431–2
reduction   66, 140
reduplication   110, 466
reflexive pronouns   17
regional variation   139, 141–55, 155–9
register   95–7
relative clauses   28, 39–40

relative pronouns   18
religion, language of *see* Church language
repertoire   139, 163
repetition   44, 80
reported clauses   241
rhetoric   74–6
  lexical choice   75
  rhyme   76
  sound patterning   75–6
rhotic accent   56
rhyming couplets   308
rhythm   69–71
rising-falling tones   68
rounding *see* lip rounding
RP *see* Received Pronunciation
runes   120

schwa   65
scientific language   435–6
selective perception   238, 240, 256
semi-vowels   53, 56
sentences   37–41
  analysing a sentence   41
  complex   39–41, 81
  compound   37–8
  compound-complex   40–1
  major *vs* minor   41
  simple   37, 81
sermons   357–65
sexist language   104–8
similes   78
slogans   260, 261–2
social variation   139, 140–1, 155–6
South Wales accent   152–4
speech   97–101, 194
  manner   194
spelling
  American *vs* British   114, 115, 300
  Early Modern English   127
  Middle English   123
  Modern English   132
  non-standard   258, 300, 302–3
  reform   128, 132
split infinitives   94
Spoken Corpus project   193
spoken language   194–228
  grammar   199–200
  lexis   199
  manner   194–5
  prosodic features   197–9
  repairs   201–3
  structure   195–6

topics   195, 401
vocal effects   199
see also broadcasting language; legal
  language; normal non-fluency
  features; political language
spoken narrative   204–6
sports commentary   216–26
Standard English (SE)   91, 138–9
standard international English   115
stative verbs   8
statutes   330–4
stereotypes   258, 261
stress   69–70, 198
style   72–82
subjects (grammatical)   33–4, 35–6
subjunctives   135
subordinate clauses   38–9
substitution   38, 44
suffixes   22, 23–4, 24–5
superlatives   7, 15
superordinates   44
symbolism   78
synchronic approach   102, 117
synecdoche   78

tag questions   105, 166
tautology *see* pleonasm
telegraphic style   171, 175, 237
telephone conversations   206–10
  vs interviews   215–16
television *see* broadcasting
tenses   10, 158–9
tetrameter   310
textbooks   435–6
themes   72
thorn   121
tone units   70–1, 198
topic shifts   195
transitive verbs   9
trimeter   310
trochee   310
turn-taking   196–7
typography   128–9, 230, 256, 265, 281,
  312, 326, 327–8, 352, 449

under-extension   169
understatement   79
unparliamentary language   369–70

velars   54
verbless clauses   40
verb phrases   30–1

verbs   8–12, 158
  as clause elements   34, 35–6
  auxiliary *vs* lexical   9–10
  finite *vs* non-finite   12
  in Old English   121
  modal   11
  phrasal   31
  prepositional   31
  regular *vs* irregular   9
  stative *vs* dynamic   8
  transitive *vs* intransitive   8
  see also aspect; future time; passive;
    tense
vocatives   43

voice *see* passive voice
voicing   50, 52
volume   69, 198
vowels   57–62
  compound   60–2
  pure   57–60

wh- questions   18, 170, 172, 174
wills   334–7
word class   4–21
writing *vs* speech   97–101

yes/no questions   372, 393, 394
Yorkshire accent   143–6